NORTON SCORES

An Anthology for Listening

Fourth Edition • Expanded

Volume II

THE NORTON SCORES

An Anthology for Listening

FOURTH EDITION • EXPANDED
IN TWO VOLUMES

VOLUME II:
SCHUBERT TO GLASS

EDITED BY

ROGER KAMIEN

ASSOCIATE PROFESSOR OF MUSIC, QUEENS COLLEGE
OF THE CITY UNIVERSITY OF NEW YORK

W · W · NORTON & COMPANY

New York · London

Acknowledgments

The texts for items 1, 11, and 19 are from *The Ring of Words* by Philip L. Miller. Reprinted by permission of Doubleday & Company, Inc., and Philip L. Miller.

The text translation for item 31 is reprinted through the courtesy of London Records, a Division of PolyGram Classics, Inc.

The text translation for item 37 is from Federico García Lorca, *Selected Poems.* Copyright 1955 by New Directions Publishing Corporation. Reprinted by permission of New Directions Publishing Corporation.

Page makeup and highlighting by Roberta Flechner.

PRINTED IN THE UNITED STATES OF AMERICA.
Library of Congress Cataloging in Publication Data
Main entry under title:
The Norton scores.
Includes index.
Contents: v. 1. Gregorian chant to Beethoven—v. 2. Schubert to Glass.
1. Music appreciation—Music collections. I. Kamien, Roger.
MT6.5.N7 1984b 83-19428

ISBN 0-393-95310-6

W. W. Norton & Company, Inc., 500 Fifth Avenue, New York, N. Y. 10110
W. W. Norton & Company Ltd., 37 Great Russell Street, London WC1B 3NU

5 6 7 8 9 0

Contents

Preface

This anthology is designed for use in introductory music courses, where the ability to read music is not a prerequisite. The unique system of highlighting employed in this book enables students to follow full orchestral scores after about one hour of instruction. This system also has the advantage of permitting students who *can* read music to perceive every aspect of the score. It is felt that our system of highlighting will be of greater pedagogical value than artificially condensed scores, which restrict the student's vision to pre-selected elements of the music. The use of scores in introductory courses makes the student's listening experience more intense and meaningful, and permits the instructor to discuss music in greater depth.

The works included in this Fourth Edition have been chosen from among those most frequently studied in introductory courses. The selections range from Gregorian chant to the present day, and represent a wide variety of forms, genres, and performing media. To make this Fourth Edition reflect today's concert repertory more closely, increased emphasis has been placed on instrumental and secular music of earlier periods and on music of the present century. A majority of the pieces are given in their entirety, while the others are represented by complete movements or sections particularly suitable for classroom study. Scenes from operas and some choral works are presented in vocal score, while all others are reprinted in their full original form. This anthology may be used independently, or along with any introductory text. The publishers have prepared a set of recordings to accompany *The Norton Scores.*

A few words about the highlighting system employed in the full scores: Each system of score is covered with a light gray screen, and the most prominent line in the music at any given point is spotlighted by a white band (see No. 1 in sample on page *x*). In cases where two or more simultaneous lines are equally prominent, they are each highlighted. When a musical line continues from one system or page to the next, the white highlighting band ends with a wedge shape at the right-hand margin, and its continuation begins with a reverse wedge shape (see No. 2 in sample). By following these white bands in sequence through the score, the listener will perceive the notes corresponding to the most audible lines. Naturally, the highlighting will not *always* correspond with the most prominent instruments in a specific recording, for performances differ in their emphasis of particular lines. In such cases, we have highlighted those parts that, in our opinion, *should* emerge most clearly. (There are occasional passages in complex twentieth-century works where no single line represents the musical continuity. In such passages we have drawn the listener's attention to the most audible musical events while endeavoring to keep the highlighting as simple as possible.) To facilitate the following of highlighted scores, a narrow white band running the full width of the page has been placed between systems when there is more than one on a page.

It must be emphasized that we do not seek here to *analyze* melodic structure, contrapuntal texture, or any other aspect of the music. The highlighting may break off before the end of a phrase when the entrance of another part is more audible, and during long-held notes the attention will usually be drawn to more rhythmically active parts. The highlighting technique has been used primarily for instrumental music; in vocal works, the text printed under the music provides a firm guideline for the novice score-reader.

A few suggestions for the use of this anthology may be found useful:

1. The rudiments of musical notation should be introduced with a view to preparing the student to associate audible melodic contours with their written equivalents. It is more important for beginning students to recognize rising and falling lines, and long and short notes, than to identify specific pitches or rhythms. It is helpful to explain the function of a tie, and the layout of a full score.

2. Before listening to a work, it is best for students to familiarize themselves with the names and abbreviations for instruments used in that particular score (a glossary of instrumental names and abbreviations will be found at the conclusion of the book). We have retained the Italian, German, French, and English names used in the scores reproduced in this anthology. This exposure to a wide range of terminology will prepare students for later encounters with scores.

3. Students should be careful to notice whether there is more than one system on a page of score. They should be alerted for tempo changes, repeat signs, and *da capo* indications. Since performances often differ, it is helpful for the instructor to forewarn the class about the specific repeats made or not made in the recordings used for listening.

4. When a piece is very fast or difficult, it is helpful to listen once without a score.

5. It is best to begin with music that is relatively simple to follow: e.g. (in approximate order of difficulty) Handel, *Comfort ye* from *Messiah;* the first and third movements of Mozart's *Eine kleine Nachtmusik;* the Air from Bach's *Suite No. 3 in D major;* and the second movement of Haydn's *Symphony No. 104 in D major* (*London*).

6. Important thematic material and passages that are difficult to follow should be pointed out in advance and played either on the recording or at the piano. (We have found that rapid sections featuring two simultaneously highlighted instruments sometimes present difficulties for the students—e.g. Beethoven, *Symphony No. 5,* first movement, m. 65 ff.)

We have attempted to keep the highlighted bands simple in shape while showing as much of the essential slurs and dynamic indication as possible. Occasionally, because of the layout of the original score, stray stems and slurs will intrude upon the white area and instrumental directions will be excluded from the highlighting. (Naturally, the beginning of a highlighted area will not always carry a dynamic or similar indication, as the indication may have occurred measures earlier when the instrument in question was not the most prominent.) As students become more experienced in following the scores, they can be encouraged to direct their attention outside the highlighted areas, and with practice should eventually develop the skill to read conventional scores.

I should like to record here my great debt to the late Nathan Broder, who originated the system of highlighting employed here and whose advice and counsel were invaluable. My thanks go also to Mr. David Hamilton, and to Claire Brook and Kathleen Wilson Spillane of W. W. Norton, for many helpful suggestions. I am most grateful to my wife, Anita, who worked with me on every aspect of the book. She is truly the co-editor of this anthology.

1
2
5
310
320
330
1.
Fl.
Ob.
Fg.
Cor.
(Es)
Timp
Vl.
Vla.
Vc.
Cb.
Cl.
cresc.

How to Follow the Highlighted Scores

1. The most prominent line in the music at any given time is highlighted by a white band.

2. When a musical line continues from one system (group of staffs) or page to the next, the white highlighted band ends with a wedge shape, and its continuation begins with a reverse wedge shape.

3. By following the highlighted bands in sequence through the score, the listener will perceive the notes corresponding to the most audible lines.

4. A narrow white band running the full width of the page separates one system from another when there is more than one on a page. It is very important to be alert for these separating bands.

5. When two or more lines are equally prominent, they are each highlighted. When encountering such passages for the first time, it is sometimes best to focus on only one of the lines.

THE
NORTON SCORES
An Anthology for Listening

Fourth Edition • Expanded

Volume II

1. FRANZ SCHUBERT (1797-1828),
Erlkönig (1815)

Kind; er hat den Kna - ben wohl in dem Arm, er fasst ihn
sicher, er hält ihn warm.
Mein
Sohn, was birgst du so bang dein Ge-sicht?
Siehst, Va - - ter,
du den Erl - kö - nig nicht?
den Er - - len -
kö - nig mit Kron' und Schweif?
Mein Sohn, es ist ein
f
pp
(pp)
mf
p

Ne - belstreif. „Du lie - - bes Kind, komm,
(ppp)
geh mit mir! gar schö - - ne Spie - le
spiel' ich mit dir; manch bun - - - - te Blu - men sind
an dem Strand; mei - ne Mut - ter hat manch'
gül - - den Ge - wand". Mein Va - ter, mein Va - ter, und hö - rest du
f

nicht, was Er-len-könig mir lei - se verspricht? Sei ru-hig, bleibe
p
decresc.
ru-hig, mein Kind; in dür-ren Blättern säu-selt der Wind. „Willst,
fei - ner Kna - be, du mit mir gehn? mei-ne Töch - ter sol - len dich
ppp
war - ten schön; mei-ne Töch - ter füh - ren den nächt - li-chen Reihn, und
wie - gen und tan - zen und sin - gen dich ein, sie wie-gen und tan - zen und sin - gen dich ein".
f

Mein Va - ter, mein Va - ter, und siehst du nicht dort Erl -

kö - nigs Töchter am dü - stern Ort? Mein Sohn, mein Sohn, ich

decresc.

seh' es ge - nau; es scheinen die al - ten Wei - den so grau.

cresc. *ff*

„Ich lie - be dich, mich

p *pp*

reizt dei - ne schö - ne Ge - stalt; und bist du nicht wil - lig, so brauch' ich Ge -

walt". Mein Va - ter, mein Va - ter, jetzt fasst er mich an! Erl - kö - nig
fff
fz fz
hat mir ein Leids ge - than! Dem Va - ter
fz fz fz fz
f
accelerando
grau - set's, er rei - tet geschwind, er hält in Ar - men das
cresc.
äch - zen - de Kind, er - reicht den
ff
fz
Recit.
Hof mit Müh' und Noth; in seinen Armen das Kind war todt.
Andante.
fz
fp
pp
p
f

Translation

Wer reitet so spät durch Nacht
und Wind?
Es ist der Vater mit seinem Kind;
er hat den Knaben wohl in dem Arm,
er fasst ihn sicher, er hält ihn warm.

"Mein Sohn, was birgst du so bang dein
Gesicht?"
"Siehst, Vater, du den Erlkönig nicht?
den Erlenkönig mit Kron' und Schweif?"
"Mein Sohn, es ist ein Nebelstreif."

"Du liebes Kind, komm, geh' mit mir!
gar schöne Spiele spiel' ich mit dir;
manch' bunte Blumen sind an dem Strand;
meine Mutter hat manch' gülden Gewand."

"Mein Vater, mein Vater, und hörest du
nicht,
was Erlenkönig mir leise verspricht?"
"Sei ruhig, bleibe ruhig, mein Kind;
in dürren Blättern säuselt der Wind."

"Willst, feiner Knage, du mit mir geh'n?
meine Töchter sollen dich warten schön;
meine Töchter führen den nächtlichen
Reih'n
und wiegen und tanzen und singen dich ein."

"Mein Vater, mein Vater, und siehst du nicht
dort
Erlkönigs Töchter am düstern Ort?"
"Mein Sohn, mein Sohn, ich seh' es genau,
es scheinen die alten Weiden so grau."

"Ich liebe dich, mich reizt deine schöne
Gestalt,
und bist du nicht willig, so brauch' ich
Gewalt."
"Mein Vater, mein Vater, jetzt fasst er
mich an!
Erlkönig hat mir ein Leid's gethan!"

Dem Vater grauset's, er reitet geschwind,
er hält in Armen das ächzende Kind,
erreicht den Hof mit Müh' und Noth:
in seinem Armen das Kind war todt!

JOHANN WOLFGANG VON GOETHE

Who rides so late through the night
and the wind?
It is the father with his child;
he folds the boy close in his arms,
he clasps him securely, he holds him warmly.

'My son, who do you hide your face so
anxiously?"
"Father, don't you see the Erlking?
The Erlking with his crown and his train?"
"My son, it is a streak of mist."

"Dear child, come, go with me!
I'll play the prettiest games with you.
Many colored flowers grow along the shore;
my mother has many golden garments."

"My father, my father, and don't you
hear
the Erlking whispering promises to me?"
"Be quiet, stay quiet, my child;
the wind is rustling in the dead leaves."

"My handsome boy, will you come with me?
My daughters shall wait upon you;
my daughters lead off in the dance every
night,
and cradle and dance and sing you to sleep."

"My father, my father, and don't you
see there
the Erlking's daughters in the shadows?"
"My son, my son, I see it clearly;
the old willows look so gray."

"I love you, your beautiful figure
delights me!
And if you are not willing, then I
shall use force!"
"My father, my father, now he is taking
hold of me!
The Erlking has hurt me!"

The father shudders, he rides swiftly on;
he holds in his arms the groaning child,
he reaches the courtyard weary and anxious:
in his arms the child was dead.

PHILIP L. MILLER

2. SCHUBERT, Fourth movement (Theme and Variations) from *Quintet in A major (Trout)* for Violin, Viola, Cello, Double Bass, and Piano (1819?)

Var. I
pp
p
pizz.
p
tr
1.
2.
30

tr
40
Var. II
p
arco
mf

1.
2.
50

fp
fp
60
Var. III
p
p
p
p
tr
f tr

1.

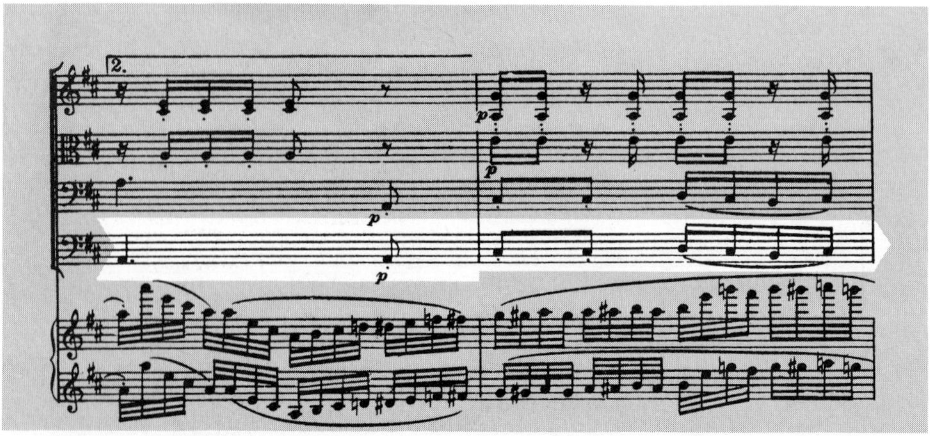

8

80

Var. IV
ff
fp
pp

tr
pp
90
decresc.
cresc.
p

tr
100
dim.
pp
p
decresc.
Var. V
1.

2.
110
pp
pp
p
pp
cresc.
cresc.
cresc.
cresc.
pp
pp
p
pp
pp
120
3
dim.

p
decresc.
decresc.
dim
dim.
dim.
dim.
dim.
Allegretto
130
p
p
p
p
p

140

160
decresc.
decresc.
p
decresc.
170
pp
dim.
pp
dim.
pp
dim.
pp
dim.
pp
dim.

3. SCHUBERT, First movement from *Symphony No. 8 in B minor* (*Unfinished*) (1822)

I

Allegro moderato.

10

Flutes

Oboes

Clarinets in A

Bassoons

Horns in D

Trumpets in E

Trombones: Alto, Tenor, Bass

Timpani in B, F♯

Violin I *pp*

Violin II *pp*

Viola pizz. *pp*

Cello *pp* pizz.

Bass *pp* pizz.

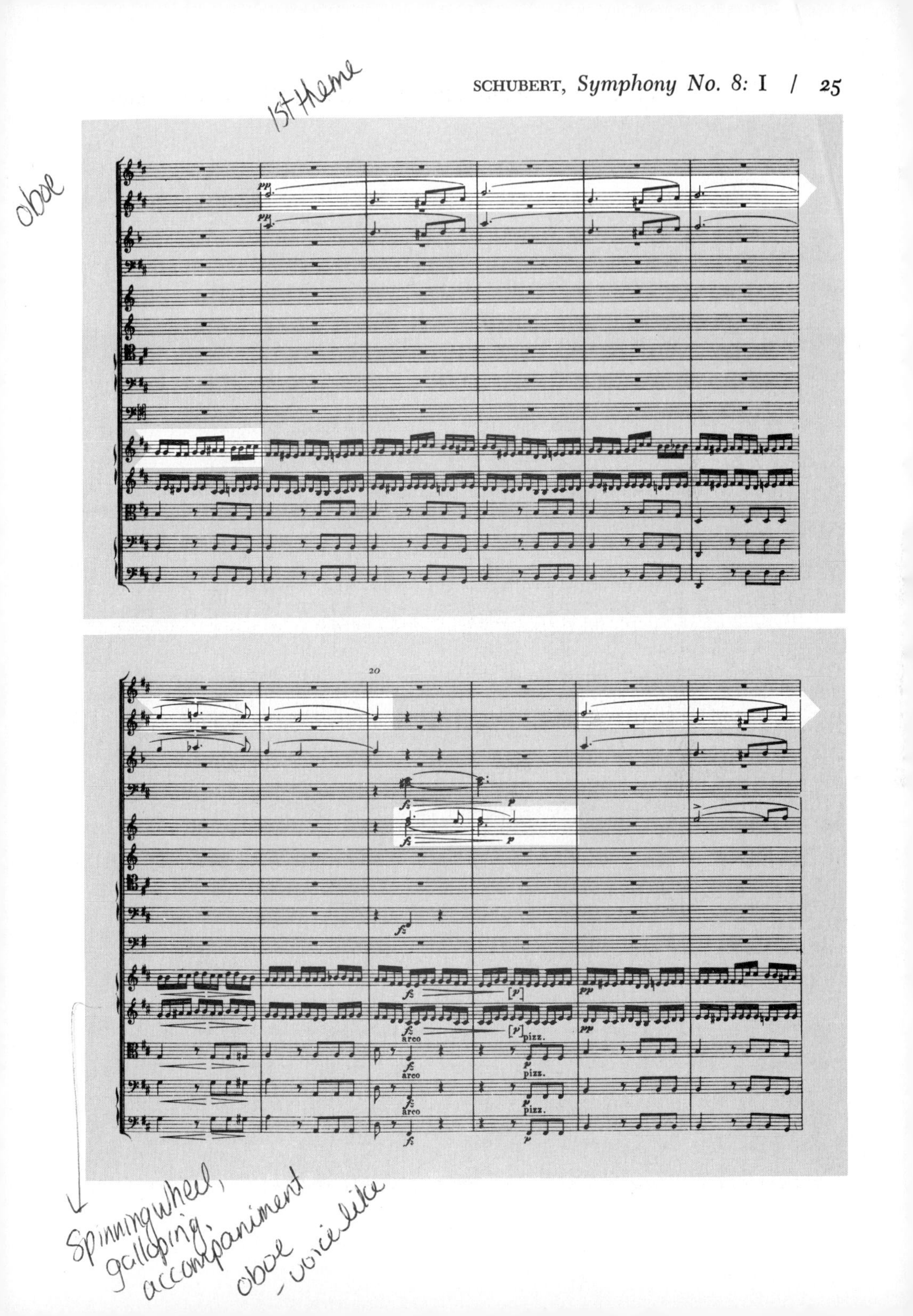

cresc.
p
fz
fp
arco

30
p
cresc.
a 2.
f
ff

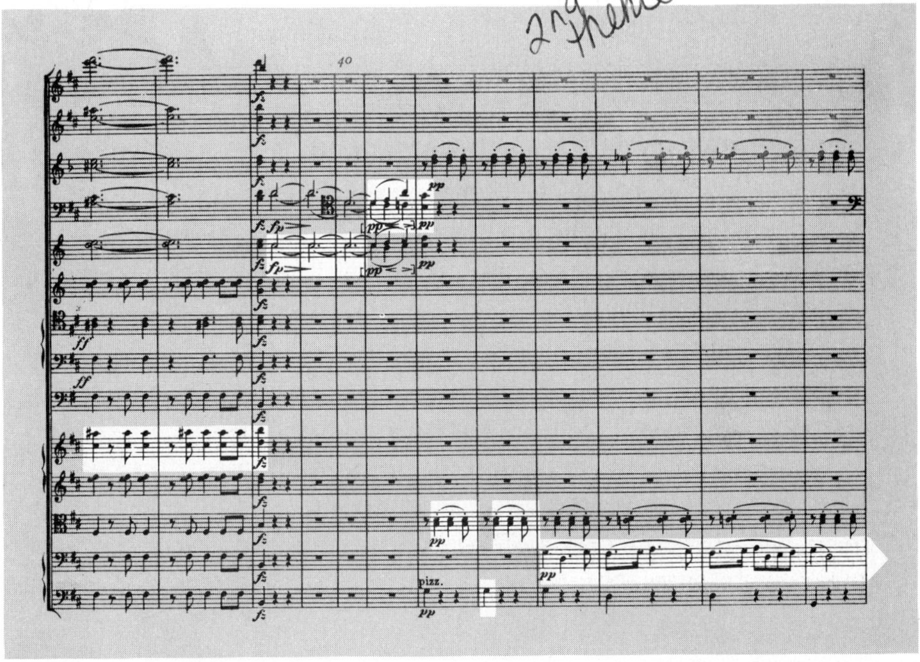

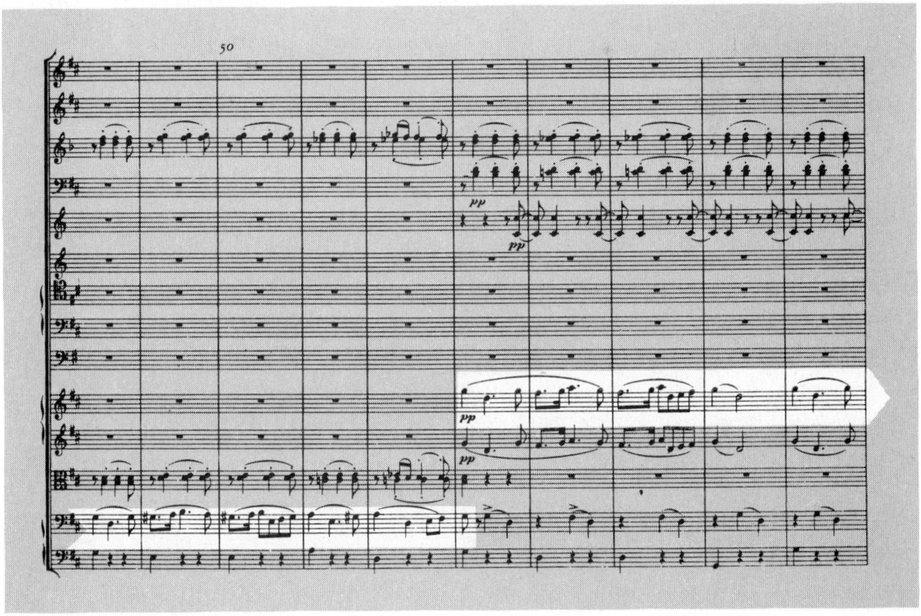

development of 2nd theme

100
110a
110b
a 2.
pizz.
arco

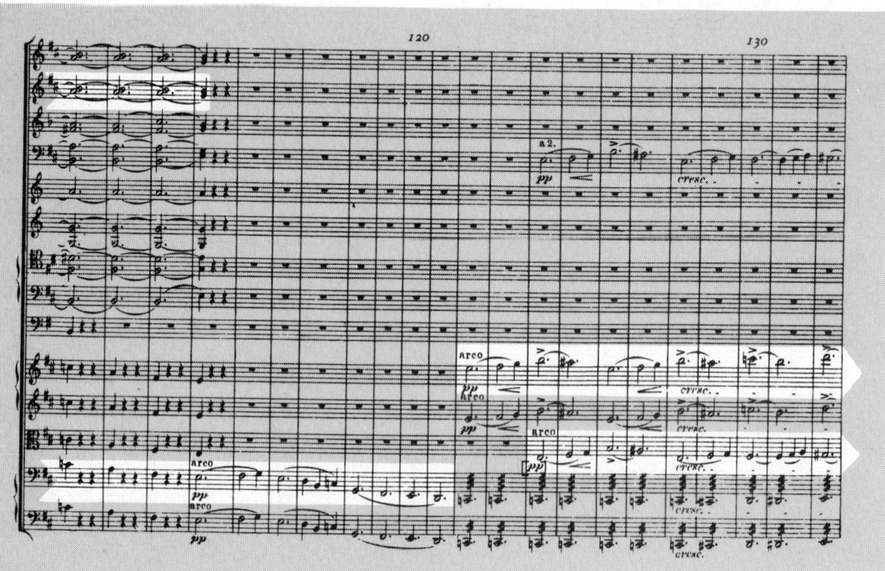
120
130
a 2.
arco
cresc.

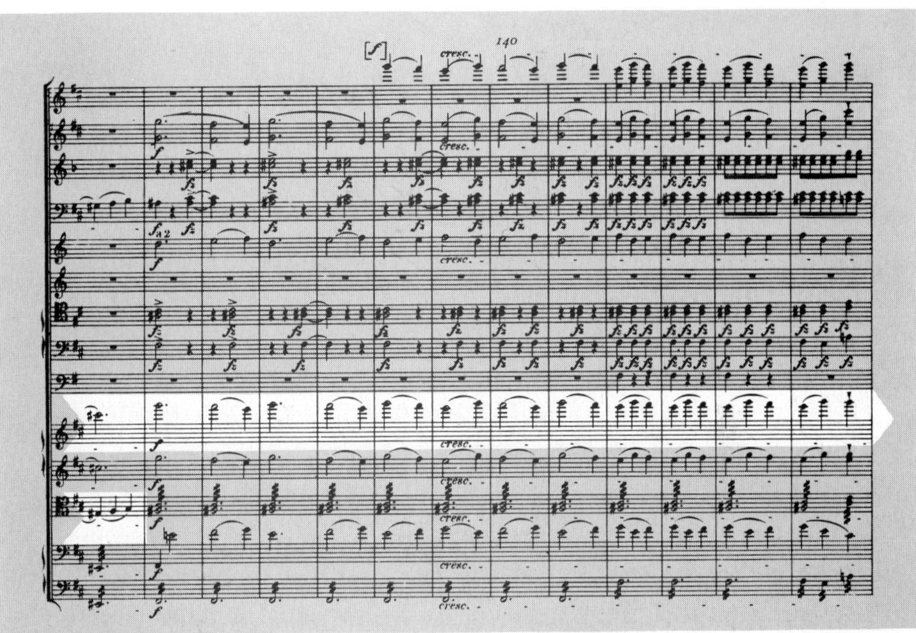

dramatic dynamic contrasts

160

170

contrasting
tone colour

a 2.

190
a 2.

recap.

220

240
cresc.
f
fz
fp
arco
p

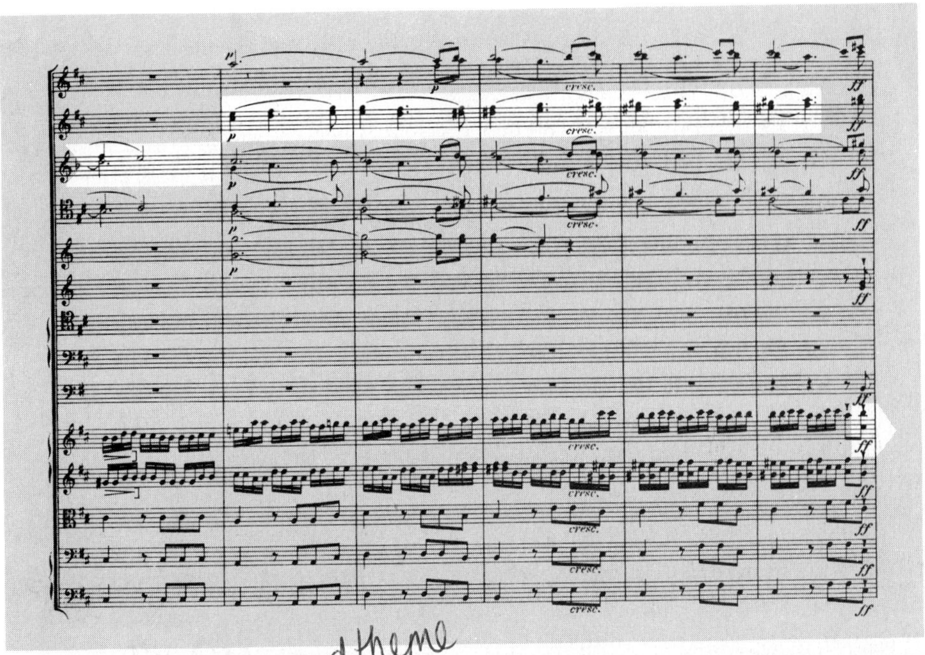

2nd theme

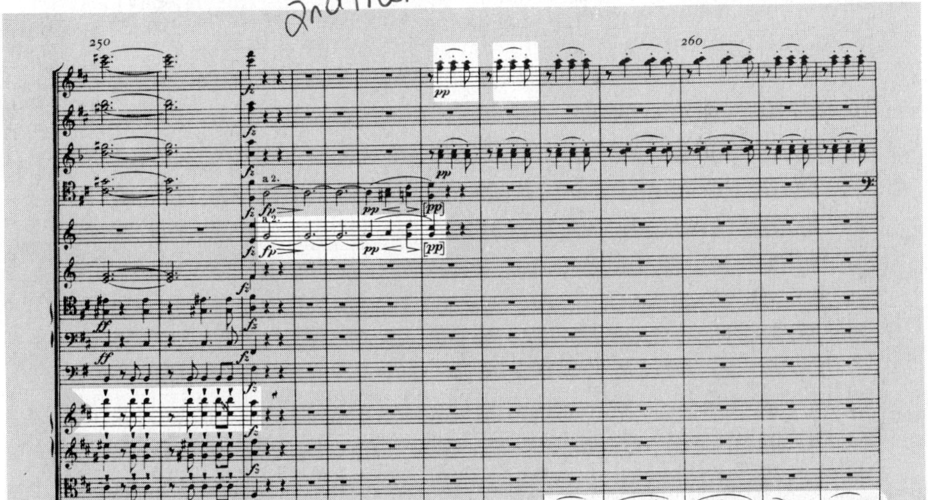

Favorite (melancholy)
cello
↓
violin

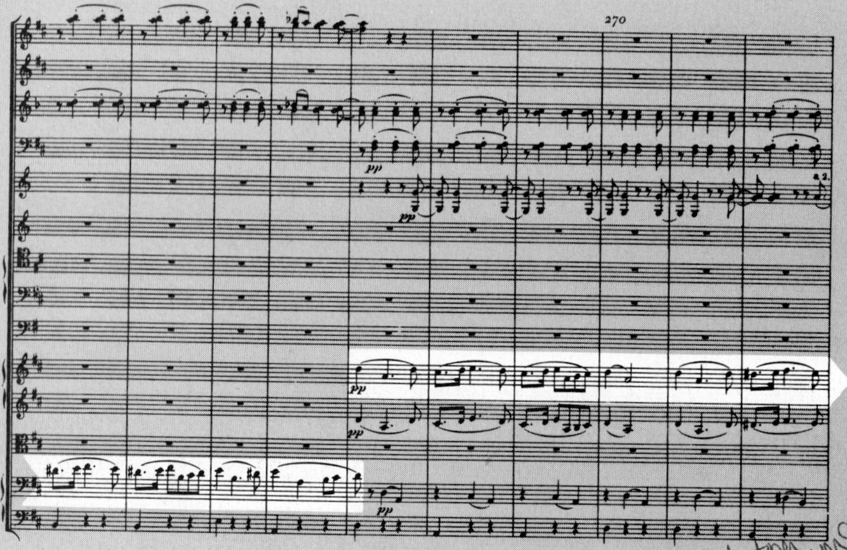
270
pp
a 2.

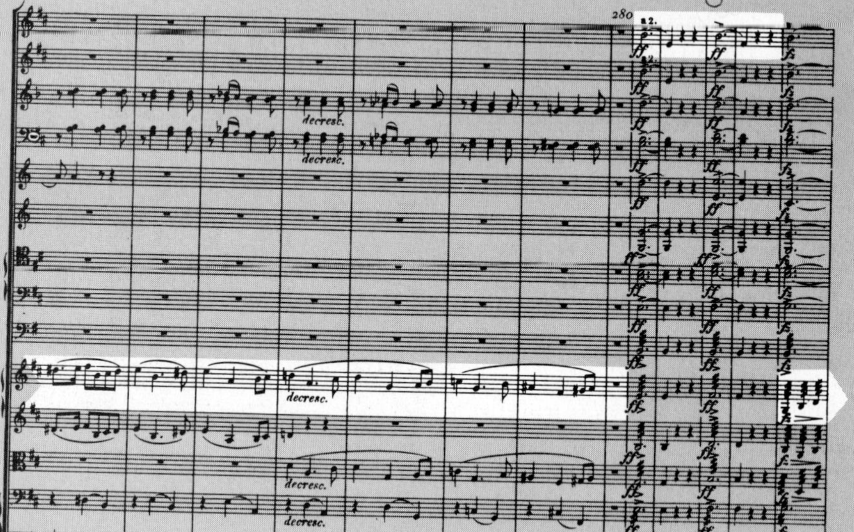
280
a 2.
decresc.
ff
f

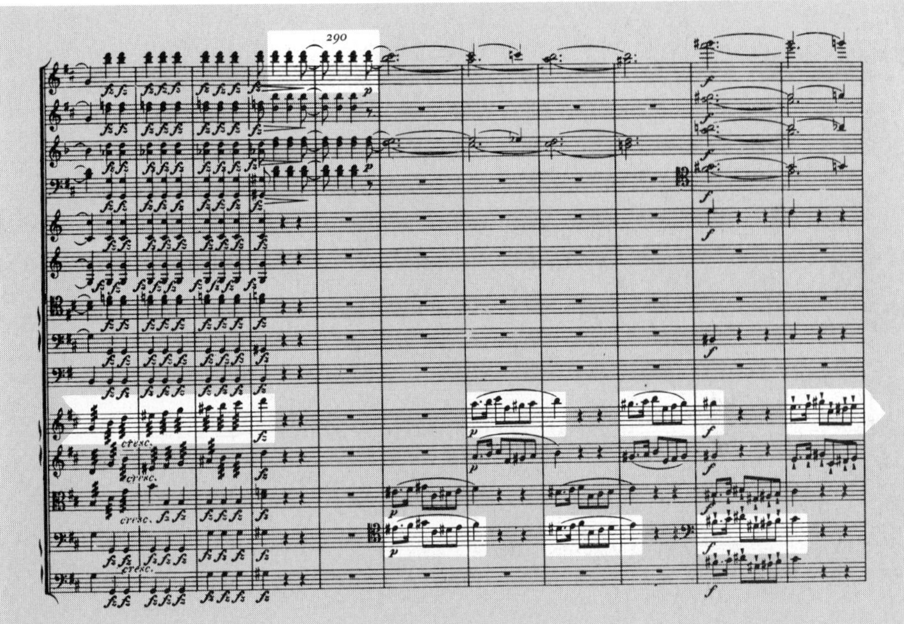
290
p
f
cresc.
fz

300
ff
fz

310
fz
p
pp
Coda
320
330
ff
a 2.
pizz.
arco

coda cont'd

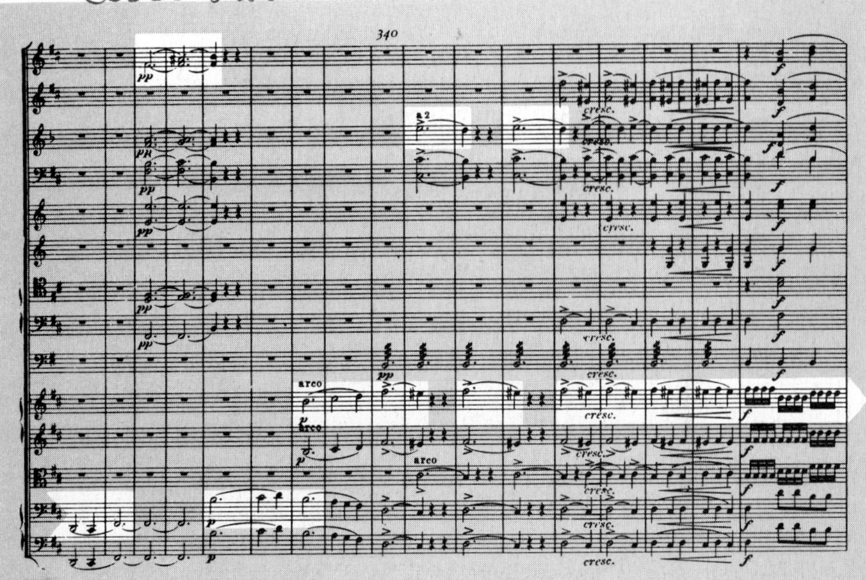

4. HECTOR BERLIOZ (1803-1869), Fifth movement from *Symphonie fantastique* (1830)

Dream of a Witches' Sabbath

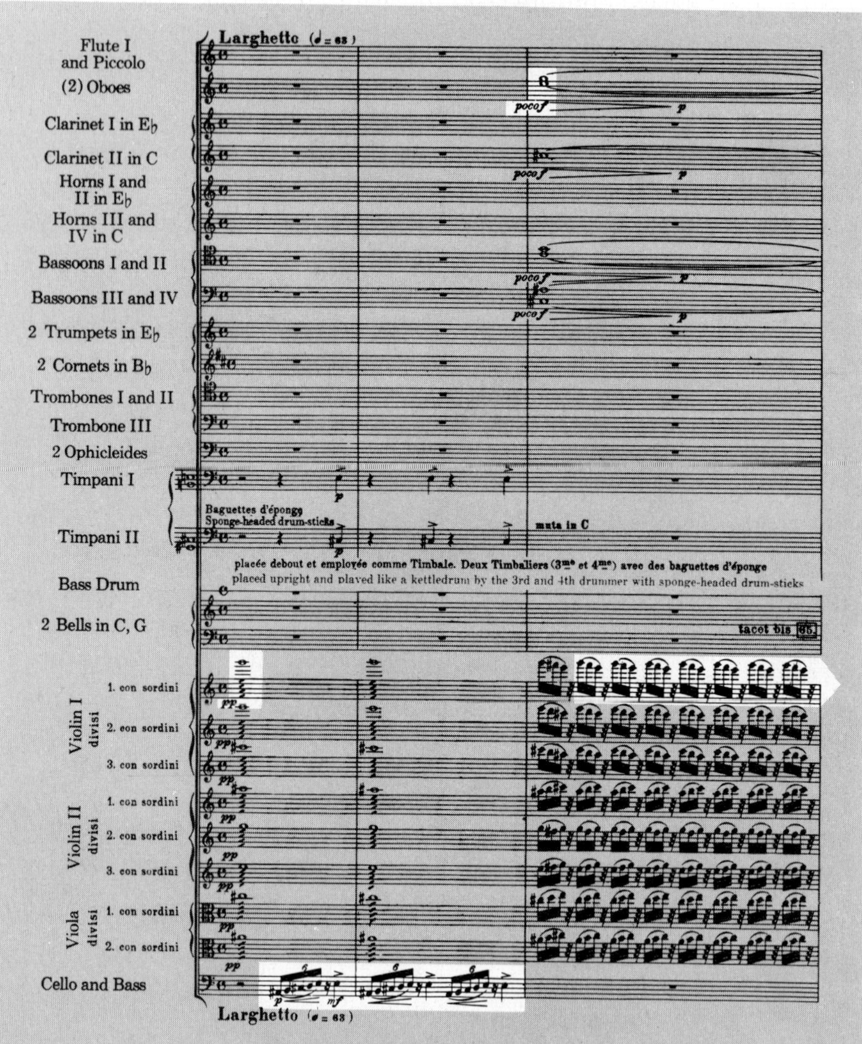

4
60
f
dim.
p
I.
pizz.
ppp
Vcllo.
C.B.
div.
mf
60

Fl. Solo
Fl. picc. Solo
a 2.
Soli
dim.
61
I. Solo
Solo III. bouché avec les cylindres
ppp stopped, with valves
II.
Deux timbaliers, roulement avec des baguettes à tête d'éponge sur la Grande Caisse placée debout
Two timpanists, rolling with sponge-headed sticks on the upright Bass Drum.
arco
unis.

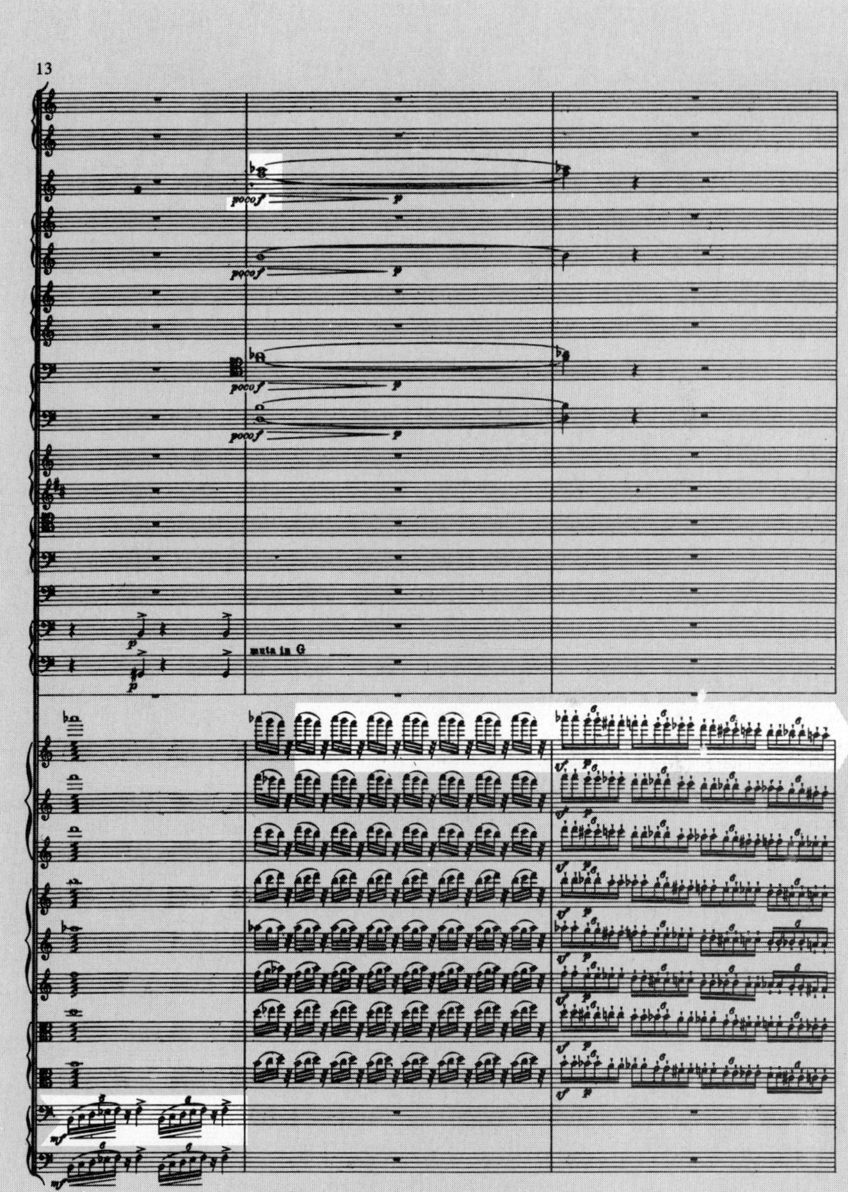
13
poco f
p
poco f
p
poco f
p
poco f
p
p
p
muta in G
mf
mf

16
62
Solo I
mf
dim.
sf>pp
Solo. III. bouché avec les cylindres
pppp
éponges
f
pp
sf>p
ôtez les sourdines
ôtez les sourdines
ôtez les sourdines
ôtez les sourdines
ôtez les sourdines
ôtez les sourdines
div.
div.
62

21

Allegro (♩. = 112)

Solo lointain distant

ppp

cresc.

ouvert avec les cylindres

open, with valves

p cresc. poco a poco

Sur les deux timbales

p

cresc. poco a poco

cresc. poco a poco

sans sourdine

sans sourdine

Allegro (♩. = 112)

Allegro assai (𝅝 = 76)

a 2.

I.

Allegro assai (𝅝 = 76)

32

63
40
Allegro (♩. = 104)
Fl. picc.
mf
Ob.
poco f
Clar. I in E♭
Solo
poco f
cresc.
Clar. II in C
poco f
Fag.
unis.
mf
Viol. I unis.
Viol. II unis.
Viola unis.
Vcllo.
C.B.
Allegro (♩. = 104)
63

49
Fl. picc.
Ob.
Clar.
Fag.
Viol.
pp
pp

55
Fl.
Fl. picc.
Ob.
Clar.
Cor.
Fag.
Viol.
a2

61
64
Fl.
Fl. pic.
Ob.
Clar.
Cor.
Fag.
(cresc.)
Viol.
cresc.
64

67
Fl.
Fl. picc.
Ob.
Clar.
a 2.
Cor.
a 2.
unis.
Fag.
Tr.
C^tti
Tromb.
Oph.
Timp.
Viol.

74

𝅗𝅥 = 𝅗𝅥.

a 2.

a 2.

a 2.

unis.

a 2.

a 2.

𝅗𝅥 = 𝅗𝅥.

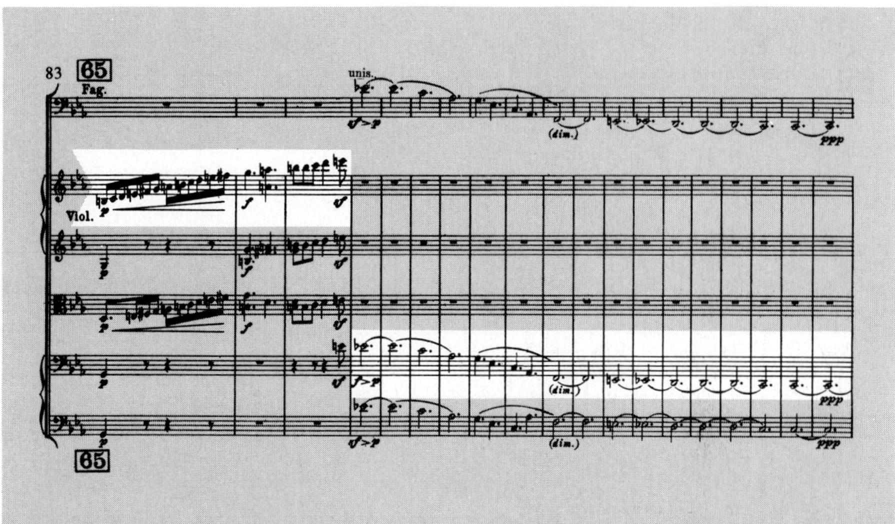
83
65
Fag.
unis.
sf>p
(dim.)
ppp
Viol.
p
f
sf
65

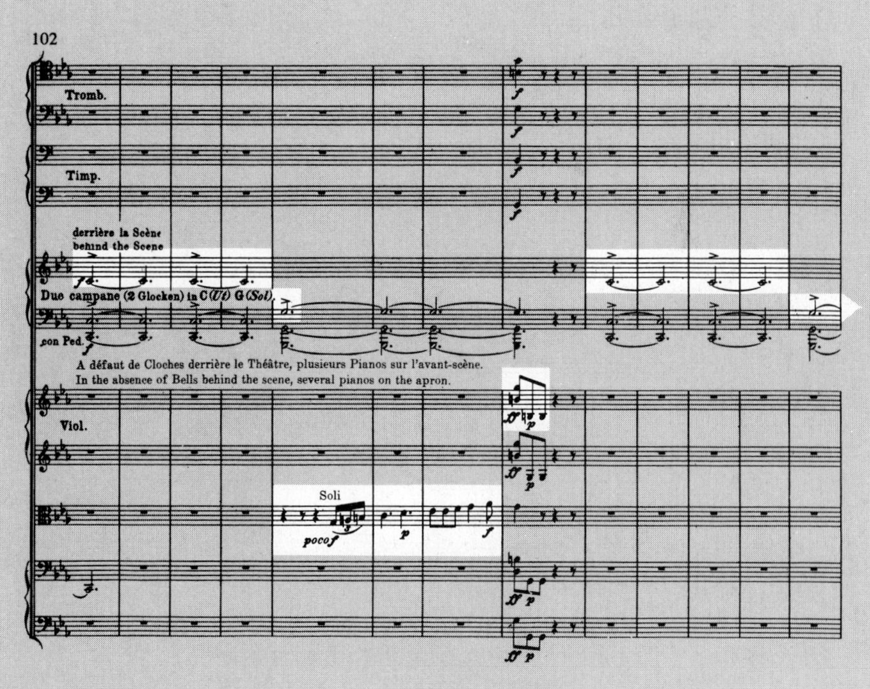
102
Tromb.
Timp.
derrière la Scène
behind the Scene
Due campane (2 Glocken) in C (Ut) G (Sol).
con Ped.
A défaut de Cloches derrière le Théâtre, plusieurs Pianos sur l'avant-scène.
In the absence of Bells behind the scene, several pianos on the apron.
Viol.
Soli
poco f
ff
p

115
66
Ob. I. Solo
mf
a 2.
Cor.
Tr.
Tromb.
Timp.
Camp.
p
pp
Viol.
66

Dies iræ
127 sans presser
Fag. unis.
Oph. a 2.
Soli
f
Camp.
Viol.
sans presser

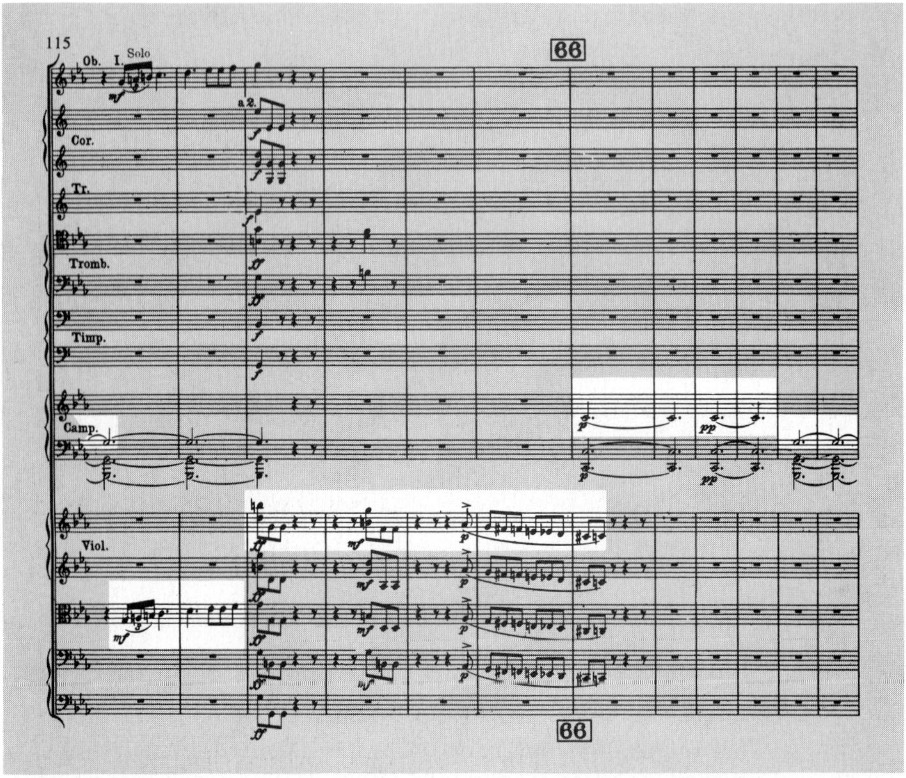

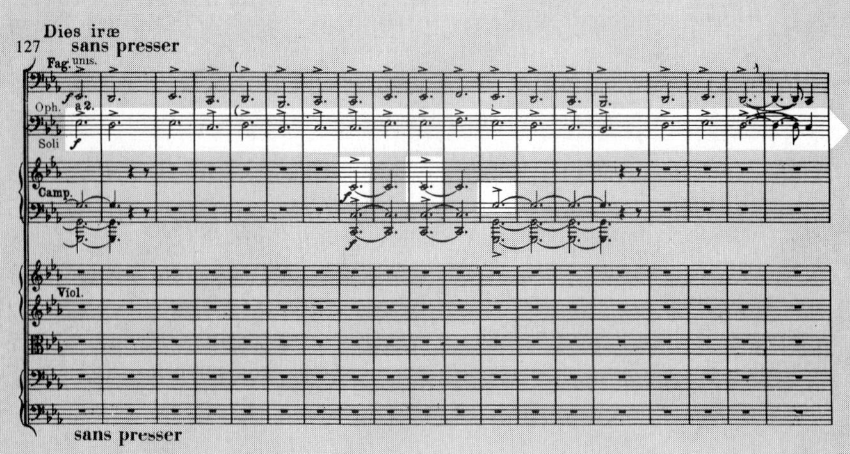

146
Fl.
Fl. picc.
Ob.
Clar.
Cor.
Fag.
Tr.
Ctti
Tromb
Oph.
Gr. Tamb.
Camp.
pizz.
Viol.
pizz.
pizz.

159
67
arco
arco
arco
pizz.
pizz.
67

171
pizz.
pizz.
pizz.

184
68
arco
arco
arco
arco
arco
tenu
tenu
68

196

209
pizz.
pizz.
pizz.

221 69

a2.

a2.

G-Caisse roulante, deux Timbaliers

Bass-Drum roll, two timpanists

arco

arco

arco

69

231
70
Fl.
Fl. picc.
Ob.
Clar.
Cor.
Fag.
Tr.
Ctti
Tromb.
Oph.
Baguettes d'éponge
Sponge-headed sticks
Timp.
Baguettes d'éponge
Sponge-headed sticks
Viol.
cresc.
a 2
a 4.
70

Ronde du Sabbat
Witches' round dance
241 **Un peu retenu**

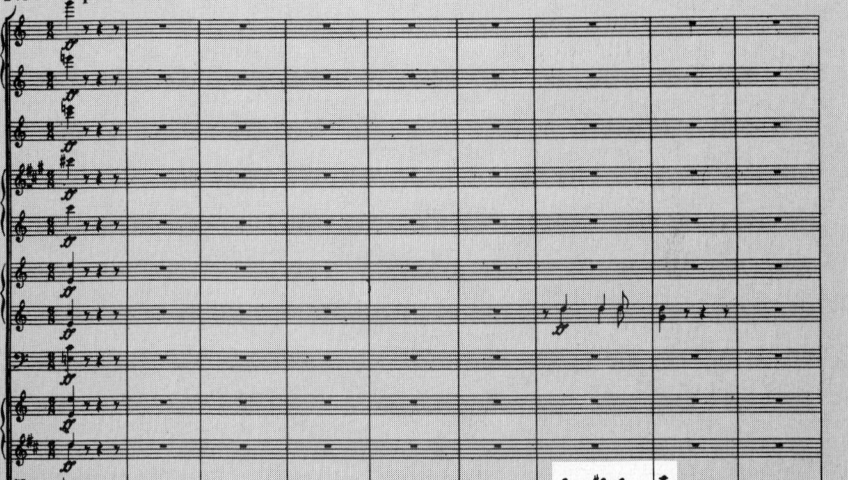

I.

Un peu retenu

250
71
I.
71

257
I.
a 2.
a 2.
unis.

265
72
unis.
a 2.
a 2.
mf
cresc.
72

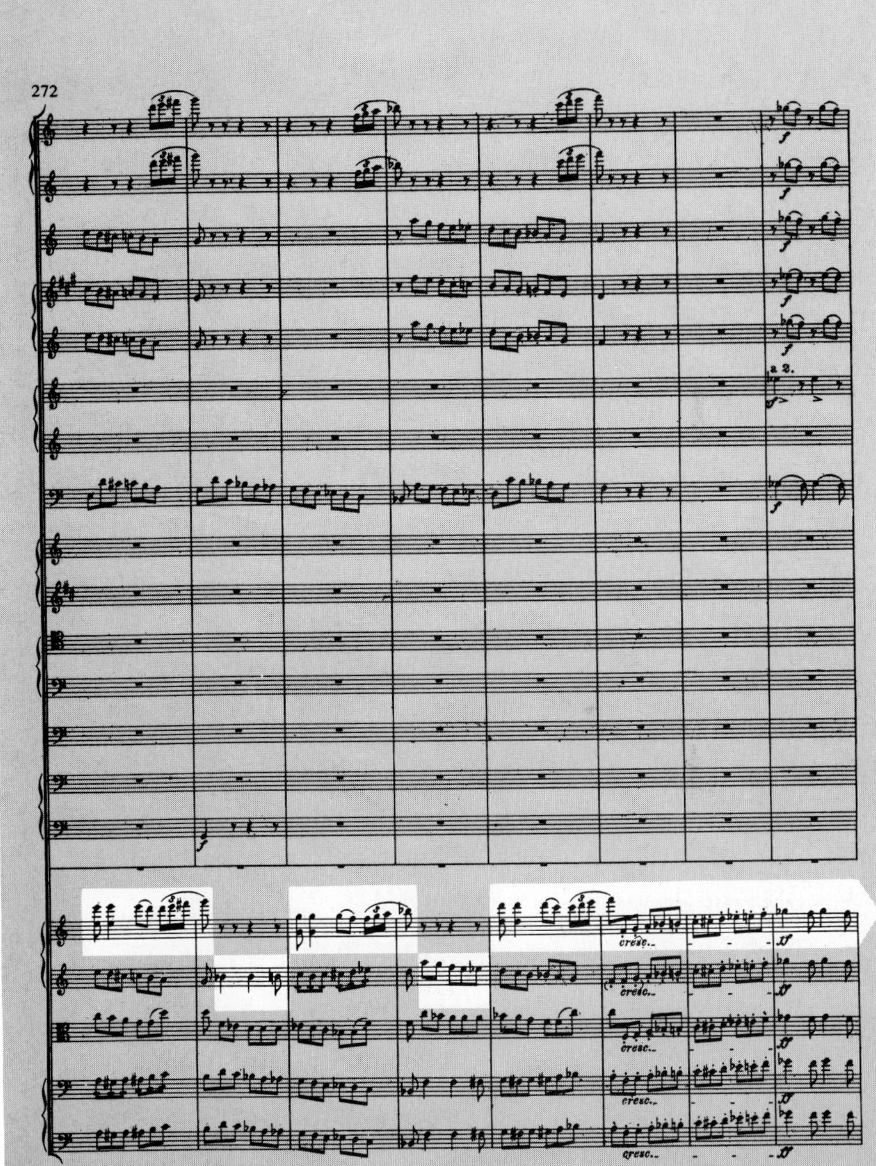
272
a 2.
cresc.
cresc.
cresc.
cresc.
cresc.

280

73

III.

a 2.

a 2.

a 2.

f

p *cresc.*

ff

73

289
I.
(cresc.)
(cresc.)

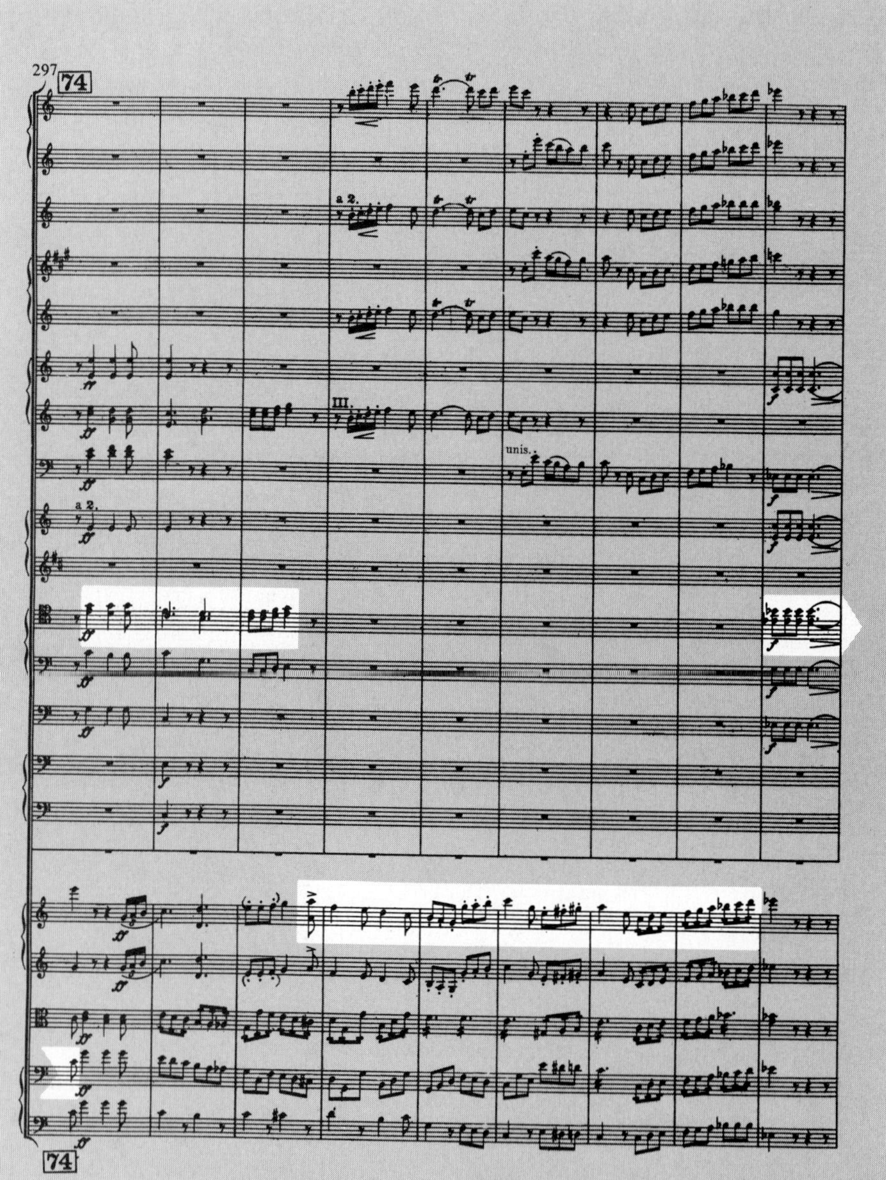
297
74
a 2.
III.
unis.
a 2.
74

306
Soli
éponges
pizz.
arco
pizz.
arco
pizz.
arco

313
f dimin.
f dimin.
f (dimin.
f dimin.
f dimin.
a 2.
ff
p
a 2.
ff
p
ff
pp
pizz.
arco
f
ff

320 75

a 2.

unis.

a 2.

a 2.

a 2.

pizz.

pizz.

75

327
76
I.
III.
Soli
dim.
pp
sf
Soli
unis. Soli
arco
arco
en dim. toujours
en dim. toujours
(en dim. toujours)
pizz.
poco f
pizz.
poco f
76

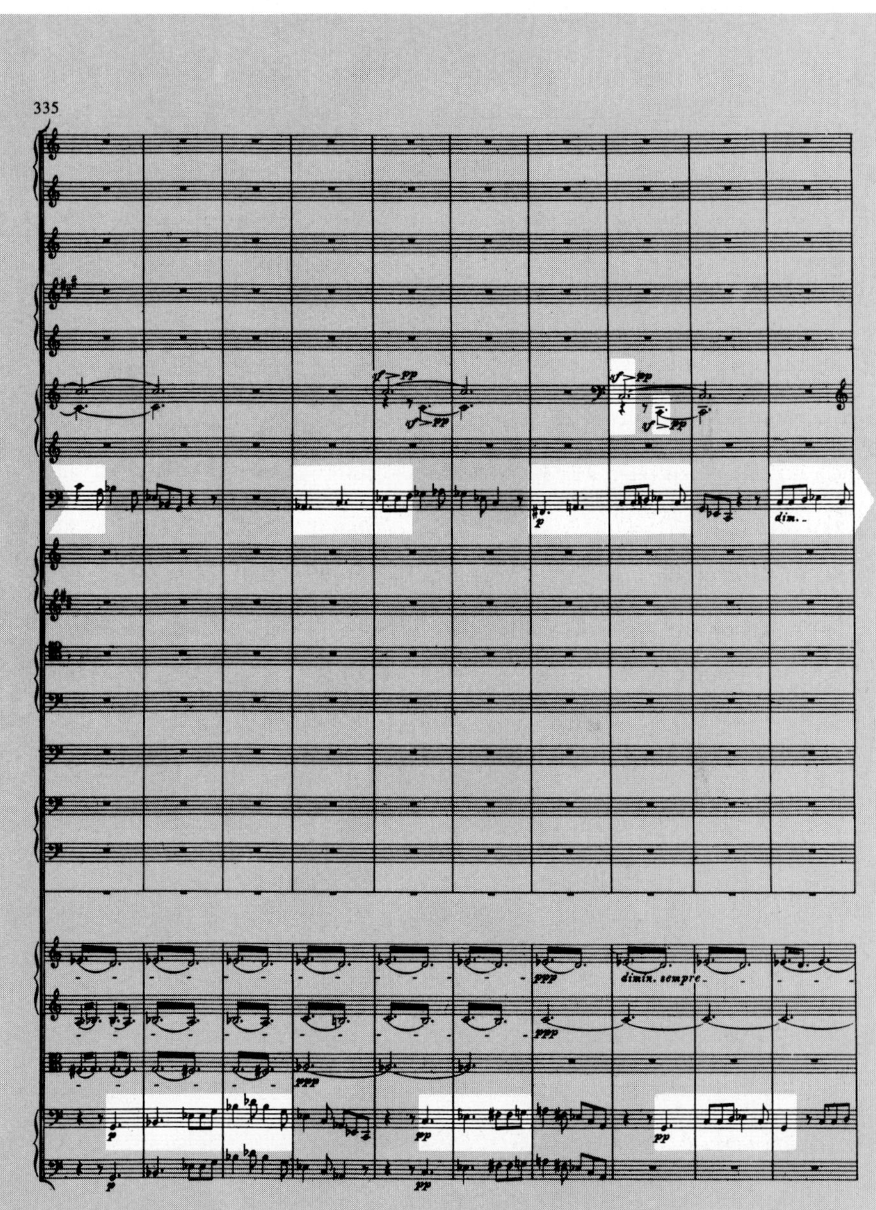
335
sf > pp
sf > pp
sf > pp
sf > pp
p
dim.
ppp
dimin. sempre
ppp
ppp
p
pp
pp
p
pp

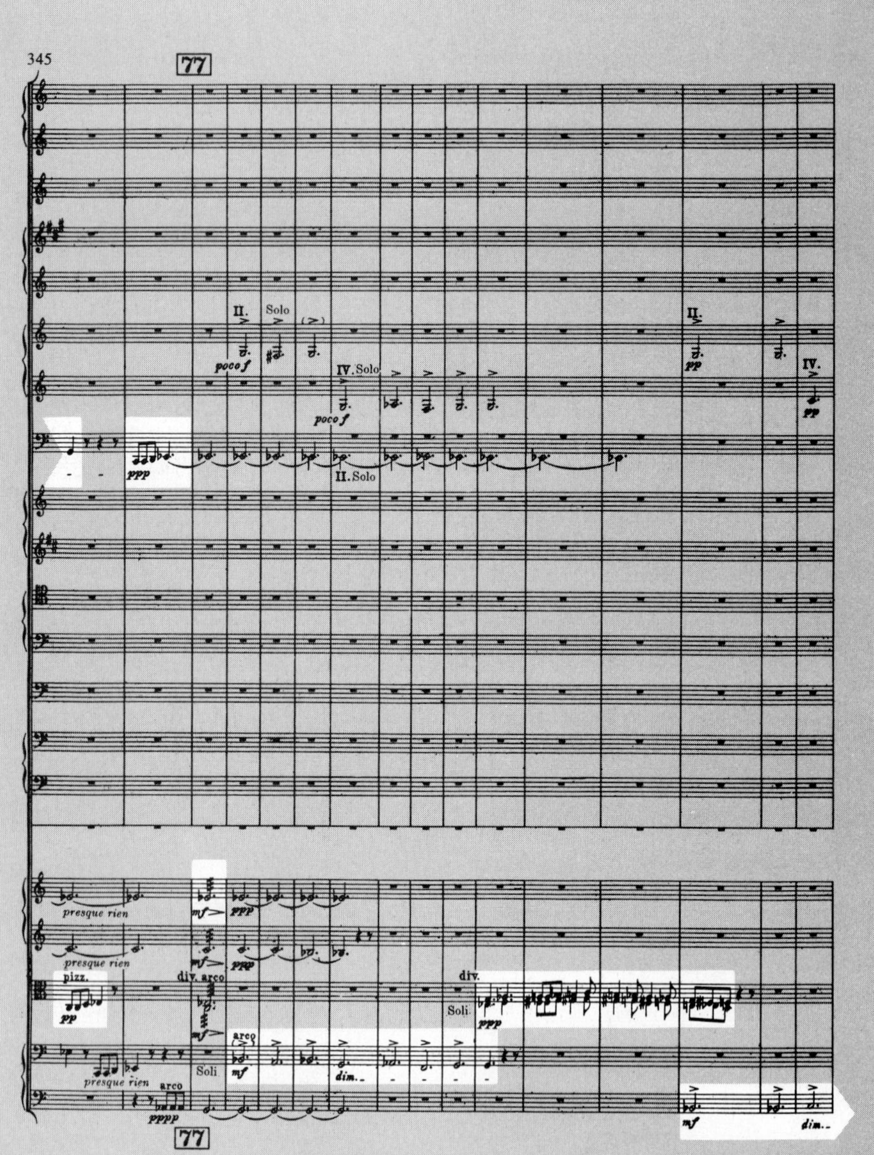
345
77
II.
Solo
poco f
IV. Solo
poco f
II.
pp
IV.
pp
ppp
II. Solo
presque rien
mf
ppp
presque rien
pizz.
pp
div. arco
div.
Soli
ppp
arco
Soli
mf
dim.
presque rien
arco
pppp
mf
dim.
77

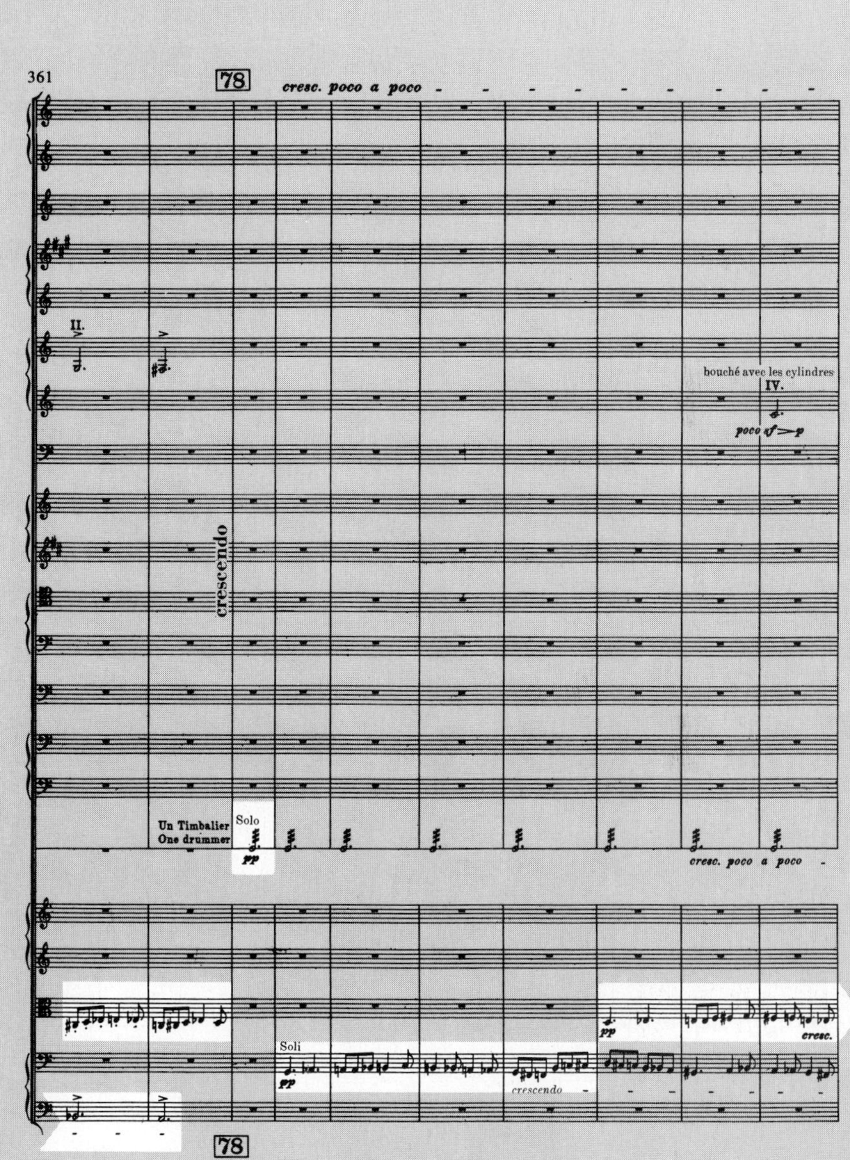
361
78
cresc. poco a poco
II.
bouché avec les cylindres
IV.
poco sf > p
crescendo
Un Timbalier
One drummer
Solo
pp
cresc. poco a poco
Soli
pp
crescendo
pp
cresc.
78

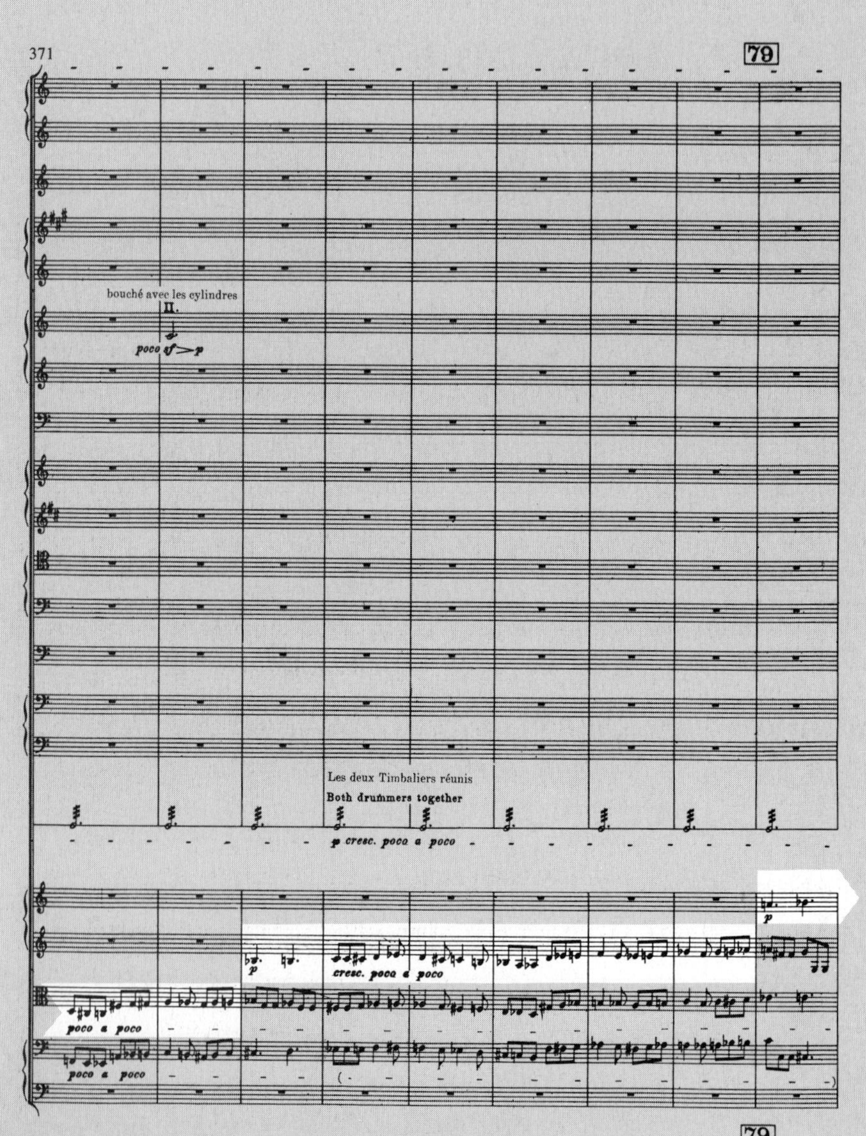
371
79
bouché avec les cylindres
II.
poco sf > p
Les deux Timbaliers réunis
Both drummers together
p cresc. poco a poco
p
p
cresc. poco a poco
poco a poco
poco a poco
79

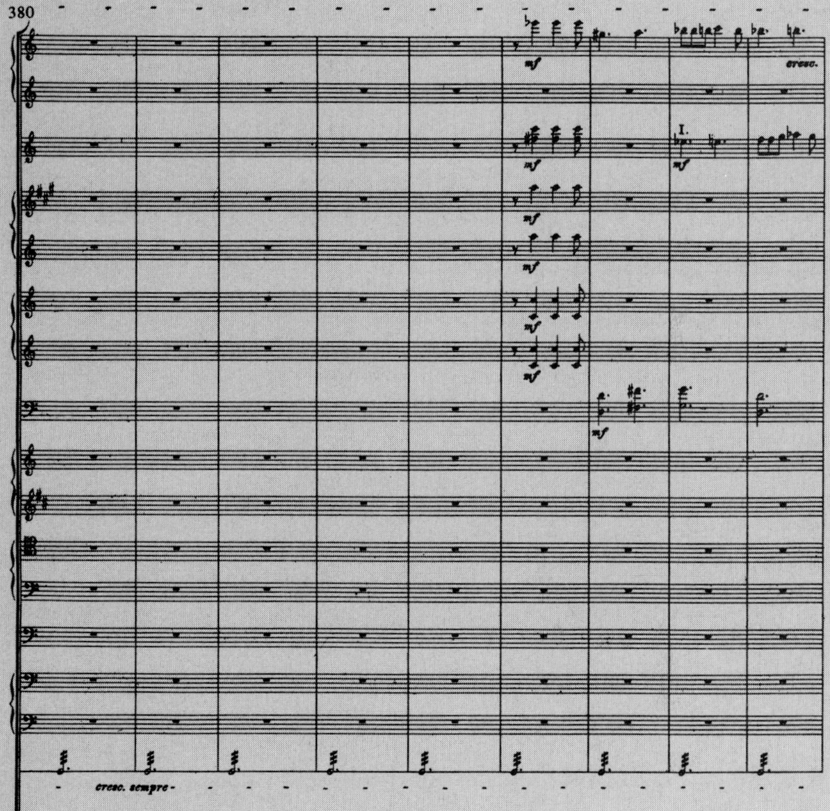

380

mf cresc.

mf

cresc. sempre

cresc. poco a poco

cresc. (poco a poco)

(cresc. poco a poco)

mf cresc sempre

f cresc. sempre

cresc. sempre

389
80
ff
mf
mf
f
unis.
a 2.
cresc. molto
div.
unis.
80

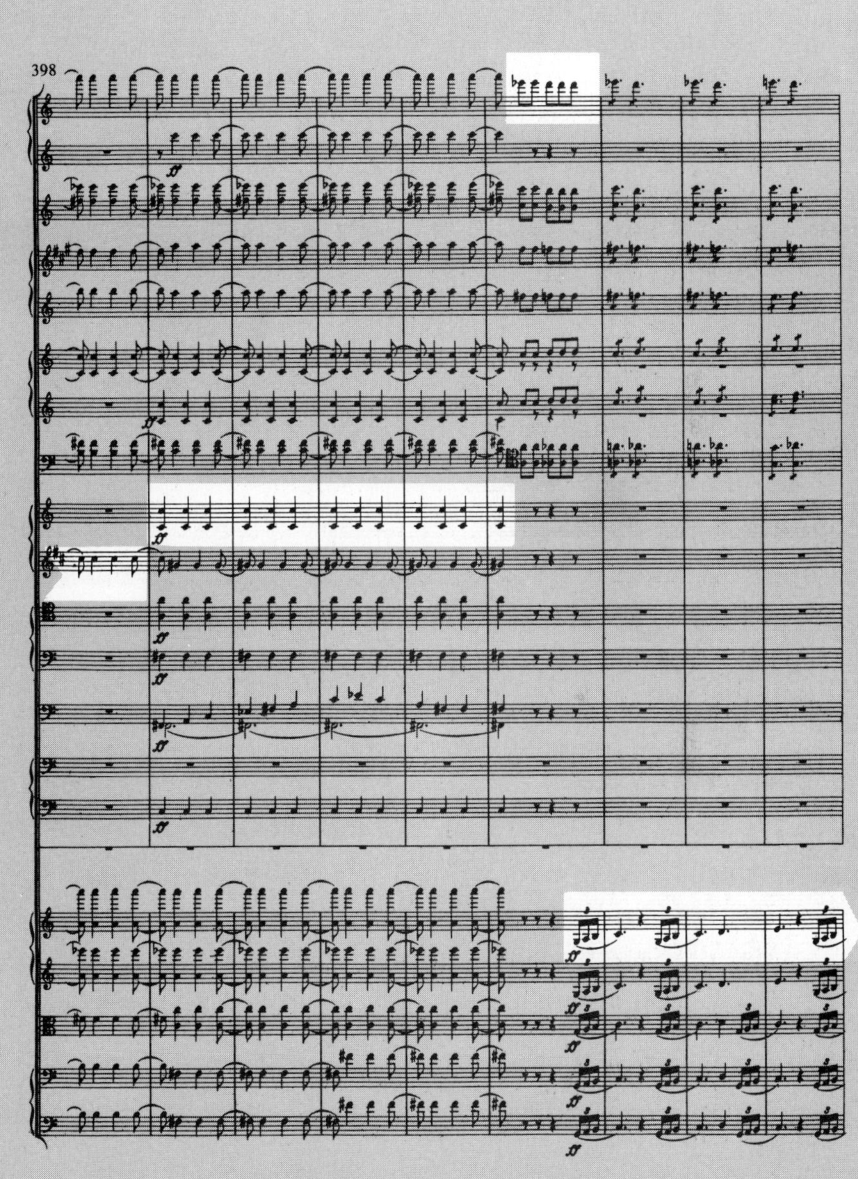
398

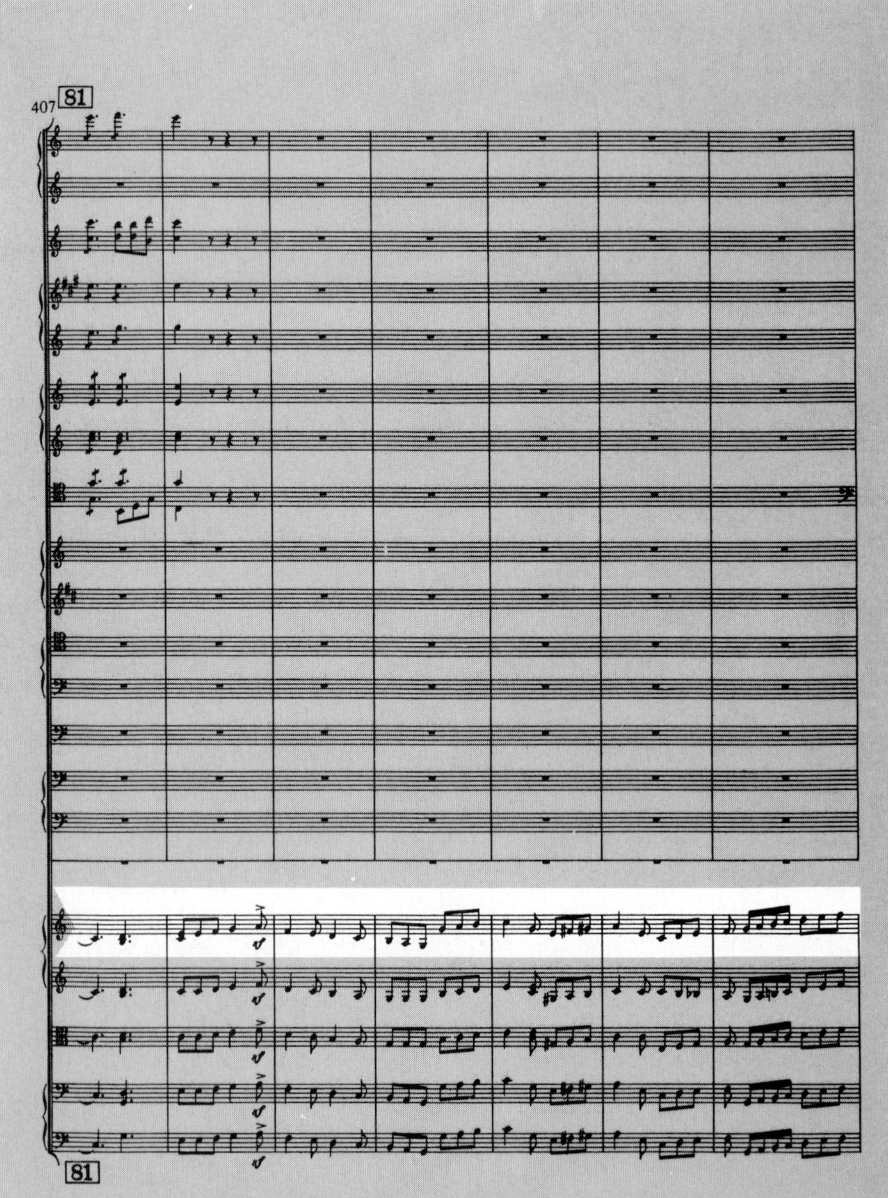
407
81
81

414 Dies irae et Ronde du Sabbat ensemble
Dies irae and witches' round dance together

a 2.

unis.

a 2.

a 2.

a 2.

423

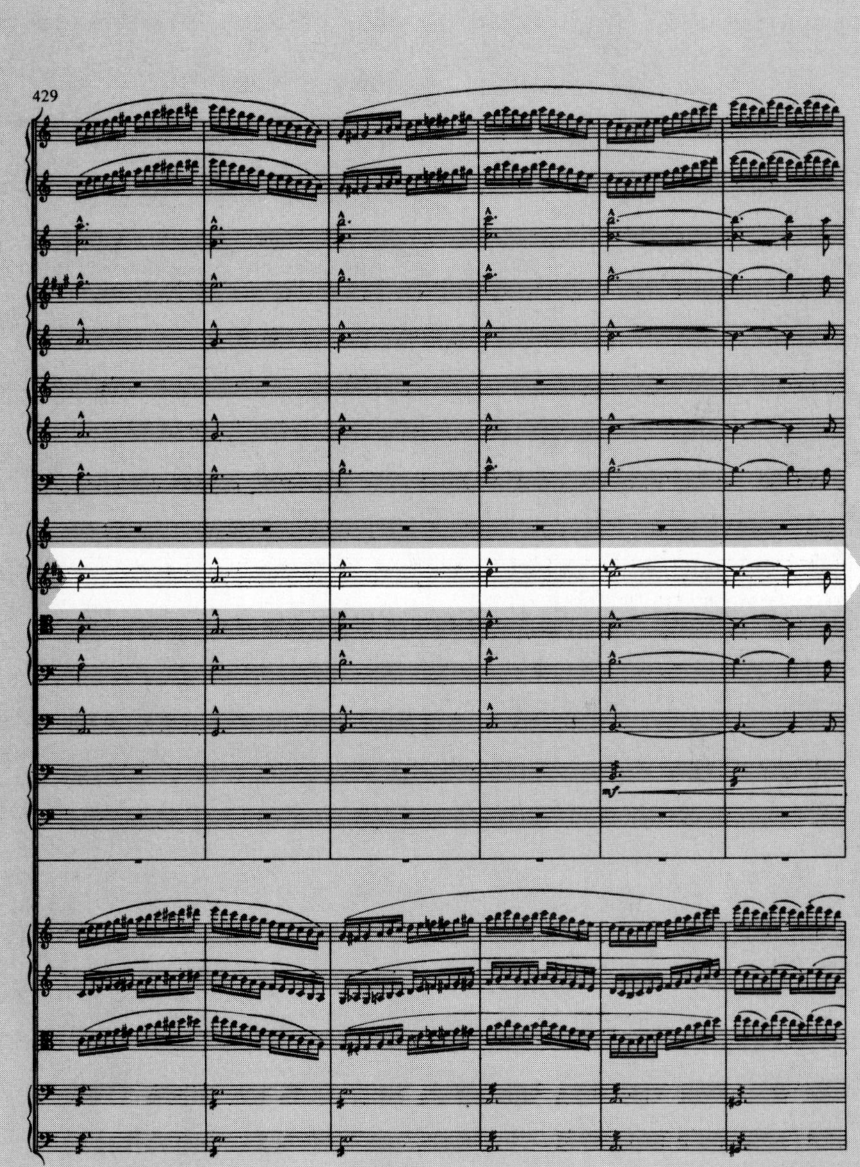
429

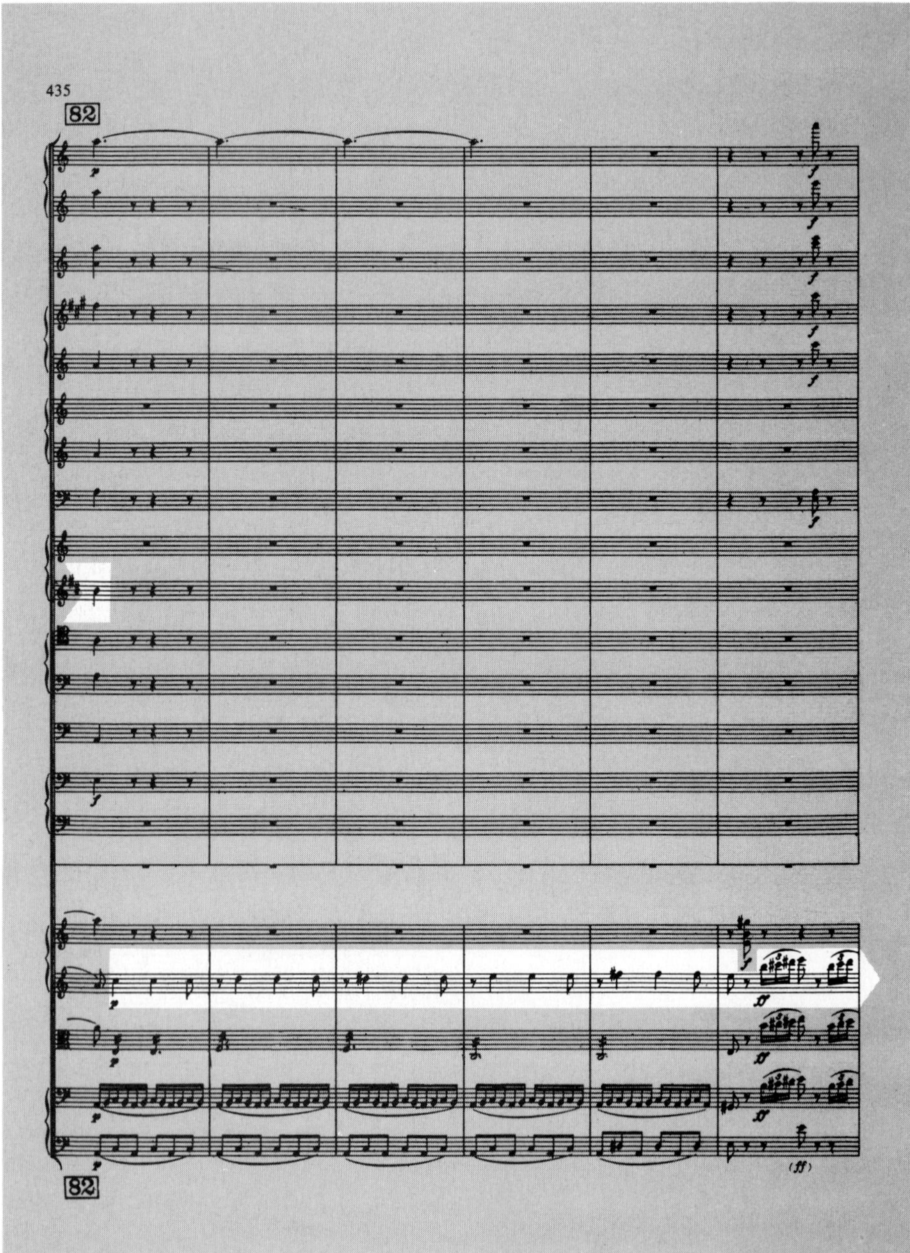

435
82
82

441
83
a 2.
mf
unis.
frappez avec les bois de l'archet
frappez avec les bois de l'archet
frappez avec les bois de l'archet
(col legno battuta)
div.
83

448

pizz.
pp
pizz.
pp

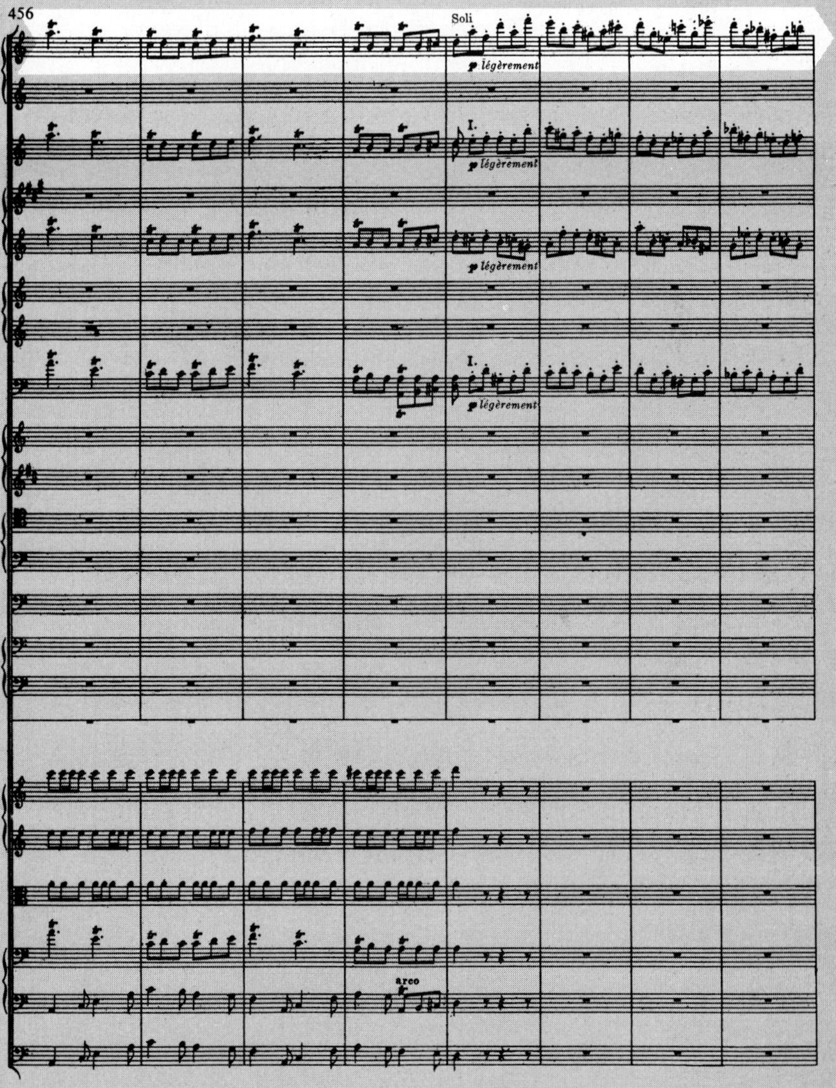

456

Soli

p légèrement

I.

p légèrement

p légèrement

I.

p légèrement

arco

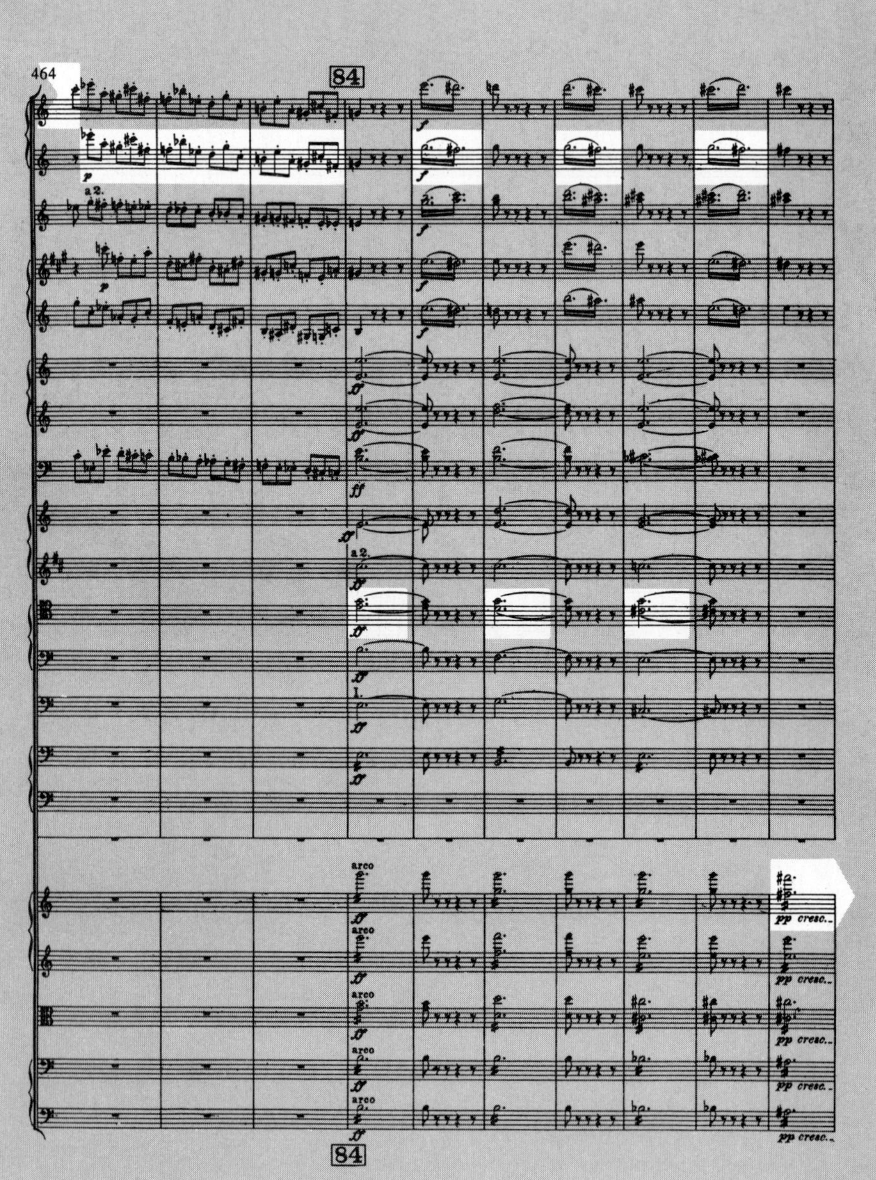
464
84
a 2.
p
f
ff
a 2.
1.
arco
pp cresc.
84

474
Soli
I.
a 2.
unis.
cresc.

85
483
a 2.
Solo II.
unis.
a 2.
cresc. molto
a 2.
85

animez un peu

493

animez un peu

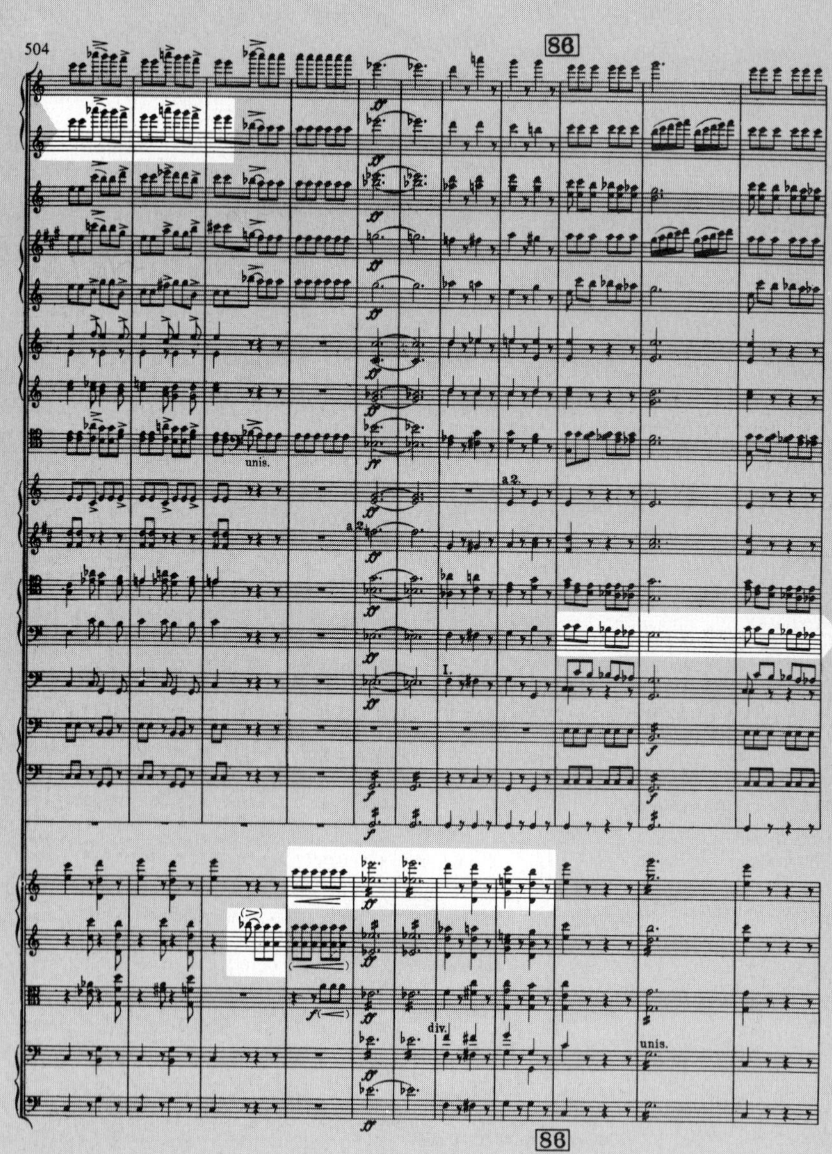
504
86
unis.
a 2.
a 2.
I.
div.
unis.
86

515

tenu

unis.

Coup frappé sur une Cymbale avec une baguette couverte d'éponge ou un tampon

Struck on a cymbal with a sponge-headed drum-stick or a padded stick

Cinelli.

5. FELIX MENDELSSOHN (1809-1847), Overture to *A Midsummer Night's Dream* (1826)

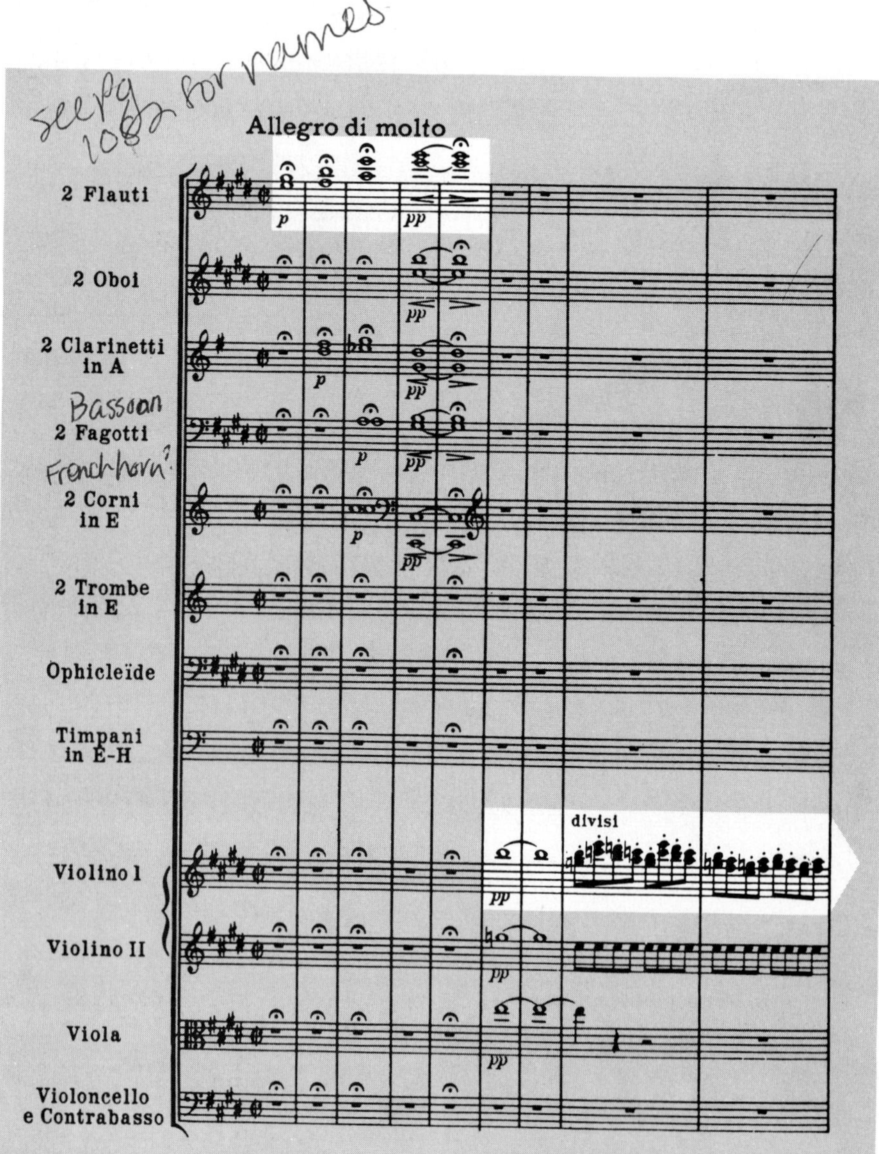

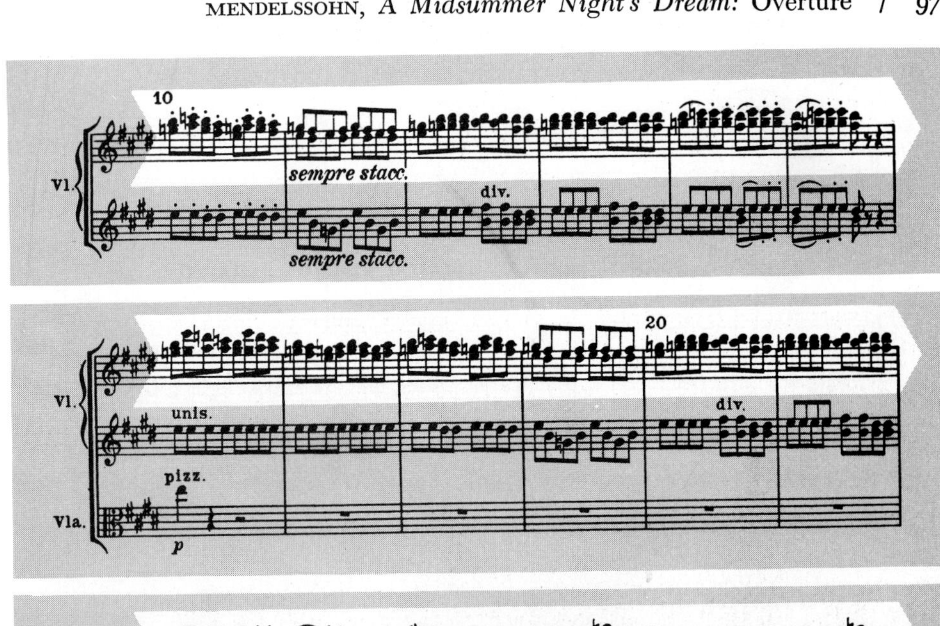
10
Vl.
sempre stacc.
div.
sempre stacc.
20
unis.
div.
pizz.
Vla.
p

Vl.
pp stacc.
stacc.
pp pizz.
pizz.
Vla.
pp

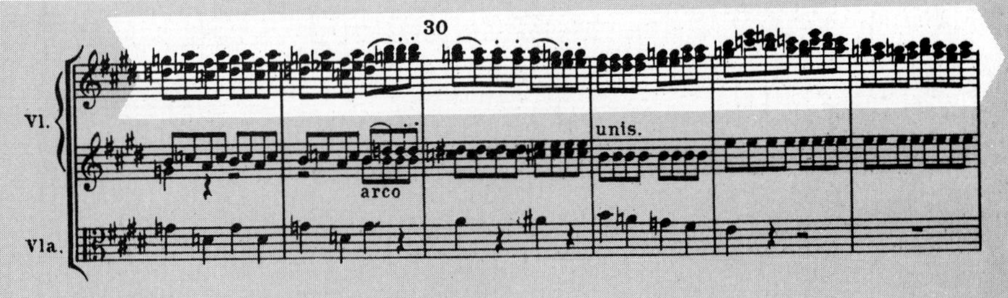
30
Vl.
unis.
arco
Vla.

Vl.
div.

40

Fl. *pp*

Cl. (A) *pp*

Fg. *pp*

Cor. (E) *pp*

Vl. div. arco pizz.

Vla. pizz.

50

Vl. arco unis. div.

Vla.

Fl. *pp*

Cl. (A)

Fg.

Cor. (E) *pp*

Vl. *pp* *pp*

60
Fl.
Ob.
Cl. (A)
Fg.
Cor. (E)
Tr. (E)
Oph.
Timp.
Vl.
Vla.
Vc. e Cb.
ff
tr
unis.
arco

70
Fl.
Ob.
Cl. (A)
Fg.
Cor. (E)
Tr. (E)
Oph.
Timp.
Vl.
Vla.
Vc. e Cb.
ff
sf
tr

80
Fl.
Ob.
Cl. (A)
Fg.
Cor. (E)
Tr. (E)
Oph.
Timp.
Vl.
Vla.
Vc. e Cb.
sf
ff
a 2
tr

a 2
Fl.
sf
ff
a 2
Ob.
sf
ff
Cl. (A)
ff
Fg.
ff
Cor. (E)
ff
Tr. (E)
ff
Oph.
ff
ff
Timp.
ff
Vl.
ff
ff
Vla.
ff
Vc. e Cb.
ff

90
a 2
a 2
a 2
Fl.
Ob.
Cl. (A)
Fg.
Cor. (E)
Tr. (E)
Oph.
Timp.
Vl.
Vla.
Vc. e Cb.
sf
f

Ob.
Cl. (A)
Fg.
Cor. (E)
Vl.
Vla.
Vc.
Cb.
a 2
1.
cresc.
ff
f

100
Fl.
Ob.
Cl. (A)
Fg.
Cor. (E)
Oph.
Vl.
Vla.
Vc.
1.
f
ff

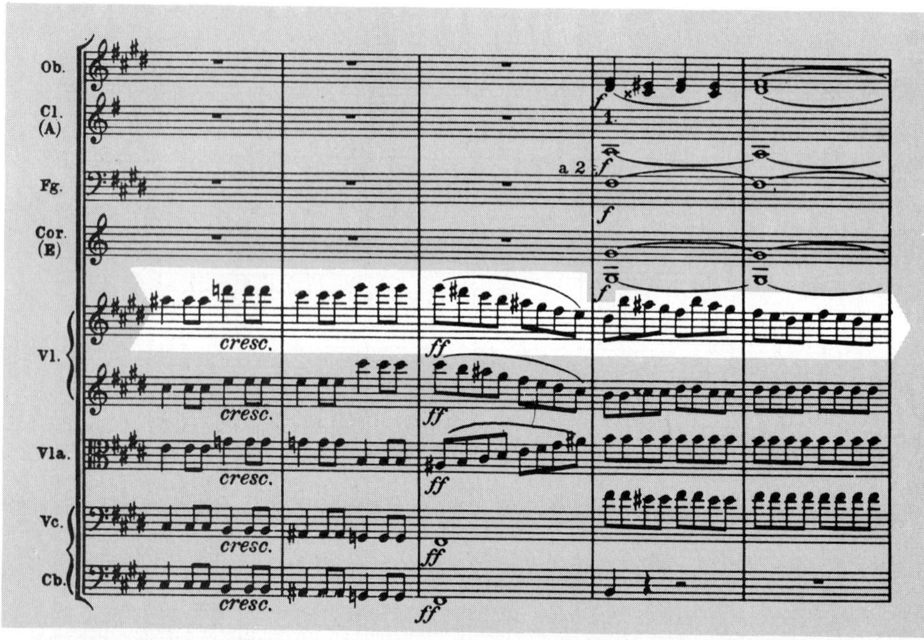

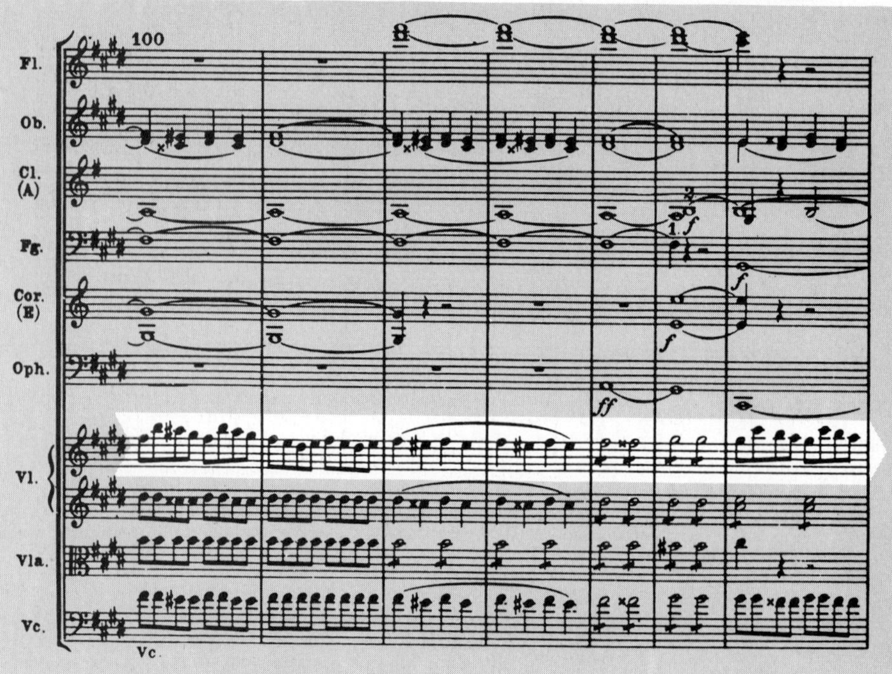

cresc.
Ob.
cresc.
Cl.
(A)
cresc.
Fg.
Cor.
(E)
f
Tr.
(E)
Oph.
Timp.
tr.
tr.
Vl.
Vla.
Vc.
Cb.
cresc.
ff
ff
ff
ff
ff
ff
ff
ff
ff
ff
ff
ff
ff

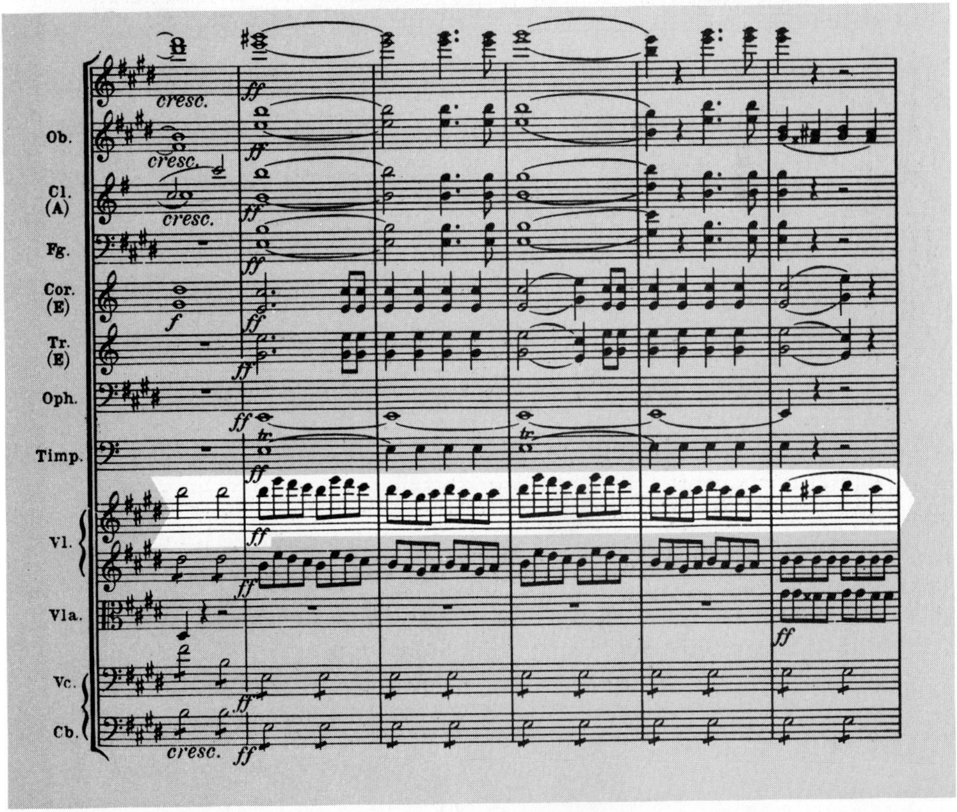

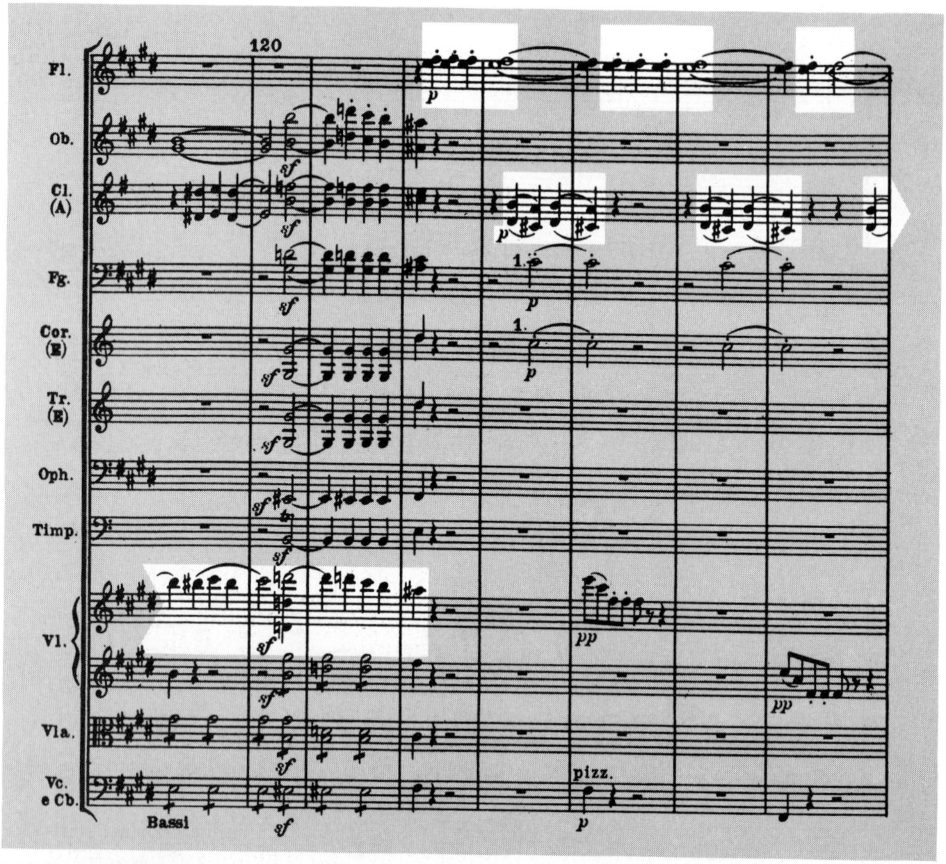

120
Fl.
Ob.
Cl. (A)
Fg.
Cor. (E)
Tr. (E)
Oph.
Timp.
Vl.
Vla.
Vc. e Cb.
Bassi
p
sf
1.
pizz.
pp

140
Fl.
Cl. (A)
Fg.
Cor. (E)
Vl.
Vla.
Vc.
Bassi
div.
150
Vc. e Cb.
160

170
Fl.
Ob.
Cl. (A)
a 2
Fg.
Cor. (E)
Tr. (E)
Oph.
Timp.
Vl.
Vla.
Vc.
Cb.
cresc.
p
dolce
f
mf
pizz.

180
Fl.
Ob.
Cl. (A)
Fg.
Cor. (E)
Tr. (E)
Timp.
Vl.
Vla.
Vc.
Cb.
f
mf
pp
p
cresc.
arco

Cl. (A)
Fg.
Cor. (E)
Vl.
Vla.
Vc. e Cb.
Bassi
mf
cresc.
f
più f

190
Ob.
Cl. (A)
Fg.
Cor. (E)
Tr. (E)
Oph.
Timp.
Vl.
Vla.
Vc. e Cb.
a 2
cresc.
f
ff

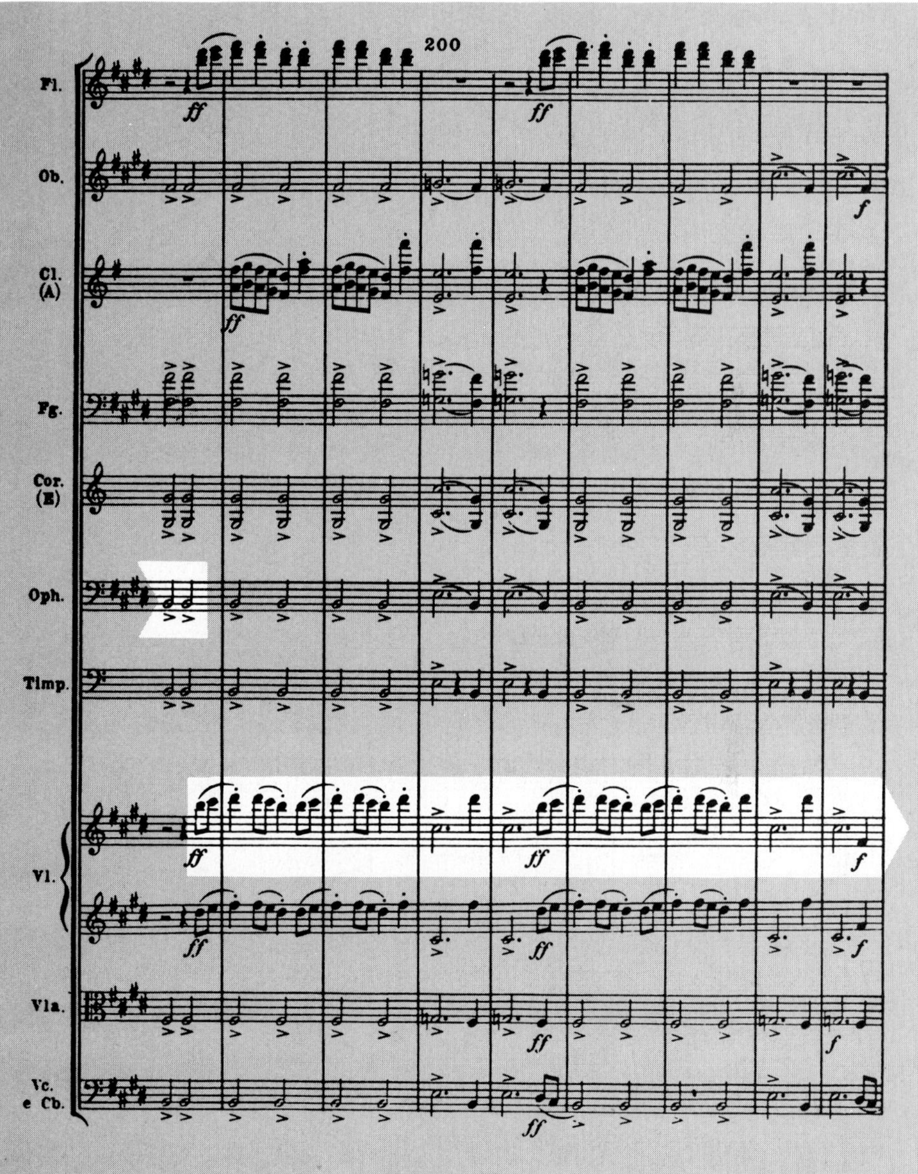

clowns

210
Fl.
Ob.
Cl. (A)
Fg.
Cor. (E)
Oph.
Timp.
Vl.
Vla.
Vc. e Cb.
f
ff

220
Fl.
Ob.
ff
f
Cl. (A)
Fg.
Cor. (E)
Tr. (E)
Oph.
Timp.
Vl.
Vla.
Vc. e Cb.

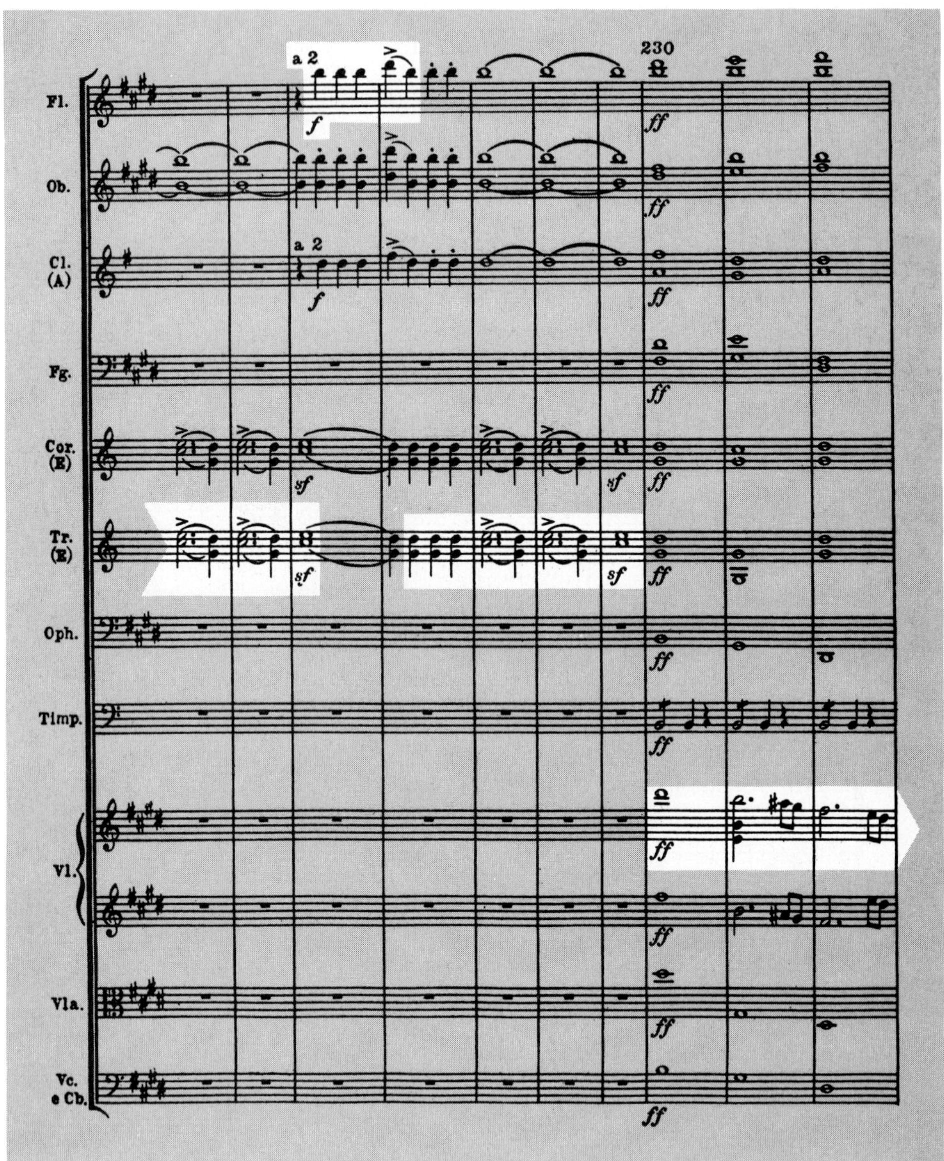
230
a 2
Fl.
Ob.
Cl. (A)
Fg.
Cor. (E)
Tr. (E)
Oph.
Timp.
Vl.
Vla.
Vc. e Cb.
f
sf
ff

240
Fl.
Ob.
Cl. (A)
Fg.
Cor. (E)
Tr. (E)
a 2
Oph.
Timp.
tr
Vl.
Vla.
Vc. e Cb.
sf
f

a 2 250

Fl.

Ob.

Cl. (A)

Fg.

Cor. (E)

Tr. (E)

Oph.

Timp.

Vl.

Vla.

Vc. e Cb.

ff *f* *sf* div. *pp stacc.*

260
Fl.
pp
Ob.
pp
Cl. (A)
pp
Fg.
pp
Cor. (E)
pp
Timp.
pp
unis.
Vl.
pp
unis.
pp
Vla.
pp

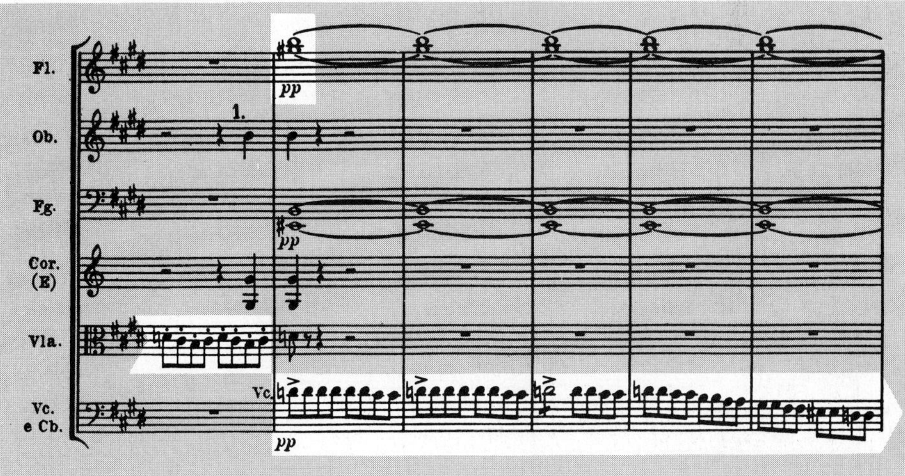

280
Fl.
Ob.
Cl. (A)
Fg.
Cor. (E)
Vl.
Vc. e Cb.
1.
pp
unis.
Bassi

Fl.
pp
Ob.
p
pp
Cl. (A)
pp
Fg.
pp
Cor. (E)
pp
pp
a 2
Tr. (E)
pp
Timp.
pp
Vl.
pp
pp
Vla.
pp
pp
Tutti
Vc.
pp
Tutti
Cb.
pp

290
Fl.
1.
pp
Ob.
2.
pp
Cl. (A)
Fg.
Cor. (E)
Tr. (E)
1.
pp
Timp.
pp
Vl.
pp
pp
Vc.
Cb.

Fl.
pp
pp
Ob.
1.
pp
con tutta la forza
a 2
Cor. (E)
ff
dim. poco a poco
Timp.
tr
pp
Vl.
pp
pp
div.
Vla.
pp
Vc.
sempre pp
Cb.

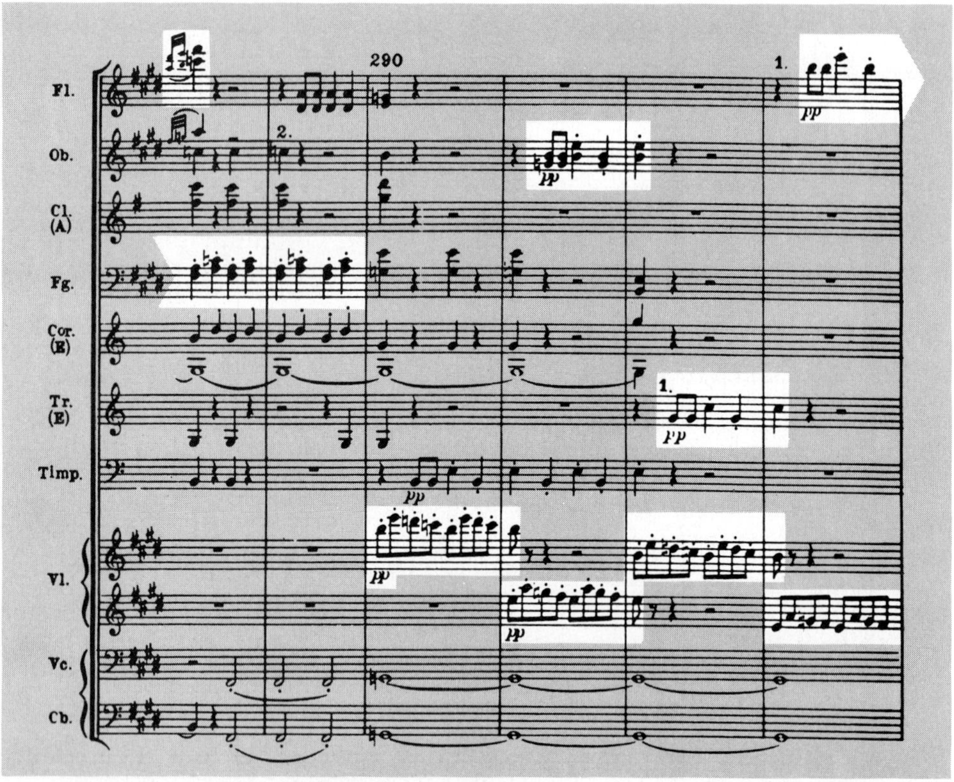

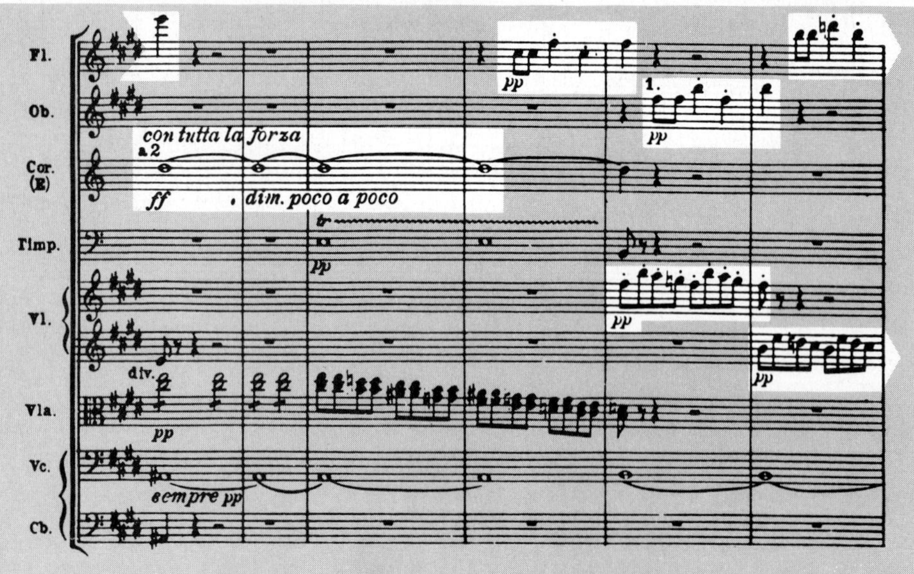

300

Fl.
Cl. (A)
Fg.
Cor. (E)
Timp.
Vl.
Vla.
Vc.
Cb.

pp
ff
dim. poco a poco
tr

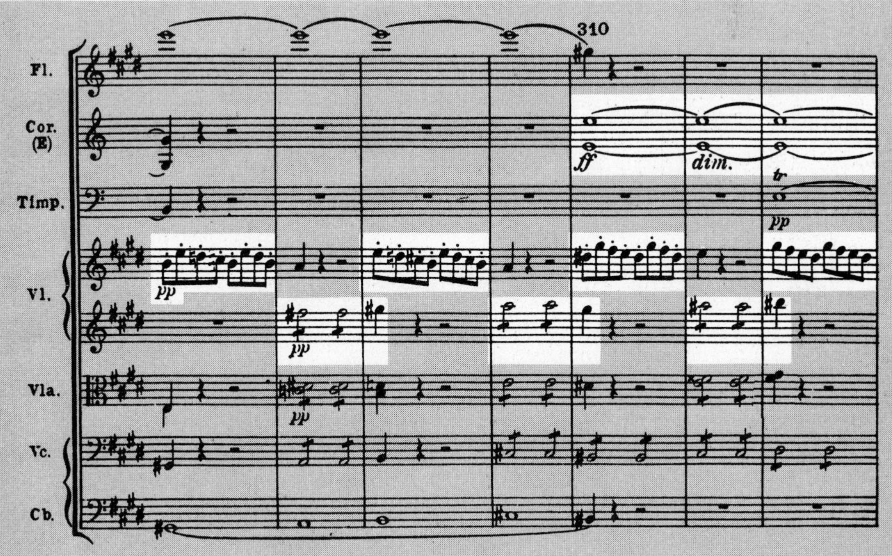

Fl.
pp
Ob.
pp
Cl. (A)
1.
pp
pp
Fg.
pp
pp
Cor. (E)
pp
a 2
p
Tr. (E)
1.
pp
Timp.
tr
Vl.
pp
pp
pp
Vla.
pp
Vc.
pp
Cb.
pp

320
Fl.
Ob.
Cl. (A)
Fg
Cor. (E)
Tr. (E)
Vl.
Vla.
Vc. e Cb.
p
Vc.

330
Fl.
Ob.
Cl. (A)
Fg.
Cor. (E)
a 2
Vla.
Vc.

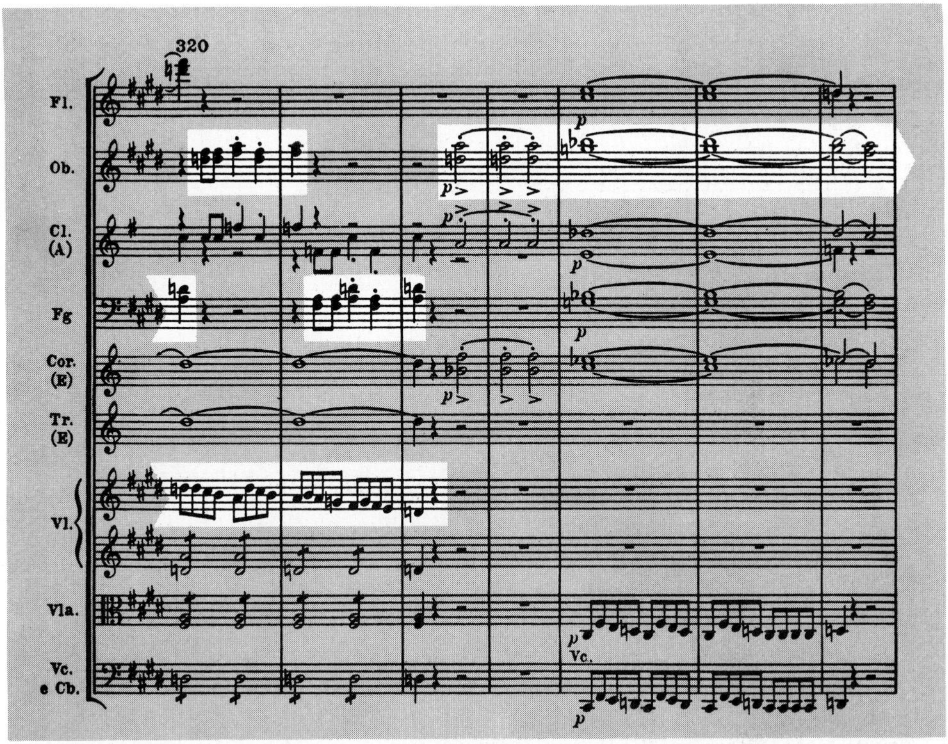

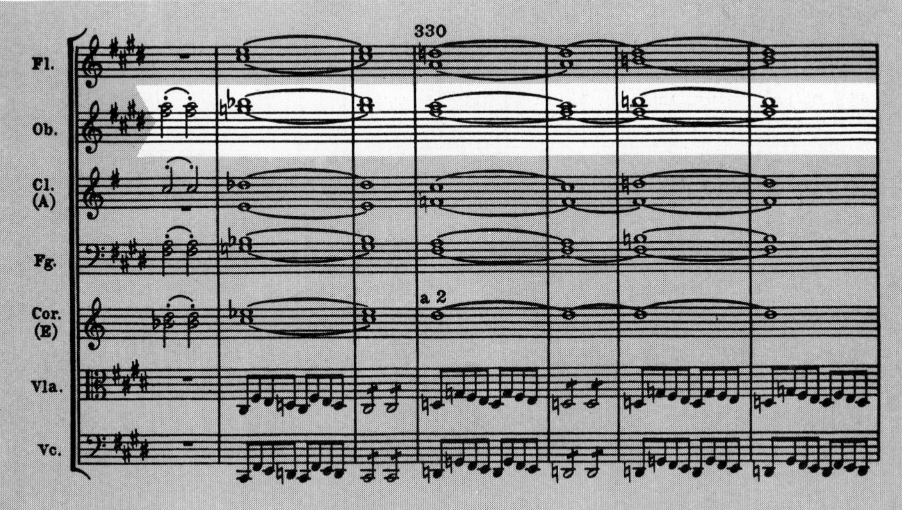

Fl.
Ob.
Cl. (A)
Fg.
Cor. (E)
Timp.
Vl.
Vla.
Vc.
340
a 2
pp
1.
div.
pizz.
arco
Bassi pizz.

350

Fl.
Ob.
Cl. (A)
Fg.
Cor. (E)
Timp.
Vl.
Vla.
Vc.

pp *pp* 1. *pp* *pp* *pp*
pizz. arco pizz. Bassi (pizz.) (pizz.)

370
1.
Fl.
Cl. (A)
Fg.
Cor. (E)
Vl.
Vla.
Vc.
Cb.
pp

380
Fl.
Cl. (A)
Fg.
Cor. (E)
Vl.
Vla.
Vc. e Cb.
dim.
p espress.
p
pp

ritard.
390
Vl.
Vla.
Vc.
e Cb.
pp

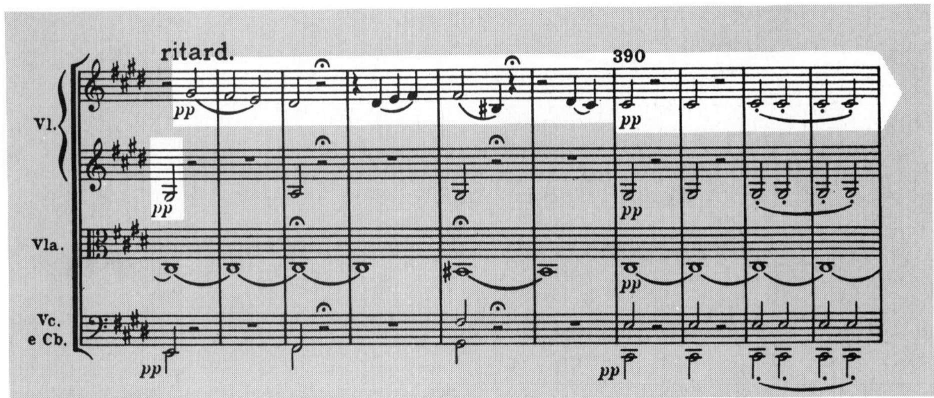

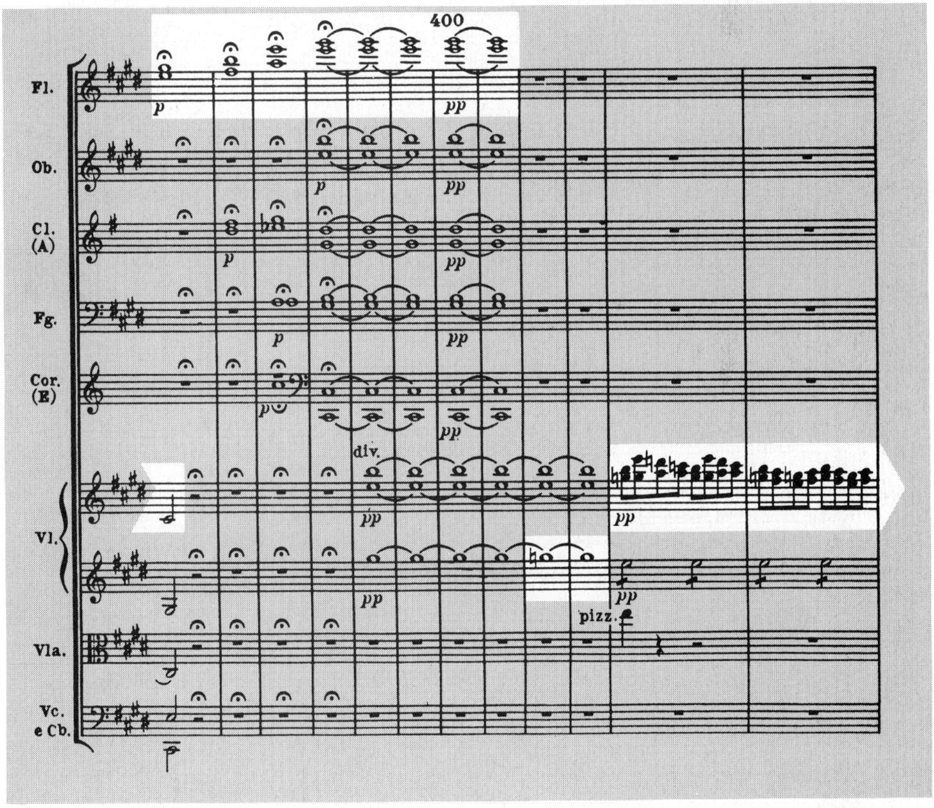

400
Fl.
Ob.
Cl.
(A)
Fg.
Cor.
(E)
Vl.
Vla.
Vc.
e Cb.
div.
pizz.
p
pp

recap

410
Fl.
Ob.
Cl. (A)
Vl.
div.
Fg.
Cor. (E)
Oph.
unis.
420
Timp.
arco
pizz.

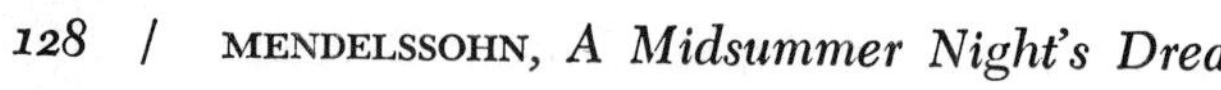

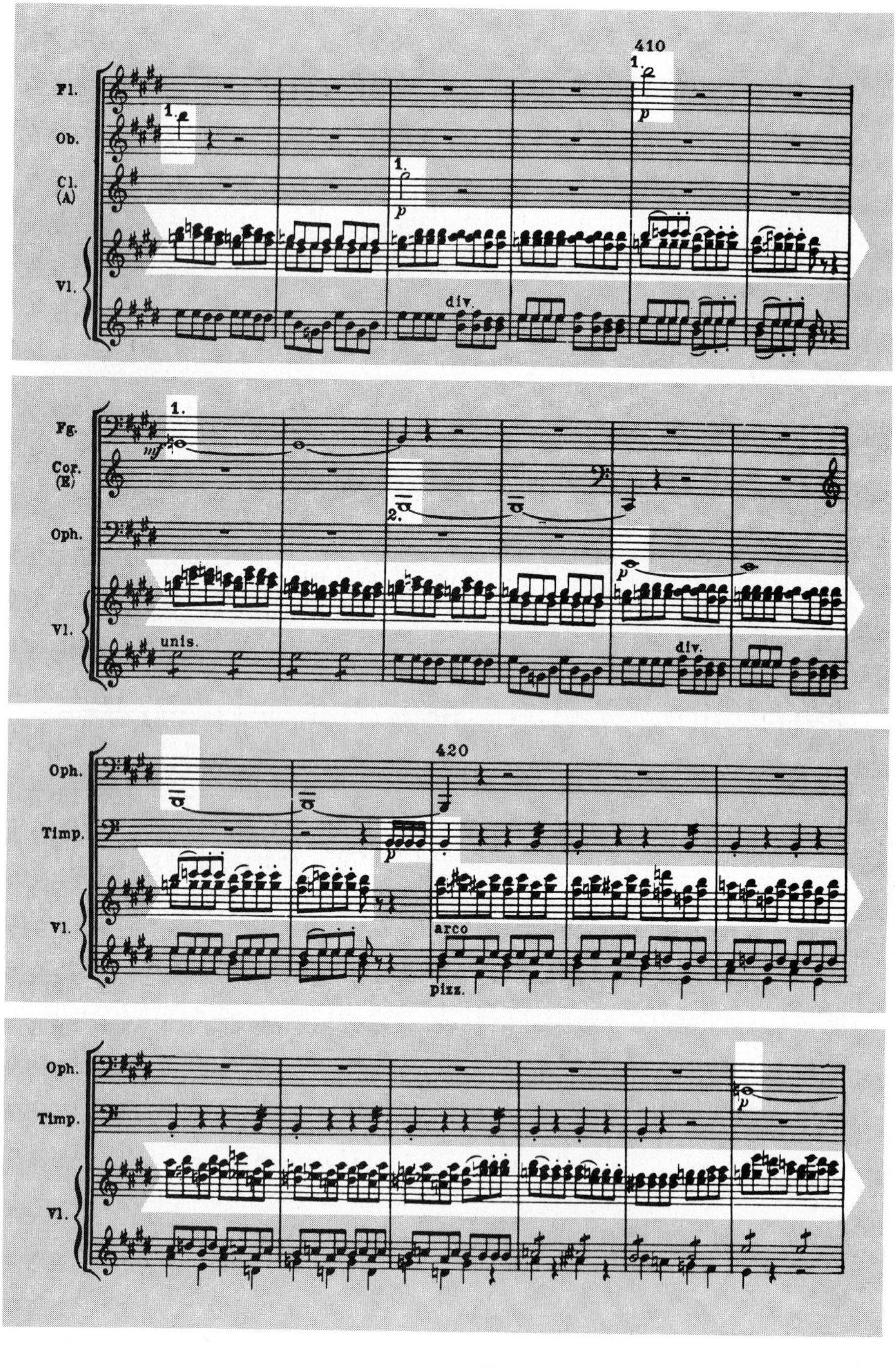

430
Fl.
Ob.
Cor. (E)
Oph.
Timp.
Vl.
Vc. e Cb.
pp
tr
unis.
arco
pizz.

440
Fl.
Ob.
Cl. (A)
Cor. (E)
Oph.
Timp.
Vl.
Vc. e Cb.
1.
pp
tr
div.

Fl.
Ob.
Cl. (A)
Cor. (E)
Vl.
Vla.
Vc. e Cb.
p
unis.
pp
arco
pp

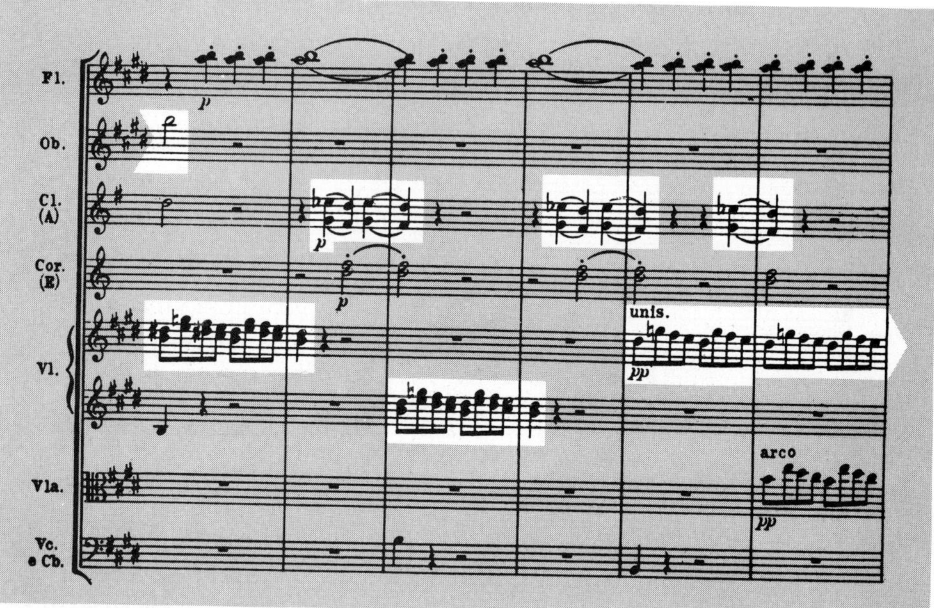

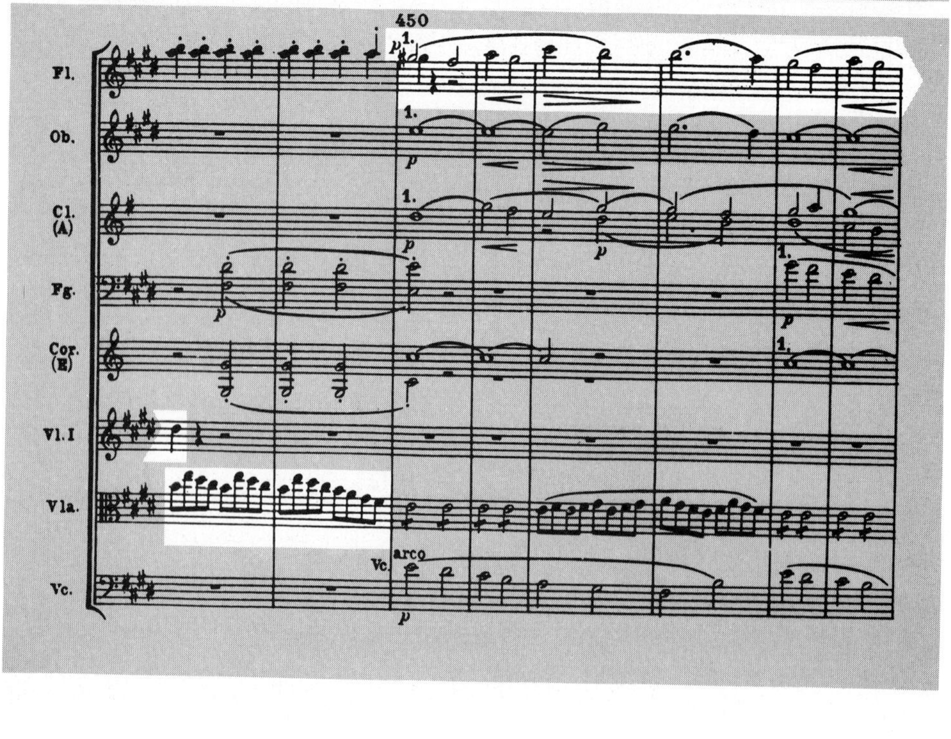

450
Fl.
Ob.
Cl. (A)
Fg.
Cor. (E)
Vl. I
Vla.
Vc.
1.
p
arco

460

Fl.

Ob.

Cl. (A)

p

Fg.

Cor. (E)

Vl.

p

p

div.

Vla.

p

Bassi

Vc. e Cb.

p arco

480
Fl.
Ob.
Cl. (A)
Fg.
Cor. (E)
Tr. (E)
Oph.
Timp.
Vl.
Vla.
Vc. e Cb.
a 2
cresc.
sf cresc.

490
Fl.
Ob.
Cl.
(A)
Fg.
Cor.
(E)
Tr.
(E)
Oph.
Timp.
Vl.
Vla.
Vc.
e Cb.
Vc.
Bassi
f
mf
pp
p

500
Cl. (A)
Fg.
Cor. (E)
Vl.
Vla.
Vc. e Cb.
mf
cresc.
f
più f

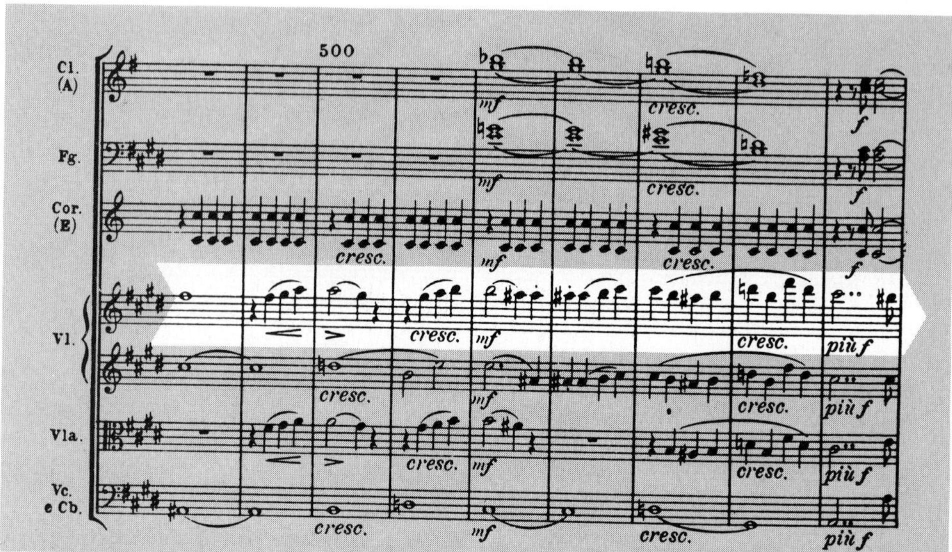

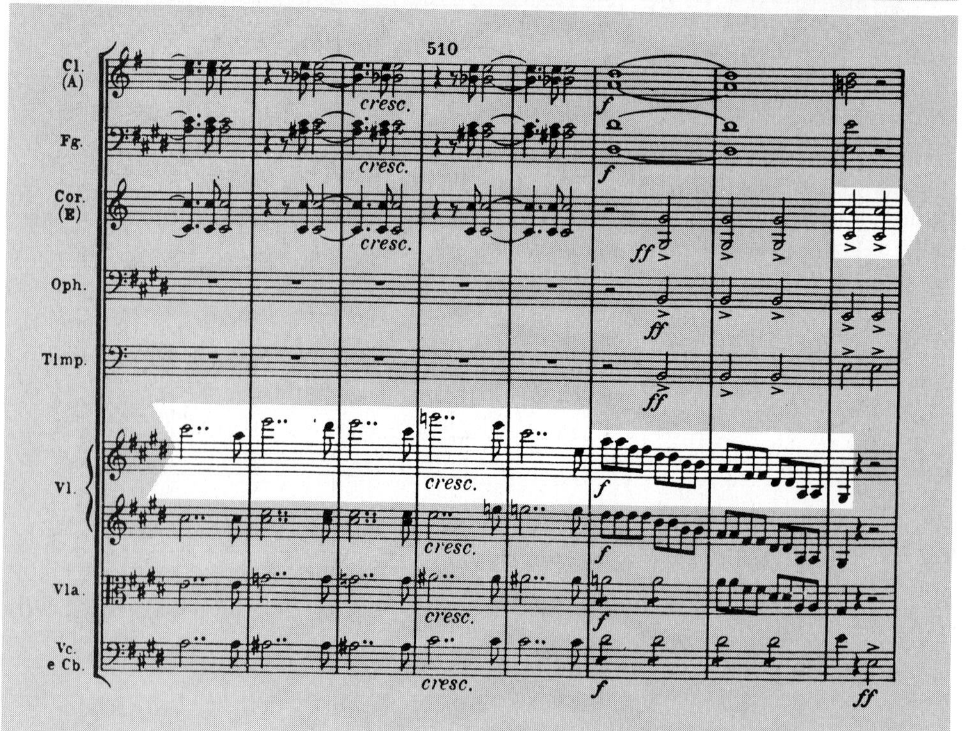

510
Cl. (A)
Fg.
Cor. (E)
Oph.
Timp.
Vl.
Vla.
Vc. e Cb.
cresc.
f
ff

520
Fl.
Ob.
Cl. (A)
Fg.
Cor. (E)
Oph.
Timp.
Vl.
Vla.
Vc. e Cb.
a 2
ff

530
Fl.
Ob.
Cl. (A)
Fg.
a 2
Cor. (E)
Oph.
Timp.
Vl.
Vla.
Vc. e Cb.

540
Fl.
Ob.
Cl. (A)
Fg.
Cor. (E)
Oph.
Timp.
Vl.
Vla.
Vc. e Cb.
a 2
a 2
a 2
ff

Fl.
Ob.
Cl. (A)
Fg.
Cor. (E)
Tr. (E)
Oph.
Timp.
Vl.
Vla.
Vc. e Cb.
a 2
f
sf
tr

550
Fl.
a 2
Ob.
Cl. (A)
Fg.
Cor. (E)
Tr. (E)
Oph.
Timp.
Vl.
Vla.
Vc. e Cb.

560
Fl.
Ob.
a 2
f sempre
Cl. (A)
f
sf
f sempre
Fg.
f sempre
Cor. (E)
a 2
f
f sempre
Oph.
f sempre
Timp.
tr
Vl.
f
Vla.
Vc. e Cb.

Fl.
a 2
f
Ob.
a 2
f
Cl. (A)
a 2
f
Fg.
a 2
f
Cor. (E)
f
Tr. (E)
f
Oph.
f
Timp.
f
Vl.
f
f sempre
f sempre
Vla.
f sempre
Vc. e Cb.
f sempre

570
580
Fl.
Ob.
Cl. (A)
Fg.
Cor. (E)
a 2
Tr. (E)
Oph.
Timp.
Vl.
Vla.
Vc. e Cb.

590
Fl.
Ob.
a 2
Cl.
(A)
Fg.
Cor.
(E)
Tr.
(E)
Oph.
Timp.
Vl.
Vla.
Vc.
e Cb.
sf
ff
tr

Fl.
Ob.
Cl. (A)
Fg.
Cor. (E)
Tr. (E)
a 2
Oph.
Timp.
Vl.
Vla.
Vc. e Cb.

600
610
Fl.
Ob.
Cl. (A)
Fg.
Cor. (E)
Tr. (E)
a 2
Oph.
Timp.
Vl.
Vla.
Vc. e Cb.
f
ff

620

Fl. a 2 *ff* *ff* *sf*

Ob. a 2 *ff* *ff* *sf*

Cl. (A) a 2 *ff* *ff* *sf*

Fg. a 2 *ff* *ff* *sf*

Cor. (E) *ff* *ff* *sf*

Tr. (E) *ff* *ff* *sf*

Oph. *ff* *ff* *sf*

Timp. *ff* tr *con tutta la forza* *ff*

Vl. div. *pp* *pp*

Vla. *ff* *ff* *sf*

Vc. *ff* *ff* *sf*

Cb. *ff* *ff* *sf*

Vl.
unis.
Ob.
1.
p
630
Cl. (A)
1.
pp
Vl.
div.
pp
pp
Fl.
1.
pp
Cl. (A)
Vl.
Fl.
1.
pp
640
Ob.
1.
pp
Cl. (A)
1.
pp
Vl.
div.

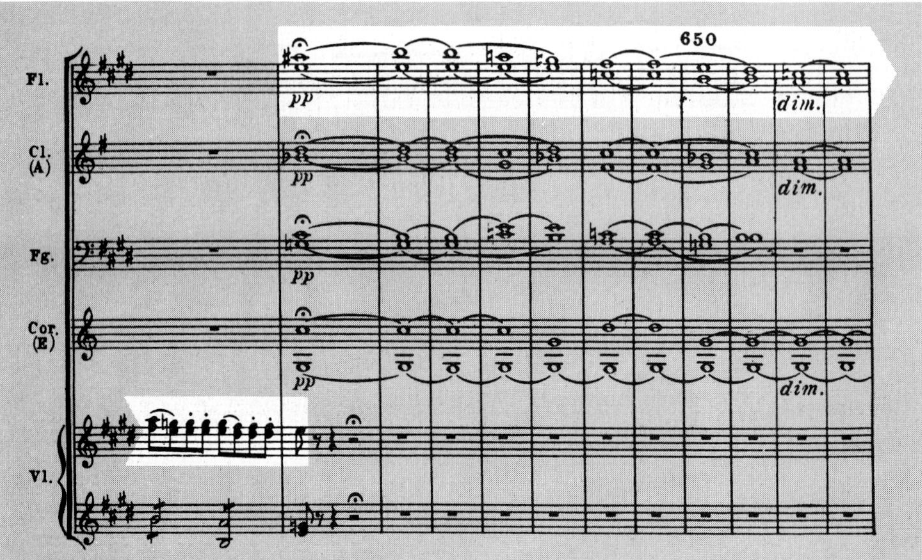
650
Fl.
pp
dim.
Cl. (A)
pp
dim.
Fg.
pp
Cor. (E)
pp
dim.
Vl.

poco riten.
660
Fl.
Cl. (A)
pp
dolce
Fg.
pp
Cor. (E)
pp
pp
Vl.
pp
pp
pizz.
Vc. e Cb.

670
Fg.
pp dolce
Cor. (E)
pp dolce
Vl.
Vc. e Cb.

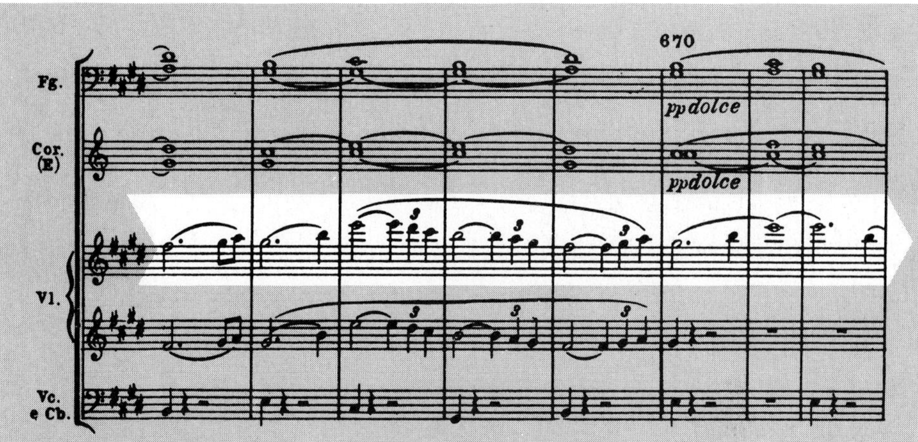

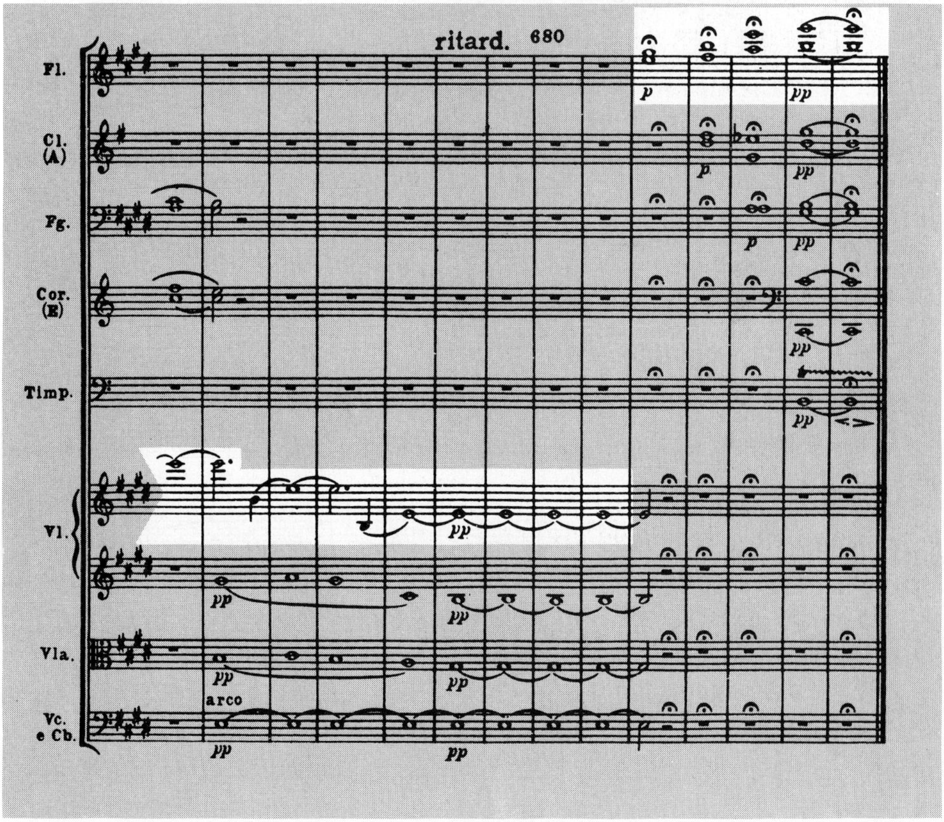

ritard.
680
Fl.
p
pp
Cl. (A)
p
pp
Fg.
p
pp
Cor. (E)
pp
Timp.
pp
Vl.
pp
pp
pp
Vla.
pp
pp
arco
Vc. e Cb.
pp
pp

6. MENDELSSOHN,
First movement from *Violin Concerto in E minor* (1844)

10
1.
Fl.
p
Cl.
p
Fg.
p
Cor.
(E)
p
Timp.
p
Vl. pr.
Vl.
Vla.
Vc.
e Cb.

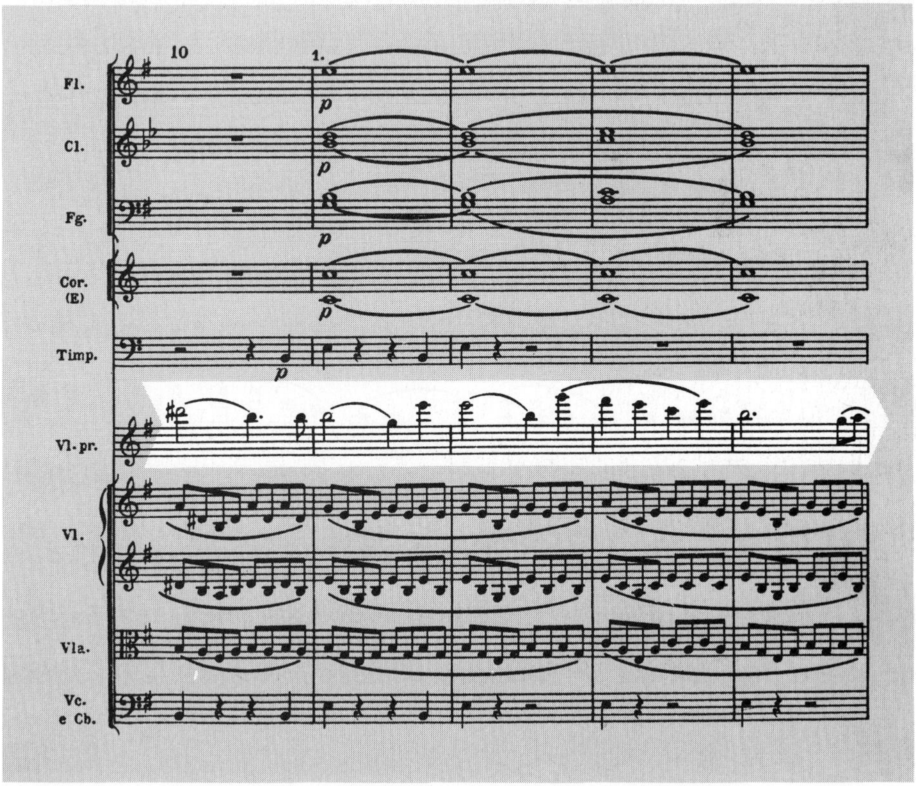

Fl.
Fg.
Vl. pr.
Vl.
Vla.
Vc. e Cb.
arco
get.
20
Ob.
Cl.
Cor. (E)
Timp.
zu 2
cresc.
p
f

Fl.
Ob.
Cl.
Fg.
Cor. (E)
Timp.
Vl. pr.
Vl.
Vla.
Vc. e Cb.
virtuosic playing
30
zu 2

Fl.
Ob.
Cl.
Fg.
Cor. (E)
Timp.
Vl. pr.
Vl.
Vla.
Vc. e Cb.
mf
4ta
cresc.
1.
p
fp
40
sf
tr
f

double stopping

Tutti
50
zu 2
Fl.
ff
zu 2
Ob.
ff
Cl.
ff
Fg.
ff
Cor. (E)
ff
sf
sf
sf
zu 2
Tbe. (E)
ff
sf
sf
sf
tr
tr
tr
Timp.
ff
sf
sf
sf
Vl. pr.
Vl.
ff
ff
Vla.
ff
Vc. e Cb.
ff

Fl.
Ob.
Cl.
Fg.
zu 2
Cor. (E)
Tbe. (E)
Timp.
Vl.
Vla.
Vc. e Cb.
60

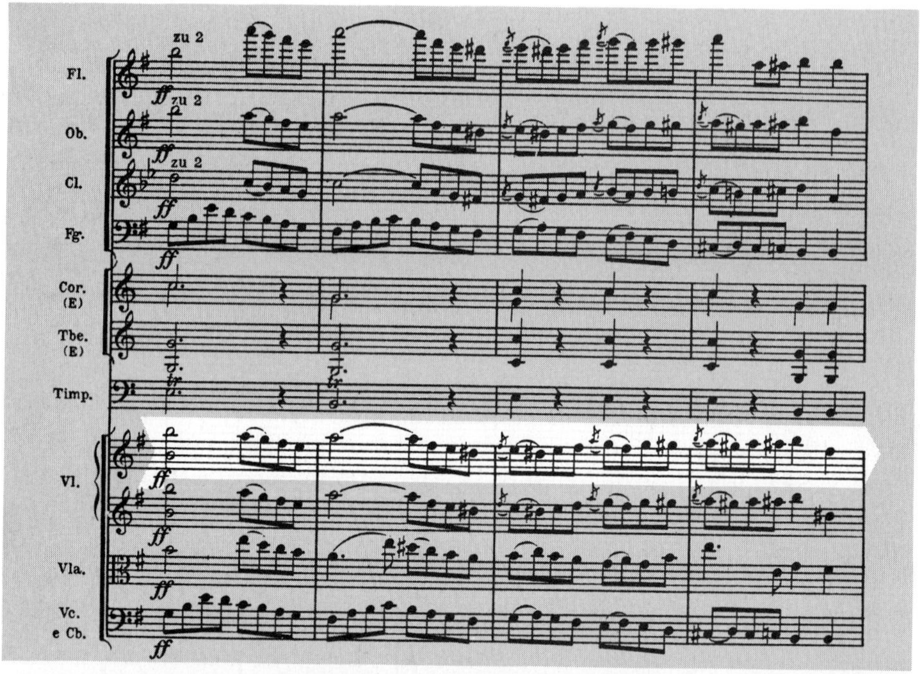

zu 2
Fl.
ff
zu 2
Ob.
ff
zu 2
Cl.
ff
Fg.
ff
Cor. (E)
Tbe. (E)
tr
Timp.
Vl.
ff
ff
Vla.
ff
Vc. e Cb.
ff
Fl.
Ob.
Cl.
Fg.
sf
Cor. (E)
zu 2
Tbe. (E)
tr
Timp.
Vl.
Vla.
Vc. e Cb.
sf

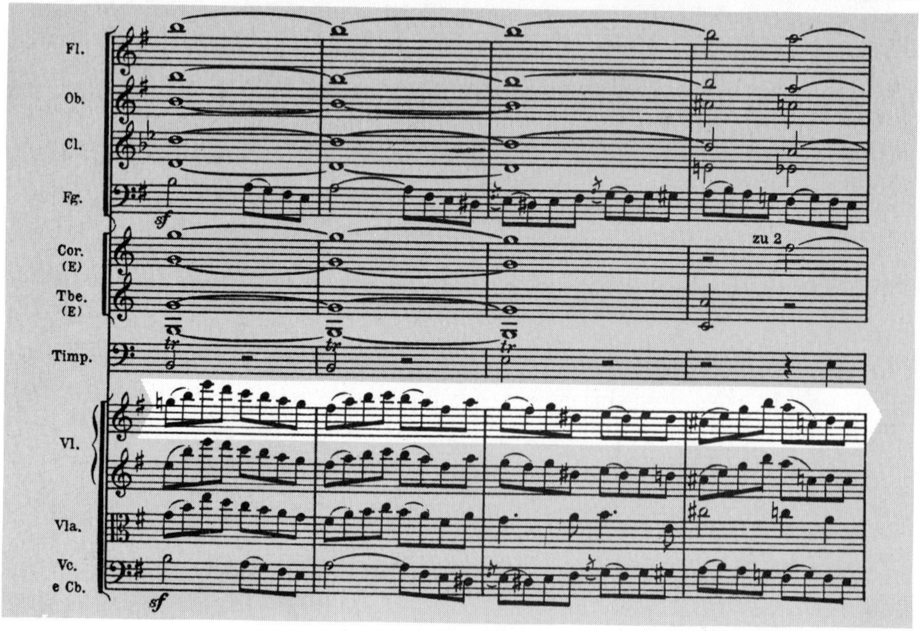

70
Fl.
Ob.
Cl.
Fg.
Cor. (E)
Tbe. (E)
Timp.
Vl.
Vla.
Vc. e Cb.
zu 2
Solo
80
Vl. pr.

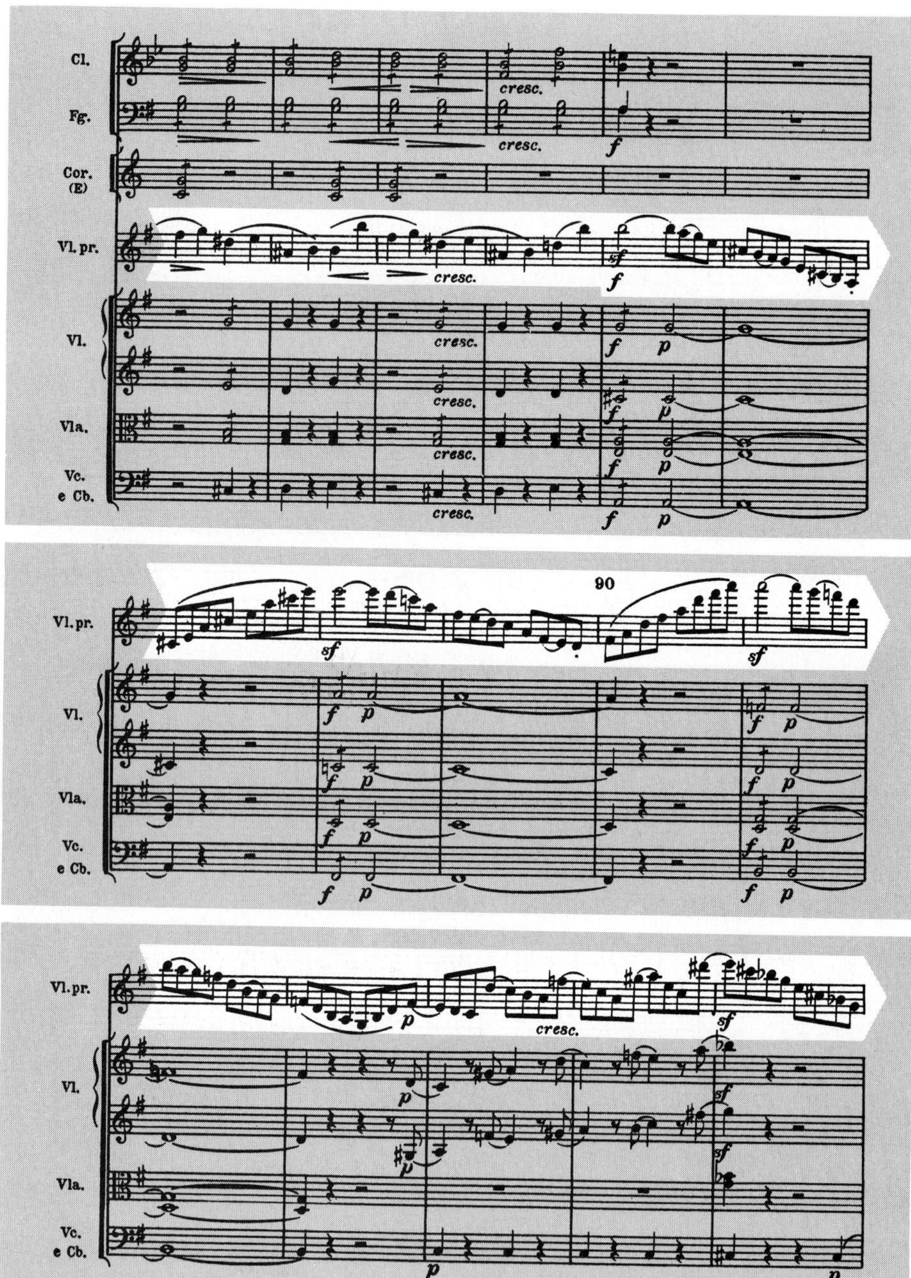
Cl.
Fg.
Cor. (E)
Vl. pr.
Vl.
Vla.
Vc. e Cb.
cresc.
f
p
sf
90

1.
Fl.
p
3
Vl. pr.
cresc.
Vl.
p
p
Vla.
p
Vc.
e Cb.

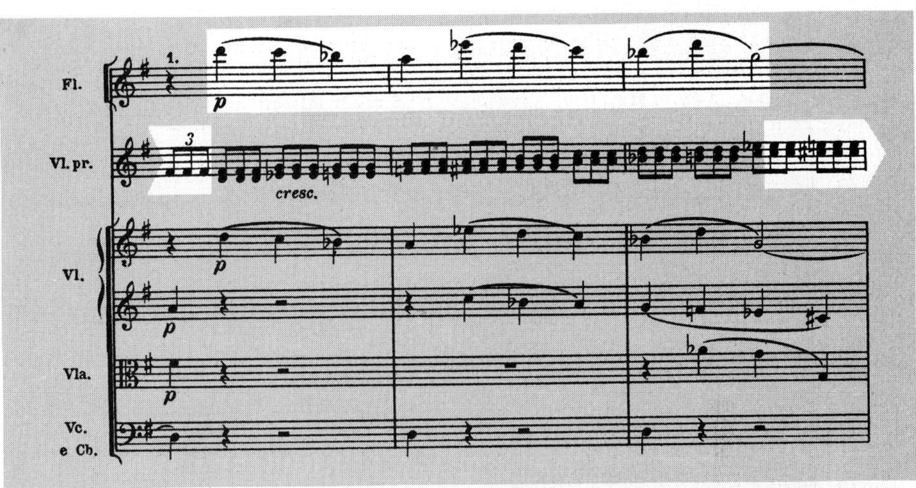

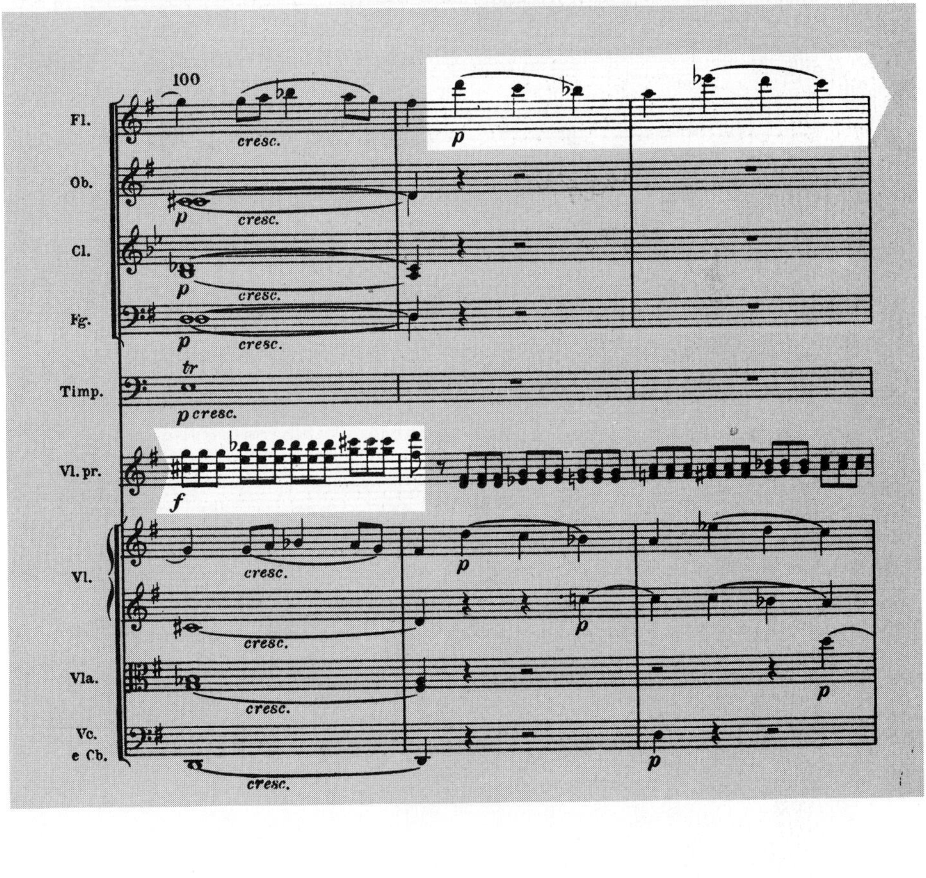

100
Fl.
cresc.
p
Ob.
p
cresc.
Cl.
p
cresc.
Fg.
p
cresc.
tr
Timp.
p cresc.
Vl. pr.
f
Vl.
cresc.
p
cresc.
p
Vla.
cresc.
p
Vc.
e Cb.
cresc.
p

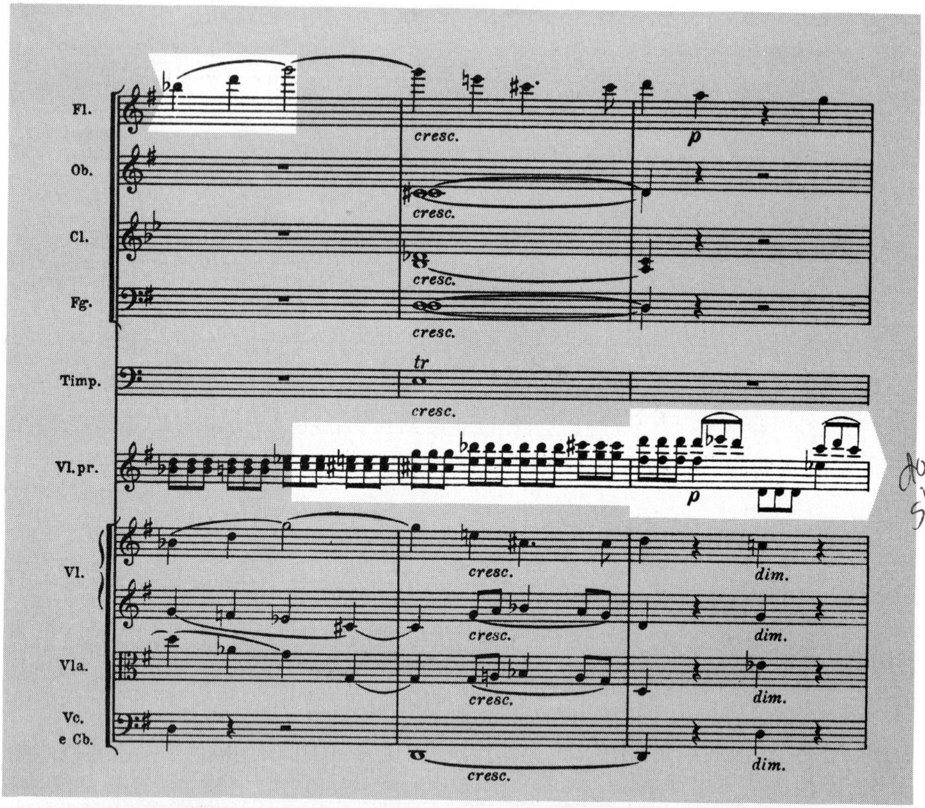

Fl.
cresc.
p
Ob.
cresc.
Cl.
cresc.
Fg.
cresc.
Timp.
tr
cresc.
Vl. pr.
p
Vl.
cresc.
dim.
cresc.
dim.
Vla.
cresc.
dim.
Vc. e Cb.
dim.
cresc.

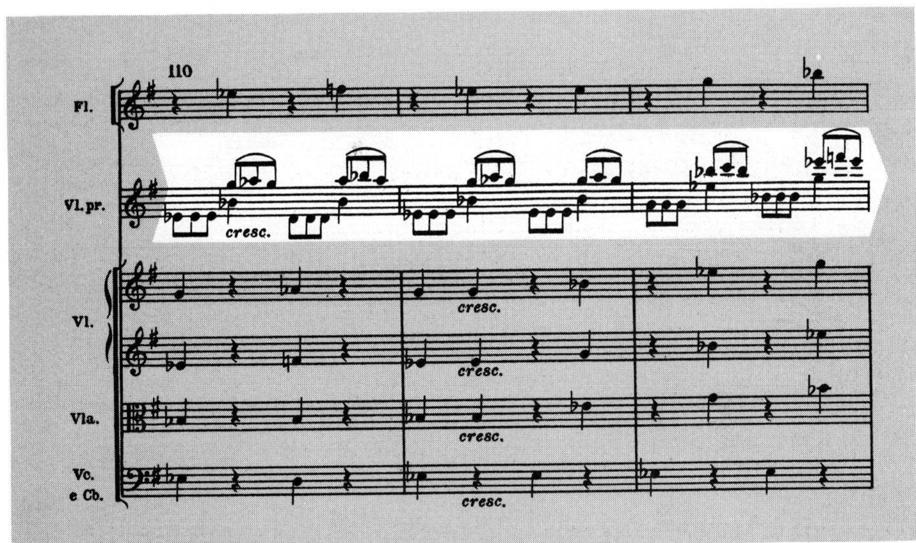

Fl.
Ob.
Cl.
Fg.
Vl. pr.
Vl.
Vla.
Vc.
e Cb.

120
Ob.
Cl.
Fg.
dim.
Vl. pr.
Vl.
f
Vla.
Vc.
e Cb.
sempre dim.
p
130
tranquillo
Fl.
pp
pp tranquillo
p tranquillo
new theme contrasting

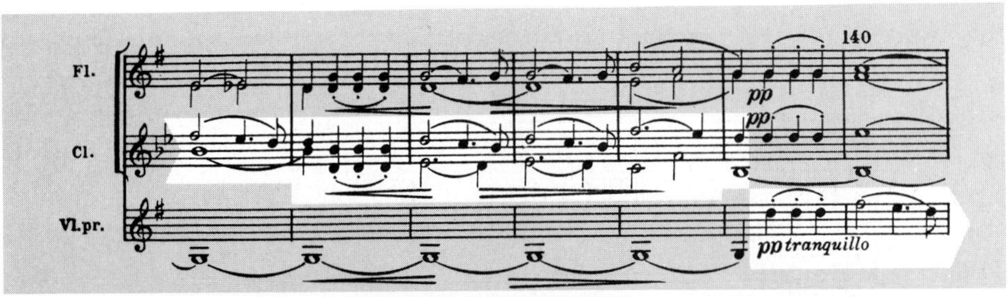

140

Fl.

Cl.

pp

Vl. pr.

pp tranquillo

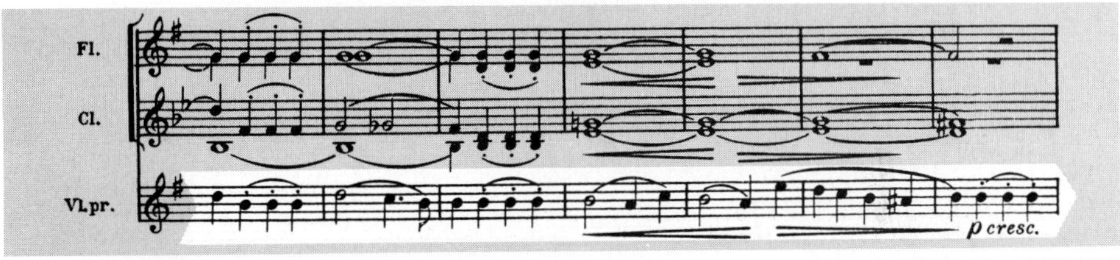

Fl.

Cl.

Vl. pr.

p cresc.

150

Vl. pr.

sf

Vl.

pp

Vla.

Vc.

160

Fl.

Cl.

p

Vl. pr.

cresc.

Vl.

Vla.

Vc.

pp

end of 1st Section of movement: Development

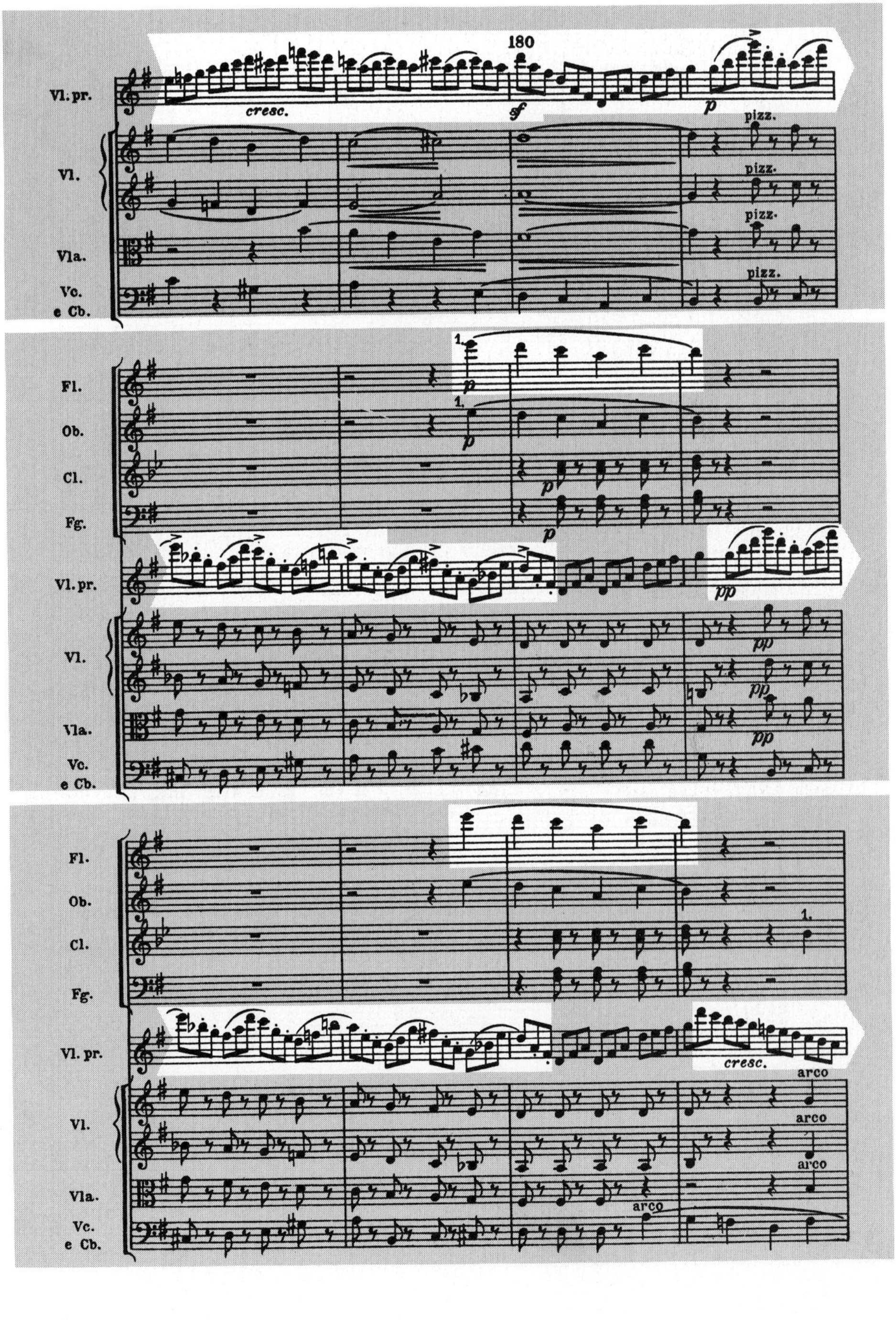
180
Vl. pr.
cresc.
sf
p
pizz.
Vl.
Vla.
Vc.
e Cb.
Fl.
Ob.
Cl.
Fg.
1.
pp
arco

190
Cl.
Fg.
Vl. pr.
Vl.
Vla.
Vc.
e Cb.
sf

Cl.
Fg.
Vl. pr.
Vl.
Vla.
Vc.
e Cb.
cresc.
f
sf
pp
p leggiero

200
1.
Fl.
Ob.
Cl.
Fg.
Vl. pr.
Vl.
Vla.
Vc. e Cb.
p
pp

Fl.
Ob.
Cl.
Fg.
Vl. pr.
Vl.
Vla.
Vc. e Cb.
cresc.

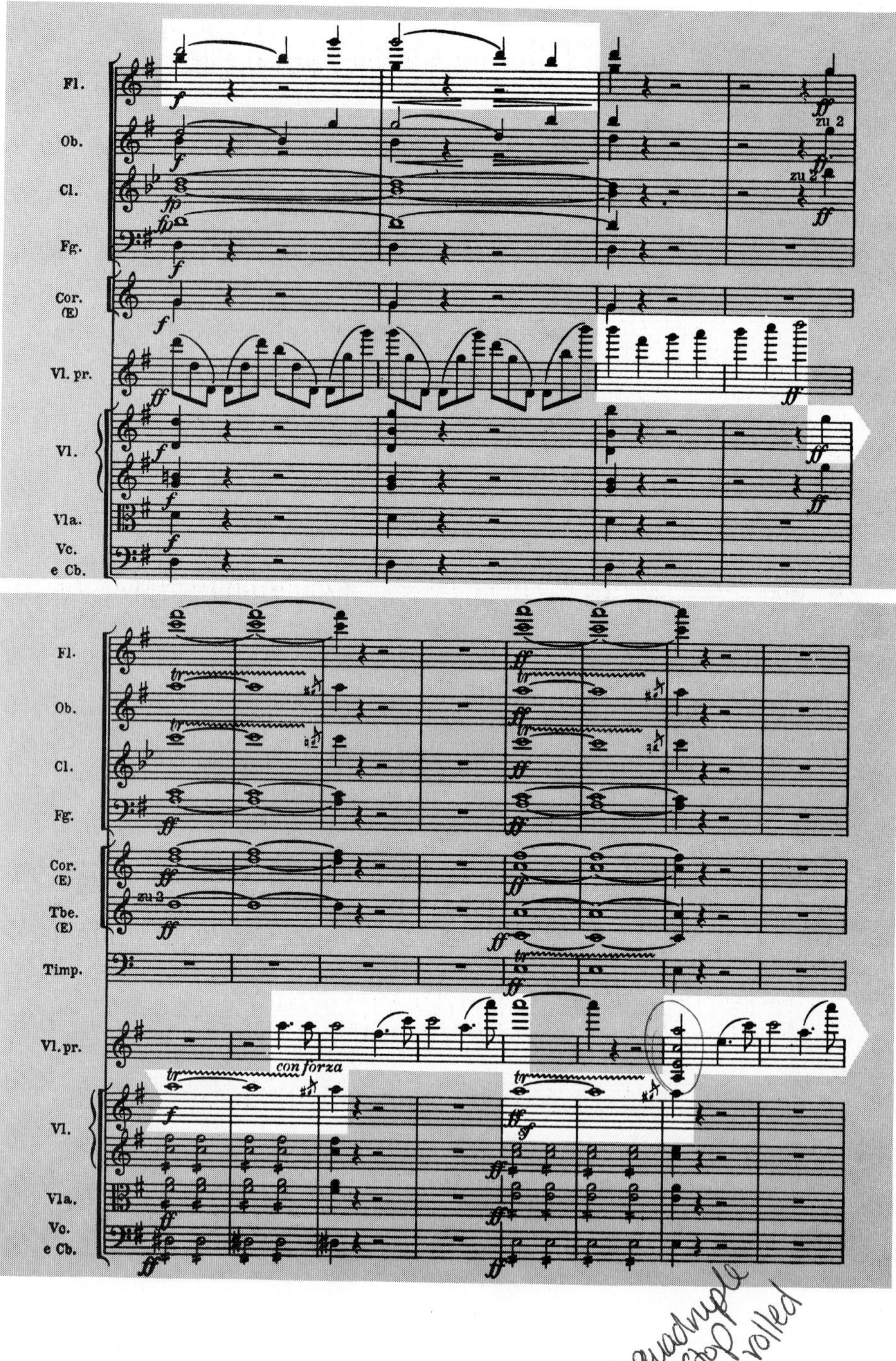
Fl.
Ob.
Cl.
Fg.
Cor. (E)
Vl. pr.
Vl.
Vla.
Vc. e Cb.
zu 2
Tbe. (E)
Timp.
con forza
quadruple stop is rolled

220
Fl.
Ob.
Cl.
Fg.
Cor. (E)
Tbe. (E)
Timp.
Vl. pr.
Vl.
Vla.
Vc. e Cb.
zu 2
dim.
230
agitato
pizz.
cresc.

Tutti
zu 2
Solo
Fl.
Ob.
Cl.
Fg.
zu 2
Cor. (E)
Tbe. (E)
Timp.
Vl. pr.
ppranq.
Vl.
Vla.
arco
Vc. e Cb.
240
1.
Fl.
Cl.
Vl. pr.
Vl.
Vla.
Vc.
Vc. e Cb.
Bassi

Fl.
p
Ob.
p
Cl.
Vl.pr.
Vl.
Vla.
Vc.
Vc.
e Cb.

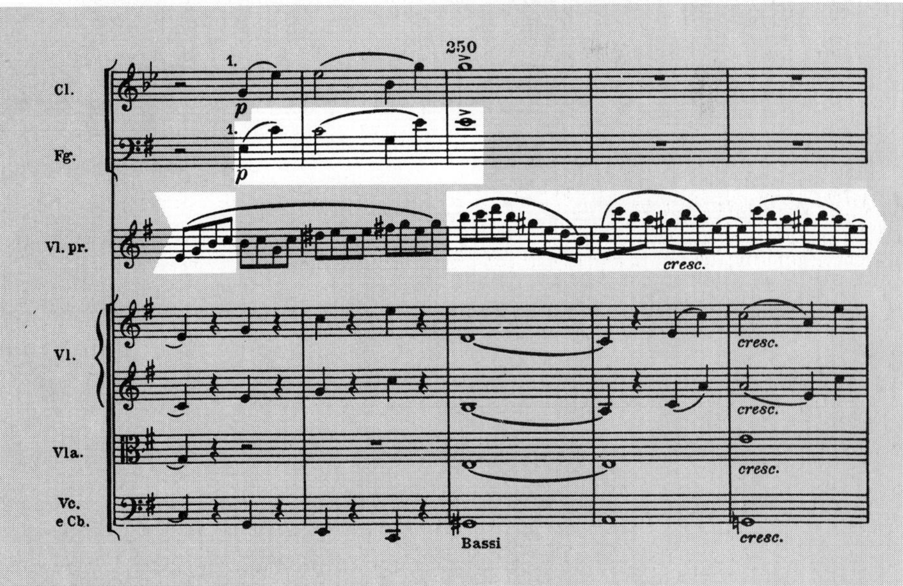
250
Cl.
1.
p
Fg.
1.
p
Vl. pr.
cresc.
Vl.
cresc.
cresc.
Vla.
cresc.
Vc.
e Cb.
Bassi
cresc.

zu 2
Fl.
Ob.
Cl.
Fg.
Cor. (E)
Tbe. (E)
Timp.
Vl. pr.
Vl.
Vla.
Vc. e Cb.

260
Fl.
Ob.
Cl.
Fg.
Cor. (E)
Tbe. (E)
Timp.
Vl. pr.
Vl.
Vla.
Vc. e Cb.
f
p
dim.

Cl.
Fg.
Timp.
Vl. pr.
Vl.
Vla.
Vc. e Cb.
pp
pp
pp
p dim.
p
p
p
p

270
Cl.
Fg.
Timp.
Vl. pr.
Vl.
Vla.
Vc. e Cb.
pp
sempre più p
dim.
sempre dim.
dim.
sempre dim.
dim.
sempre dim.
dim.
sempre dim.

Sense of anticipation (tempo is slow) (pp then poco cres.)

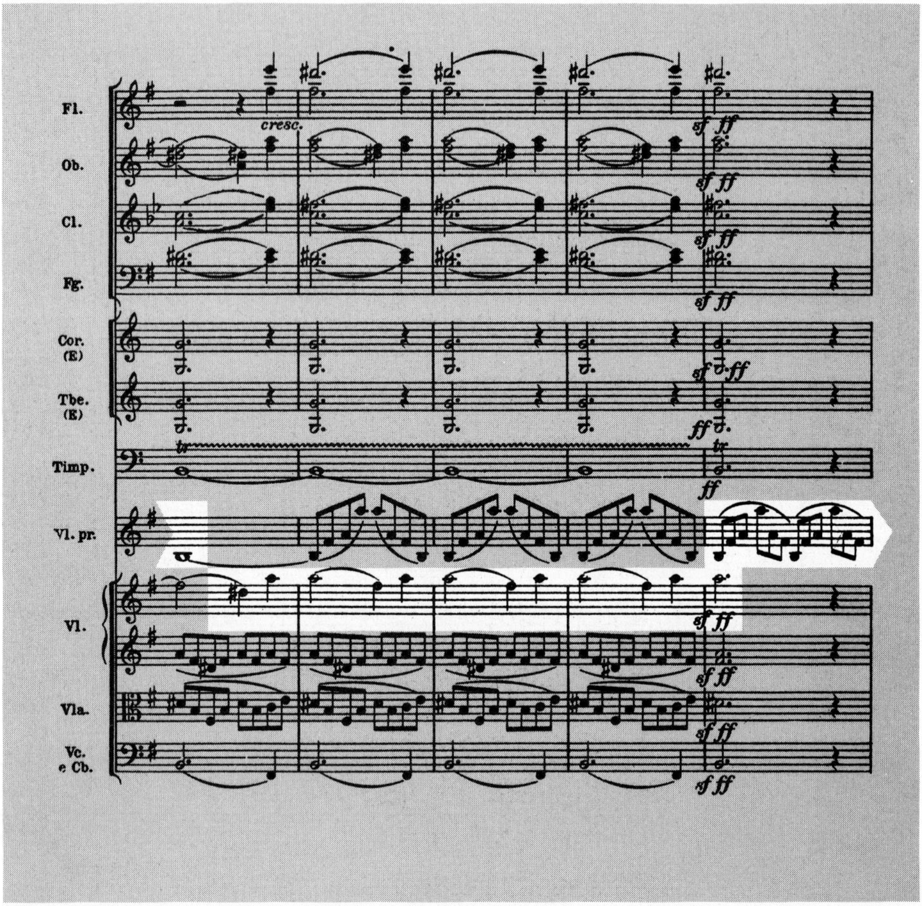

Fl.
cresc.
sf ff
Ob.
sf ff
Cl.
sf ff
Fg.
sf ff
Cor. (E)
sf ff
Tbe. (E)
ff
Timp.
tr
ff
Vl. pr.
Vl.
sf ff
sf ff
Vla.
sf ff
Vc. e Cb.
sf ff

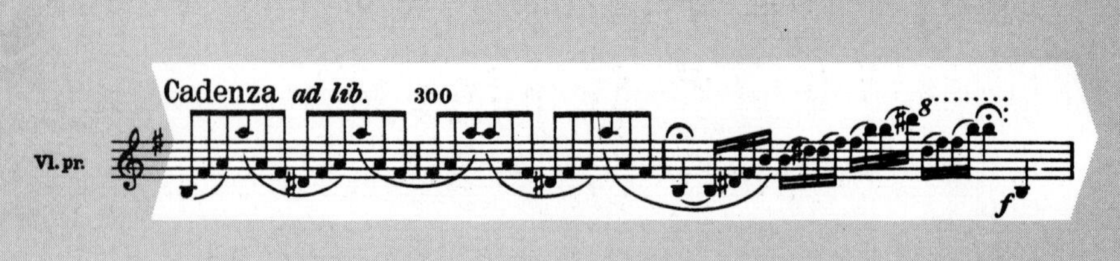

Vl. pr.
8
f

Vl. pr.
8
Tempo I
tr
f

310
Vl. pr.
tr tr tr tr
cresc.
f

320
8
a tempo
Vl. pr.
tr
3 3
f
cresc.

Vl. pr.

330
Vl. pr.
poco a poco dimin.

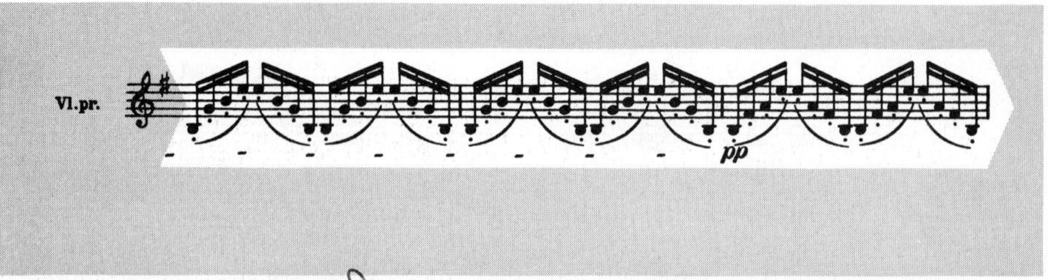

Recap.

Fl.
1.
Ob.
1.
pp
Cl.
pp
Fg.
pp
Cor. (E)
zu 2
pp
Timp.
pp
Vl. pr.
segue
Vl.
pp
pp
Vla.
pp
Vc. e Cb.
pp

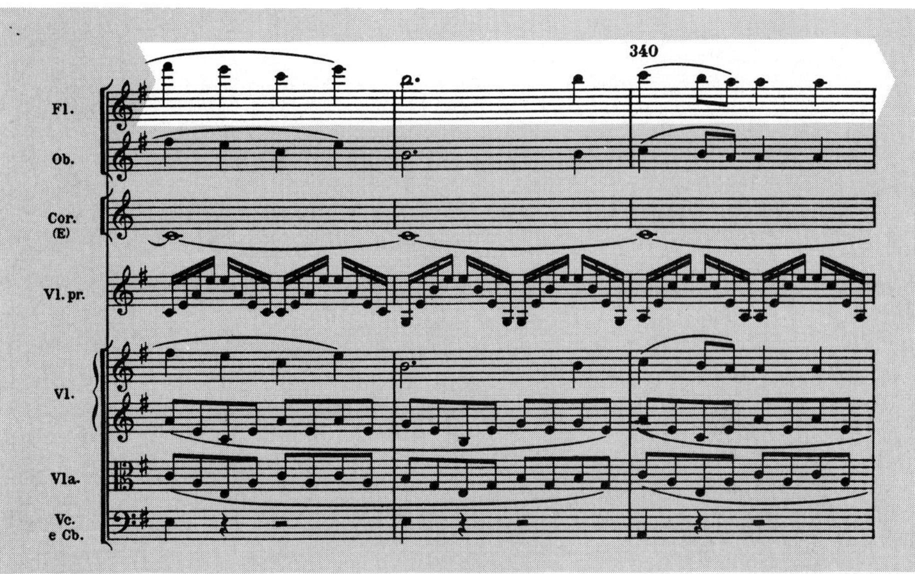

Fl.
cresc.
Ob.
cresc.
Cl.
cresc.
Fg.
cresc.
Cor. (E)
Timp.
p
Vl. pr.
cresc.
Vl.
cresc.
cresc.
Vla.
cresc.
Vc. cresc.
Vc. e Cb.
Cb.

Fl.
Ob.
Cl.
Fg.
Cor. (E)
Timp.
Vl. pr.
Vl.
Vla.
Vc. e Cb.
Fl.
Ob.
Cl.
Fg.
Cor. (E)
Vl. pr.
ff
Vl.
cresc.
Vla.
cresc.
Vc. e Cb.
cresc.

bridge theme

360

Fl.
Ob.
Cl.
Fg.
Cor. (E)
Tbe. (E)
Timp.
Vl. pr.
Vl.
Vla.
Vc. e Cb.

zu 2
ff
sfp
mf
sf

bridge theme

370

Cl.
Vl. pr.
Vc. e Cb.

dim.
sempre più tranquillo

Cl.
Cor. (E)
Vl. pr.
Vc. e Cb.

pp

2nd theme

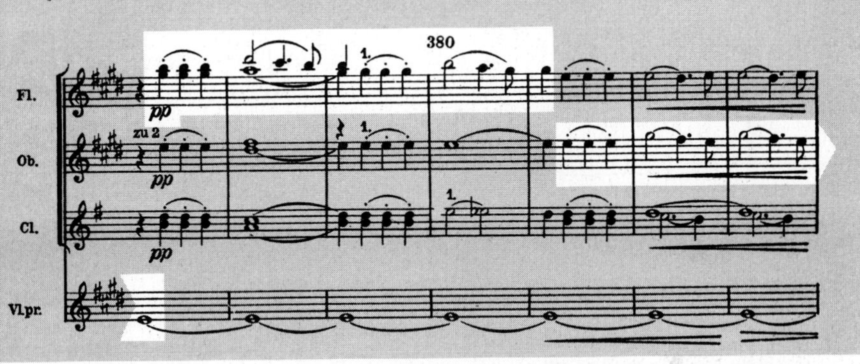
380
Fl.
Ob.
Cl.
Vl.pr.
zu 2
pp

390
Fl.
Ob.
Cl.
Cor. (E)
Vl.pr.
pp

Ob.
Cl.
Vl.pr.
cresc.
Vl.
Vla.
Vc. e Cb.
p

400
Fl.
Ob.
Cl.
Cor. (E)
Vl.pr.
Vl.
Vla.
Vc. e Cb.
pp
1.
zu 2
Vc.

410
Vl. pr.
Vl.
Vla.
Vc. e Cb.
dim.
pp
Bassi

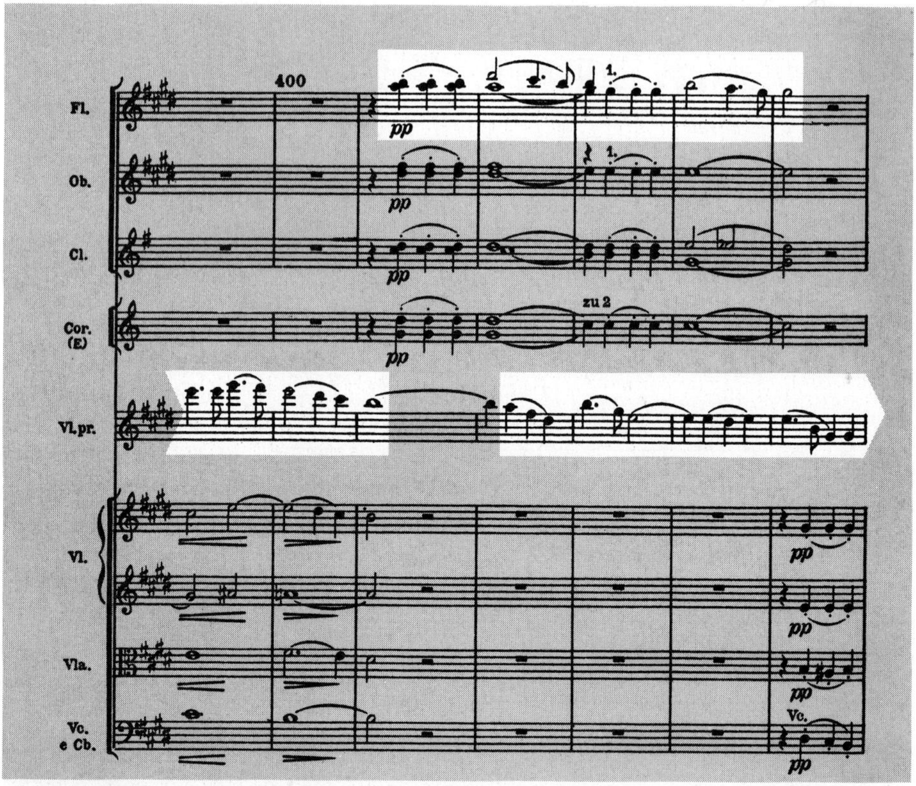

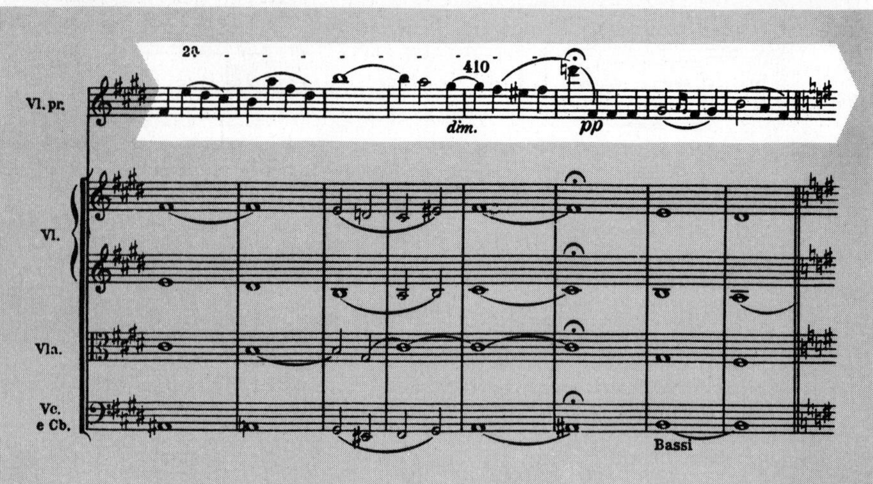

zu 2
Cor. (E)
pp
1.
Tbe. (E)
pp
Timp.
pp
Vl. pr.
3
cresc.
Vl.
pp
fsf
pp
fsf
Vla.
pp
fsf
Vc. e Cb.
pp
fsf
p

420
Cl.
1.
p
Fg.
1.
p
Vl.pr.
3
3
Vl.
p
p
Vla.
Vc. e Cb.

Cl.
Fg.
Vl. pr.
3
cresc.
Vl.
cresc.
cresc.
Vla.
cresc.
Vc. e Cb.
cresc.

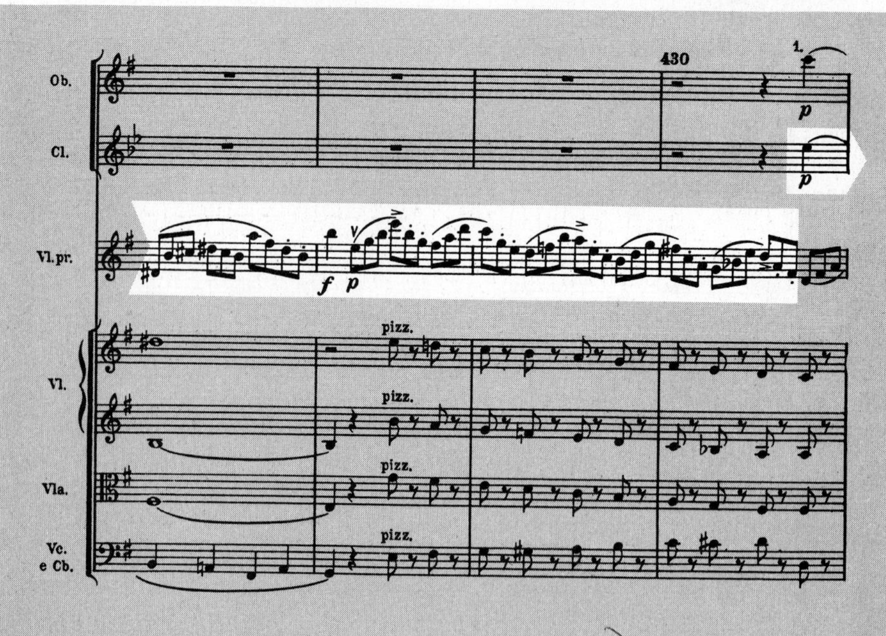
Ob.
430
1.
p
Cl.
p
Vl. pr.
f
p
Vl.
pizz.
pizz.
Vla.
pizz.
Vc. e Cb.
pizz.

1.
Ob.
1.
Cl.
Cor. (E)
pp
Tbe. (E)
pp
Timp.
pp
Vl.pr.
pp
Vl.
pp
pp
Vla.
pp
Vc. e Cb.
pp

Ob.
Cl.
Cor. (E)
Tbe. (E)
Timp.
pp
Vl.pr.
cresc.
sf
sf
Vl.
arco
arco
arco
Vla.
Vc. e Cb.
arco

440
Cor. (E)
cresc.
Vl. pr.
sf
sf
più cresc.
Vl.
cresc.
cresc.
Vla.
cresc.
Vc. e Cb.
cresc.

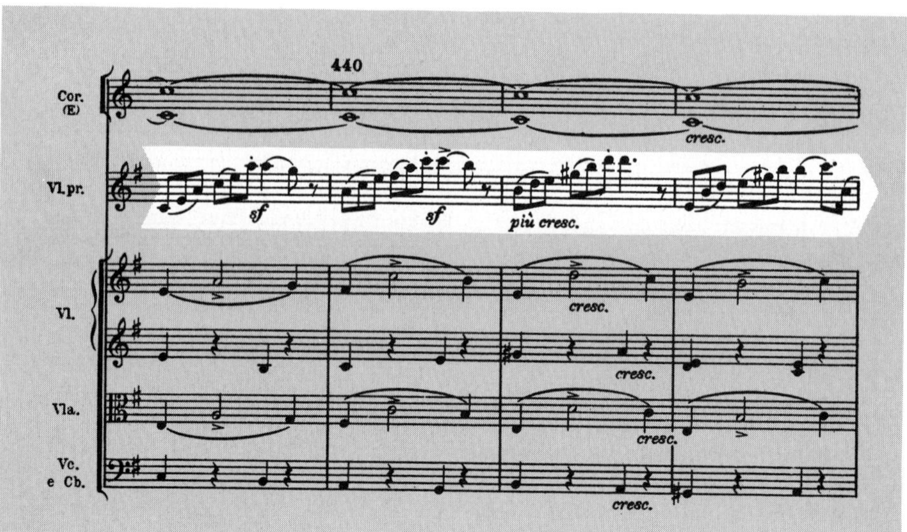

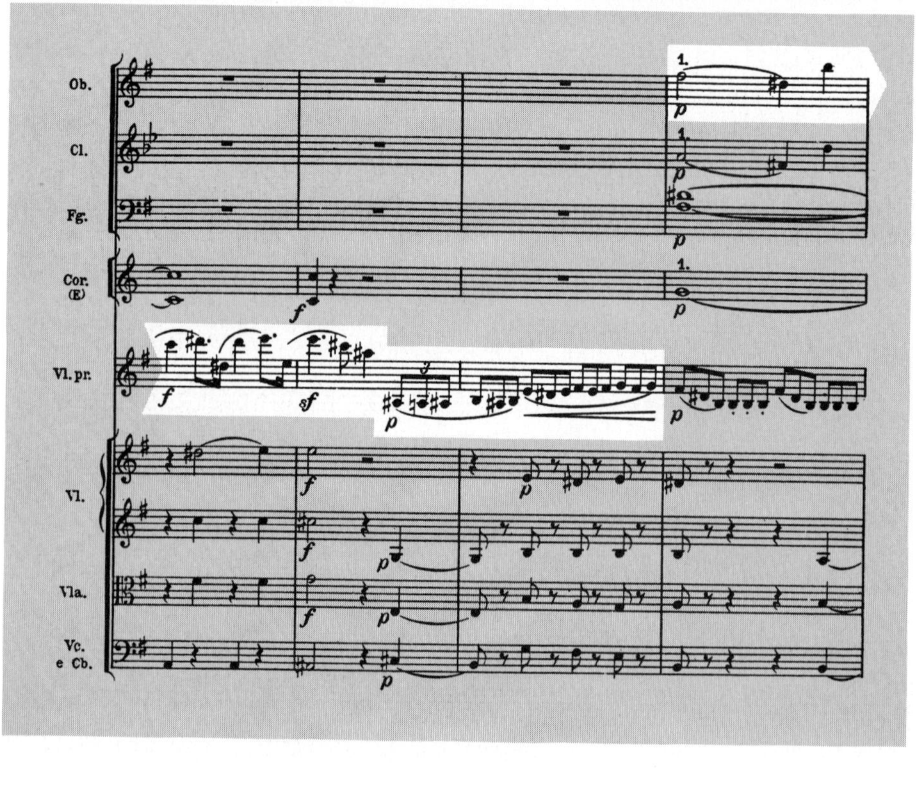

Ob.
1.
p
Cl.
1.
p
Fg.
p
Cor. (E)
f
1.
p
Vl. pr.
f
sf
p
p
Vl.
f
p
f
p
Vla.
f
p
Vc. e Cb.
p

450
Ob.
Cl.
Fg.
Cor. (E)
Vl.pr.
p
cresc.
Vl.
Vla.
Vc. e Cb.
Fl.
Timp.
Tbe. (E)
zu 2
2a e 3a corda
ff
f

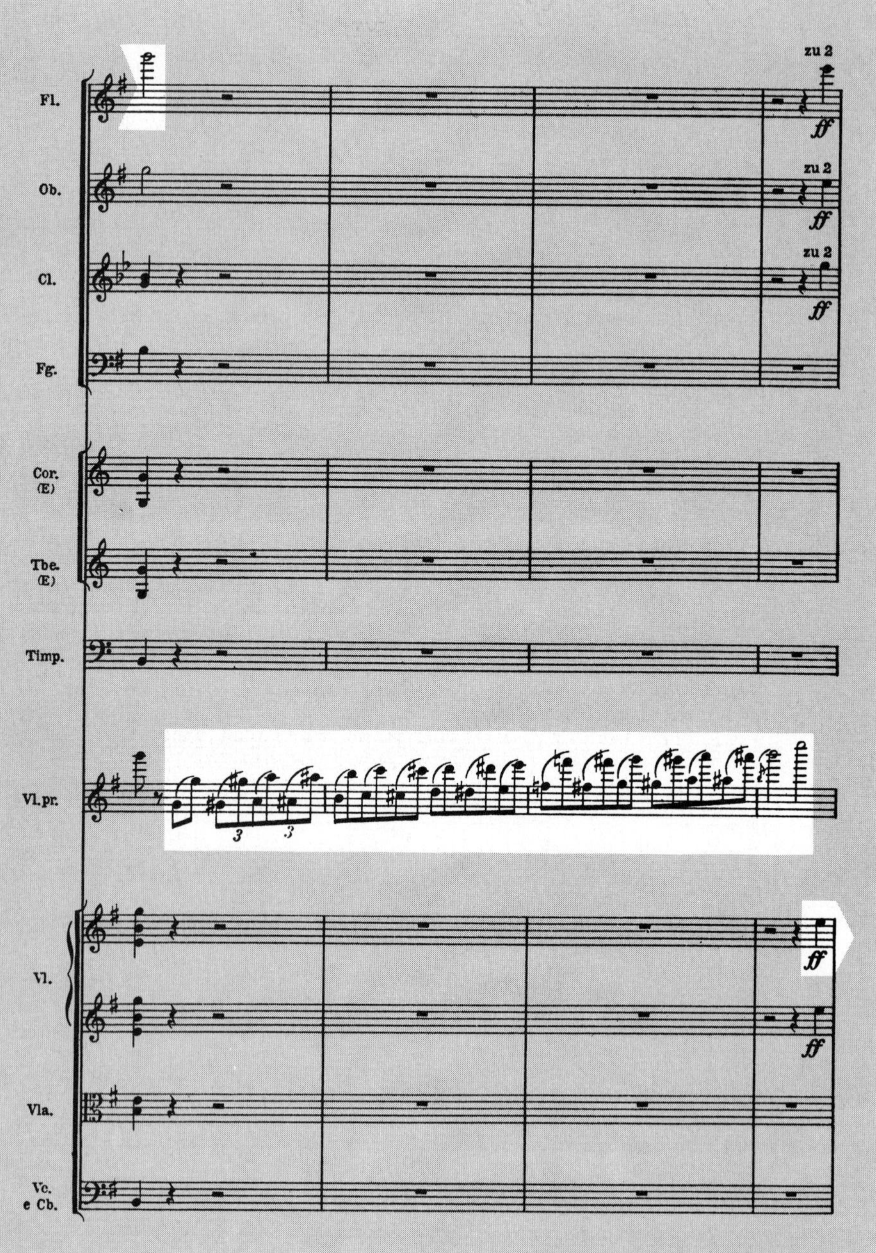
Fl.
zu 2
ff
Ob.
zu 2
ff
Cl.
zu 2
ff
Fg.
Cor.
(E)
Tbe.
(E)
Timp.
Vl. pr.
3
3
Vl.
ff
ff
Vla.
Vc.
e Cb.

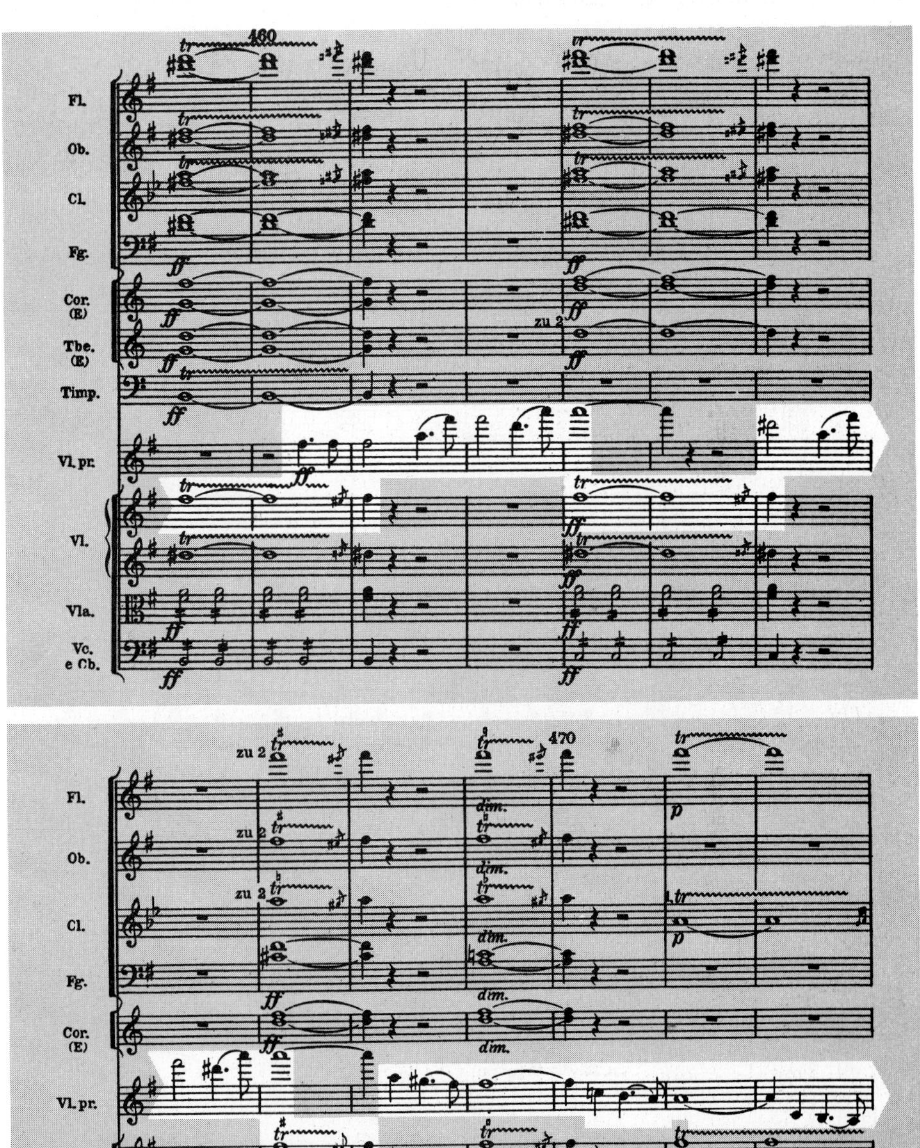
460
tr
Fl.
Ob.
Cl.
Fg.
ff
Cor. (E)
Tbe. (E)
zu 2
Timp.
Vl. pr.
Vl.
Vla.
Vc. e Cb.
470
dim.
p

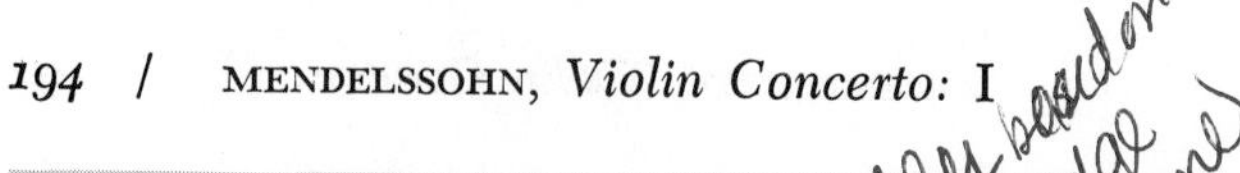

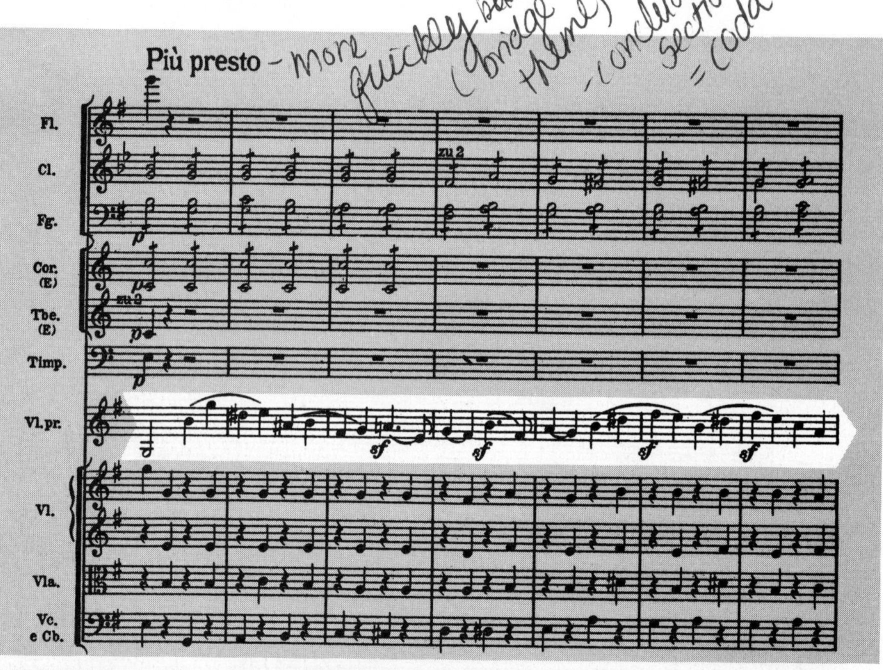
Più presto
Fl.
Cl.
Fg.
Cor. (E)
Tbe. (E)
Timp.
Vl. pr.
Vl.
Vla.
Vc. e Cb.
zu 2
p
sf

Sempre più presto
480
Fl.
Ob.
Cl.
Fg.
Cor. (E)
Tbe. (E)
Timp.
Vl. pr.
Vl.
Vla.
Vc. e Cb.
zu 2
p
sf cresc.
sf

490
Fl.
Ob.
Cl.
Fg.
Vl. pr.
Vl.
Vla.
Vc. e Cb.
cresc.
zu 2
p
sf
ff

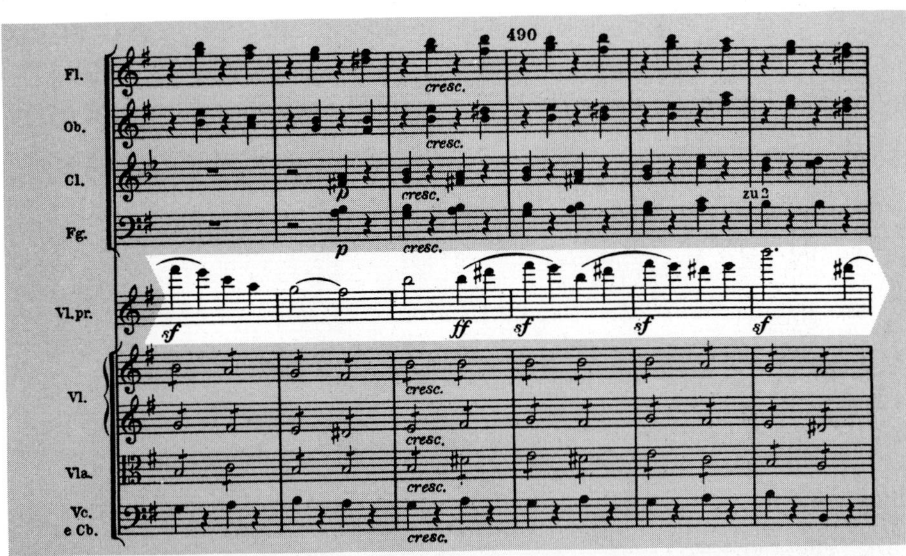

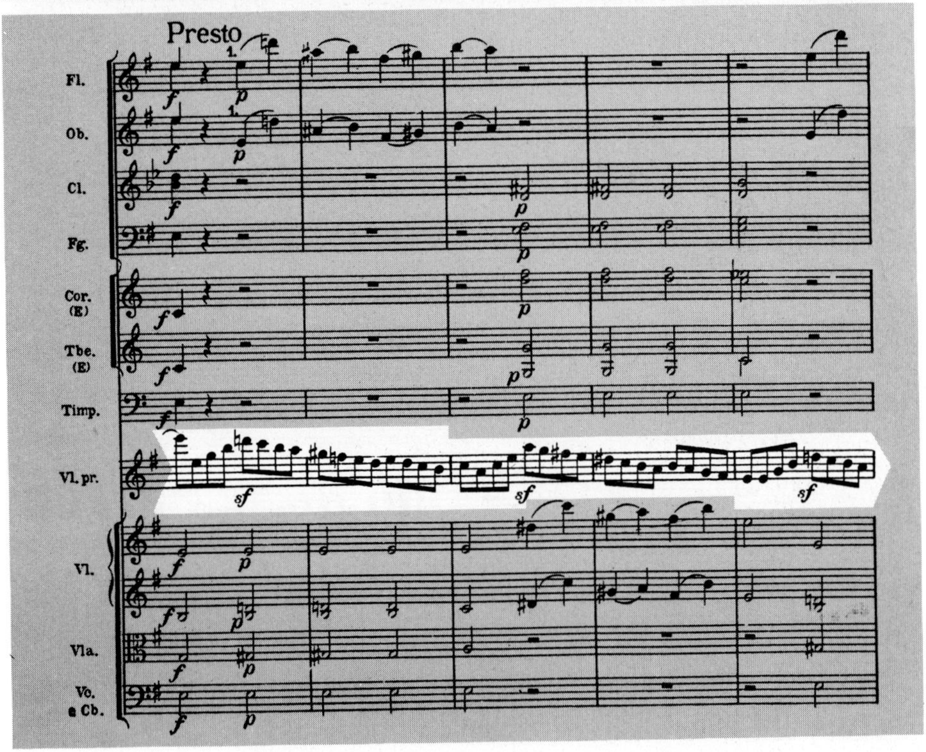

Presto
Fl.
Ob.
Cl.
Fg.
Cor. (E)
Tbe. (E)
Timp.
Vl. pr.
Vl.
Vla.
Vc. e Cb.
f
p
sf

500
Fl.
Ob.
Cl.
Fg.
Cor. (E)
Tbe. (E)
Timp.
Vl. pr.
f
cresc.
Vl.
cresc.
cresc.
Vla.
cresc.
Vc. e Cb.
cresc.
1.
zu 2
zu 2
ff
p
p
p
p
cresc.
cresc.
cresc.

510
Ob.
Cl.
Fg.
zu 2
1.
cresc.
Vl. pr.
Vl.
Vla.
Vc. e Cb.
Tutti
Fl.
Ob.
Cl.
Fg.
Cor. (E)
Tbe. (E)
Timp.
Vl. pr.
Vl.
Vla.
Vc. e Cb.

48
520
Fl.
Ob.
Cl.
Fg.
Cor. (E)
Tbe. (E)
Timp.
Vl.
Vla.
Vc. e Cb.
zu 2
sf
tr

7. FRÉDÉRIC FRANÇOIS CHOPIN (1810-1849), *Polonaise in A-flat major*, Op. 53 (1842)

tr
cresc.
ff
8

tr
tr
Ped.
8
sf
sostenuto
f

sotto voce
staccato
poco
a
poco
cresc.
cresc.

sf pp
staccato
poco
a
poco
cresc.
f
cresc.
ff
Ped.

Singing Section

tr
tr
tr
Ped.
sf
6
smorz.

cresc.
A
f
tr
8
Ped.
*

8. CHOPIN, *Etude in A minor*, Op. 25, No. 11 (PUBL. 1837)

f
dim.

f
Ped.
8

2b
f
8
Ped.
f
marcato
Ped.
8
Ped.

f
ff
ff
fz
fz

p
cre
scen
do
f
f
Ped.
dimin.
Ped.
Ped.
marcato
Ped.
Ped.
Ped.
Ped.
f
Ped.
Ped.

cresc.
ff
p
cresc.
f
ff
dimin.
ff
marcatissimo
fff

9. CHOPIN, *Prelude in E minor*, Op. 28, No. 4 (PUBL. 1839)

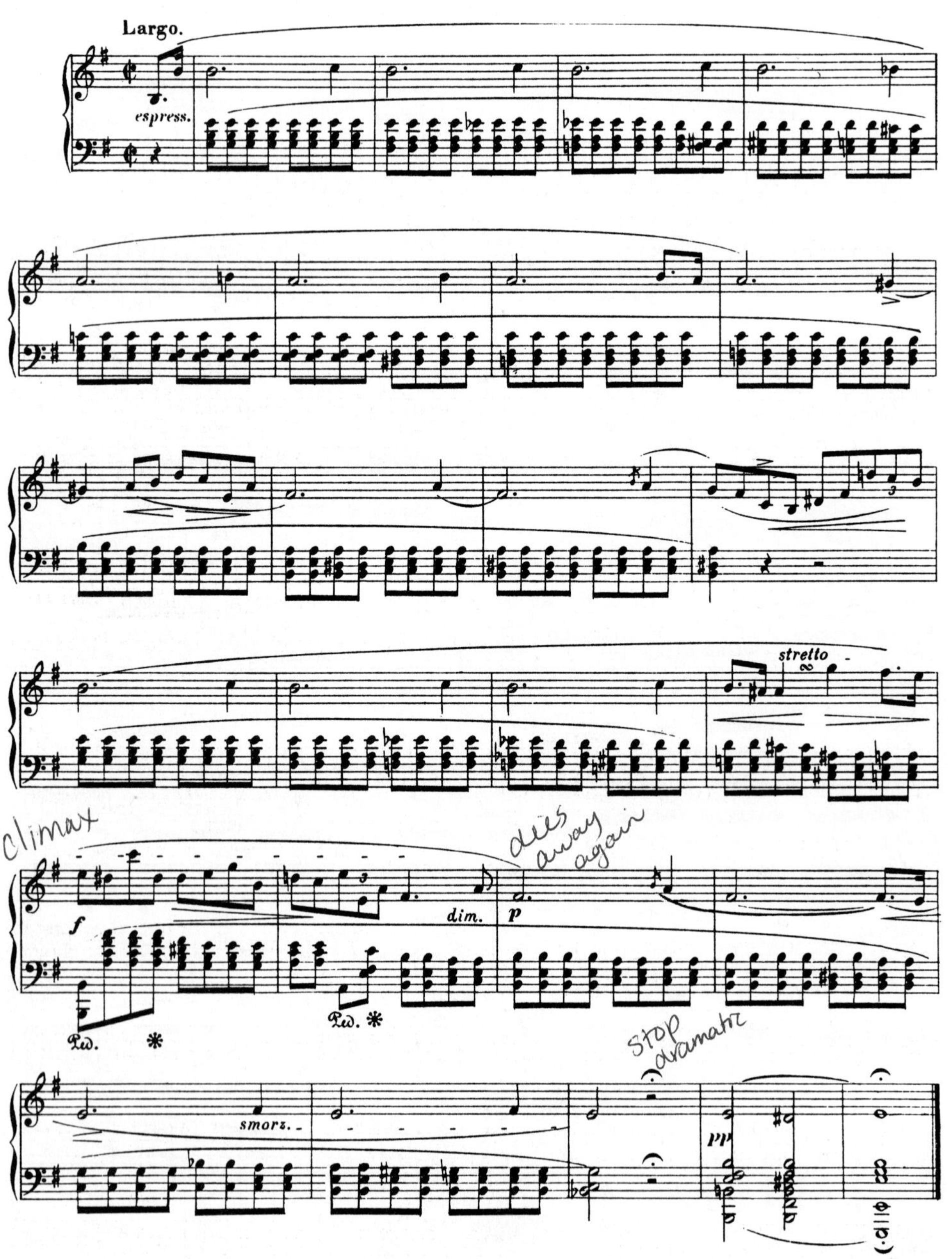

10. ROBERT SCHUMANN (1810-1856), *Aufschwung* from *Fantasiestücke* (1837)

ritard.
mf
L.H.
sf
ff
f
(sost.)
espr.

poco rit.
a tempo
ritard.
sf
mf
p scherz.
ritard.
p ma pesante

sf
ff
sf
f
sf
Ped.
p

pp

ritard.

mf

Ped. Ped. Ped. Ped. Ped.

Ped. Ped. Ped.

sf *f* *sf* *sf*

Ped. Ped.

sf *sf* *ff* *f* *f*

Ped. Ped. Ped. Ped.

11. SCHUMANN, *Ich grolle nicht* from *Dichterliebe* (1840)

Translation

Ich grolle nicht und wenn das Herz
auch bricht.
Ewig verlor'nes Lieb, ich grolle nicht.
Wie du auch strahlst in
Diamantenpracht,
Es fällt kein Strahl in deines
Herzens Nacht.

Das weiss ich längst. Ich sah dich ja im
Traume,
Und sah die Nacht in deines Herzens
Raume,
Und sah die Schlang', die dir am
Herzen frisst,
Ich sah, mein Lieb, wie sehr du elend
bist.

HEINRICH HEINE

I bear no grudge, even though my
heart may break,
eternally lost love! I bear no grudge.
However you may shine in the
splendor of your diamonds,
no ray of light falls in the darkness
of your heart.

I have long known this. I saw you in
a dream,
and saw the night within the void of
your heart,
and saw the serpent that is eating
your heart—
I saw, my love, how very miserable
you are.

PHILIP L. MILLER

12. FRANZ LISZT, (1811-1886), *Sonetto 104 del Petrarca* (PUBL. 1858)

cantabile con passione senza slentare
f
p
Ossia
più facile
etc.
cresc.
ff
accel.
rinforz.

cresc. molto
molto appassionato
ff
poco rall.
dimin.
f
non legato
ff
Ossia
cresc. e rinfz.
cresc. e rinfz.
riten.
p
stringendo
ff vibrato
poco rall.

rallent.
dolce dolente
una corda
poco rall.
dimin.
smorzando
ritenuto a piacere
agitato
molto espr.
marcato
cresc.
rinfz.

dimin.
perdendo
rallent.
un poco più lento
accentuato assai
Adagio.
a tempo
molto sostenuto
languendo
smorzando

13. LISZT, *Les Préludes* (1856)

A very long introduction

Poco ritenuto
Più rit.
10
Fl.
Kl. (C)
Fg.
smorz. pp
1.V.
2.V.
Br.
Vc.
Kb.
pizz.
arco

Poco ritenuto
Fl.
Kl. (C)
Fg.
dim.
1.V.
2.V.
Br.
Vc.
Kb.
arco

20
Fl.
pp
Hb.
Kl.
(C)
Fg.
Hr.
(C)
Tr.
(C)
Tps.
pp legato
Hps.
Tb.
Hrf.
p
1. V.
2. V.
Br.
Vc.
Kb.

Fl.
Hb.
Kl. (C)
Fg.
Hr. (C).
Tr. (C)
Tps.
Bps. Tb.
Hrf
1 V
2 V.
Br.
Vc.
Kb.
pp
pp
pp
pp
p
p
p
p
p

Fl.
poco a poco cresc.
poco a poco cresc.
Hb.
poco a poco cresc.
Kl. (C)
poco a poco cresc.
Fg.
poco a poco cresc.
Hr. (C)
p
p
Tr. (C)
Tps.
poco cresc.
Bps. Tb.
poco cresc.
Hrf.
(cresc.
1.V.
poco a poco cresc.
2.V.
poco a poco cresc.
Br.
poco a poco cresc.
Vc.
poco a poco cresc.
Kb.
poco a poco cresc.

30
Fl.
più cresc.
Hb
p
Kl. (C)
Fg.
Hr. (C)
Tr. (C)
Tps.
Rps. Tb.
f
Hf
1 V
2 V
Br
Vc
Kb

end of intro.

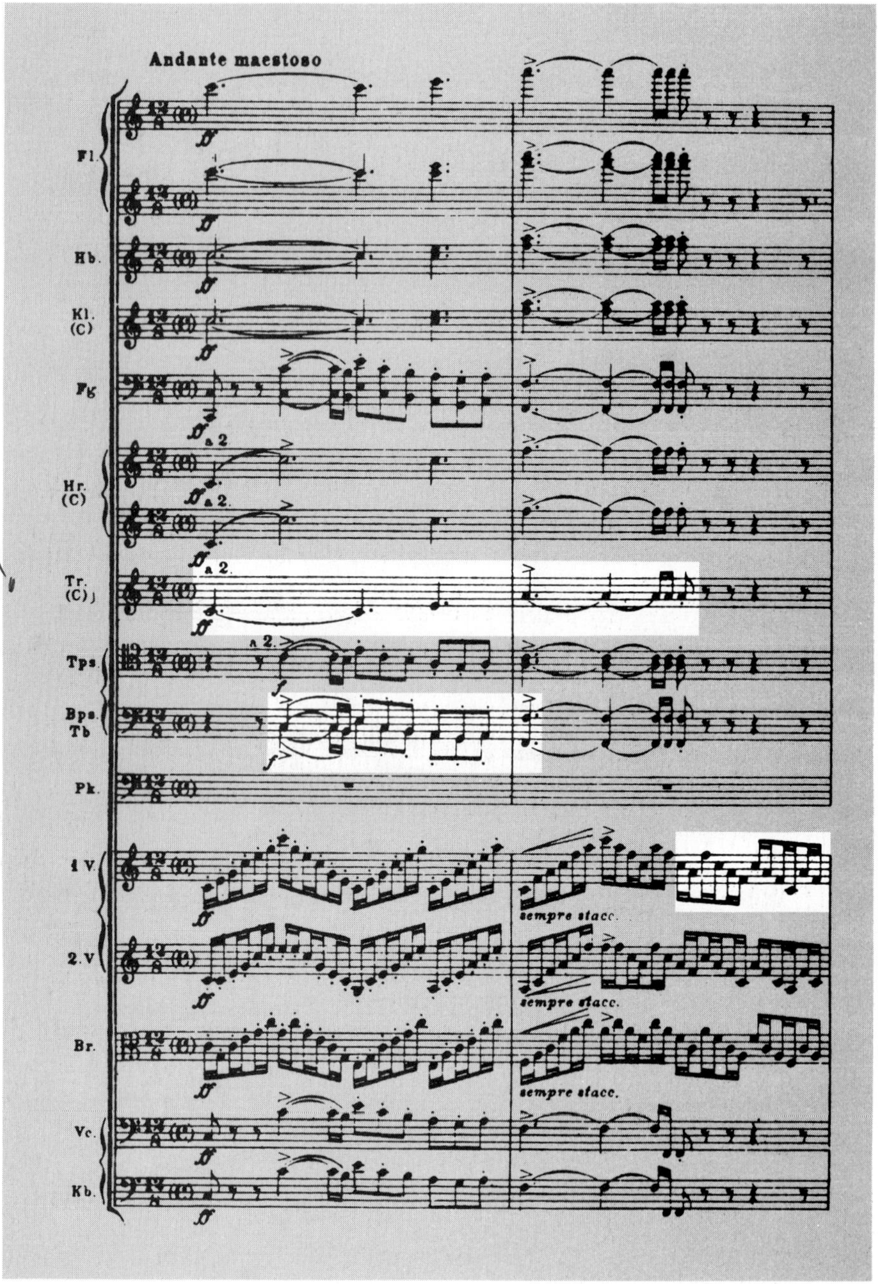

Andante maestoso

Fl.

Hb.

Kl. (C)

Fg

Hr. (C)

a 2

Tr. (C)

a 2

Tps.

a 2

Bps. Tb

Pk.

1 V.

sempre stacc.

2. V

sempre stacc.

Br.

sempre stacc.

Vc.

Kb.

Fl.
Hb.
Kl. (C)
Fg.
a 2.
Hr. (C)
Tr. (C)
Tps.
Bps. Tb.
Pk.
1.V.
2.V.
Br.
Vc
Kb.

40
Fl.
a 2.
Hb.
Kl. (C)
Fg.
Hr. (C)
Tr. (C)
Tps.
Bps. Tb.
Pk.
1. V.
2. V.
Br.
Vc.
Kb.

Fl.
a 2.
Hb.
Kl. (C)
Fg.
Hr. (C)
a 2.
a 2.
ff
Tr. (C)
a 2.
Tps.
Bps. Tb.
Pk.
ff
1. V.
2. V.
Br.
Vc.
Kb.

B
Fl.
a 2.
Hb.
Kl. (C)
Fg.
a 2.
Hr. (C)
a 2.
a 2.
Tr. (C)
Tps.
Bps. Tb.
Pk.
1 V
2. V
Br.
Vc.
Kb.

Fl.

a 2.

dim.

dim.

Hb.

dim.

Kl. (C)

dim.

Fg.

dim.

Hr. (C)

dim.

muta in E.

dim.

muta in E.

Tr. (C)

Tps.

Bps. Tb.

Pk.

muta in A.C.E.

1. V.

dim.

2. V.

Br.

dim.

Vc.

Kb.

dim.

"Dawn of life"

L'istesso tempo
1.V.
2.V.
Br.
Vc.
Kb.
p dolce (egualmente)
p cantando
mf
mf espress. cantando
pizz.
p

50
a 2
Fg.
1.V.
2.V.
Br.
Vc.
Kb.
p
arco
pizz.

Poco rall.
a 2.
Fg.
1.V.
2.V.
Br.
Vc.
Kb.
sempre dolce
arco
p

a 2.
Fg.
Solo
1.2. p dolce espressivo
Hr. (E)
1.V.
2.V.
Br.
Vc.
pizz.
Kb.
p
60
arco
div.

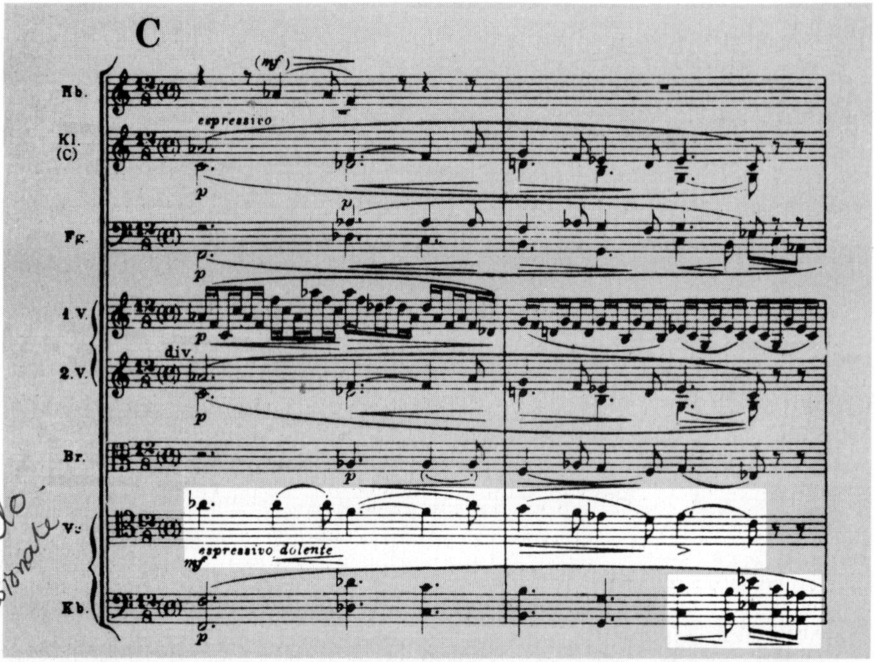

C

Hb.
(mf)
espressivo
Kl. (C)
p
Fg.
p
1. V.
p
div.
2. V.
p
Br.
p
Vc.
espressivo dolente
mf
Kb.
p

cello - passionate

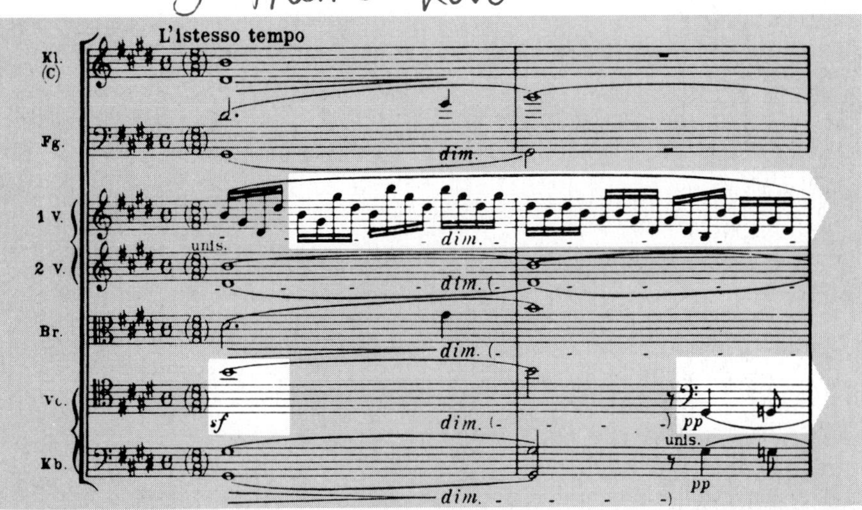

Fg.
70
espressivo ma tranquillo
Hr. (E)
(p) dolce
(p) dolce
espressivo ma tranquillo
(Vl. p)
Hrf.
p
1. V.
smorzando
(pp) dolcissimo
2. V.
(pp) dolcissimo
Br.
div. in 2 parti
con Sordino
(p) dolce
espressivo ma tranquillo
Vc.
Kb.

Hr. (E)
Hrf.
1. V.
2. V.
Br.
Vc.
Kb.
Hr. (E)
Hrf.
1. V.
2. V.
Br.
Vc.
Kb.
espress.
espress.

Oboe's-theme violins-counter melody

(I. p)
Fl.
Hb.
Kl. (C)
a 2.
Fg.
(I p)
Hr. (E)
(p)
Bps. Tb.
Hrf.
unis.
1 V
p
2. V
p
unis.
Br.
Vc.
Kb.

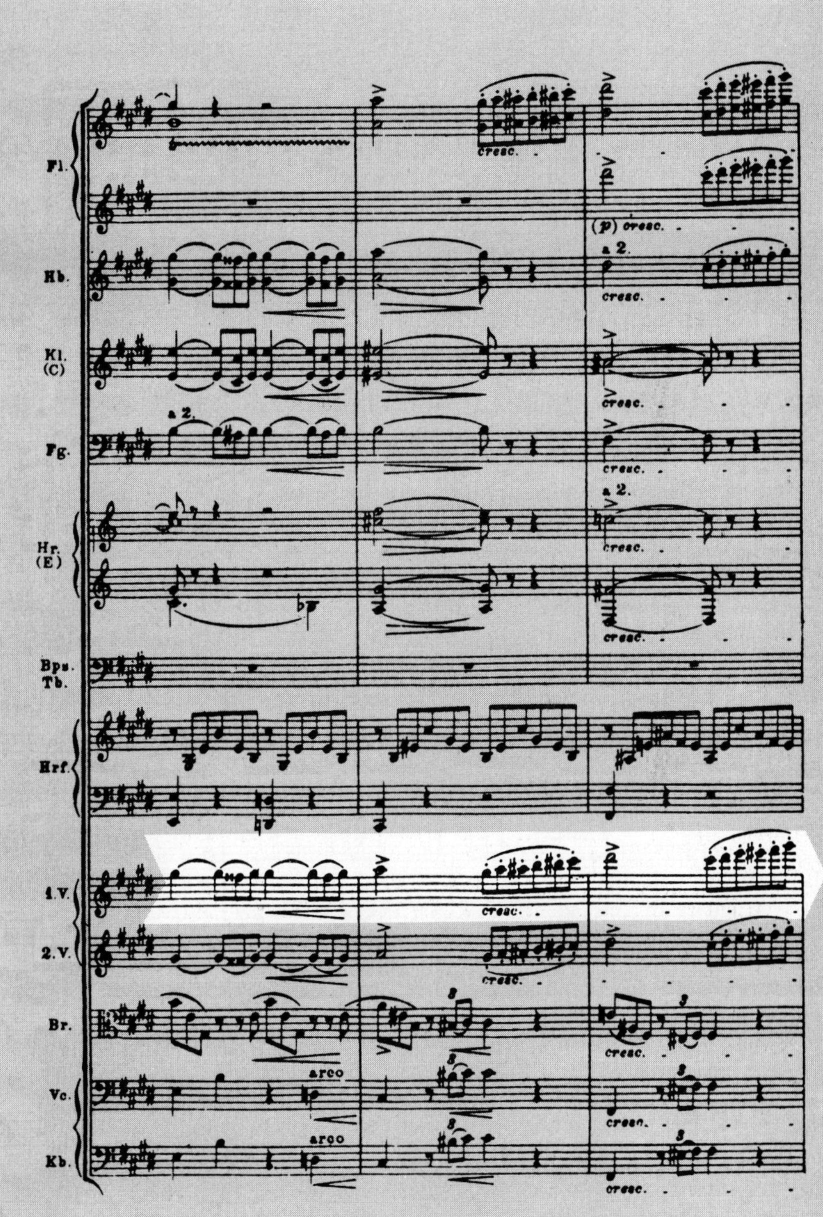
Fl.
Hb.
Kl. (C)
Fg.
Hr. (E)
Bps. Tb.
Hrf.
1. V.
2. V.
Br.
Vc.
Kb.
cresc.
(p) cresc.
a 2.
arco

Fl.
Hb.
Kl. (C)
Fg.
Hr. (E)
Bps. Tb.
Hrf.
1 V
2. V
Br.
Vc.
Kb.
più cresc.
a 2.
(p) cresc.
ff

90
Poco rall.
Fl.
p dolce
pp
Hb.
amors.
dim.
p
Kl. (C)
p dolce
pp
Fg.
dim
pp
a 2.
Hr. (E)
Bps. Tb.
Sons harmoniques
Hrf.
(p)
1.V.
(f)
2.V.
(f)
Br.
Vc.
pizz.
arco
Kb.
pizz.
arco

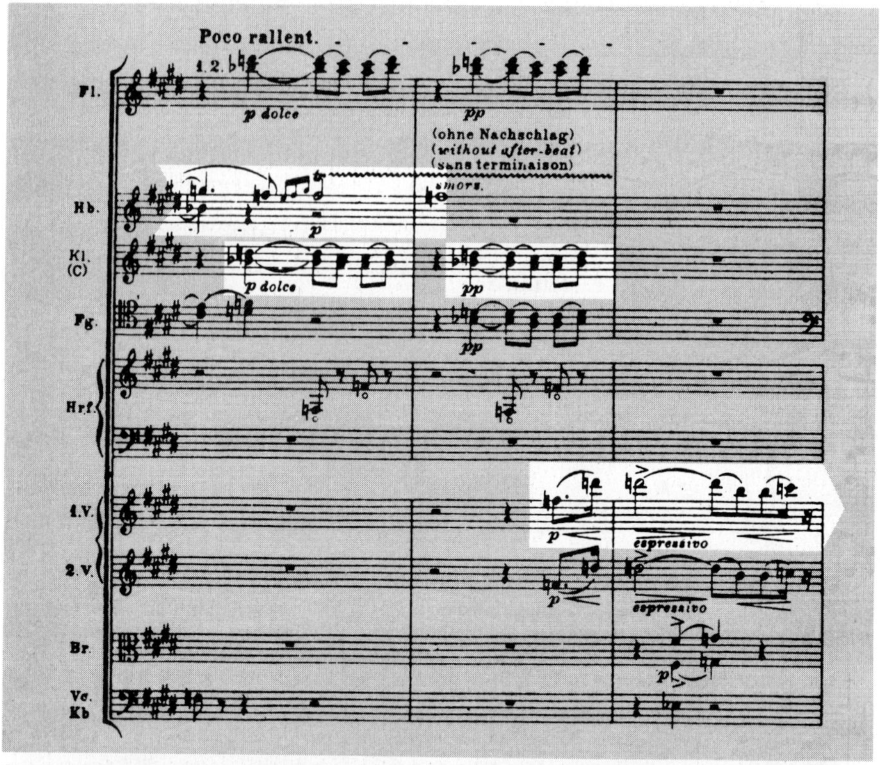

Poco rallent.
1.2.
Fl.
p dolce
pp
(ohne Nachschlag)
(without after-beat)
(sans terminaison)
smorz.
Hb.
p
Kl. (C)
p dolce
pp
Fg.
pp
Hrf.
1.V.
p
espressivo
2.V.
p
espressivo
Br.
p
Vc. Kb

rit.
100
pp
Kl. (C)
Fg.
pp
1.2.
Solo
(p) dolce
Hr. (E)
1.V.
dim.
pp
2.V.
pizz.
dim.
pp
Br.
pp
Vc. Kb.
rit.
pp

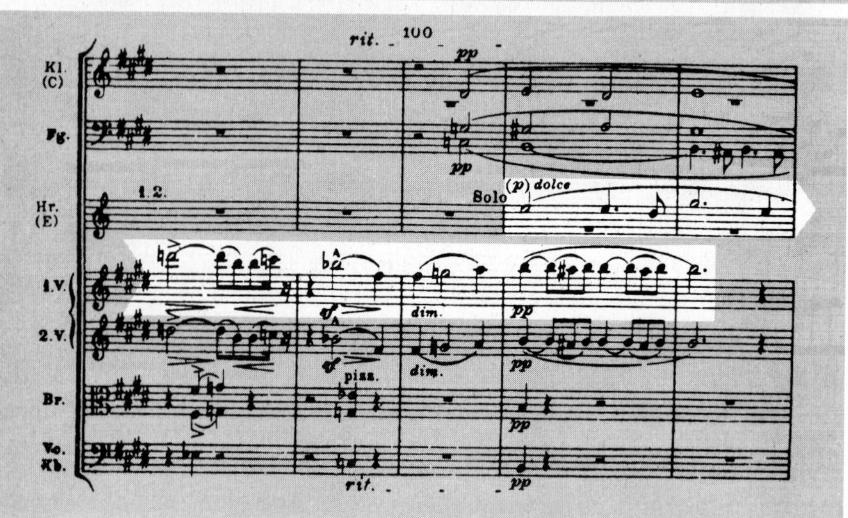

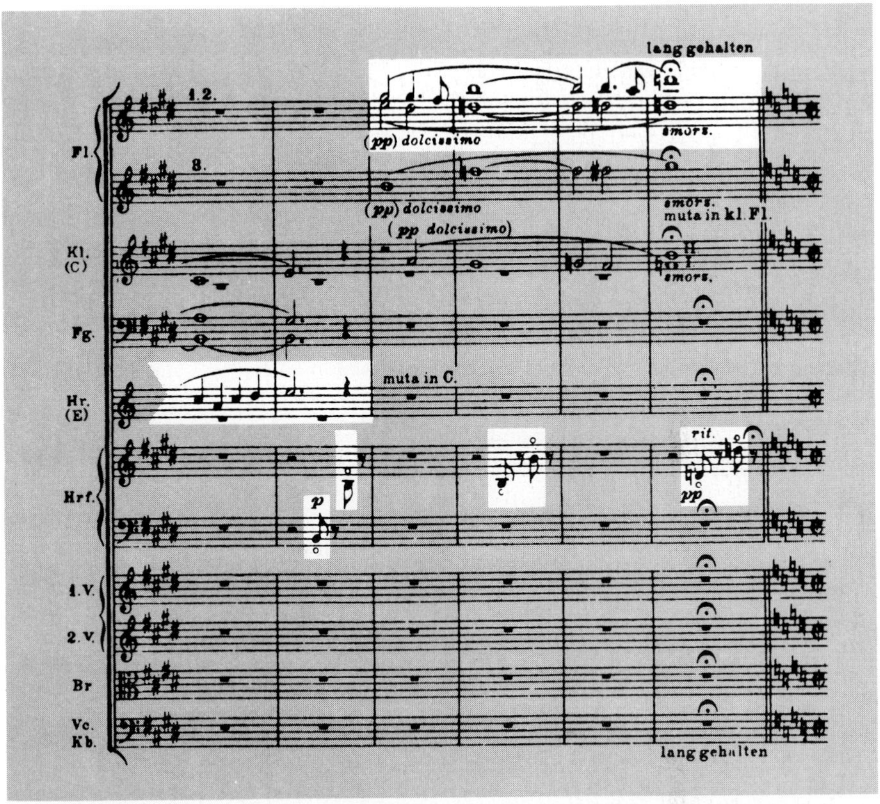

lang gehalten

Fl.

1.2.

(*pp*) *dolcissimo*

smorz.

8.

(*pp*) *dolcissimo*

smorz.

muta in kl. Fl.

Kl. (C)

(*pp dolcissimo*)

smorz.

Fg.

Hr. (E)

muta in C.

Hrf.

p

rit.

pp

1. V.

2. V.

Br

Vc. Kb.

lang gehalten

Kl. (C)
1.V.
2.V.
Br.
Vc.
(II. mf)
(12)
p
120
Fg.

E
Fl.
1.2.
a 2.
(p) cresc. e stringendo
Hb.
(p) cresc. e stringendo
Kl.
(C)
cresc. e stringendo
Fg.
a 2.
cresc. e stringendo
1.V.
cresc. e stringendo
2.V.
cresc. e stringendo
Br.
cresc. e stringendo
Vc.
cresc. e stringendo

130
Fl.
a 2.
Hb.
Kl.
(C)
a 2.
Fg.
in C.
a 2.
(C)
Hr.
(E)
a 2.
ff
1.V.
2.V.
Br.
Vc.

Allegro tempestoso.
Kl. Fl.
Fl.
Hb.
Kl. (C)
a 2.
Fg.
(C)
Hr.
(E)
a 2.
Tr. (C)
a 2.
Tpe.
Bps. Tb.
in A. C. E.
Pk.
1. V
2. V.
Br.
Vc.
arco
Kb.

Kl.Fl.
Fl.
Hb.
Kl. (C)
Fg.
a 2.
f
(C)
Hr.
(E)
a 2.
Tr. (C)
a 2.
Tps.
Bps. Tb.
Pk.
tr
1.V.
sempre f
2.V.
sempre f
Br.
sempre f
Vc.
sempre f
Kb.

Kl.Fl.
Fl.
Hb.
Kl. (C)
Fg.
(C) Hr. (E)
Tr. (C)
Tps.
Bps. Tb.
Pk.
1 V
2 V
Br
Vc.
Kb.
a 2.
sempre f

140
Kl Fl.
Fl.
Hb.
Kl. (C)
Fg.
(C) Hr. (E)
Tr. (C)
Tps.
Bps Tb.
Pk.
1.V.
2.V.
Br.
Vc.
Kb
a 2.
cresc.
molto agitato
pizz.
arco

Kl Fl.
Fl.
a 2
Hb.
Kl. (C)
Fg.
(C) Hr. (E)
Tr. (C)
Tps.
Bps Tb.
Pk
1. V.
div.
2. V.
div.
Br.
div.
Vc.
Kb.
pizz.
cresc.

F
Kl.Fl.
(mf) cresc.
a 2
Fl.
cresc.
Hb.
Kl. (C)
Fg.
a 2
(C)
Hr.
(E)
a 2
Tr. (C)
Tpk.
Bps. Tb.
Pk.
unis.
1 V.
unis.
2 V.
unis.
Br.
Vc
arco
Kb.

150
Kl.Fl.
Fl.
Hb.
Kl (C)
Fg
(C)
Hr.
(E)
Tr. (C)
Tps.
Bps. Tb.
Pk.
1 V
2.V
Br.
Vc.
Kb

Kl.Fl.
a 2.
Fl.
Hb.
Kl.
(C)
Fg.
(C)
Hr.
(E)
a 2
a 2.
Tr.
(C)
Tpa.
Bpa.
Tb.
Pk.
1.V.
2.V.
Br
Vc
Kb.

Kl.Fl
Fl.
a 2.
Hb.
Kl.
(C)
Fg.
(C)
Hr
(E)
a 2.
Tr.
(C)
Tps.
Bps.
Tb.
Pk.
1.V.
2.V.
Br.
Vo.
marcato
Kb.
marcato

Kl.Fl.
Fl.
Hb.
Kl. (C)
Fg.
(C) Hr. (E)
Tr. (C)
Tps.
Bps. Tb.
Pk.
1. V.
2. V.
Br.
Vc.
Kb.
a 2.
(f)
f
cresc. molto
cresc. molto

new theme

160
Kl. Fl.
muta in 3. Fl.
a 2.
Fl.
Hb.
a 2.
Kl. (C)
1. Klar. muta in B.
2. Klar. muta in A.
a 2.
Fg
a 2.
(C)
Hr.
(E)
f marcatiss
a 2.
f marcatiss.
a 2.
Tr. (C)
f marcatiss.
Tps.
Bps. Tb.
Pk
1. V.
2. V.
Br.
Vc.
Kb.

Fl.
Hb.
a 2.
Kl.
(C)
Fg.
a 2.
(C)
Hr.
(F)
a 2.
a 2.
Tr.
(C)
a 2.
Tps
Bps.
Tb.
(Tb. *f*)
Pk.
1. V.
2. V.
Br.
Vc.
Kb.

Fl.
a 2
Hb.
marc.
Kl. (C)
a 2
Fg.
marc.
a 2
(C)
Hr.
(E)
a 2
Tr. (C)
Tps.
Bps. Tb.
Pk.
1.V.
2.V.
Br.
Vc.
Kb

G
170
Hb.
a 2
Fg.
a 2
(C)
Hr.
(E)
a 2
sf
1. muta in B basso
2. muta in E
Tr.
(C)
a 2
sf
Tps.
sf
Bps.
Tb.
sf
Pk
sf
1. V.
ff e marcatissimo sempre
2. V.
Br.
Vc.
Kb.
Hb.
Fg.
Pk.
mf
1. V.
2. V.
staccato sempre
Br.
staccato sempre
Vc.
Kb.
staccato sempre

Hb.
Fg.
Pk.
muta in G.C.E.
1.V.
2.V.
Br.
Vc.
Kb.

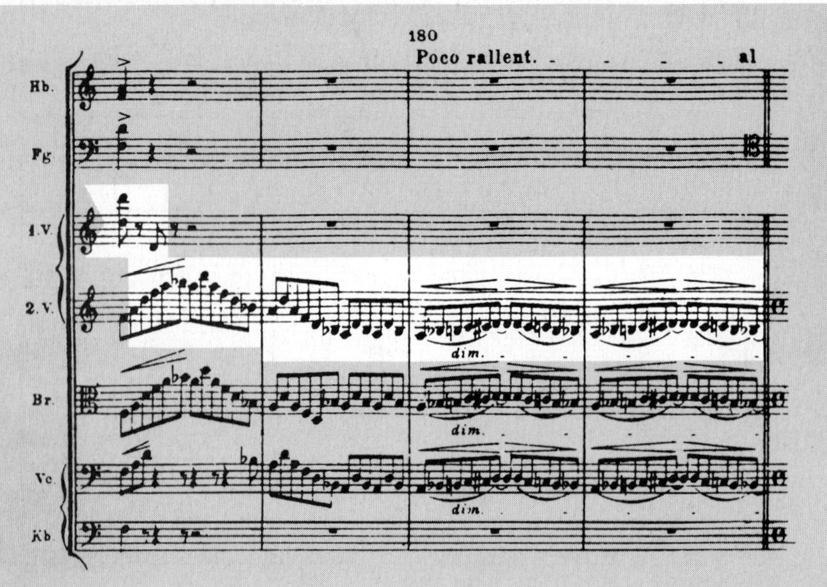
180
Poco rallent. - - - - al
Hb.
Fg
1.V.
2.V.
dim.
Br.
dim.
Vc.
dim.
Kb.

Un poco più moderato.
(p) dolce espressivo
rit.
a tempo
Hb
in B
Kl. (B)
Fg.
Hr. (B)
1. V
2. V
Br.
Vc
Kb

Fl.
Hb.
Kl. (B)
Fg.
Hr. (B)
muta in E.
1. V.
2. V.
Br
Vc.

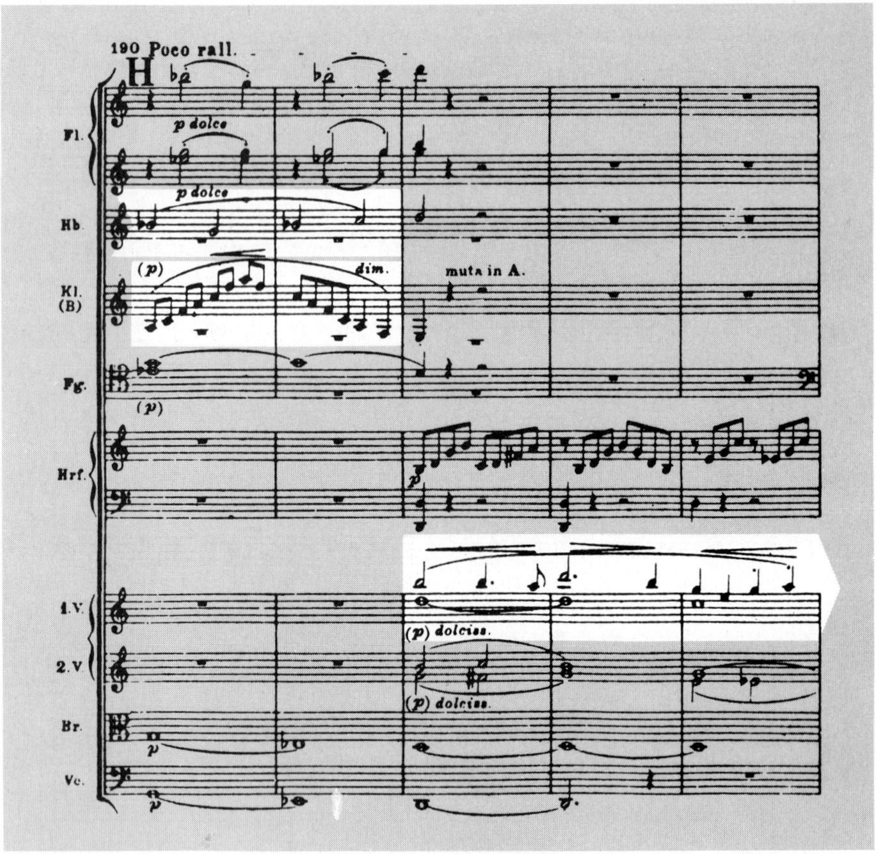

190 Poco rall.
H
p dolce
p dolce
Fl.
Hb.
(p)
dim.
muta in A.
Kl. (B)
Fg.
(p)
Hrf.
p
1.V.
(p) dolciss.
2.V.
(p) dolciss.
Br.
p
Vc.
p

Poco rall.
Hrf.
1.V.
smorzando
2.V.
morzando
Br.
smorzando
Solo
Vc.
(p)
smorzando

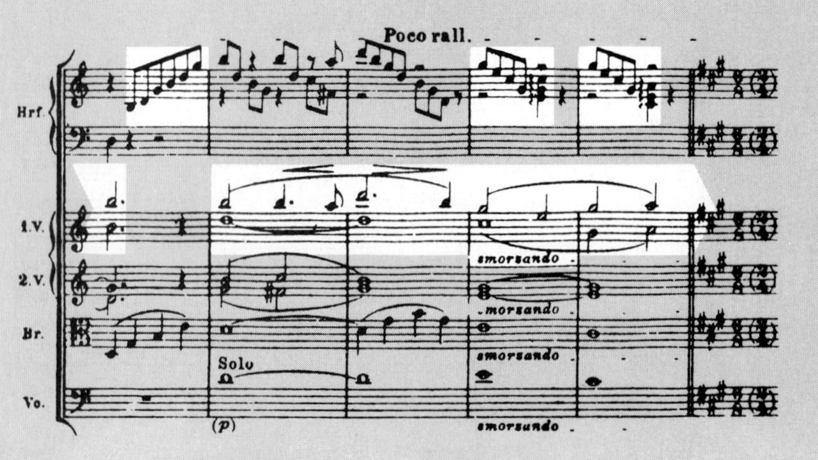

new
section

200
Allegretto pastorale
Hb.
Hr.
(E)
Hrf.
1.V.
2.V.
Br.
Vc.
1.Solo
(p) dolciss.
p
pp
1.Solo
(p) dolciss.

Hb.
Kl.
(A)
1.V.
2.V.
Br.
Vc.
210
(p) un poco marc.
1.Solo
sempre pp
sempre pp
sempre pp
div.
sempre pp

Fl.
Kl.
(A)
Hr
(E)
1.V.
2.V.
Br.
Vc.
p
dim.
1
p
(dim.)
1.
p
(dim.)
(p)
1.
p
(dim.)
(pp)
(pp)
(pp)
(pp)

220
Hb.
pp
dim.
Kl. (A)
dim.
p
(dim.)
Fg.
1 V.
2 V.
Br.
Vc.

I
230
Fl.
p grazioso
Hb.
p grazioso
p
Kl. (A)
con grazia
p
Fg.
p
1 V.
con grazia
p
2 V.
Br.
Vc.

Fl.
p
p
sempre dolce
sempre dolce
Hb.
Kl. (A)
sempre dolce
p
Fg.
1. V.
pp
2. V.
Br.
Vc.

240
Fl.
Kl. (A)
Fg.
1. V.
2. V.
Br.
pizz.
p
Vc

Fl.
Kl. (A)
Fg.
1.2.
Hr. (E)
(p)
1. V.
pizz.
p
arco
2. V.
(p)
Br.
pizz.
Vc.
(p)
Kb.

250
Solo
p
Solo
p
Fl.
Hb.
Kl. (A)
Fg.
1.2.
Hr. (E)
1. V.
2. V.
Br.
Vc.
Kb.

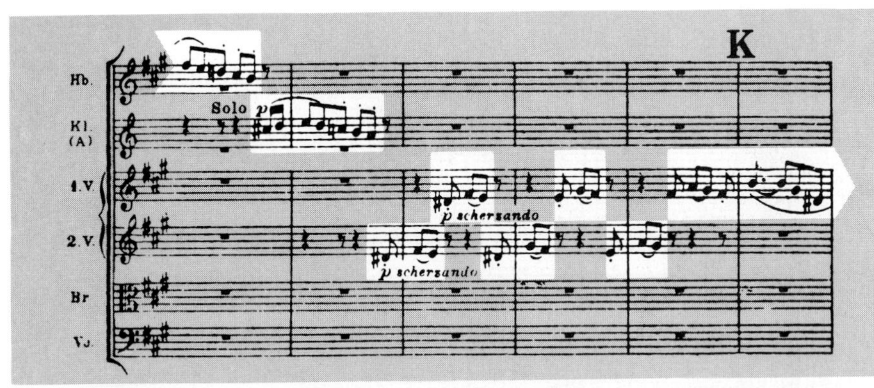
K
Hb.
Solo
Kl. (A)
1.V.
p scherzando
2.V.
p scherzando
Br
Vc.

260
Fg.
p
1.V.
dolce espressivo
2.V.
dolce espressivo
Br.
p marcato
Solo
p marcato
Vc.
div.
div.
p

Fg.
1.V.
2.V.
Br.
Vc.
div.

270
Fg.
1.V.
2.V.
Br.
Vc.
div.
pizz.
pizz.
Kb.
p

1.2.
Fl.
p
Fg.
Hr.
(E)
(mf)
(mf)
1.V.
rf.
(dim.)
2.V.
rf
(dim.)
Br.
rf
(p)
Vc.
rf
(p) dolce
div.
arco
(rf)
(p) dolce
Kb.
(rf)

(Poco a poco più mosso)
280
Fl.
dolce
(p) dolce
Kl. (A)
a 2
(p) dolce, un poco marc.
Fg.
a 2
(p) dolce, un poco marc.
Hr. (F)
muta in C
(p)
muta in C
(p)
Hrf.
mf
1. V.
(p) dolce
2. V.
(p) dolce
Br.
tranquillo
Vc.
unis.
Kb.
(p)

290
Fl.
a 2
Kl. (A)
a 2
Fg.
Hrf.
1. V.
2. V.
Br.
Vc.
Kb.

L
Fl.
cresc.
cresc.
Kl. (A)
a 2
cresc.
Fg.
a 2
cresc.
Hr. (C)
1. 2.
in C
mf
Hrf.
1. V.
div.
(p) dolce
2. V.
Br.
Vc.
div.
mf
Kb.

Poco a poco più di moto sino al Allegro marziale
Fl.
Hb.
mf
a 2. muta in C.
Kl. (A)
a 2.
Fg.
Hr. (C)
espress.
in C.
mf espress.
Tr. (C)
Tps.
Bps. Tb.
Hrf.
mf
1.V.
div.
p grazioso
pizz.
2.V.
poco f
Br.
p
div.
p
espress.
Vc.
div.
p tranquillo
arco
Kb.

300
Fl.
Hb.
Kl. (C)
Fg
Hr (C)
Tr. (C)
Tps.
Bps Tb
Hrf
1.V.
div.
2.V
Br
div.
Vc.
div.
Kb.

Fl.
Hb.
Kl. (C)
Fg.
Hr. (C)
Tr. (C)
Tps.
Bps. Tb.
Hrf.
1. V.
div.
2. V.
Br.
div.
Vc.
div.
Kb.

310
Fl.
Hb
Kl. (C)
Fg.
Hr. (C)
Tr. (C)
Tps
Bps. Tb
Hrf.
1. V.
div.
2. V.
Br.
div.
Vc.
div.
Kb.

Fl.
Hb.
Kl. (C)
Fg.
Hr. (C)
Tr. (C)
Tps.
Bps. Tb.
Pk.
Hrf.
1.V.
2.V.
Br.
Vc.
Kb.
a 3.
in C.
a 2.
cresc.
(p)
in G.C.E.
(mf)
unis.
arco
div.

M
a 8.
320
Fl.
Hb.
a 2.
Kl.
(C)
Fg.
Hr.
(C)
Tr.
(C)
Tps
Bps.
Tb
Pk
Hrf.
1. V
2. V
Br.
div.
Vc.
div.
Kb.
marcato

a 8.
Fl.
Hb.
a 2.
Kl. (C)
Fg.
Hr. (C)
Tr. (C)
Tps.
Bpv. Tb.
Pk.
Hrf.
1. V.
2. V.
unis.
Br.
unis.
Vc.
Kb.

330
a 8.
Fl.
Hb.
a 2.
Kl. (C)
Fg.
Hr. (C)
Tr. (C)
Tps
Bps. Tb.
Pk.
Hrf.
1. V.
2. V.
Br.
Vc.
Kb.
più cresc.
(f) più cresc.

Fl.
Hb.
Kl. (C)
Fg.
Hr. (C)
Tr. (C)
Tps.
Bps. Tb.
Pk.
Hrf.
1. V.
2. V.
Br.
Vc.
Kb.

Fl.
Hb.
Kl. (C)
Fg.
Hr. (C)
Tr. (C)
Tps
Bps Tb.
Pk
Hrf
1. V.
2. V.
Br.
Vc.
Kb.
a 8.
a 2.

340
a 3.
Fl.
Hb.
a 2.
Kl. (C)
a 2.
Fg.
Hr. (C)
a 2.
Tr. (C)
Tps.
Bps. Tb.
Pk.
(f)
Hrf.
1. V.
2. V.
Br.
Vc.
Kb.

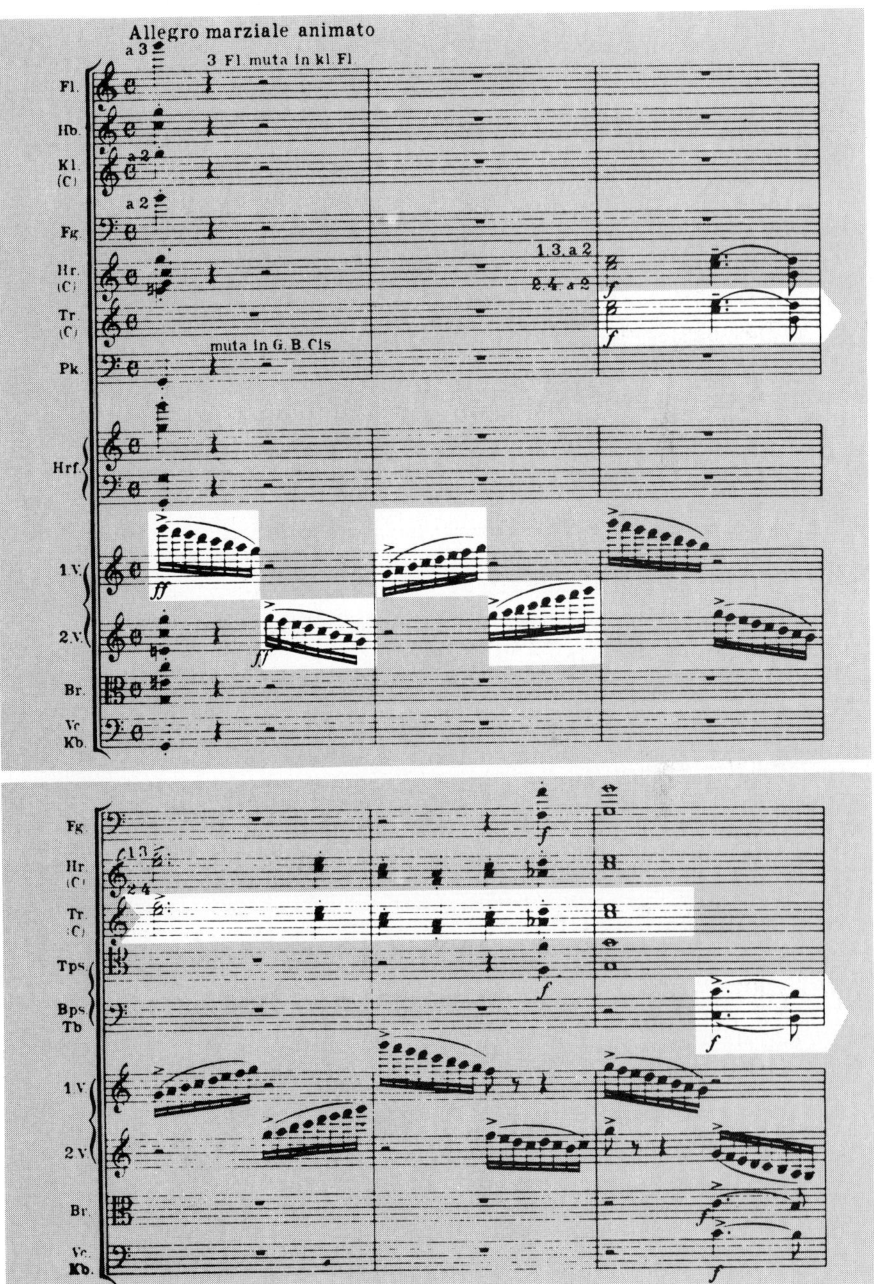
Allegro marziale animato
a 3
3 Fl muta in kl Fl.
Fl.
Hb.
Kl. (C)
a 2
a 2
Fg.
Hr. (C)
1.3. a 2
2.4. a 2
Tr. (C)
muta in G. B. Cis
Pk.
Hrf.
ff
1 V.
2 V.
Br.
Vc. Kb.
Fg.
Hr. (C)
Tr. (C)
Tps.
Bps. Tb
Br.
Vc. Kb.

350
Hr. (C)
Tr. (C)
Bps. Tb.
1. V.
2. V.
Br.
Vc. Kb.

N
Fg.
Hr. (C)
Tr. (C)
Tps.
Bps. Tb.
1. V.
2. V.
Br.
Vc. Kb.

(mf)
Fl.
(mf)
Hb.
mf
Kl. C
a 2.
mf
a 2.
Fg.
f
Solo
Tr. C
f
(II. f)
Bps. Tb.
p
1. 2. V.
p
fp
Br.
p
Vc.
p
Kb.
p

360
Fl.
Hb.
a 2.
Kl. C
Fg.
a 2.
Tr. C
p
1. 2. V.
fp
cresc.
Br.
Vc.
cresc.

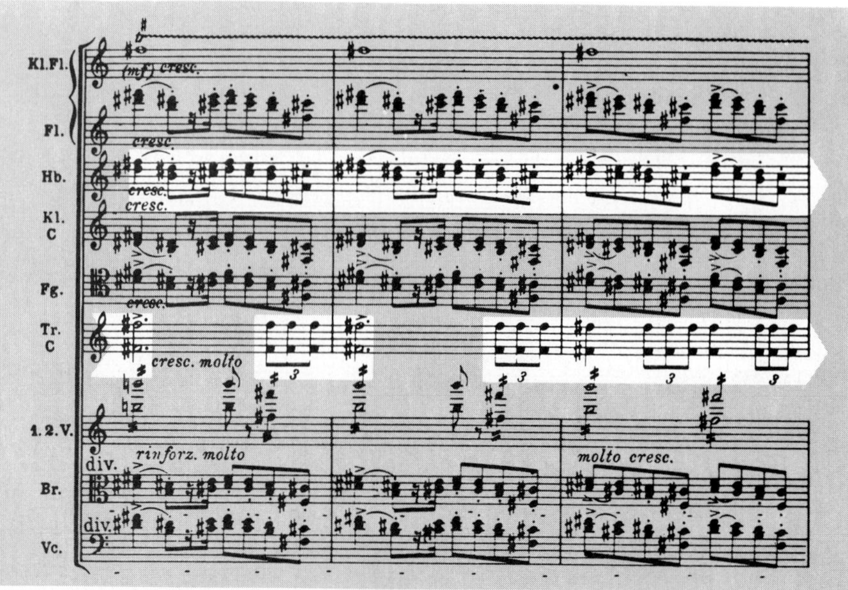
Kl.Fl.
(mf) cresc.
Fl.
cresc.
Hb.
cresc.
Kl. C
cresc.
Fg.
cresc.
Tr. C
cresc. molto
1.2.V.
rinforz. molto
molto cresc.
div.
Br.
div.
Vc.

O
(poco riten.)
Kl.Fl.
più cresc.
Fl.
più cresc.
Hb.
più cresc.
Kl. C
più cresc.
Fg.
a 2.
più cresc.
Hr. C
3.4.
ff
Tr. C
Bps. Tb.
ff
unis.
1.2.V.
Br.
unis.
Vc.

370 (Tempo di marcia.)
Kl.Fl.
Fl.
Hb.
Kl. (C)
Fg.
Hr. (C)
Tr. (C)
Tps.
Bps. Tb.
in G. B. Cis.
Pk.
Mtr.
Bk.
Gr.Tr.
1. V.
2. V.
Br.
unis.
Vc.
Kb.

Kl.Fl.
Fl.
a 2.
Hb.
Kl. (C)
Fg.
Hr. (C)
Tr. (C)
Tps.
Bps. Tb.
Pk.
Mtr.
Bk.
Gr.Tr.
1.V.
2.V.
Br.
Vc.
Kb.

(Più maestoso)
Kl.Fl.
Fl.
Hb.
Kl. (C)
Fg.
Hr. (C)
Tr. (C)
Tps.
Bps Tb.
Pk.
Mtr.
Bk.
Gr Tr.
1. V.
2. V.
Br.
Vc.
Kb.
a 2.

380
Kl Fl
a 2
Fl.
Hb.
Kl.
(C)
Fg.
Hr.
(C)
Tr.
(C)
Tps.
Bps.
Tb.
Pk.
Mtr.
Bk.
Gr.Tr.
1. V.
2. V.
Br.
Vc.
Kb.

P
Kl.Fl
a 2.
Fl.
Hb.
Kl. (C)
Fg.
Hr. (C)
Tr. (C)
Tps.
Bps. Tb
Pa.
muta Cis in C.
Mtr
Bk
Gr.Tr.
1 V
2 V
Br
Vc
Kb

(Vivace)
Kl. Fl.
Fl.
Hb.
Kl (C)
Fg.
Hr. (C)
Tr. (C)
Tps.
Bps. Tb.
Pk.
Bk.
1. V.
2. V.
Br.
Vc.
Kb.
(I. mf)
(mf)
mf
f
(II. f)
p
fp
div.
pizz.
arco

390
Kl.Fl.
Fl.
Hb.
Kl. (C)
a 2.
Fg.
(II. mf)
Hr. (C)
Tr. (C)
Tps.
Bps. Tb.
Pk.
Bk.
1. V.
2. V.
Br.
Vc.
pizz.
arco
Kb.

Kl.Fl.
Fl.
Hb.
Kl. (C)
Fg.
Hr. (C)
Tr. (C)
Tps.
Bps. Tb.
Pk.
Bk.
1.V.
2.V.
Br.
Vc.
Kb.
a 2.
(mf)
cresc.
fp
div.
arco
pizz.
cresc. molto

Kl. Fl.
Fl.
Hb.
Kl. (C)
Fg.
Hr. (C)
Tr. (C)
Tpe.
Bpe. Tb.
Pk.
Bk.
1. V.
2. V.
Br.
Vc.
Kb.
a 2.
cresc. molto
div.

Q
400
Kl.Fl.
a 2.
Fl.
a 2.
Hb.
a 2.
Kl. (C)
Fg.
a 2.
Hr. (C)
a 2.
Tr. (C)
Tps.
(mf cresc.
Bps. Tb.
(mf cresc.
in G. B. C
Pk.
(mf cresc.
Bk.
unis.
1. V.
unis.
2. V.
unis.
Br.
Vc.
Kb.

poco ritard.
Kl.Fl.
a 2.
Fl.
Hb.
Kl.
(C)
Fg.
Hr.
(C)
Tr.
(C)
Tps.
Bps.
Tb.
Pk.
1.V.
2.V.
Br.
Vc.
Kb.

Andante maestoso
Kl.Fl.
Fl.
Hb.
Kl. (C)
Fg.
Hr. (C)
Hr. (C)
Tp.
Hps Tb
Pk
Mtr
Bk
Gr Tr
1 V
2 V
Br
Vc.
Kb

Kl.Fl.
Fl.
Hb.
Kl. (C)
Fg.
a 2.
Hr. (C)
Tr. (C)
Tp.
Bps Tb
Pk.
Mtr
Bk.
Gr Tr.
1. V.
sempre stacc.
2. V.
sempre stacc.
Br.
sempre stacc.
Vc.
Kb.

410
Kl. Fl.
Fl.
Hb.
Kl. (C)
Fg.
Hr. (C)
Tr. (C)
Tpn.
Bps. Tb.
Pk.
Mtr.
Bk.
Gr. Tr.
1. V.
2. V.
Br.
Vc.
Kb.

Kl.Fl.
Fl.
Hb.
Kl. (C)
Fg.
Hr. (C)
Tr. (C)
Tps.
Bps. Tb.
Pk.
Mtr.
Bk.
Gr.Tr.
1.V.
2.V.
Br.
Vc.
Kb.
a 2.

Kl.Fl.
Fl.
Hb.
Kl. (C)
Fg.
Hr. (C)
Tr (C)
Tps.
Bps. Tb.
Pk.
Mtr.
Bk.
Gr.Tr
1 V
2 V.
Br.
Vc
Kb.
a 2.
sempre ff

Kl. Fl.
Fl.
Hb.
Kl. (C)
Fg.
Hr. (C)
Tr. (C)
Tps.
Bps., Tb.
Pk.
Mtr.
Bk.
Gr. Tr.
1. V.
2. V.
Br.
Vc.
Kb.

Kl Fl.
Fl.
Hb.
Kl. (C)
Fg.
Hr. (C)
Tr. (C)
Tps.
Bps. Tb.
Pk.
Mtr.
Bk.
Gr. Tr.
1. V.
2. V.
B.
Vc
Kb

14. RICHARD WAGNER (1813-1883), Excerpts from *Tristan und Isolde* (1859)

Prelude

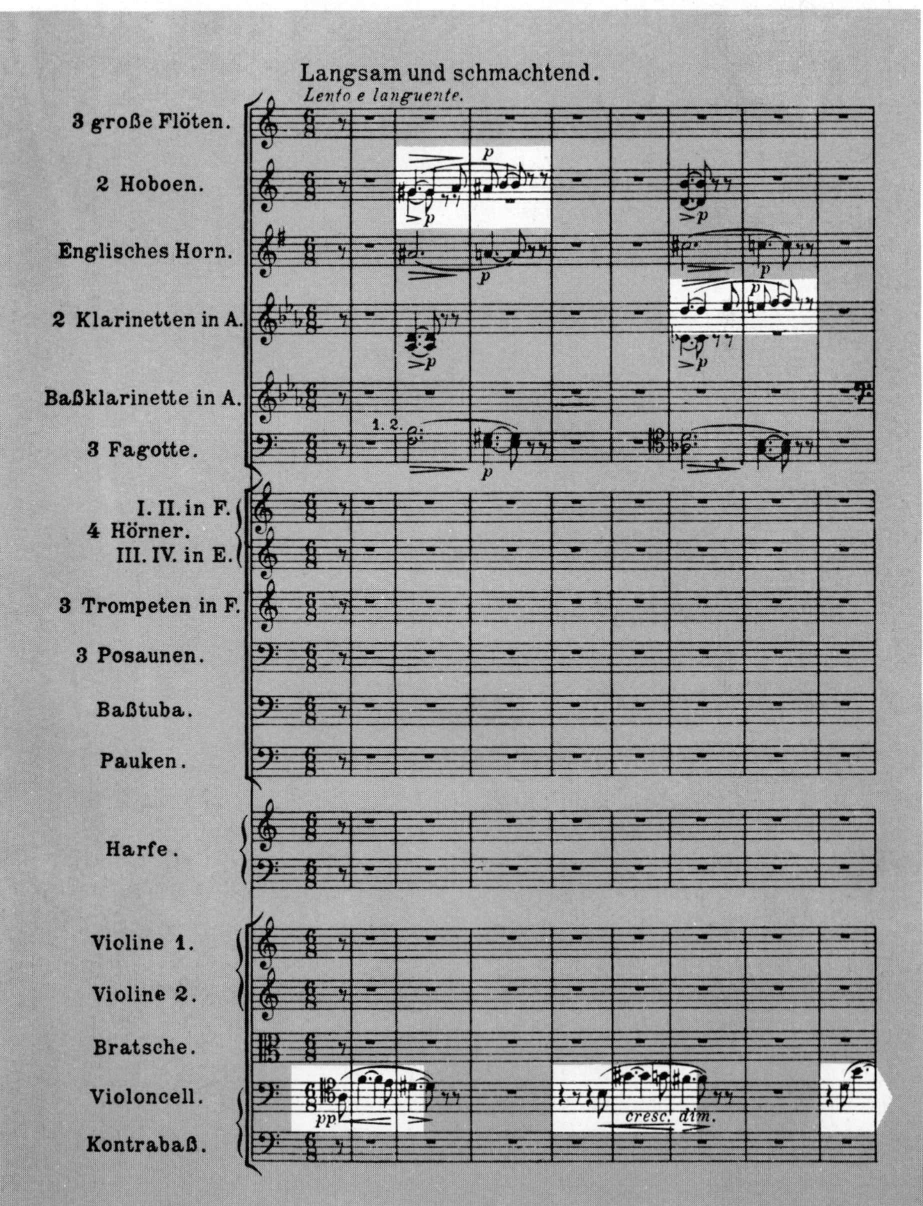

tristan chord

again

again

lovedeath motif

riten. a tempo

30

E. H.

Bkl.

Fg.

F Hr. E

1. V.

2. V.

Br.

Vc.

Kb.

1.2.

zu 3

ten.

f dim. p

sf

p cresc.

zart. dolce

Continuous melody

Hb.
E.H.
Kl.
Bkl.
Fg.
F.
Hr.
E.
1. V.
2. V.
Br.
Vc.
1.
cresc.
dim.
1. 2. zus.
p cresc.
8.
ten.
1. p
zart.
dolce
ten.
get.
più p
pp
p dim.

back & forth — strings & winds

rallent.
a tempo
Fl.
Hb.
E.H.
Kl.
Bkl.
Fg.
F. Hr.
E.
1. V.
2. V.
Br.
Vc.
Kb.
zart
dolce
dim.
cresc.
1. 2. zus.
più p
ff dim.

50
1.
1.2.
zu 3
1.
Fl.
p
sf
<sf
cresc.
f
dim.
Hb.
sf
E.H.
p
Kl.
zu 2
Bkl.
cresc.
p cresc.
1.2.
Fg.
F.
Hr.
E.
1. V.
p cresc.
2. V.
Br.
Vc.
Kb.

1.
zu 8
60
Fl.
p
f
più f
Hb.
zu 2
p
f
più f
E.H.
f
più f
Kl.
zu 2
p
f
più f
Bkl.
f
più f
1. 2.
zu 2
Fg.
8.
p
f
più f
F.
Hr.
E.
f
dim.
più f
1.V.
f
più f
2.V.
f
più f
Br.
f
più f
Vc.
f
più f
Kb.
f
più f

zu 8
Fl.
ff
zu 2
Hb.
ff
E. H.
ff
zu 2
espress.
Kl.
ff
Bkl.
ff
meno f
1.2.zus.
espress.
Fg.
ff
meno f
f
p
8.
ff
meno f
zu 2
espress.
F.
Hr.
E.
ff
zu 2
espress.
meno f
f
ff
1.V.
meno f
2.V.
ff
dim.
meno f
Br.
ff
meno f
Vc.
ff
meno f
Kb.
ff
meno f

Fl.
Hb.
E. H.
Kl.
Bkl.
Fg.
F. Hr. E.
Ps.
1. V.
2. V.
Br.
Vc.
Kb.
1. 2.
zu 2
3.
p cresc.
molto cresc.
f
p
sempre più f

70
1.2.
Fl.
p cresc..
f
zu 2
Hb.
molto cresc.
f
più f
E.H.
molto cresc.
f
più f
zu 2
Kl.
molto cresc.
Bkl.
molto cresc..
Fg.
f
cresc.
molto cresc.
molto cresc.
1.
F.
2.
Hr. F.
f
p cresc.
molto cresc.
3.
E.
molto cresc.
f
3.4.zus.
Ps.
p
cresc.
1.V.
f
2.V.
f
p
f
Br.
f
p
f
Vc.
f
Kb.
f

1. 2.
Fl.
p cresc.
3.
più f
zu 2
Hb.
ff
f
più f
E. H.
ff
f
più f
zu 2
Kl.
ff
f
più f
Bkl.
Fg.
1.
F.
molto cresc.
2.
Hr. F.
3. 4. zus.
E.
f
f
più f
Ps.
cresc.
1. V.
più f
2. V.
p
f
più f
Br.
più f
Vc.
più f
Kb.
più f

zu 3
Fl.
zu 2
Hb.
E. H.
zu 2
Kl.
Bkl.
più f
Fg.
F.
Hr.
E.
Ps.
Btb.
C.
Pk.
p cresc.
1. V.
2. V.
a. d. G.
Br.
Vc.
Kb.
ff

zu 8
Fl.
sempre f
più f
zu 2
Hb.
più f
E.H.
sempre f
più f
zu 2
Kl.
sempre f
più f
Bkl.
ff
Fg.
sempre f
sempre f
dim.
F.
Hr.
E.
sempre f
dim.
sempre f
Btb.
sempre f
Pk.
tr
mf
1.V.
sempre f
2.V.
sempre f
trem.
Br.
sempre f
Vc.
dim.
Kb.
sempre f

zu 8
80
Fl.
Hb.
E. H.
Kl
Bkl.
ff espress.
Fg.
più f
f espress.
F.
Hr.
E.
f espress.
più f
Tr. F.
f
Ps.
f
Btb.
F.
Pk.
tr
p cresc.
1. V.
più f
2. V.
più f
Br.
più f
espress.
Vc.
f
più f
Kb.
più f

zu 3
Fl.
Hb.
E. H.
Kl.
Bkl.
Fg.
F.
Hr.
E.
Tr. F.
Ps.
Btb.
Pk.
1. V.
2. V.
Br.
Vc.
Kb.
ff
più f
1.2. zus.
tr
trem.

allmählich im Zeitmaß etwas zurückhaltend
poco a poco ritenuto
zu 2
Fl.
Hb.
E. H.
Kl.
Bkl.
Fg.
F. Hr. E.
Pk.
1. V.
2. V.
Br.
Vc.
Kb.
dim.
p
più p
espress.
tr
E.
tristan chord

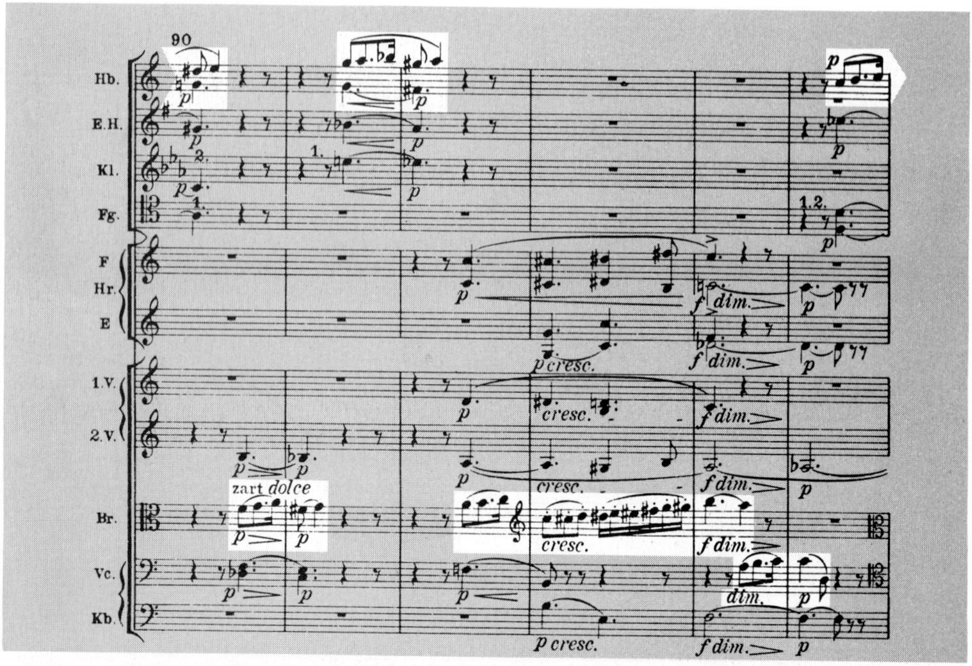

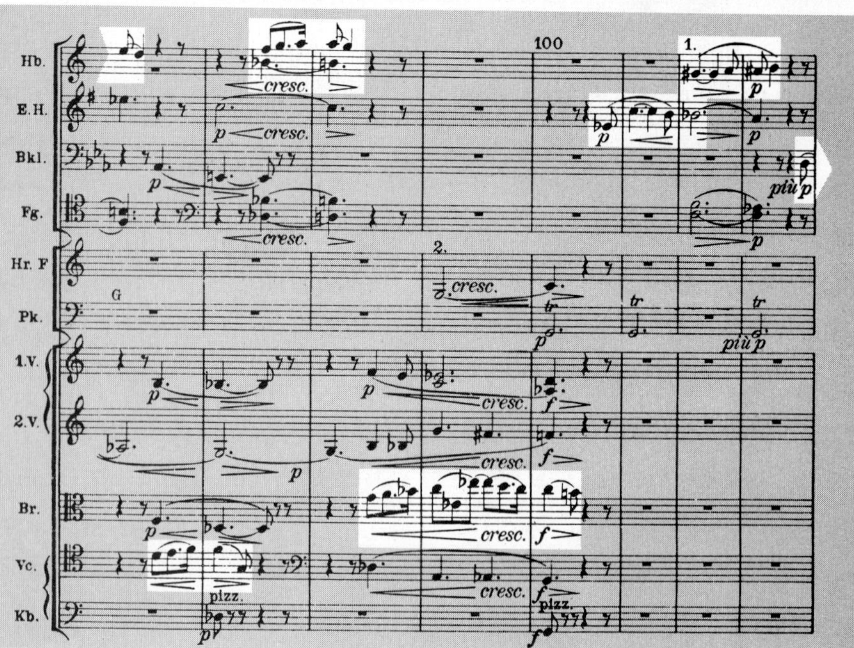

90
Hb.
E.H.
Kl.
Fg.
F
Hr.
E
1.V.
2.V.
Br.
Vc.
Kb.
zart dolce
p cresc.
f dim.
dim.
1.2.

100
Hb.
E.H.
Bkl.
Fg.
Hr. F
Pk.
G
1.V.
2.V.
Br.
Vc.
Kb.
cresc.
più p
pizz.
tr

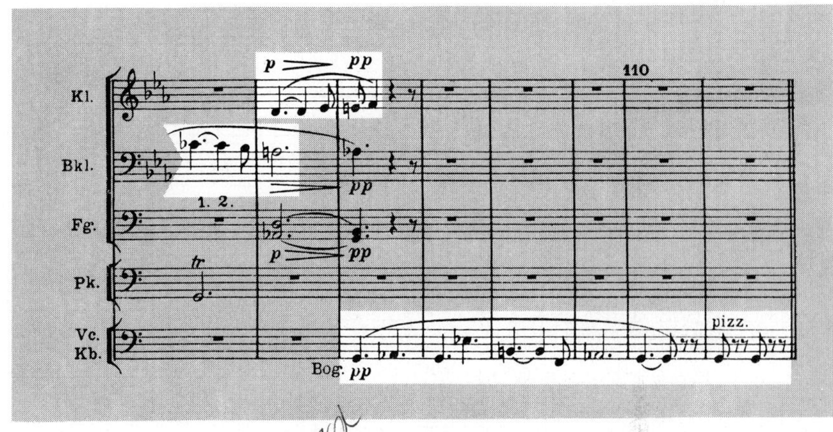

chord

Isolda.
O
De-

Tristan.
O sink' her- nie- -der, Nacht der
De - scend up - on us, night of

pp

I.
gieb__ Ver-ges - sen, dass_ ich le- - -be,
let__ us live,__ our life__ for - get- - -ting,

T.
le- - -be, nimm mich auf___ in dei- -nen
get- - -ting, lift,__ oh! lift___ us up__ to

dim.

orchestra is continuous too

I.
heil'- -ger Dämm' - rung heh- -res
ho- -ly twi- -light's sweet- -est
T.
heil'- -ger Dämm'- -rung heh- -res Ah- -nen
ho- -ly twi- -light's sweet- -est hop- -ing,
p
poco cresc.
poco f
I.
Ah- -nen löscht des Wäh- -nens Graus
hop- -ing, let false fears be hurled
T.
löscht des Wäh- -nens Graus welt-
let false fears be hurled from
cresc.
molto cresc.
Breiter.
Allargando.
Sehr breit und zurückhaltend.
Ritenuto e largo.
riten.
I.
welt- -er-lö- -send aus.
from a van- -ished world.
T.
er-lö- -send aus.
a van- -ished world.
ff
dim.
p riten.

Wieder mässig langsam.
Lento moderato, come prima.

Isolda. *ruhig* *p* *tranquillo*

I. Barg im Bu - sen uns sich die Son - ne, leuch - ten la -
Could our hearts the sun but im - pris - on, laugh - ing stars

Sehr ruhig.
Molto tranquillo.

p 3 3 3 3 *p*

I. - chend Ster - ne der Won - ne.
of love were a - ris - en.

Tristan.
Von dei - nem Zau - ber sanft um -
While thus thy power is through us

3 3 3 3 *immer* *sempre* *p*

T. spon - nen, vor dei - nen Au - gen süss zer - ron - nen,
flow - ing, thine eyes a - bove us soft - ly glow - ing,

p

Isolda.

I. Herz an Herz dir, Mund an Mund;
Heart to heart and lips to lips,

T. ei - nes A - thems ein' - ger
One the breath that 'twixt them

p dolce *p dolce*

I.
bricht mein Blick sich wonn' - er - blin - det, er - bleicht die Welt
Breaks my glance at glo - ry blind - ing, and pales the earth

T.
p
Bund; bricht mein Blick sich wonn' - er - blin - det, er-
slips, breaks my glance at glo - ry blind - ing, and

p dolce
più p

I.
più p
mit ih - rem Blen - den: die uns der Tag trü-gend er-
to ra - diance bend - ing, that once the day lit with its

T.
p
bleicht die Welt mit ih - rem Blen-den:
pales the earth to ra - diance bend-ing:

pp
p

I.
accel.
hellt, selbst dann bin
lies. I then, I

T.
accel.
zu täuschendem Wahn entge-genge - stellt, selbst dann bin
At fraud-u - lent dreams de-fi-ance I've hurled: I then, I

accel.
p
cresc. -
Ped. * Ped. * Ped. *

Erstes Tempo.
Tempo primo.

I. ich die Welt: Won- - - - -ne -
am the world. Joy life's

T. ich die Welt: Won- - - -ne- -
am the world. Joy life's

Erstes Tempo.
Tempo primo.

ff *dim.*

I. *p* hehr- - - - - -stes We- - - - - - -
won- - - - - -drous weav- - - - - - -

T. *p* hehr- - - - -stes We- - - - - - -
won- - - - -drous weav- - - - - - -

p

I. *ff* - - - - -ben, Lie- - -be-hei- -lig- stes
- - - - -ing, Love life's ho- -li- est

T. *f* - - - - -ben, Lie- - -be-hei- -lig- stes
- - - - -ing, Love life's ho- -li- est

molto cresc. *ff* *(sehr ausdrucksvoll)* *(molto espress.)* *dim.*

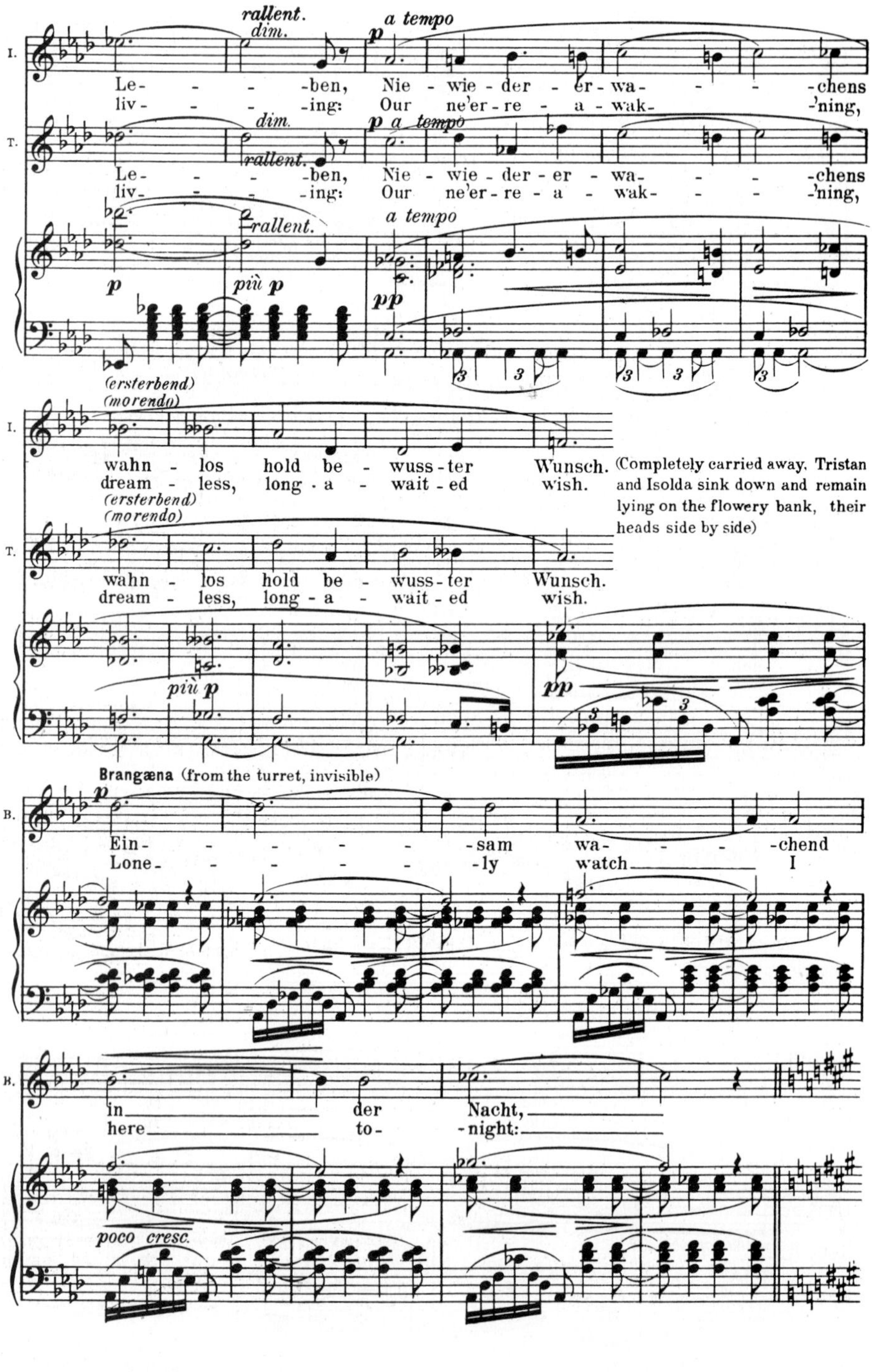

rallent. dim. a tempo

I. Le- - - - -ben, Nie - wie - der - er - wa- - - - -chens
liv- - - - -ing: Our ne'er - re - a - wak- -'ning,

T. Le- - - - -ben, Nie - wie - der - er - wa- - - - -chens
liv- - - - -ing: Our ne'er - re - a - wak- - - - -'ning,

(ersterbend) (morendo)

I. wahn - los hold be - wuss - ter Wunsch.
dream - less, long - a - wait - ed wish.

T. wahn - los hold be - wuss - ter Wunsch.
dream - less, long - a - wait - ed wish.

(Completely carried away, Tristan and Isolda sink down and remain lying on the flowery bank, their heads side by side)

Brangæna (from the turret, invisible)

B. Ein- - - - - - - - -sam wa- - - - -chend
Lone- - - - - - - -ly watch I

B. in der Nacht,
here to- -night:

B.
wem der Traum der Lie-
Ye that dream of love-
dim.
più p
be lacht,
-de- -light,
ausdrucksvoll
p espressivo
dim.
(gesteigert)
(appassionato)
hab' der Ei-
let your ears
p
dim.
ausdrucksvoll
p espressivo
-nen Ruf in
my call re-
dim.
p
dim.

B.
Acht, die den Schlä- -fern
quite, call that should your
sehr zart und ausdrucksvoll
dolcissimo e molto espressivo
p
p
B.
Schlim- -mes ahnt, ban-
slum- -ber shake, warn-
dim.
p
B.
-ge zum Er- -wa-
-ing you to fear,
p
dim.
p
Sehr ruhig.
Molto tranquillo.
B.
-chen mahnt!
to wake!
dolce

B.
f
Ha- -bet Acht!
Have a care!
mf
pp

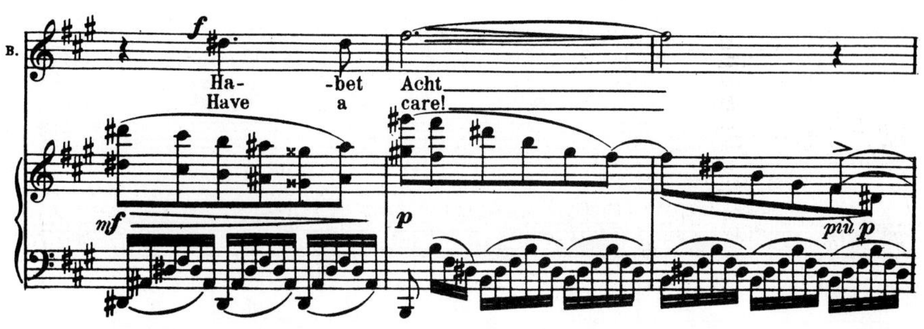
B.
f
Ha- -bet Acht
Have a care!
mf
p
più p

B.
Bald ent- -weicht die
Day- - -light comes! be-
morendo

verhallend
morendo
B.
Nacht!
ware!
morendo

15. GIUSEPPE VERDI (1813-1901), Opening of Act III from *Aïda* (1871)

Shores of the Nile.– Granite rocks overgrown with palm-trees. On the summit of the rocks, a temple dedicated to Isis, half hidden in foliage. Night; stars and a bright moon.

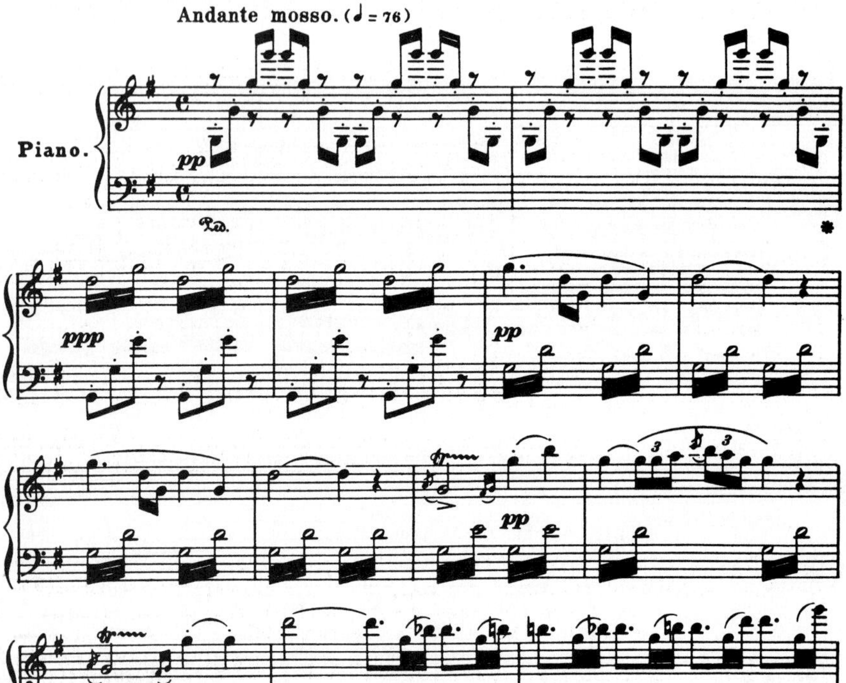

Andante mosso. (♩ = 76)

Piano.

pp

Ped.

ppp

pp

pp

morendo

Chorus (in the Temple).
Tutti.
TENOR.
O tu che sei d'O-si-ri - de madre immorta - le e spo - sa,
Oh, Thou who bore O-si - ris, Con-sort and ho - ly mother - er,
BASS.
O tu che sei d'O-si-ri - de madre immorta - le e spo - sa,
Oh, Thou who bore O-si - ris, Con-sort and ho - ly moth - er,
p
Ped.
Di - va che i ca - sti pal - pi - ti de-sti a - gli u-ma-ni in cor;
God-dess of love and chas - ti - ty, Font of e - ter-nal law,
Di - va che i ca - sti pal - pi - ti de-sti a - gli u-ma-ni in cor;
God-dess of love and chas - ti - ty, Font of e - ter-nal law,
High Priestess.
ben legato
f
ff
Soc - cor - ri, soc-cor - ri a noi,
Lend us Thy com - fort, Oh God - dess on high!
Soc-cor-ri a noi, pie -
Lend us Thine aid and
Soc-cor-ri a noi, pie -
Lend us Thine aid and

(From a boat which approaches the shore descend Amneris and Ramphis, followed by some women closely veiled. Guards.)
portando la voce
soc - cor - - ri a
Oh, Lend us Thy
to - sa, ma - dre d'im - men - so a - mor, soc - cor - - ri a
com - fort, Lead us who stand in awe! Oh, Lend us Thy
to - sa, ma - dre d'im - men - so a - mor, soc - cor - - ri a
com - fort, Lead us who stand in awe! Oh, Lend us Thy
Ramphis.
Meno mosso.
(to Amneris)
Vie - ni d'I - si - de al tempio: al - la vi -
Come, let us pray to I - sis! Before her
noi, soc - cor - ri a noi.
com - fort, Oh God - dess on high.
noi, soc - cor - ri a noi.
com - fort, Oh God - dess on high.
noi, soc - cor - ri a noi.
com - fort, Oh God - dess on high.
Meno mosso. (♩ = 60)
pp lunga
con calma
gi - lia del - le tue noz - ze in - vo - ca del - la Di - va il fa - vo - re.
al - tar ask for her - bless - ing up - on the ho - ly bond which a - waits you.

pp
I-si-de leg-ge de' mor-ta-li nel co-re; o-gni mi-ste-ro
Well read is I-sis in the heart of a mor-tal. No one can hide a
Amneris.
cantabile
de-gli u-ma-ni a le-i no-to. Sì; io pre-ghe-
thought or pas-sion be-fore the god-dess. Yes, and I will
pp
pp
rò che Ra-da-mès mi do-ni tut-to il suo cor, co-me il mio
pray that Ra-da-mès may tru-ly give me his heart, be-cause my
cor a lui sa-cro è per sem-pre.
own be-longs to him for-ev-er.
Ramphis.
An-diamo. Pre-ghe-rai fi-no al-
Come with me! You will pray till the
p>
ppp
Ped.

(all enter the temple)
l'al-ba; io sa-rò te-co.
sun-rise, while I'll stay near you.
Chorus: Priestesses.
Soc - - cor - ri, soc-cor - ri a noi,
Lend us Thy com - fort, Oh God - dess on high.
Chorus
portando la voce
Soc-
Oh,
TENOR.
Soc-cor-ri a noi, pie - to - sa, ma-dre d'immenso a - mor, soc-
Lend us Thine aid and com - fort, God-dess of love and law. Oh,
BASS.
Soc-cor-ri a noi, pie- to - sa, ma-dre d'immenso a - mor,
Lend us Thine aid and com - fort, God-dess of love and law. Oh,
p
ff
morendo
cor - - ri a noi, soc - cor - ri a noi.
Lend us Thy com - fort, Oh God - dess on high!
cor - - ri a noi, soc - cor - ri a noi.
Lend us Thy com - fort, Oh God - dess on high!
Lend us Thy com - fort, Oh God - dess on high!

orchestral interlude

vie-ni a re-car-mi o cru-del, l'ul-ti-mo ad-di-o, del
came for a fi-nal fare-well, cruel-ly to leave me... The
Ni-lo i cu-pi vor-ti-ci
Nile soon will be a tomb to me,
mi da-ran tom-ba
end my de-spair for-ev-er.
morendo
e pa-ce for-se e pa-ce for-se e o-bli-o.
Si-lent and som-ber, calm of the deep, re-ceive me!
morendo
Andante mosso. (♩ = 92.)
p legato
oboe
beginning of Aida's "Oh my country" "Oh patria mia"

a piacere

Oh pa-tria mia, mai più, mai più_ ti ri-ve-

Land of my fa-thers, you, my home,_ I'll see no

col canto

drò!

more.

p

mai più!

Nev-er,...

mai più ti ri-ve-drò!

I'll see you nev-er more.

dim. dolcissimo

Lo stesso movimento. (♩. = 92.)

cantabile

O cieli az-zur-ri, o dol-ci au-re na-ti-

Ah, blue ho-ri-zon A-shim-mer in the

pppp

sfumato il do♯.

ve, do-ve se-re-no il mio mat-tin bril-

breeze! Mem-ries of child-hood, Re-call my na-tive

16 24 16 16

dolciss.
lò
shore!
o ver - di
Green were my
col - li
moun - tains,
o pro - fu - ma - te
Fra - grant in flor - id
poco cresc.
ri - ve
beau - ty.
o pa - tria
Land of my
mi - a,
fa - thers,
mai più ti ri - ve -
You I shall see no
lunga
drò!
more!
espress.
oh pa - tria mi - a,
Land of my fa - thers,
mai
Oh
legato

più, ah! mai più, ma - i
land I knew, I
pp
più ti ri-ve - drò! oh pa-tria mia, oh pa-tria
knew and see no more! Oh land I love, land of my
p
cresc.
f
mi - a, mai più ti ri-ve - drò!
fa - thers, oh, you I'll see no more.
pp
rall.
ppp col canto
pp parlante
mai più!
Nev-er...
parlato
no no mai più, mai più!
no, no, not ev-er-more!...
Cantabile.
O fre-sche
Cool were the
ten.
ppp
2nd verse/stanza
-structural cohesion
-oboe keeps it together

dolciss.
sfumate
val - li, o que - to a - sil be - a - - to che un di pro -
val - leys Where I hid in won - - der, Weav - ing a
dol.
mes - so dal - l'a - mor mi fu - Or che d'a -
dream — Of love and ten - der hue. Torn is the
poco più f
- mo - - re il so - gno è di - le - gua - - to — o pa - tria
veil, My heart now is rent a - sun - - der. Land of my
mi - - a, non ti ve - drò mai più!
dreams, I can - not re - turn to you,
espr.
legato
pp
oh pa - tria mi - a, non ti ve - drò mai più! no, — mai
Land of — my — dreams, I can - not re - turn to you, not — to

dol.
senza affrett.
più ___ non ti ve-drò, non ti ve-drò mai più!
you, ___ Re-turn no more, No more re-turn to you.
pp
col canto
pp
legato
pp con forza dim. allarg. ppp
oh ___ pa-tria mia, mai più ___ ti ri-ve-
Oh ___ land of mine, 'tis you ___ I'll see ___ no
pp
smorz.
drò! ___
more! ___
allarg.
ppp

Allegro vivo. (♩ = 138)
Aïda.
Amonasro.
Ciel! mio pa - dre!
Heav-ens! My fa - ther!
A
For weight-y
Piano.
ff
te gra - ve ca - gion m'ad - du - ce, A - i - da.
cause I had to find you here, A - ï - da.
Nul - la
I know
p
sfug - ge al mio sguar - do.
all that has hap - pened.
pp
Presto parlante.
D'a - mor ti strug - gi per Ra - da -
You pine in pas - sion for Ra - da -
mès ei t'a - ma qui lo at - ten - di. Dei Fa - ra - on la fi - glia è tua ri -
mès . . . he loves you . . . he will come here. The Phar-aoh's on-ly daugh-ter is your

declamato.

va - le__ raz - za_in - fa - me, ab - bor - ri - ta e_a noi fa -
ri - val, a child of ty - rants, vile and vi - cious, who would de -

Aïda. *fiero.*

E_in suo po - te - re_io sto!__ Io d'A - mo - na - sro fi - glia!
And yet I am her slave, I, A - mo - na - sro's daugh - ter!

ta - le! In po - ter di
stroy us. You, a slave to

lei! No! se lo bra - mi, la pos - sen - te ri - val tu vin - ce - ra - i, e
her? No. If you're will - ing to de - feat her to - night, your might - y ri - val . . . your

pp *ff*

morendo.

pa - tria, e tro - no, e_a - mor, tut - to tu_a - vra - i.
coun - try, your king - dom, your love . . . all lie be - fore you.

p *p* *pp*

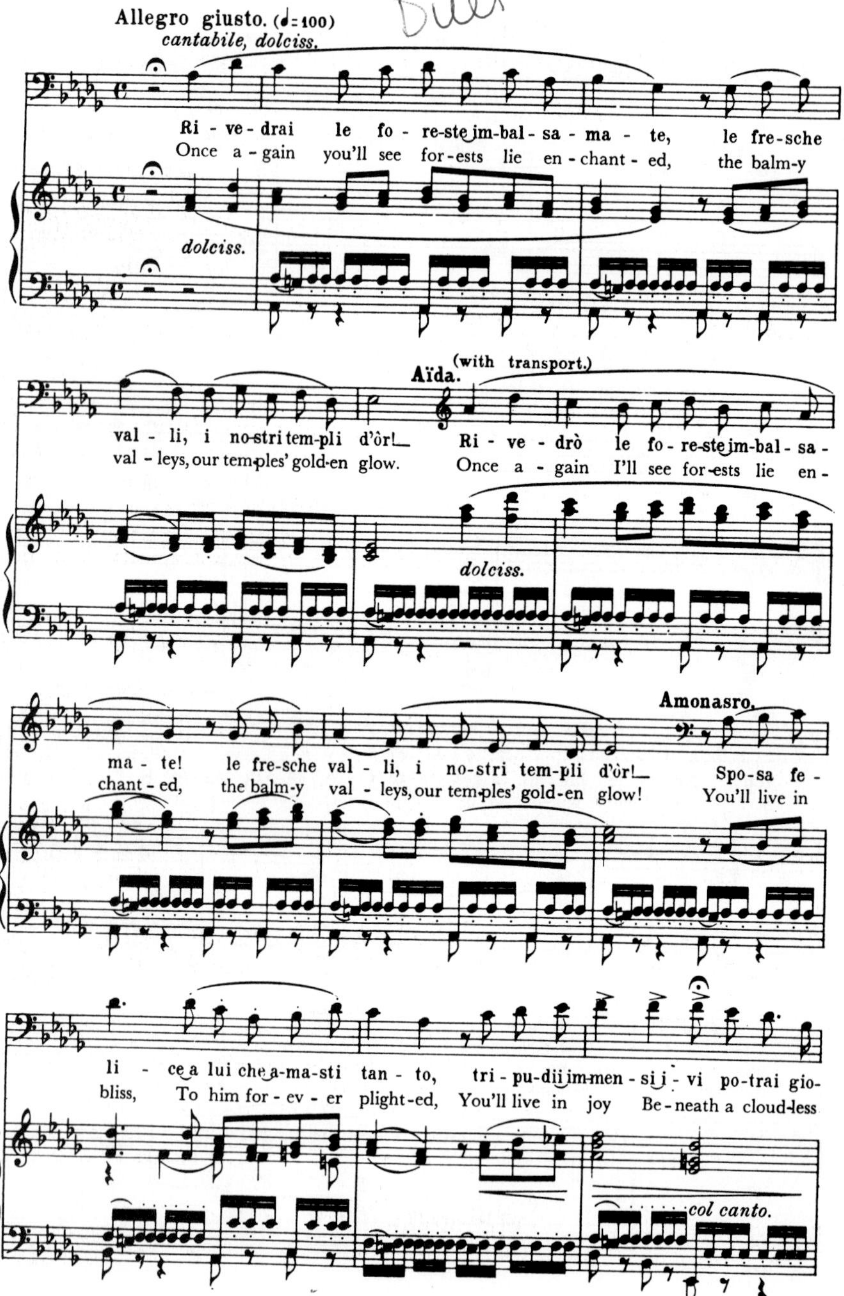

Allegro giusto. (♩=100)

cantabile, dolciss.

Ri - ve - drai le fo - re-ste im-bal - sa - ma - te, le fre-sche
Once a - gain you'll see for - ests lie en - chant - ed, the balm-y

dolciss.

val - li, i no-stri tem-pli d'òr!
val - leys, our tem-ples' gold-en glow.

Aïda. (with transport.)

Ri - ve - drò le fo - re-ste im-bal - sa -
Once a - gain I'll see for - ests lie en -

dolciss.

ma - te! le fre-sche val - li, i no-stri tem-pli d'òr!
chant - ed, the balm-y val - leys, our tem-ples' gold-en glow!

Amonasro.

Spo-sa fe -
You'll live in

li - ce a lui che a-ma-sti tan - to, tri - pu-dii im-men - si i - vi po-trai gio-
bliss, To him for - ev - er plight-ed, You'll live in joy Be-neath a cloud-less

col canto.

Aida. (with transport.)

ir.— Un gior-no so - lo di sì dol-ce in-can - to— u-n' o - ra, u-
sky! Oh, for a day In love to be u - nit - ed, One sin-gle

cresc.

Amonasro. *cupo.*

n'o - ra di— tal— gio - ia, e poi mo-rir! e poi mo - rir! Pur ram-
hour — of joy— sub— - lime And then to die, And then to die! Yet re -

men - ti che a noi l'E - gi-zio im-mi - te, le ca - se, i tem-pii e l'a - re pro - fa -
mem - ber the hang-men he com-mand-ed! No tem-ple, no al-tar, could stay their sav-age

pp

nò— tras-se in cep - pi le ver - gi - ni ra - pi - te— ma - dri -
horde. Shamed, in fet - ters, our wives and daugh-ters brand - ed, Moth-ers,

p

ten.
Aïda. appassionato.
vec - chi fan - ciul - li ei tru - ci - dò. Ah! ben ram -
chil - dren, dis - mem - bered by their sword! Ah, I re -
col canto.
ff
dolcissimo.
men - to quegl' in - fau - sti gior - ni! ram - men - to i
mem - ber how I had to suf - fer Tor - ment un -
Cantabile.
pp
lut - ti che il mio cor sof - fri! Deh!
end - ing, pain be - yond be - lief. Heav'n a -
dolcissimo.
fa - te o Nu - mi, che per
bove, Oh hear me, hear the

noi ri - tor- - ni, che per
prayer I — of - - fer, hear the
Amonasro.
Rammen - ta!
Re-mem - ber!
noi ri - tor - ni l'al-ba in-vo-ca-ta de' se-re-ni
prayer I — of - fer: Grant us a dawn with-out de-spair and
Non fia che tar -
Soon you will find re -
dì.
grief!
parlante
dì.
lief!
In ar-mi o-ra si de-sta il po-pol
Our forc-es have re-armed and lie in
Poco più animato. (♩= 116)
fz
pp

nos-tro; tut-to è pron-to già_ Vit-to-ria a-
wait-ing, ea-ger to at-tack. We shall not
vrem,_ So-lo a sa-per mi re-sta qual sen-
fail. One thing I must dis-cov-er: 'Tis the
Aïda.
Chi sco-prir-lo po-
Who is here who could
tier il ne-mi-co se-gui-rà._
path of the en-e-my's ad-vance.
tri-a? chi mai?
know it? Who?
Tu stes-sa!
A-ï-da!

I-o!
I?...
sotto voce.
Ra-da-mès so che qui at-tendi.
Ra-da-mès will come to see you . . .
col canto.
ppp
ppp
Amonasro.
Ei t'a-ma
he loves you . . .
ei con-du-ce gli E-gi-zii
he commands the E-gyp-tians . . .
Aïda.
Or-ro- - -re! Che mi con-si-gli
Oh ter- - -ror! What would you have me
In-ten-di?
you sure-ly . . .
ff
tu?
do?
No! no! giam-mai!
No, no, not I!
Su
A-
ff

Allegro. (♩. = 96)
(with savage fury)
dun - - que! sor - get - te e - gi - zie co - rise, men of E - gypt, De - stroy us and
or - ti! col fuo - co strug - ge - te le no - stre cit - tà. -
plun - der And rend us a - sun - der In hor - ri - ble wrath!
tutta forza.
Spar - ge - - - te il ter-
In ter - - - - ror and
ro - re, le stragi, le mor - ti al vos - tro fu - ro - re più fre - no non
fu - ry Our tem - ples shall tum - ble! To piec - es shall crum - ble What lies in your
ff
mf

Aïda.
Ah! pa-dre! pa-dre!
Fa-ther, my fa-ther!
(repulsing her)
Pie-tà! pie-
Not that, not
v'ha.
path!
Mia fi-glia ti chiami!
Be-trayed by my daugh-ter!
mf
ff
tà! pie-tà!
that, oh fa - ther!
mezza voce
Flut-ti di san - gue scor - ro - no
Tor-rents of blood flow end - less - ly,
8
ff
dim.
sul-le cit-tà dei vin - ti.
Min-gling with dust and em - ber.
Ve-di? dai ne - gri
Down in the dark and
vor - ti - ci si le-va-no gli e-stin - ti
crim - son flood Ghosts of the dead re-mem - ber, . . .
3

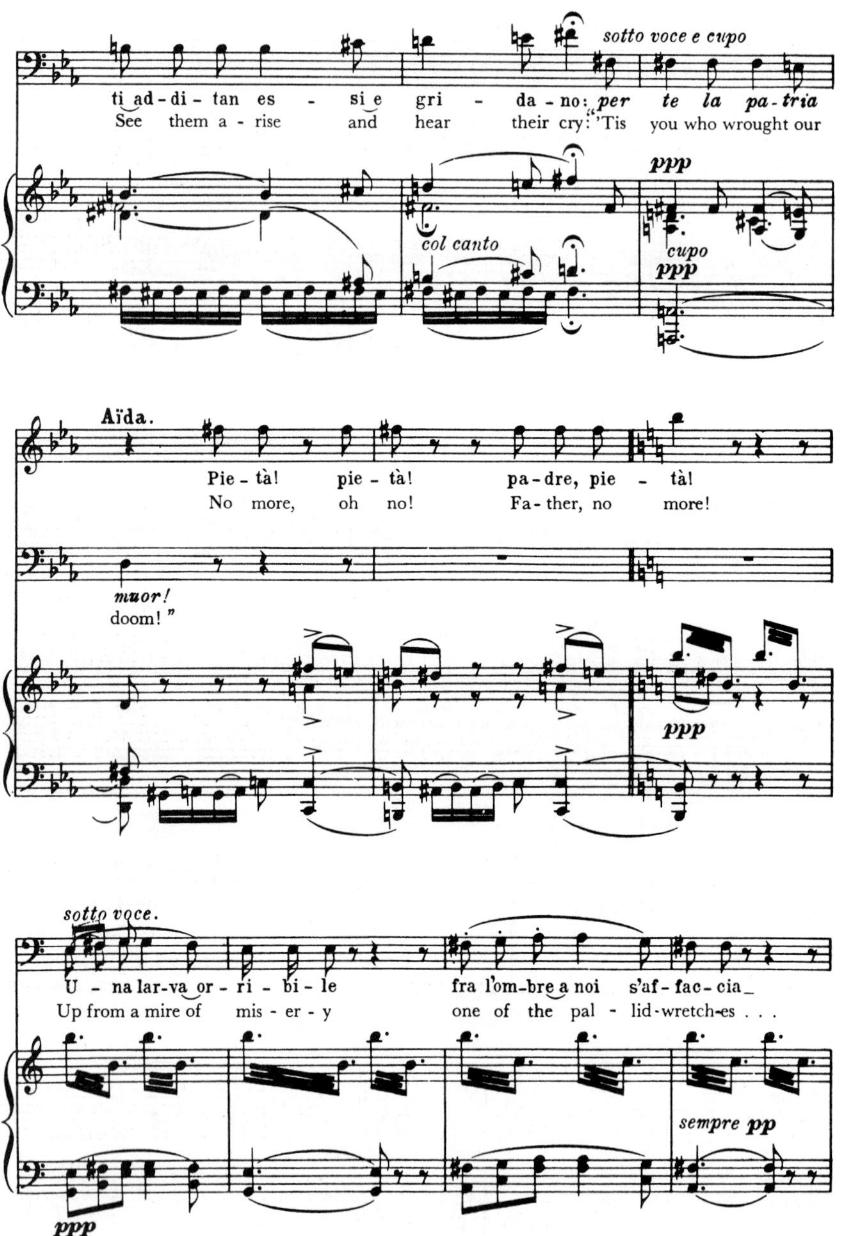
sotto voce e cupo
ti ad - di - tan es - si e gri - da - no: per te la pa - tria
See them a - rise and hear their cry: "'Tis you who wrought our
ppp
col canto
cupo
ppp
Aïda.
Pie - tà! pie - tà! pa - dre, pie - tà!
No more, oh no! Fa - ther, no more!
muor!
doom!"
ppp
sotto voce.
U - na lar - va or - ri - bi - le fra l'om - bre a noi s'af - fac - cia
Up from a mire of mis - er - y one of the pal - lid - wretch - es . . .
sempre pp
ppp

Aïda
senza suono.
Ah!
Ah
Amonasro.
tre-ma! le scar-ne brac-cia sul ca-po tuo le-vò
watch her! she sways and stretch-es, grop-ing to find your brow!
Padre! No! Ah!
fa-ther,... no, ah!
Tua madre ell' è rav-vi-sa-la ti ma-le-
Yes, 'tis your moth-er... You're shud-der-ing, hear-ing her
poco cresc.
(with the utmost terror.)
Ah! no! Ah! no! pa-dre, pie-tà! pie-tà! pie-
Ah no, my fa-ther, ah, no more, no more... not
di-ce.
curs-es!
ff

tà! pie-tà! pie - tà!
that! Ah no! Ah no!

(repulsing her)

Non sei mia
You're not my

ff

fi - glia!_ Dei Fa - ra - o - ni tu sei la
daugh-ter. You are no more than a slave of

Aïda.

(uttering a cry.)

Ah! pie-
Ah, for-

schiava!
E - gypt.

fff

un poco allarg.

p

tà! pie - tà! pie -
give,... my fa-ther, for -

ppp

Andante assai sostenuto. (♩ = 76)
(dragging herself to her father's feet.)
tà!
give!
ppp con espress.
pp con espress.
molto sotto voce e cupo
Pa-dre!__ a co - sto-ro__ schiava__ non
Fa-ther,... in their bond-age am I no
so-no__ Non ma-le - dir - mi__ non im - pre-
long-er... Ah, do not curse me, nor chide and
repeated notes
in acc.
- a kind of
tension

car - mi_ an - cor tua
scold me! Still as a
fi - glia po - trai chia -
daugh - ter your arms en -
mar - - mi_ del - la mia
fold me.... Un - to my
pa - tria, del - la mia pa - tria de - gna sa -
fa - thers, to king and coun - try my life shall be

rò.
sworn!
Amonasro.
Pen - sa che un po - po -
Think, oh my child, of
pp
lo vin - to, stra - zia - to
all our grief and sor - row!
per te sol - tan - to, per te sol -
You, you a - lone can set us free once
tan - to ri - sor - ger può.
more, in a land re - born.
Aïda.
Oh pa - tria! oh
Land of my
cresc. poco a poco

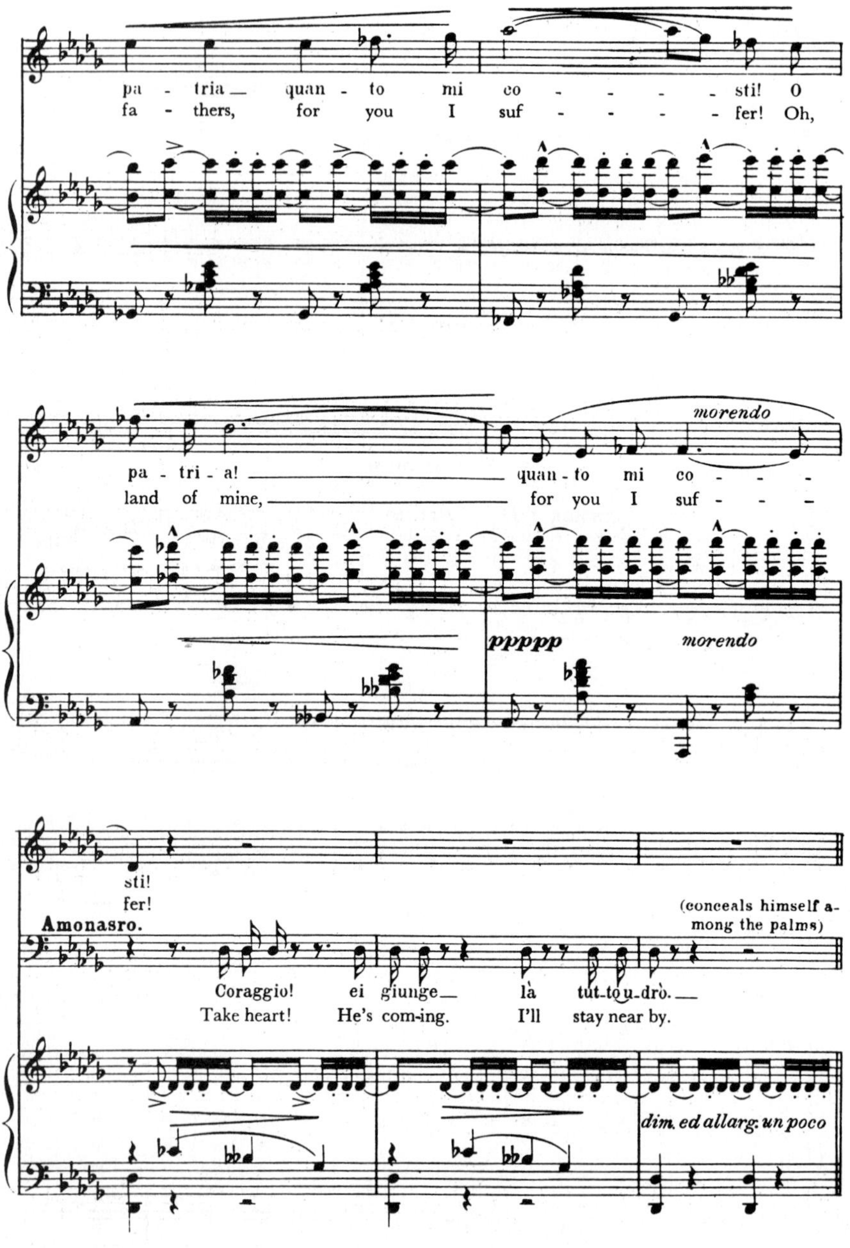

pa - tria — quan - to mi co - - - - - sti! O
fa - thers, for you I suf - - - - - fer! Oh,
pa - tri - a! — quan - to mi co - - - -
land of mine, — for you I suf - - - -
morendo
ppppp
morendo
sti!
fer!
(conceals himself among the palms)
Amonasro.
Coraggio! ei giunge — là tut-to u-drò. —
Take heart! He's com-ing. I'll stay near by.
dim. ed allarg. un poco

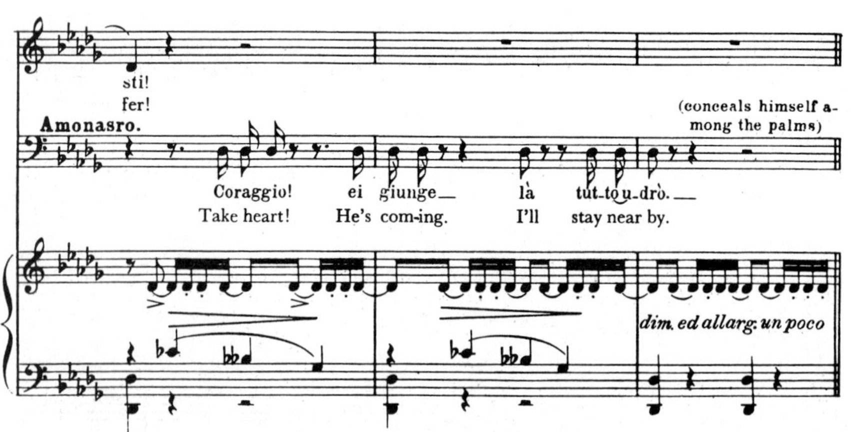

16. VERDI, Opening of the Dies irae from *Messa da Requiem* (1874)

Reprinted Courtesy of G. Schirmer, Inc.

ger;
rae,
ger;
rae,
ger;
rae,
ger;
rae,
ger;
rae,
ger;
rae,
ger;
rae,
ff
Day of troub - le, day of
Di - es il - - la, di - es
ff
ff
8

troub - - - - le,
il - - - - la,
ff
Day of troub - - - - le,
Di - es il - - - - la,
troub - - - - - le,
il - - - - - la,
ff
Day of troub - - - le,
Di - es il - - - - la,
troub - - - - - le,
il - - - - - la,
troub - le, day of troub - - - le,
il - la, di - es il - - - la,
troub - - - - - le,
il - - - - - la,
f
Time shall per - ish like a
Sol - vet sae - clum in fa -
f
f
Time shall, Time shall per - ish like a
Sol - vet, Sol - vet sae-clum in fa -
ff
Time shall, Time shall per - ish like a
Sol - - vet, Sol - - vet sae-clum in fa -

bub - - - ble, So spake Da - vid and the
vil - - - la: Te - ste, Da - vid cum Si-
bub - - - ble, So spake, so spake David and the
vil - - - la: Te - ste, Te - ste David cum Si-
So spake, so spake David and the
Te - ste, Te - ste David cum Si-
ff
Sib - - - yl: Day of
byl - - - la. Di - es
ff
f
ff
Sib - - - yl: Day of, day of
byl - - - la. Di - es, Di - es
f
ff
Sib - - - yl: Day of an - ger, day of
byl - - - la. Di - es i - rae, Di - es
f
ff

an - ger, Day of troub - le,
i - rae, Di - es il - la,
an - ger, Day of troub - le,
i - rae, Di - es il - la,
Time shall per - ish, per - ish like a
Sol - vet sae - clum, Sol - vet in fa-
Time shall per - ish, per - ish like a
Sol - vet sae - clum, Sol - vet in fa-

bub - ble,
vil - la:
Day of,
Di - es,
day of
Di - es
an - ger,
i - rae,
bub - ble,
vil - la:
Day of,
Di - es,
day of
Di - es
an - ger,
i - rae,
bub - ble, Day of an - ger, day of troub-le, Time shall per - ish like a
vil - la: Di-es i - rae, Di - es il - la, Sol-vet sae-clum in fa-
pesante
stent.
a tempo
bub - ble, So spake Da - vid and the Sib - yl.
vil - la: Te - ste Da - vid cum Si - byl - la.
stent. un poco
a tempo

A
ff
Day— of an - ger, Day— of troub - le,
Di - es i - rae, Di - es il - la,
ff
Day of an - ger, Day of troub - le,
Di - es i - rae, Di - es il - la,
ff
Day— of an - ger, Day— of troub - le,
Di - es i - rae, Di - es il - la,
ff
Day of an - ger, Day of troub - le,
Di - es i - rae, Di - es il - la,
ff
Time— shall per - ish like— a bub - ble,
Sol - vet sae - clum in— fa - vil - la,
Time shall per - ish like a bub - ble,
Sol - vet sae - clum in fa - vil - la,
Time— shall per - ish like— a bub - ble,
Sol - vet sae - clum in— fa - vil - la,
Time shall per - ish like a bub - ble,
Sol - vet sae - clum in fa - - vil - la,

p
Day of an - ger, Day of
Di - es i - rae, Di - es
dim.
p
Time shall per - ish like a bub - ble,
Sol - vet sae - clum in fa - vil - la:
p dim.
Time shall per - ish like a bub - ble,
Sol - vet sae - clum in fa - vil - la:
Time shall per - ish like a bub - ble,
Sol - vet sae - clum in fa - vil - la:
p
dim.
sempre pppp
troub - le, Day of an - ger, Day of
il - la, Di - es i - rae, Di - es
p
pp
So spake Da - vid and the Sib - yl.
Te - ste Da - vid cum Si - byl - la.
p
pp
So spake Da - vid and the Sib - yl.
Te - ste Da - vid cum Si - byl - la.
p
pp
So spake Da - vid and the Sib - yl.
Te - ste Da - vid cum Si - byl - la.
ancora più p
ancora dim.

SOPRANO
TENOR
ppp cupo
troub - le;
il - la;
Day of
Di - - es
ppp
an - ger,
i - rae,
CONTRALTO
cupo
pp
Day of an - ger,
Di - - es i - rae,
SOPRANO
pp cupo
B
Day of an - ger!
Di - es i - rae!
ppp

SOPRANO
CONTRALTO
TENOR
BASS
Chorus
pp sotto voce
How each heart shall
Quan - tus tre-mor
pp sotto voce
How each heart shall
Quan - tus tre-mor
beat with ter-ror, When the judge comes, truth to
est fu-tu-rus, Quan-do Ju - dex est ven-
beat with ter-ror, When the judge comes, truth to
est fu-tu-rus, Quan-do Ju - dex est ven-

mir-ror,
Strict - ly weigh - ing mor - tal er -
tu-rus,
Cun - cta stri - cte dis - cus - su -
mir-ror,
Strict - ly weigh - ing mor - tal er -
tu-rus,
Cun - cta stri - cte dis - cus - su -
ppp
C
Allegro sostenuto
ror!
rus!
ror!
rus!
Allegro sostenuto (♩= 88)
(Trumpets in the Orchestra)
pp (Trumpets afar)
(in the Orch.)
pp (afar)

(afar)
m.s.
p (in the Orch.)
pp
(afar)
(in the Orch.)
poco cresc.
m.s.
m.s.
m.s.
m.d.
animando a poco
cresc. a poco a poco
tutta la forza
fff
sempre animando a poco a poco

SOPRANO
CONTRALTO
TENOR
BASS
Chorus
Hark!
Tu -
Hark the trum - pet sounds ap-pall - ing,
Tu - - ba mi - rum spargens so - num,
(afar)
the trum - - pet
ba mi - - rum
Hark! the trum - pet sounds ap -
Tu - ba mi - rum spar - gens

sounds ap - - pall - - -
spar - - gens so - - -
ff
sounds ap - pall - - -
spar - gens so - - -
ff
sounds ap - pall - - -
spar - gens so - - -
pall - ing, Earth's se - pul - tur'd dead up - call - - -
so - num Per se - pul - chra re - gi - o - - -
ff animando sempre sino
- - - ing,
- - - num,
E
- - - ing,
- - - num,
- - - ing,
- - - num,
- - - ing, Hark! the
- - - num, Tu - ba
(Trumpet afar)
(Orchestra)
alla fine ma a poco a poco.

sounds ap - pall - ing,
spar - gens so - num,
sounds ap-
spar- -gens
trum - pet!
mi- -rum.
(afar)
dead up - call - ing,
reg - i - o - num,
palling,
sonum,
Round the
Co - get
Earth's se - pul - tur'd
Per se - pul - chra
(afar)

call -
o -
Lord's throne
o - mnes
pros - trate
au - te
fall -
thro-
call -
o -
fff
Molto meno mosso
1
ing.
mnes.
ing.
num.
ing.
mnes.
ppp Solo
Death, with
Mors stu-
Molto meno mosso (♩ = 72)
ppp
ppp
con 8a sotto
con 8a sotto

wonder, Death, with won - der is en - chain - ed When man
pe-bit, Mors stu - pe - bit et na - tu- -ra, Cum re-
ppp
con 8a sotto
from his grasp, re - gain - ed, Stands be - fore the judge ar-
sur - get cre - a - tu - ra, Ju - di - can - ti re - spon-
raign- - ed. Death,
su - -ra. Mors,
pp
1
cupo.
Death, Death en-chain - ed.
Mors, Mors stu - pe - bit.
pppp

17. BEDŘICH SMETANA (1824-1884), *The Moldau* from *Má Vlast* (1874-1879)

*Smaller notes indicate an alternate version for reduced orchestra.

5
Fl.
Harfe
1.Viol.
2.Viol.
Br.

10
Fl.
1.Viol.
2.Viol.

15
Fl.
Klar. (C)
p
1.Viol.
2.Viol.

20
Fl.
Klar. (C)
1.Viol.
2.Viol.
Br.
p

25
Fl.
Klar. (C)
1.Viol.
2.Viol.
Br.
p
30
Fl.
Klar. (C)
1.Viol.
2.Viol.
Br.
35
A
Fl.
Ob.
Klar. (C)
*2.Ob.
I.II.
a 2
Hr. (C)
Trgl.
p elegante
1.Viol.
2.Viol.
arco
p dolce
lusingando
arco
ondeggiante
Br.
lusingando
p lusingando
*2.Vcll.
p lusingando
Vcll.
pizz.
K.-B.

40
Fl.
Ob.
Klar. (C)
Fag.
Hr. (C)
Trpt. (C)
Pos. Tuba
Pk.
Trgl.
1.Viol.
2.Viol.
Br.
Vcll.
K-B.
*1.Ob.
*2.Ob.
*3. Hr.
*2. Fag.
dolce
p dolce
a 2
ppp
sf
p
f
dim.
sempre ondeggiante

45
Fl.
Ob.
Klar. (C)
Fag.
Hr. (C)
Trpt. (C)
Pos. Tuba
Pk.
Trgl.
I.Viol.
2.Viol.
Br.
Vcll
K.-B.
dolce
*2. Ob.
p glockenartig
sempre ondeggiante

50
Fl.
Ob.
Klar. (C)
Fag.
Hr. (C)
Trpt. (C)
Pos. Tuba
Pk.
1.Viol.
2.Viol.
Br.
Vcll.
K.-B.
sf
p
dim.

55
Fl.
a 2
mf
cresc.
sf
Ob.
mf cresc.
Klar. (C)
Fag.
Hr. (C)
p
*4 Hr.
Trpt. (C)
Pos.
Tuba
p cresc.
Pk.
Trgl.
Harfe
1.Viol.
2.Viol.
Br.
Vcll.
K.-B.

60
a 2
Fl.
Ob.
*2.Ob.
Klar. (C)
*2.Fl.
*2.Ob.
Fag.
Hr. (C)
*4.Hr.
Trpt. (C)
Pos. Tuba
Pk.
Trgl.
Harfe
1.Viol.
2.Viol.
Br.
Vcll.
K.-B.
sf
p
cresc.

65
B
Fl.
Ob.
Klar. (C)
*2.Fl.2.Ob.
Fag.
Hr. (C)
Trpt. (C)
Pos. Tuba
Pk.
Trgl.
1.Viol.
2.Viol.
Br.
Vell.
K.-B.
cresc.
arco
pizz.

70
Fl.
Ob.
Klar. (C)
Fag.
Hr. (C)
Trpt. (C)
Pos. Tuba
Pk.
Trgl.
Harfe
1.Viol.
2.Viol.
Br.
Vcll.
K.-B.
*2.Vcll.
*2.Ob.
*4.Hr.
*3.Hr.
*2.Fag.
dopo la repetizione muta in C.G.
pizz.

75
Fl.
Ob.
Klar. (C)
Fag.
Hr. (C)
Trpt. (C)
Pos. Tuba
Pk.
Trgl.
Harfe
1.Viol.
2.Viol.
Br.
Vcll.
K.-B.
sf
dim.
p

80
Forest Hunt
Fl.
Ob.
Klar. (C)
Fag.
Hr. (C)
Trpt. (C)
*2 Ob.
Pos. Tuba
*4. Hr.
Pk.
Trgl.
Harfe
1. Viol.
2. Viol.
Br.
Vcll.
arco
K.-B.

86
Fl.
Ob.
Klar. (C)
*2. Ob.
Fag.
Hr. (C)
Trpt. (C)
*3. Hr.
Pos. Tuba
*4. Hr.
Pk.
Trgl.
1.Viol.
2.Viol.
Br.
Vcll.
K.-B.

92
Fl.
Ob.
Klar. (C)
Fag.
Hr. (C)
Trpt. (C)
Pos. Tuba
*4. Hr.
Pk.
muta in A. D.
Trgl.
1.Viol.
2.Viol.
Br.
Vcll.
K.-B.

97

Fl.

Ob.

2. Ob.

Klar. (C)

Fag.

Hr. (C)

Trpt. (C)

3. Hr.

Pos. Tuba

Pk.

1.Viol.

2.Viol.

Br.

Vcll.

K.-B.

C
102
Fl.
Ob.
Klar. (C)
*2 Ob.
Fag.
Hr. (C)
Trpt. (C)
muta in E
*3. Hr.
Pos. Tuba
*3. Hr.
*4. Hr.
Pk.
Trgl.
1.Viol.
2.Viol.
Br.
Vcll.
K.-B.
f dim.

107
Fl.
Ob.
Klar. (C)
dim.
sempre dim.
Fag.
dim.
sempre dim.
Hr. (C)
dim.
p dim.
sempre dim.
sempre dim.
Trpt. (E)
sempre dim.
Pos. Tuba
dim.
sempre dim.
Pk.
1.Viol
dim.
sempre dim.
2.Viol.
dim.
sempre dim.
Br.
dim.
sempre dim.
Vcll.
dim.
sempre dim.
dim.
sempre dim.
K.-B.
dim.
sempre dim

112
Fl.
Ob.
Klar. (C)
a 2
Fag.
Hr. (C)
Trpt. (E)
Pos. Tuba
Pk.
1.Viol.
2.Viol.
Br.
Vcll.
K.-B.
pp
ppp

– rustic dance

Peasant Wedding

118 **L'istesso tempo, ma moderato** ♩ = ♩.

Klar. (C)
a 2
mf
p

Fag.
mf
p

Hr. (C)
p
p

Trpt. (E)

3. Pos.

1. Viol.
mf
p

2. Viol.
cresc.
mf
p

Br.
cresc.
mf
p

Vcll.
mf
p
mf
p

K.-B.
mf
p

136
D
Fl.
Ob.
Klar. (C)
Fag.
Hr. (C)
Trpt. (A)
*3.u.4.Hr.
Pos. Tuba
*2.Fag.
*2.Vell.
Pk.
Trgl.
1.Viol.
2.Viol.
Br.
Vcll.
K.-B.

144
Fl.
Ob.
Klar. (C)
Fag.
Hr. (C)
Trpt. (A)
Pos. Tuba
Pk.
Trgl.
1.Viol.
2.Viol.
Br.
Vcll.
K.-B.
dim.
p

152
Fl.
a 2
p
Ob.
Klar. (C)
Fag.
*3.u.4. Hr.
Hr. (C)
Trpt. (A)
Pos. Tuba
Pk.
più p
Trgl.
1.Viol.
2.Viol.
Br.
Vcll.
K.-B.

160

Fl. a 2 dim. sempre dim.
Ob. II. più p dim. sempre dim.
Klar. (C) più p dim. sempre dim.
Fag. più p dim. sempre dim.
Hr. (C) II. *4. Hr. più p IV. più p dim. dim.
Pk. muta in E H
1. Viol. più p dim. sempre dim.
2. Viol. più p dim. sempre dim.
Br. più p dim. sempre dim.
Vcll. più p dim. sempre dim.
K.-B. più p dim. sempre dim.

Moonlight: Nymphs' Dance
181
L'istesso tempo
Fl.
Ob.
Klar. (B)
Fag.
Hr. (Es)
Trpt. (B)
1. Viol.
2. Viol.
Br.
Vcll.
K.-B.
plusingando
pp
ppp
*2. Ob.
*Die 1. Stimme blasen
in B
*2. Ob. mit Dämpfer
tranquillo
con sordini
pp ondeggiante
dolciss.

188
Fl.
Klar. (B)
(Es) Hr. (F)
Trpt. (B)
3. Pos.
Harfe
1. Viol.
2. Viol.
Br.
Vcll.
ppp
pp
*2. Hr. ohne Dämpfer
*4. Hr.

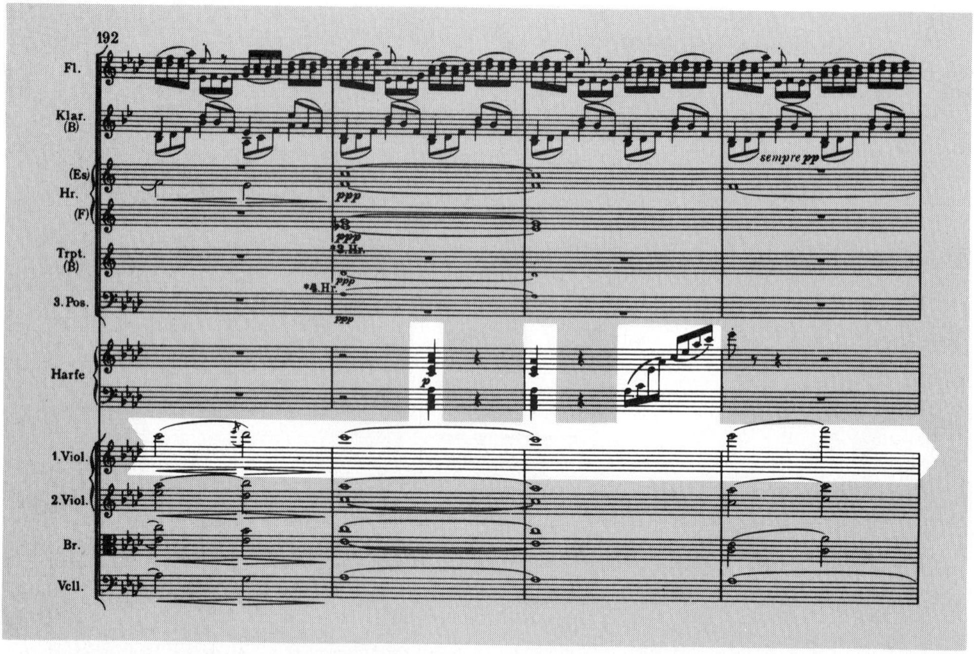

196
Fl.
Klar. (B)
(Es) Hr. (F)
Trpt. (B)
3. Hr.
ppp
*4. Hr.
3. Pos.
ppp
Harfe
p
1. Viol.
2. Viol.
Br.
Vcll.

200

Fl.

Klar. (B)

(Es) Hr. (F)

sempre pp

sempre pp

*3. Hr.

Trpt. (B)

sempre pp

*4. Hr.

3. Pos.

sempre pp

Harfe

p

p

*3 Hr.

pp

1. Viol.

2. Viol.

Br.

*Die 1. Stimme spielen

Vcll.

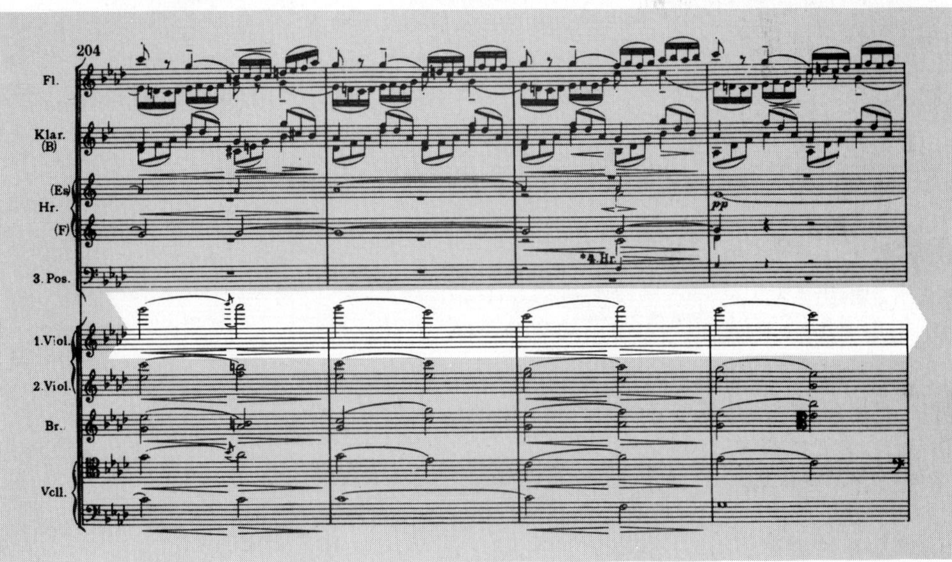

208
F
Fl.
Ob.
Klar. (B)
Fag.
(Es)
Hr.
(F)
Trpt. (B)
Pos. Tuba
Pk.
Harfe
1. Viol.
2. Viol.
Br.
Vell
K B
dim.
più pp
pp
*3.u.4. Hr.
*3. Hr.
*4. Hr.
p

212
Fl.
Ob.
Klar. (B)
*4. Hr.
Fag.
ppp possibile
(Es)
Hr.
(F)
ppp possibile
ppp possibile
*3. Hr.
*4. Pos.
Trpt. (B)
ppp possibile
Pos. Tuba
ppp possibile
*3. Pos. bläst die Tubastimme
ppp possibile
Pk.
Harfe
p
1. Viol.
2. Viol.
Br.
Vcll.
*2. Vcll.
K.-B.
pp

216
Fl.
Ob.
Klar. (B)
Fag.
ppp
sempre pp
(Es)
Hr.
(F)
ppp
sempre pp
Trpt. (B)
*1.u.2. Pos.
ppp
sempre pp
Pos. Tuba
ppp
*3. Pos. bläst die Tubastimme
ppp
sempre pp
Pk.
Harfe
p
1.Viol.
pp
2.Viol.
pp
Br.
pp
Vcll.
pp
K.-B.
pp

220
Fl.
Ob.
Klar. (B)
Fag.
*2. Hr.
(Es)
Hr.
(F)
*3. Hr.
sempre pp
sempre pp
Trpt. (B)
sempre pp
Pos. Tuba
sempre pp
sempre pp
Pk.
Harfe
p
p
1. Viol.
sempre pp
2. Viol.
sempre pp
Br.
sempre pp
Vll.
sempre pp
sempre pp
K-B.
sempre pp

brass

224
Fl.
Ob.
Klar. (B)
Fag.
(Es)
Hr.
(F)
Trpt. (B)
Pos. Tuba
Pk.
Harfe
1. Viol.
2. Viol.
Br.
Vcll.
K.-B.
pp
p

228
G
Fl.
Die obere Stimme
Ob.
Klar. (B)
Die obere Stimme
Fag.
3.u.4.Hr.
(Es)
Hr.
(F)
in E a 2
Trpt. (B)
Pos. Tuba
Pk.
Trgl.
p cresc.
pp cresc.
Harfe
1.Viol.
cresc.
2.Viol.
Br.
1.Vcll.
2.Vcll. K.-B.
pp

231
Fl.
Ob.
Klar. (B)
Fag.
pp
(Es) Hr. (F)
Trpt. (E)
a 2
Pos. Tuba
Pk.
Trgl.
Harfe
sf
1.Viol.
2.Viol.
Br.
1.Vcll.
2.Vcll. K.-B.
cresc.

234
Fl.
cresc.
Ob.
Klar. (B)
cresc.
Fag.
(Es)
Hr.
(F)
muta in C
muta in C
Trpt. (E)
Pos. Tuba
*2. Fag.
Pk.
1.Viol.
2.Viol.
Br.
1.Vcll.
2.Vcll. K.-B.

river scene again
237
Tempo I
*2. Ob.
dolce
Fl.
*Die obere Stimme
Ob.
dolce
Klar. (B)
muta in C
Fag.
p dolce
Hr. (C)
Trpt. (E)
Pos. Tuba
*2. Fag.
pp dolce
Pk.
Trgl.
senza sordini
1.Viol.
dolce
2.Viol.
senza sordini
sempre ondeggiante
Br.
senza sordini
sempre ondeggiante
senza sordini
Vcll.
*2 Vcll.
senza sordini
sempre ondeggiante
sempre ondeggiante
K.-B.
pizz.

241
Fl.
Ob.
dim.
Klar. (C)
Fag.
Hr. (C)
Trpt. (E)
* 3. Hr.
Pos. Tuba
Pk.
1.Viol.
2.Viol.
Br.
Vcll.
K.-B.

246
Fl.
a 2
mf cresc.
sf
Ob.
• 2. Ob.
Klar. (C)
Fag.
mf cresc.
Hr. (C)
p
Trpt. (E)
• 3. Hr.
Pos. Tuba
mf cresc.
Pk.
Trgl.
Harfe
cresc.
1. Viol.
2. Viol.
Br.
Vcll.
K.-B.

251
a 2
Fl.
Ob.
*2.Ob.
Klar. (C)
Fag.
Hr. (C)
Trpt. (E)
Pos. Tuba
Pk.
Trgl.
Harfe
1.Viol.
2.Viol.
Br.
Vcll.
K.-B.
sf
cresc.
p
f
* Die obere Stimme
*2.Ob.

256
Fl.
Ob.
Klar. (C)
Fag.
Hr. (C)
Trpt. (E)
Pos. Tuba
Pk.
Trgl.
1.Viol.
2.Viol.
Br.
Vcll.
K.-B.
cresc.
arco
pizz.
arco

261
Fl.
Ob.
Klar. (C)
Fag.
Hr. (C)
Trpt. (E)
Pos. Tuba
Pk.
Trgl.
Harfe
1.Viol.
2.Viol.
Br.
Vcll.
K.-B.
*2.Vcll.
*2.Ob.
*2.Fag.
dim.
pp
mf
p
sf
pizz.

266
Fl.
Ob.
Klar. (C)
Fag.
Hr. (C)
Trpt. (E)
Pos. Tuba
Pk.
Trgl.
Harfe
1.Viol.
2.Viol.
Br.
Vcll.
K.-B.
*2.Ob.
sf
dim.
p
f

271 H St. John's Rapids
bei kl. Bes. *1. Fl. nimmt Kl. Fl. bis Schluß
Fl.
Ob.
Klar. (C)
Fag.
Hr. (C)
Trpt. (E)
Pos. Tuba
*4. Hr.
Pk.
Trgl.
Gr. Tr.
Solo mit Paukenschlägel
Harfe
1. Viol.
2. Viol.
Br.
1. Vcll.
2. Vcll. K.-B.
cresc.

276
Kl.Fl.
1.Fl.
*1. Fl.
2.Fl.
Ob.
Klar. (C)
Fag.
Hr. (C)
Trpt. (E)
*1. Pos.
*1.u.2. Pos.
Pos. Tuba
Pk.
Gr. Tr.
mit Paukenschlägel
1.Viol.
2.Viol.
Br.
1.Vcll.
2.Vcll. K.-B.

281
Kl. Fl.
1. Fl.
*1. Fl.
2. Fl.
Ob.
*2. Ob.
Klar. (C)
Fag.
cresc.
Hr. (C)
Trpt. (E)
Pos. Tuba
*4. Hr.
Pk.
1. Viol.
2. Viol.
Br.
1. Vcll.
2. Vcll. K.-B.

286
Kl. Fl.
1. Fl.
2. Fl.
Ob.
*2. Ob.
Klar. (C)
Fag.
Hr. (C)
Trpt. (E)
*1. Pos.
Pos. Tuba
Pk.
1. Viol.
2. Viol.
Br.
1. Vcll.
2. Vcll. K.-B.

291
I
Kl.Fl.
1.Fl.
2.Fl.
Ob.
Klar. (C)
Fag.
Hr. (C)
Trpt. (E)
Pos. Tuba
Pk.
Bck.
1.Viol.
2.Viol.
Br.
1.Vcll.
2.Vcll. K B.
*1.Fl.
*1.u.3.Hr.

296
Kl. Fl.
1. Fl.
2. Fl.
Ob.
Klar. (C)
Fag.
Hr. (C)
Trpt. (E)
Pos. Tuba
Pk.
1. Viol.
2. Viol.
Br.
1. Vcll.
2. Vcll. K-B.
* Kl. Fl. loco
cresc.
sf
marc.
* 3. Hr.
* 4. Hr.
f * 3. Pos. bläst die Tubastimme

303

Kl. Fl.

1. Fl.

*1. Fl.

2. Fl.

Ob.

Klar. (C)

Fag.

Hr. (C)

Trpt. (E)

Pos. Tuba

Pk.

Bck.

Kl. Fl. loco

cresc.

*3. Hr.

*4. Hr.

*3. Pos. bläst die Tubastimme

1. Viol.

2. Viol.

Br.

1. Vcll.

2. Vcll. K.-B.

cresc.

309
Kl. Fl.
1. Fl.
2. Fl.
Ob.
Klar. (C)
Fag.
marc.
Hr. (C)
Trpt. (E)
*1. u. 2. Pos.
rfz
Pos. Tuba
sf
*3. Pos. bläst die Tubastimme
Pk.
Gr. Tr.
Bck.
1. Viol.
2. Viol.
Br.
1. Vcll.
2. Vcll. K.-B.
marc.

315
Kl. Fl.
1. Fl.
2. Fl.
Ob.
Klar. (C)
Fag.
Hr. (C)
Trpt. (E)
Pos. Tuba
Pk.
Gr. Tr.
Bck.
1. Viol.
2. Viol.
Br.
1. Vcll.
2. Vcll. K.-B.
sempre cresc.
cresc.

K
321
Kl. Fl.
1. Fl.
2. Fl.
Ob.
Klar. (C)
muta in A
Fag.
Hr. (C)
muta in E
Trpt. (E)
4. Hr.
Pos. Tuba
Pk.
dim.
sub. pp
Gr. Tr.
mit Schlägeln
Bck.
1. Viol.
2. Viol.
Br.
1. Vcll.
2. Vcll. K.-B.

328

Kl. Fl. *ff*

1. Fl. *ff*

2. Fl. *ff*

Ob. *ff*

Klar. (A) *ff*

Fag. *ff*

Hr. (E)

Trpt. (E)

Pos. Tuba

Pk. *pp* *sub. cresc.*

1. Viol. *pp* *sub. cresc. molto*

2. Viol. *pp* *sub. cresc. molto*

Br. *cresc. molto*

1. Vcll.

2. Vcll. K.-B.

The Moldau in its Greatest Breadth
333
Più moto
Kl. Fl.
1. Fl.
2. Fl.
Ob.
Klar. (A)
Fag.
Hr. (E)
Trpt. (E)
Pos. Tuba
Pk.
Trgl.
Harfe
1. Viol.
2. Viol.
Br.
1. Vcll.
2. Vcll.
K.-B.

341
Kl. Fl.
*Kl. Fl. loco
1. Fl.
*Kl. Fl. Okt. höher
2. Fl.
1. Fl.
Ob.
Klar. (A)
Fag.
Hr. (E)
Trpt. (E)
Pos. Tuba
Pk.
Trgl.
Harfe
1. Viol.
2. Viol.
Br.
1. Vcll.
2. Vcll.
K.-B.

350
Kl.Fl.
1.Fl.
2.Fl.
Ob.
Klar. (A)
Fag.
Hr. (E)
Trpt. (E)
Pos. Tuba
Pk.
Trgl.
Harfe
1.Viol.
2.Viol.
Br.
1.Vcll.
2.Vcll.
K.-B.
fz
marcatiss.
cresc.
f

Vyšehrad Motive (Symphonic Poem No. 1)
359
L
Kl. Fl.
1. Fl.
2. Fl.
Ob.
Klar. (A)
Fag.
Hr. (E)
Trpt. (E)
Pos. Tuba
Pk.
Trgl.
Gr. Tr.
Bck.
Harfe
1. Viol.
2. Viol.
Br.
1. Vcll.
2. Vcll.
K.-B.

364
Kl. Fl.
1. Fl.
2. Fl.
Ob.
Klar. (A)
Fag.
Hr. (E)
Trpt. (E)
Pos. Tuba
Pk.
Trgl.
Gr. Tr.
Bck.
1. Viol.
2. Viol.
Br.
1. Vcll.
2. Vcll.
K.-B.
fz
7
8

369
Kl. Fl.
1. Fl.
2. Fl.
Ob.
Klar. (A)
Fag.
Hr. (E)
Trpt. (E)
Pos. Tuba
Pk.
Trgl.
Gr. Tr.
Bck.
1. Viol.
2. Viol.
Br.
1. Vcll.
2. Vcll.
K.-B.
fz
rinf

374
sempre ff
Kl. Fl.
1. Fl.
2. Fl.
Ob.
Klar. (A)
Fag.
Hr. (E)
Trpt. (E)
Pos. Tuba
Pk.
Trgl.
Gr. Tr.
Bck.
1. Viol.
2. Viol.
Br.
Vcll.
K B.
fz
rfz
ff
*Kl. Fl. loco

383
Kl. Fl.
1. Fl.
2. Fl.
Ob.
Klar. (A)
Fag.
Hr. (E)
Trpt. (E)
Pos. Tuba
Pk.
Trgl.
Gr. Tr.
Bck.
1. Viol.
2. Viol.
Br.
Vcll.
K.-B.

392
Kl. Fl.
1. Fl.
2. Fl.
1. Fl.
Ob.
Klar. (A)
Fag.
Hr. (E)
Trpt. (E)
Pos. Tuba
Pk.
Trgl.
Gr. Tr.
Bck.
1. Viol.
2. Viol.
Br.
Vcll.
K.-B.

401
Kl.Fl.
1. Fl.
2. Fl.
Ob.
Klar. (A)
Fag.
Hr. (E)
Trpt. (E)
Pos. Tuba
Pk.
Trgl.
Gr.Tr.
Bck.
1.Viol.
2.Viol.
Br.
1.Vcll.
2.Vcll.
K. B.
fz
sf dim.
sempre dim.
*1. Fl.
*3. Hr.
*2. Fag.
fff
ff
f
*Die 2. Stimme bis Schluß

410
Kl. Fl.
1. Fl.
2. Fl.
Ob.
Klar. (A)
Fag.
Hr. (E)
Trpt. (E)
Pos. Tuba
Pk.
1. Viol.
2. Viol.
Br.
1. Vcll.
2. Vcll.
K.-B.
pp
p dim.
ppp
ff
dim.
sempre dim. al

419
rall.
Kl.Fl.
1.Fl.
2.Fl.
Ob.
Klar. (A)
Fag.
Hr. (E)
Trpt. (E)
Pos. Tuba
Pk.
1.Viol.
2.Viol.
Br.
1.Vcll.
2.Vcll.
K.-B.
pp
dim. al ppp
smorz.
ff
fz
rall.

18. JOHANNES BRAHMS (1833-1896), Fourth movement from *Symphony No. 2 in D major* (1877)

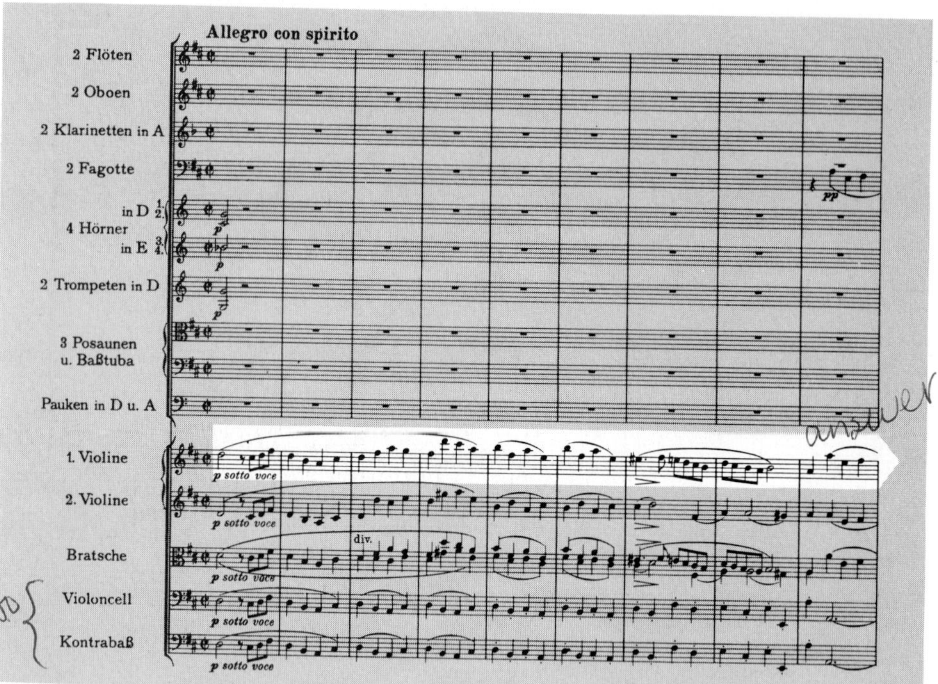

Allegro con spirito
2 Flöten
2 Oboen
2 Klarinetten in A
2 Fagotte
4 Hörner
in D 1. 2.
in E 3. 4.
2 Trompeten in D
3 Posaunen u. Baßtuba
Pauken in D u. A
1. Violine
2. Violine
Bratsche
Violoncell
Kontrabaß
p sotto voce
div.
pp
answer
ostinato

Allegro con spirito
10
Fl.
Ob.
Klar. (A)
Fag.
1. Viol.
2. Viol.
Br.
Vcl.
K.-B.
pp
p dolce
dim.

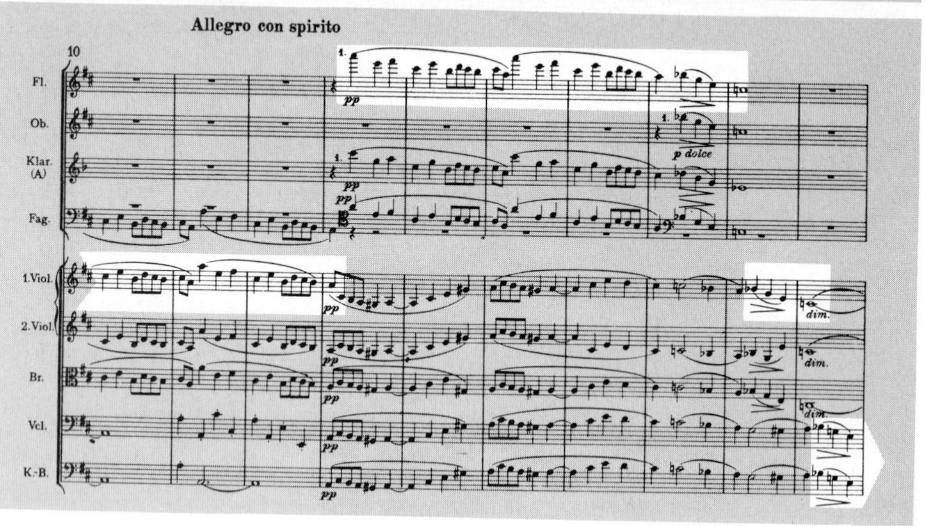

20
A
Fl.
Ob.
Klar. (A)
Fag.
(D) Hr. (E)
Trpt. (D)
Pk.
1. Viol.
2. Viol.
Br.
Vcl.
K.-B.
a 2
dim.
29

37
Fl.
Ob.
Klar. (A)
Fag.
a 2
(D)
Hr.
(E)
Trpt. (D)
Pk.
1. Viol.
2. Viol.
Br.
Vcl.
K.-B.

45
Fl.
Ob.
Klar. (A)
Fag.
(D)
Hr.
(E)
Trpt. (D)
Pk.
1. Viol.
2. Viol.
Br.
Vcl.
K.-B.
cresc.

53
B
Fl.
Ob.
Klar. (A)
Fag.
(D)
Hr.
(E)
Trpt. (D)
Pk.
1. Viol.
2. Viol.
Br.
Vcl.
K.-B.
ff
sf
tr
2.
pp
f dim.
dim.
B

62
Fl.
Ob.
Klar. (A)
Fag.
(D)
Hr.
(E)
Trpt. (D)
1. Viol.
2. Viol.
Br.
Vcl.
K.-B.
1.
dolce
2.
pizz.
arco
pp legg.
legg.
p
pp
f

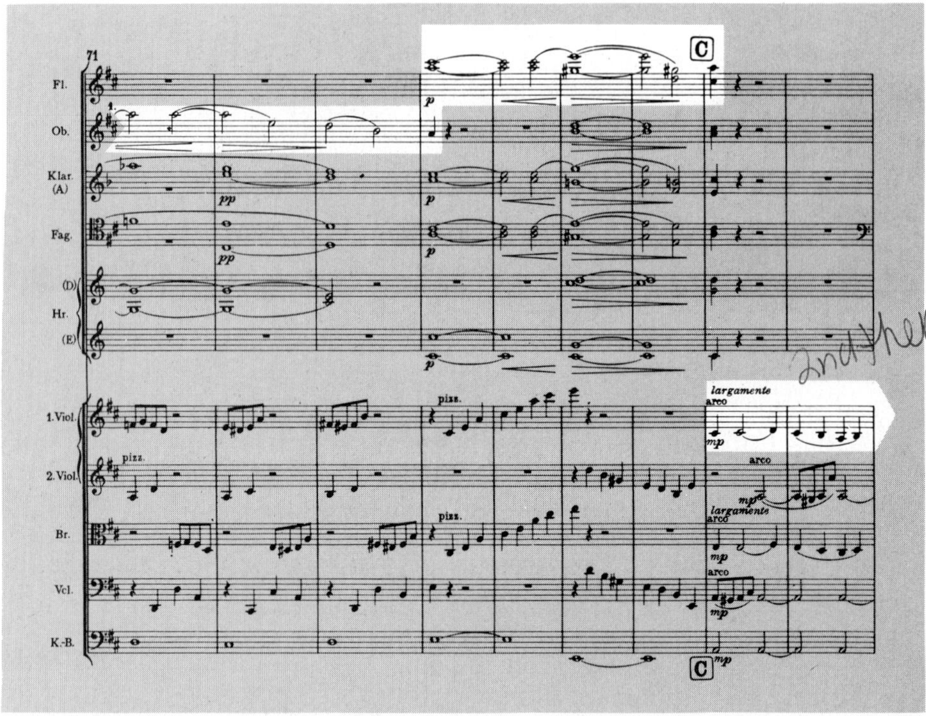

71
C
Fl.
Ob.
Klar. (A)
Fag.
(D)
Hr.
(E)
1. Viol.
2. Viol.
Br.
Vcl.
K.-B.
pp
p
pizz.
largamente
arco
mp
2nd theme

80
Fl.
Ob.
Klar. (A)
Fag.
1. Viol.
2. Viol.
Br.
Vcl.
K.-B.
p
cresc.

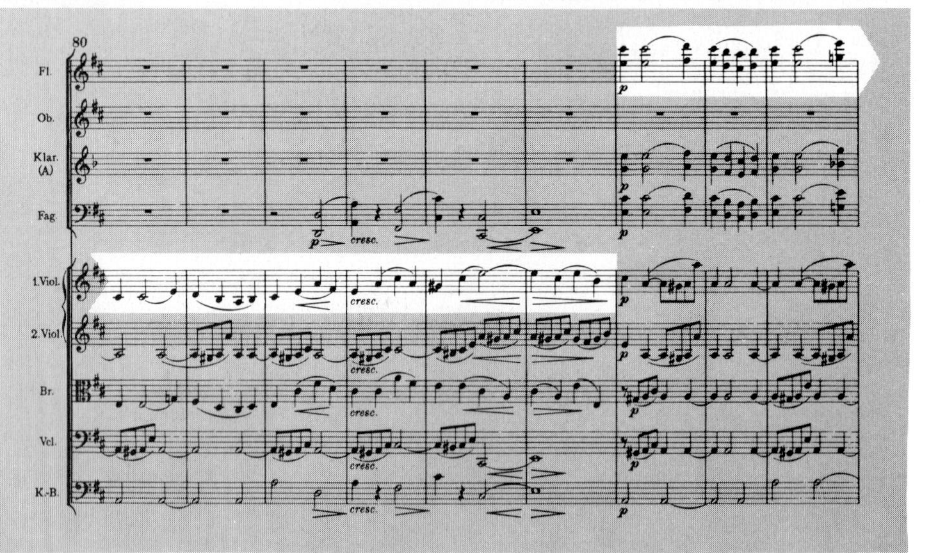

89
Fl.
Ob.
Klar. (A)
Fag.
(D) Hr. (E)
1. Viol.
2. Viol.
Br.
Vcl.
K.-B.
cresc.
p cresc.
f

97
D
a 2
Fl.
Ob.
Klar. (A)
Fag.
(D) Hr. (E)
1. Viol.
2. Viol.
Br.
Vcl.
K.-B.
f
sf

105
Fl.
Ob.
Klar. (A)
Fag.
(D)
Hr.
(E)
1.Viol.
2.Viol.
div.
Br.
Vcl.
K.-B.

112
Fl.
a 2
Ob.
Klar. (A)
Fag.
(D)
Hr.
(E)
Trpt. (D)
Pk.
1.Viol.
ben marc.
2.Viol.
Br.
Vcl.
K.-B

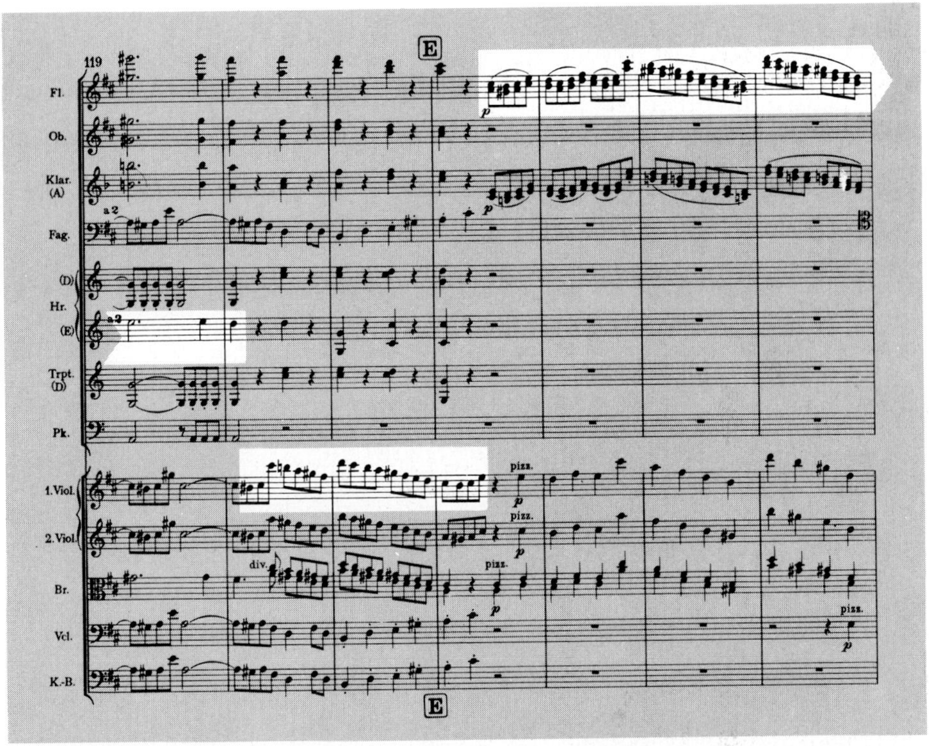

119

E

Fl.
Ob.
Klar. (A)
a 2
Fag.
(D)
Hr.
(E)
a 2
Trpt. (D)
Pk.
1. Viol.
2. Viol.
Br.
Vcl.
K.-B.
p
pizz.
div.
pizz.
pizz.
p

E

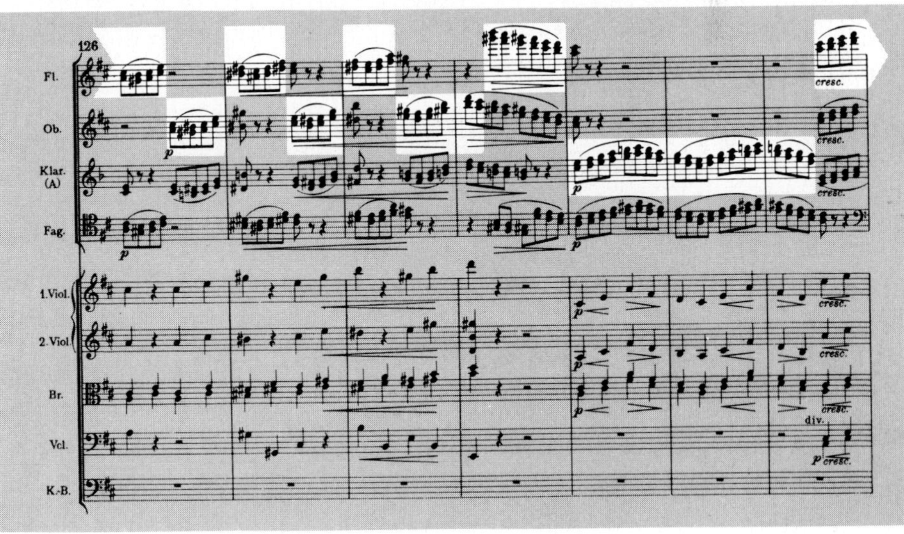

133
F
Fl.
Ob.
Klar. (A)
Fag.
Hr.
1.Viol.
2.Viol.
Br.
Vcl.
K.-B.
cresc.
arco
p cresc.
unis.
f

141
Fl.
Ob.
Klar. (A)
Fag.
Hr.
Trpt. (D)
Pk.
1.Viol.
2.Viol.
Br.
Vcl.
K.-B.
a 2
f
p

Development

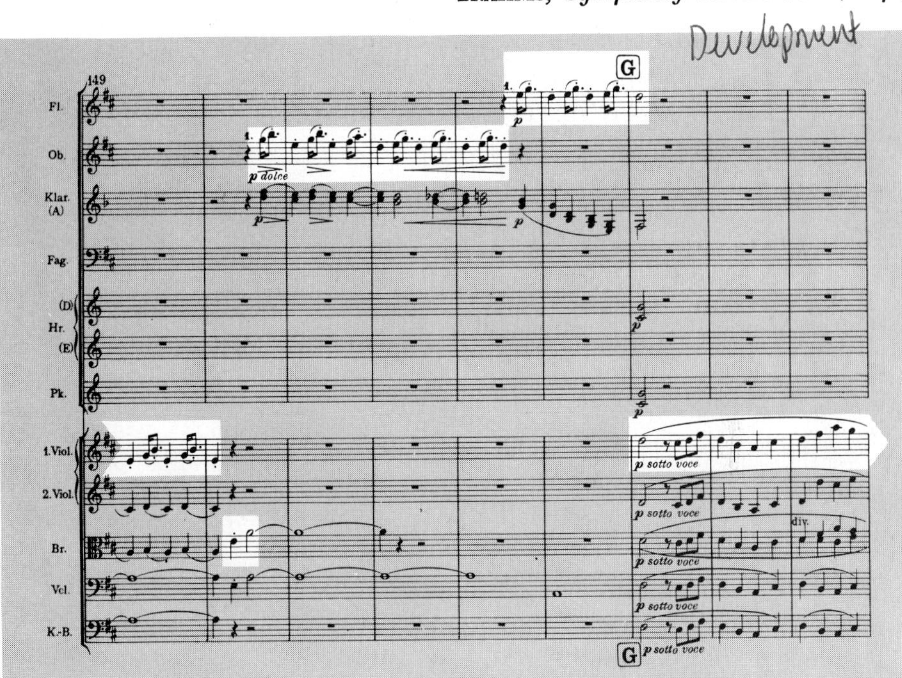

168
H
Fl.
Ob.
Klar. (A)
Fag.
(D)
Hr.
(E)
1. Viol.
2. Viol.
Br.
Vcl.
K.-B.
legg.
H

175
Fl.
Ob.
Klar. (A)
Fag.
(D)
Hr.
(E)
1. Viol.
2. Viol.
Br.
Vcl.
K B.

182
Fl.
Ob.
Klar. (A)
Fag.
Hr. (D)
Hr. (E)
Trpt. (D)
1. Viol.
2. Viol.
Br.
Vcl.
K.-B.
pizz.
arco
f marc.
sf marc.
Very strong accents - on off beats

189
Fl.
Ob.
Klar. (A)
Fag.
Hr. (D)
1.2.
Trpt. (D)
1. Viol.
2. Viol.
Br.
Vcl.
K.-B.

196
Fl.
Ob.
Klar. (A)
Fag.
(D) Hr. (E)
Trpt. (D)
Pos. u. Btb.
1.Viol.
2.Viol.
Br.
Vcl.
K.-B.
cresc.
marc.
a 2
ff
f

204
I Tranquillo
Fl.
Ob.
Klar. (A)
Fag.
(D) Hr. (E)
Pos. u. Btb.
1.Viol.
2.Viol.
Br.
Vcl.
K.-B.
p dolce
I Tranquillo

leading passage back to recap.

228
Fl.
Ob.
Klar. (A)
Fag.
(D) Hr. (E)
Pos. u. Btb.
1.Viol.
2.Viol.
Br.
Vcl.
K.-B.
div.
pp sempre più
Recap.
238
in tempo
Trpt. (D)
Pk.
pp sempre
in tempo

250
L
Fl.
Ob.
Klar. (A)
Fag.
(D)
Hr.
(E)
Trpt. (D)
1. Viol.
2. Viol.
Br.
Vcl.
K.-B.
pp
pp sempre
L

258
Fl.
Ob.
Klar. (A)
Fag.
(D)
Hr.
(E)
Trpt. (D)
Pk.
1. Viol.
2. Viol.
Br.
Vcl.
K.-B.
dim.
a 2
f sempre più
ff

267

Fl. a 2
Ob. a 2
Klar. (A) a 2
Fag. a 2
Hr. (D) (E)
f sempre più
Trpt. (D)
Pk.
1. Viol.
2. Viol.
Br.
Vcl.
K.-B.

builds up momentum by emph. musical pattern
rhythm
- like beethoven

274

Fl.
Ob.
Klar. (A)
Fag. a 2
Hr. (D) (E)
Trpt. (D)
Pos. u. Btb.
Pk.
1. Viol.
2. Viol.
Br.
Vcl.
K.-B.

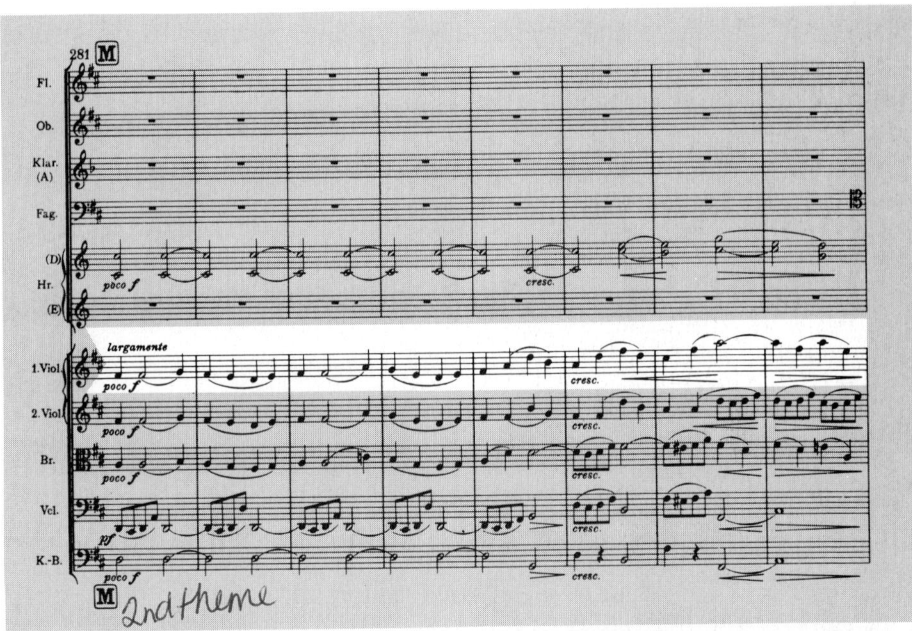
281
M
Fl.
Ob.
Klar. (A)
Fag.
(D)
Hr.
(E)
poco f
cresc.
largamente
1.Viol.
2.Viol.
Br.
Vcl.
K.-B.
pf
M
2nd theme

289
Fl.
Ob.
Klar. (A)
Fag.
(D)
Hr.
(E)
1.Viol.
2.Viol.
Br.
Vcl.
K.-B.
p
cresc.
p cresc.

297
Fl.
Ob.
Klar. (A)
Fag.
(D) Hr. (E)
1.Viol.
2.Viol.
Br.
Vcl.
K.-B.

306
Fl.
Ob.
Klar. (A)
Fag.
(D) Hr. (E)
Trpt. (D)
1.Viol.
2.Viol.
Br.
Vcl.
K.-B.

Woodwind solo

335
Fl.
cresc.
Ob.
p cresc.
a 2
Klar. (A)
Fag.
(D) Hr. (E)
p cresc.
1. Viol.
arco
2. Viol.
Br.
div.
Vcl.
K.-B.
p cresc.

343
Fl.
Ob.
Klar. (A)
Fag.
(D) Hr. (E)
Trpt. (D)
Pk.
1. Viol.
2. Viol.
Br.
Vcl.
K.-B.
a 2
più f

350
O
Fl.
Ob.
Klar. (A)
Fag.
Hr. (D)
Pos. u. Btb.
1. Viol.
2. Viol.
Br.
Vcl.
K.-B.
a 2
ff
p
pp
fp
fpp
molto pp e legg.

358
Fl.
Ob.
Klar. (A)
Fag.
Hr. (D)
Pos. u. Btb.
1. Viol.
2. Viol.
Br.
Vcl.
K.-B.
p
pp sempre
pp
f
ff

367
Fl.
Ob.
Klar. (A)
Fag.
(D)
Hr.
(E)
Trpt. (D)
Pos. u. Btb.
Pk.
1. Viol.
2. Viol.
Br.
Vcl. u. K.-B. unis.
a 2
p cresc.
cresc.
p
f

377
Fl.
Ob.
Klar. (A)
Fag.
(D) Hr. (E)
Trpt. (D)
Pk.
1. Viol.
2. Viol.
Br.
Vcl. u.K.-B.
p cresc.
cresc.
p cresc.
a 2

P
387
a 2
Fl.
Ob.
Klar. (A)
Fag.
(D) Hr. (E)
Trpt. (D)
Pos. u. Btb.
Pk.
1. Viol.
2. Viol.
Br.
Vcl. u.K.-B.
cresc.

395

Fl.
Ob.
Klar. (A)
Fag.
(D) Hr. (E)
Trpt. (D)
Pos. u. Btb.
Pk.
1. Viol.
2. Viol.
Br.
Vcl. u. K.-B.

404

Fl.
Ob.
Klar. (A)
Fag.
(D) Hr. (E)
Trpt. (D)
Pos. u. Btb.
Pk.
1. Viol.
2. Viol.
Br.
Vcl. u. K.-B.

419
Fl.
Ob.
Klar. (A)
Fag.
(D)
Hr.
a 2
(E)
Trpt. (D)
Pos. u. Btb.
Pk.
8
1. Viol.
2. Viol.
Br.
Vcl. u. K.-B.

19. BRAHMS, *Vergebliches Ständchen* (PUBL. 1882)

(Sie.)
Mein' Tür ist ver - schlos - sen, ich lass' dich nicht
ein, ich lass' dich nicht ein;
p
Mut - ter, die rät mir klug, wärst du her - ein mit Fug, wär's mit mir vor -
pp
bei, wär's mit mir, wär's mit mir, wär's mit mir vor - bei!
poco f

(Er.)
So kalt ist die Nacht, so ei-sig der Wind,
so ei-sig der Wind,
dass mir das Herz er-friert, mein' Lieb' er-lö-schen wird, öff-ne mir, mein Kind,
öff-ne mir, öff-ne mir, öff-ne mir, mein Kind!
Lebhafter.
Lebhafter.
p
p
f

(Sie.)
Löschet dein' Lieb', lass sie lö - schen nur, lass sie
f
lö - schen nur! Lö - schet sie im - mer - zu, geh' heim zu
p legg.
Bett, zur Ruh', gu - te Nacht, mein Knab', gu - te Nacht, gu - te Nacht,
gu - te Nacht, mein Knab'!
f
sf

Translation

Guten Abend, mein Schatz,
Guten Abend, mein Kind!
Ich komm' aus Lieb' zu dir,
Ach, mach' mir auf die Tür!

"Meine Tür ist verschlossen,
Ich lass dich nicht ein;
Mutter die rät' mir klug,
Wär'st du herein mit Fug,
Wär's mit mir vorbei!"

So kalt ist die Nacht,
So eisig der Wind,
Dass mir das Herz erfriert,
Mein' Lieb' erlöschen wird;
Öffne mir, mein Kind!

"Löschet dein Lieb',
Lass sie löschen nur!
Löschet sie immer zu,
Geh' heim zu Bett zur Ruh',
Gute Nacht, mein Knab'!"

TRADITIONAL

Good evening, my dear
good evening, my child!
I come out of love for you,
ah, open the door for me!
Open the door for me!

"My door is locked,
I will not let you in.
Mother warned me
that if I let you in willingly
all would be over with me!"

The night is so cold,
the wind is so icy,
that my heart is freezing.
My love will be extinguished;
open up for me, child!

"If your love is extinguished,
just let it go out!
Just keep on extinguishing it;
go home to bed, to rest!
Good night, my boy!"

PHILIP L. MILLER

20. PETER ILYICH TCHAIKOVSKY (1840-1893), Excerpts from *The Nutcracker* (1892)

Fl.
Gr. Fl.
Ob.
Cl.
Fg.
Cor. (F)
Trbe. (A)
Tbni.
Tuba
Mit Paukenschlägel.
Piat.
Vl.
Vle.
pizz.
Celli
pizz.
C.-B.

10
Fl.
Ob.
Cl.
Fg.
Cor. (F)
Trbe. (A)
Tbni.
Tuba
Piat.
Vl.
Vle.
Celli
C.-B.
p
mf
pp
pizz.

Fl.
Ob.
Cl.
cre - - - scen - - - do
f
Fg.
Cor. (F)
Trbe. (A)
Tbni. Tuba
Mit Paukenschlägel.
Piat.
Vl.
Vle.
Celli
C.-B.

20
Fl.
Ob.
Cl.
Fg.
Cor. (F)
Trbe. (A)
Tbni. Tuba
Piat.
Vl.
Vle.
Celli
C.-B.
pizz.
pizz.
arco
arco
arco

Fl.
Ob.
Cl.
Fg.
Cor. (F)
Trbe. (A)
Tbni. Tuba
Piat.
Vl.
Vle.
Celli
C.-B.

30
Fl.
Ob.
Cl.
Fg.
Cor. (F)
Trbe. (A)
Tbni. Tuba
Piat.
Vl.
Vle.
Celli
C.-B.
mf
p
pp
pizz.

Fl.

Ob.

Cl.

Fg.

Cor. (F)

Trbe. (A)

Tbni. Tuba

Mit Paukenschlägel.

Piat.

Vl.

Vle.

Celli

C.-B.

40
Fl.
Ob.
Cl.
pp
cre - - scen - - do
f
ff
Fg.
Cor. (F)
Trbe. (A)
Tbni.
Tuba
Mit Paukenschlägel.
Piat.
Vl.
Vle.
pizz.
Celli
C.-B.
p

Fl.
Ob.
Cl.
Fg.
Cor. (F)
Trbe. (A)
Tbni. Tuba
Piat.
Vl.
Vle.
Celli
C.-B.
mf
marcato
arco

Fl.
Ob.
Cl.
Fg.
Cor. (F)
Trbe. (A)
Tbni. Tuba
Piat.
Vl.
Vle.
Celli
C.-B.

Fl.
Ob.
Cl.
Fg.
marcato
marcato
Cor. (F)
Trbe. (A)
Tbni.
Tuba
Piat.
Vl.
Vle.
Celli
C.-B.

50
Fl.
Ob.
Cl.
Fg.
Cor. (F)
Trbe. (A)
Tbni. Tuba
Piat.
Vl.
Vle.
Celli
C.-B.

Fl.
Ob.
Cl.
Fg.
Cor. (F)
Trbe. (A)
Tbni. Tuba
Piat.
Vl.
Vle.
Celli
C.-B.
mf
cresc.
pizz.

Fl.
Ob.
Cl.
Fg.
Cor. (F)
Trbe. (A)
Tbni. Tuba
Mit Paukenschlägel.
Piat.
Vl.
Vle.
arco
Celli
arco
C.-B.

60
Fl.
Ob.
Cl.
Fg.
Cor.
(F)
Trbe.
(A)
Tbni.
Tuba
Piat.
Vl.
Vle.
Celli
C.-B.
pizz.
pizz.

Fl.
mf cresc.
mf cresc.
mf cresc.
ff
Ob.
cresc.
Cl.
cresc.
cresc.
Fg.
cresc.
cresc.
Cor. (F)
cresc.
Trbe. (A)
Tbni. Tuba
Mit Paukenschlägel.
Piat.
Vl.
cresc.
cresc.
Vle.
cresc.
Celli
cresc.
C.-B.
cresc.

Fl.
Ob.
Cl.
Fg.
Cor.
(F)
Trbe.
(A)
Tbni.
Tuba
Piat.
Vl.
Vle.
Celli
C.-B.
pizz.
pizz.

70
Fl.
Ob.
Cl.
Fg.
Cor. (F)
Trbe. (A)
Tbni. Tuba
Piat.
Vl.
Vle.
Celli
C.-B.
arco
arco
arco

Fl.
Ob.
Cl.
Fg.
Cor. (F)
Trbe. (A)
Tbni. Tuba
Piat.
Vl.
Vle.
Celli
C.-B.

Fl.
Ob.
Cl.
Fg.
Cor. (F)
Trbe. (A)
Tbni. Tuba
Piat.
Vl.
Vle.
Celli
C.-B.
mf
cresc.
pizz.

80
Fl.
Ob.
Cl.
Fg.
Cor. (F)
Trbe. (A)
Tbni.
Tuba
Mit Paukenschlägel.
Piat.
Vl.
Vle.
Celli
C.-B.
arco
arco

Fl.
Ob.
Cl.
Fg.
Cor. (F)
Trbe. (A)
Tbni. Tuba
Piat.
Vl.
Vle.
Celli
C.-B.
pizz.
pizz.

Fl.
Ob.
Cl.
Fg.
Cor. (F)
Trbe. (A)
Tbni. Tuba
Piat.
Vl.
Vle.
Celli
C.-B.
mf cresc.
cresc.
f
ff
Mit Paukenschlägel.
arco

Arabian Dance

10
C.Ingl.
Cl.
Vl.
Vle.
Celli
5

C.Ingl.
Cl.
Vl.
Vle.
Celli
con sordini
p
p molto espress.
più f
5

20
Cl.
Tamb.
pp
p
Vl.
pp
cresc.
Vle.
Celli

30
Cl.
Tamb.
pp
Vl.
mf
p
Vle.
Celli

C.Ingl.
Cl.
Fg.
Tamb.
Vl.
Vle.
Celli
p

40
C.Ingl.
Fg.
Tamb.
Vl.
Vle.
Celli
pp

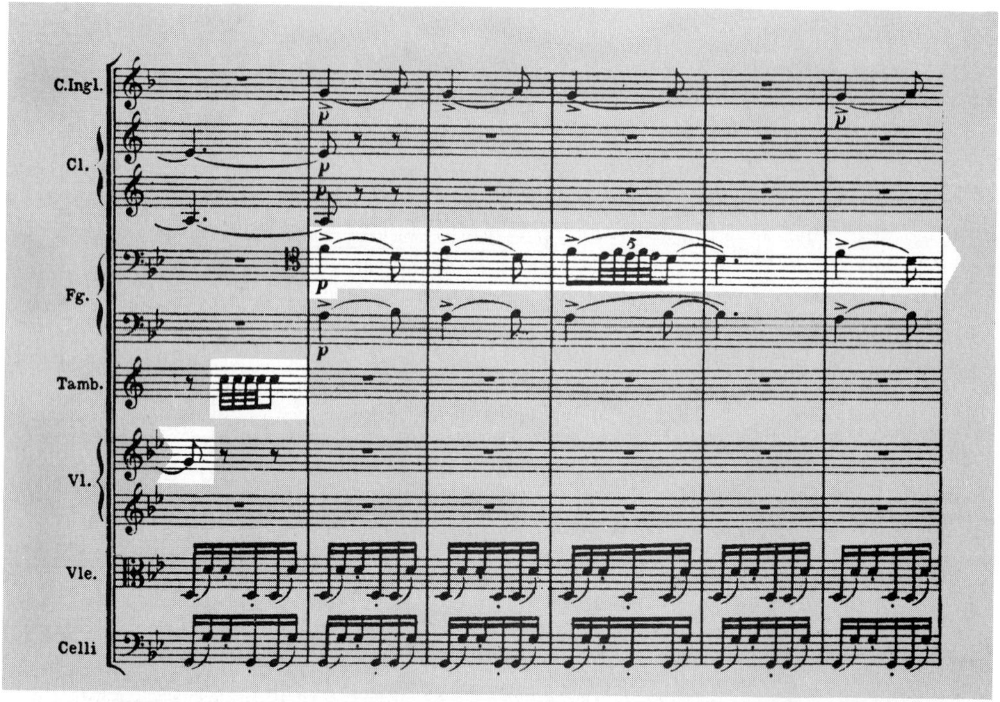

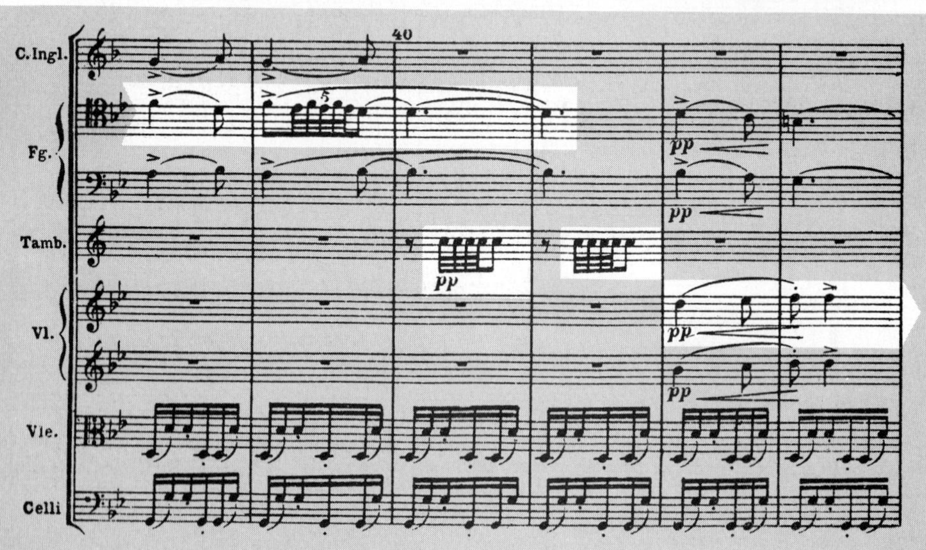

Fg.
Vl.
Vle.
Celli
cresc.
mf
dim.
50
p
Tamb.
pp
60

C. Ingl.
Cl.
p
Tamb.
pp
Vl.
pp
Vle.
Celli
pp
con sordini
C.-B.
pp div.
con sordini
70 
Ob.
mf
f
C.Ingl.
Cl.
Tamb.
pp
Vl.
p
Vle.
p
Celli
C.-B.

Fl.
Ob.
C.Ingl.
Cl.
Cl.b.
Fg.
Tamb.
Vl.
Vle.
Celli
C.-B.
mp
p
mf
f
pp

80
Fl.
Ob.
C.Ingl.
Cl.
Cl. b.
Fg.
Tamb.
Vl.
Vle.
Celli
C.-B.
p
pp
mp
5

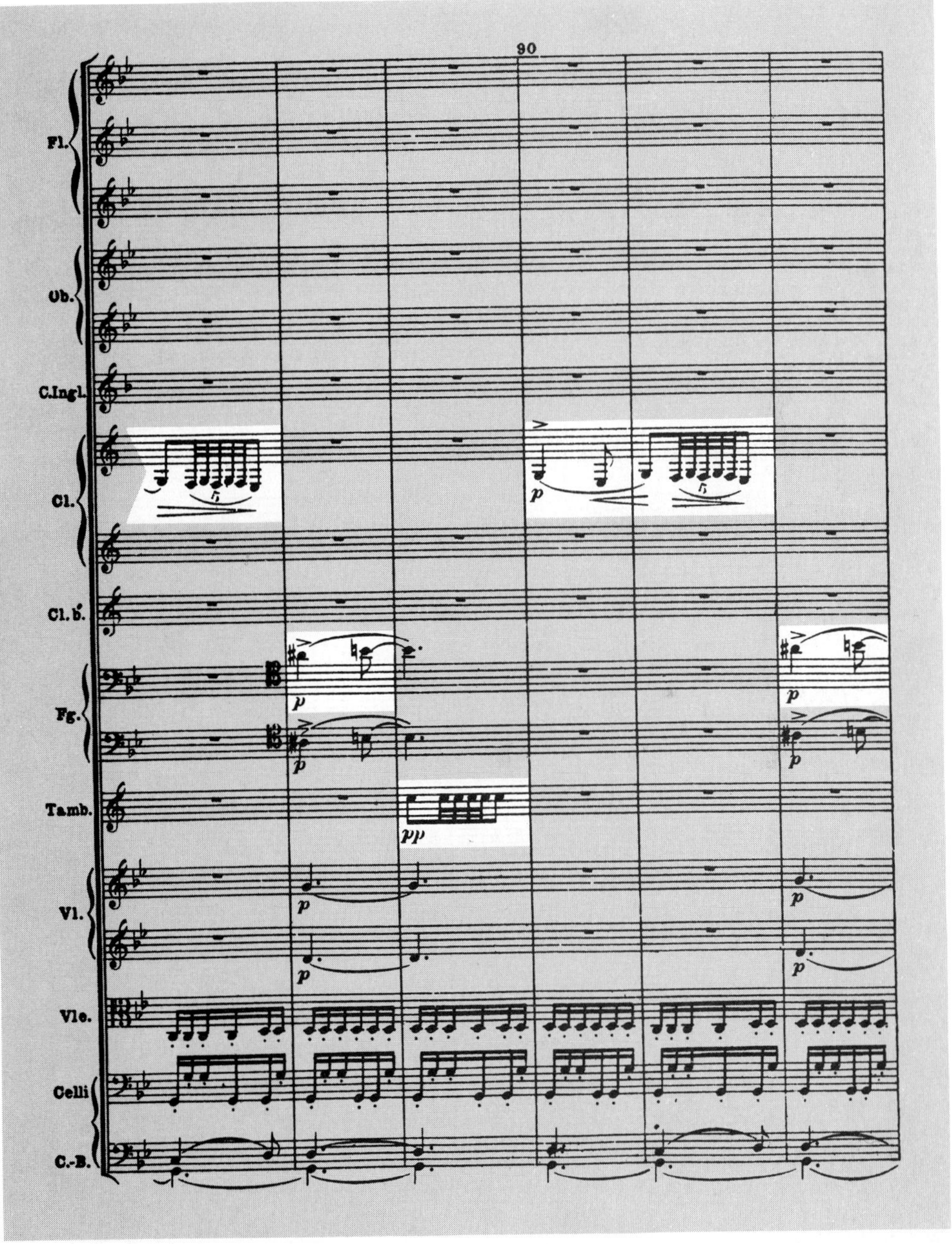

90

Fl.

Ob.

C.Ingl.

Cl.

Cl. b.

Fg.

Tamb.

Vl.

Vle.

Celli

C.-B.

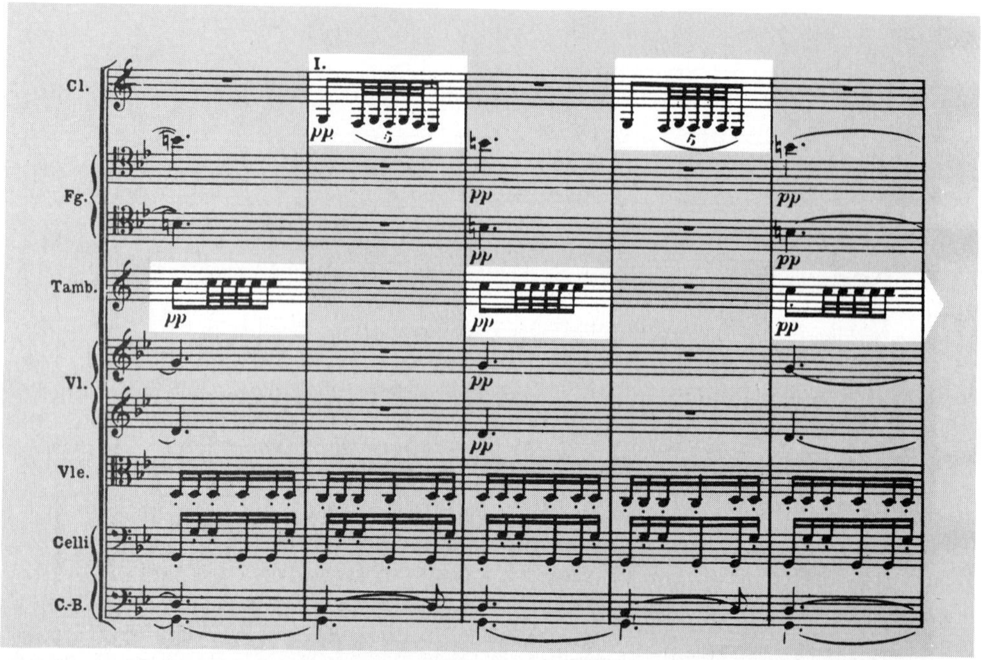

Cl.
I.
pp
Fg.
pp
pp
Tamb.
pp
Vl.
pp
pp
Vle.
Celli
C.-B.

Dance of the Toy Flutes

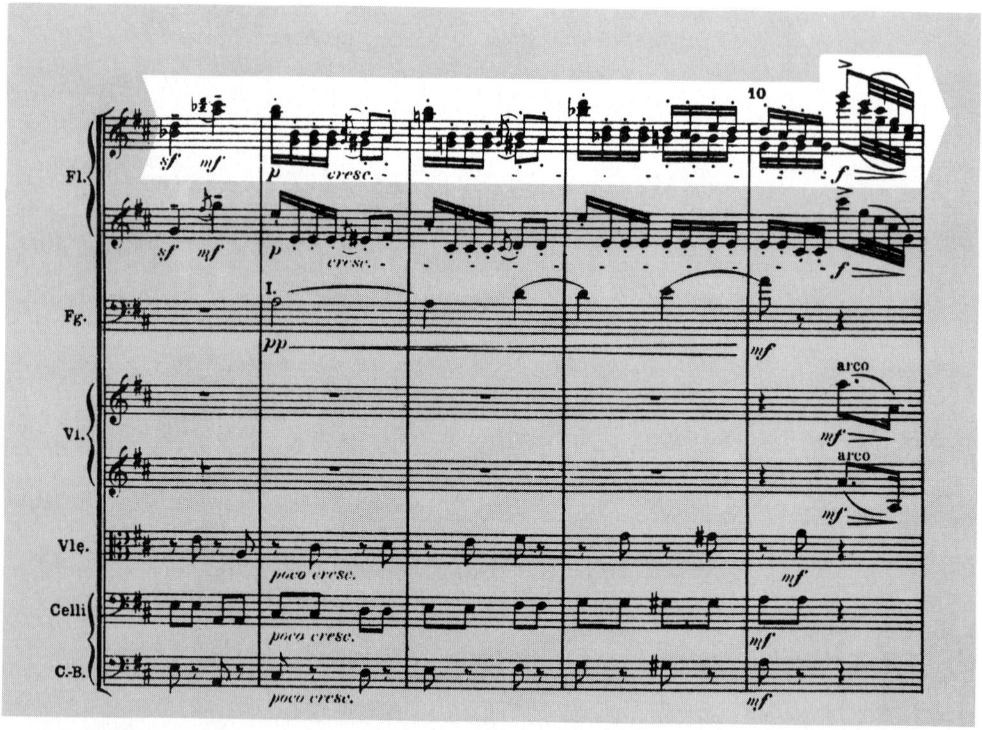

10
Fl.
sf
mf
p
cresc.
f
I.
Fg.
pp
mf
arco
Vl.
arco
mf
Vle.
poco cresc.
Celli
poco cresc.
C.-B.
poco cresc.

Fl.
p
mf
sf
mf
p
Vl.
Vle.
p
Celli
p
C.-B.
p

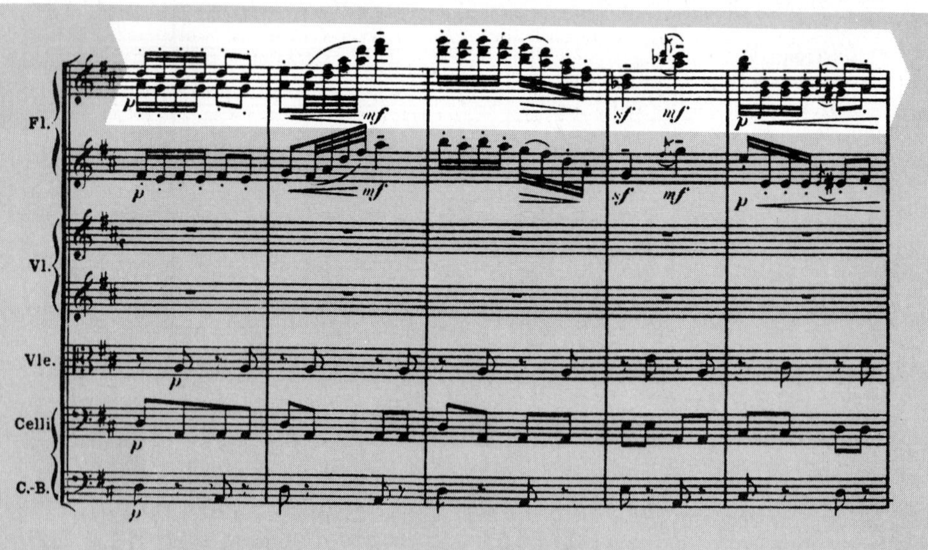

20
Fl.
mf cresc.
ff
ff espress.
C.Ingl.
f
Vle.
cresc.
mf
Celli
C.-B.
Cl. b.
p
pizz.
arco
Vl.
sempre
mf

30
Fl.
sf
mf
p
cresc.
Vl.
poco più f
cresc.
Vle.
poco più f
cresc.
Celli
p
cresc.
C.-B.
p
cresc.

Fl.
f
p
mf
Cor.
(F)
mf
p
Vl.
mf
p
poco più f
Vle.
mf
p
poco più f
Celli
mf
p
C.-B.
mf
p

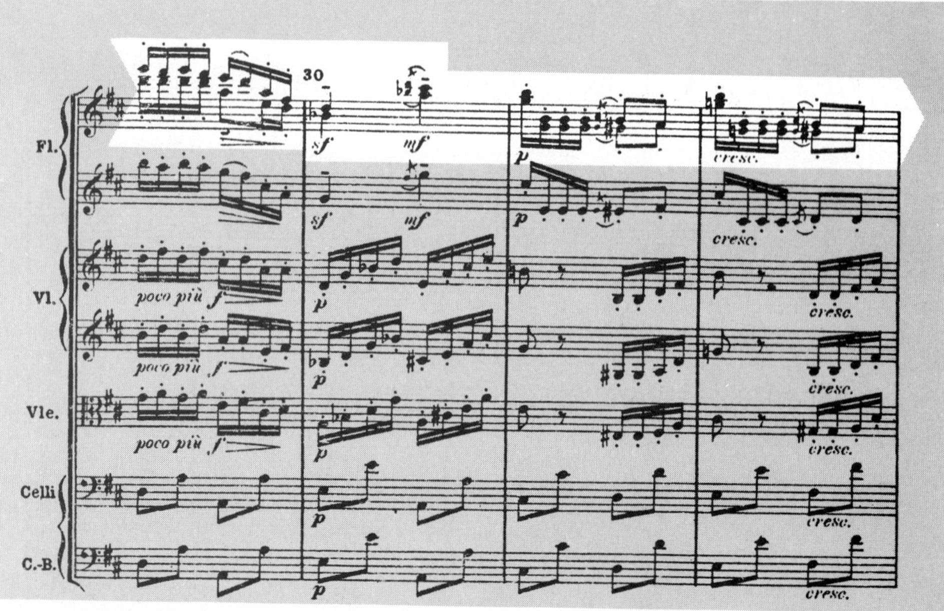

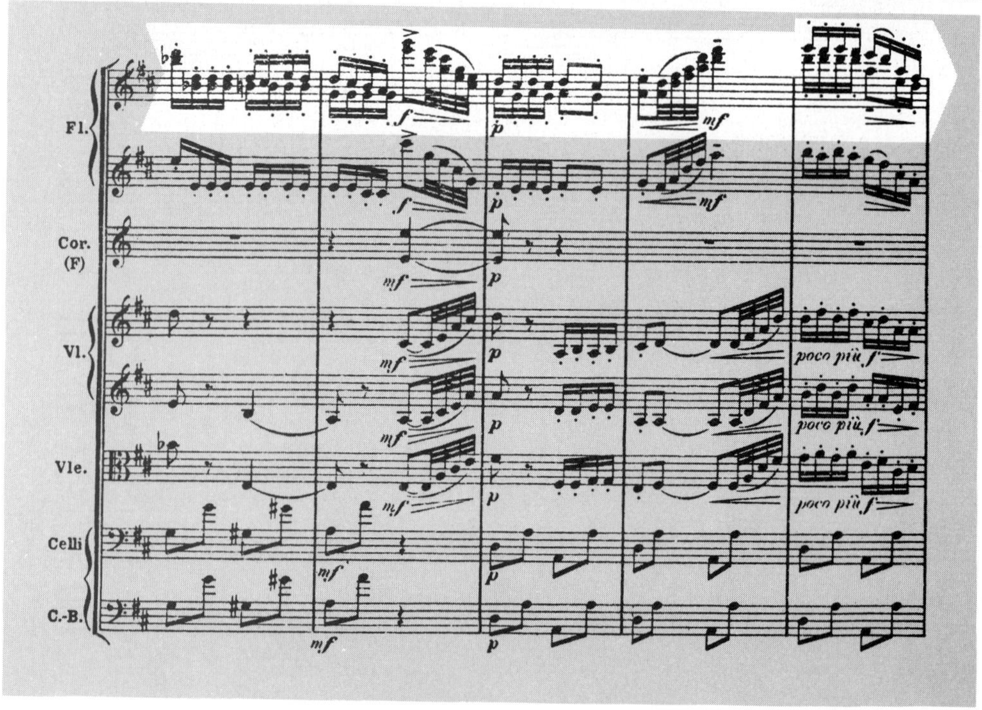

40
Fl.
Ob.
C.Ingl.
Cl.
Cl. b.
Fg.
Cor. (F)
Trbe. (A)
Tbni. Tuba
Timp.
Piat.
Vl.
Vle.
Celli
C.-B.
sf
mf
p cresc.
f
p
cresc.

Fl.
Ob.
C.Ingl.
Cl.
Cl.b.
Fg.
Cor. (F)
Trbe. (A)
Tbni. Tuba
Timp.
Piat.
Vl.
Vle.
Celli
C.-B.

pizz.
pizz.
pizz.

50
Fl.
Ob.
C.Ingl.
Cl.
Cl.b.
Fg.
Cor. (F)
Trbe. (A)
Tbni. Tuba
Timp.
Piat.
Vl.
Vle.
Celli
C.-B.
arco
divisi arco

Fl.
Ob.
C.Ingl.
Cl.
Cl. b.
Fg.
Cor. (F)
Trbe. (A)
Tbni. Tuba
Timp.
Piat.
Vl.
sempre spiccato
sempre spiccato
Vle.
sempre spiccato
Celli
C.-B.

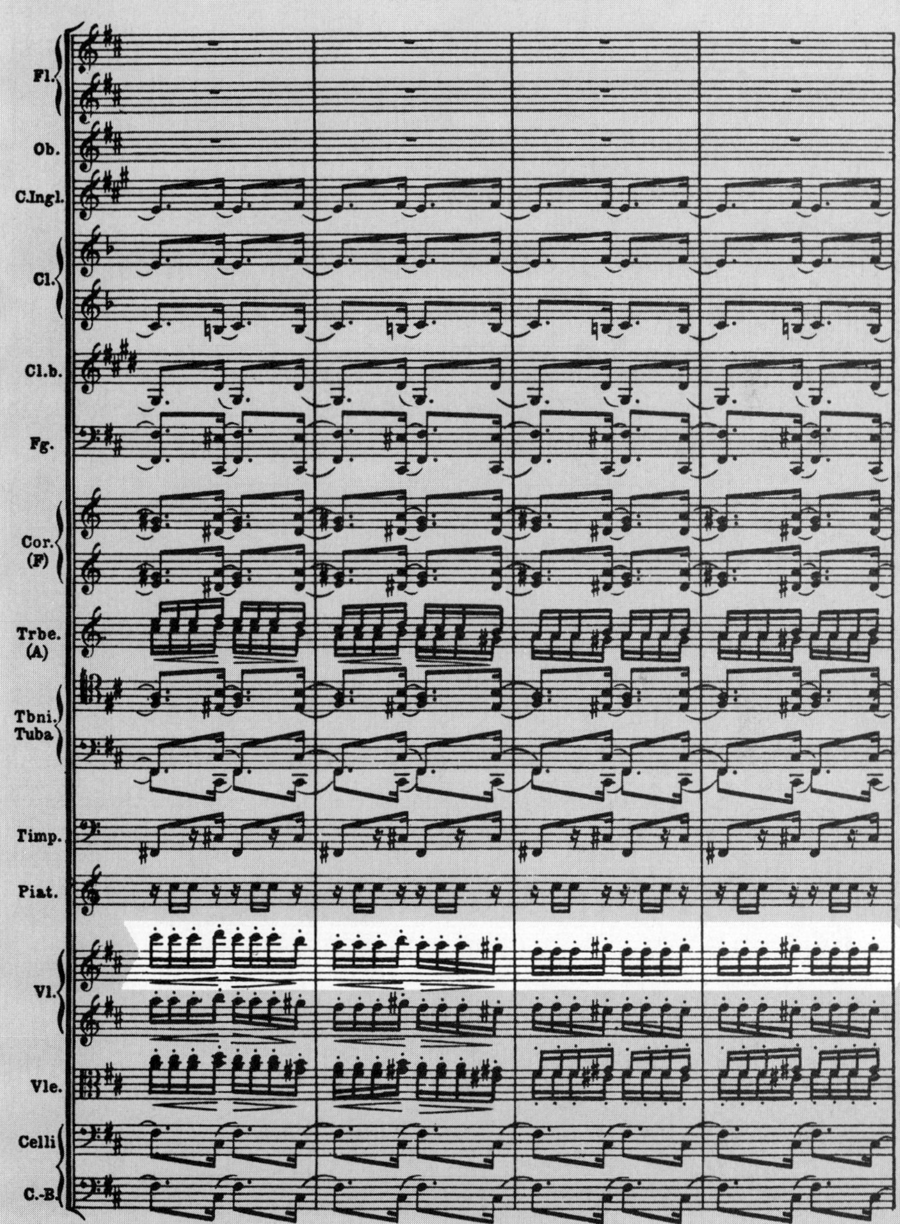
Fl.
Ob.
C.Ingl.
Cl.
Cl.b.
Fg.
Cor. (F)
Trbe. (A)
Tbni. Tuba
Timp.
Piat.
Vl.
Vle.
Celli
C.-B.

60
Fl.
Ob.
C.Ingl.
Cl.
Cl.b.
Fg.
Cor.
(F)
Trbe.
(A)
Tbni.
Tuba
Timp.
Piat.
Vl.
Vle.
Celli
C.-B.
pizz.
arco
unis. pizz.
sempre pizz.
poco più f
mf
p

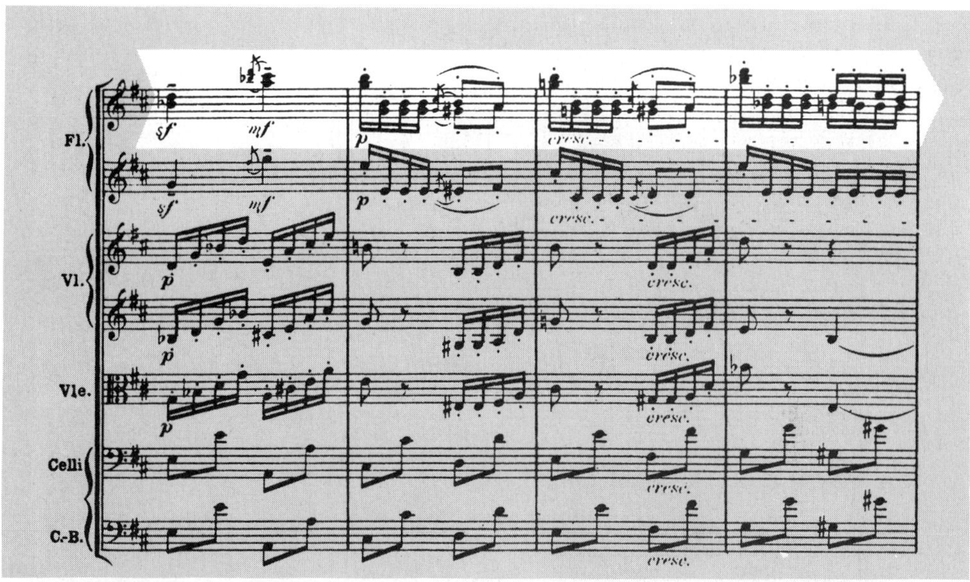

Fl.
70
f
p
mf
Cor.
(F)
1.3
2.4
Vl.
poco più f
Vle.
Celli
C.-B.

Fl.
Ob.
C.Ingl.
Cl.
Cl.b.
Fg.
Cor. (F)
Trbe. (A)
Tbni. Tuba
Timp.
Piat.
Vl.
Vle.
Celli
C.-B.
sf
mf
p cresc.
cresc.
f
p
pizz.

21. TCHAIKOVSKY, *Symphony No. 6 in B minor (Pathétique)* (1893)

ritenuto
Ob.1.2
1.in A
Klar.
2.in A
Fag.1
Hrn.
1.2.in F
Vla.
div.
Kb.
div.
ritenuto
ritenuto

Allegro non troppo (♩= 116)
1.
Fl.
2.
1.in A
Klar.
2.in A
Allegro non troppo (♩= 116)
Vla.
div.
Vc.
div.
Allegro non troppo (♩= 116)

1.
Fl.
2.
1. in A
Klar.
2. in A
1.
Fag.
2.
Vla.
div.
Vc.
div.
Kb.
div.
p

Klar.
1 in A
A
1. Hälfte
Viol. 1
Vla.
div.
Vc.
div.
Kb.
div.
pp

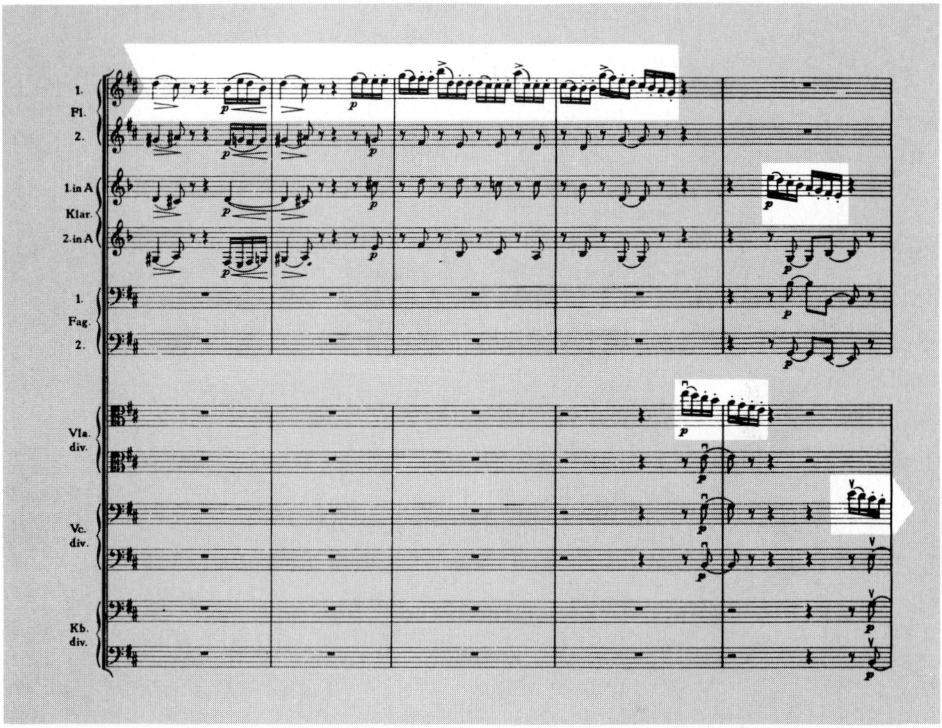

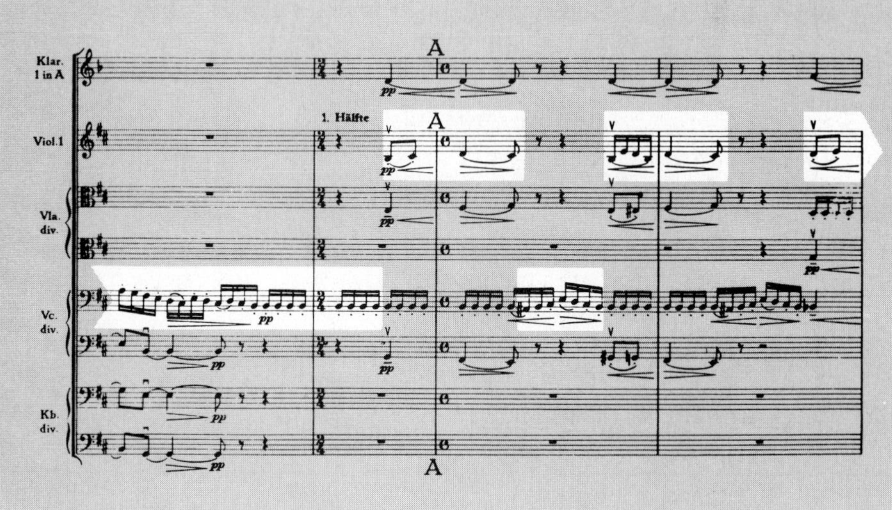

Klar. 1 in A
1.2. in F
Hrn.
3.4. in F
Viol. 1 div.
cresc.
restez
Viol. 2 div.
div.
Vla. div.
cresc.
Vc.
div.
Kb. div.

Fl.1
Ob.1
Klar.
1 in A
Fag.1
Hrn.
3.4 in F
Viol.1
Viol.2
Vla.
div.
Vc.
div.
Kb.
div.
unis.
saltando
pp
p

1.
Fl.
2.
Kl.Fl.
Ob.1
Klar.
1 in A
Fag.1
Viol.1
Viol.2
Vla.
Vc.
Kb.
unis.
p

B
Fl.
Kl. Fl.
Ob. 1
Klar. 1 in A
Fag. 1
1.2. in F
Hrn.
3. in F
Viol. 1
Viol. 2
Vla.
Vc.
Kb.

Fl.
Ob. 1.2
1. in A
Klar.
2. in A
Fag. 1
1.2. in F
Hrn.
3. in F
Viol. 1
Viol. 2
Vla.
Vc.
Kb.
Solo

1. Fl. 2.
Ob.1.2
1.in A Klar. 2.in A
Fag.1
1.2.in F Hrn. 4.in F
Viol.1
Viol.2
Vla.
Vc.
Kb.
pizz.
arco
espr.

C
Ob.1.2
1.in A Klar. 2.in A
Solo
Fag.1.2
1.2.in F Hrn. 4.in F
Viol.1
Viol.2
Vla.
Vc.
Kb.

Un poco animando
Solo
1.
Fl.
2.
Kl.Fl.
Ob.1.2
1. in A
Klar.
2. in A
Fag.1.2
1.2.in F
Hrn.
3.4.in F
Trp.1.2 in B
A.T.
Pos.
B.
Btb.
Un poco animando
Viol.1
Viol.2
Vla.
Vc.
Kb.
Un poco animando

1.
Fl.
2.
Kl.Fl.
Ob.1.2
1.in A
Klar.
2.in A
Fag.1.2
1.2.in F
Hrn.
3.4.in F
Trp.1.2 in B
A.T.
Pos.
B.
Btb.
Pk.
Viol.1
ff détaché
Viol.2
ff détaché
div.
Vla.
détaché
Vc.
Kb.

Un poco più animato (♩ = 132)

1. Fl. 2.

Kl. Fl.

Große Flöte vorbereiten

Ob. 1.2

1. in A Klar. 2. in A

Fag. 1.2

1.2. in F Hrn. 3.4. in F

Trp. 1.2 in B

A. T. Pos. B.

Btb.

Pk.

muta in C, D, E

Un poco più animato (♩ = 132)

Viol. 1

Viol. 2 div.

unis.

Vla.

Vc.

Kb.

Un poco più animato (♩ = 132)

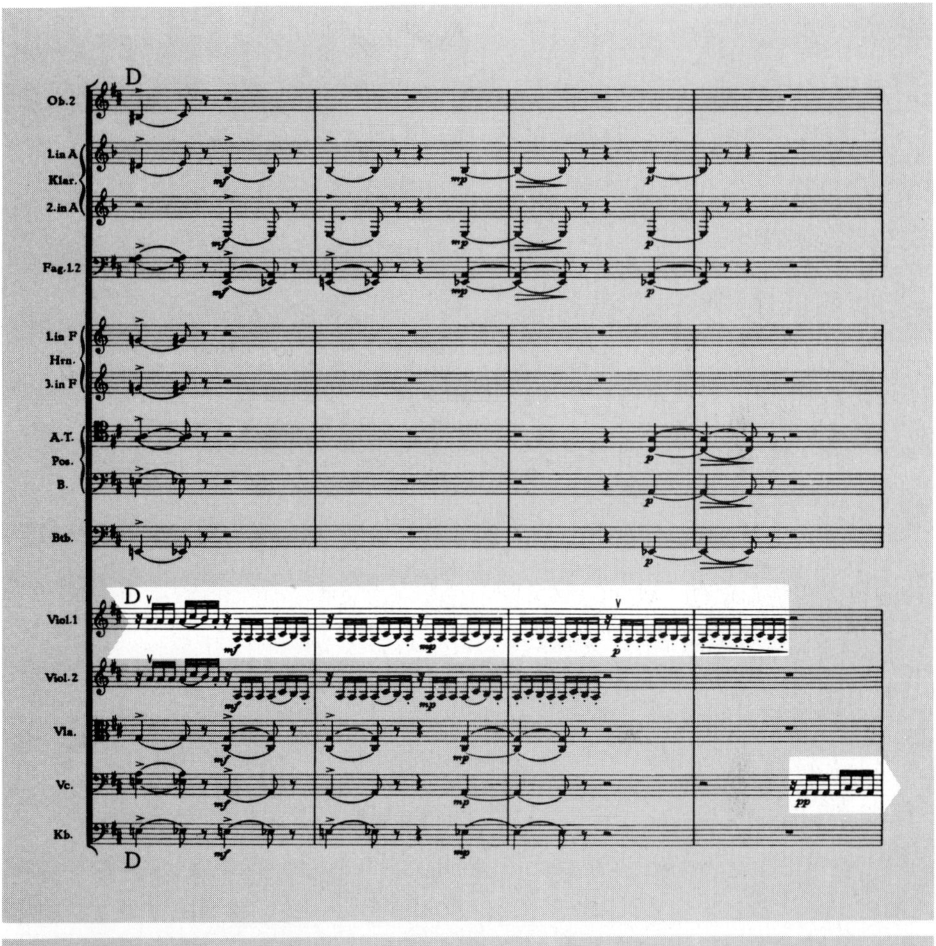

D
Ob. 2
1. in A
Klar.
2. in A
Fag. 1. 2
1. in F
Hrn.
3. in F
A. T.
Pos.
B.
Btb.
D
Viol. 1
Viol. 2
Vla.
Vc.
Kb.
D

T.
Pos.
B.
Btb.
Vc.
ritardando molto
ritardando molto

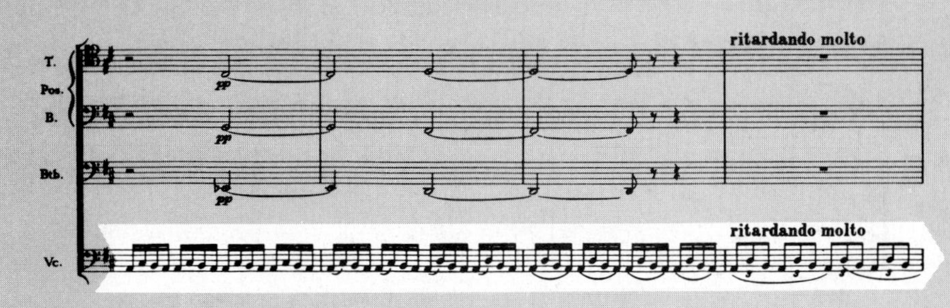

theme 2 – in rel. major D+

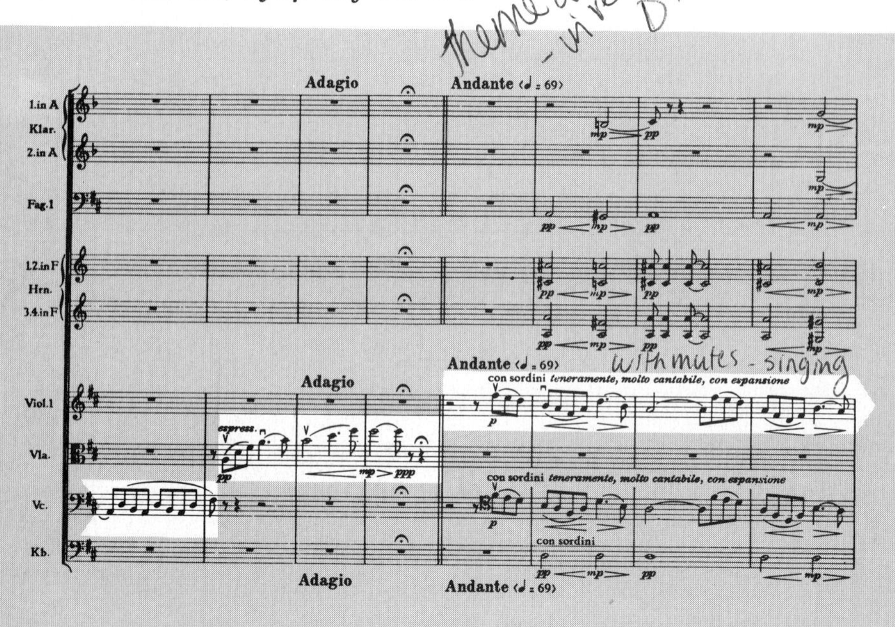

Moderato mosso (♩ = 100)
Fl. 1
Fag. 1
1.2. in F
Hrn.
3.4. in F
Moderato mosso (♩ = 100)
saltando
Viol. 1
saltando
Viol. 2
Vla.
saltando
Vc.
pizz.
arco
Kb.
pizz.
Moderato mosso (♩ = 100)

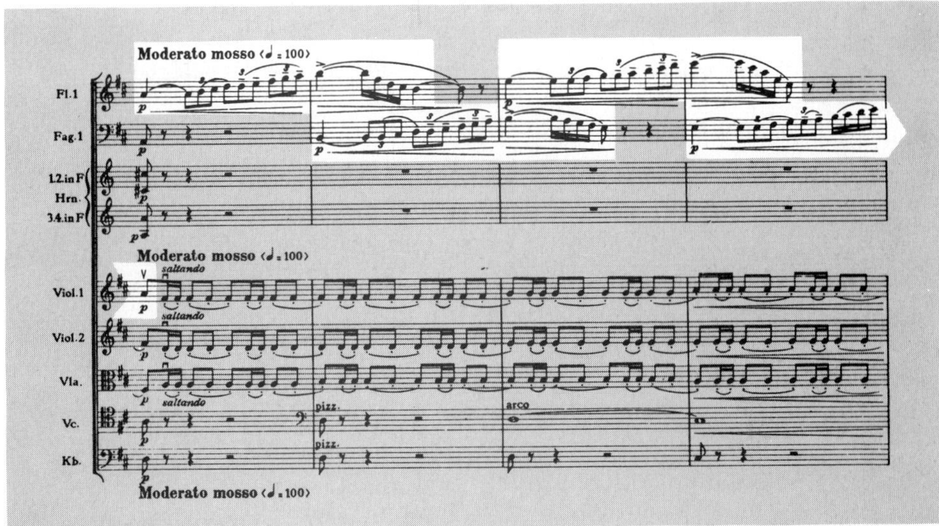

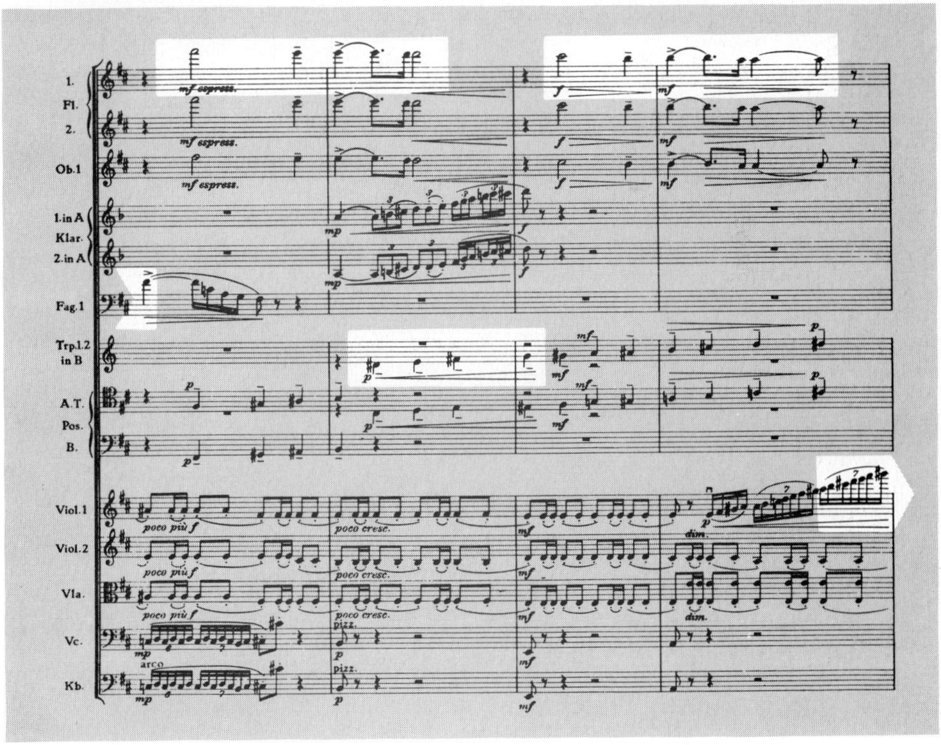

1.
Fl.
2.
mf espress.
mf espress.
Ob. 1
mf espress.
1. in A
Klar.
2. in A
Fag. 1
Trp. 1.2 in B
A. T.
Pos.
B.
Viol. 1
poco più f
poco cresc.
dim.
Viol. 2
poco più f
poco cresc.
Vla.
poco più f
poco cresc.
dim.
Vc.
pizz.
arco
Kb.
pizz.

counterpoint

E
Klar. 1 in A
Fag. 1
Viol. 1
saltando
Viol. 2
Vla.
Vc.
arco
Kb.

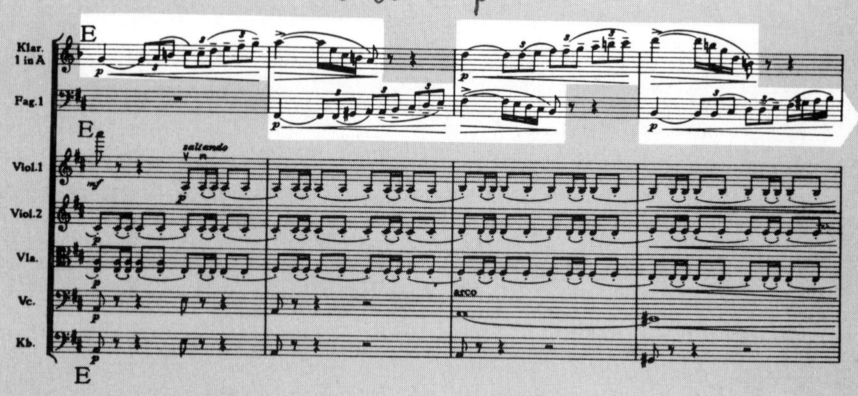

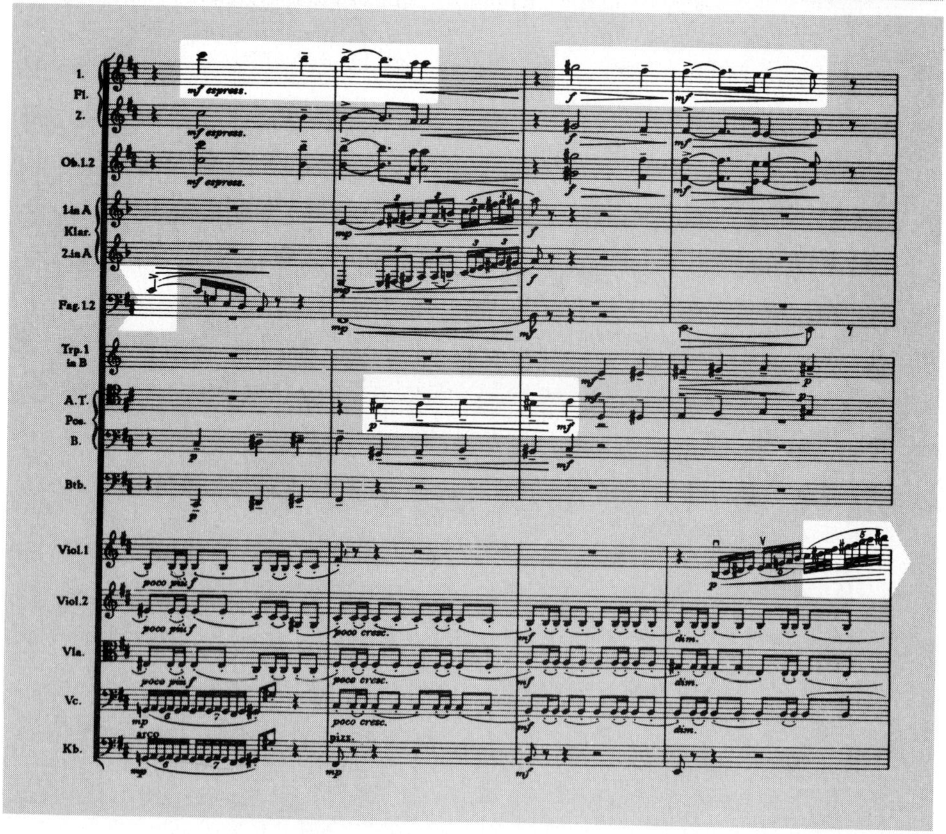

1. Fl. 2.
mf espress.
Ob. 1. 2
1. in A Klar. 2. in A
Fag. 1. 2
Trp. 1 in B
A. T. Pos. B.
Btb.
Viol. 1
Viol. 2
Vla.
Vc.
Kb.
poco più f
poco cresc.
dim.
arco
pizz.

F
1.
Fl.
2.
3.
Gr.Fl.
1.in A
Klar.
2.in A
Fag.1.2
a 2
più f
Viol.1
Viol.2
Vla.
Vc.
Kb.
saltando
cresc.
pizz.
arco

1.
Fl.
2.
3.
Ob.1.2
a 2
1.in A
Klar.
2.in A
Fag.1.2
1.in F
Hrn.
3.in F
espress.
Viol.1
Viol.2
Vla.
Vc.
Kb.
simile
poco cresc.
arco
cresc.

basically repeat of 2nd theme -without mutes.

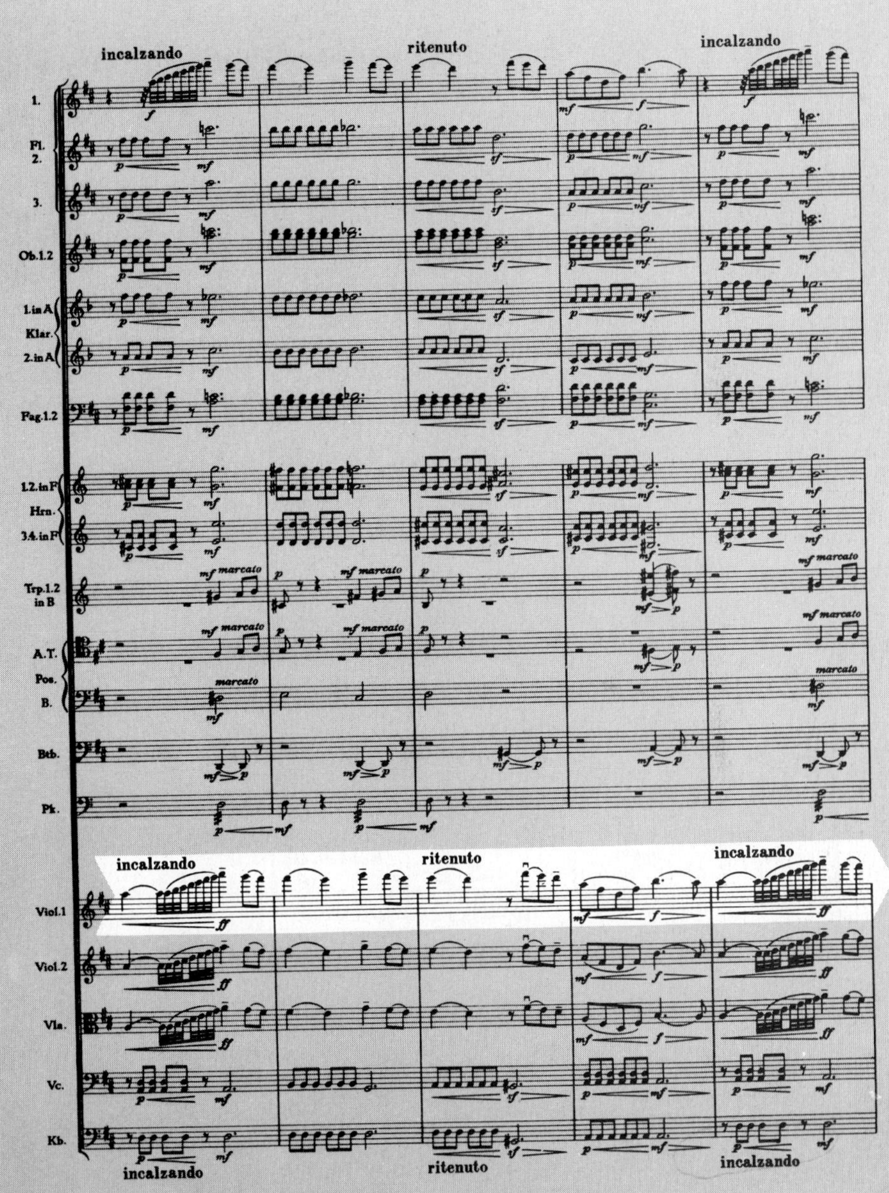

incalzando
ritenuto
incalzando
1.
Fl.
2.
3.
Ob.1.2
1.in A
Klar.
2.in A
Fag.1.2
1.2.in F
Hrn.
3.4.in F
Trp.1.2 in B
marcato
A.T.
Pos.
B.
Btb.
Pk.
Viol.1
Viol.2
Vla.
Vc.
Kb.
incalzando
ritenuto
incalzando

ritenuto
Moderato assai (♩ = 88)
1.
Fl.
2.
3.
Ob.1.2
1.in A
Klar.
2.in A
Fag.1.2
a 2
1.2.in F
Hrn.
3.4.in F
Trp.1.2
in B
mf marcato
A.T.
Pos.
B.
Btb.
Pk.
ritenuto
Moderato assai (♩ = 88)
Viol.1
Viol.2
Vla.
Vc.
Kb.
ritenuto
Moderato assai (♩ = 88)

G
rallentando
Ob. 1.2
1. in A
Klar.
2. in A
a 2
Fag. 1.2
1.2. in F
Hrn.
3.4. in F
Trp. 1.2
in B
T.-Pos.
Pk.
poco a poco smorz.
G
rallentando
Viol. 1
Viol. 2
Vla.
Vc.
Kb.
dim.
G
rallentando

Development (2nd theme)
Adagio mosso (♩ = 60)
Solo
dolce possibile
ritardando molto
Klar.
1 in A
a 2
Fag. 1.2
1. Solo
1.2. in F
Hrn.
4. in F
Pk.
Adagio mosso (♩ = 60)
ritardando molto
Viol. 1
divisi
Vla.
divisi
Vc.
divisi
pizz.
Kb.
Adagio mosso (♩ = 60)
ritardando molto

Development
Allegro vivo (♩ = 144)
Fl. 1. 2. 3.
Ob. 1. 2
a 2
Klar. 1. in A 2. in A
Fag. 1. 2
sempre ff
Hrn. 1. 2. in F 3. 4. in F
Trp. 1. 2 in B
Pos. A. T. B.
Btb.
Pk.
Allegro vivo (♩ = 144)
Viol. 1
Viol. 2
arco unis.
Vla.
unis. arco
Vc.
Kb.
sempre ff
Allegro vivo (♩ = 144)

H
1.
Fl.
2.
3.
Ob. 1.2
1. in A
Klar.
2. in A
Fag. 1.2
1.2. in F
Hrn.
3.4. in F
Trp. 1.2 in B
A. T.
Pos.
B.
Btb.
Pk.
muta in G, D, A
sul G
feroce
Viol. 1
Viol. 2
Vla.
feroce
Vc.
Kb.
H

1.
Fl.
2.
3.
Ob. 1.2
1. in A
Klar.
2. in A
1.2. in F
Hrn.
3.4. in F
Trp. 1.2 in B
A.T.
Pos.
B.
Btb.
Viol. 1
Viol. 2
Vla.
Vc.
Kb.
forcе
forcе
forcе

1.
Fl.
2.
3.
Ob. 1.2
1. in A
Klar.
2. in A
Fag. 1.2
1.2. in F
Hrn.
3.4. in F
Trp. 1.2 in B
A.T.
Pos.
B.
Btb.
Viol. 1
Viol. 2
Vla.
Vc.
Kb.
sul G
ff come prima
come prima

I
1.
Fl.
2.
3.
Ob. 1. 2
1. in A
Klar.
2. in A
Fag. 1. 2
1. 2. in F
Hrn.
3. 4. in F
Trp. 1. 2 in B
A. T.
Pos.
B.
Btb.
Viol. 1
Viol. 2
Vla.
Vc.
Kb.
sempre ff
sempre ff
sempre ff
sempre ff
sempre ff
I

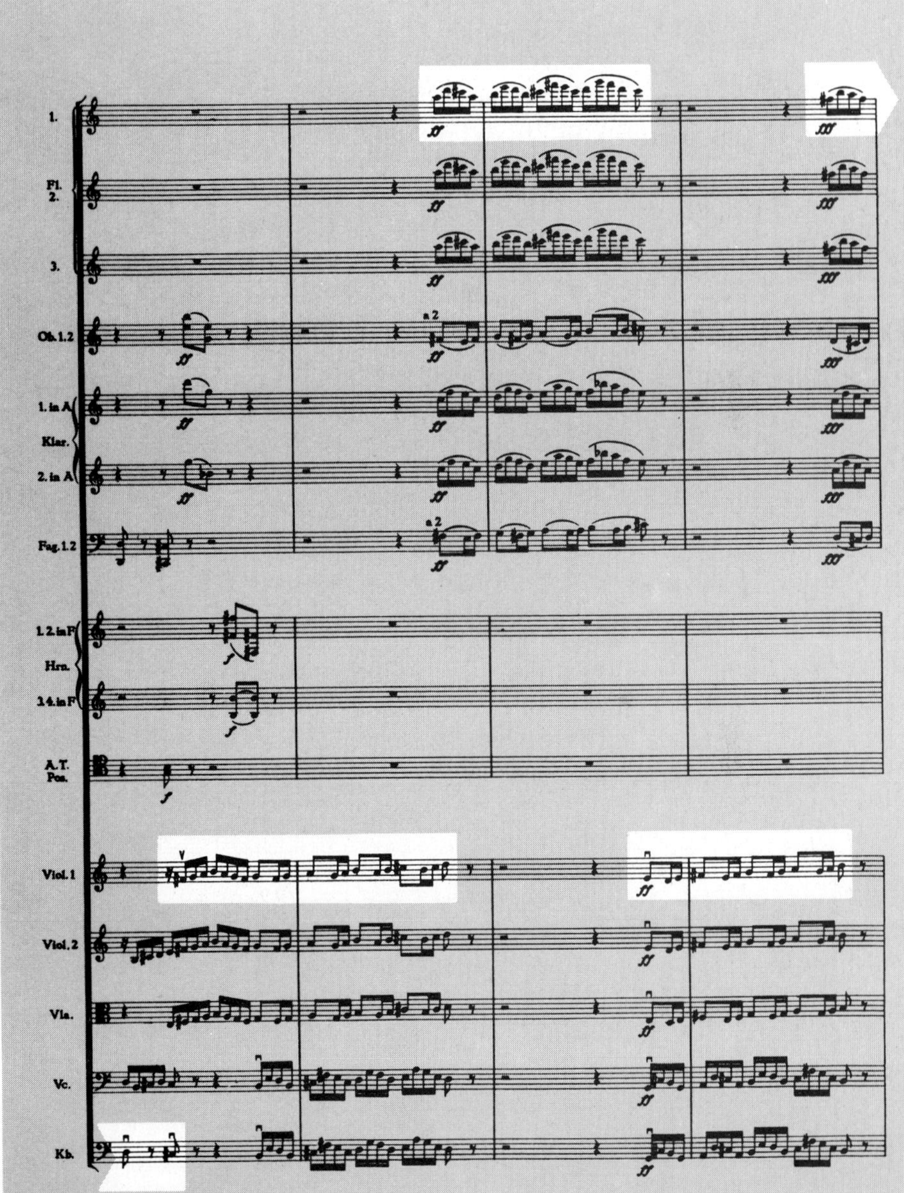
1.
Fl.
2.
3.
Ob. 1.2
1. in A
Klar.
2. in A
Fag. 1.2
1.2. in F
Hrn.
3.4. in F
A.T.
Pos.
Viol. 1
Viol. 2
Vla.
Vc.
Kb.
a 2
ff
fff
f

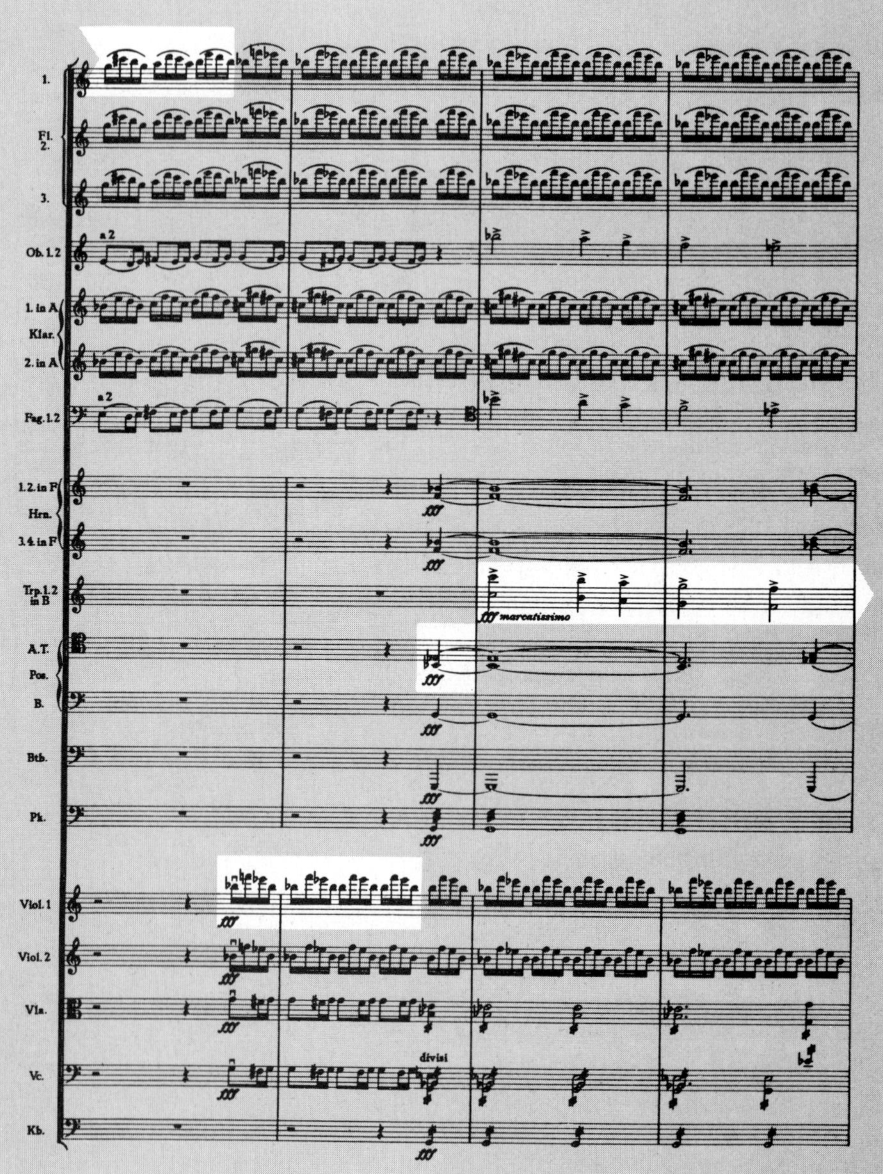

1.
Fl.
2.
3.
Ob. 1.2
a 2
1. in A
Klar.
2. in A
Fag. 1.2
a 2
1.2. in F
Hrn.
3.4. in F
fff
Trp. 1.2 in B
fff marcatissimo
A.T.
Pos.
B.
Btb.
Pk.
Viol. 1
Viol. 2
Vla.
Vc.
divisi
Kb.

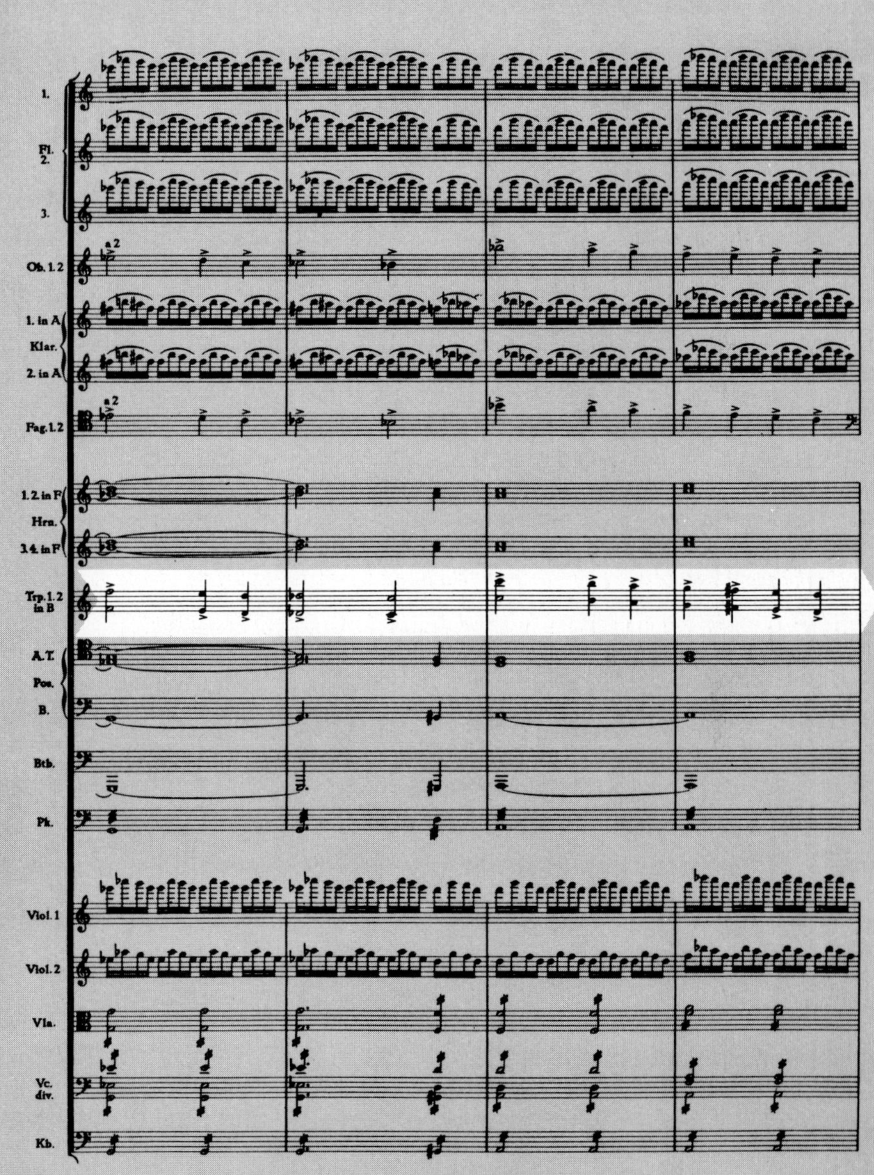
a 2
a 2
1.
Fl.
2.
3.
Ob. 1.2
1. in A
Klar.
2. in A
Fag. 1.2
1.2. in F
Hrn.
3.4. in F
Trp. 1.2 in B
A.T.
Pos.
B.
Btb.
Pk.
Viol. 1
Viol. 2
Vla.
Vc. div.
Kb.

K
Fl. 1.
Fl. 2.
3.
Ob. 1. 2
a 2
1. in A
Klar.
2. in A
Fag. 1. 2
a 2
1. 2. in F
Hrn.
3. 4. in F
Trp. 1. 2 in B
A. T.
Pos.
B.
Btb.
Pk.
muta in Fis, H, E
Viol. 1
Viol. 2
Vla.
Vc. div.
unis.
ff
dim.
Kb.

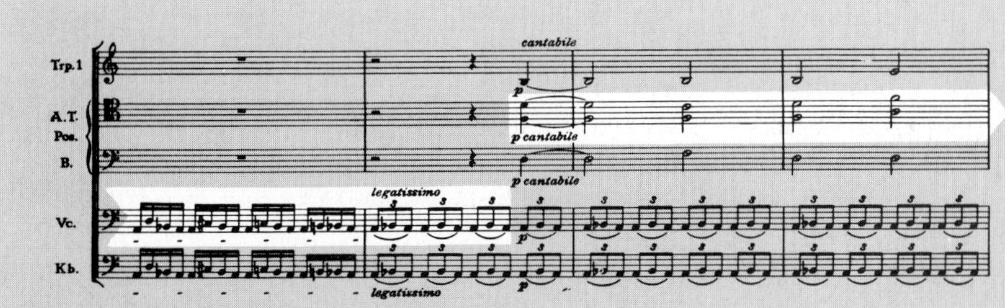

1.
Fl. 2.
3.
Kleine Flöte vorbereiten
Ob. 1. 2
1. in A
Klar.
2. in A
Fag. 1. 2
poco a poco cresc..
1. 2. in F
Hrn.
3. 4. in F
poco a poco cresc..
Trp. 1. 2 in B
poco a poco cresc..
A. T.
Pos.
B.
poco a poco cresc..
Btb.
poco a poco cresc..
Viol. 1
Viol. 2
Vla.
Vc.
poco a poco cresc..
Kb.
poco a poco cresc..

Ob. 1.2
1. in A
Klar.
2. in A
Fag. 1.2
1.2. in F
Hrn.
3.4. in F
Trp. 1.2 in B
A. T.
Pos.
B.
Btb.
Viol. 1
Viol. 2
Vla.
Vc.
Kb.
mf
poco cresc.
più f
cresc.
f

L
1.
Fl.
2.
ff
dim. un poco
Ob. 1. 2
a 2
1. in A
Klar.
2. in A
Fag. 1. 2
1. 2. in F
Hrn.
3. 4. in F
Trp. 1. 2 in B
A. T.
Pos.
B.
Btb.
Viol. 1
Viol. 2
Vla.
Vc.
Kb.
div.

1.
Fl.
2.
a 2
Ob. 1. 2
1. in A
Klar.
2. in A
Fag. 1. 2
1. 2. in F
Hrn.
3. 4. in F
A.
Pos.
B.
Btb.
Viol. 1
Viol. 2
Vla.
Vc.
Kb. div.
f
dim.
dim. un poco
mf

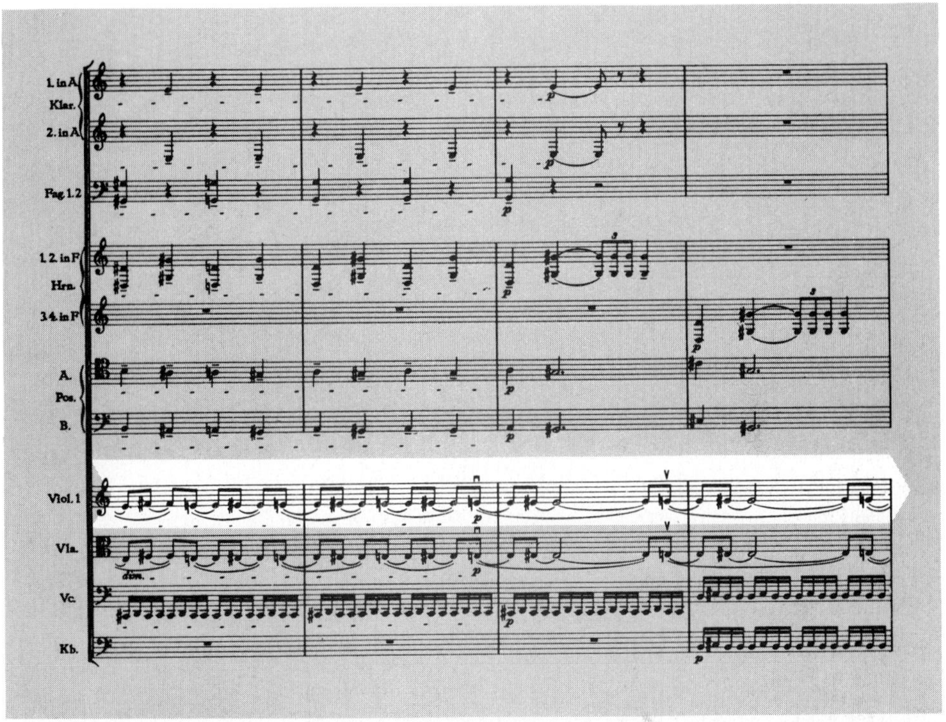

1. in A
Klar.
2. in A
Fag. 1.2
1.2. in F
Hrn.
3.4. in F
A.
Pos.
B.
Viol. 1
Vla.
Vc.
Kb.
p
dim.

1.2. in F
Hrn.
3.4. in F
A.
Pos.
B.
Viol. 1
Vla.
Vc.
Kb.
p
dim.
pp

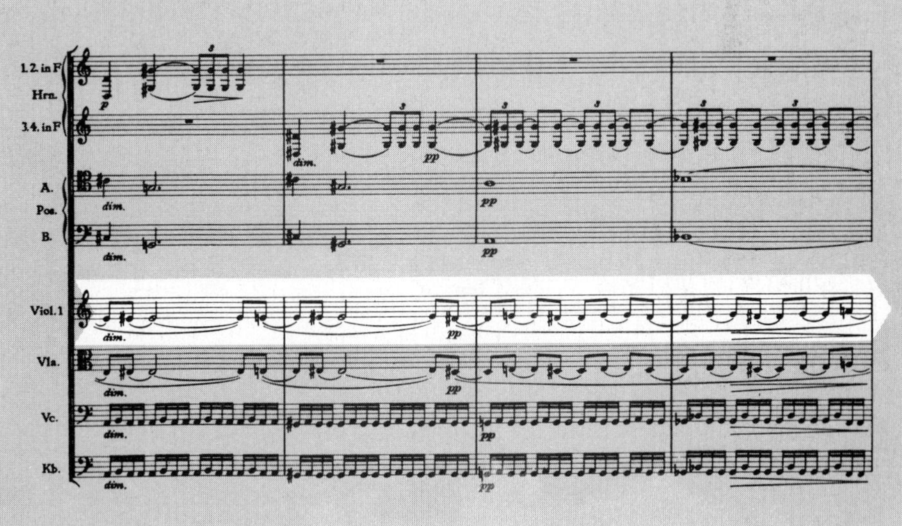

M

1. 2. in F
Hrn.
3. 4. in F
A. T.
Pos.
B.
M
Viol. 1
Vla.
Vc.
Kb.
M
pp
pizz.

1.
Fl.
2.
Kl. Fl.
Ob. 1
1. in A
Klar.
2. in A
Fag. 1.2
1.2. in F
Hrn.
3.4. in F
Trp. 1 in B
A.
Pos.
B.
Viol. 1
Viol. 2
Vla.
Vc.
Kb.
cresc.
f
mf
ff
mf cresc.

N
1.
Fl.
2.
Kl.Fl.
Ob. 1. 2
1. in A
Klar.
2. in A
Fag. 1. 2
1. 2. in F
Hrn.
3. 4. in F
Trp. 1. 2 in B
A. T.
Pos.
B.
Btb.
Pk.
N
Viol. 1
Viol. 2
Vla.
Vc.
Kb.
N

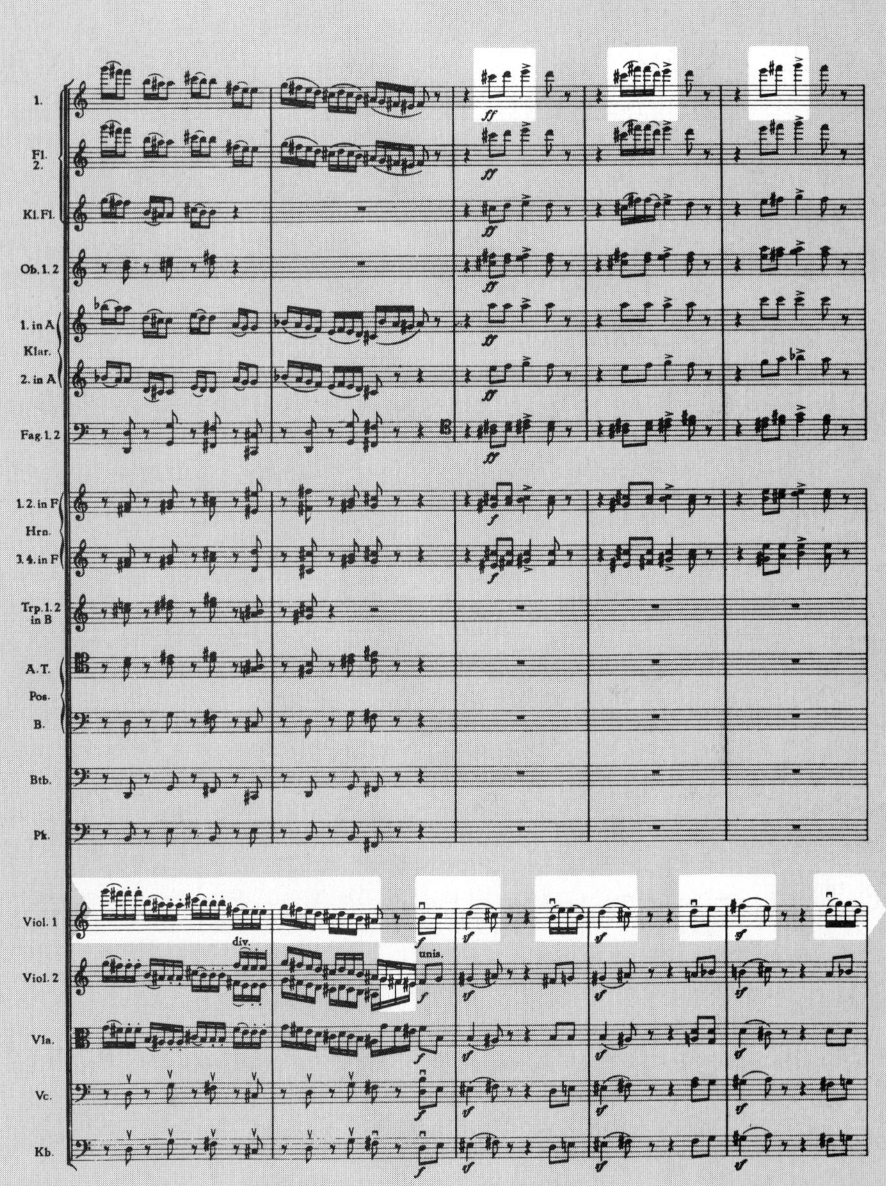

1st motive coming back

1.
Fl.
2.
Kl.Fl.
Ob. 1. 2
1. in A
Klar.
2. in A
Fag. 1. 2
1. 2. in F
Hrn.
3. 4. in F
Viol. 1
Viol. 2
Vla.
Vc.
Kb.

1.
Fl.
2.
Kl. Fl.
Ob. 1.2
1. in A
Klar.
2. in A
Fag. 1.2
1.2. in F
Hrn.
3.4. in F
Trp. 1.2
in B
A.T.
Pos.
B.
Btb.
Viol. 1
Viol. 2
Vla.
Vc.
Kb.
pp
cresc.
p cresc.
mf
a 2
p
mp
poco cresc.

1.
Fl.
2.
Kl.Fl.
f cresc.
Ob. 1.2
cresc.
1. in A
Klar.
2. in A
cresc.
Fag. 1.2
cresc.
1. 2. in F
Hrn.
3. 4. in F
cresc.
Trp. 1.2 in B
cresc.
A. T.
Pos.
B.
cresc.
a2
Btb.
cresc.
ff
Viol. 1
molto
Viol. 2
molto
Vla.
molto
Vc.
molto
Kb.
molto

P
1.
Fl.
2.
Kl. Fl.
Gr. Flöte vorbereiten
Ob. 1. 2
a 2
fff pesante
1. in A
Klar.
2. in A
Fag. 1. 2
1. 2. in F
Hrn.
3. 4. in F
Trp. 1. 2
in B
pesante
a 2
fff
a 2
fff pesante
A. T.
Pos.
B.
pesante
Btb.
Pk.
Viol. 1
Viol. 2
div.
Vla.
Vc.
Kb.
P

1.
Fl.
2.
Ob. 1. 2
1. in A
Klar.
2. in A
Fag. 1. 2
1. 2. in F
Hrn.
3. 4. in F
Trp. 1. 2 in B
A. T.
Pos.
B.
Btb.
Pk.
Viol. 1
Viol. 2
Vla.
Vc.
Kb.
a 2
cresc.
ff pesante
unis.

Q
1. Fl. 2.
a 2
Ob. 1. 2
1. in A Klar. 2. in A
Fag. 1. 2
1. 2. in F Hrn. 3. 4. in F
sempre ff
Trp. 1. 2 in B
B.-Pos.
Btb.
Pk.
Viol. 1
Viol. 2
Vla.
Vc.
Kb.
sempre ff

1.
Fl. 2.
Gr. Fl.
3.
Ob. 1. 2
1. in A
Klar.
2. in A
a 2
Fag. 1. 2
1. 2. in F
Hrn.
3. 4. in F
Trp. 1. 2 in B
a 2 marcato
A. T.
Pos.
marcato
B.
marcato
Btb.
Pk.
Viol. 1
largamente, forte possibile
Viol. 2
largamente, forte possibile
div.
Vla.
largamente, forte possibile
unis.
Vc.
largamente, forte possibile
Kb.

R
1.
Fl.
2.
3.
Ob. 1
1. in A
Klar.
2. in A
a 2
Fag. 1. 2
1. 2. in F
Hrn.
3. 4. in F
Trp. 1. 2 in B
T.
Pos.
B.
Btb.
Pk.
Viol. 1
Viol. 2
Vla.
Vc.
Kb.
pizz.

2nd theme
Andante come prima (♩. 69)
con dolcezza
Fl. 1.
2.
3.
Ob. 1. 2
a 2
1. in A
Klar.
2. in A
Fag. 1. 2
1. 2. in F
Hrn.
3. 4. in F
B.-Pos.
Viol. 1
Viol. 2
Vla.
Vc.
arco
Kb.
Andante come prima (♩. 69)

incalzando
ritenuto
incalzando
S
Fl. 1. 2. 3.
Ob. 1. 2
a 2
Klar. 1. in A 2. in A
Fag. 1. 2
Hrn. 1. 2. in F 3. 4. in F
Trp. 1. 2 in B
Pos. A. T. B.
Btb.
Pk.
Viol. 1
Viol. 2
Vla.
Vc.
Kb.
poco cresc.
p poco cresc.
mp poco cresc.
div.
incalzando
ritenuto
S incalzando

ritenuto
Tempo I
1.
Fl. 2.
3.
Ob. 1. 2
1. in A
Klar.
2. in A
Fag. 1. 2
a 2
1. 2. in F
Hrn.
3. 4. in F
Trp. 1. 2 in B
A. T.
Pos.
B.
Btb.
Pk.
ritenuto
Tempo I
Viol. 1
Viol. 2
Vla. div.
unis.
Vc.
Kb. div.
ritenuto
Tempo I

T ritenuto
1.
Fl.
2.
3.
Ob. 1. 2
1. in A
Klar.
2. in A
a 2
Fag. 1. 2
1. 2 in F
Hrn.
3. 4. in F
B.-Pos.
Btb.
Pk.
Solo
ppp
T ritenuto
Viol. 1
div.
Viol. 2
Vla.
Vc.
Kb.
T ritenuto

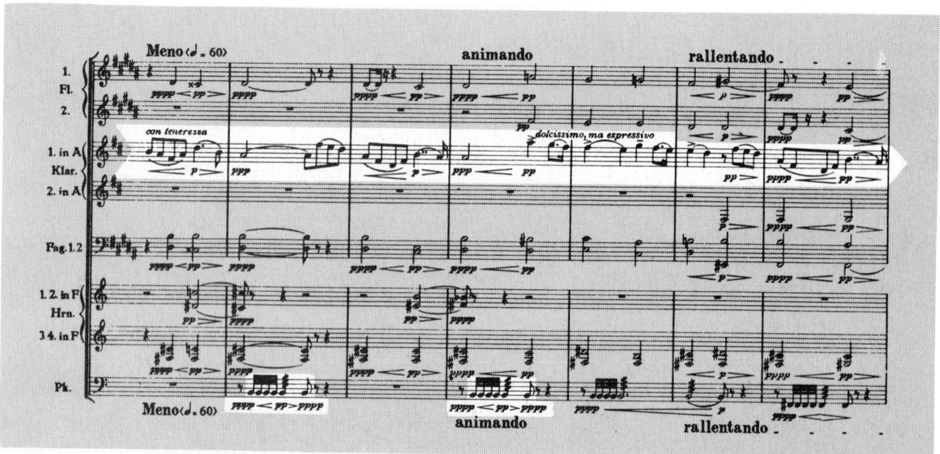

quasi adagio
Andante mosso (♩. 80)
1. Fl. 2.
1. in A Klar. 2. in A
Fag. 1. 2
1. in F Hrn. 3. 4. in F
Trp 1. 2 in B
cantabile
A. T. Pos. B.
cantabile
cantabile
Pk.
quasi adagio
Andante mosso (♩. 80)
Viol. 1
pizz.
Viol. 2
pizz.
Vla.
pizz.
Vc.
pizz.
Kb.
pizz.
quasi adagio
Andante mosso (♩. 80)

- almost march
- long ending section

Fag. 1
1. 2. in F Hrn. 3. 4. in F
A. T. Pos. B.
Btb.
Pk.
Viol. 1
Viol. 2
Vla.
Vc.
Kb.
morendo
pp morendo
sempre pp

II
Allegro con grazia (♩=144)
1.
Flöten
2.
3.
Oboen 1.2
1. in A
Klarinetten
2. in A
Fagotte 1.2
1.2. in F
Hörner
3.4. in F
Trompeten 1.2 in A
Alt, Tenor
Posaunen
Baß
Baßtuba
Pauken in A, D, E
Allegro con grazia (♩=144)
Violine 1
Violine 2
Viola
Violoncell
Kontrabaß
pizz.
mf
f
Allegro con grazia (♩=144)

1.
Fl. 2.
3.
Ob. 1.2
a 2
1. in A
Klar.
2. in A
Fag. 1.2
1.2. in F
Hrn.
3.4. in F
Viol. 1
Viol. 2
Vla.
Vc.
Kb.
mf
f
ff
arco
pizz.
div.
unis.
gliss.

1.
Fl. 2.
3.
Ob. 1.2
a 2
1. in A
Klar.
2. in A
Fag. 1
1.2. in F
Hrn.
3.4. in F
Viol. 1 div.
Viol. 2 div.
Vla.
Vc.
Kb.
più f
mf
pizz.
arco
unis.
sempre mf
div.
1.
2.

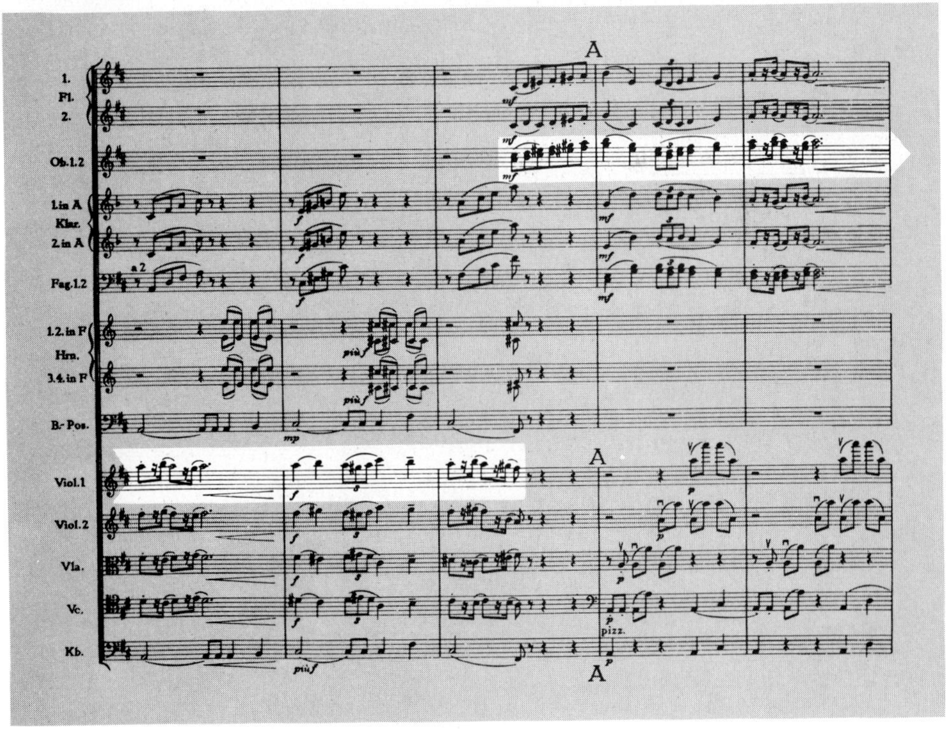

A

1.
Fl.
2.
Ob. 1.2
1. in A
Klar.
2. in A
a 2
Fag. 1.2
1.2. in F
Hrn.
3.4. in F
più f
B-Pos.
Viol. 1
Viol. 2
Vla.
Vc.
pizz.
Kb.
più f

A

1.
Fl.
2.
Ob. 1.2
1. in A
Klar.
2. in A
Fag. 1.2
Viol. 1
Viol. 2
Vla.
Vc.
Kb.
più f
mf
f
mp

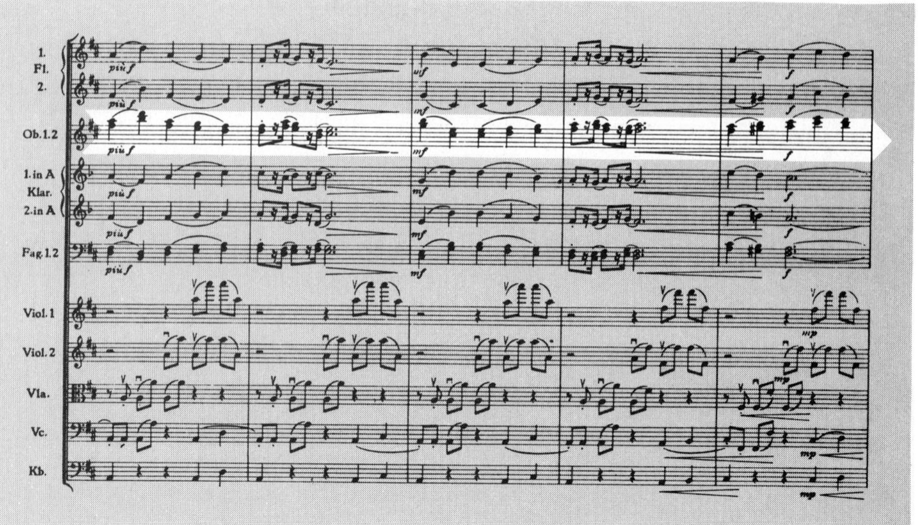

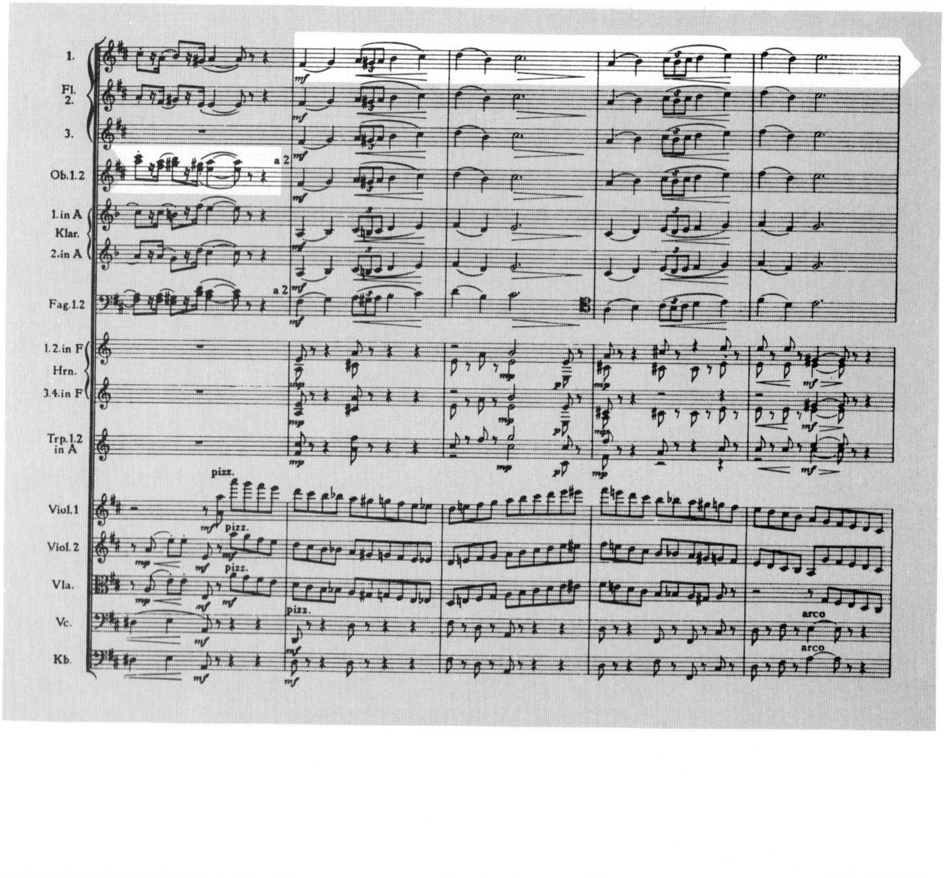

1.
Fl.
2.
3.
Ob. 1.2
a 2
1. in A
Klar.
2. in A
Fag. 1.2
1.2. in F
Hrn.
3.4. in F
Trp. 1.2
in A
Viol. 1
Viol. 2
Vla.
Vc.
Kb.
pizz.
arco
mf
mp
pf

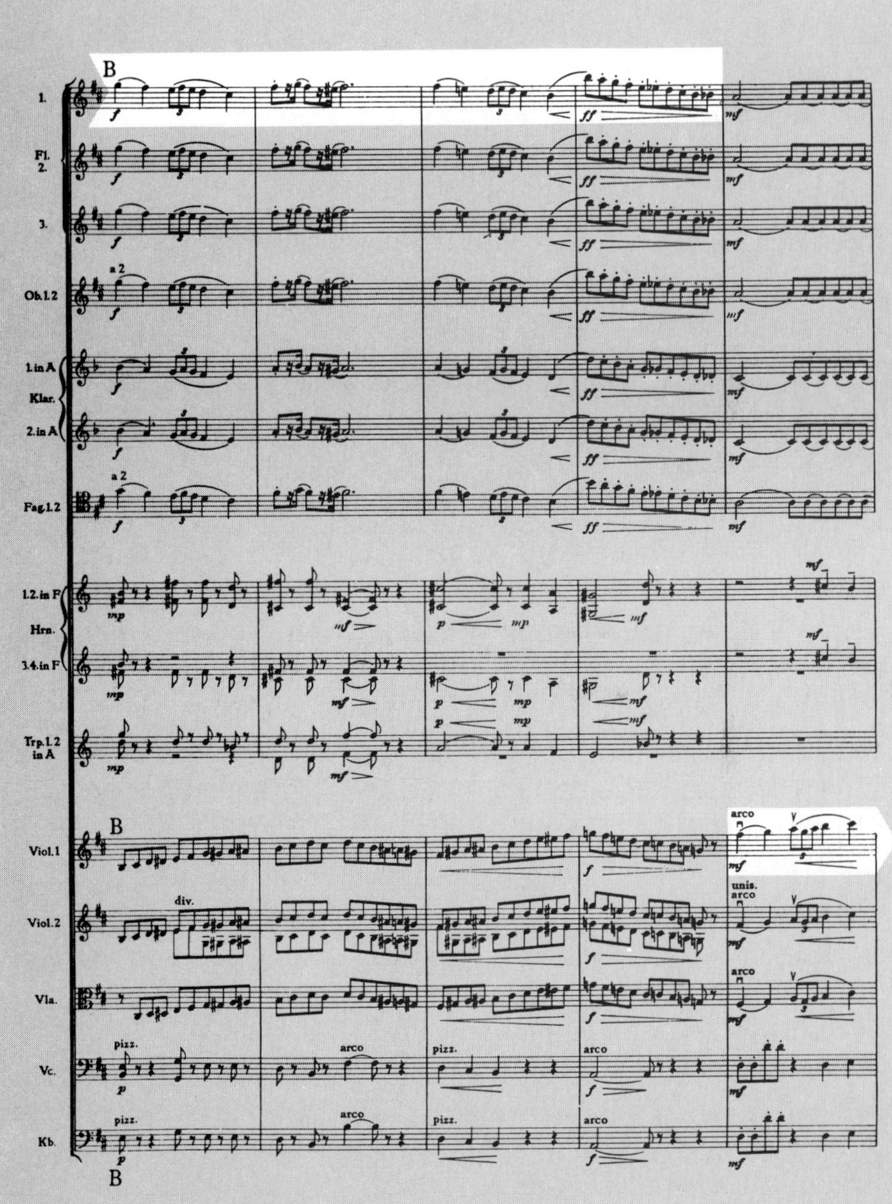
B
1.
Fl. 2.
3.
a 2
Ob.1.2
1.in A
Klar.
2.in A
a 2
Fag.1.2
1.2.in F
Hrn.
3.4.in F
Trp.1.2 in A
B
Viol.1
div.
Viol.2
Vla.
pizz.
Vc.
pizz.
Kb.
B
arco
unis.
arco
arco
arco
pizz.
arco
arco
pizz.
arco

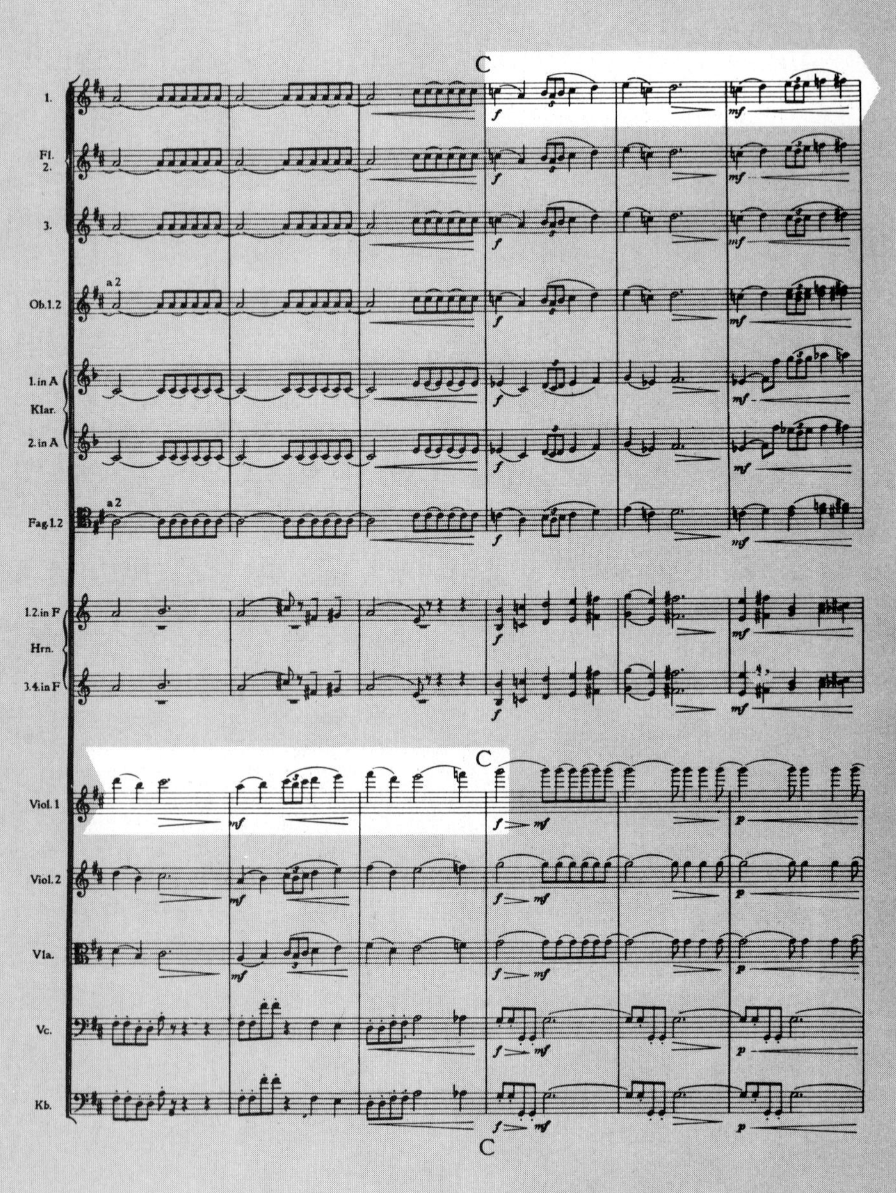
C
1.
Fl.
2.
3.
a 2
Ob.1.2
1. in A
Klar.
2. in A
a 2
Fag.1.2
1.2. in F
Hrn.
3.4. in F
C
Viol. 1
Viol. 2
Vla.
Vc.
Kb.
C

1.
Fl.
2.
3.
Ob. 1.2
1. in A
Klar.
2. in A
Fag. 1.2
1.2. in F
Hrn.
3.4. in F
Trp. 1.2 in A
A.T.
Pos.
B.
Btb.
Pk.
Viol. 1
Viol. 2
Vla.
Vc.
Kb.
a 2
ff
f
p

D
con dolcezza e flebile
1.
Fl. 2.
3.
Ob. 1.2
a 2
1. in A
Klar.
2. in A
Fag. 1.2
1.2. in F
Hrn.
3.4. in F
Br.-Pos.
Btb.
Pk.
Viol. 1
Viol. 2
Vla.
Vc.
Kb.
pizz.
arco

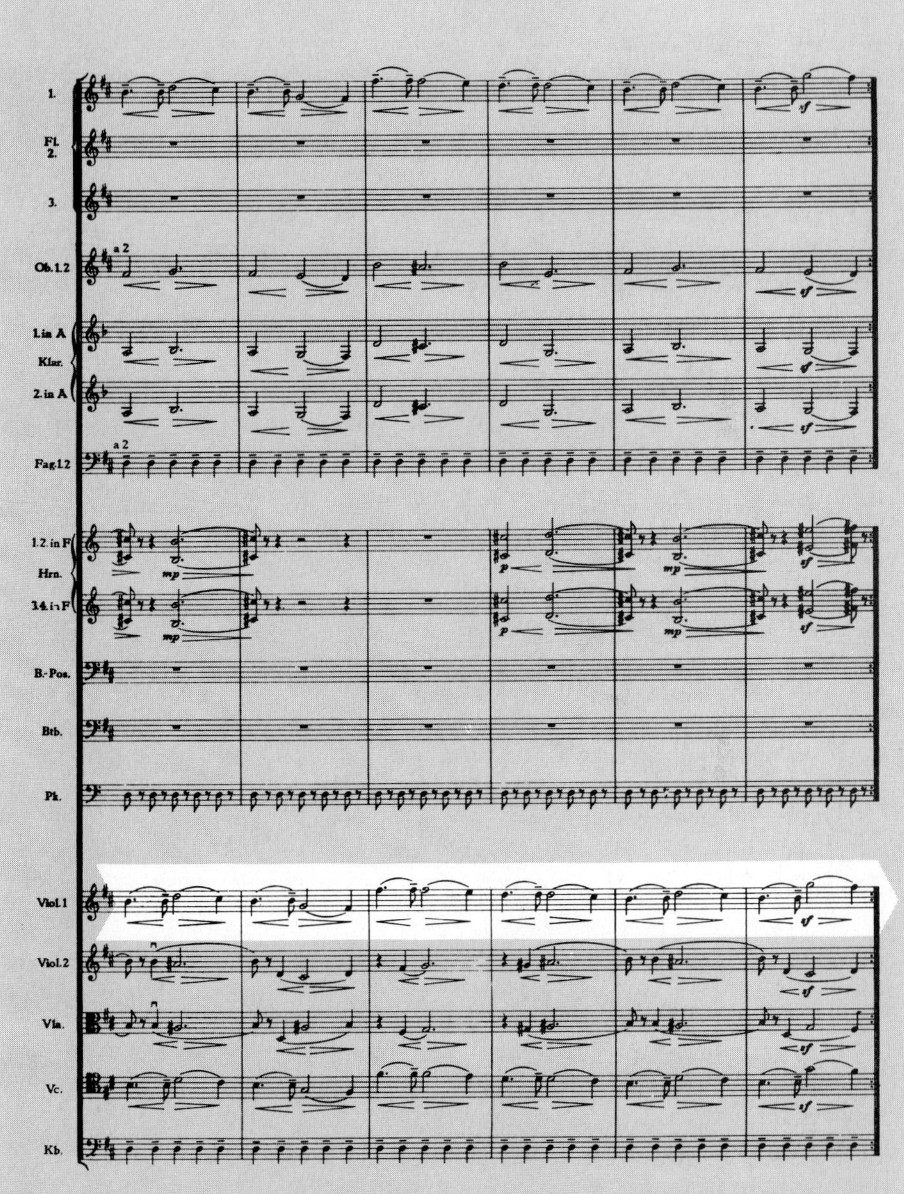
1.
Fl.
2.
3.
Ob. 1.2
a 2
1. in A
Klar.
2. in A
Fag. 1.2
a 2
1.2. in F
Hrn.
3.4. in F
mp
p
sf
B.-Pos.
Btb.
Pk.
Viol. 1
Viol. 2
Vla.
Vc.
Kb.

E
1.
Fl.
2.
3.
Ob.1.2
1.in A
Klar.
2.in A
a 2
Fag.1.2
1.2.in F
Hrn.
3.4.in F
Trp.1.2
in A
A.-T.-
Pos.
Pk.
E
div.
Viol.1
Viol.2
Vla.
Vc.
Kb.
E
p
pp cresc.
pp

F
Fl. 1. 2. 3.
Ob. 1. 2
a 2
Klar. 1. in A 2. in A
Fag. 1. 2
Hrn. 1. 2. in F 3. 4. in F
Trp. 1. 2 in A
A.-T.-Pos.
Pk.
Viol. 1
Viol. 2
unis.
Vla.
Vc.
Kb.
mf
f
p
mp

G
1.
Fl.
2.
3.
Ob. 1.2
a 2
1. in A
Klar.
2. in A
Fag. 1.2
1.2. in F
Hrn.
3.4. in F
Trp. 1
in A
A.T.
Pos.
B.
Btb.
Pk.
Viol. 1
div.
Viol. 2
Vla.
Vc.
Kb.

1.
Fl.
2.
3.
Ob.1.2
1.in A
Klar.
2.in A
Fag.1.2
1.2.in F
Hrn.
3.4.in F
Trp.1
in A
A.T.
Pos.
B.
Btb.
Pk.
Viol.1
Viol.2
div.
Vla.
Vc.
Kb.

1.
Fl.
2.
3.
Ob. 1.2
a 2
1. in A
Klar.
2. in A
Fag. 1.2
1.2. in F
Hrn.
3.4. in F
Trp. 1.2 in A
A.T.
Pos.
B.
Btb.
Pk.
Viol. 1
Viol. 2 div.
Vla.
div.
Vc.
Kb.

H
a 2
Ob.1.2
mf
1.in A
Klar.
2.in A
a 2
Fag.1.2
1.2.in F
Hrn.
3.4.in F
mp
Trp.1.2 in A
A.-T.-Pos.
Btb.
Pk
H
Viol.1
p
mf
f
Viol.2
unis.
pizz.
Vla.
Vc.
Kb.
pizz.
H

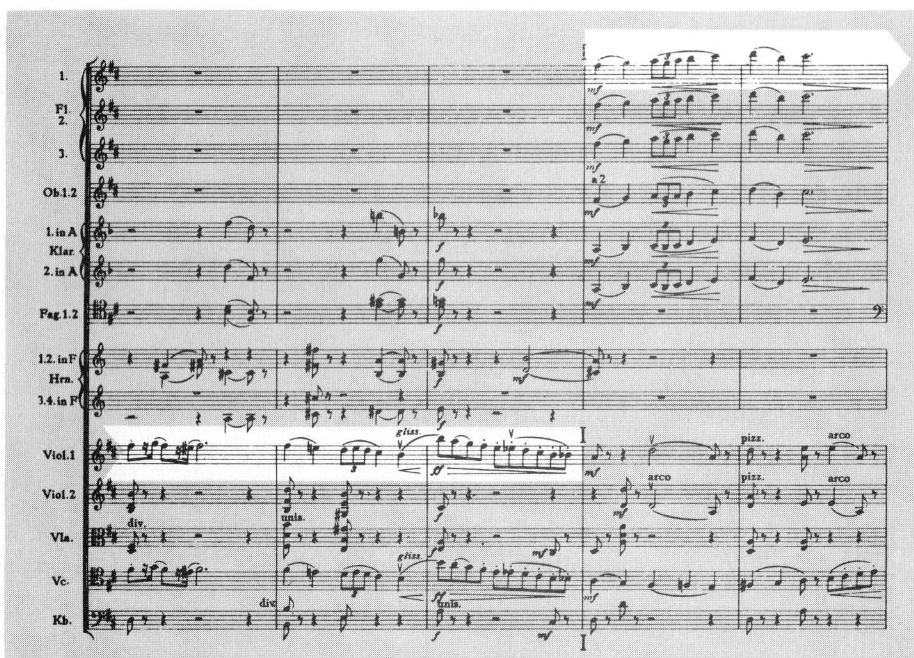
Fl.
1.
2.
3.
Ob.1.2
Klar.
1. in A
2. in A
Fag. 1.2
Hrn.
1.2. in F
3.4. in F
Viol. 1
Viol. 2
Vla.
Vc.
Kb.
a 2
gliss.
pizz.
arco
div.
unis.
mf
f
ff
I

Fl.
1.
2.
3.
Ob.1.2
Klar.
1.in A
2.in A
Fag. 1
Viol. 1
Viol. 2
Vla.
Vc.
Kb.
a 2
più f
pizz.
div.
arco
unis.
mf sempre
mf

1.
Fl.
2.
3.
Ob. 1.2
a2
1. in A
Klar.
2. in A
Fag. 1.2
1.2. in F
Hrn.
3.4. in F
B Pos.
Viol. 1
Viol. 2
Vla.
Vc.
Kb.
div.
unis.
pizz.
arco
più f

K
1.
Fl.
2.
Ob. 1.2
1. in A
Klar.
2. in A
Fag. 1.2
1.2. in F
Hrn.
3.4. in F
B.-Pos.
Viol. 1
Viol. 2
Vla.
Vc.
Kb.
pizz.
più f

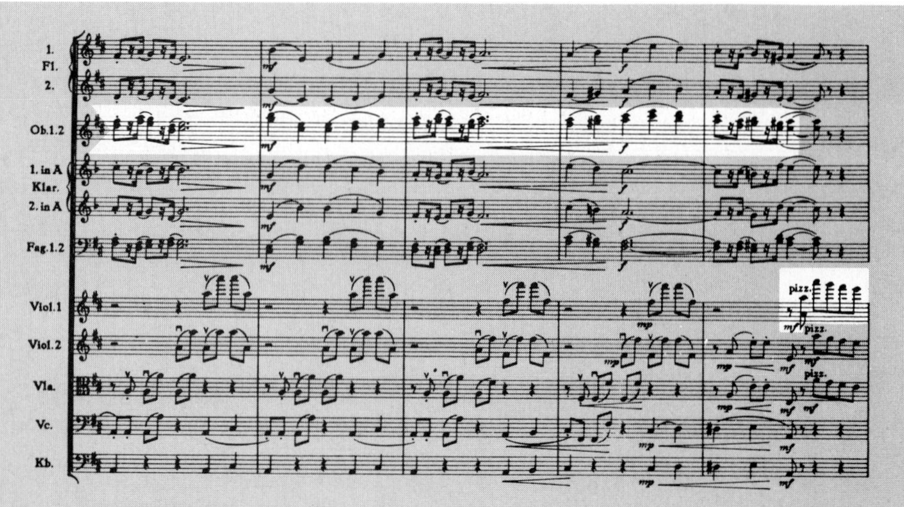

1.
Fl.
2.
Ob.1.2
1. in A
Klar.
2. in A
Fag.1.2
Viol.1
Viol.2
Vla.
Vc.
Kb.
pizz.
pizz.
pizz.

L
1.
Fl.
2.
3.
Ob.1.2
a 2
1.in A
Klar.
2.in A
Fag.1.2
a 2
1.2.in F
Hrn.
3.4.in F
Trp.1.2
in A
Viol.1
Viol.2
divisi
Vla.
Vc.
pizz.
arco
pizz.
Kb.
arco
pizz.
L

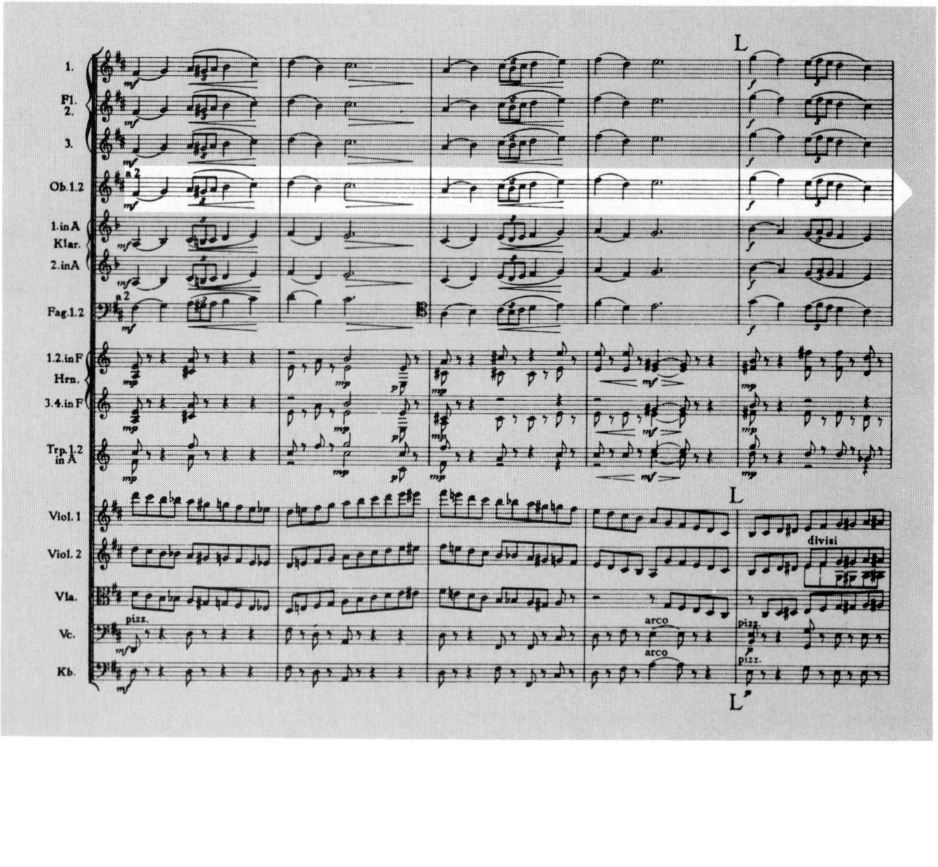

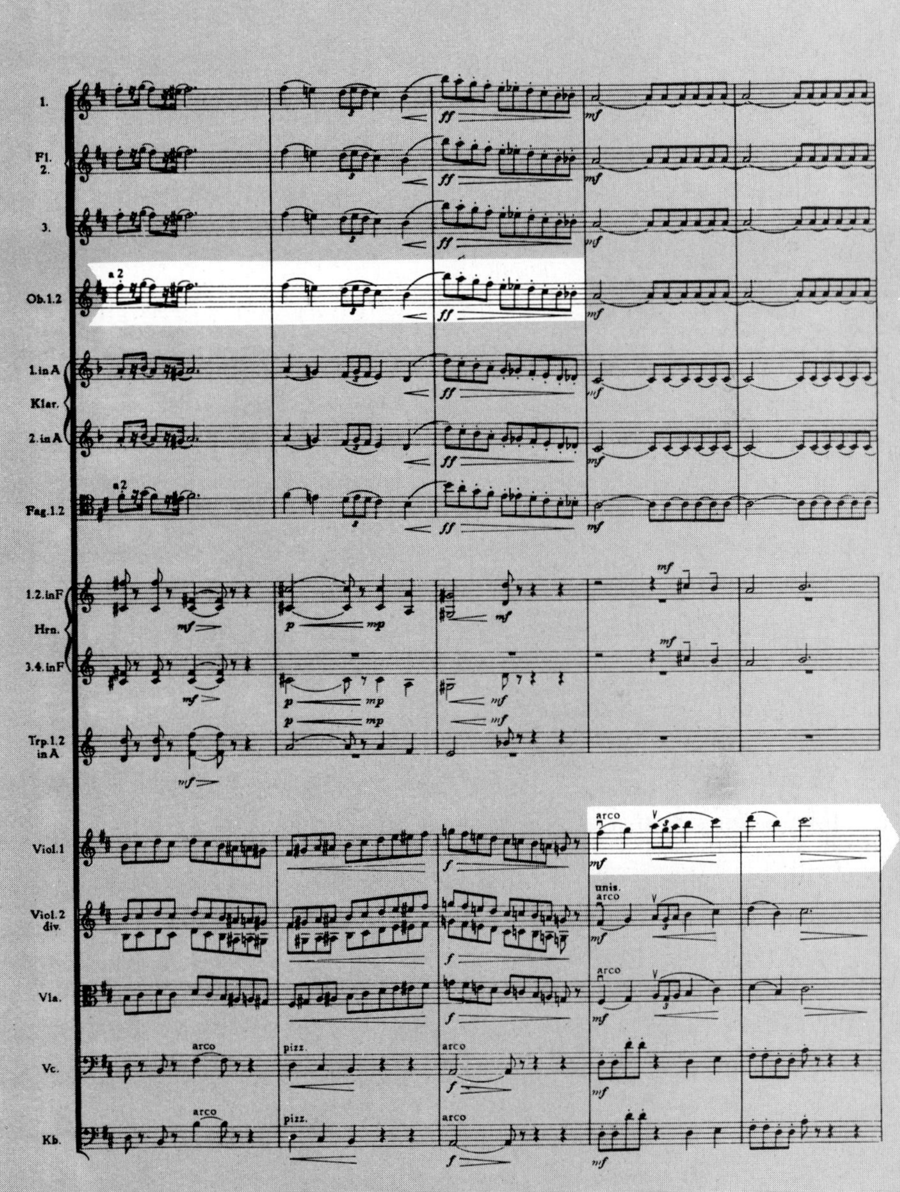
Fl. 1.
Fl. 2.
3.
a 2
Ob. 1.2
1. in A
Klar.
2. in A
a 2
Fag. 1.2
1.2. in F
Hrn.
3.4. in F
Trp. 1.2 in A
Viol. 1
Viol. 2 div.
Vla.
Vc.
Kb.
arco
pizz.
unis.
mf
ff
p
mp
f

M

Fl. 1. 2. 3.

Ob. 1. 2 a 2

Klar. 1. in A 2. in A

Fag. 1. 2 a 2

Hrn. 1. 2. in F 3. 4. in F

Viol. 1

Viol. 2

Vla.

Vc.

Kb.

M

1.
Fl.
2
3.
Ob.1.2
1.in A
Klar.
2.in A
Fag.1.2
1.2.in F
Hrn.
3.4.in F
Trp.1.2
in A
A. T.
Pos.
B.
Btb.
Pk.
Viol.1
Viol.2
Vla.
Vc.
Kb.
a2
ff
f
p

N
1.
Fl.
2.
3.
Ob. 1.2
1. in A
Klar.
2. in A
Fag. 1.2
1.2. in F
Hrn.
3.4. in F
B.-Pos.
Btb.
Pk.
Viol. 1
Viol. 2
Vla.
Vc.
Kb.
mf
mp
f
p
pizz.
arco

Ob. 1.2
1. in A
Klar.
2. in A
Fag. 1.2
1.2. in F
Hrn.
3. in F
Trp. 1.2 in A
A.-T.-Pos.
Pk.
Viol. 1
Viol. 2
Vla.
Vc.
Kb.
arco
arco

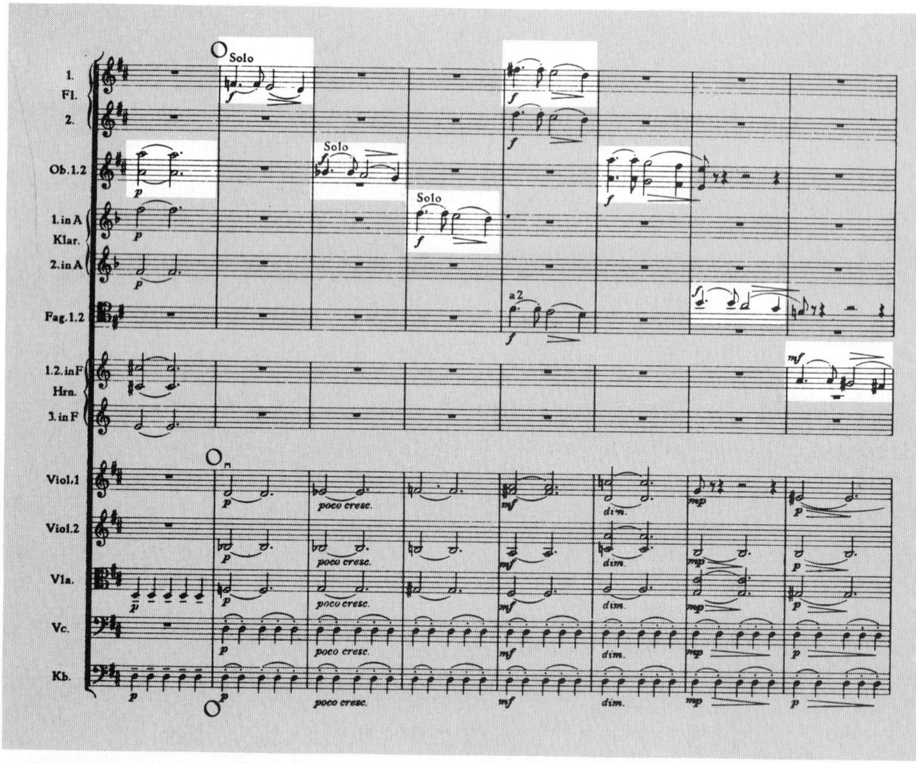

O Solo

1. Fl. 2.

Ob. 1.2

1. in A Klar. 2. in A

Fag. 1.2

1.2. in F Hrn. 3. in F

Viol. 1

Viol. 2

Vla.

Vc.

Kb.

p f Solo f Solo f a2 f mf

p poco cresc. mf dim. mp p

O

III

Allegro molto vivace (♩. = 152)

1. Flöten 2.
Kleine Flöte
Oboen 1.2
1. in A Klarinetten 2. in A
Fagotte 1.2
1.2. in F Hörner 3.4. in F
Trompeten 1.2 in A
Alt, Tenor Posaunen Baß
Baßtuba
Pauken in Fis, G, H
Gr. Trommel u. Becken

Allegro molto vivace (♩. = 152)

Violine 1 divisi
Violine 2 divisi
Viola divisi
Violoncell divisi
Kontrabaß divisi

Allegro molto vivace (♩. = 152)

A
1.
Fl.
2.
Ob.1.2
1. in A
Klar.
2. in A
Fag.1.2
Hrn.
1.2. in F
A
Viol.1
div.
Viol.2
div.
Vla.
div.
Vc.
div.
Kb.
div.
A

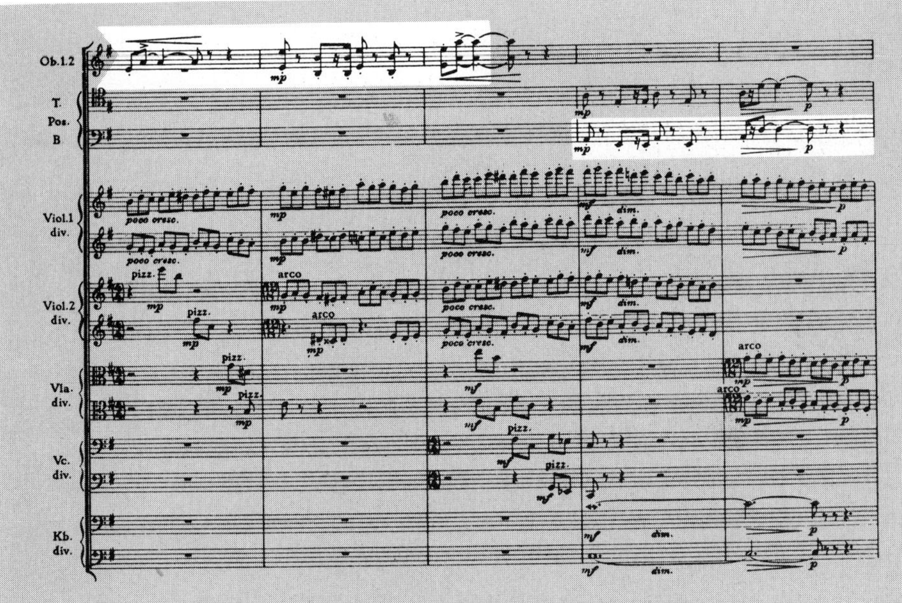

B

Ob.1.2
Hrn.
2.in F
Trp.1
in A
Viol.1
div.
Viol.2
div.
Vla.
div.
Vc.
div.
Kb.
div.
p
pp
dim.
pizz.
mf
mp
arco
p leggiero

B

Ob.1.2
p
Hrn. 1.2 in F
un poco marcato
p
Trp.1.2 in A
pp
p
C
Viol.1 div.
p
p
Viol.2 div.
arco
p arco
p
Vla. div.
p
p
Vc. div.
sempre p
Kb. div.
sempre p
C

D
1. Fl. 2.
Ob.1.2
1. in A Klar. 2. in A
Fag.1.2
1.2.in F Hrn. 3.4.in F
Trp.1.2 in A
Viol.1 div.
Viol.2 div.
Vla. div.
Vc. div.
Kb. div.
un poco cresc.
arco

1.in A
Klar.
2.in A
Fag.1.2
1.2.in F
Hrn.
4.in F
Viol.1
div.
Viol.2
div.
Vla.
div.
Vc.
div.
Kb.
div.
arco
pizz.
diminuendo

1.
Fl.
2.
Kl. Fl.
1. in A
Klar.
2. in A
Fag. 1.2
Viol. 1 div.
pizz.
Viol. 2 div.
Vla. div.
Vc. div.
arco
Kb. div.
p
mf

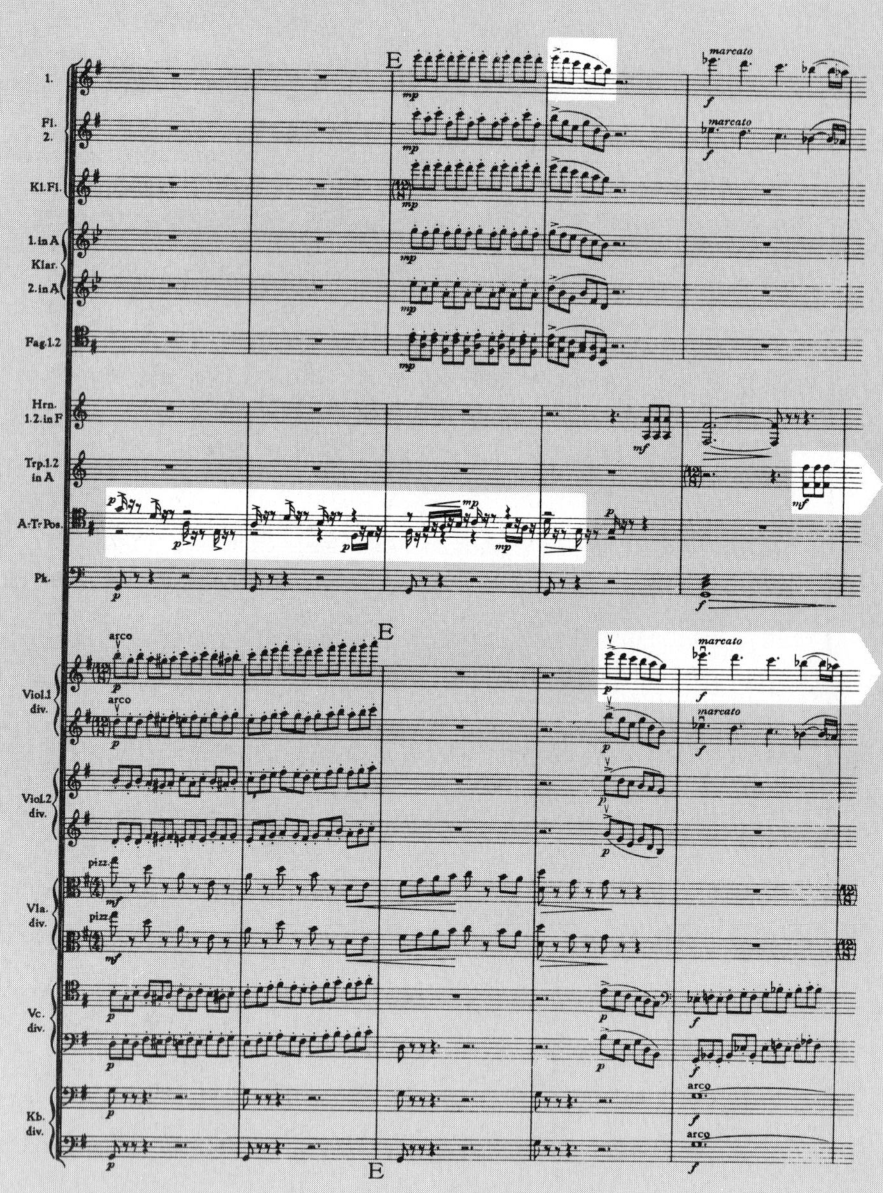

E
Fl. 1. 2.
Kl. Fl.
1. in A Klar. 2. in A
Fag. 1.2
Hrn. 1.2. in F
Trp. 1.2 in A
A.-T.-Pos.
Pk.
Viol. 1 div.
Viol. 2 div.
Vla. div.
Vc. div.
Kb. div.
marcato
arco
pizz.

Fl. 1. 2.
Kl. Fl.
Ob. 1.2
Klar. 1. in A 2. in A
Fag. 1.2
Hrn. 1.2. in F 3.4. in F
Trp. 1.2 in A
Pos. T. B.
Pk.
Viol. 1 div.
Viol. 2 div.
Vla. div.
Vc. div.
Kb.
marcato
a 2
arco
unis.

F
1.
Fl.
2.
Ob.1.2
a 2
1.in A
Klar.
2.in A
Fag.1.2
pp crescendo
1.2.in F
Hrn.
3.4.in F
Trp.2 in A
A.
Pos.
B.
Pk.
pp crescendo
F unis.
sul G
Viol.1
Viol.2
unis.
Vla.
Vc.
Kb.
crescendo
F

Fl. 1. 2.

Kl. Fl.

Ob. 1. 2 a 2

Klar. 1. in A 2. in A

Fag. 1. 2 a 2

pp crescendo

Hrn. 1. 2. in F 3. 4. in F

Trp. 1. 2 in A

Pos. A. B.

Pk.

pp crescendo

Viol. 1

Viol. 2

Vla.

Vc.

Kb.

pp crescendo

G
Fl. 1. 2.
Kl.Fl.
Ob.1.2
Klar. 1.in A 2.in A
Fag.1.2
Hrn. 1.2.in F 3.in F
Trp.1.2 in A
Pos. A.T. B.
Btb.
Pk.
G
Viol.1
Viol.2
Vla.
Vc.
Kb.
G
a 2
p
mp
mf
poco a poco crescendo
p crescendo
mf crescendo
crescendo poco a poco

1. Fl. 2.
Kl. Fl.
Ob. 1.2
1. in A Klar. 2. in A
Fag. 1.2
1.2. in F Hrn. 3.4. in F
Trp. 1.2. in A
A.T. Pos. B.
Btb.
Pk.
Gr. Tr.
Viol. 1
Viol. 2
Vla.
Vc.
Kb.

a 2
f cresc.
ff
diminuendo
mf
f
muta in G, A, D
dim.

H
leggieramente
1. in A
Klar.
2. in A
a 2
Fag. 1.2
1.2. in F
Hrn.
3.4. in F
Vla.
Vc.
sempre pp
Kb.

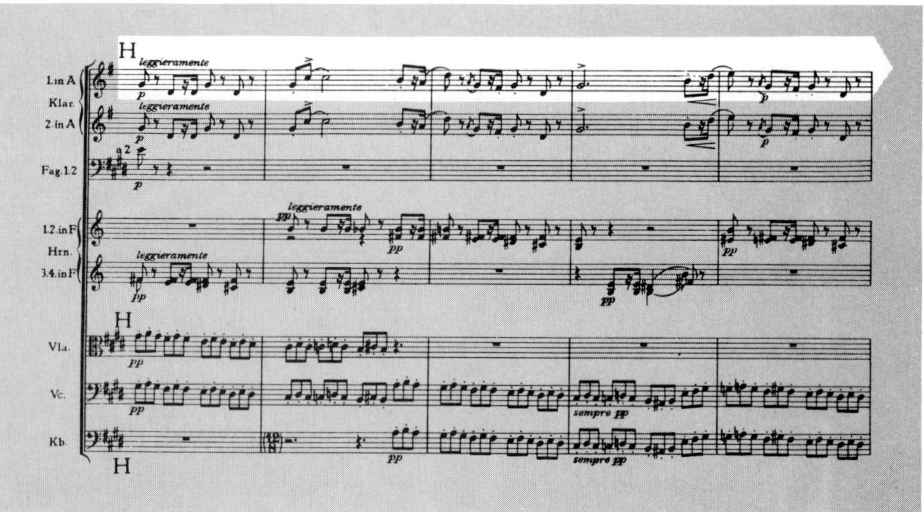

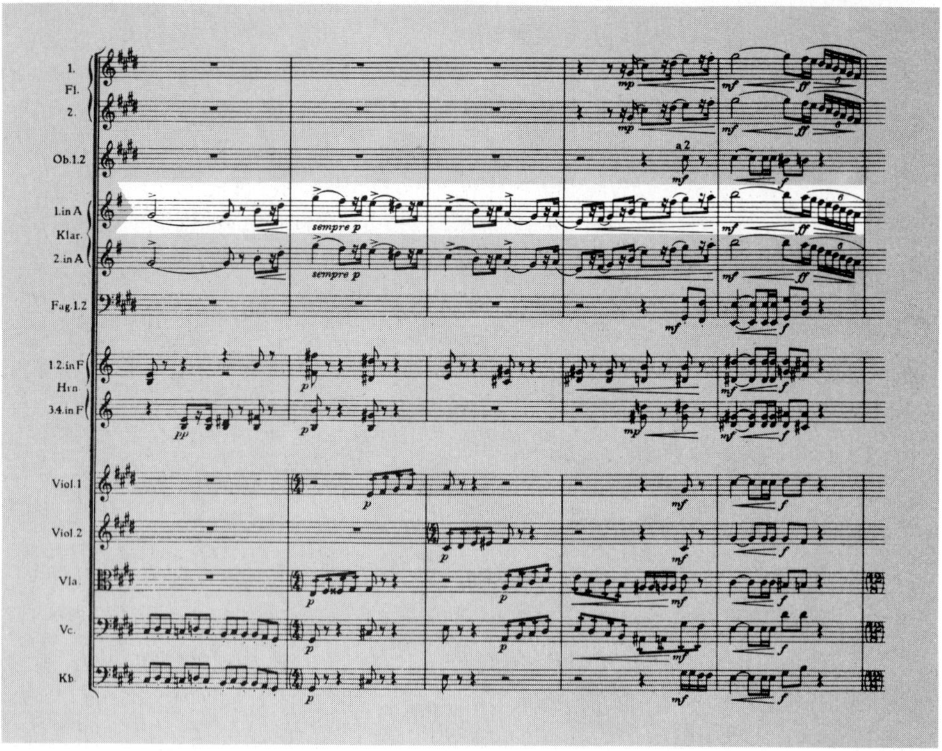

1.
Fl.
2.
Ob. 1.2
a 2
1. in A
Klar.
2. in A
sempre p
Fag. 1.2
1.2. in F
Hrn.
3.4. in F
Viol. 1
Viol. 2
Vla.
Vc.
Kb.

I
1. Fl. 2.
1. in A Klar. 2. in A
Fag. 1.2
1.2. in F Hrn. 3.4. in F
leggieramente
Viol. 1
Viol. 2
Vla.
Vc.
Kb.
un poco cresc.

1. Fl. 2.
Ob. 1.2
1. in A Klar. 2. in A
Fag. 1.2
1.2. in F Hrn. 3.4. in F
B.-Pos.
Btb.
Viol. 1
Viol. 2
Vla.
Vc.
Kb.
cresc.
div.

K
1.
Fl.
2.
Ob.1.2
1.in A
Klar.
2.in A
Fag.1.2
a 2
1.2.in F
Hrn.
3.4.in F
Trp.1.2
in A
Viol.1
Viol.2
div.
Vla.
Vc.
Kb.
cresc.
ff
f

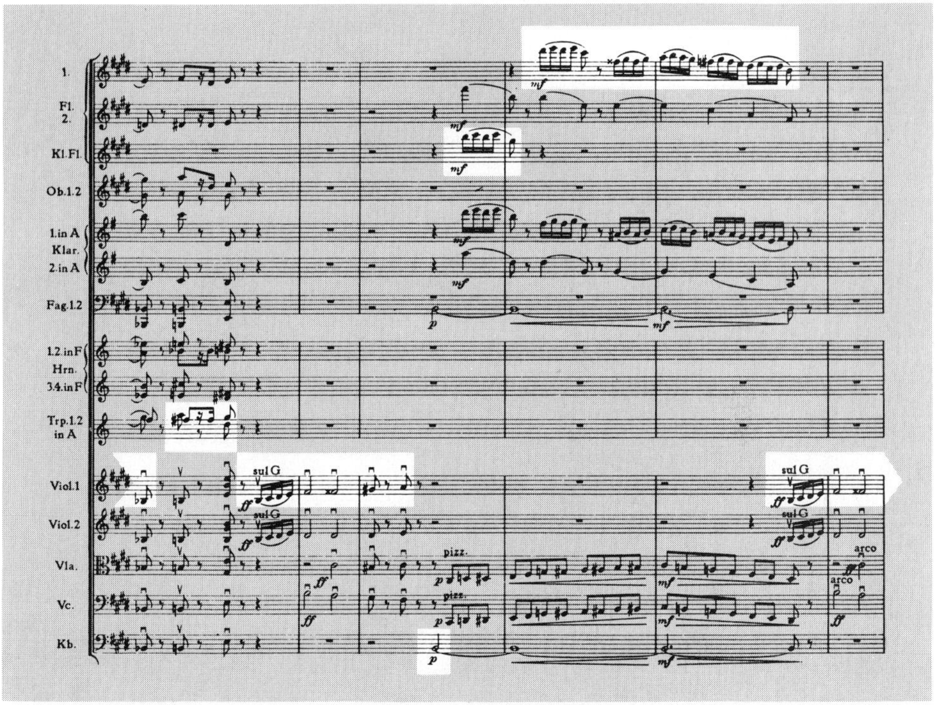

1.
Fl.
2.
Kl. Fl.
Ob. 1.2
1. in A
Klar.
2. in A
Fag. 1.2
1.2. in F
Hrn.
3.4. in F
Trp. 1.2
in A
Viol. 1
Viol. 2
Vla.
Vc.
Kb.
mf
p
ff
sul G
pizz.
arco

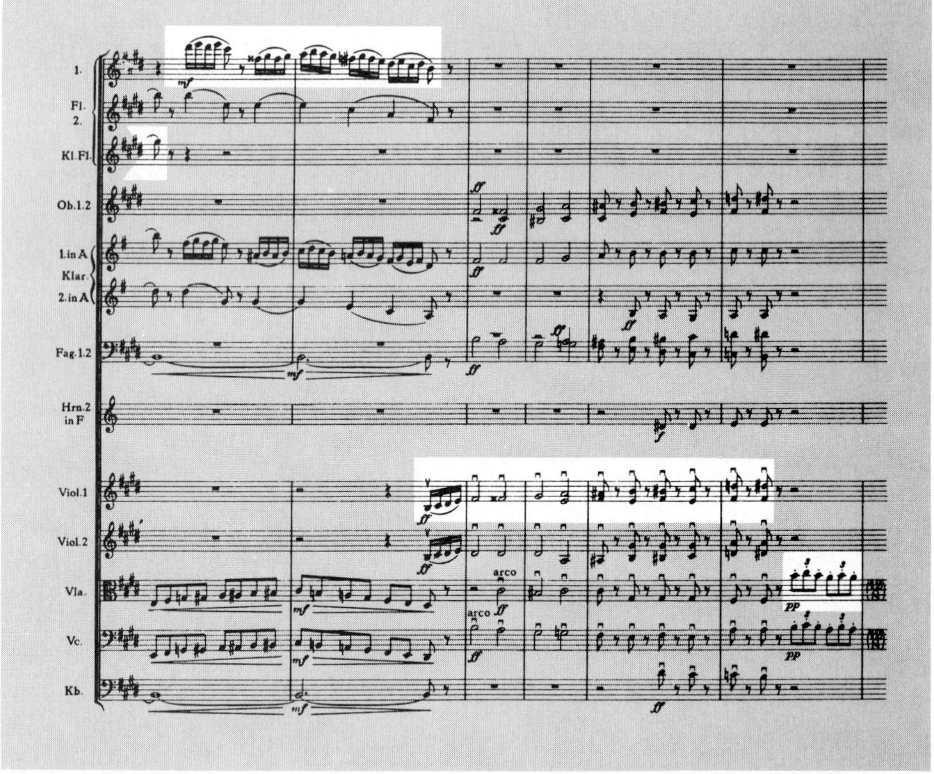

1. Fl. 2.
Kl.Fl.
Ob.1.2
1.in A Klar. 2.in A
Fag.1.2
Hrn.2 in F
Viol.1
Viol.2
Vla.
arco
Vc.
arco
Kb.

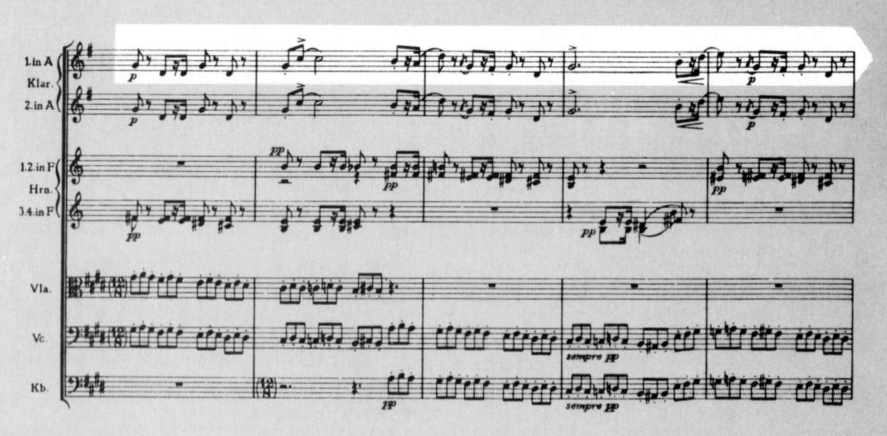

M
1. Fl. 2.
Ob. 1.2
a2
1. in A Klar. 2. in A
sempre p
Fag. 1.2
1.2. in F Hrn. 3.4. in F
M
Viol. 1
Viol. 2
Vla.
Vc.
Kb.
M

1. Fl. 2.
1. in A Klar. 2. in A
un poco cresc.
Fag. 1.2
1.2. in F Hrn. 3.4. in F
Viol. 1
Viol. 2
Vla.
Vc.
Kb.

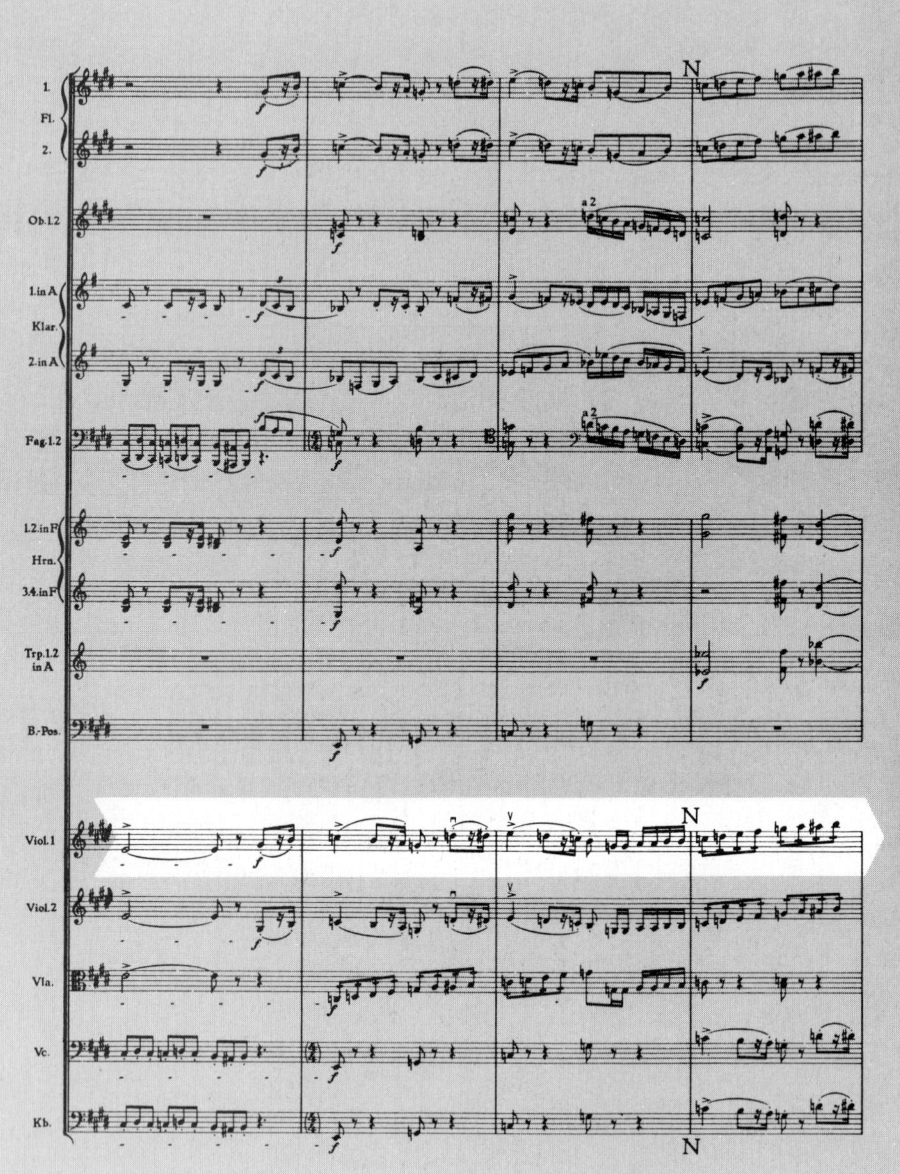
N
1.
Fl.
2.
Ob.1.2
a 2
1.in A
Klar.
2.in A
Fag.1.2
1.2.in F
Hrn.
3.4.in F
Trp.1.2
in A
B.-Pos.
Viol.1
Viol.2
Vla.
Vc.
Kb.
N

1.
Fl.
2.
a 2
Ob.1.2
1.in A
Klar.
2.in A
Fag.1.2
1.2.in F
Hrn.
3.4.in F
Trp.1.2
in A
B.-Pos.
Viol.1
Viol.2
Vla.
Vc.
Kb.

1.
Fl.
2.
Kl.Fl.
Ob.1.2
a 2
1.in A
Klar.
2.in A
Fag.1.2
a 2
1.2.in F
Hrn.
3.4.in F
Trp.1.2
in A
Viol.1
div.
Viol.2
div.
Vla.
div.
Vc.
div.
Kb.

1.
Fl.
2.
Ob.1.2
1.in A
Klar.
2.in A
Fag.1.2
Hrn.1.2 in A
Viol.1 div.
Viol.2 div.
Vla. div.
Vc. div.
Kb.
pizz.
arco
div.

1.
Fl.
2.
Ob.1.2
1.in A
Klar.
2.in A
Fag.1.2
Hrn.1.2 in F
Viol.1 div.
poco cresc.
Viol.2 div.
pizz.
arco
Vla. div.
Vc. div.
Kb.

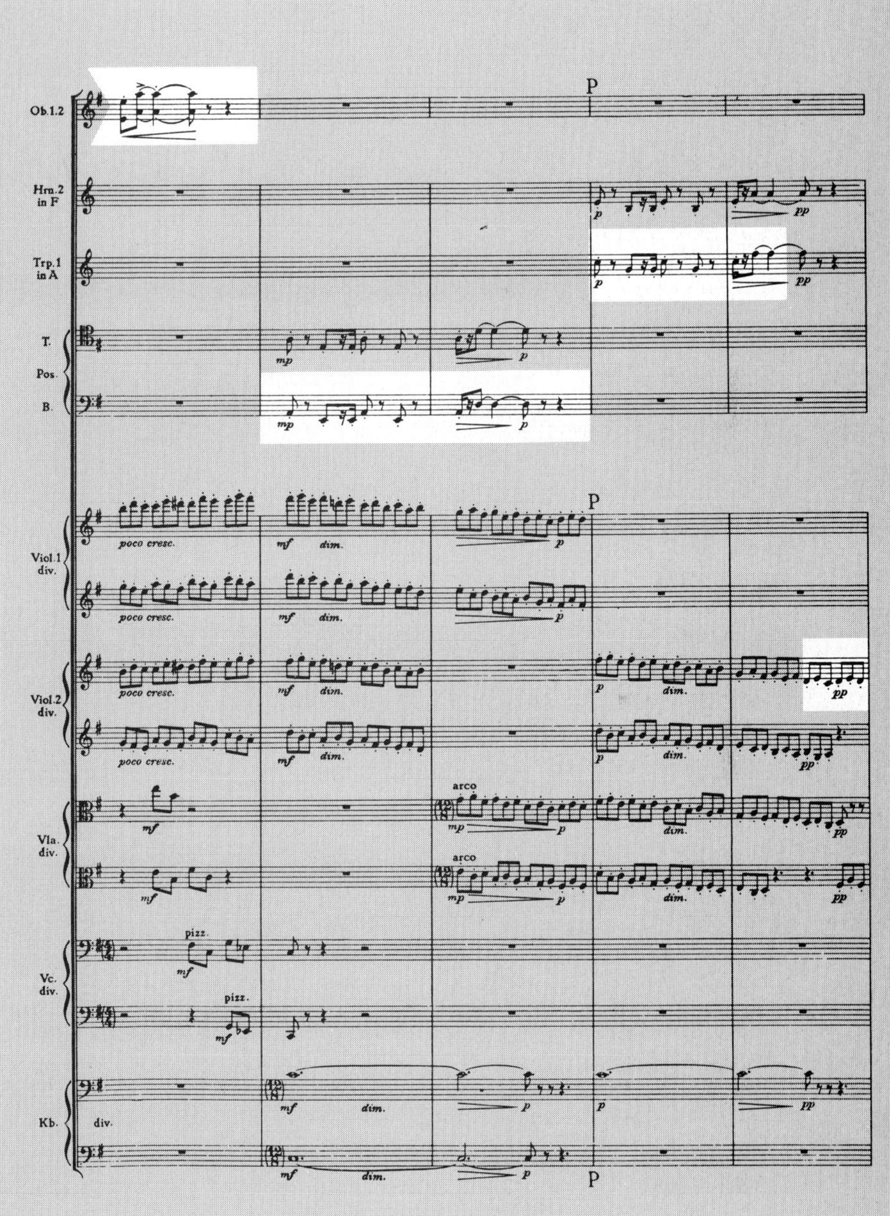
Ob.1.2
Hrn.2 in F
Trp.1 in A
T.
Pos.
B.
Viol.1 div.
Viol.2 div.
Vla. div.
Vc. div.
Kb.
div.
P
poco cresc.
mf
dim.
p
pp
mp
arco
pizz.

Ob.1.2
Viol.1 div.
Viol.2 div.
Vla. div.
Vc. div.
Kb. div.
pizz.
mf
mp
p
pp
arco
p leggiero
7
sempre p

Q
Ob.1.2
Hrn.1.2 in F
Trp.1.2 in A
Viol.1 div.
Viol.2 div.
Vla. div.
Vc. div.
Kb. div.
un poco marcato
p
pp
3
7

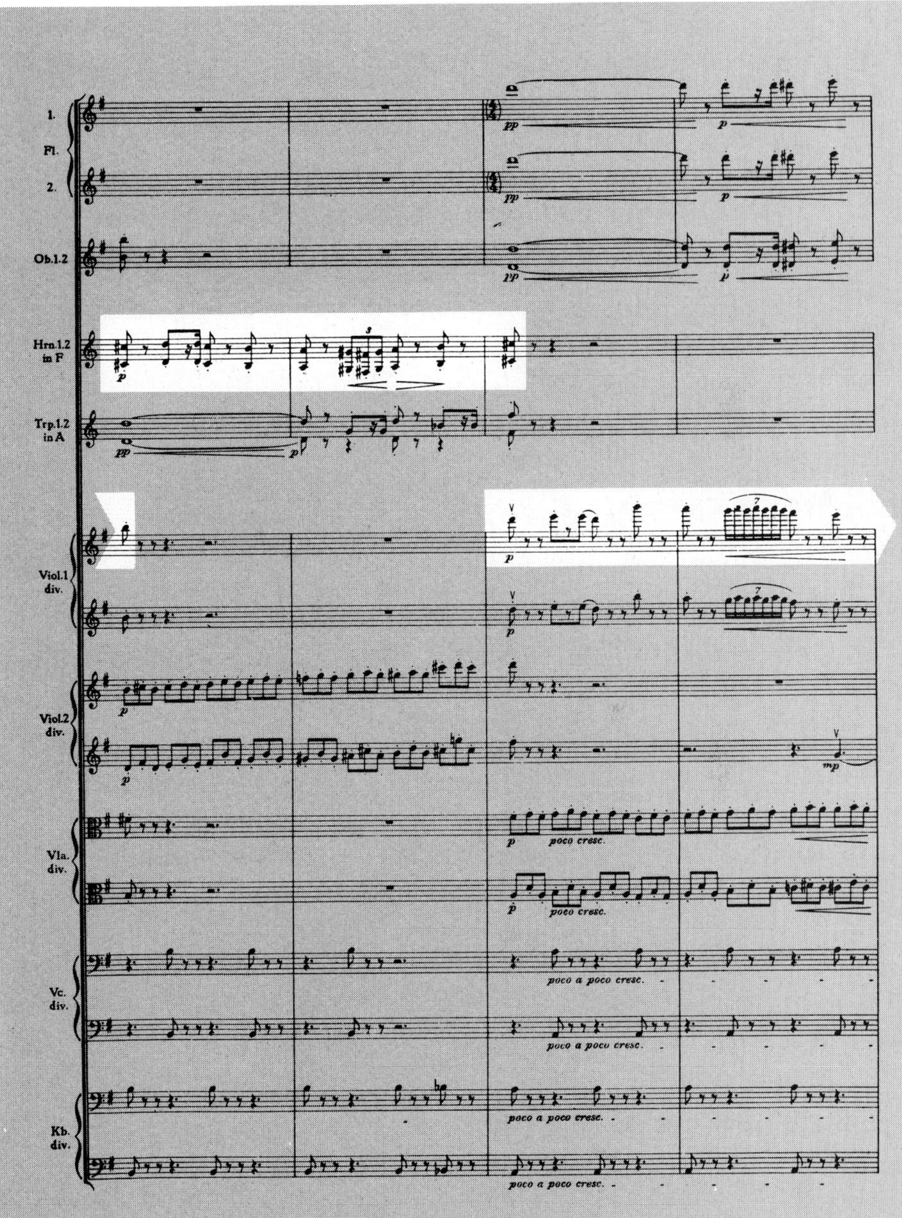
1.
Fl.
2.
Ob.1.2
Hrn.1.2 in F
Trp.1.2 in A
Viol.1 div.
Viol.2 div.
Vla. div.
Vc. div.
Kb. div.
pp
p
mp
poco cresc.
poco a poco cresc.

R

1. Fl. 2.

Ob. 1.2

1. in A Klar. 2. in A

Fag. 1.2

1.2. in F Hrn. 3.4. in F

mp un poco cresc.

Trp. 1.2 in A

Viol. 1 div.

Viol. 2 div.

Vla. div.

Vc. div.

arco

Kb. div.

R

1. in A
Klar.
2. in A
Fag. 1.2
1.2. in F
Hrn.
4. in F
Viol. 1 div.
Viol. 2 div.
Vla. div.
Vc. div.
Kb. div.
mf
mp
p
pizz.
arco
diminuendo

1. Fl. 2.

Kl. Fl.

1. in A Klar. 2. in A

Fag. 1. 2

A.-T.-Pos.

Pk.

Viol. 1 div.

Viol. 2 div.

Vla. div.

Vc. div.

Kb. div.

p mf arco pizz.

1.
Fl.
2.
Kl. Fl.
1. in A
Klar.
2. in A
Fag. 1.2
Hrn. 1.2 in F
Trp. 1.2 in A
A.-T.-Pos.
Pk.
Viol. 1 div.
Viol. 2 div.
Vla. div.
Vc. div.
Kb. div.
mp
f marcato
mf
p
f
arco
S

1.
Fl.
2.
Kl. Fl.
Ob. 1. 2
a 2
1. in A
Klar.
2. in A
f marcato
Fag. 1. 2
Hrn. 3. 4 in F
Trp. 1. 2 in A
Pk.
Viol. 1 div.
Viol. 2 div.
Vla. div.
arco
Vc. div.
Kb. div.

1.
Fl.
2.
Kl. Fl.
Ob. 1. 2
1. in A
Klar.
2. in A
Fag. 1. 2
1. 2. in F
Hrn.
3. 4. in F
Trp. 1. 2
in A
A. T.
Pos.
B.
Btb.
Pk.
Viol. 1
div.
Viol. 2
div.
Vla.
div.
Vc.
div.
Kb.
div.
T

1. Fl. 2.
Ob. 1.2
1. in A Klar. 2. in A
Fag. 1.2
1.2. in F Hrn. 3.4. in F
Trp. 1.2 in A
A. T. Pos. B.
Btb.
Pk.
Viol. 1
Viol. 2
Vla.
Vc.
Kb.

leggieramente
pp
a 2
unis.

U

Fl. 1.
Fl. 2.
Kl. Fl.
Ob. 1. 2
Klar. 1. in A
Klar. 2. in A
Fag. 1. 2
Hrn. 1. 2. in F
Hrn. 3. 4. in F
Trp. 1. 2 in A
Pos. A. T.
Pos. B.
Btb.
Pk.

p leggieramente
leggieramente
a 2
poco a poco cresc.
poco a poco

U

Viol. 1
Viol. 2
div.
Vla.
Vc.
Kb.

U

V

1. Fl. 2.

Ob. 1.2

1. in A Klar. 2. in A

Fag. 1.2

a 2

1. 2. in F Hrn. 3. 4. in F

Trp. 1.2 in A

A. T. Pos. B.

mp leggieramente

Btb.

Pk.

Viol. 1

Viol. 2

unis.

mf poco a poco cresc.

Vla.

mf poco a poco cresc.

Vc.

Kb.

cresc.

V

1.
Fl.
2.
Kl. Fl.
Ob. 1. 2
1. in A
Klar.
2. in A
Fag. 1. 2
1. 2. in F
Hrn.
3. 4. in F
Trp. 1. 2 in A
A. T.
Pos.
B.
Btb.
Pk.
Viol. 1
Viol. 2
Vla.
Vc.
Kb.

a 2
div.
f ff fff mf

W

Fl. 1. 2.
Kl. Fl.
Ob. 1. 2
Klar. 1. in A 2. in A
Fag. 1. 2
Hrn. 1. 2. in F 3. 4. in F
Trp. 1. 2 in A
Pos. A. T. B.
Btb.
Pk.
Viol. 1
Viol. 2
Vla.
Vc.
Kb.

W

X
1.
Fl.
2.
Kl. Fl.
Ob. 1. 2
1. in A
Klar.
2. in A
Fag. 1. 2
1. 2. in F
Hrn.
3. 4. in F
Trp. 1. 2 in A
A. T.
Pos.
B.
Btb.
Pk.
Gr. Tr.
Viol. 1
Viol. 2
Vla.
Vc.
Kb.
a2
sempre fff
fff

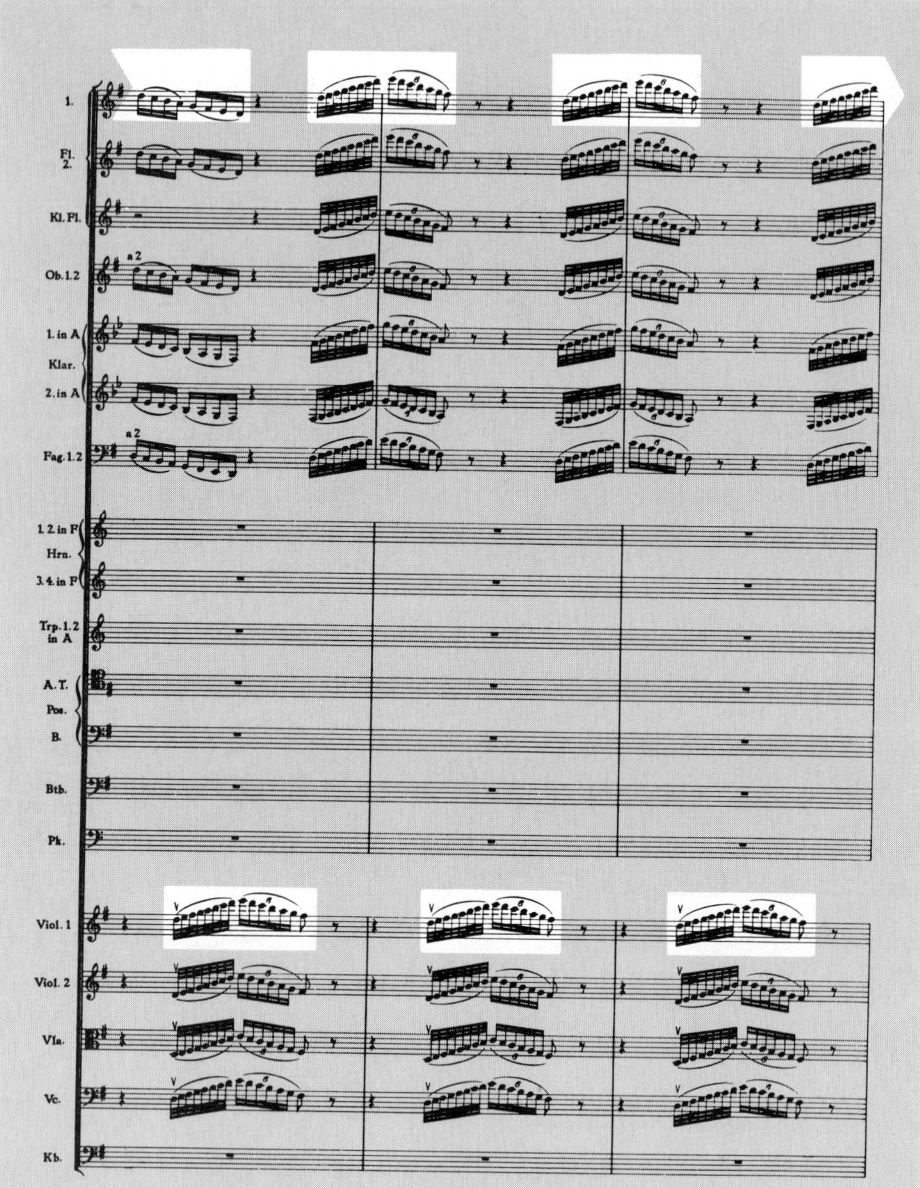
1.
Fl.
2.
Kl. Fl.
a 2
Ob. 1.2
1. in A
Klar.
2. in A
a 2
Fag. 1.2
1.2. in F
Hrn.
3.4. in F
Trp. 1.2
in A
A. T.
Pos.
B.
Btb.
Pk.
Viol. 1
Viol. 2
Vla.
Vc.
Kb.

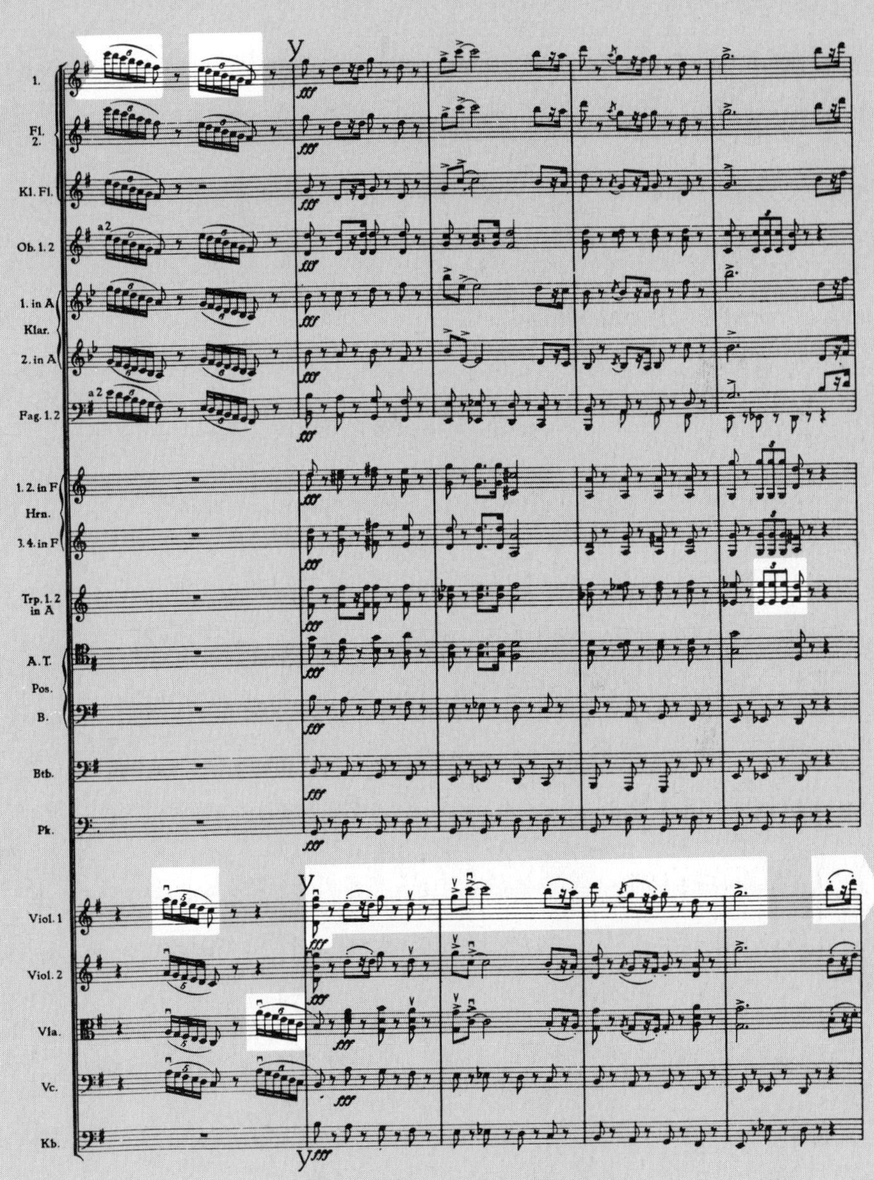

1.
Fl.
2.
Kl. Fl.
a2
Ob. 1. 2
1. in A
Klar.
2. in A
a2
Fag. 1. 2
1. 2. in F
Hrn.
3. 4. in F
Trp. 1. 2
in A
A. T.
Pos.
B.
Btb.
Pk.
Viol. 1
Viol. 2
Vla.
Vc.
Kb.
y
fff

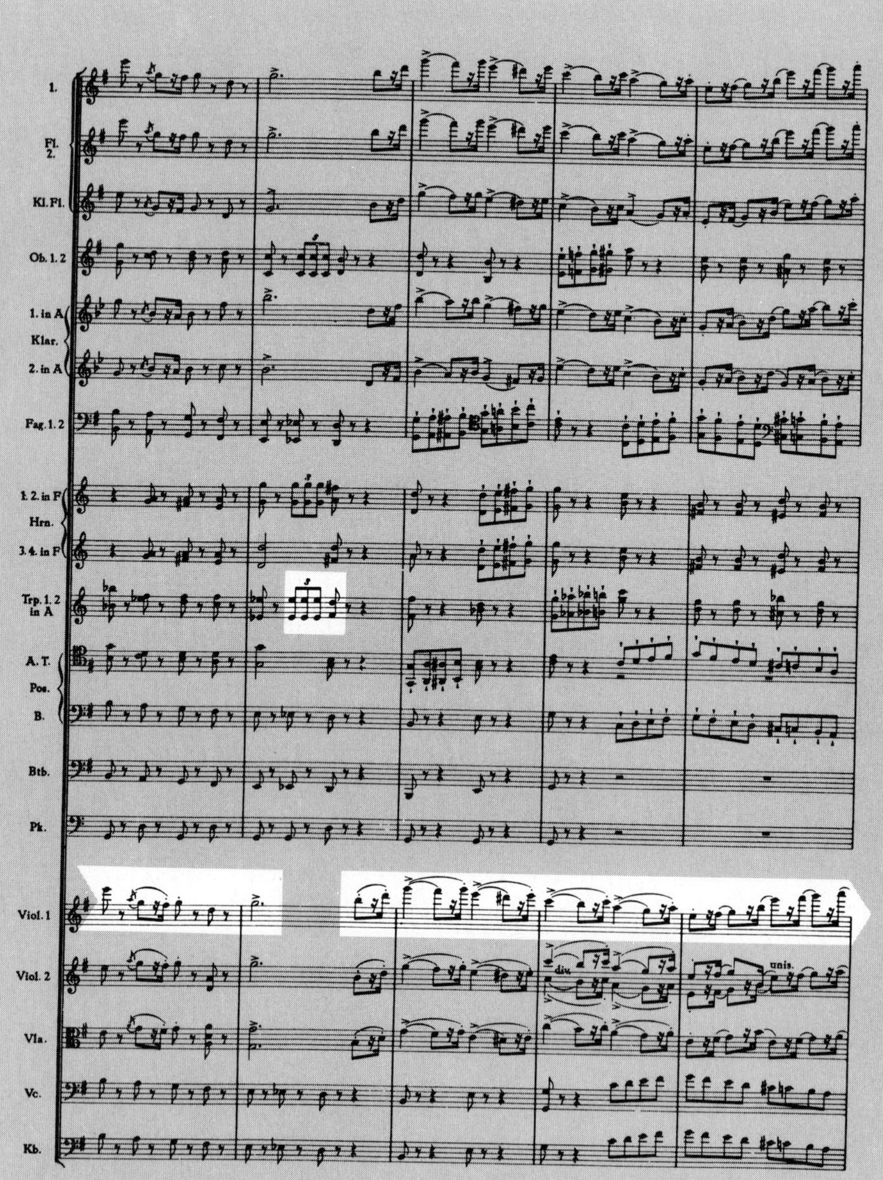

1.
Fl.
2.
Kl. Fl.
Ob. 1. 2
1. in A
Klar.
2. in A
Fag. 1. 2
1. 2. in F
Hrn.
3. 4. in F
Trp. 1. 2
in A
A. T.
Pos.
B.
Btb.
Pk.
Viol. 1
Viol. 2
div.
unis.
Vla.
Vc.
Kb.

Z
1.
Fl.
2.
Kl. Fl.
Ob. 1. 2
1. in A
Klar.
2. in A
Fag. 1. 2
1. 2. in F
Hrn.
3. 4. in F
Trp. 1. 2 in A
A. T.
Pos.
B.
Btb.
Pk.
(Die Becken dürfen nicht angebunden sein)
Beck.
Gr. Tr.
Viol. 1
Viol. 2
Vla.
Vc.
Kb.

AA
1.
Fl.
2.
Kl. Fl.
Ob. 1. 2
1. in A
Klar.
2. in A
Fag. 1. 2
1. 2. in F
Hrn.
3. 4. in F
Trp. 1. 2
in A
A. T.
Pos.
B.
Btb.
Pk.
muta A in C
AA
Viol. 1
Viol. 2
Vla.
Vc.
Kb.
AA

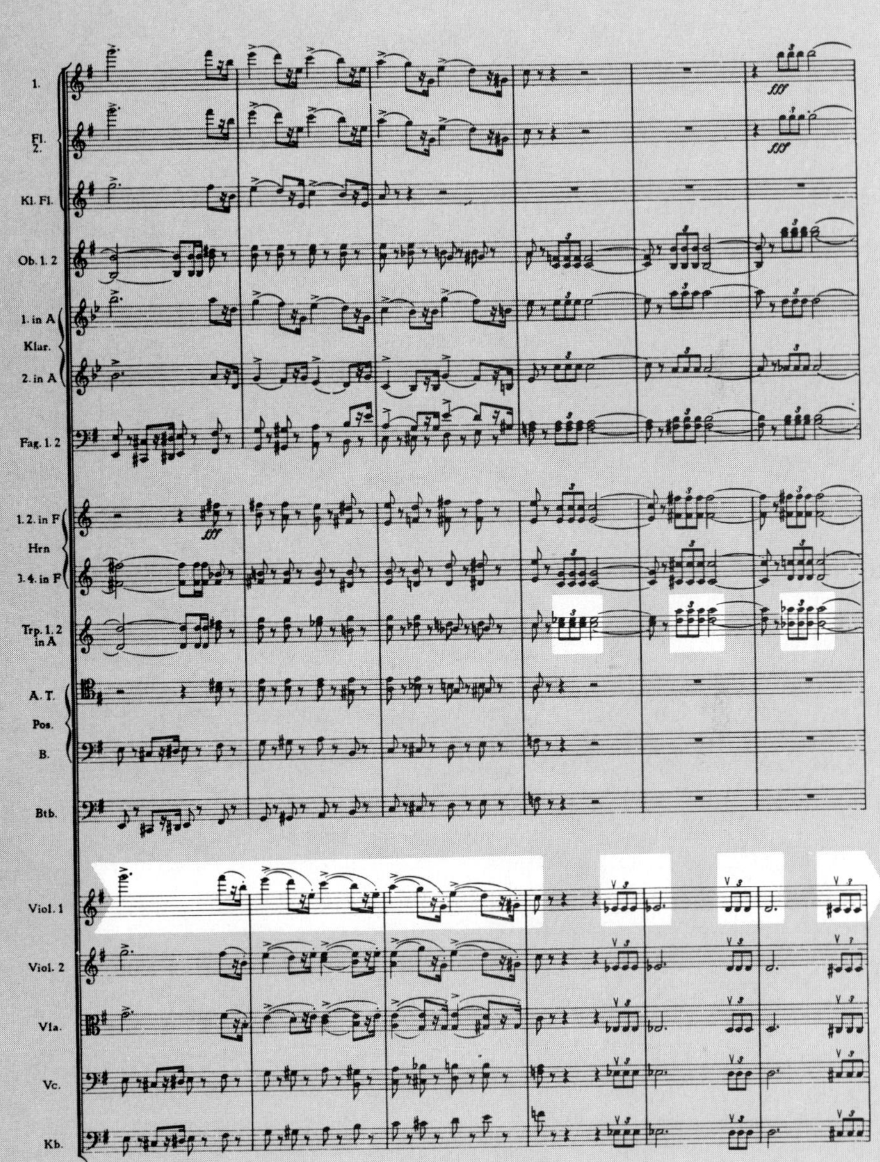
1.
Fl. 2.
Kl. Fl.
Ob. 1. 2
1. in A
Klar.
2. in A
Fag. 1. 2
1. 2. in F
Hrn
3. 4. in F
Trp. 1. 2 in A
A. T.
Pos.
B.
Btb.
Viol. 1
Viol. 2
Vla.
Vc.
Kb.

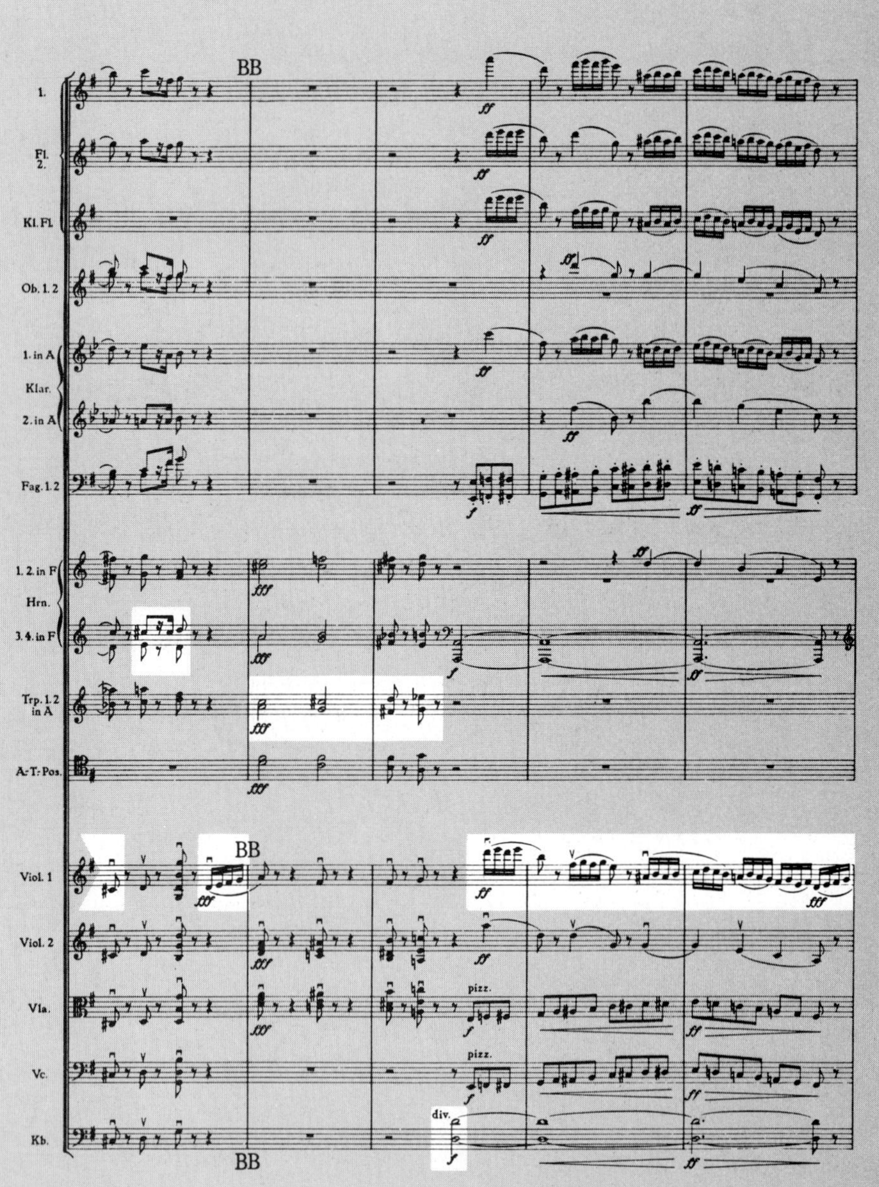
BB
1.
Fl. 2.
Kl. Fl.
Ob. 1. 2
1. in A
Klar.
2. in A
Fag. 1. 2
1. 2. in F
Hrn.
3. 4. in F
Trp. 1. 2 in A
A-T. Pos.
BB
Viol. 1
Viol. 2
Vla.
pizz.
Vc.
pizz.
div.
Kb.
BB

1.
Fl. 2.
Kl. Fl.
Ob. 1.2
1. in A
Klar.
2. in A
Fag. 1.2
1. 2. in F
Hrn.
3. 4. in F
Trp. 1.2 in A
A. T.
Pos.
B.
Btb.
Viol. 1
Viol. 2
Vla.
Vc.
Kb.
arco
pizz.
div.

CC
1.
Fl.
2.
Kl. Fl.
Ob. 1.2
1. in A
Klar.
2. in A
Fag. 1.2
1. 2. in F
Hrn.
3. 4. in F
Trp. 1.2
in A
A. T.
Pos.
B.
Viol. 1
Viol. 2
Vla.
Vc.
Kb.
pizz.
arco
CC

1.
Fl.
2.
Kl. Fl.
Ob. 1. 2
1. in A
Klar.
2. in A
Fag. 1. 2
1. 2. in F
Hrn.
3. 4. in F
Trp. 1. 2 in A
A. T.
Pos.
B.
Btb.
Viol. 1
Viol. 2
Vla.
Vc.
Kb.

DD

1. Fl. 2.

Kl. Fl.

Ob. 1.2

1. in A Klar. 2. in A

Fag. 1.2

1.2. in F Hrn. 3.4. in F

Trp. 1.2 in A

A. T. Pos. B.

Btb.

Pk.

Gr. Tr.

a 2

fff

marcato assai

DD

Viol. 1

Viol. 2

Vla.

Vc.

Kb.

DD

EE
1.
Fl.
2.
Kl. Fl.
Ob. 1.2
1. in A
Klar.
2. in A
Fag. 1.2
a 2
1.2. in F
Hrn.
3.4. in F
Trp. 1.2
in A
A. T.
Pos.
B.
Btb.
Pk.
Beck.
Gr. Tr.
EE
Viol. 1
Viol. 2
Vla.
Vc.
Kb.
EE

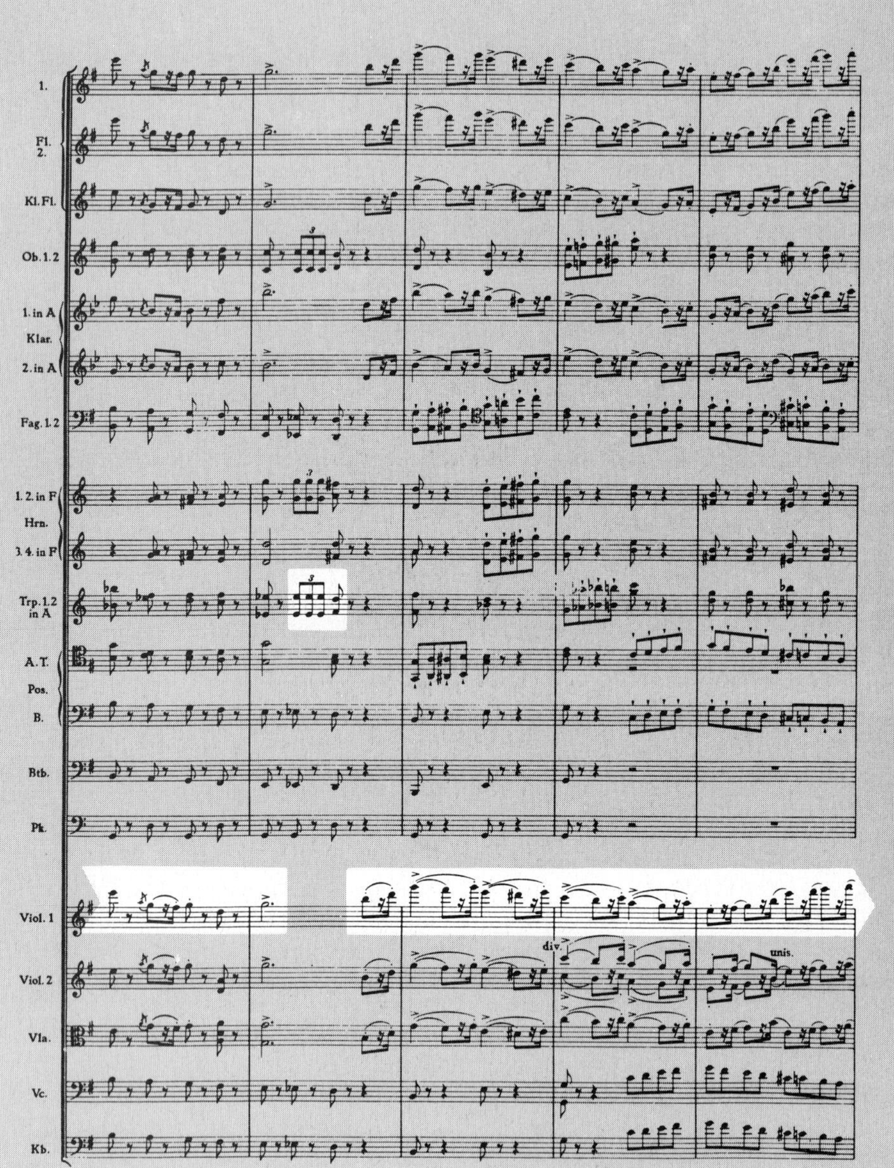
1.
Fl.
2.
Kl. Fl.
Ob. 1. 2
1. in A
Klar.
2. in A
Fag. 1. 2
1. 2. in F
Hrn.
3. 4. in F
Trp. 1. 2
in A
A. T.
Pos.
B.
Btb.
Pk.
Viol. 1
Viol. 2
Vla.
Vc.
Kb.
div.
unis.

FF
1.
Fl.
2.
Kl. Fl.
Ob. 1. 2
1. in A
Klar.
2. in A
Fag. 1. 2
1. 2. in F
Hrn.
3. 4. in F
Trp. 1. 2
in A
A. T.
Pos.
B.
Btb.
Pk.
Beck.
Gr. Tr.
fff
FF
Viol. 1
Viol. 2
Vla.
Vc.
Kb.
FF

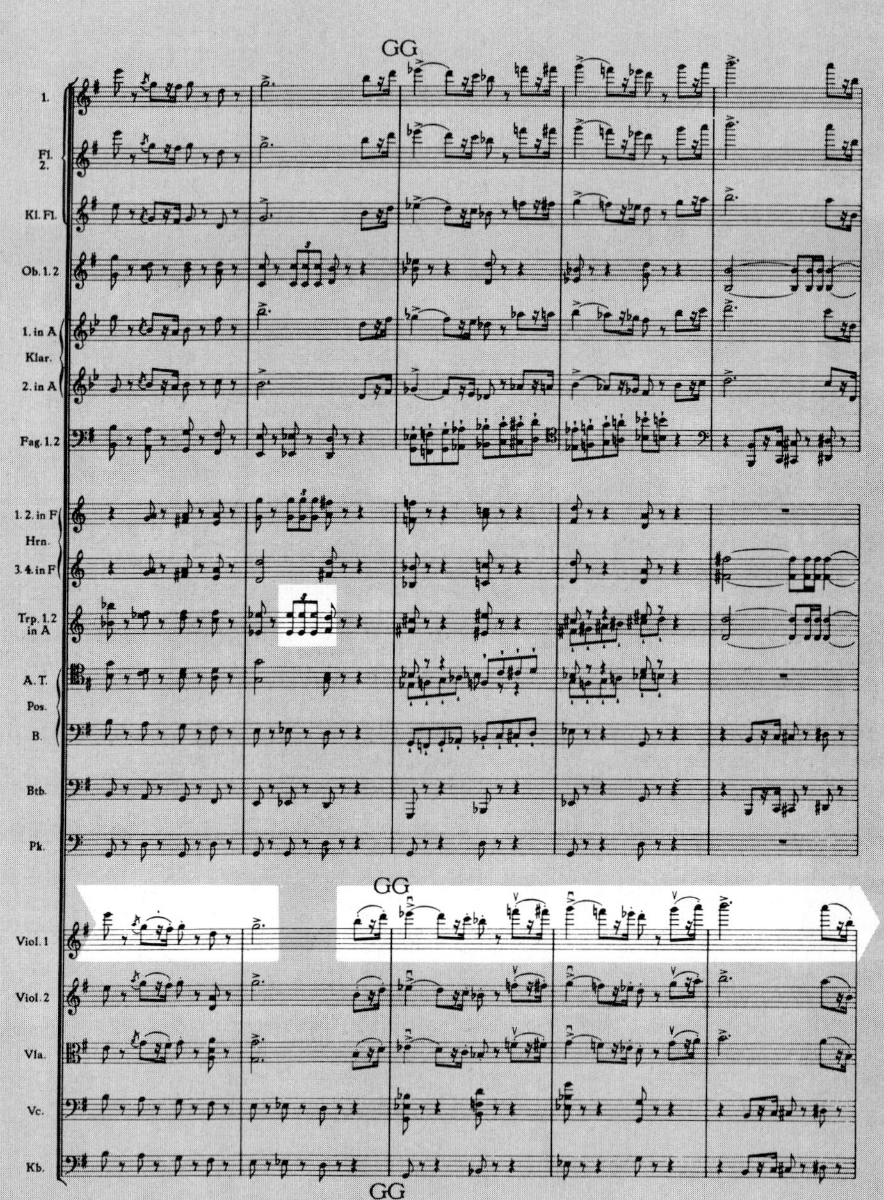
GG
1.
Fl.
2.
Kl. Fl.
Ob. 1.2
1. in A
Klar.
2. in A
Fag. 1.2
1. 2. in F
Hrn.
3. 4. in F
Trp. 1.2
in A
A. T.
Pos.
B.
Btb.
Pk.
GG
Viol. 1
Viol. 2
Vla.
Vc.
Kb.
GG

HH
1.
Fl.
2.
Kl. Fl.
Ob. 1. 2
1. in A
Klar.
2. in A
Fag. 1. 2
1. 2. in F
Hrn.
3. 4. in F
Trp. 1. 2 in A
A. T.
Pos.
B.
Btb.
Viol. 1
Viol. 2
Vla.
Vc.
Kb.
sempre fff
fff

1.
Fl.
2.
Kl. Fl.
Ob. 1. 2
1. in A
Klar.
2. in A
Fag. 1. 2
1. 2. in F
Hrn.
3. 4. in F
Trp. 1. 2 in A
A. T.
Pos.
B.
Btb.
Pk.
Gr. Tr.
Viol. 1
Viol. 2
Vla.
Vc.
Kb.

II
1.
Fl.
2.
Kl. Fl.
Ob. 1. 2
1. in A
Klar.
2. in A
Fag. 1. 2
1. 2. in F
Hrn.
3. 4. in F
Trp. 1. 2 in A
A. T.
Pos.
B.
Btb.
Pk.
Beck.
Viol. 1
Viol. 2
Vla.
Vc.
Kb.
a 2
p cresc.
mf cresc.
mp
mf
p
fff
II

KK
1.
Fl.
2.
Kl. Fl.
Ob. 1.2
1. in A
Klar.
2. in A
Fag. 1.2
1. 2. in F
Hrn.
3. 4. in F
Trp. 1. 2
in A
a 2
A. T.
Pos.
B.
Btb.
Pk.
Gr. Tr.
KK
div.
div.
Viol. 1
Viol. 2
Vla.
Vc.
Kb.
KK
ff cresc.
f cresc.
cresc
f
ff
fff

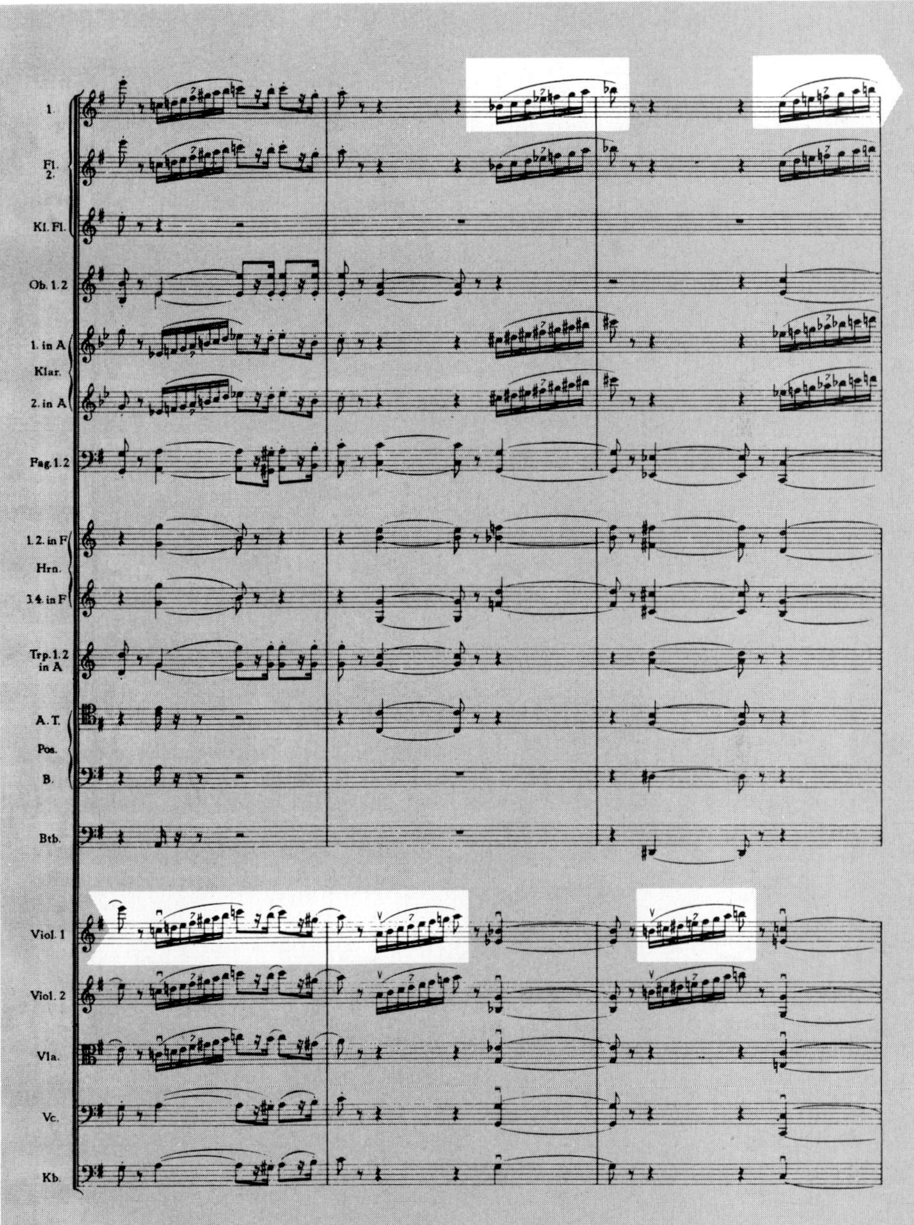
1.
Fl. 2.
Kl. Fl.
Ob. 1. 2
1. in A
Klar.
2. in A
Fag. 1. 2
1. 2. in F
Hrn.
3. 4. in F
Trp. 1. 2 in A
A. T.
Pos.
B.
Btb.
Viol. 1
Viol. 2
Vla.
Vc.
Kb.

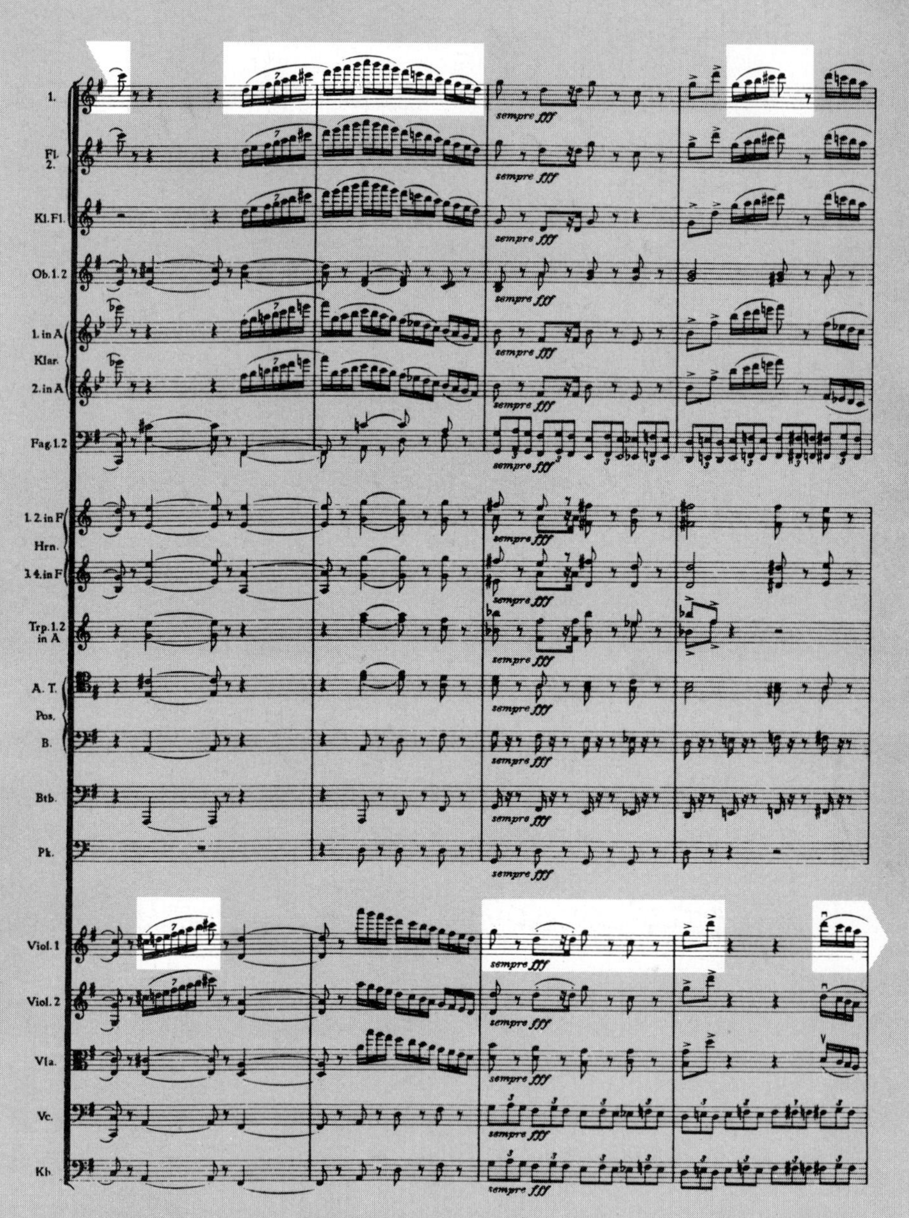
1.
Fl.
2.
Kl. Fl.
Ob. 1. 2
1. in A
Klar.
2. in A
Fag. 1. 2
1. 2. in F
Hrn.
3. 4. in F
Trp. 1. 2
in A
A. T.
Pos.
B.
Btb.
Pk.
Viol. 1
Viol. 2
Vla.
Vc.
Kb.
sempre fff

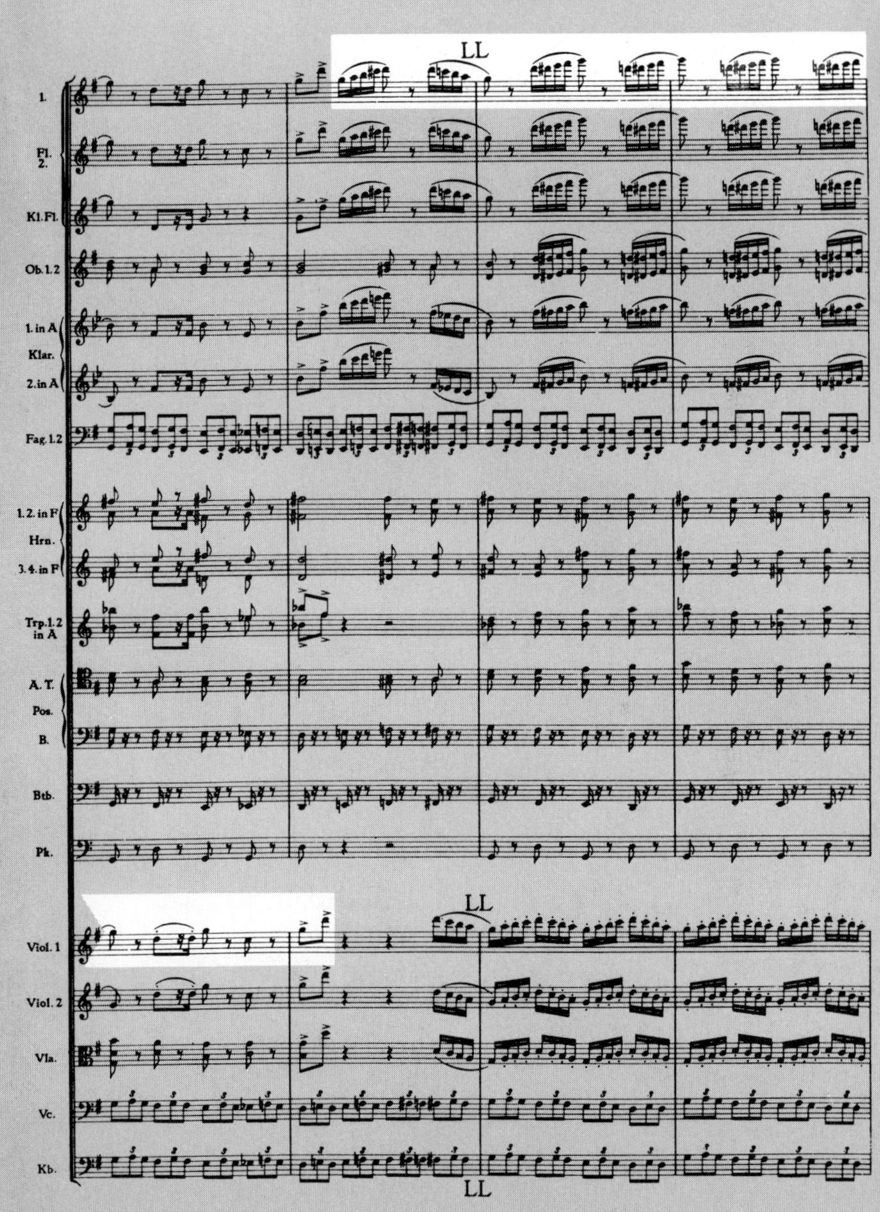
LL
1.
Fl.
2.
Kl.Fl.
Ob.1.2
1. in A
Klar.
2. in A
Fag.1.2
1.2. in F
Hrn.
3.4. in F
Trp.1.2
in A
A.T.
Pos.
B.
Btb.
Pk.
LL
Viol. 1
Viol. 2
Vla.
Vc.
Kb.
LL

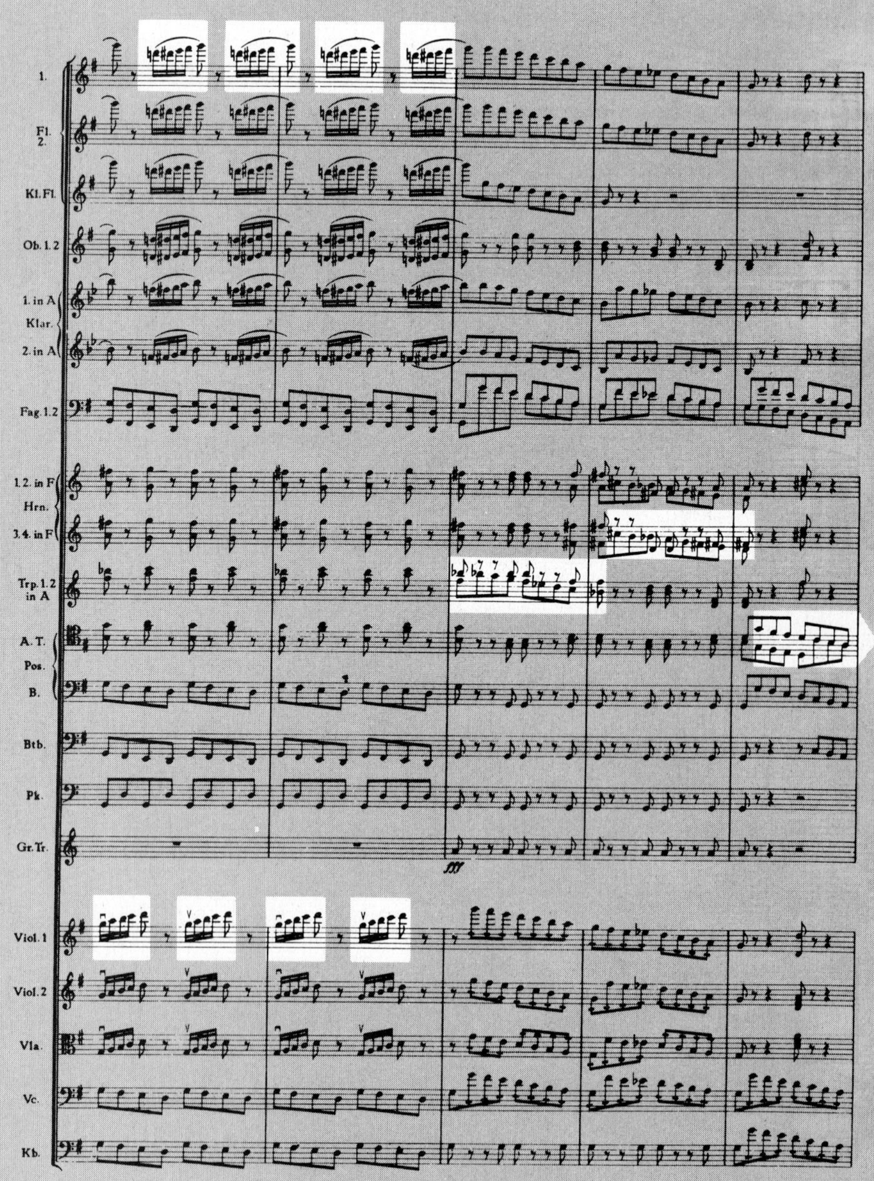
1.
Fl.
2.
Kl. Fl.
Ob. 1.2
1. in A
Klar.
2. in A
Fag. 1.2
1.2. in F
Hrn.
3.4. in F
Trp. 1.2 in A
A. T.
Pos.
B.
Btb.
Pk.
Gr. Tr.
fff
Viol. 1
Viol. 2
Vla.
Vc.
Kb.

1.
Fl.
2.
Kl. Fl.
Ob. 1.2
1. in A
Klar.
2. in A
Fag. 1.2
a 2
1.2. in F
Hrn.
3.4. in F
Trp. 1.2 in A
A. T.
Pos.
B.
Btb.
Pk.
Gr. Tr.
fff
Viol. 1
Viol. 2
Vla.
Vc.
Kb.

IV. Finale
Adagio lamentoso (♩. = 54)
affrettando
1.
Flöten
2.
3.
Oboen 1. 2
1. in A
Klarinetten
2. in A
a 2
Fagotte 1. 2
1. 2. in F
Hörner
3. 4. in F
Trompeten 1. 2 in A
Alt, Tenor
Posaunen
Baß
Baßtuba
Pauken in Fis, C, D
Tamtam (ad libitum)
largamente
Violine 1
Violine 2
Viola
Violoncell
Kontrabaß

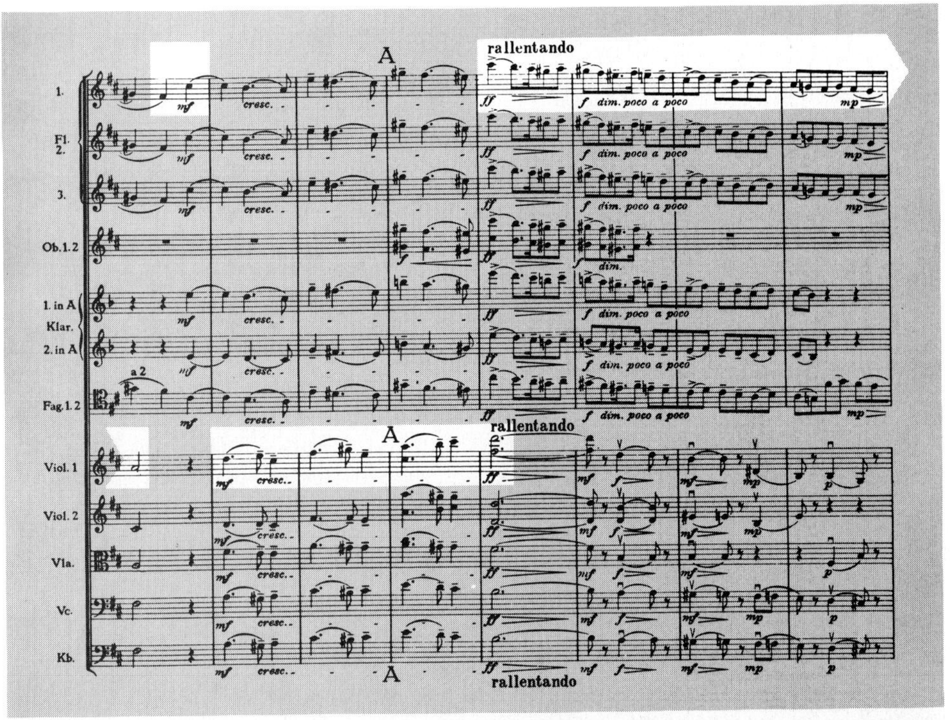

A

rallentando

1. Fl. 2. 3. Ob. 1.2 1. in A Klar. 2. in A Fag. 1.2 Viol. 1 Viol. 2 Vla. Vc. Kb.

cresc. f dim. poco a poco mp

rallentando

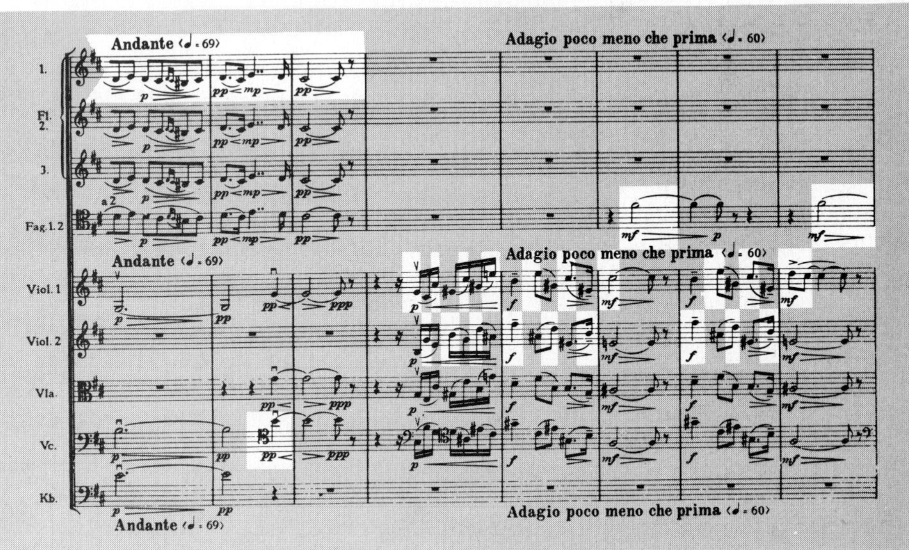

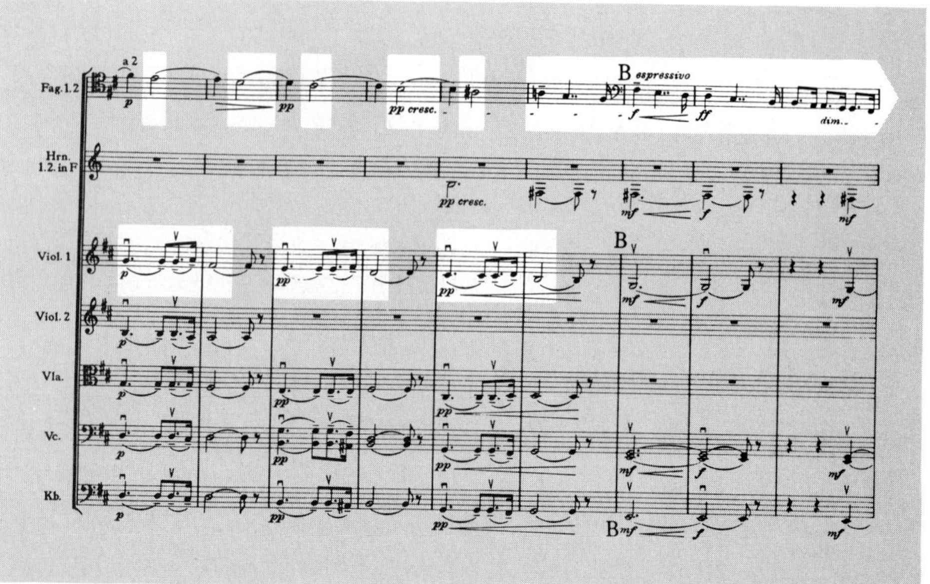
Fag. 1.2
a 2
B espressivo
Hrn. 1.2. in F
Viol. 1
Viol. 2
Vla.
Vc.
Kb.
B

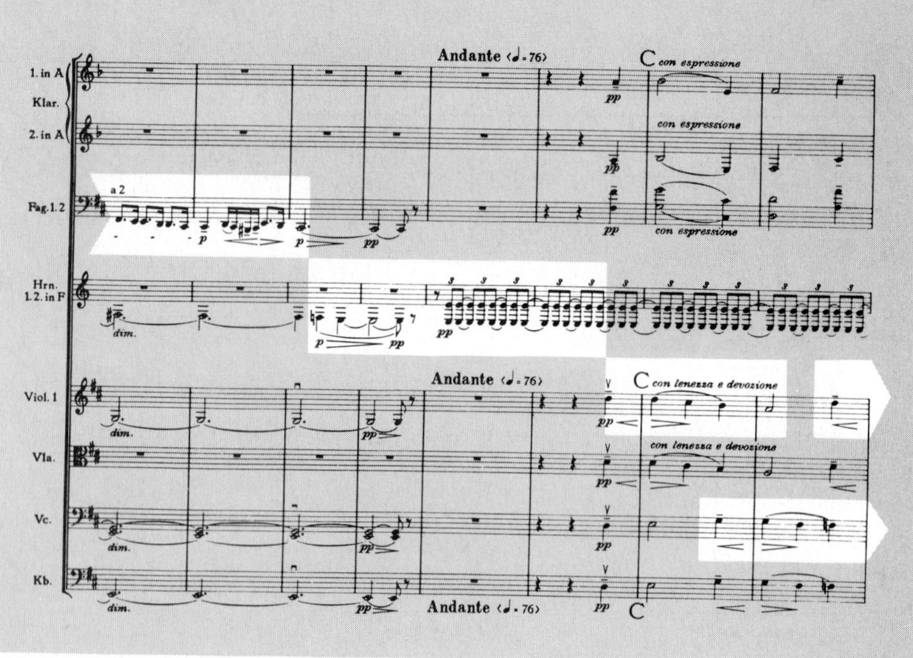
Andante (♩= 76)
C con espressione
1. in A
Klar.
2. in A
Fag. 1.2
Hrn. 1.2. in F
Viol. 1
C con tenezza e devozione
Vla.
Vc.
Kb.
C

poco animando
ritenuto
1. in A
Klar.
2. in A
Fag. 1.2
Hrn. 1.2. in F
Viol. 1
Viol. 2
Vla.
Vc.
Kb.
cresc.
mf
p
a 2
div.

Tempo I
D poco animando
1. in A
Klar.
2. in A
Fag. 1.2
Hrn. 3.4. in F
Trp. 1 in A
A.-T.-Pos.
con sentimento
Viol. 1
Viol. 2 div.
Vla.
Vc.
Kb.
cresc.
p
mp

ritenuto
Tempo I
1.
Fl. 2.
3.
Ob. 1. 2
1. in A
Klar.
2. in A
Fag. 1. 2
a 2
1. 2. in F
Hrn.
3. 4. in F
Trp. 1 in A
A.-T.-Pos.
Viol. 1
Viol. 2 div.
unis.
Vla.
Vc.
Kb.
cresc.
mf

poco animando
ritenuto
E Tempo I
1.
Fl.
2
3.
Ob. 1. 2
1. in A
Klar.
2. in A
a 2
Fag. 1. 2
1. 2. in F
Hrn.
3. 4. in F
cresc.
Trp. 1. 2
in A
a 2
espressivo
A. T.
Pos.
B.
Viol. 1
Viol. 2
div.
Vla.
Vc.
Kb.
cresc.

animando
1.
Fl.
2.
3.
Ob. 1.2
1. in A
Klar.
2. in A
Fag. 1.2
a 2
cresc.
ff
1. 2. in F
Hrn.
3.4. in F
f
p
Trp. 1.2
in A
A. T.
Pos.
B.
Btb.
mf
animando
Viol. 1
Viol. 2
div.
Vla.
div.
Vc.
Kb.
div.
animando

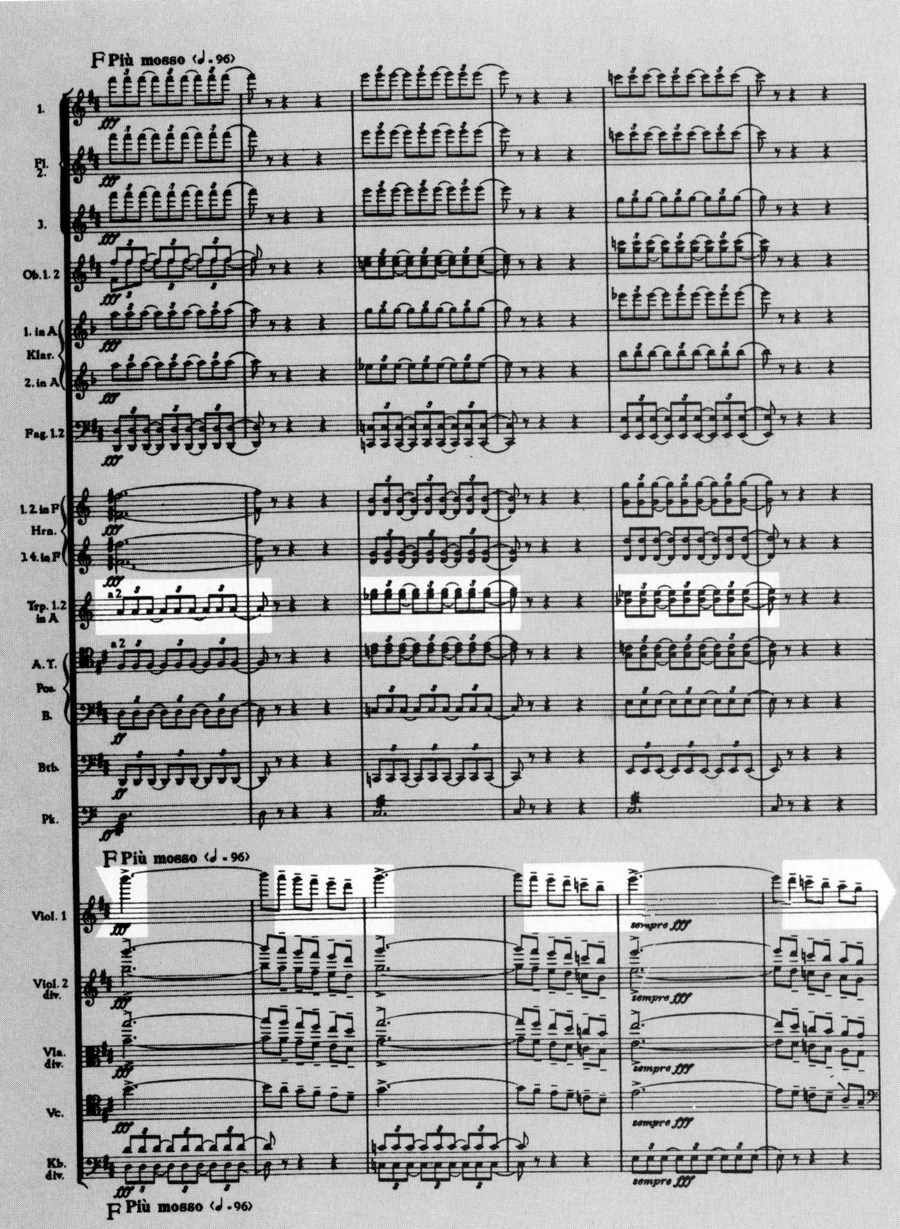
F Più mosso (♩. 96)
1.
Fl. 2.
3.
Ob. 1. 2
1. in A
Klar.
2. in A
Fag. 1. 2
1. 2. in F
Hrn.
3. 4. in F
Trp. 1. 2 in A
a 2
A. T.
Pos.
B.
Btb.
Pk.
F Più mosso (♩. 96)
Viol. 1
Viol. 2 div.
Vla. div.
Vc.
Kb. div.
sempre fff
F Più mosso (♩. 96)

stringendo
Vivace
Fl.
Ob. 1. 2
1. in A
Klar.
2. in A
Fag. 1. 2
a 2
1. 2. in F
Hrn.
3. 4. in F
Trp. 1. 2 in A
A. T.
Pos.
B.
Btb.
muta D in E
Pk.
sempre fff
Viol. 1
Viol. 2 div.
unis.
Vla. div.
Vc.
Kb.

Andante (♩ = 76)
Ob. 1. 2
a 2
1. in A
Klar.
2. in A
Fag. 1. 2
Viol. 1
Viol. 2
Vla.
Vc.
Kb.

G Andante non tanto (♩ = 60)
1. 2. in F
Hrn.
3. 4. in F
Viol. 1
Viol. 2
Vla.
Vc.
Kb.
mf cresc.

stringendo molto

1.
Fl. 2.
3.
Ob. 1.2
a 2
1. in A
Klar
2. in A
Fag. 1.2
a 2
1.2. in F
Hrn.
3.4. in F
Trp. 1.2 in A
muta C in H
Pk.

stringendo molto

Viol. 1
Viol. 2
Vla.
Vc.
Kb.

cresc.

stringendo molto

Moderato assai (♩ = 88)
pesante
cresc.
fff
Fl. 1. 2. 3.
Ob. 1. 2
1. in A
Klar.
2. in A
a2 pesante
ff cresc.
marcato e pesante
Fag. 1. 2
1. 2. in F
Hrn.
3. 4. in F
Trp. 1. 2 in A
A. T.
Pos.
B.
ff
Btb.
f cresc.
Pk.
Viol. 1
Viol. 2
Vla.
Vc.
Kb.

1.
Fl.
2.
3.
Ob. 1. 2
1. in A
Klar
2. in A
Fag. 1. 2
1. 2. in F
Hrn.
3. 4. in F
Trp. 1. 2 in A
A. T.
Pos.
B.
Btb.
Pk.
ff marcato e pesante
Viol. 1
Viol. 2
Vla.
Vc.
Kb.
div.
div.

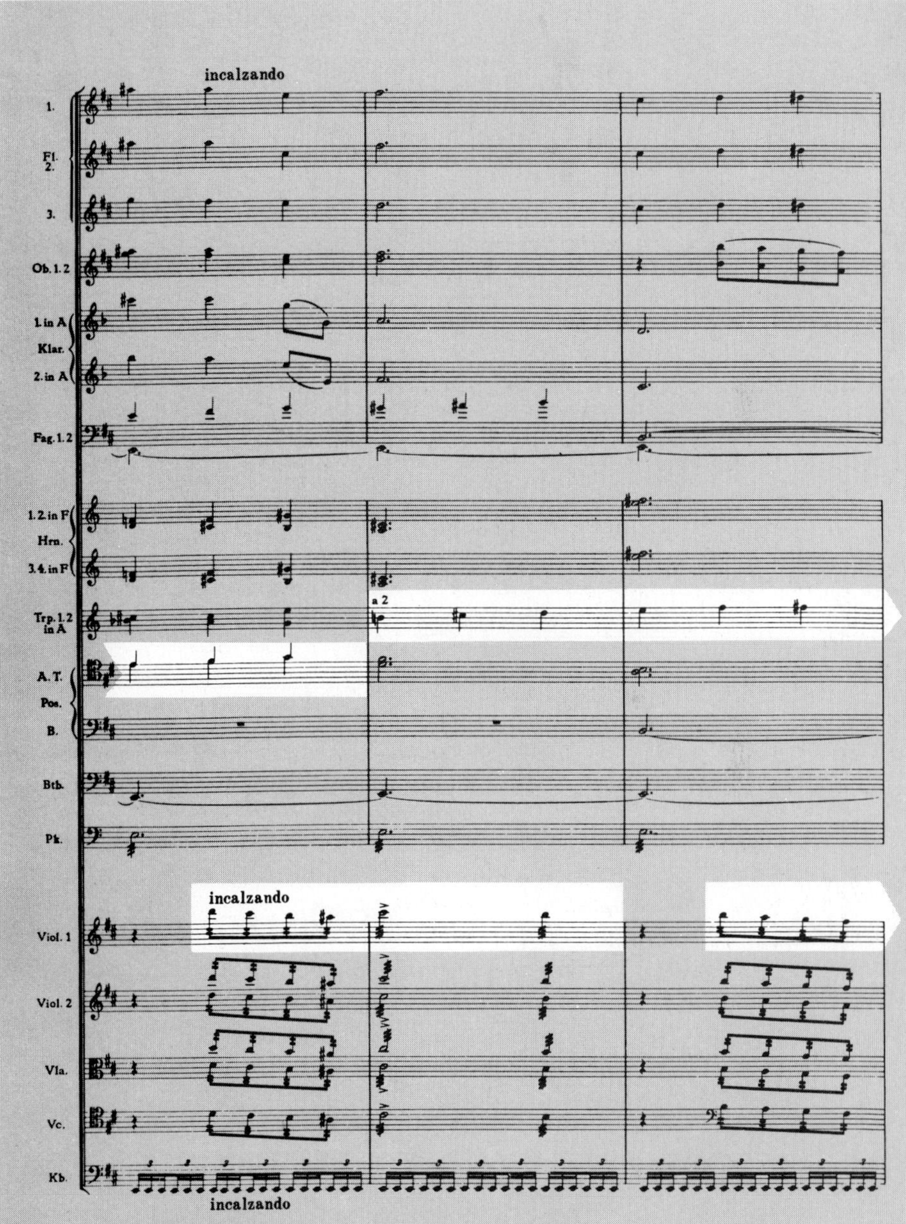
incalzando
1.
Fl.
2.
3.
Ob. 1.2
1. in A
Klar.
2. in A
Fag. 1.2
1.2. in F
Hrn.
3.4. in F
a 2
Trp. 1.2 in A
A. T.
Pos.
B.
Btb.
Pk.
incalzando
Viol. 1
Viol. 2
Vla.
Vc.
Kb.
incalzando

ritenuto
K Andante (♩. = 80)
Fl. 1. 2. 3.
Ob. 1. 2
a 2
fff
1. in A
Klar.
2. in A
Fag. 1. 2
1. 2. in F
Hrn.
3. 4. in F
ff gestopft
Trp. 1. 2 in A
A. T.
Pos.
B.
Btb.
Pk.
mf
Viol. 1
Viol. 2 div.
unis.
Vla. div.
Vc.
Kb.

1.
Fl.
2.
3.
Ob. 1. 2
a 2
1. in A
Klar.
2. in A
Fag. 1. 2
a 2
1. 2. in F
Hrn.
3. 4. in F
B.-Pos.
p
Btb.
p
Pk.
sempre mf
dim.
Viol. 1
Viol. 2
Vla.
div.
unis.
Vc.
Kb.
dim.

L
poco rallentando
quasi adagio
1. in A
Klar.
2. in A
Fag. 1.2
1.2. in F
Hrn.
3.4. in F
f dim.
A. T.
Pos.
B.
Btb.
Pk.
Tamt.
Viol. 1
Viol. 2
Vla.
Vc.
Kb.

M Andante giusto (♩. 76)
Fl.
Ob. 1. 2
1. in A
Klar.
2. in A
Fag. 1. 2
1. 2. in F
Hrn.
3. 4. in F
p nicht gest.
A.-T.-Pos.
M Andante giusto (♩. 76)
con sordini
sul G
Viol. 1
Viol. 2
Vla.
Vc.
Kb.
M Andante giusto (♩. 76)

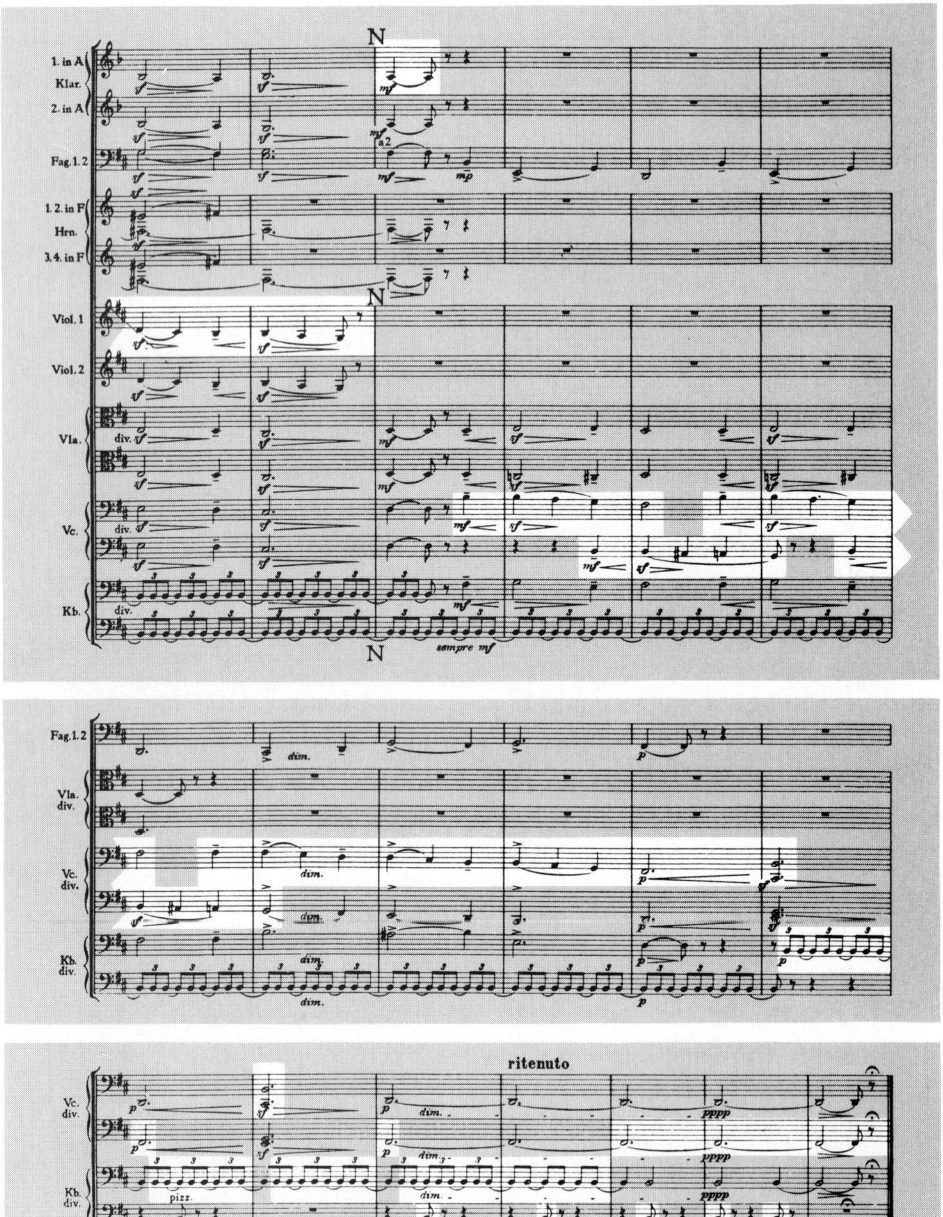

N

1. in A
Klar.
2. in A
Fag. 1. 2
1. 2. in F
Hrn.
3. 4. in F
Viol. 1
Viol. 2
Vla.
Vc.
Kb.
div.
a2
sempre mf
N

22. GUSTAV MAHLER (1860-1911),
Fourth movement from Symphony No. 4 (1900)

10
Poco rit.
Fl.
Ob.
Cor. ingl.
Cl. (B)
Cl.b. (B)
Fg.
Cor.
Trgl.
Arp.
Vl.I
Vl.II
Vla.
Vlc.
Cb.
dim.
2.3.a 2
a 2
1. 2.
pp subito
Poco rit.
senza sord.
pizz.
10

NB Singstimme mit kindlich heiterem Ausdruck; durchaus ohne Parodie!
Il canto con espressione infantile e serena, sempre senza parodia!

Fl.
Ob.
Cor. ingl.
Cl. (B)
Cl.b. (B)
Fg.
Cor.
Timp.
Trgl.
Arp.
Canto
Vl.I
Vl.II
Vla.
Vlc.
Cb.
3.4. mutano in Picc.
3. Cl. in B-Sib
1.2. a 2
pizz.
arco
mei - den.
noy us,
Kein welt - lich' Ge-tüm - mel hört man nicht im
in heav-en not a rus - tle heard is of earth's

20
Fl.
Ob.
Cor. ingl.
Cl. (B)
Fg.
Cor.
Arp.
Canto
Him - mel! Lebt Al - les in sanf - te-ster Ruh', in
bus - tle, in deep - est of peace all goes on, in
Vl.I
Vl.II
Vla.
Vlc.
Cb.
1.2.a 2
con sord.
arco
pizz.
20

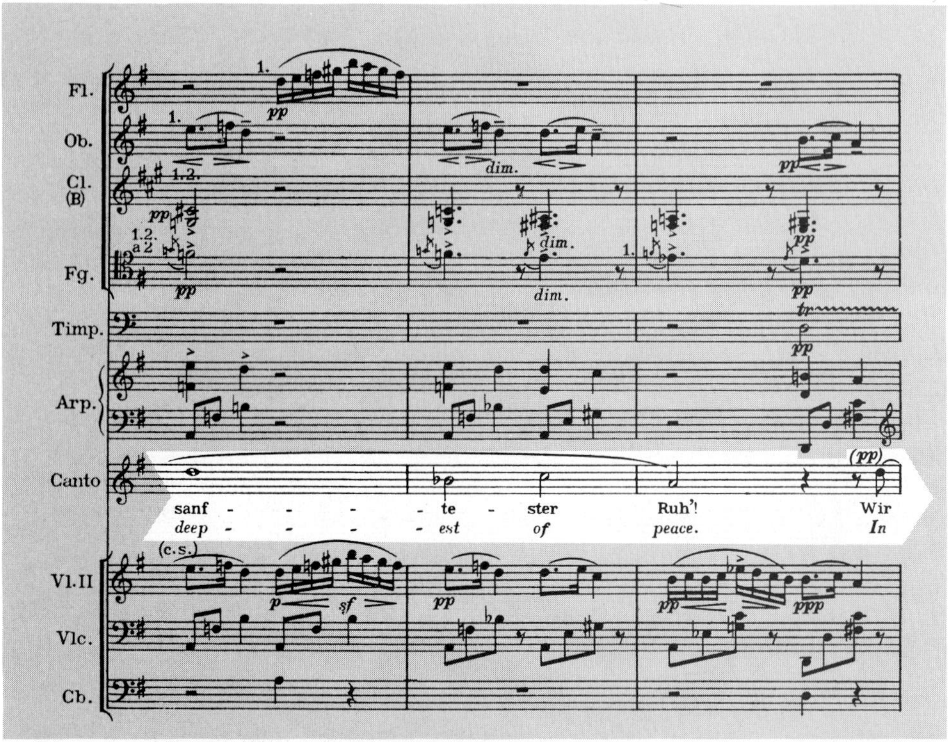

Fl.
Ob.
Cl. (B)
Fg.
Timp.
Arp.
Canto
sanf - - - - - te - ster Ruh'! Wir
deep - - - - - est of peace. In
(c.s.)
Vl.II
Vlc.
Cb.

Fließend
2 Scorrevole
25
Fl.
etwas hervortretend
un poco rilevato
Cor. ingl.
Cl. (B)
staccatiss.
Canto
füh - ren ein eng - li-sches Le - ben! Sind den-noch ganz lu - stig, ganz
way that's an - gel - ic we're liv - - ing, it's due though to mer - ri-ment, to
Vl.I
Vla.
pizz.
2 25

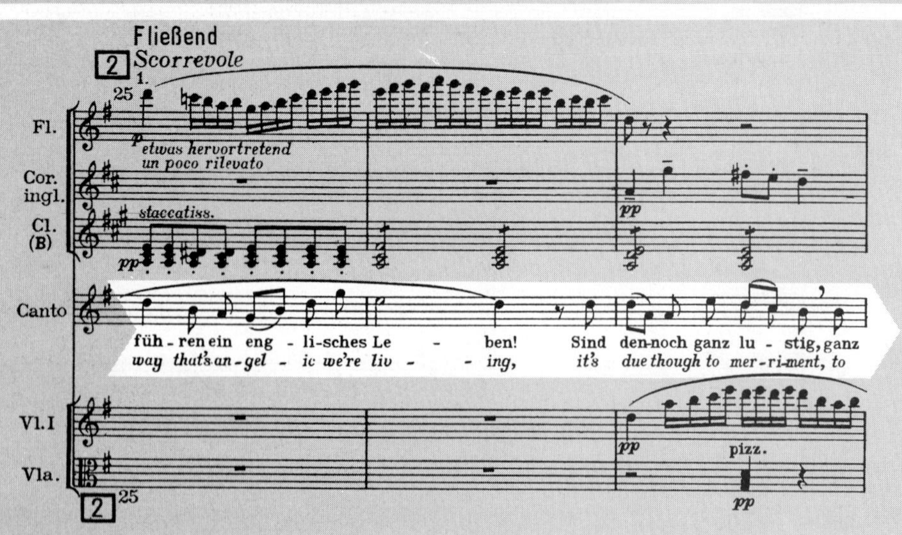

30
Fl.
Picc.
Cl. (B)
Cor.
Canto
lu - stig da - ne - ben! Wir füh-ren ein en - gli-sches Le - ben, wir
mer-ri-ment e'er giv - ing, in way that's an-gel - ic we're liv - ing, a -
con sord.
Vl. I
Vla.
Vlc.
arco
div.
stacc.
3. muta in Cl.b. in B-Sib
30

Nicht schleppen
Non stentare
Fl.
Picc.
Ob.
con sord.
Cor.
Trgl.
Arp.
Canto
tan - zen und sprin-gen, wir hüp - fen und sin - gen, wir sin - - - - -
danc - ing and spring-ing, a - skip - ping and sing - ing, yes sing - - - -
Nicht schleppen
Vl.-S.
senza sord.
Vl. I
(c.s.)
arco
Vl. II
senza sord.
stacc.
Vla.
dim.

Etwas drängend
Poco stringendo
Plötzlich zurückhaltend
Ritardando subito
rit.
35
Fl.
Picc.
Ob.
Cor.
(c.s.)
con sord.
senza sord.
a 2 offen
Ptti.
mit Schwammschlägel
con bacchetta di spugna
Arp.
Canto
gen!
ing.
Sankt
Saint
Pe-ter im Himmel sieht zu!
Pe-ter in heav-en looks on.
Etwas drängend
Plötzlich zurückhaltend rit.
Vl.S.
Vl.I
Vl.II
Vla.
Vlc.
Cb.
(con sord.)
morendo
div.
arco

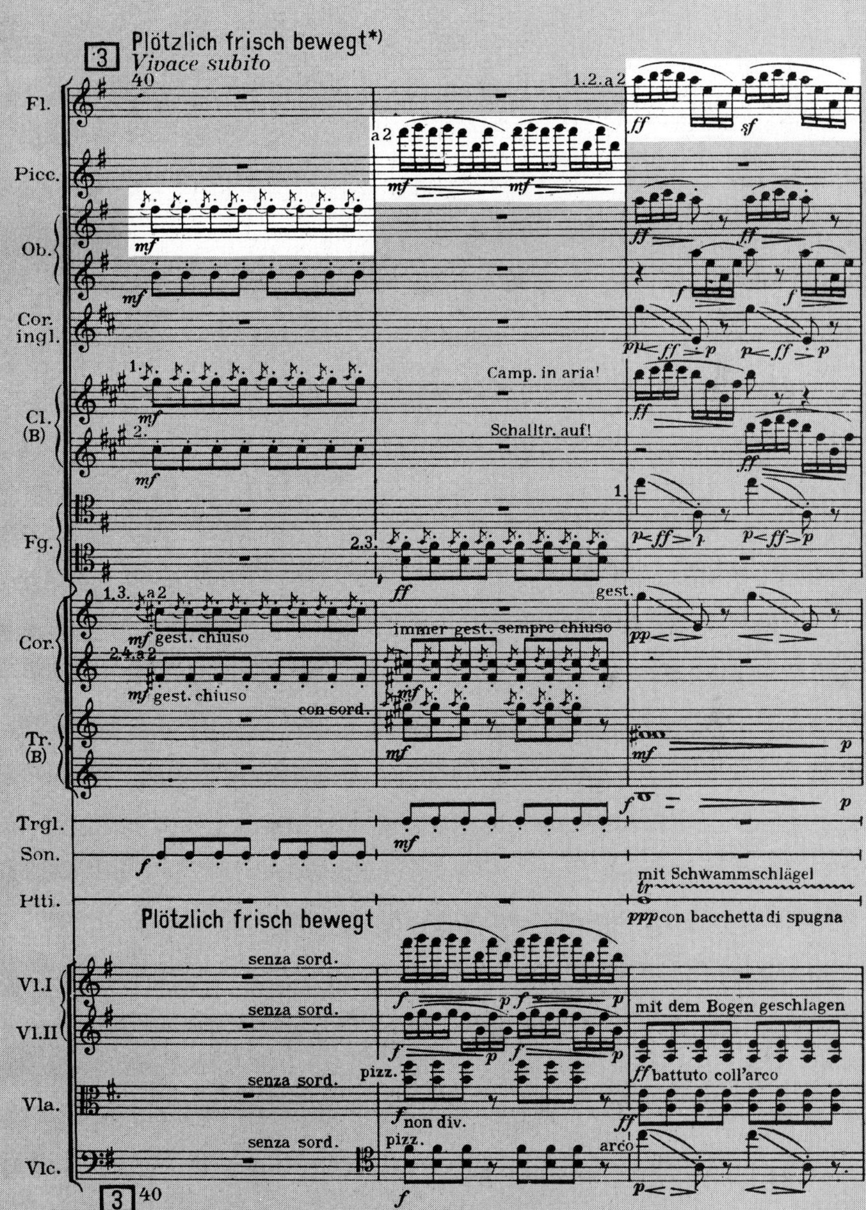
3
Plötzlich frisch bewegt*)
Vivace subito
40
Fl.
Picc.
Ob.
Cor. ingl.
Cl. (B)
Fg.
Cor.
Tr. (B)
Trgl.
Son.
Ptti.
Camp. in aria!
Schalltr. auf!
gest. chiuso
immer gest. sempre chiuso
con sord.
mit Schwammschlägel
ppp con bacchetta di spugna
Plötzlich frisch bewegt
senza sord.
Vl.I
Vl.II
Vla.
Vlc.
mit dem Bogen geschlagen
ff battuto coll'arco
pizz.
non div.
arco
3 40
*) Hier muß dieses Tempo bewegter genommen werden, als an den korrespondierenden Stellen im ersten Satze
*) Questo tempo deve essere portato più mosso che nel primo movimento

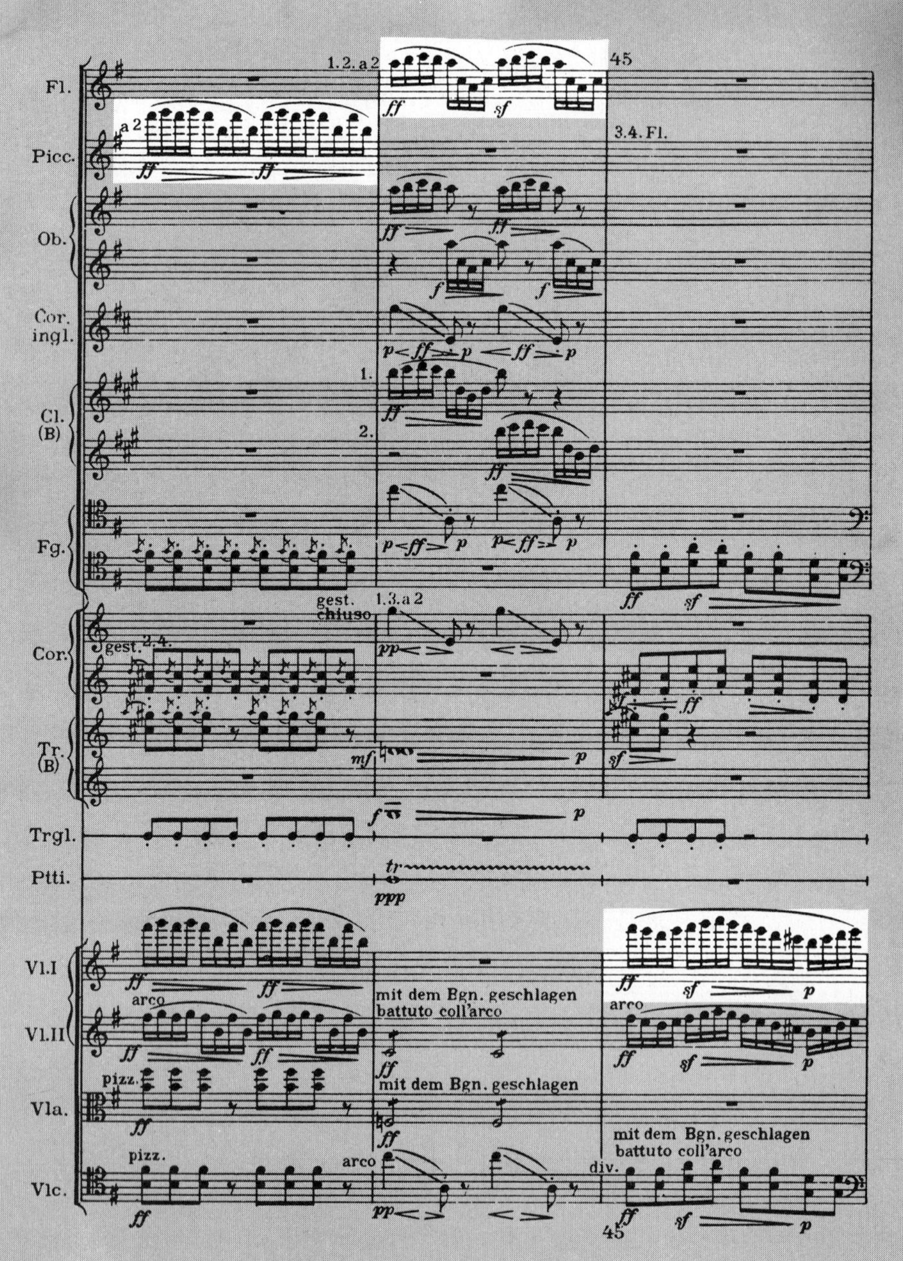

Fl.
1.2. a 2
45
Picc.
a 2
3.4. Fl.
Ob.
Cor. ingl.
Cl. (B)
1.
2.
Fg.
Cor.
gest.
chiuso
1.3. a 2
gest. 2.4.
Tr. (B)
Trgl.
Ptti.
Vl. I
Vl. II
arco
mit dem Bgn. geschlagen
battuto coll'arco
Vla.
pizz.
Vlc.
div.
45

4
1.2. a 2
ff sf p
Fl.
3.4. a 2
ff p
ff p
1.2. a 2
Ob.
ff sf p
f
Cor. ingl.
ff sf p
1.2.
a 2
Cl. (B)
ff sf p
f
Cl.b. (B)
ff
1.-3. a 3
Fg.
ff
1. offen
f
2. 4. gest. chiuso
aperto
Cor.
f
ff
3. offen
ff
Trgl.
mf p pp
div.
Vl.II
f p
Vla.
f p
Vlc.
f p
4
f

50
1. 2. a 2
Fl.
1. 2. a 2
Ob.
Cor. ingl.
1. 2. a 2
Cl. (B)
Cl. b. (B)
1. 2. a 2
Fg.
3.
1.
Cor.
2. 4.
3.
2.
3. 4. a 2
Tr. (B)
3. con sord.
Pk.
Arp.
Vlc.
50

Fl.
1.2. a 2
fp
ff
3.4. a 2
p
Ob.
1.2. a 2
a 2
f
p
Cor. ingl.
fp
ff
p
Cl. (B)
1.2. a 2
Cl.b. (B)
ff
Fg.
1.2.a 2
2.
1.
3.
ff
f
p
1.2.a 2
Cor.
1.2.a 2
3.4.a 2
gest.
chiuso
gest.
mf
offen-aperto
in F - Fa
Tr. (B)
fp
f
p
Trgl.
Son.
Ptti.
tr
p mit Schwammschlägel
con bacchetta di spugna
Vl.I
mf col legno
Vl.II
mf col legno
Vla.
con sord.
arco
senza sord.
Vlc.
con sord.
arco
senza sord.
ff

55
5 Etwas zurückhaltend
Poco ritardando
Fl.
Ob.
Cor. ingl.
Cl. (B)
Cl.b. (B)
Fg.
Pk.
Ptti.
Canto
Jo - han - nes das Lämm - lein aus-
Saint John and his lamb have been
mit dem Bogen schlagen
battere coll'arco
Etwas zurückhaltend
Vl. I
Vl. II
con sord.
Vla
con sord.
mit dem Bogen schlagen
battere coll'arco
Vlc.
Cb.
pizz.
55
5

1.2.3.
60
Fl.
Ob.
Cor. ingl.
Cl. (B)
Fg.
Canto
las - set, der Metz - ger He-ro - des drauf pas - set! Wir
part - ed, and Her - od to catch it has start - ed. An
Vl. II
Vla.
c.s. div.
pp stacc.

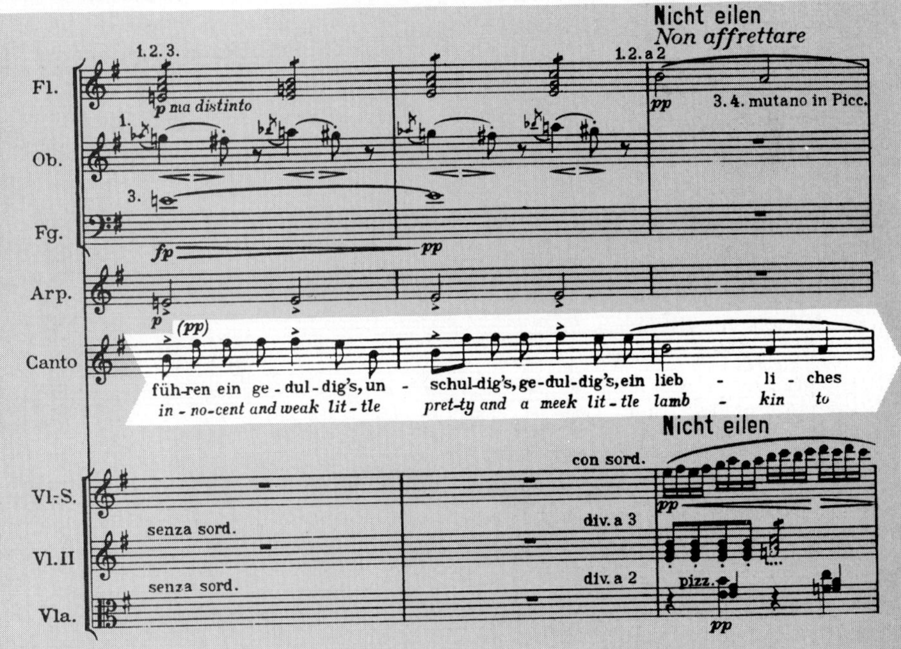
Nicht eilen
Non affrettare
p ma distinto
3.4. mutano in Picc.
Fl.
Ob.
Fg.
Arp.
Canto
füh-ren ein ge-dul-dig's, un - schul-dig's, ge-dul-dig's, ein lieb - li - ches
in-no-cent and weak lit-tle pret-ty and a meek lit-tle lamb - kin to
Nicht eilen
con sord.
Vl. S.
senza sord.
div. a 3
Vl. II
senza sord.
div. a 2
pizz.
Vla.

1.2. a 2
65
6
Fl.
Picc.
Cl. (B)
Fg.
Canto
Lämm - lein zu Tod! Sanct Lu - cas den Och - sen tät
slaugh - ter is led. Saint Luke is the ox - en a -
Vl.-S.
Vl.II
Vla.
Vlc.
con sord.
arco
pp
65
6
1.2. a 2
Fl.
Picc.
Cl. (B)
Cl.b. (B)
Fg.
offen aperto
Cor.
Canto
schlach - ten ohn' ei - nig's Be - den - ken und Ach - ten, der
slay - ing, he does it wi - thout all de - lay - ing, in
arco
con sord. non div.
Vla.
pp stacc.
con sord. non div.
Vlc.
Cb. Solo con sord. arco
Cb.

Wieder zurückhaltend
Di nuovo ritardando
70
75
1.2.
Fl.
Picc.
Cl. (B)
Cl.b. (B)
Fg.
Cor.
4. offen
Trgl.
Arp.
non arpegg.
Canto
Wein kost kein Hel-ler im himm-lischen Kel-ler, die Eng-lein, die bak-ken das Brot.
heav-en - ly cel-lar the wine costs no hel-ler! The an - gels they bake all the bread.
Wieder zurückhaltend
con sord.
senza sord.
Vl.I
Vl.II
Vla.
Vlc.
Cb.
(c.s.)
Solo
Tutti

7
Wieder lebhaft
Di nuovo vivace
Fl.
Picc.
Ob.
Cor. ingl.
Cl. (B)
Cl.b. (B)
Fg.
Cor.
Tr. (F)
Trgl.
Son.
Ptti.
1.2. a 2
3.4. Fl.
Schalltrichter auf!
(3. Cl. in B-Sib)
gest. chiuso
3.4. gest.
con sord.
(c. s.)
a 2
mit Schwammschl.
con baccetta di spugna
Wieder lebhaft
col legno
Vl. I
Vl. II
Vla.
Vlc.
Cb.
arco
7

Tempo I.
1.2. a 2
80
Fl.
ff
Solo
Ob.
1.
pp
Cor. ingl.
pp
Cl. (B)
1.
Cor.
ff
p
Son.
Arp.
pp
Canto
Gut' Kräu - ter von al - - ler-hand
All man - ner of herbs u - ro -
Tempo I.
con sord.
arco
Vl. I
pp
Vl. II
con sord.
arco
pp
Vla.
con sord.
arco
pp
Vlc.
con sord.
arco
pp
Cb.
pizz.
pp
80

1.
85
Ob.
Cor. ingl.
morendo
1.2.
Cl. (B)
3.
Arp.
Canto
Ar - ten, die wach-sen im himm-li-schen Gar - ten! Gut' Spar-gel, Fi-
mat - ic, they grow in our gar - den ec - stat - ic. As-par - a-gus
(c. s.)
div.
Vl. I
Vl. II
Vla.
Vlc.
85

8
Allmählich, aber sehr unmerklich bewegter
Poco a poco insensibilmente più mosso
Fl.
Cor. ingl.
Cl. (B)
offen 1.
aperto
3.4. offen
2.offen
aperto
Cor.
Timp.
Arp.
Canto
so - len und was wir nur wol-len! Gan-ze Schüsseln voll sind uns be - reit!
sal-ad, de-lights to the pal-ate! On great platters for us there a - bound.
Allmählich, aber sehr unmerklich bewegter
Vl. I
sempre pp
pizz.
senza sord.
Vl. II
Vla.
senza sord.
pizz.
senza sord.
Vlc.
div.
Cb.
8

90
Fl.
Ob.
Cl. (B)
Fg.
Cor.
Tr. (F)
Trgl.
Son.
Canto
Vl. I
Vl. II
Vla.
Vlc.
Cb.
1.2.
2.
sempre stacc.
con sord.
keck!
arditamente
Gut' Äp-fel, gut' Birn' und gut' Trau - ben! die Gärt-ner, die Al - les er -
Good ap-ples good pears and good peach - es, to eat them the garden-ers be -
sempre con sord.
non div.
Doppelgriff
pizz.
col legno
90

Etwas bewegter
Poco più mosso
95
Fl.
3.4. mutano in Picc.
Ob.
Cor. ingl.
Cl. (B)
Fg.
gest. chiuso
Cor.
Tr. (F)
1.2.
in B-Sib
mit Schwammschlägel, klingen lassen
con bacch. di spugna, lasci vibrare
Ptti.
Son.
Arp.
non arpeggiato
Canto
lau - ben! Willst Reh - bock, willst Ha - sen auf of - fe - ner
seech us. Wouldst roe - buck, wouldst pheas - ant, in num - bers they're
Etwas bewegter
Vl. I
Vl. II
Vla.
Vlc.
col legno
pizz.
95

9
Nicht schleppen
Non strascinare
Fl.
1.
2.
Ob.
Cor. ingl.
Cl. (B)
Cor.
1.2. offen-aperto
4. offen-aperto
Arp.
Canto
Stra-ßen sie lau - fen her-bei! Sollt ein Festtag et-wa kommen al-le Fische gleich mit
pres-ent and run - ning a - round. If for fast day food one wish-es, then with joy there come a -
Nicht schleppen
Vl. I
arco
Vl. II
arco
9

100
Fl.
1.
p
Ob.
1.
pp
Cor. ingl.
pp
Cl. (B)
pp
pp
Cor.
1.2.
4.
Trgl.
p
Arp.
p
Canto
Freu-den an-ge-schwommen! Dort läuft schon Sankt Pe - ter mit Netz und mit Kö - der zum
swimming all the fish - es. See yon-der Saint Pe - ter with nets runn-ing fleet - er than
senza sord.
pp
Vl. I
div.
con sord.
pp mit dem Bogen geschlagen
batťuto coll'arco
sempre pp
con sord.
Vl. II
pp mit dem Bogen geschlagen
battuto coll'arco
con sord.
Vla.
pp mit dem Bogen geschlagen
battuto coll'arco
con sord.
Vlc.
pp
100

105
Fl.
Ob.
Cor. ingl.
Cl. (B)
Timp.
Arp.
Canto
himm - li-schenWei - her hin - ein.
wind to the heav - en - ly brook.
Sankt
Saint
Vl. I
Vl. II
Vla.
Vlc.
morendo
105

10
Wieder plötzlich zurückhaltend
Di nuovo ritardando subito
110
rit.
Luftpause!
Respiro!
Fl.
Cl. (B)
Cor.
con sord.
senza sord.
deutlich
distinto
senza sord.
Tr. (B)
in F-Fa
Timp.
rein stimmen
ben accordato
Mit Schwammschlägel, klingen lassen
Ptti.
con bacch. di spugna, lasci vibrare
Arp.
Canto
Mar-tha die Kö-chin muß sein! Sankt Mar-tha die Kö-chin muß sein!
Mar-tha there must be the cook. Saint Mar-tha there must be the cook.
Wieder plötzlich zurückhaltend
Tutti div.
con sord.
Vl. I
Vl. II
Vla.
div. a 3
Vlc.
con sord. arco
Cb.
10

11
115
Wieder lebhaft
Di nuovo vivace
a 2
Fl.
Picc.
Ob.
Cor. ingl.
Cl. (B)
2.3. a 2
Fg.
1.2. a 2
gest. chiuso
offen - aperto
Cor.
mf stacc.
2.4. a 2 gest. chiuso
mf con sord.
Tr. (F)
mf con sord.
Trgl.
Son.
Wieder lebhaft
senza sord.
Vl. I
non div. Doppelgr.
mit dem Bogen geschlagen
battuto coll'arco
Vl. II
Vla.
Vlc.
div.
11
115

1.2.a 2
120
Fl.
Ob.
Cor. ingl.
Cl. (B)
1.
2.3.a 2
2.
Fg.
a 2
Cor.
1.3.a 2
2.4.a 2
a 2
Trgl.
Son.
Vl. I
Vl. II
Vla.
Vlc.
Cb.
senza sord.
p mit dem Bogen geschlagen
battuto coll'arco
120

12
Tempo I. Sehr zart und geheimnisvoll bis zum
Molto tenero e misterioso sino al fine
Cor. ingl.
mf
pp
1.2. a 2
1.2. in A-La
Cl. (B)
3. muta in Cl.b. in B-Sib
Son.
Arp.
sempre p
Tempo I. Sehr zart und geheimnisvoll bis zum
pizz.
Vlc.
ppp
Cb.
12

Schluß
125
Fl.
ppp
Cor. ingl.
Arp.
Schluß
con sord.
Vl. I
ppp
Vla.
con sord.
ppp
Vlc.
125

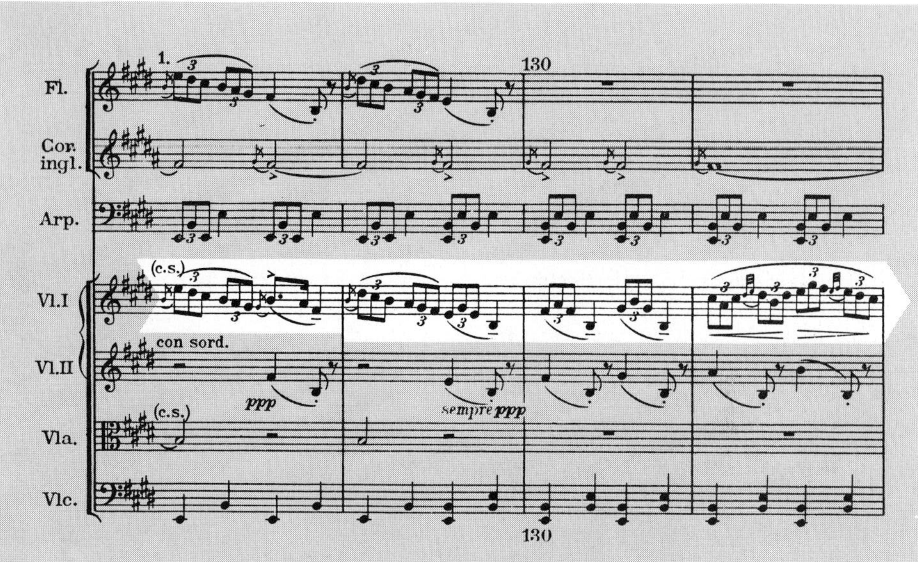
1.
130
Fl.
Cor. ingl.
Arp.
(c.s.)
Vl. I
con sord.
Vl. II
ppp
sempre ppp
(c.s.)
Vla.
Vlc.
130

1.
135
Fl.
pp
Cor. ingl.
morendo
2.4.a 2
Cor.
pp
Arp.
(c.s.)
Vl. I
(c.s.)
Vl. II
sf
(c.s.)
Vla.
pp
con sord.
arco
Vlc.
ppp
arco
Cb.
ppp
135

Cor. ingl.
Cl. (A)
Cl.b. (B)
Cor.
Arp.
Vl.I
Vl.II
Vla.
Vlc.
Cb.
1.
2.4.a 2
(c.s.)
pizz.
pp
p

13

140

Fl. 1. *pp*

Cor. ingl. *ppp*

Cl. (A) 1. *pp*

Cl. b. (B) *pp* *dim.*

Fg. 1. *pp*

Cor. 2.4. a 2

Arp.

Sehr zart und geheimnisvoll bis zum Schluß

Molto tenero e misterioso sino al fine

Canto

Kein Mu-sik ist ja ______ nicht auf Er-den, die

No mu-sic on earth ______ e'er so stirring with

Vl. I sempre sord. *ppp*

Vl. II sempre sord. *ppp*

Vla. sempre sord. *ppp*

Vlc. sempre sord. *ppp*

Cb. arco *ppp*

140

13

145
Cor. ingl.
Cl. (A)
1.
mf
p
Cl. b. (B)
pp
Arp.
Canto
uns-rer ver-gli-chen kann wer-den.
ours — can stand the com - pa-ring.
Elf - tau - send Jung-frau - en zu
Ten thou - sand young vir - gins to
Vl. I
(c.s.)
ppp
Vl. II
(c.s.)
Vla.
(c.s.)
Vlc.
(c.s.)
Cb.
pizz.
145

150
riten.
Cl. b. (B)
1.3. a 2
Cor.
2.4. a 2
Trgl.
Arp.
Canto
tan - zen sich trau - en!
danc - ing it ur - ges!
Sankt Ur - - - - -
With laugh - - - - -
(c. s.)
Vl. I
Vl. II
Vla.
pizz.
arco
Vlc.
Cb.
150

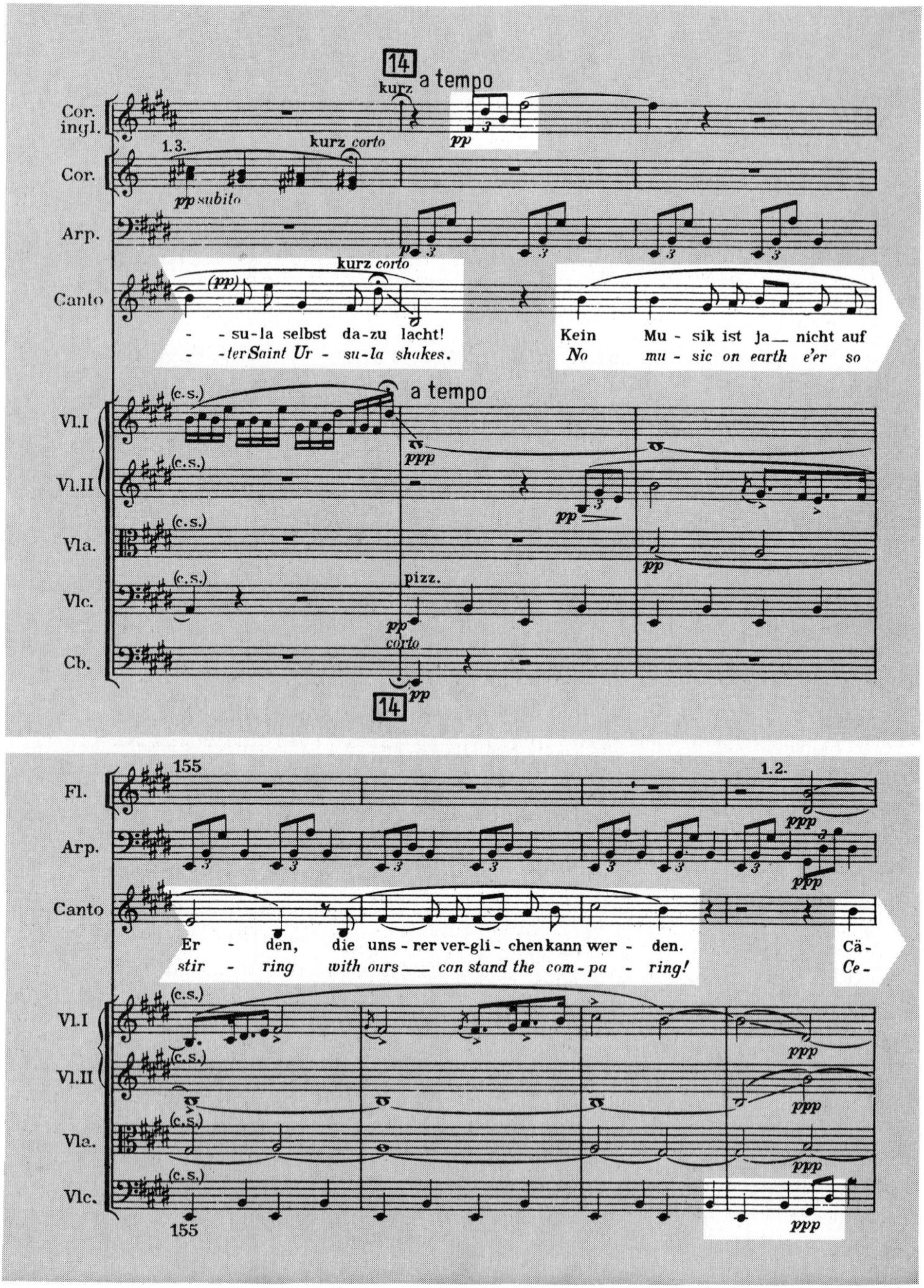

14 a tempo

- - su-la selbst da-zu lacht! Kein Mu - sik ist ja nicht auf
- - ter Saint Ur - su-la shakes. No mu - sic on earth e'er so

Fl.
Ob.
Cor. ingl.
Arp.
Canto
Vl.I
Vl.II
Vla.
Vlc.
1.2.
160
ppp
pp
sf
(c.s.)
ci - lia mit ih - ren Ver - wand - - - - - - ten sind
ci - lia with all her re la- - - - - - - tions are

Ob.
Cor. ingl.
Cl. (A)
Arp.
Canto
Vl.I
Vl.II
Vla.
Vlc.
Cb.
1.2.
div.
ppp
pp
(c.s.)
treff - li-che Hof - mu - si - kan - ten!
ex - cel-lent court mu - si - cians.
Die
Of

15 165
Fl.
Cor. ingl.
Cl. (A)
Arp.
Canto
eng - li-schen Stim-men er - mun - tern die Sin - nen, er - mun- tern die Sin - nen!
sweet an-gels' voi - ces a cho - rus re-joic - es, a cho - rus re - joic - es!
Vl.I
Vl.II
Vla.
Vlc.
Cb.
15 165
1.2.a 2
170
Fl.
Cor. ingl.
Cl. (A)
Arp.
Canto
daß al - les für Freu - den, für Freu -
To pleas - ure, to pleas - ure it all
Vl.I
Vl.II
Vla.
Vlc.
Cb.
170

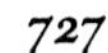

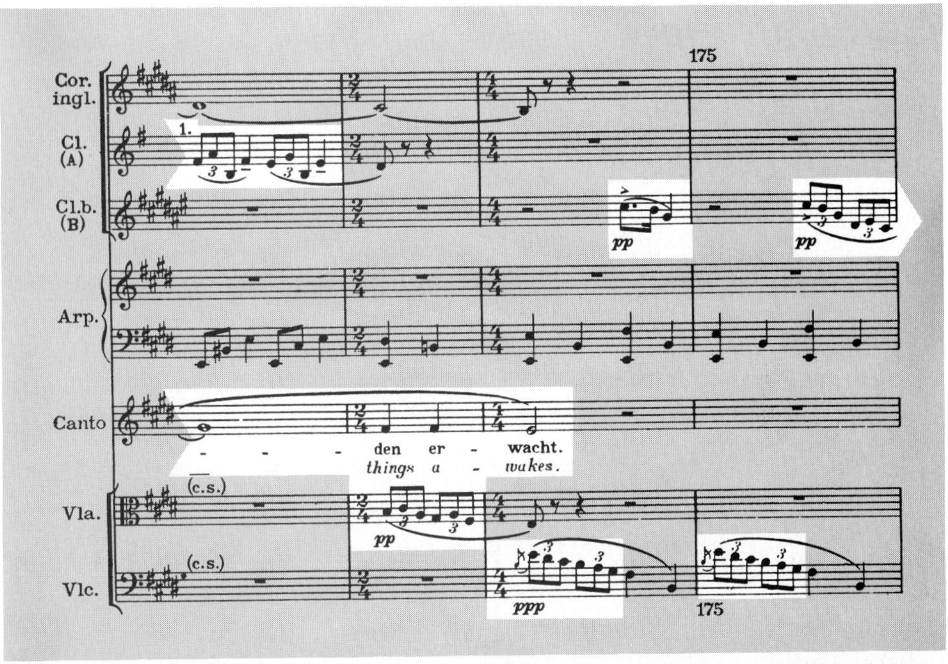

175
Cor. ingl.
Cl. (A)
1.
Cl.b. (B)
pp
pp
Arp.
Canto
den er wacht.
things a wakes.
(c.s.)
Vla.
pp
(c.s.)
Vlc.
ppp
175

180
Cor. ingl.
ppp
morendo
Cl.b. (B)
morendo
2.4.
Cor.
pp morendo
Arp.
sich Zeit lassen!
non affrettare!
morendo
pp
c.s.
Vlc.
morendo
arco
Cb.
180
ppp
morendo

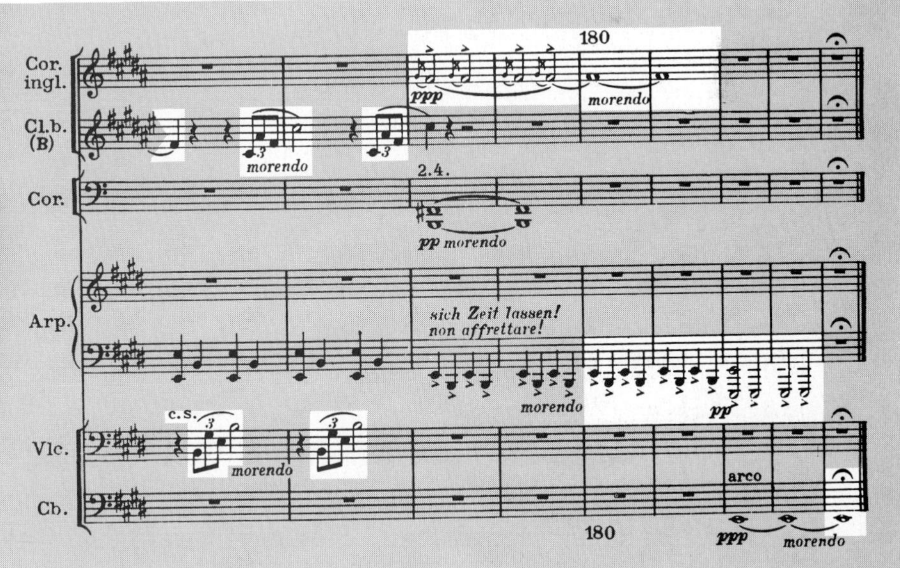

23. CLAUDE DEBUSSY (1862-1918), *Prelude to "The Afternoon of a Faun"* (1894)

HAUTB.
CL.
CORS
1re HARPE
glissando
2e HARPE
(sourdine)
Div.
pp
p
ppp

1
1re FL.
SOLO
p
HAUTB.
p
expressif
CL.
pp
pp
Bons
1o
p
1o
p
CORS
3o
p
1
Div. (sur la touche)
pp
(sur la touche)
pp
(sur la touche)
pp
à 2
pp

Fl.
1° et 2°
p cre - scen - do f
Hautb.
à 2
Cor Angl.
Cl.
dim. et retenu
Bons
Cors
1. 2.
3. 4.
dim.
Div.
cresc.
position nat.
Unies.

2

1re FL. SOLO *légèrement et expressif*

p

2°

CORS

pp

4°

pp

1re HARPE

pp

2e HARPE

pp

2

pp

pp

Div.

pp

pizz.

pp

1er FL.
Cl.
Bons
1o
1er COR
1o
1re HARPE
pp
2e HARPE
pp
Unis
pizz.
pp
Unis.

Fl.
2°
Cl.
Bons
Cors
2e et 4o
1re Harpe
2e Harpe p
Div.
arco
Div.
arco
arco

Fl.
Bons
Div.
Unis
Unis
tim.
dim.
Div.
dim.
Div.
arco

3
1re Fl.
Cl
1o
sourdines
sourdines
Cors
1re Harpe
3
ôtez vite les sourdines
ôtez vite les sourdines
ôtez vite les sourdines
pizz.

1re FL.
CL.
Bons
1o
CORS
1re HARPE
pizz.
arco
Div.
tr
mf
p
sfz
pp

4
En animant
1re FL.
f
HAUTB.
1° SOLO
doux et expressif
CL.
Bons
1°
p
p
CORS
1re HARPE
p
f
p
4
En animant
pizz.
sfz
Div.
arco
pizz.
sfz
p
p
pizz
sfz
arco
p
p
pizz.
sfz
p
Unis
p

HAUTB.
(à 2)
cre - - scen - - do *mf*

COR ANGL.
cre - - scen - - do *mf*

CL.
1°
cresc.
(2)

B^ons
cresc.
mf

1. 2.
cresc.

CORS

3. 4.
p
3°
mf

arco
cresc.
mf

cre - - scen - - do *mf*

cre - - scen - - do *mf*

arco
cre - - scen - - do *mf*

Div.
p
arco
mf

5
Toujours en animant
1°
FL.
2° 3°
cresc.
HAUTB.
2°
COR ANGL.
CL.
Changez en Sib
à 2
Bons
CORS
Div.
Div.
Unis

FL.
HAUTB.
COR ANGL.
CL.
BONS
CORS
Div.
mf
f
f très en dehors
f (en dehors)
3o (en dehors)
1o
più f
dim.

retenu
6
1.er mouv!
1°
dim.
FL.
2° 3°
2°
ppp
HAUTB.
1°
COR ANGL.
Solo
CL.
p doux et expressif
B.ons
CORS
dim.
1.re HARPE
2.e HARPE
Div.
pizz.

Même mouvt et très soutenu
p expressif et très soutenu
mf
Fl.
Hautb.
p expressif et très soutenu
mf
Cor Angl.
p expressif et très soutenu
mf
Cl.
p expressif et très soutenu
mf
Bons
pp
pp
p
Cors
(3. 4.)
pp
pp
Même mouvt et très soutenu
p
pp
pp
pp
arco
pp
pp
pp
pp

7
p cre - - scen - do f
FL. 2° et 3°
HAUTB.
à 2
COR ANGL.
CL.
B^ons
1°
cresc
mf
1.2.
CORS
3.4.
4°
7
cresc
pp
Unis
Div.
do

cre
pp subito
Fl.
pp subito
cre
Hautb.
pp subito
Cor Angl.
pp subito
Cl.
pp subito
cre
Bons
pp
à 2
pp
Cors
cre
1re Harpe
pp
cre
2e Harpe
pp
cre
Unis
très expressif et très soutenu
pp subito
cre
pp subito
cre
pp subito
cre
pp subito
cre
Div.
pp
cre

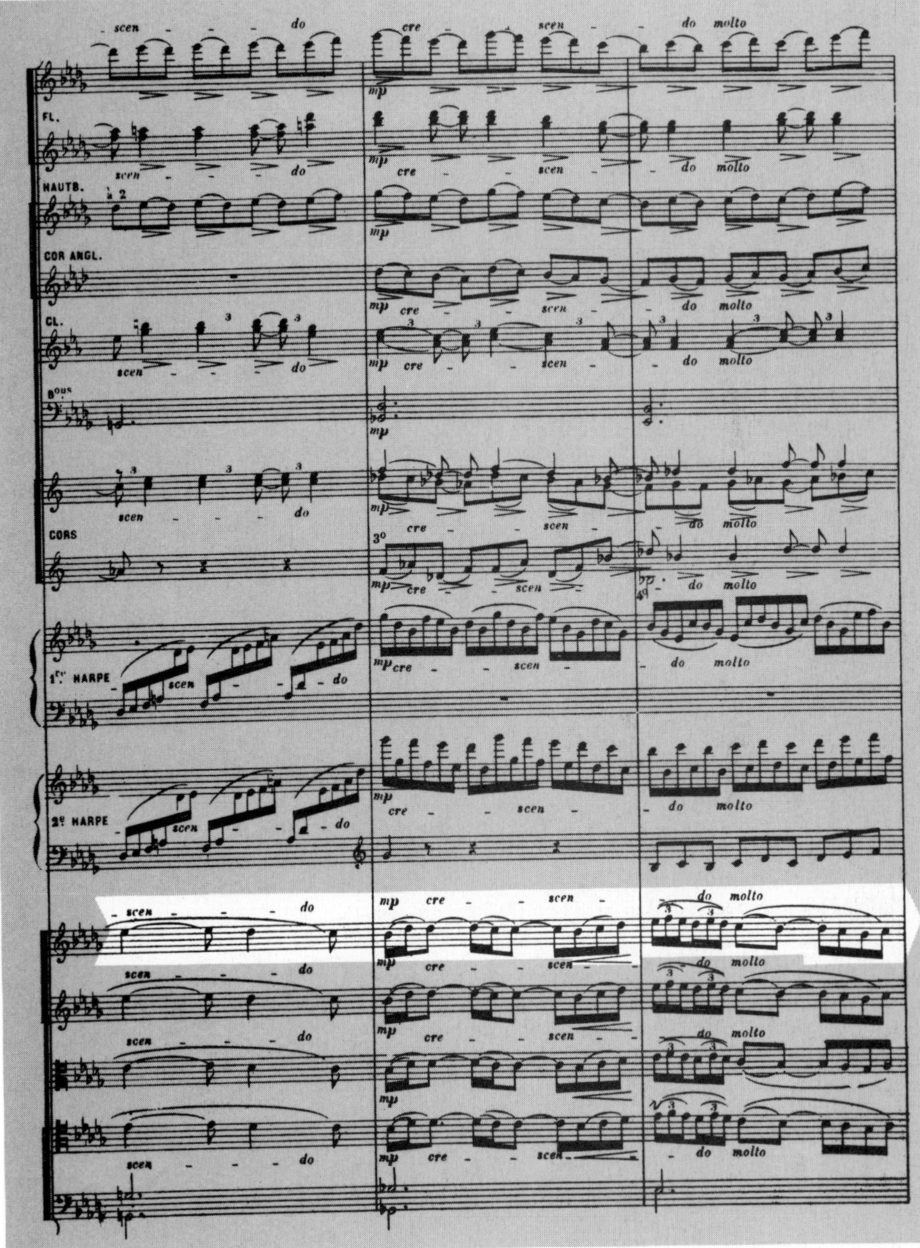
FL.
HAUTB.
à 2
COR ANGL.
CL.
Bons
CORS
3o
1re HARPE
2e HARPE
scen - - - do
cre - scen - - do molto
mp

FL.
HAUTB.
COR ANGL.
CL.
BONS
à 2
CORS
1re HARPE
2e HARPE

Fl.
Cl.
1°
mf
Bons
Cors
2°
1re Harpe
f
sfz
1er Von solo
p très doux
p espressif et doux
p doux et expressif
sourdines
Div.
p
pp

1rs FL. **8** **Mouvt du Début**

doux et expressif

p

HAUTB.

CL.

CORS

pp

1re HARPE

Vons SOLO **8** **Mouvt du Début** (1rs Vns)

Div.

pp

Div.

pp

Div.

pp

Div.

pp

Un peu plus animé
1re FL.
HAUTB.
CL.
Bons
sourdines
CORS
1. 2.
3. 4.
3°
1re HARPE
préparez le ton de Mib
Un peu plus animé
pizz.

1
FL.
2. 3.
pp
HAUTB.
p
sfz
pp
COR ANGL.
pp
CL.
p
pp
pp
pp
B^ous
p
pp
pp
1°
pp
pp
pp
CORS
pp
pp
sur la touche
pp
arco
sur la touche
pp
arco
sur la touche
pp
pp
arco
pp
pizz
arco
sur la touche
Div.
pp
pp
arco
pp
pizz
arco
pp

9 1er mouvt
HAUTB.
doux et expressif
p
CORS
pp
1re HARPE
2e HARPE accordez sur SI#-DO♮, RÉ#-MI♭, FA#-SOL♭, LA#-SI♭
9
1er mouvt
pos. nat.
pos. nat.
Div.
pos. nat.
Unis.
Div.
Div.

dans le mouvt plus animé
1.
FL.
2. 3.
HAUTB.
COR ANGL.
CL.
Changez en La♮
Bons
CORS
3o
1re HARPE
2e HARPE
glissando
dans le mouvt plus animé
pizz.
pizz.
pizz.
pizz.

1.
FL.
2. 3.
HAUTB.
COR ANGL.
CL.
BONS
CORS
1o cuivré
glissando
2e HARPE
arco
Div.
Unis.
pizz.

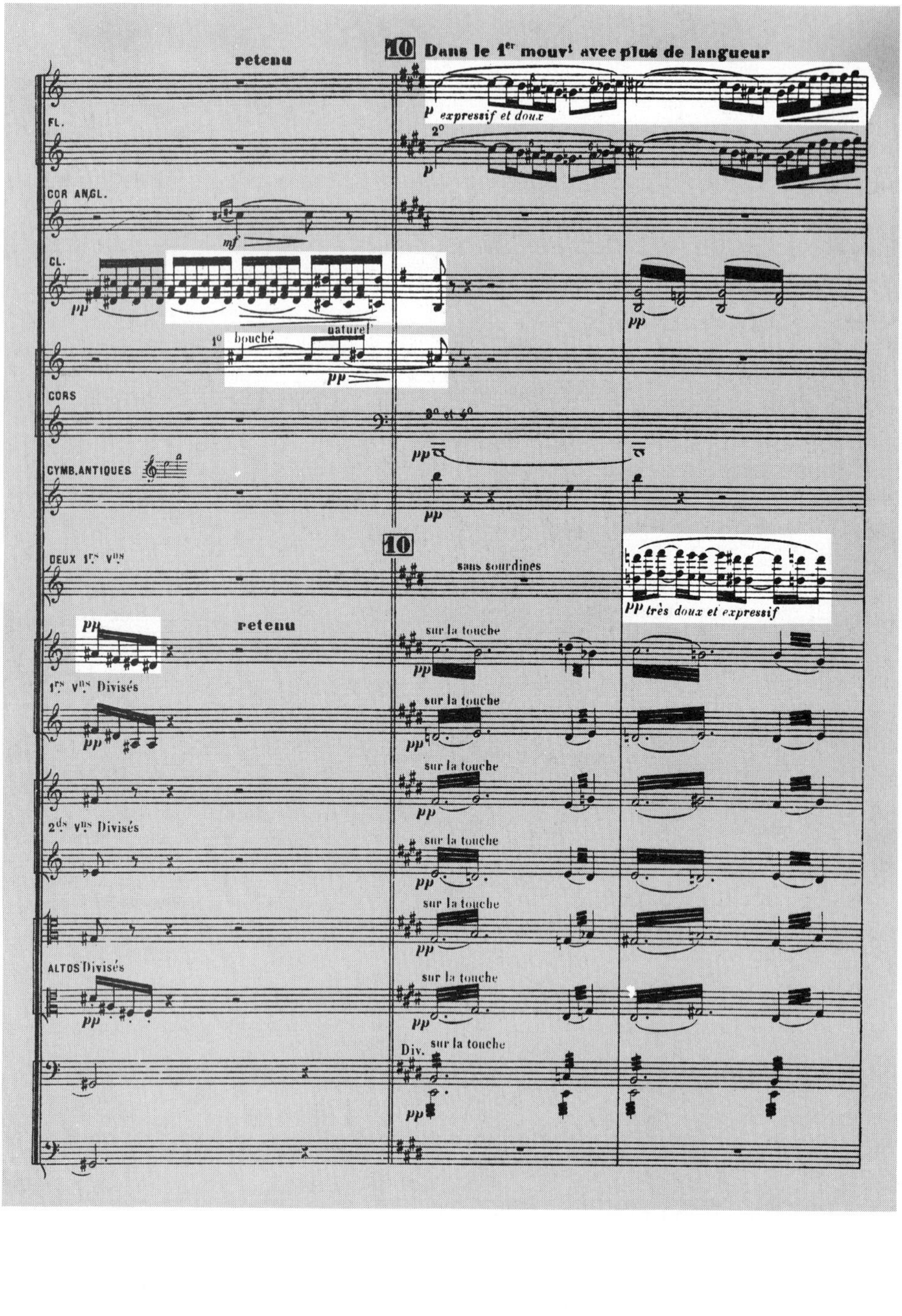

retenu

10 Dans le 1er mouvt avec plus de langueur

Fl.

p expressif et doux

2o

p

Cor angl.

mf

Cl.

pp

1o bouché

naturel

pp

Cors

3o et 4o

pp

Cymb. antiques

pp

10

Deux 1rs Vns

sans sourdines

pp très doux et expressif

pp

retenu

sur la touche

pp

1rs Vns Divisés

sur la touche

pp

sur la touche

pp

2ds Vns Divisés

sur la touche

pp

sur la touche

pp

Altos Divisés

sur la touche

pp

Div. sur la touche

pp

FL.
HAUTB.
CL.
à 2
B^ONS
1° sourdine
CORS
3° et 4°
CYMB. ANT.
1 V^lle SOLO

FL.
HAUTB.
CL.
B^ons
CORS
sourdine
CYMB. ANT.
1re HARPE
pos. nat.
pos. nat.
pos. nat.
pos. nat.
pos. nat.
pos. nat.
1 v^lle SOLO

11
Retenu
(a tempo)
Très retenu
1er FL.
HAUTB.
SOLO
COR ANGL.
CL.
Bons
CORS
2o
11
Très retenu
Retenu
(a tempo)

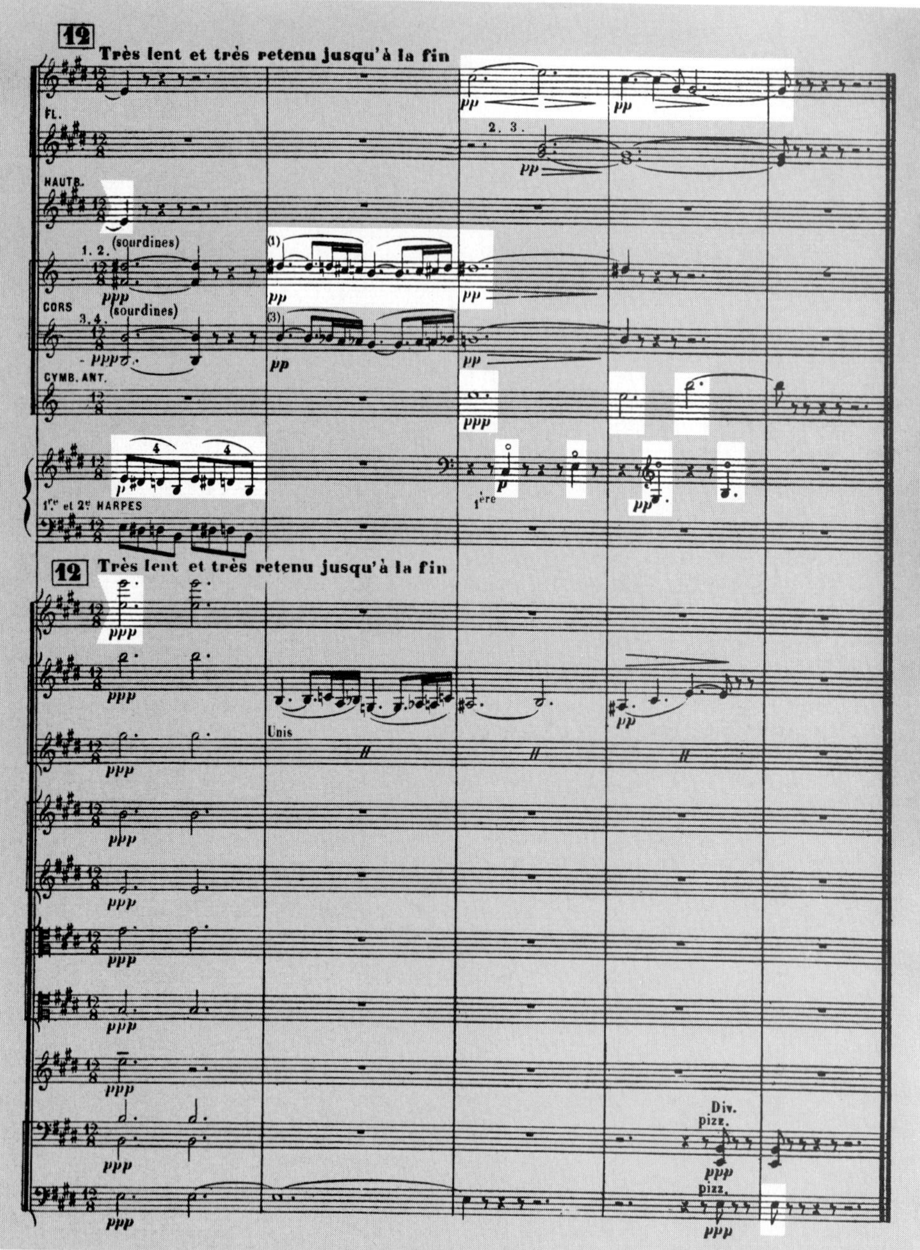
12
Très lent et très retenu jusqu'à la fin
FL.
2. 3.
HAUTB.
1. 2.
(sourdines)
CORS
3. 4.
(sourdines)
CYMB. ANT.
1ère
1re et 2e HARPES
12
Très lent et très retenu jusqu'à la fin
Unis
Div.
pizz.
pizz.

24. ARNOLD SCHOENBERG (1874-1951),
Excerpts from *Five Pieces for Orchestra*, Op. 16 (1909, REV. 1949)

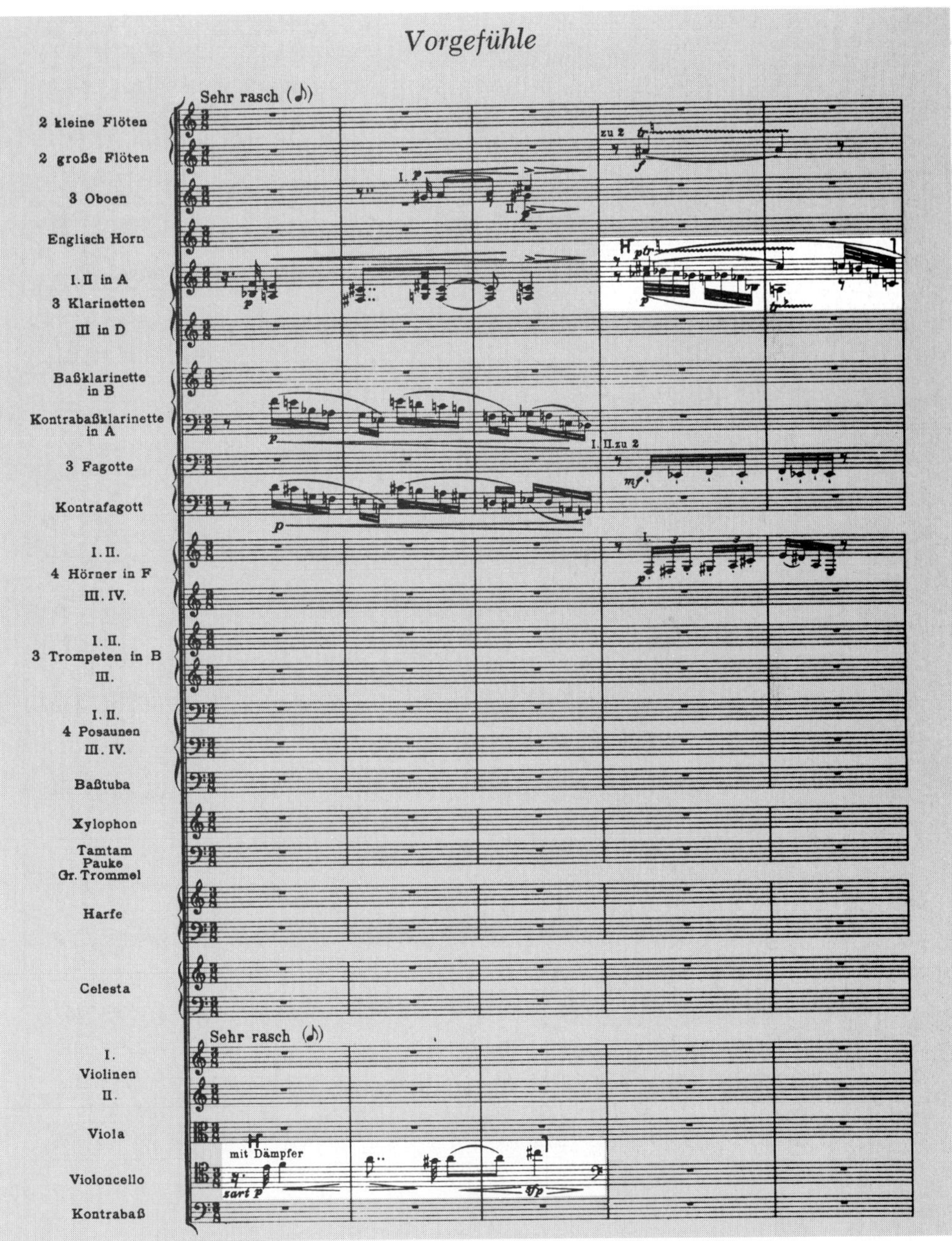

langsamer
rit.
sehr rasch
rit.
langsamer
Kl. Fl. I
Ob. I. II
Kbkl. in A
Fag. I. II
Hr. III in F
Pos. III
III mit Dämpfer
III. (Baß-Pos) mit Dämpfer
mit Dämpfer
pizz.
Viol.
Vcello.
Kb.
rasch
langsam
Fl. I. II
Ob. I
Engl. H.
Kl. in A
Bkl. in B
Fag. I. II
Kfag.
Hr. in F
Trp. I in B
Pos. II
III. u. Btba.
Hrfe.
alle 4 mit Dämpfer
alle 3 mit Dämpfer
arco
ohne Dämpfer
get. pizz.

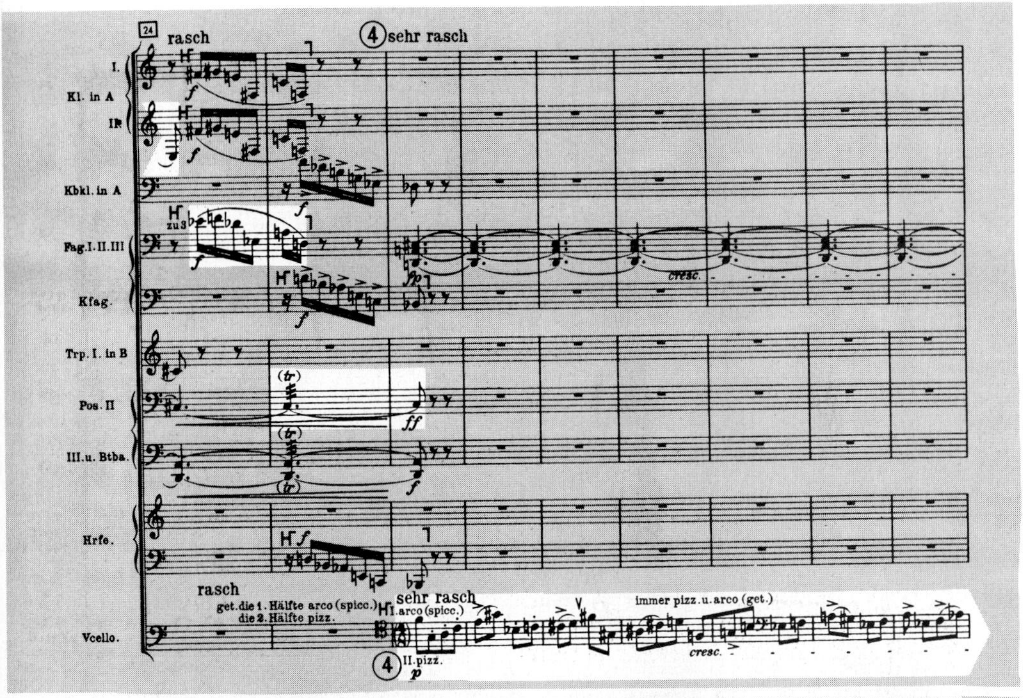

24
rasch
4 sehr rasch
I.
Kl. in A
II.
Kbkl. in A
zu 3
Fag. I. II. III
Kfag.
cresc.
Trp. I. in B
Pos. II
(tr)
III. u. Btba.
Hrfe.
rasch
get. die 1. Hälfte arco (spicc.)
die 2. Hälfte pizz.
sehr rasch
I. arco (spicc.)
immer pizz. u. arco (get.)
Vcello.
II. pizz.
cresc.

33
5
Kl. Fl. I. II
Gr. Fl. I. II
zu 2
Ob. I. II
Kl. I. II. in A
Fag. I. II. III
mit Dämpfer
Hr. III. IV. in F
mit Dämpfer
I. II.
Trp. in B
III.
alle 3 mit Dämpfer
get. die 1. Hälfte arco (kurz, spiccato) mit Dämpfer
die 2. Hälfte pizz.
arco (spicc.)
pizz.
Viola
Vcello.
4 fach
get. arco
pizz.

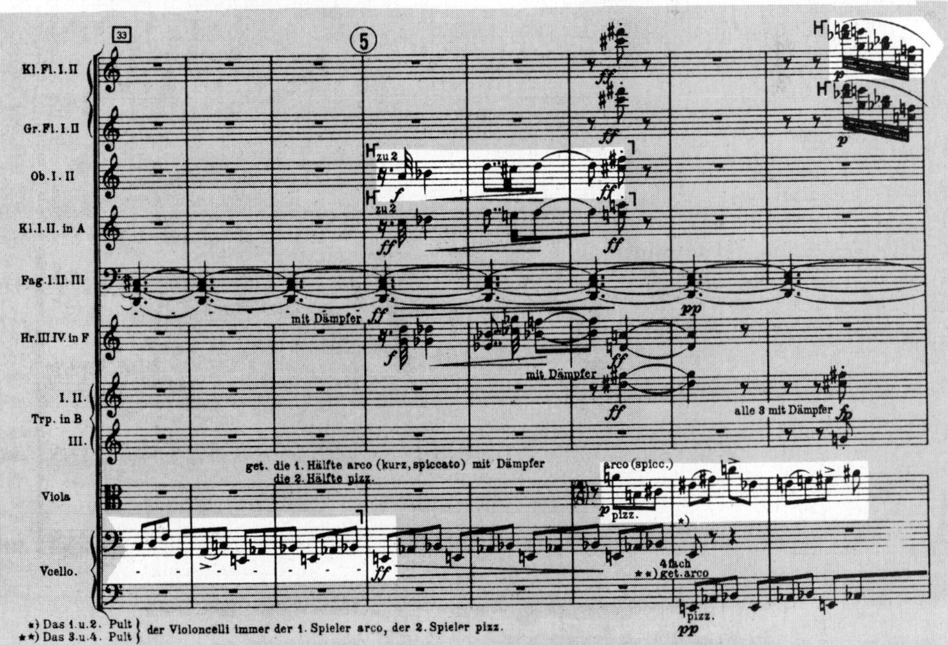

*) Das 1. u. 2. Pult
**) Das 3. u. 4. Pult } der Violoncelli immer der 1. Spieler arco, der 2. Spieler pizz.

41
6
Kl. Fl. I. II
Gr. Fl. I. II
I. II.
Ob.
III.
Engl. H.
Kl. I. II. in A
Kl. III. in D
Fag. I. II. III
cresc.
Hr. III. in F
mit Dämpfer
I. II.
Trp. in B
III.
Pos. I. II
III. u. Btba.
alle 4 mit Dämpfer
Viol. I.
pizz.
get.
ohne Dämpfer
3 fach get.
Viola
I.
Vcello.
II.
4 fach get.
get. der 1. arco
get. der 2. pizz.
arco
pizz.
Kb.
ohne Dämpfer
3 fach get.
arco
I.
II. III.
6

49
Kl. Fl. I. II
Gr. Fl. I. II
I. II.
Ob.
III.
Engl. H.
Kl. I. II. in A
Kl. III. in D
Fag. I. II. III
Hr. III. IV. in F
Trp. I. II. III. in B
Pos. III. IV
Xyl.
Tamt.
Celesta
I.
Viol.
II.
Viola
I. II.
Vcello.
III. IV.
zu 2
mit Dämpfer
mit Dämpfer
mit Dämpfer
mit Dämpfer
die 1. Hälfte arco
get.
die 2. Hälfte pizz.
get.
arco
pizz.
4 fach get.
arco
pizz.

7
57
Kl.Fl. I.II
Gr.Fl. I.II
I. II.
Ob.
III.
Engl. H.
Kl.I.II. in A
Kl.III. in D
Bkl. in B
Kbkl. in A
Fag. I.II.III
Kfag.
I. II.
Hr. in F
III. IV.
alle 4 mit Dämpfer
I. II
Trp. in B
III.
I. II.
Pos.
III. IV.
mit Dämpfer, so stark wie möglich
Btba.
Xyl.
hart
Pk.
I.
Viol.
II.
alle arco
arco
Viola
der 1. Sp. arco
alle arco
der 2. Sp. pizz.
I. II.
Vcello.
III. IV.
pizz.
Kb.
zu 2 I. III.
II. IV.
8
*) Das tiefe d muß dabei sein!

64
9
zu 2
Kl. Fl. I. II
Gr. Fl. I. II
I. II.
Ob.
III.
Engl. H.
Kl. I. II. in A
Kl. III. in D
Bkl. in B
Kbkl. in A
Fag. I. II. III
Kfag.
I. III.
Hr. in F
II. IV.
mit Dämpfer
Trp. I. II. in B
Pos. I. II
Xyl.
Viol. II
I. II.
Viola
III. IV.
Vcello.
Kb.
3 fach get.

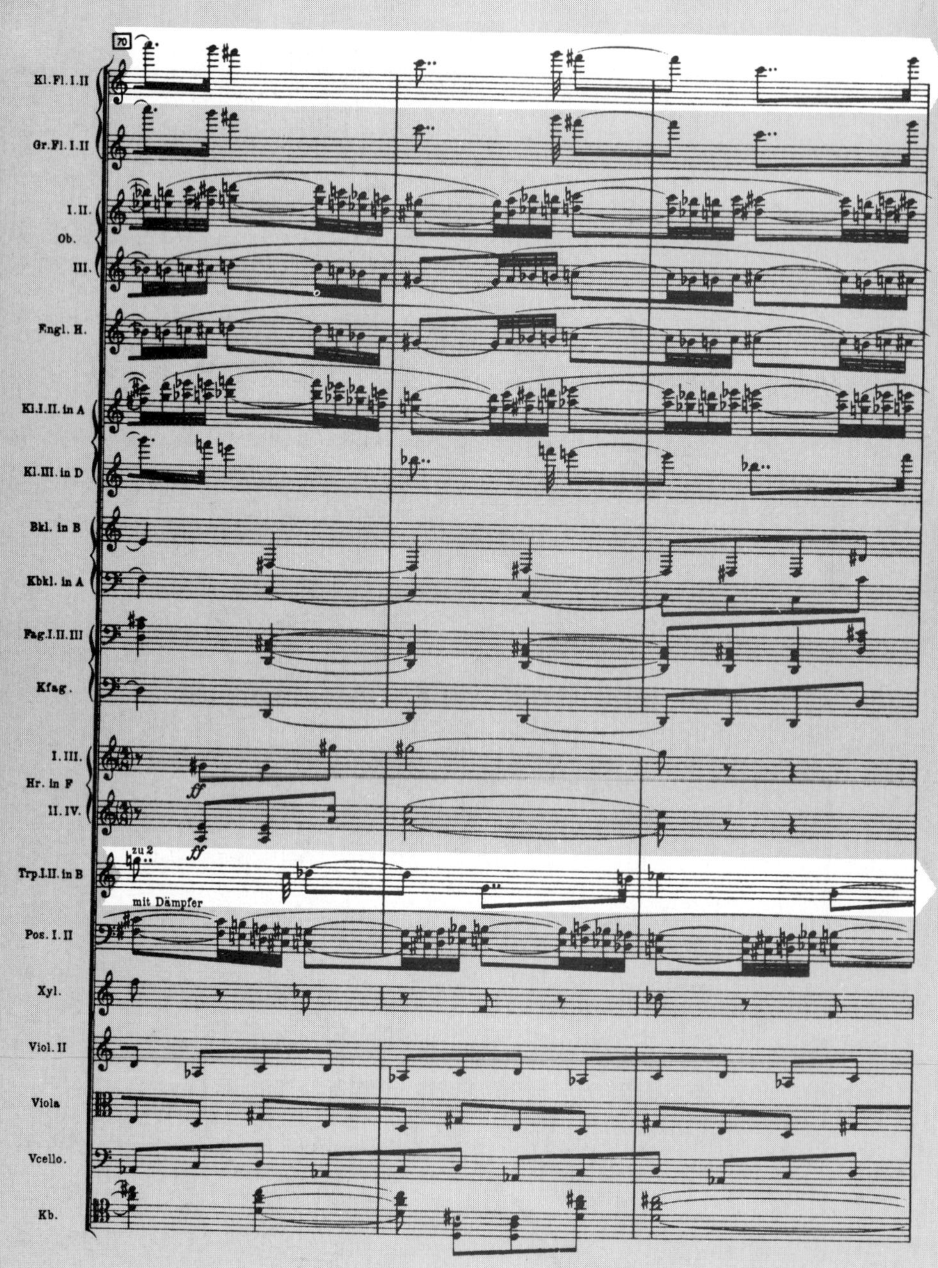
70
Kl. Fl. I. II
Gr. Fl. I. II
I. II.
Ob.
III.
Engl. H.
Kl. I. II. in A
Kl. III. in D
Bkl. in B
Kbkl. in A
Fag. I. II. III
Kfag.
I. III.
Hr. in F
II. IV.
ff
ff
zu 2
Trp. I. II. in B
mit Dämpfer
Pos. I. II
Xyl.
Viol. II
Viola
Vcello.
Kb.

73
rit.
zu 2
Kl. Fl. I. II
Gr. Fl. I. II
I. II.
Ob.
III.
Engl. H.
Kl. I. II. in A
Kl. III. in D
Bkl. in B
Kbkl. in A
Fag. I. II. III
zu 3
Flatterzunge
Kfag.
I. III.
Hr. in F.
II. IV.
mit Dämpfer
Trp. I. II. in B.
I. II.
Pos.
III. IV.
immer pp
rasch anschwellend
Btba.
Xyl.
Pk.
Viol.
Viola
get.
Vcello.
Kb.
unis.

78 ⑩

I. II. Fag. III.

ff

I. III. Hr. in F II. IV.

mit Dämpfer fff

III. I. III.

Trp. I. in B

I. allein mit Dämpfer

ff Flatterzunge

I. ohne Dämpfer zu 2

I. II. Pos. III. IV.

II. mit Dpf. fff

mit Dämpfer

Btba.

mit Dämpfer fff

Tamt. ff

Xyl.

Gr. Trom.

auf beiden Fellen ff

Pk. ff

Hrfe. ff

I. Viol. II. fff

Viola fff

Vcello. pizz. fff

Kb. pizz. fff

⑩

87
11
Kl. Fl. I. II
Gr. Fl. I. II
Ob. I. II. III
Kl. I. II. in A
I. II.
Fag.
III.
I. III.
Hr. in F
II. IV.
Trp. I. II. III in B
Pos. I. II
III. IV.
Xyl.
Pk.
Hrfe.
I.
Viol.
II.
Viola.
Vcello.
Kb.
zu 2
p cresc.
zu 3
mit Dämpfer
molto cresc.
I. allein mit Dämpfer
alle 3 mit Dämpfer
ff
I. ohne Dämpfer
zu 4
II. mit Dämpfer
II. III. IV. mit Dämpfer
fff
mp
arco
11

rit.
94
12
Kl. Fl. I. II
Gr. Fl. I. II
zu 2
I. II.
Ob.
III.
Engl. H.
Kl. I. II. in A
Kl. III. in D
Fag. I. II. III
I. III.
Hr. in F
II. IV.
mit Dämpfer
I. II.
Trp. in B
III.
mit Dämpfer
Schalltrichter hoch!
I. II.
Pos.
III. IV.
Pk.
Hrfe.
I.
Viol.
II.
Viola
Vcello.
Kb.

100
13
Kl.Fl.I.II
Gr.Fl.I.II
I.II
Ob.
III.
Engl. H.
Kl.I.II. in A
Kl.III. in D
Kbkl. in A
Fag.I.II.III
Kfag.
I.II.
Hr. in F
III.IV.
I.II.
Trp. in B
III.
I.II.
Pos.
III.IV.
Hrfe.
I.
Viol.
II.
Viola
Vcello.
Kb.
zu 2
mit Dämpfer
13

107
molto rit.
14
langsamer
Kbkl. in A
Fag. I. II. III
Kfag.
Hr. III. IV. in F
mit Dämpfer
IV. mit Dämpfer
stacc.
ppp
Pos. I. II. III
III. mit Dämpfer
I. II. III. mit Dämpfer
fp
Hrfe.
pp
ppp
Kb.
mit Dämpfer
f
p
14

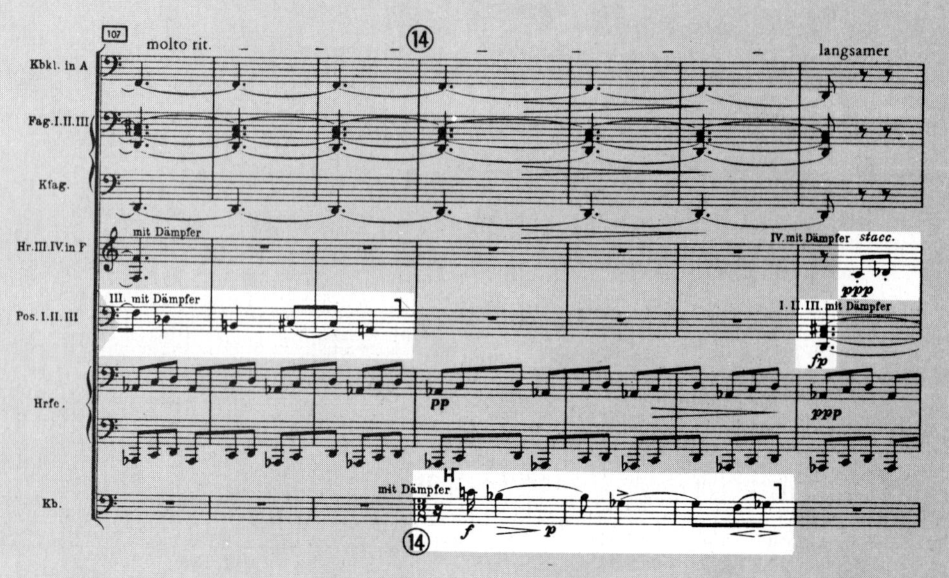

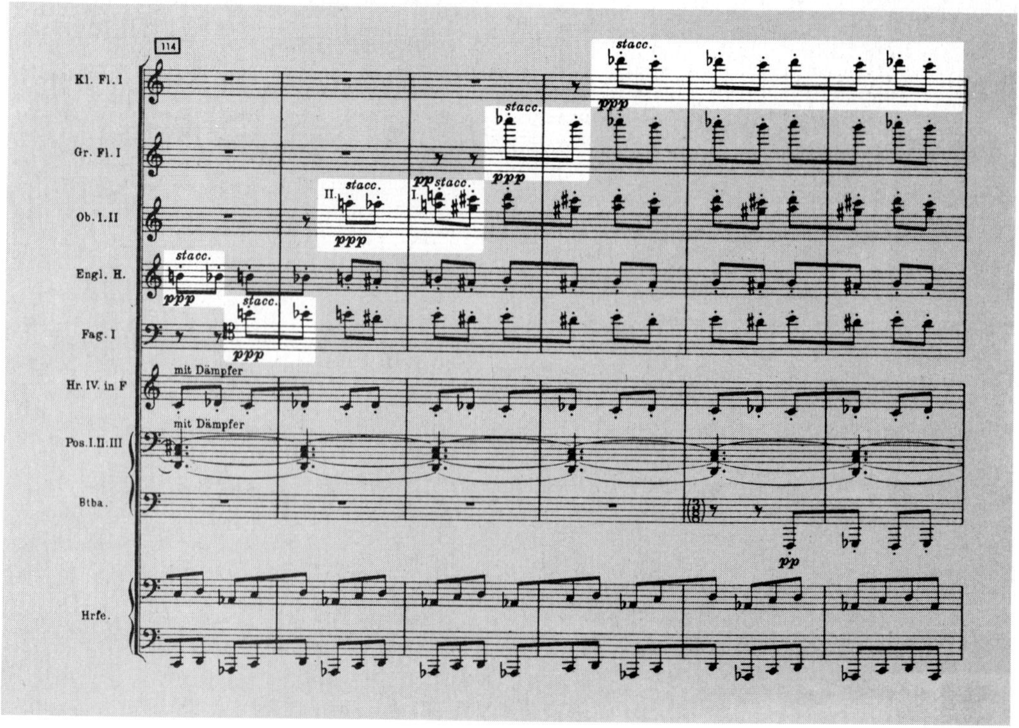

114
Kl. Fl. I
stacc.
ppp
Gr. Fl. I
stacc.
ppp
Ob. I. II
II.
stacc.
ppp
I.
pp stacc.
Engl. H.
stacc.
ppp
Fag. I
stacc.
ppp
Hr. IV. in F
mit Dämpfer
Pos. I. II. III
mit Dämpfer
Btba.
pp
Hrfe.

120
15
wieder rasch
etwas schwerer
16
I. Tempo
sehr rasch
Kl. Fl. I
Gr. Fl. I
Ob. I. II
Engl. H.
Bkl. in B
Kbkl. in A
I.
Fag.
II. III.
zu 2
Kfag.
Hr. IV. in F
mit Dämpfer
Pos. I. II. III
mit Dämpfer
IV. u. Btba.
Flatterzunge
Hrfe.
wieder rasch
etwas schwerer
I. Tempo
sehr rasch
pizz.
I.
Viol.
II.
Viola.
div. pizz.
Vcello.
die Hälfte
arco
Kb.
15
16

Vergangenes

1
135
Viertel etwas langsamer
Kl. Fl. II
Gr. Fl.
Ob. I. II
Engl. H.
Kl. I. II. in B
Kl. III. in D
Fag. I. II
II. mit Dämpfer
Hr. in F
Trp. I. II. in B
I. mit Dämpfer
espress.
II. mit Dämpfer
mit Dämpfer
Pos. IV.
Celesta
Viertel etwas langsamer
Viol.
Viola
Vcello.
Kb.
1

142
2
vom Anfang
Kl. Fl. II
Gr. Fl.
Ob. II
Engl. H.
I. II. in B
Kl.
III. in D
Bkl. in B
Fag. II
Hr. II in F
Trp. I. II in B
Celesta
mit Dämpfer
Viol.
Viola
Vcello.
Kb.
Solo-Violoncell I.
pizz.

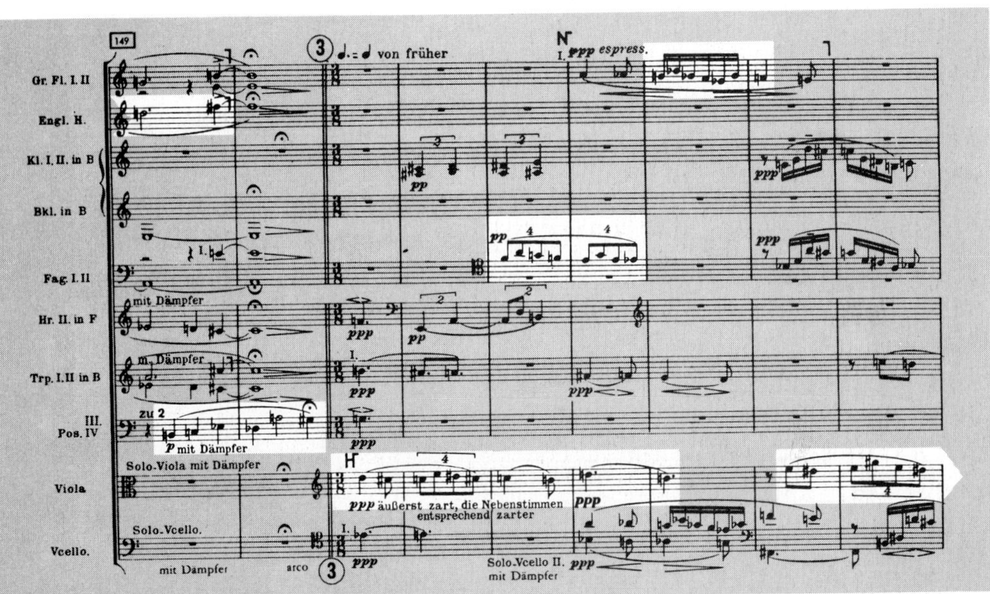

149
Gr. Fl. I. II
Engl. H.
Kl. I. II. in B
Bkl. in B
Fag. I. II
Hr. II. in F
Trp. I. II in B
III. Pos. IV
Viola
Vcello.
3
♩. = ♩ von früher
I. ppp espress.
mit Dämpfer
m. Dämpfer
zu 2
p mit Dämpfer
Solo-Viola mit Dämpfer
ppp äußerst zart, die Nebenstimmen entsprechend zarter
Solo-Vcello.
mit Dämpfer
arco
Solo-Vcello II. mit Dämpfer

158
4
Gr. Fl. I. II
Ob. II
Engl. H.
I. II. in B Kl. III. in D
Bkl. in B
Fag. I. II
Hr. I. II. in F
Trp. I. in B mit Dämpfer
Pos. IV
Viol. I. II.
Solo-Viola
Solo-Vcello. I. II
zu 2
II. in A
I. ohne Dämpfer
II. mit Dämpfer
mit Dämpfer
ohne Dämpfer
ohne Dämpfer
G-Saite
espr.

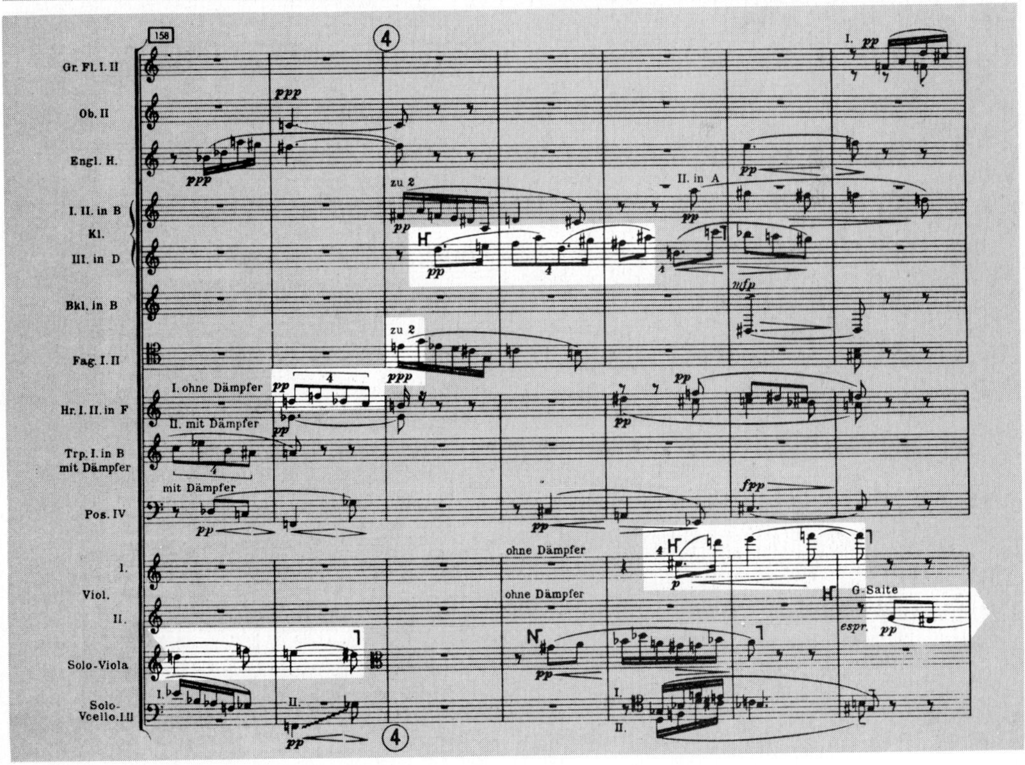

165
5
Gr. Fl. I. II
zu 2
Ob. I
I.
p espress.
Engl. H.
p
ppp
I. II. in A
Kl.
III. in D
ppp
I. in A pp
pp
Bkl. in B
Fag. I. II
pp
Hr. in F
Trp. I in B.
mit Dämpfer
p
Pos.
Celesta.
pp
Viol.
I.
II.
Viola
alle ohne Dämpfer
p
Vcello.
ohne Dämpfer
alle
p
Kb.
5

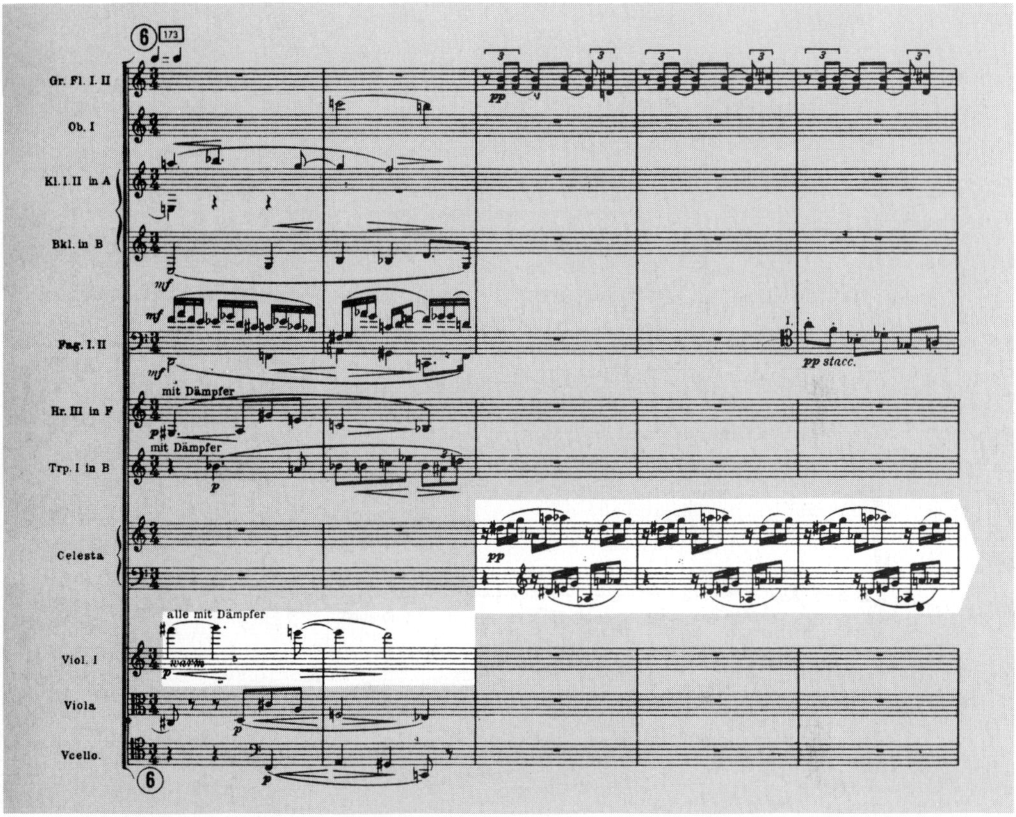

6 173

Gr. Fl. I. II

Ob. I

Kl. I. II in A

Bkl. in B

Fag. I. II

I.

pp stacc.

Hr. III in F

mit Dämpfer

Trp. I in B

mit Dämpfer

Celesta

Viol. I

alle mit Dämpfer

warm

Viola

Vcello.

6

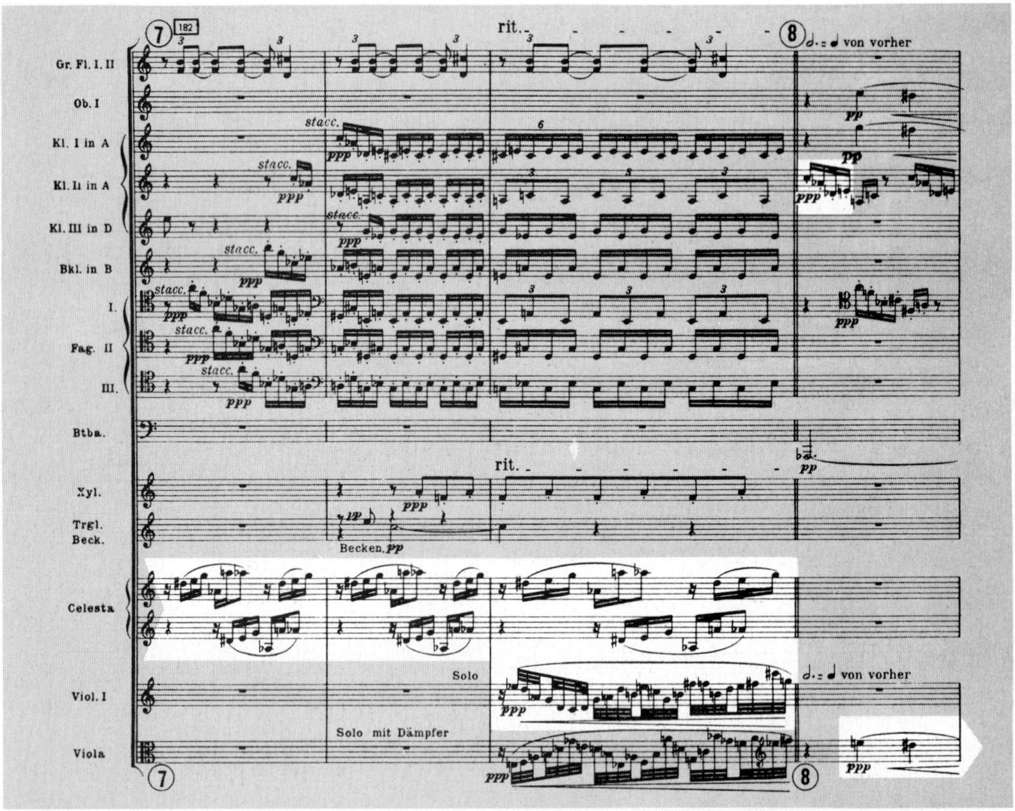

7
182
rit.
8
♩. = ♩ von vorher
Gr. Fl. I. II
Ob. I
Kl. I in A
Kl. II in A
Kl. III in D
Bkl. in B
I.
Fag. II
III.
Btba.
Xyl.
Trgl.
Beck.
Celesta
Viol. I
Viola
stacc.
ppp
pp
Becken
Solo
Solo mit Dämpfer

186
Ob. I
I. II in A
Kl.
III in D
Bkl. in B
Fag. I
Hr. I in F
Btba.
Solo-Viola
Vcello.
Kb.
immer stacc.
ohne Dämpfer
pizz.
ppp
pp

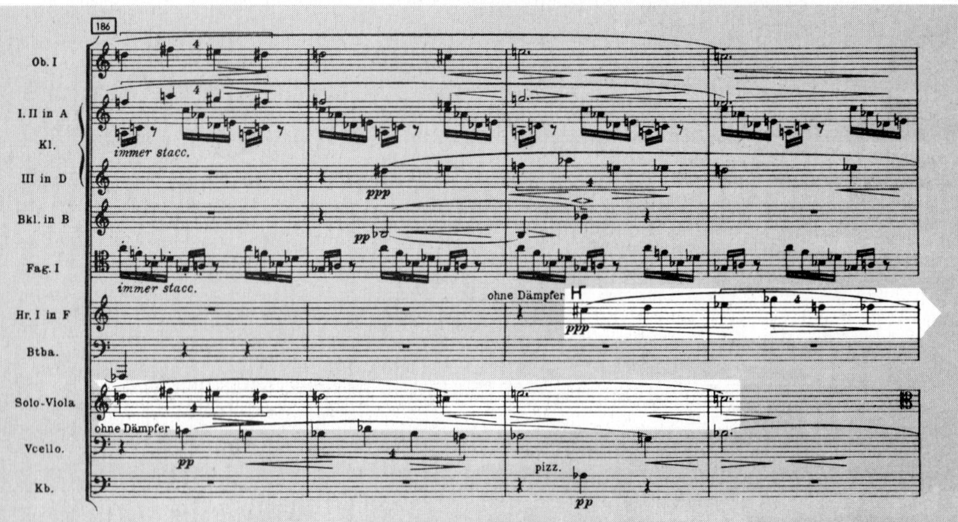

190
Kl. Fl. I
Gr. Fl. I
Ob. I. II
zu 2
immer stacc. und ppp
I. II in A
Kl.
III in D
Bkl. in B
I.
Fag.
II. III.
Hr. I in F
Btba.
Xyl.
Hrfe.
Celesta
alle mit Dämpfer
Viol. I
Vcello.
pizz.
Kb.

194
9 langsamer werden
Kl. Fl. I. II.
nimmt III. große Flöte
Gr. Fl. I. II.
Ob. I. II. III
zu 3
Engl. H.
I. II in A Kl.
III in D
Bkl. in B
Fag. I. II. III.
zu 2
Hr. in F II. III. IV.
mit Dämpfer
zu 2 mit Dämpfer
dim.
weich
Trp. I. II in B
mit Dämpfer, Flatterzunge
Pos. I II
mit Dämpfer zu 2
sehr gebunden
sehr gebunden
dim.
III. IV u. Btba.
mit Dämpfer III. IV.
Btba.
Xyl.
Hrfe.
Celesta
langsamer werden
Viol. I. II.
ohne Dämpfer
eine Solo Viol.
alle mit Dämpfer
trem. am Steg
Viola
Vcello.
Kb.
pizz.
9

198
10
Kl. Fl. I
III.
Gr. Fl. I
II.
III. gr. Fl.
Engl. H.
wenn die Stelle nicht ppp möglich ist, bleibt sie weg; sie muß schwächer klingen als die Streicher.
I II in A
Kl.
III in D
Fag. I
Kfag.
zu 2
Hr. III. IV in F
IV.
zu 2
Pos. I. II
III. IV u. Btba.
Xyl.
Hrfe.
Celesta
alle, am Steg
ohne Dämpfer
Flag.
Klang
I.
Viol.
pizz.
II.
trem. am Steg
Viola
Vcello.
Kb.
10

202
rit.
11
aber etwas langsamer
Kl. Fl. I
III.
Gr. Fl. I
II.
wieder II. kl. Fl.
Ob. I
Engl. H.
Kl. II in A
Bkl. in B
I.
Fag.
III.
Kfag.
I. II.
Hr. in F
III. IV.
mit Dämpfer
mit Dämpfer
ohne Dämpfer
Trp. I in B
Trgl.
eventuell Flag.
Hrfe.
Celesta
rit.
aber etwas langsamer
Viol. I
Flag.
ohne D.
Klang
Flag.
Viol. II
ohne D.
Klang
Flag.
Flag.
Klang
get.
Viola
ohne Dämpfer
mit Dämpfer
get.
Vcello.
4 Kontrabäße stimmen die G Saite auf Gis und spielen Flag.
Klang
Kb.
11

208
12
Kl. Fl. I
Gr. Fl. I. II
Ob. II
Engl. H.
II in A
Kl.
III in D
Bkl. in B
Kfag.
Hr. I. II in F
Trp. I. II in B
Pos. I
Celesta
I.
Viol.
II.
Violen
Vcelli.
Kb.
pp espr.
p espr.
I. mit Dämpfer
II. mit Dämpfer
pp espress.
mit Dämpfer
2 Solo-Violen mit Dämpfer
zu 2
die übrigen mit Dämpfer
2 Solo-Violoncelli mit Dämpfer

213
verlangsamend bis zum Schluß
Kl. Fl. I.II
Gr. Fl. I. II
Kl. Flöte II.
Ob. II.
Engl. H.
dim.
I. II in A
Kl.
III in D
Bkl. in B
Fag. I. II. III
zu 3
Kfag.
Hr. I. II in F
I. mit Dämpfer
mit Dämpfer
Trp. I. II in B
III. Pos. mit Dämpfer
Pos. III u. Btba.
Xyl.
Trgl.
mit Dämpfer
Hrfe.
eventuell Flag.
Celesta
verlangsamend bis zum Schluß
mit Dämpfer
Flag.
Klang
Viol. I
Viol. II.
Violen
alle in 2 gleichen Teilen mit Dämpfer
2 Solo mit Dämpfer
alle mit Dämpfer
Vcello.
pizz.
Kb.
das tiefe es!

25. CHARLES IVES (1874-1954), *Putnam's Camp, Redding, Connecticut,* from *Three Places in New England* (1903-1914)

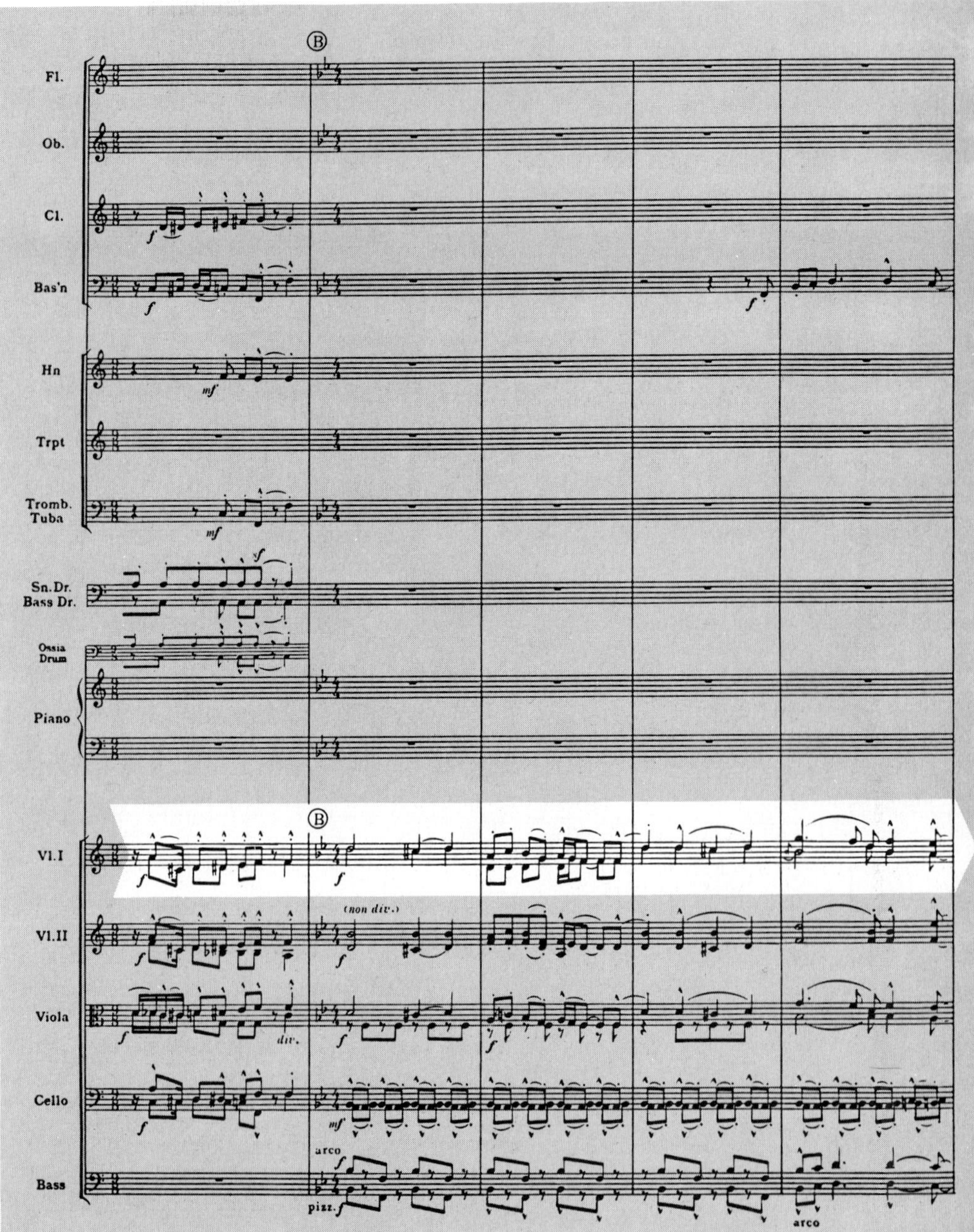
B
Fl.
Ob.
Cl.
Bas'n
Hn
Trpt
Tromb.
Tuba
Sn. Dr.
Bass Dr.
Ossia
Drum
Piano
B
Vl. I
Vl. II
(non div.)
Viola
div.
Cello
arco
Bass
pizz.
arco

C
Fl.
Ob.
Cl.
Bas'n
Hn
Trpt
Tromb.
Tuba
Sn. Dr.
Bass Dr.
Piano
Vl. I
Vl. II
Viola
Cello
Bass
poco rit.
a tempo
mf
mp
p
f
ff
(unis)
div.
pizz.

Fl.
Ob.
Cl.
Bas'n
Hn
Trpt
Tromb.
Tuba
Sn. Dr.
Bass Dr.
Piano
Vl. I
Vl. II
Viola
Cello
Bass
arco

Fl.
Ob.
Cl.
Bas'n
Hn
Trpt
Tromb.
Tuba
Sn. Dr.
Bass Dr.
Piano
Vl. I
Vl. II
Viola
Cello
Bass
(unis)
8va ad lib.
arco
pizz.

Fl.
Ob.
Cl.
Bas'n
Hn
Trpt
Tromb.
Tuba
Sn. Dr.
Bass Dr.
with Cym.
Piano
Vl. I
Vl. II
Viola
(unis.)
Cello
Bass

D
Fl.
Ob.
Cl.
Bas'n
Hn
Trpt
(with Tuba ad lib.)
Tromb.
Tuba
Sn. Dr.
Bass Dr.
(no Cym.)
Piano
D
(non div.)
Vl. I
(non div.)
Vl. II
Viola
f arco
Cello
pizz.
arco
Bass

Fl.
Ob.
Cl.
Bas'n
Hn
Trpt
Tromb.
Tuba
(no Tuba)
Sn. Dr.
Bass Dr.
Piano
Vl. I
div.
Vl. II
div.
Viola
Cello
arco
pizz.
Bass
pizz.

E
Fl.
Ob.
Cl.
Bas'n
Hn
Trpt
Tromb.
Tuba
Sn. Dr.
Bass Dr.
Piano
R. H.
Vl. I
p dolce
Vl. II
(unis.)
Viola
Cello
arco
pizz.
(unis.)
Bass
pizz.

Fl.
Ob.
Cl.
Bas'n
Hn
Trpt
Tromb.
Tuba
Sn. Dr.
Bass Dr.
Piano
Vl. I
Vl. II
Viola
Cello
Bass
mp
mf
p
ppp
(unis.)
unis.
div.
arco

F
Fl.
Ob.
Cl.
Bas'n
Hn
Trpt
Tromb.
Tuba
Sn. Dr.
Bass Dr.
Piano
Vl. I
Vl. II
Viola
Cello
Bass
p
f
mf
ff
sf
pizz.
arco
mf arco
ff pizz.

decresc. e rit.
gradually slower (about 92-88 : ♩)
Fl.
Ob.
Cl.
Bas'n
Hn
Trpt
Tromb. Tuba
Sn. Dr. Bass Dr.
(with Cym.)
Piano
R.H.
L.H.
decresc. e rit.
gradually slower (about 92-88 : ♩)
Vl. I
f (unis.)
Vl. II
f (unis.)
Viola
Cello
arco
pizz.
arco
decresc.
Bass
pizz.

rallen.
Fl.
Ob.
Cl.
pp
Bas'n
mf
pp
Hn
pp
Trpt
Tromb.
Tuba
Sn.Dr.
Bass Dr.
(no Cym.)
pp
ppp
Piano
mf
pp
(unis)
Vl.I
f
pp
(unis.)
Vl.II
mf
pp
rallen.
Viola
mf
arco
mf
Cello
pizz.
arco
Bass
pizz.
p

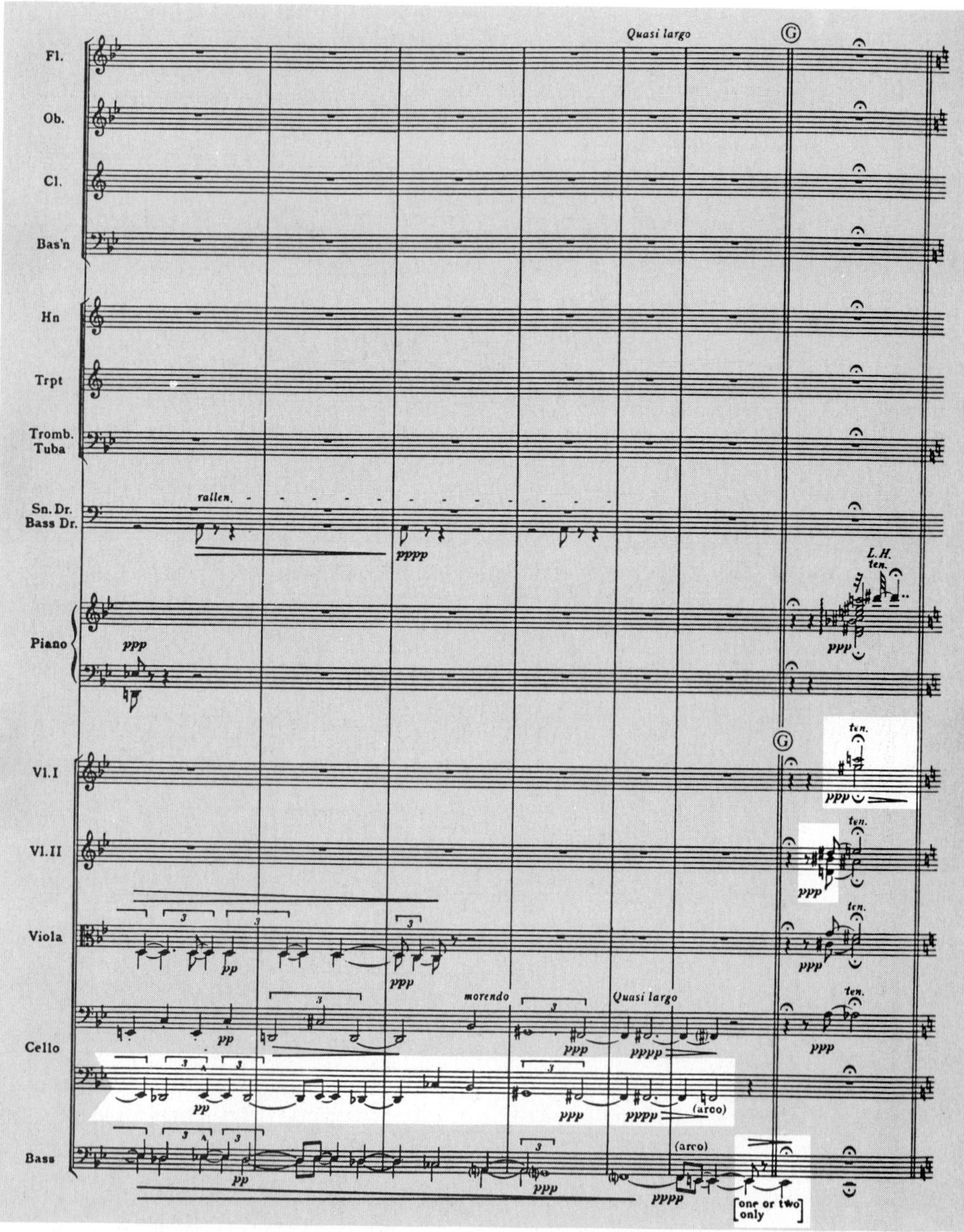
Quasi largo
G
Fl.
Ob.
Cl.
Bas'n
Hn
Trpt
Tromb.
Tuba
Sn. Dr.
Bass Dr.
rallen.
pppp
L.H.
ten.
Piano
ppp
ppp
G
Vl. I
ten.
ppp
Vl. II
ten.
ppp
Viola
ten.
pp
ppp
ppp
Cello
morendo
Quasi largo
ten.
pp
ppp
pppp
ppp
pp
ppp
pppp
(arco)
Bass
(arco)
pp
ppp
pppp
one or two only

Andante animato (about 96: ♩)
H
Poco meno mosso (about 92-88: ♩)
Fl.
pp
Ob.
Solo
mf
Cl.
Bas'n
ppp
Hn
Trpt
Tromb.
Tuba
Sn.Dr.
Bass Dr.
L.H.
Piano
ppp (as a distant drum beat)
Ossia Piano
Andante animato (about 96: ♩)
Poco meno mosso (about 92-88: ♩)
(very slightly slower)
Vl. I
Vl. II
Viola
2nd Viola ppp pizz., coll 2nd orchestra.
Cello
(unis.)
arco
Bass
pizz.

Fl.
Ob.
Cl.
Bas'n
Hn
Trpt
Tromb.
Tuba
Sn. Dr.
Bass Dr.
Piano
Vl. I
Vl. II
Viola
Cello
Bass
mp
cresc. poco a poco
pp
pp

Più mosso (about 96-100: ♩)
Fl.
Ob.
Cl.
Bas'n
Hn
Trpt
Tromb. Tuba
Sn.Dr. Bass Dr.
cresc. poco a poco
Più mosso (about 96-100: ♩)
(slightly more active)
Piano
cresc. poco a poco
Ossia Piano
Vl. I
Vl. II
Viola I
Viola
pizz.
Cello
Bass
arco

Ⓘ Più moto (about 100-104: 𝅗𝅥)
Fl.
Ob.
Cl.
Bas'n
Hn
Trpt
Tromb.
Tuba
Sn. Dr.
Bass Dr.
Ossia
Piano
(Right Hand)
Piano
Ossia
Piano
(Left Hand)
Ⓘ Più moto (about 100-104: 𝅗𝅥)
Vl. I
Vl. II
Viola
Cello
Bass
sf
f
pp
mp
mf
(unis.)
arco

decresc.
Col Clar.
Fl.
Ob.
Cl.
Col Flute
Bas'n
Hn
Trpt
Tromb.
Tuba
Sn.Dr.
Bass Dr.
Piano
Vl.I
Vl.II
arco
pizz.
Viola
Cello
pizz.
Bass
pizz.

J

Allegro moderato (about 108-112: ♩)

Fl.

Ob.

Cl.

Bas'n

Hn

Trpt

Tromb.
Tuba

Sn.Dr.
Bass Dr.

Piano

J

Allegro moderato (about 108-112: ♩)
(In a moderate march time)

Vl.I

Vl.II

Viola

Cello

pizz.

(arco)

(unis.)

pizz.

Bass

Più mosso (about 112-116 = 𝅗𝅥)
Fl.
Ob.
Cl.
Bas'n
Hn
Trpt
Tromb.
Tuba
Sn. Dr.
Bass Dr.
(with Cym.)
Piano
Più mosso (about 112-116 = 𝅗𝅥)
faster
(unis.)
Vl. I
Vl. II
Viola
Cello
Bass

Fl.
Ob.
Cl.
Bas'n
Hn
Trpt
Tromb.
Tuba
Sn.Dr.
Bass Dr.
Piano
Vl. I
Vl. II
Viola
Cello
Bass
ff
sf
p
f
mf
div.
(unis.)

K
Fl.
Ob.
mf
Cl.
f
Bas'n
sf
ff
Hn
ff
Trpt
a 2
f
Tromb.
f
Tuba
Sn. Dr.
Bass Dr.
Piano
f
K
Vl. I
sf
ff
Vl. II
ff
Viola
sf
ff
(unis.)
Cello
ff arco.
arco
Bass
ff
pizz.

L Animato (about 120: ♩)
Fl.
ff (Piccolo coll Fl.–ad lib.)
Ob.
ff
Cl.
gliss.
marcato
fff
Bas'n
fff
sf
Hn
f
sf
sf
Trpt
gliss.
(Solo)
ff
fff
Tromb.
f
sf
sf
Tuba
ff
sf
Sn.Dr.
Bass Dr.
mf
f
(with Cymb.)
Piano
ff
sf
sf
L Animato (about 120: ♩)
Vl. I
fff
Vl. II
fff
Viola
fff
Cello
div. arco
pizz.
ff
ff
arco
Bass
arco

Fl.
Ob.
Cl.
Bas'n
Hn
Trpt
Tromb.
Tuba
Sn. Dr.
Bass Dr.
Piano
Vl. I
Vl. II
Viola
Cello
Bass
marcato
marcato
marcato
ff
sf
p
div.
arco
(div.) pizz.
(div.)

con fuoco
Fl.
Ob.
Cl.
Bas'n
marcato
Hn
marcato
Trpt
marcato
Tromb.
Tuba
Sn. Dr.
Bass Dr.
con fuoco
8va
loco
Piano
con fuoco
Vl. I
Vl. II
Viola
Cello
arco
pizz.
arco
Bass

M
Fl
(no Picc.)
pp
Ob.
pp
Cl.
Bas'n
Hn
Trpt
Tromb.
Tuba
Sn. Dr.
Bass Dr.
Piano
M
pp (dolce)
Vl. I
Vl. II
Viola
ppp
pp
Cello
ppp
pp
Bass
pp
pizz.
pp

Fl.
Ob.
Cl.
Bas'n
Hn
Trpt
Tromb.
Tuba
Sn. Dr.
Bass Dr.
Piano
Vl. I
Vl. II
Viola
Cello
Bass
pizz.

[Piccolo col Fl. ad lib.]
Fl.
Ob.
Cl.
Bas'n
Hn
Trpt
Tromb.
Tuba
Sn.Dr.
Bass Dr.
(no Cym.)
Piano
Vl. I
Vl. II
unis.
div.
Viola
Cello
arco
Bass
pizz.

N
Fl.
Ob.
Cl.
Bas'n
Hn
(Solo)
Trpt
Tromb.
(Solo)
Tuba
Sn. Dr.
Bass Dr.
Piano
N
Vl. I
Vl. II
Viola
Cello
arco
pizz.
arco
Bass
arco
pizz.

Fl.
Ob.
Cl.
Bas'n
Hn
Trpt
Tromb.
Tuba
Sn. Dr.
Bass Dr.
(Cymb.)
Piano
Vl. I
(unis.)
Vl. II
(unis.)
Viola
arco.
div.
Cello
arco.
Bass
pizz.

Piccolo & Flute
(unis.)
Fl.
Ob.
Cl.
marcato
Bas'n
Hn
Trpt
Tromb.
marcato
Tuba
Sn. Dr.
Bass Dr.
Piano
Vl. I
div.
Vl. II
Viola
marcato
Cello
marcato
(unis)
arco.
Bass
pizz.

O
Fl.
Ob.
Cl.
Bas'n
Hn
Trpt
marcato
sempre
marcato
Tromb.
Tuba
Sn. Dr.
Bass Dr.
Piano
O
Vl. I
ff (non div.)
Vl. II
a2
Viola
div.
Cello
Bass

Fl.
Ob.
Cl.
Bas'n
Hn
Trpt
Tromb.
Tuba
Sn. Dr.
Bass Dr.
Piano
Vl. I
Vl. II
Viola
Cello
Bass
cresc.
div.
f

P
Fl.
Ob.
Cl.
Bas'n
Ossia Horn
ff
marcato sempre
Hn
ff
Trpt
ff
fff
sf
ff marcato sempre
Ossia
Tromb.
Tuba
Sn. Dr.
Bass Dr.
mf
Piano
mf
p
sf
P
(div. ad lib.)
Vl. I
Vl. II
Viola
Cello
Bass

Piccolo (unison with Flute)
Più moto
Q
Fl.
Ob.
Cl.
Bas'n
marcato sempre
Hn
Trpt
Tromb.
sempre marcato
Tuba
Sn. Dr.
Bass Dr.
(with Cymb.)
marcato sempre
Piano
Più moto
Q
Vl. I
Vl. II
(div. ad lib.)
Viola
marcato
Cello
arco
Bass
½ arco
½ pizz.

(lively and with a kind of a lilt)
Fl.
Ob.
Cl.
Bas'n
Hn
Trpt
Tromb.
Tuba
Sn. Dr.
Bass Dr.
Piano
(lively and with a kind of a lilt)
divisi ad lib.
Vl. I
Vl. II
div.
Viola
marcato sempre
Cello
Bass
(broken rumble)
arco

[Pic. from here to end. coll. Flute i.e. 8va higher.]
Fl.
Ob.
Cl.
Bas'n
Hn
Trpt
Tromb.
Tuba
Sn. Dr.
Bass Dr.
Piano
Vl. I
Vl. II
Viola
Cello
Bass
unis.
(non div.)
arco
pizz.

Fl.
Ob.
Cl.
Bas'n
Hn
Trpt
Tromb.
Tuba
Sn. Dr.
Bass Dr.
Piano
Vl. I
Vl. II
Viola
Cello
Bass
S
div.
arco

poco accel.
cresc.
Fl.
Ob.
Cl.
Bas'n
Hn
Trpt
Tromb.
Tuba
Sn. Dr.
Bass Dr.
Piano
Vl. I
Vl. II
Viola
Cello
Bass
div. 3
gliss.

T con fuoco
Fl.
Ob.
Cl.
Bas'n
Hn
Trpt
Tromb.
Tuba
Sn. Dr.
Bass Dr.
Piano
T con fuoco (as fast as playable)
div.
Vl. I
non divisi
Vl. II
Viola
(div.)
Cello
(div.)
arco
Bass
pizz.

Fl.
Ob.
Cl.
Bas'n
Hn
Trpt
Tromb.
Tuba
Sn. Dr.
Bass Dr.
Piano
Vl. I
Vl. II
Viola
Cello
Bass

U
poco rit.
Fl.
Ob.
Cl.
Bas'n
Hn
(if 4 Horns)
Trpt
(Solo)
Tromb.
Tuba
Sn. Dr.
Bass Dr.
Piano
U
poco rit.
(non div.)
Vl. I
div.
Vl. II
Viola
Cello
arco
Bass
arco
(pizz.)
arco

26. BÉLA BARTÓK (1881-1945), First movement from *Concerto for Orchestra* (1943)

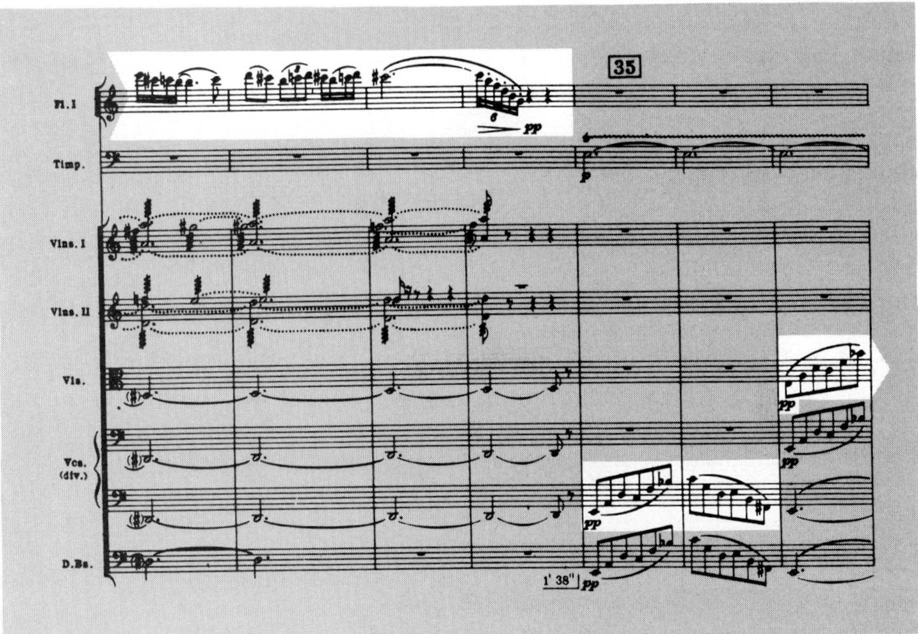
35
Fl. I
pp
Timp.
p
Vlns. I
Vlns. II
Vla.
pp
Vcs. (div.)
pp
D.Bs.
1' 38"
pp

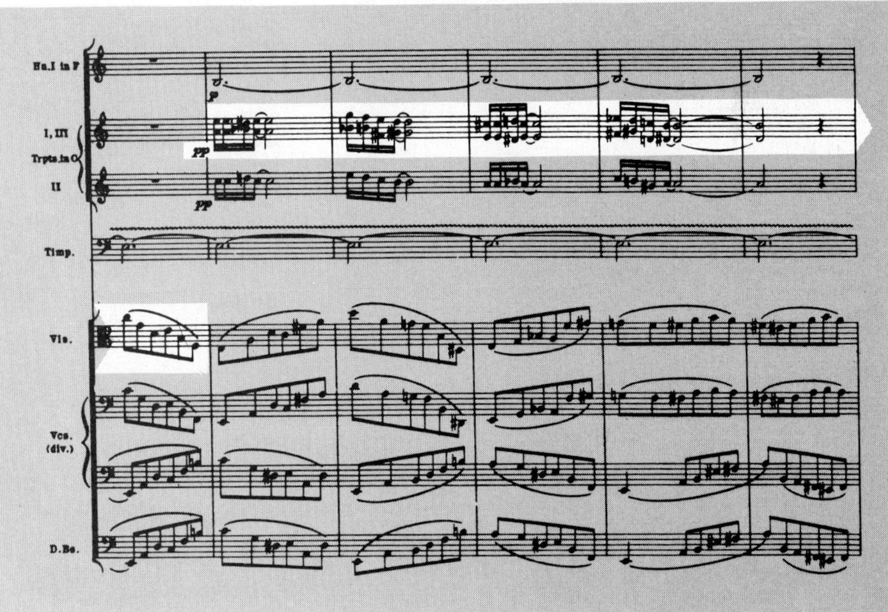
Hn. I in F
p
I, III
Trpts. in C
II
pp
pp
Timp.
Vla.
Vcs. (div.)
D.Bs.

44
Hn. I in F
I, III
Trpts. in C
II
dim.
Trb. I
p
Timp.
Vla.
Vcs. (div.)
D.Bs.
1'

51
♩ = 73
Flts. I, II
f
Obs. I, II
Clts. I, II in B♭
Hns. I, II in F
senza sord. div.
Vlns. I
senza sord. div.
Vlns. II
Vla.
unis.
Vcs.
D. Bs.

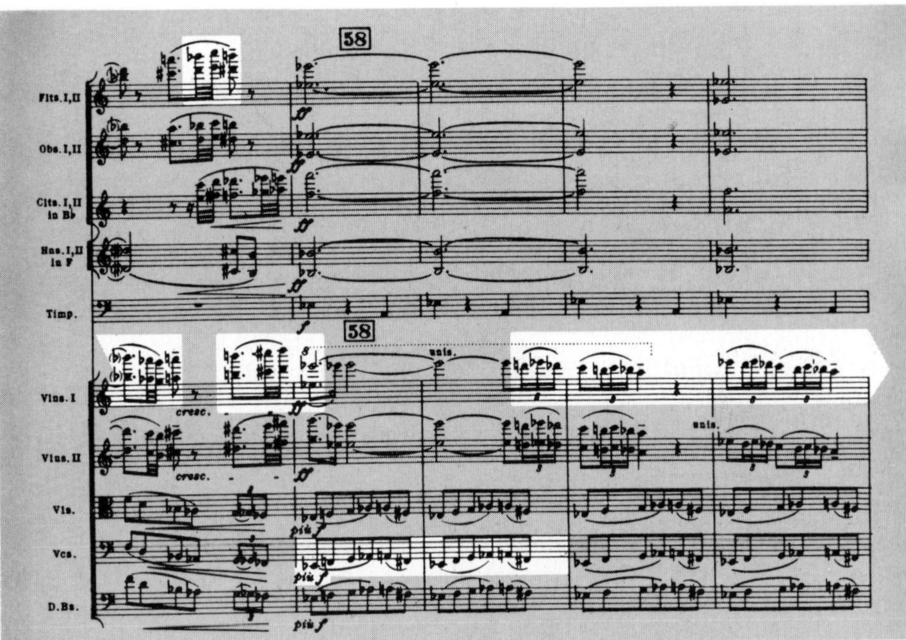
58
Flts. I, II
Obs. I, II
Clts. I, II in B♭
Hns. I, II in F
Timp.
58
unis.
Vlns. I
Vlns. II
Vla.
Vcs.
D.Bs.
cresc.
più f

poco a poco accelerando
66
Obs. I, II
Clts. I, II in B♭
Bsns. I, II
Hns. I, II in F
Trpts. I, II in C
Timp.
poco a poco accelerando
66
Vlns. I
Vlns. II
Vla.
Vcs.
D.Bs.
mf, cresc.
mf, ma marcato
p, cresc.

Flts. I,II
Obs. I,II
Clts. I,II in B♭
Bsns. I,II
Hns. I,II in F
Trpts. I,II in C
Timp.
Vla.
Vcs.
D. Bs.
a 2
cresc.
♩. = 76
50"

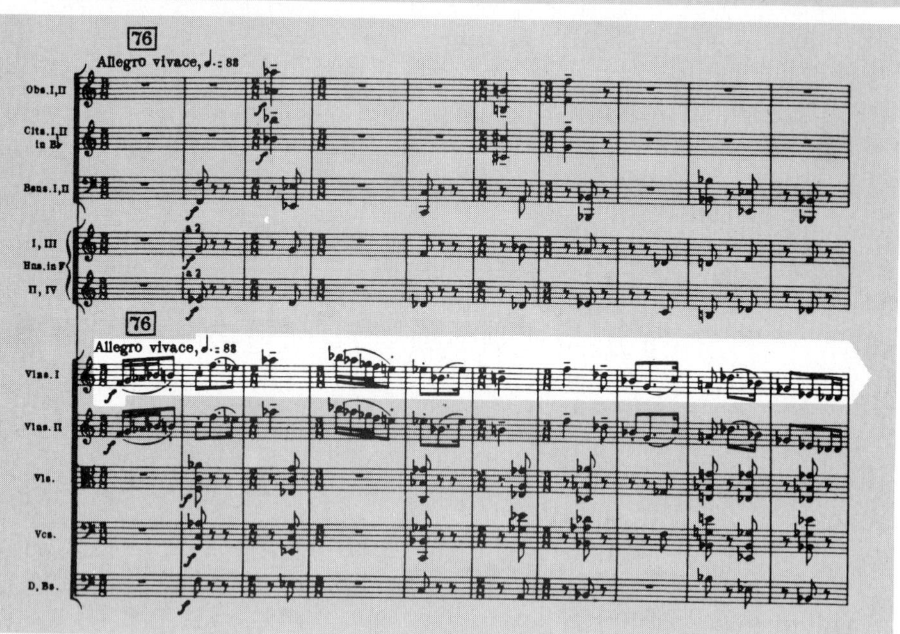
76
Allegro vivace, ♩. = 88
Obs. I,II
Clts. I,II in B♭
Bsns. I,II
I, III
Hns. in F
II, IV
a 2
Vlns. I
Vlns. II
Vla.
Vcs.
D. Bs.

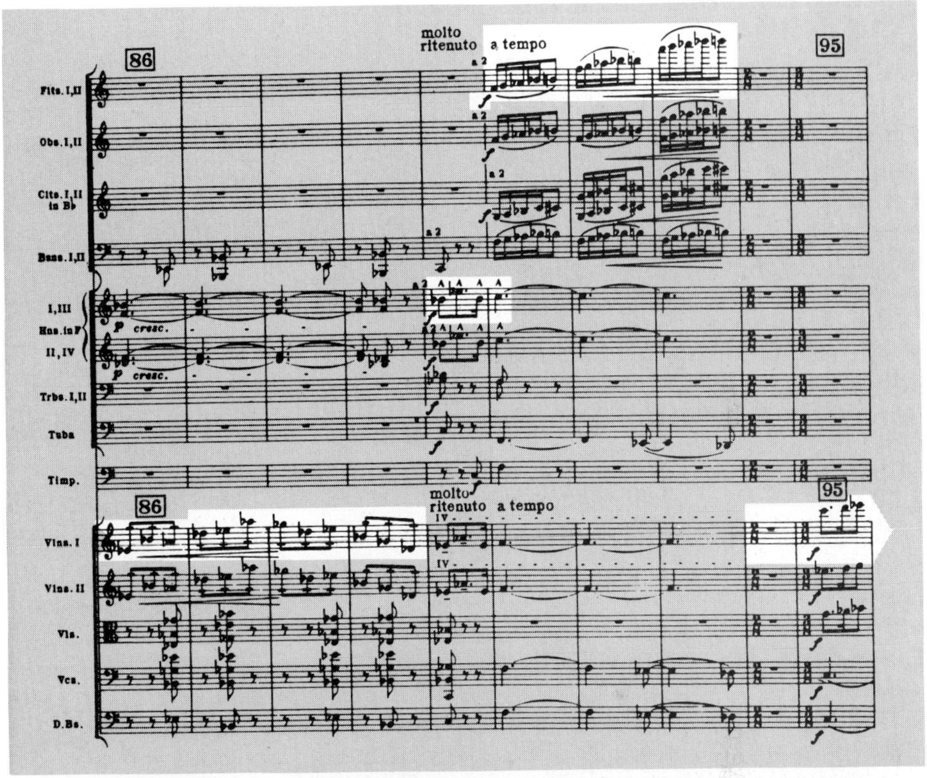

86
molto ritenuto
a tempo
95
Flts. I, II
Obs. I, II
Clts. I, II in B♭
Bsns. I, II
I, III
Hns. in F
II, IV
Trbs. I, II
Tuba
Timp.
a 2
p cresc.
Vlns. I
Vlns. II
Vls.
Vcs.
D. Bs.
IV

102
Flts. I, II
Obs. I, II
Clts. I, II in B♭
Bsns. I, II
a 2
Vlns. I
Vlns. II
Vls.
Vcs.
D. Bs.

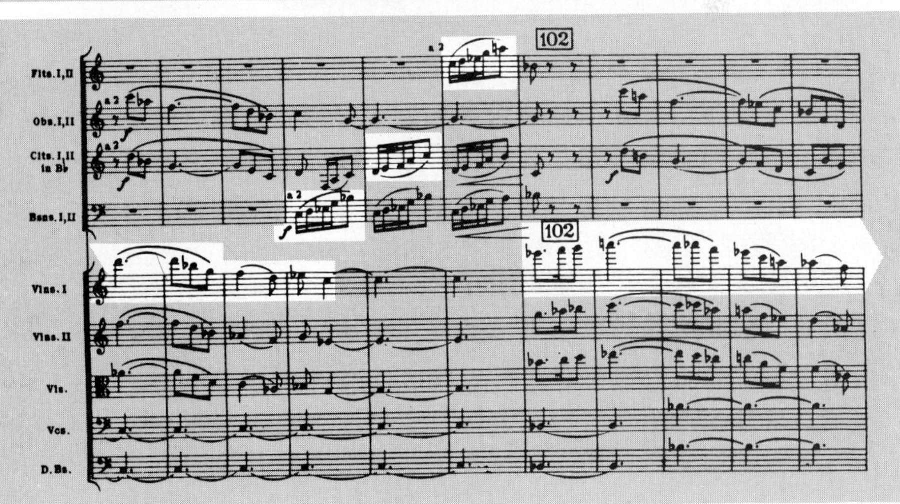

110
Obs. I,II
a 2
Clts. I,II in B♭
a 2
Vlns. I
div.
mf
unis.
Vlns. II
mf
Vla.
mf
Vcs.
mf
D. Bs.
mf

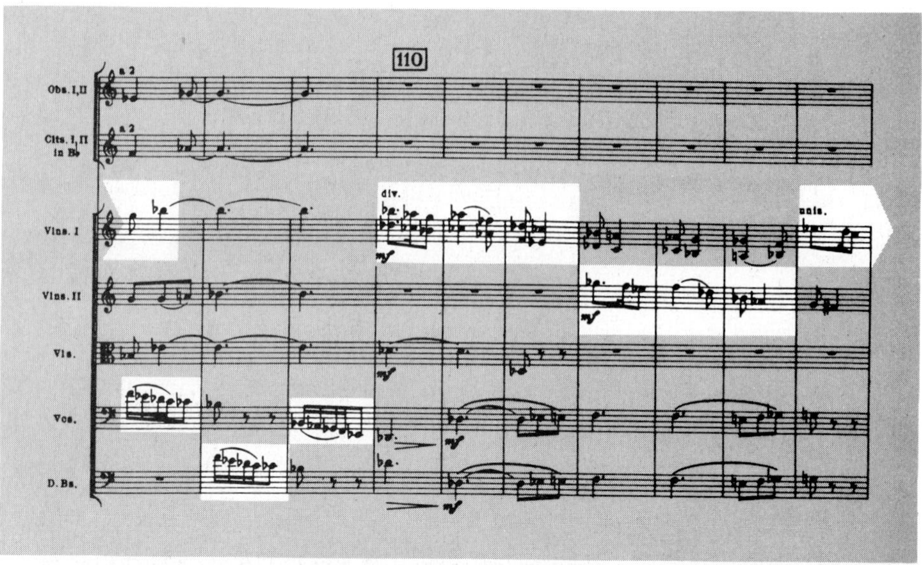

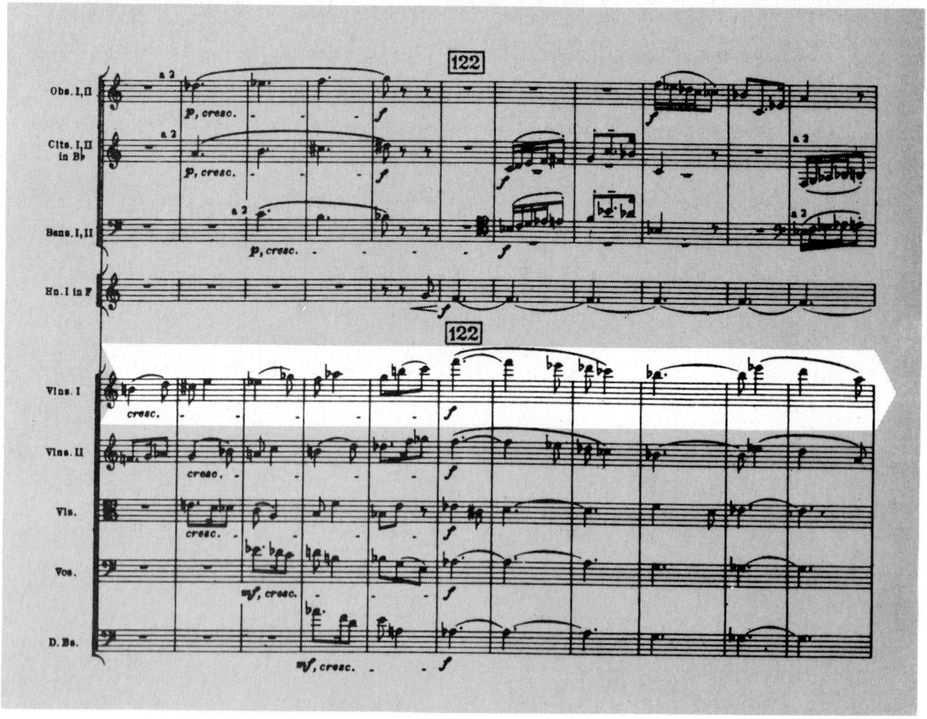

122
Obs. I,II
a 2
p, cresc.
f
Clts. I,II in B♭
a 2
p, cresc.
f
a 2
Bsns. I,II
a 2
p, cresc.
f
a 2
Hn. I in F
f
122
Vlns. I
cresc.
f
Vlns. II
cresc.
f
Vla.
cresc.
f
Vcs.
mf, cresc.
f
D. Bs.
mf, cresc.
f

135
a 2
Flts. I, II
Obs. I, II
Clts. I, II in B♭
Bsns. I, II
Hn. I in F
Trb. I
Vlns. I
Vlns. II
Vls.
Vcs.
D. Bs.
f
mf

142
Fl. I
Ob. I
Cl. I in B♭
Trb. I
Vlns. I
Vlns. II
Vls.
Vcs.
f
dim.
pp
p
1'

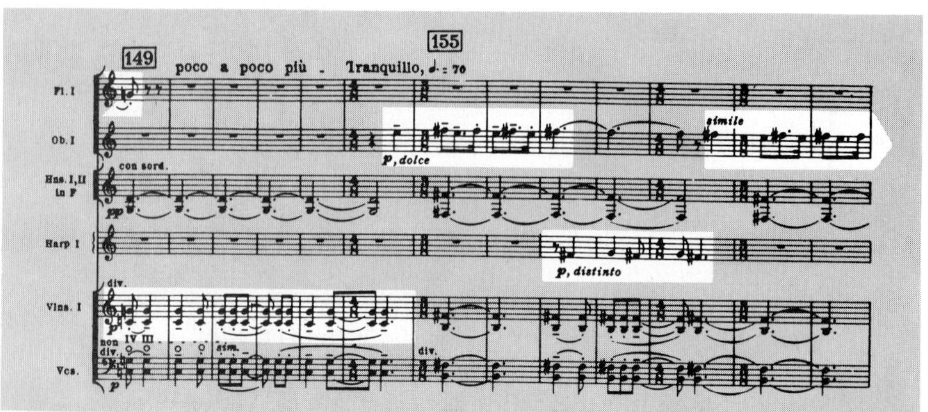
149
155
poco a poco più - Tranquillo, ♩. = 70
Fl. I
Ob. I
p, dolce
simile
con sord.
Hns. I, II in F
pp
Harp I
p, distinto
div.
Vlns. I
non IV III
div.
sim.
div.
Vcs.
p

165
Ob. I
Hns. I, II in F
Harp I
p
gliss.
Vlns. I
Vcs.

175
181
Ob. I
p
Clts. I, II in A
p, dolce
senza sord.
simile
p
Hns. I, II in F
p
Harp I
p
p
unis.
Vlns. I
p
Vlns. II
p
non div.
Vcs.
p

192
Flts. I, II
Ob. I
Clts. I, II in A
dim.
B. Cl. in B♭
I. II
Hns. in F
III
Harp I
con sord.
punta d'arco div. 2 Vlns. in each group
Vlns. I
Vlns. II
Vls.
Vcs.

198
Flts. I, II
Ob. I
Cl. I in A
B. Cl. in B♭
Harp I
Vlns. I
Vlns. II
Vls.
Vcs.

204
rallent.
a tempo
210
I, II
Flts
III
Ob. I
Clts. I, II in A
con sord.
Hn. I in F
Harp I
Vlns. II
Vls.
Vcs.
D. Bs.
p, ma poco marc.

sempre più tranquillo
220
I, II
Flts.
III
Ob. I
C. A.
Clts. I, II in A
con sord.
Trpt. I
con sord.*)
Trbs. I, II
Harp I
Vls.
Vcs.
D. Bs.
*) always use a soft (cardboard) mute.

231
Tempo I. (♩. = 88)
237
Flts. I, II
Obs. I, II, III
Clts. I, II, III in B♭
I, II
Bsns.
III
Hns. in F
I, III
II, IV
Trpts. I, II in C
Trbs. I, II
Tuba
Timp.
Vlns. I
Vlns. II
Vla.
Vcs.
D. Bs.
a 2
a 3
senza sord.
(senza sord.)
Tutti unis.
f sub.
1'25"

242
Picc.
Flts. I, II
a 2
I, II
Obs.
III
Clts. I, II, III in B♭
a 3
Bsns. I, II, III
I, III
Hns. in F
II, IV
Trpts. I, II in C
Trbs. I, II
Tuba
Timp.
Vlns. I
Vlns. II
Vls.
Vcs.
ff
f
p
mf
cresc.

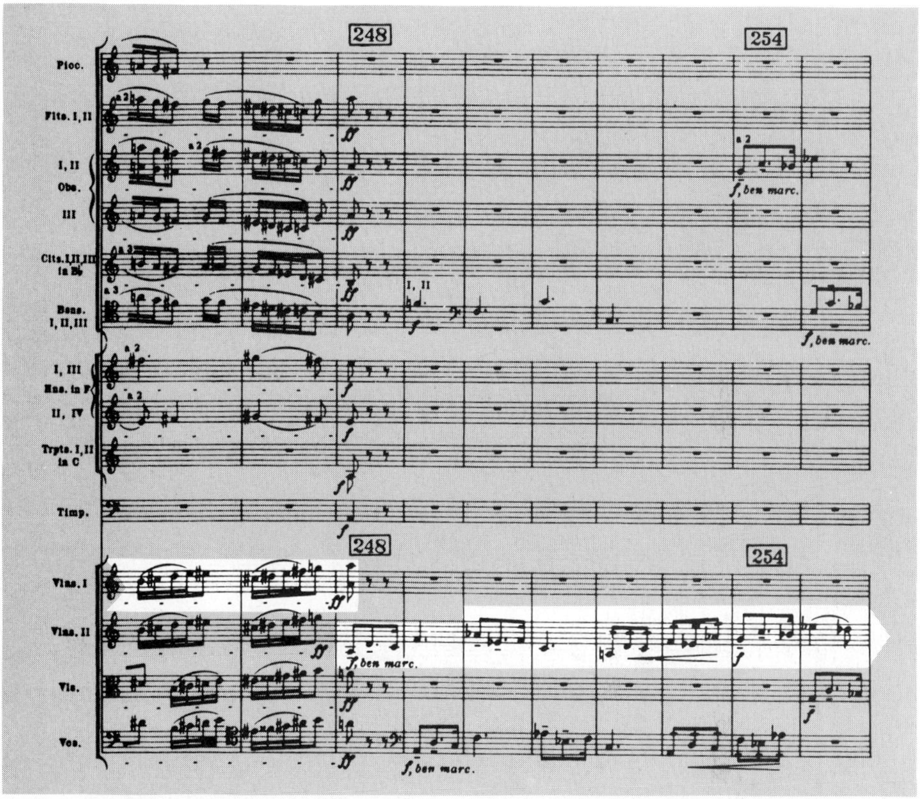

248 254

Picc.
Fls. I, II
I, II Obs. III
Clts. I, II, III in B♭
Bsns. I, II, III
I, III Hns. in F II, IV
Trpts. I, II in C
Timp.
Vlns. I
Vlns. II
Vla.
Vcs.

a 2 ff f, ben marc. I, II f

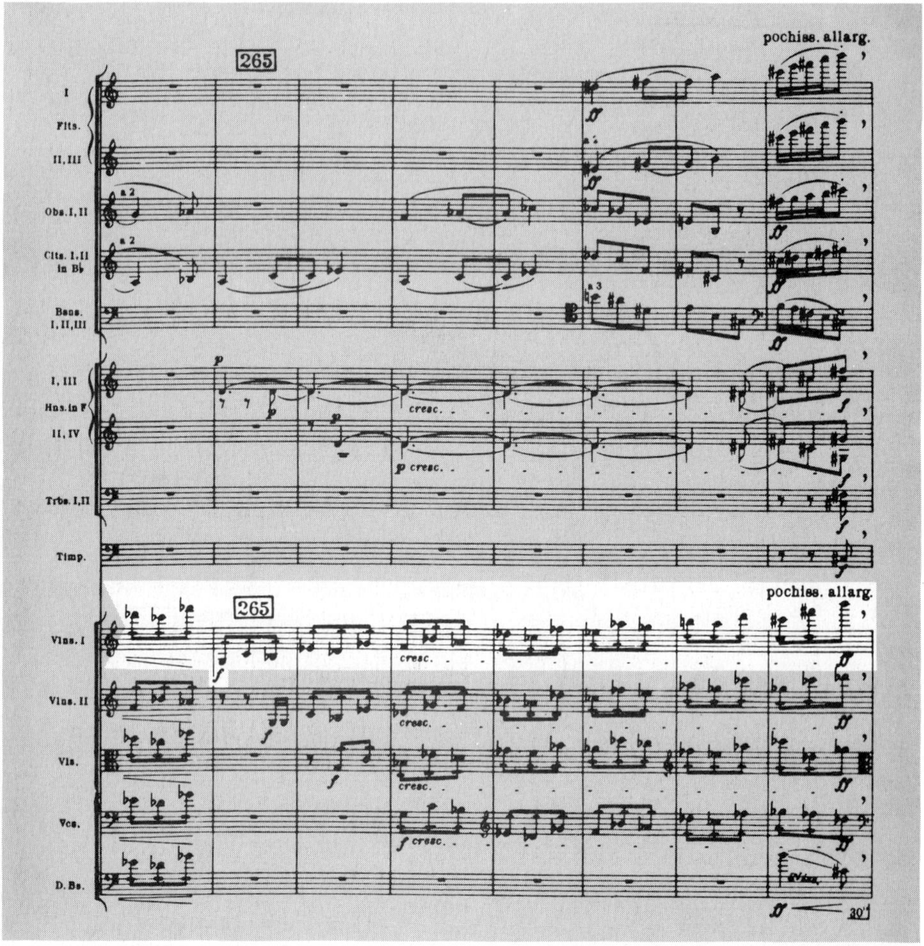

265

pochiss. allarg.

I
Flts.
II, III
Obs. I, II
a 2
Clts. I, II in B♭
a 2
Bsns. I, II, III
a 3
I, III
Hns. in F
II, IV
p
cresc.
p cresc.
Trbs. I, II
Timp.
ff
f

265

pochiss. allarg.

Vlns. I
Vlns. II
Vls.
Vcs.
D. Bs.
f
cresc.
f cresc.
ff
div.
30"

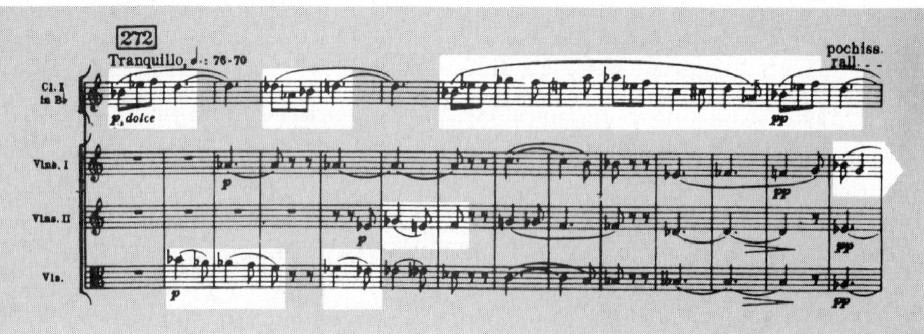

288
a tempo
Fl. I
C.A.
Cl. I in B♭
288
Vlns. I
Vlns. II
Vls.
Vcs.
pp
p, dolce
p

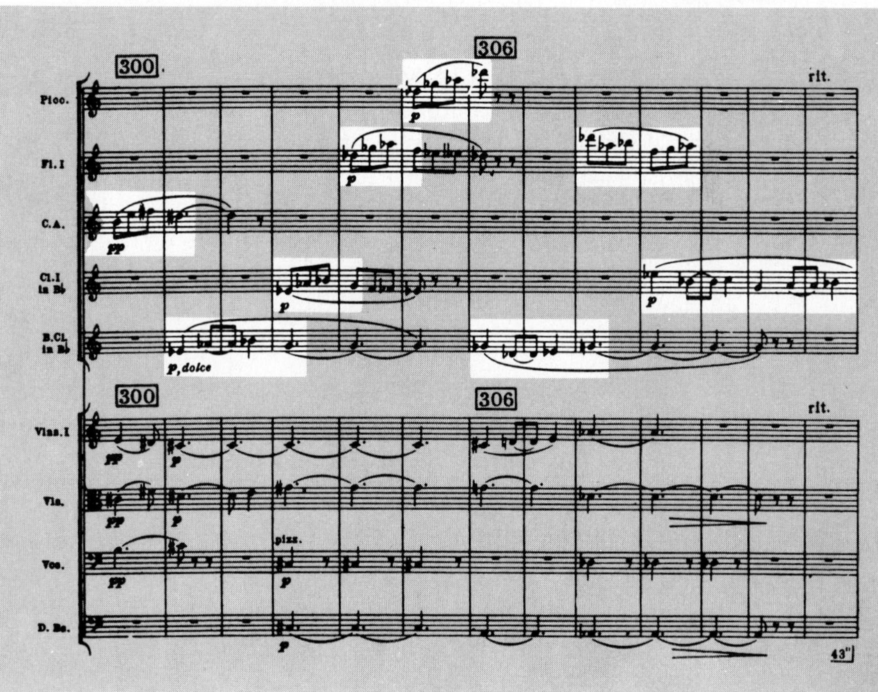
300
306
rit.
Picc.
Fl. I
C.A.
Cl. I in B♭
B. Cl. in B♭
p, dolce
300
306
rit.
Vlns. I
Vls.
Vcs.
D. Bs.
pizz.
pp
p
43"

313

Tempo I., 𝅗𝅥. = 83–90

323

Flts. I, II

Obs. I, II

Clts. I, II in B♭

Bsns. I, II

Hns. I, II in F

Trbs. I

Trbs. II

f, ben marc.

f, ben marc.

Timp.

313

Tempo I., 𝅗𝅥. = 83–90

323

Vlns. I

Vlns. II

Vls.

Vcs.

arco

D. Bs.

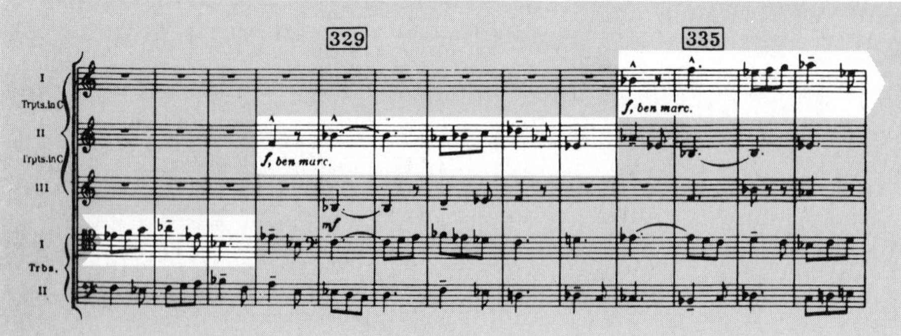

342
349
Flts. I,II,III
Obs. I,II,III
Cls. I,II,III in B♭
I
Bsns.
II,III
I,III
Hns. in F
II,IV
a 2
f, ben marc.
I,II
Trpts. in C
III
f, ben marc.
I,II
Trbs.
III
Timp.
Vlns. I
Vlns. II
Vls.
Vcs.
D.Bs.
354
359
364
Hns. I,III in F
I
Trpts. in C
II
Trpts. in C
III
f, ben marc.
marc.
II
Trbs.
III

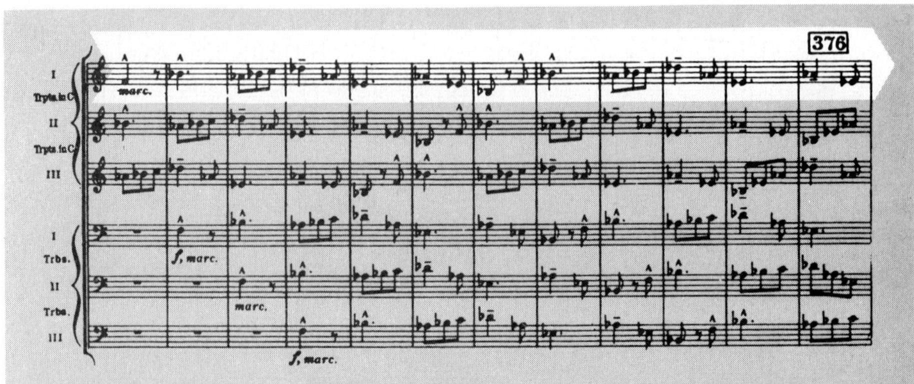

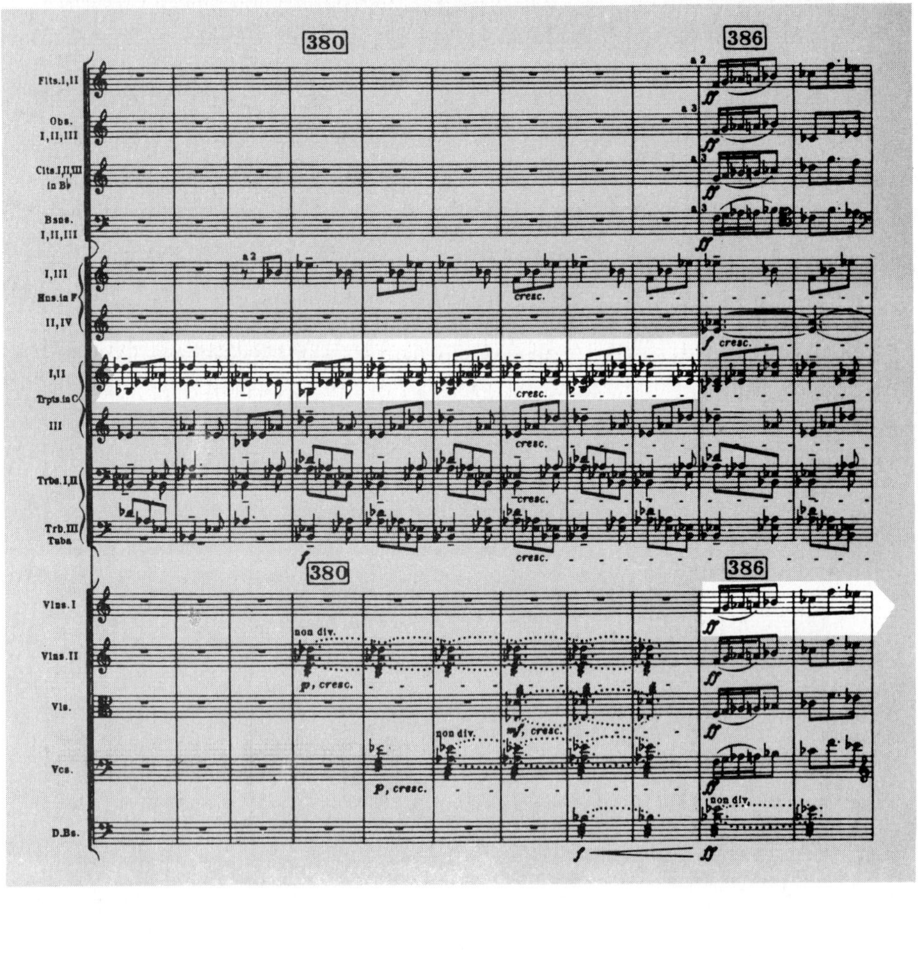

380
386
Flts. I, II
Obs. I, II, III
Clts. I, II, III in B♭
Bsns. I, II, III
a 2
a 3
ff
I, III
Hns. in F
II, IV
cresc.
f cresc.
I, II
Trpts. in C
III
Trbs. I, II
Trb. III Tuba
f
380
386
Vlns. I
Vlns. II
Vls.
Vcs.
D. Bs.
non div.
p, cresc.
mf, cresc.
f
ff

396
pochiss.allarg. Tranquillo, ♩. = 70
402
Picc.
Fls. I, II
Obs. I, II, III
Cls. I, II, III in B♭
Bsns. I, II, III
Hns. in F I, III
II, IV
Tpts. in C I, II
III
Trbs. I, II
Trb. III Tuba
Timp.
with the thick end of the Side Drum stick.
Cym.
Harp I
con sord.
p, espr.
Vlns. I
Vlns. II
Vls.
Vcs.
D.Bs
pizz.
55"

424

Flts. I, II
p, espr.
Ob. I
p, espr.
Cl. I in B♭
Hns. II, IV in F
Harp I
gliss.
p

424

Vlns. I
mf
p
con sord.
p
Vlns. II
mf
p
Vls.
pizz.
p
arco
Vcs.
mf
p
con sord.
p
D.Bs.
arco
mf
p
pizz.
div. arco

Flts.I,II
Ob.I
Cl. I in B♭
p, espr.
Harp I
Vlns.I
Vla.
Vcs.
D.Bs.

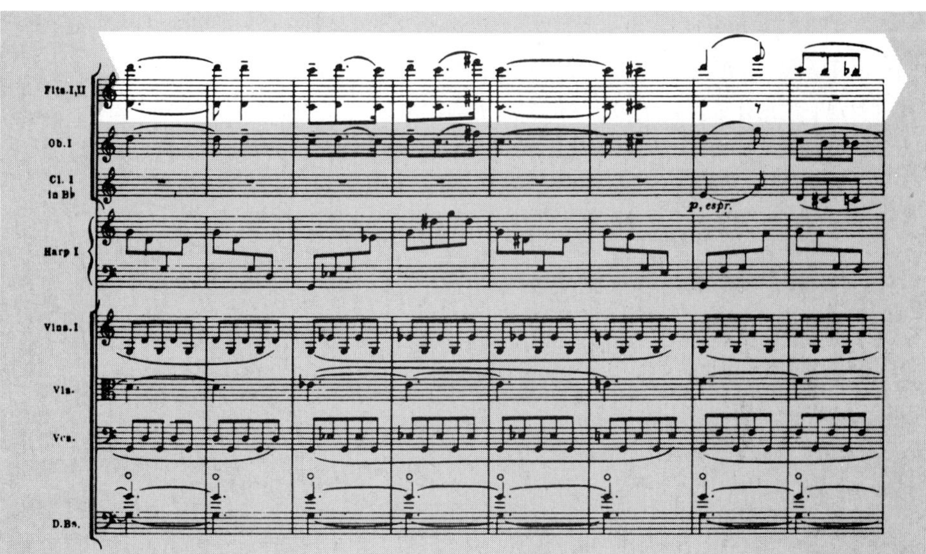

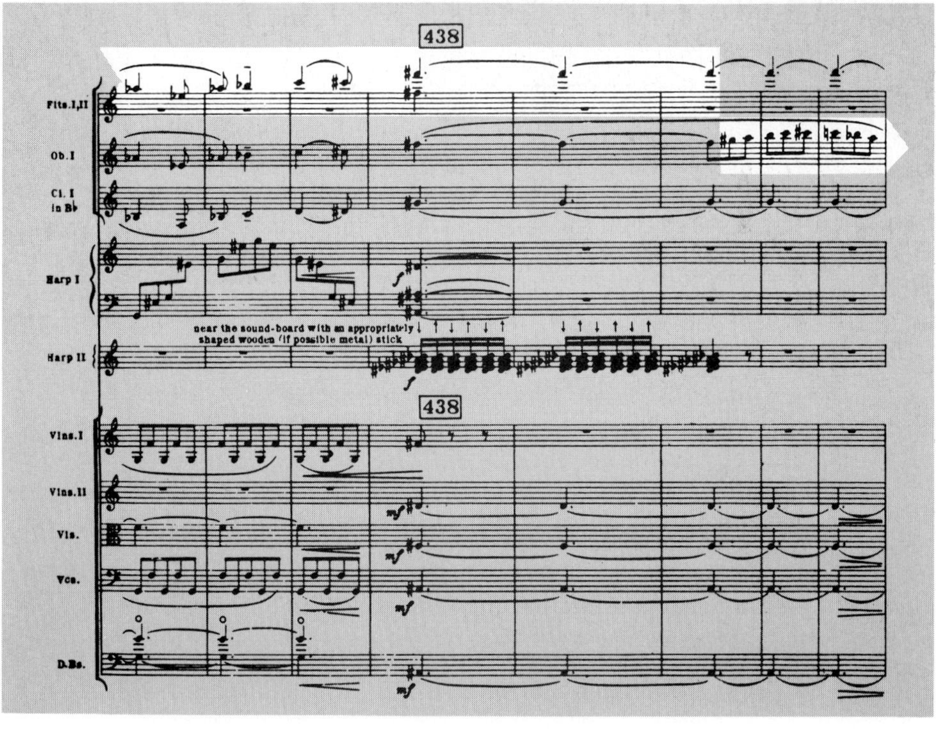

438
Flts.I,II
Ob.I
Cl. I in B♭
Harp I
near the sound-board with an appropriately shaped wooden (if possible metal) stick
Harp II
438
Vlns.I
Vlns.II
Vla.
Vcs.
D.Bs.

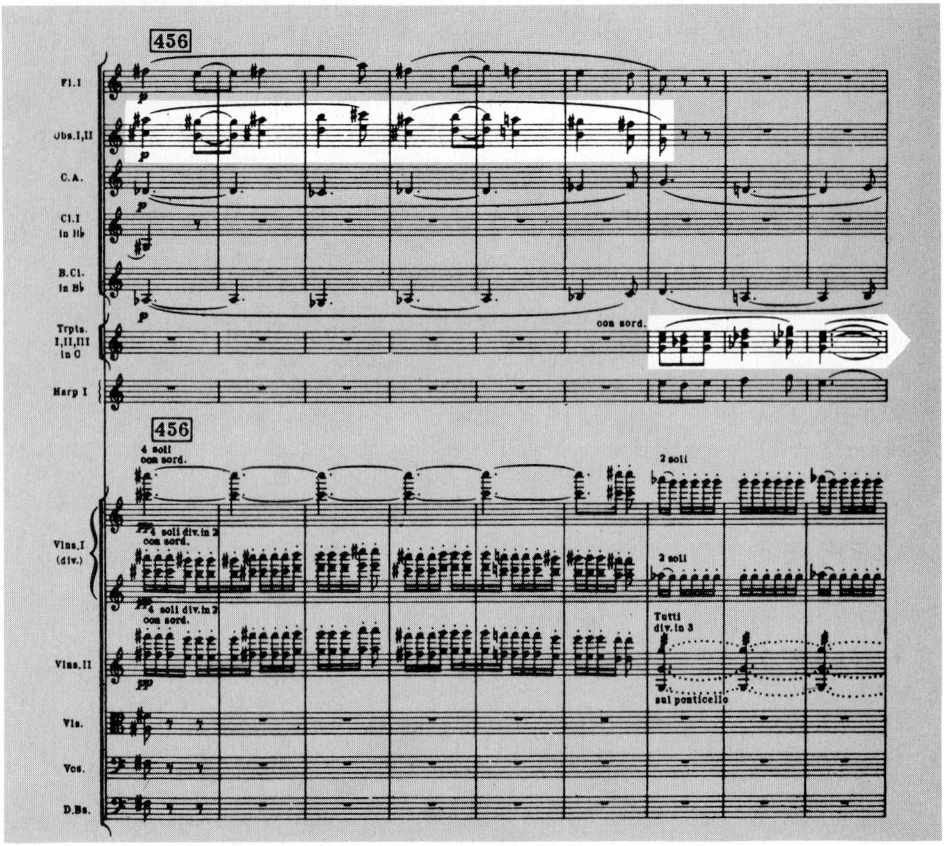

456
Fl. I
Obs. I, II
C. A.
Cl. I in B♭
B. Cl. in B♭
Trpts. I, II, III in C
Harp I
p
con sord.
456
4 soli con sord.
ppp 4 soli div. in 2 con sord.
ppp 4 soli div. in 2 con sord.
2 soli
2 soli
Tutti div. in 3
sul ponticello
Vlns. I (div.)
Vlns. II
Vla.
Vcs.
D.Bs.

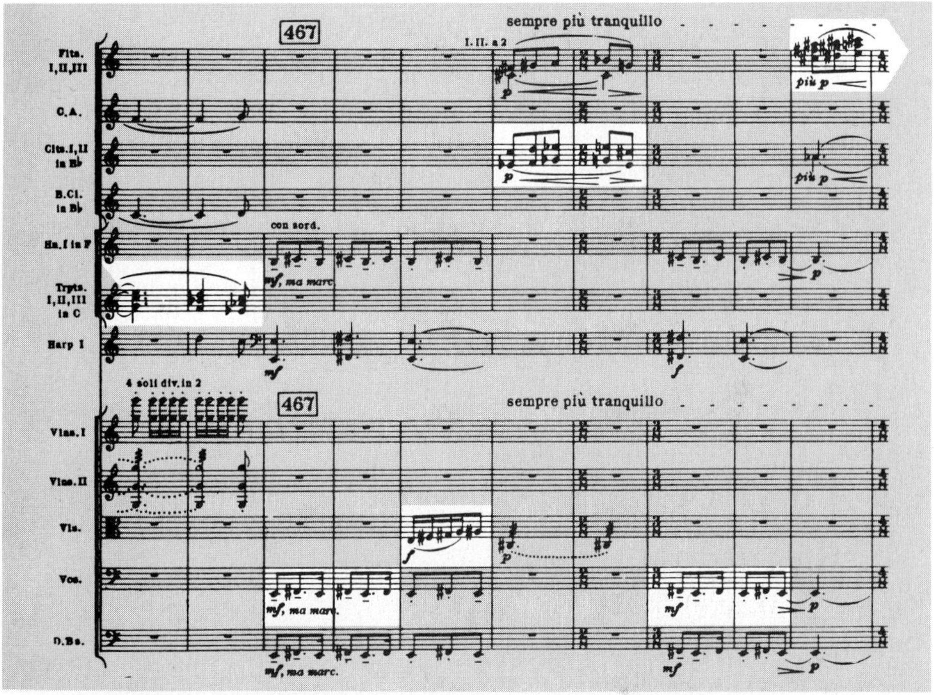

467
sempre più tranquillo
I. II. a 2
Flts. I, II, III
C. A.
Clts. I, II in B♭
B. Cl. in B♭
con sord.
Hn. I in F
mf, ma marc.
Trpts. I, II, III in C
Harp I
4 soli div. in 2
467
sempre più tranquillo
Vlns. I
Vlns. II
Vla.
Vcs.
mf, ma marc.
D. Bs.
mf, ma marc.

488
al
Tempo I. (♩. = 88)
Flts. I, II
a 2
Obs. I, II
Clts. I, II in B♭
I, II
Bsns.
III
f, cresc.
Hns. I, III in F
I, II
Trbs.
III
Tuba
Timp.
488
al
Tempo I. (♩. = 88)
Vlns. I
cresc.
ordinario senza sord.
Vlns. II
f, cresc.
Vla.
cresc.
Vcs.
cresc.
D. Bs.
cresc.
1' 27"

494
500
Flts. I,II
a 2
I,II
Obs.
III
I,II
Clts.in B♭
III
Bsns.I,II
I,III
Hns. in F
II,IV
senza sord.
Trpt.I in C
I,II
Trbs.
III
Tuba
Vlns. I
Vlns. II
Vls.
Vcs.
D.Bs.

509
I
Obs.
II
Obs.
III
I
Cl's in B♭
II
Cl's in B♭
III
a 2
I, II
Bsns.
III
f, cresc.
cresc.
f
I, III
Hns. in F
II, IV
Timp.
p, cresc.
509
Vlns. I
Vlns. II
Vls.
Vcs.
D.Bs.
ff

514
521
Picc.
I
Flts.
II
I
Obs.
II
Obs.
III
I
Cl.ta in B♭
II
Cl.ta in B♭
III
I, II
Bsns
III
I, III
Hns. in F
II, IV
Trpts. I, II, III in C
senza sord.
Trbs. I, II
Trb. III Tuba
Timp.
514
521
Vlns. I
Vlns. II
Vls.
Vcs.
D. Bs.
f, cresc.
f cresc.
ff
a 2
a 3
gliss.
Duration of 1st movement approx. 9′48″ 22″

27. IGOR STRAVINSKY (1882-1971), Opening Scene from *The Rite of Spring* (1913)

4
Oboe 2.
Cor. ingl.
Clar. picc.
Solo
espress.
Clar. (La)
Clar. basso 2
Fag.
Corni (Fa)
Viol. 2.
V-le
pizz.
dim.
4

5
Fl. gr.
Fl. c-alto in Sol
Oboi 1.2.
1. Solo
Clar. picc.
Clar. (La)
Clar. basso 1.2.
un peu en dehors
Cor. (Fa)
Viol. 2.
V-le
5

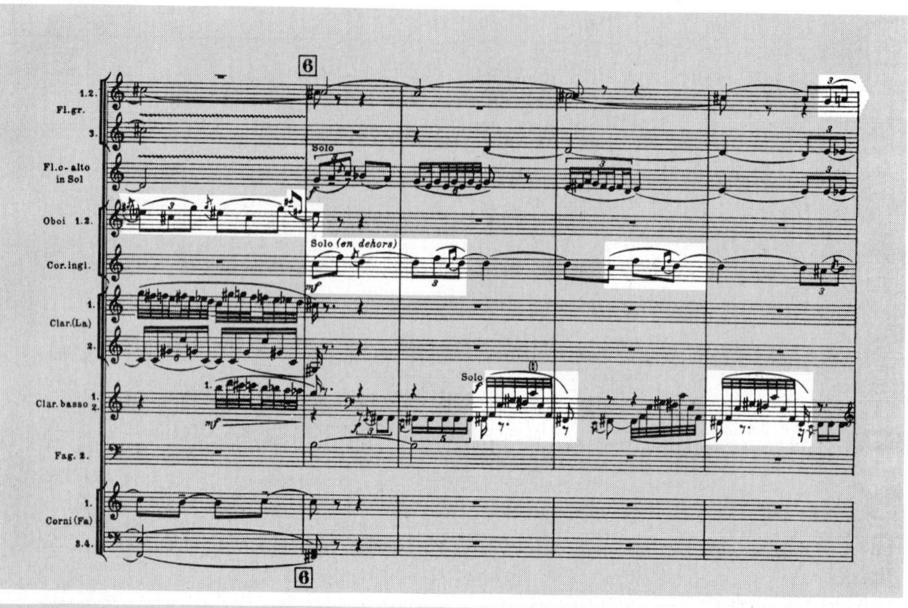
6
Fl.gr.
Fl.c-alto in Sol
Solo
Oboi 1.2.
Solo (en dehors)
mf
Cor. ingl.
Clar.(La)
Clar. basso
Solo
f
mf
Fag. 2.
Corni (Fa)
6

7
Fl.gr.
Fl. 3 : Fl. picc. 2.
Fl. in Sol
Oboi
mf
Cor. ingl.
Clar. picc.
Solo
mf espress.
Clar. 1.2. (La)
legato
mf
Clar. basso
Corni 1.2.
p
Viol. 1.
Cello Solo
pizz.
7

Fl. picc.
Fl. gr. 1.
Fl. in Sol
Oboi
Cor. ingl.
Clar. picc.
Clar. 1.2. (La)
Clar. basso
Fag. 1.
Cor. 1.2.
Cello Solo
trem.
Solo
sim.
(très en dehors)
Cl. basso 2 = Cl. 2 Sib

8
Fl. gr. 1.
Fl. in Sol
Clar. picc.
Clar. (La)
Fag.
C-Fag.
Basso Solo
dim.
poco più

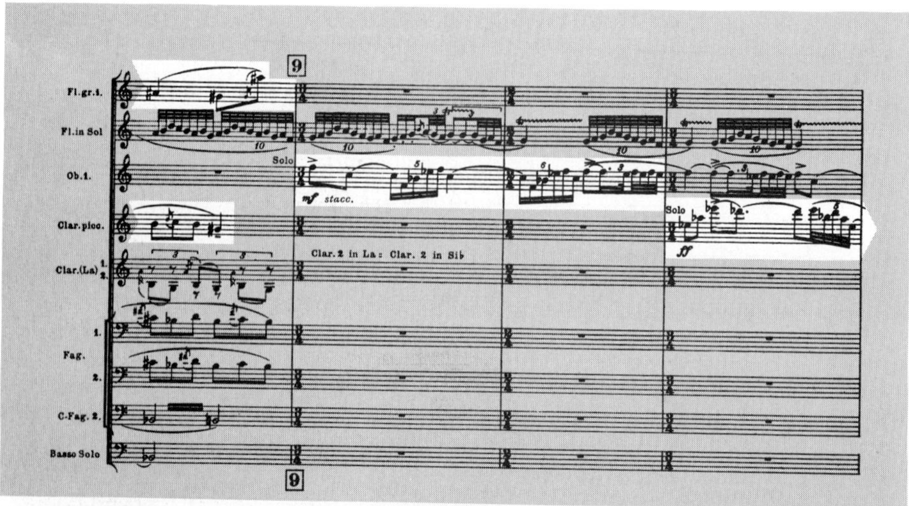

9
Fl.gr.1.
Fl.in Sol
Ob.1.
Solo
mf stacc.
Clar.picc.
Solo
ff
Clar.(La) 1. 2.
Clar. 2 in La : Clar. 2 in Si♭
Fag. 1. 2.
C-Fag. 2.
Basso Solo
9

10
Fl.gr.2.
mf
Fl.in Sol
Obol 1.
Clar.picc.
Solo
sempre ff
Clar. 1.(La)
très en dehors
Clar. 3.(Si♭)
f
C-Fag. 1. 2.
mf
Cello Solo 2.
2. con sord. (arco)
6 Contrabassi.
con sord.
pizz.
10

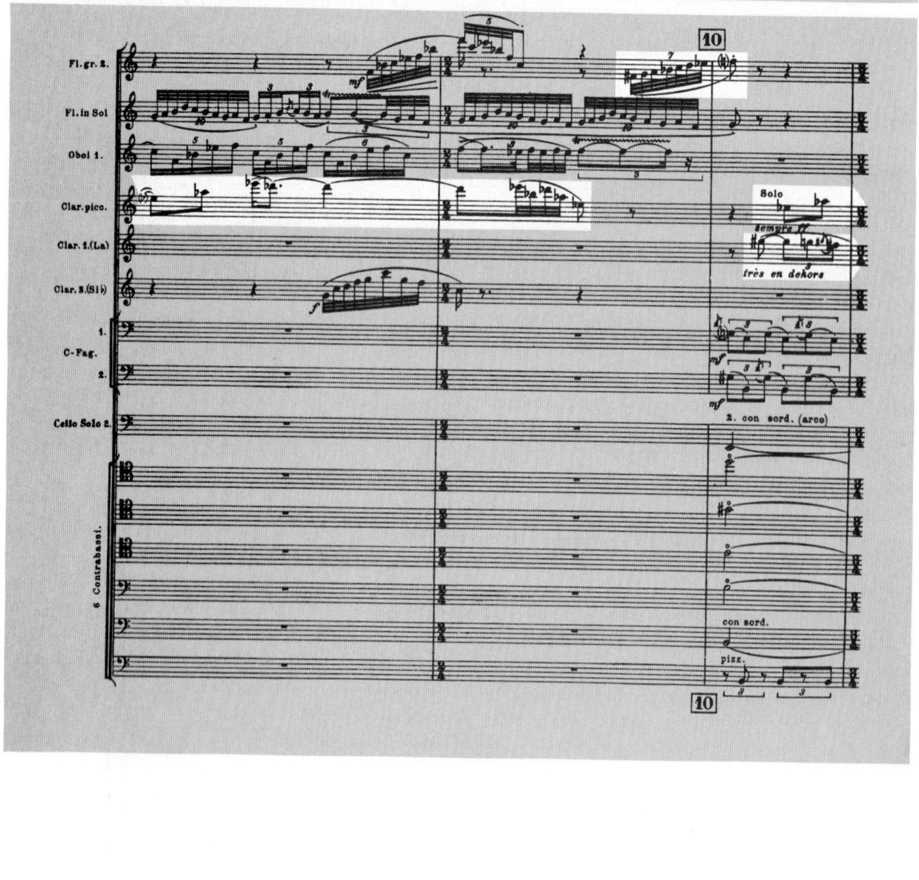

Fl. picc.
Fl. gr.
Oboi
Cor. ingl.
Clar. picc.
Clar. 1 (La)
Clar. 2 (Si♭)
C-Fag.
Tr. picc. in Re
Cello Solo
6 Contrabassi.
Solo
Flatterzunge
Solo (come sopra)
con sord.

11
Fl. picc.
Fl. gr.
Fl. in Sol
Oboi
Cor. ingl.
Clar. picc.
Clar. 1. (La)
Clar. (Sib)
Clar. basso 1.
Fag.
C-Fag.
Cor.
Tr. picc. (Re)
Viol. Solo
V-le
2 Celli
6 Contrabassi.
Flatterzunge
sul Sol
5 Viole
glissando
sul Do
arco
(pizz.)
Soli
11

12 Tempo I ♩=50
Fl. picc.
Fl. gr.
Fl. in Sol
Oboi
Cor. ingl.
Clar. picc.
Clar. 1. (La)
Clar. (Si♭)
Clar. basso 1.
Solo.
(come sopra)
Fag.
C.-Fag.
to 4th Fag.
Cor.
Tr. picc. (Re)
Viol. Solo.
Viole (div.)
2 Celli Soli.
(senza sord.)
6 Contrabassi.
(senza sord.)
12 Tempo I ♩=50

Clar. picc.
Clar. 1.(La)
Clar. 2.3. (Si♭)
Clar.basso 1.
Fag. 1.
Cor. 1.2.
Viol. 1.
6 Viole Sole
Tutti
pizz.
con sord.
Viole Tutte
Celli Tutti
C-bassi Tutti

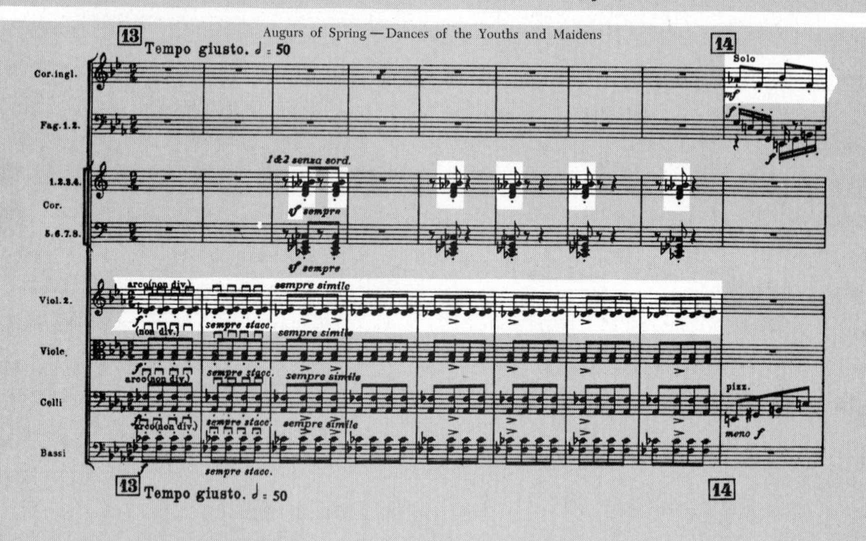
Augurs of Spring — Dances of the Youths and Maidens
13
Tempo giusto. 𝅗𝅥 = 50
14
Solo
Cor. ingl.
Fag. 1.2.
1&2 senza sord.
sf sempre
Cor.
Viol. 2.
Viole
Celli
Bassi
arco (non div.)
sempre stacc.
sempre simile
pizz.
meno f

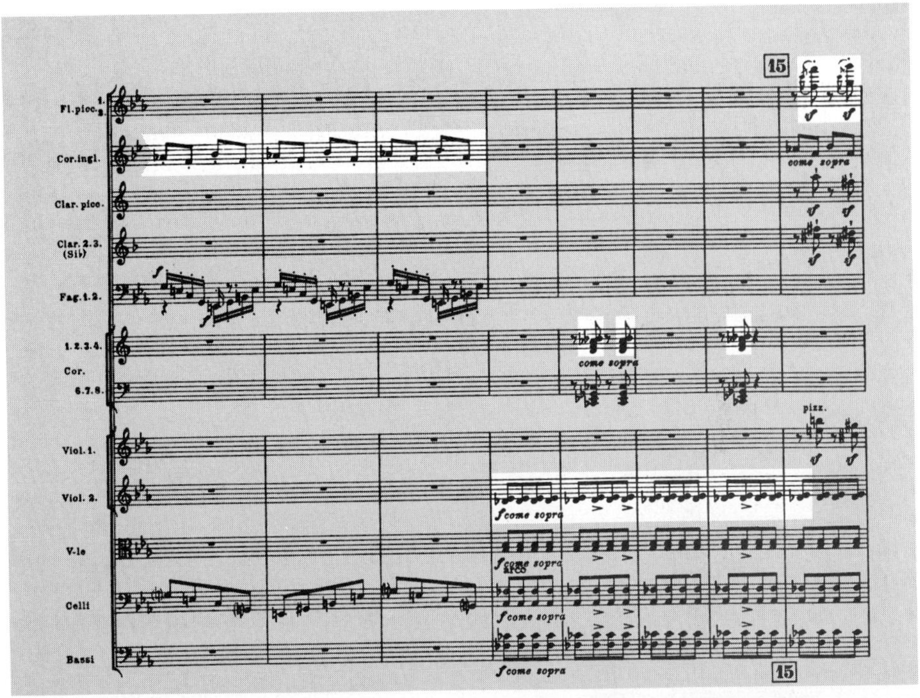

15

Fl. picc. 1. 2.

Cor. ingl.

come sopra

Clar. picc.

Clar. 2. 3. (Si♭)

Fag. 1. 2.

1. 2. 3. 4. Cor. 6. 7. 8.

come sopra

pizz.

Viol. 1.

Viol. 2.

f come sopra

V-le

f come sopra

arco

Celli

f come sopra

Bassi

f come sopra

15

17
Fl. picc.
Fl. gr.
Flatterzunge
Fl. in Sol
Flatterzunge
3 Oboi
a 2
sempre simile
Cor. ingl.
Clar. picc.
sim.
Flatterzunge
Clar. 1. (La)
Clar. (Si♭)
Flatterzunge
Fag. 1. 2.
Cor. 4.
con sord.
picc. in Re
Trombe
1. 2. 3. 4. in Do
con sord.
Viol. 1.
Viol. 2.
pizz.
V-le
Celli
sf meno f
Bassi
17

18
Fl. picc.
Fl. gr.
Fl. in Sol
2 Oboi
Cor. ingl.
Clar. picc.
Clar. 1 (La)
Clar. (Si♭)
Fag. 1.2.
8 Corni
picc. in Re
Trombe
1.2.3.4. in Do
Viol. 1.
Viol. 2.
V-le
Celli
Bassi
sim.
a2
muta in Mi♭
muta in Si♭
4º senza sord.
sf sempre
senza sord.
arco
sempre sim.
non div.
unis.
come sopra
18

19
a 2
Fag. 1.2. 3.
C-Fag. 1.
Cor.
Viol. 1.
V-le
Celli
Bassi
p sub.
f
20
piu f
Trombone 1.
mf
21
Fl. 1.
Oboi 1.2.

22
23
Fl.picc.
Fl.gr.1.
Oboi. 1.2.
Cor. ingl.
Clar.2.3.(Si♭)
Fag.2.
1.2.5.6.
Cor.
3.4.7.8.
Tr. picc.(Re)
Tr.1.(Do)
Tr-boni. 1 2
Tube. 1.2.
Timp.
Gr. C.
Viol. Solo.
Viol. 1.
Viol. 2.
V-le.
Celli.
Bassi.
sim.
Solo
stacc.
marc.
pizz.
arco

Cor. ingl.
Clar. 2.3.(Sib)
Fag.
Tr. 1. (Do)
2 Viol. Soli
Viol. 1.
Viol. 2.
V-le
Celli
Solo
marc.
sim.
24
sul Sol
col legno
col legno sino al segno
pizz.
p sub.

Fl. gr. 1.
Fag.
Cor. 1. 2.
2 Viol. Soli
Viol. 1.
Viol. 2.
V-le
Celli
25
Solo
mp (mais en dehors)

26
Fl. gr. 1.
Oboi 1. 2.
Soli
mf
1. 2.
Fag.
3. 4.
Cor. 1.
Tr. 1. (Do)
Solo
mf
2 Viol. Solo
Viol. 1.
Viol. 2.
V-le
Celli
26
27
Fl. gr. 2.
Fl. in Sol
Solo
f
mf
Clar. 2. 3. (Si♭)
p
1. 2.
Fag
3. 4.
Cor. 5.
Solo
mf
Solo con sord.
senza sord.
Tr. 2. (Do)
2. Viol. Solo
Viol. 1.
Viol. 2. div.
V-le
Celli
27

28
Fl.gr.
Fl. in Sol
Clar. picc. (Mib)
Clar. (Sib)
Clar. basso
Fag.
C-Fag.
Cor 5.
Tr-boni 1. 2.
Timp.
2 Viol. Solo.
Viol. 1.
Viol. 2. div.
V-le.
Celli.
Bassi.
pizz.
28

29
Fl. picc.
Fl. gr.
Fl. in Sol.
Oboi 1. 2.
Clar. picc. (Mi♭)
Clar. (Si♭)
Clar. basso
Fag.
C-Fag.
Tr. (Do)
Tr-boni 1. 2.
Timp.
Triang.
bag. en bois
Cymb. antique
Viol. 1.
Viol. 2.
V-le, div. en 2.
2 Soli
Celli
gli altri
Bassi
stacc.
mp cantabile
Pult 5.6. 7.8.
Tutti
div. en 2
arco
marcatiss. e molto cantabile
29

30
Fl. picc. 1. 2.
Fl. gr. 1. 2.
Fl. in Sol
Oboi 1. 2. 3.
Cor. ingl. 1. 2.
Clar. picc. (Mib)
Clar. (Sib) 1. 2. 3.
Clar. basso
Fag. 1. 2. 3. 4.
Cor. 1. 2. 3. 4. 5. 6. 7. 8.
Tr. (Do) 1. 2. 3. 4.
Tr-boni 1. 2.
Timp. 1. 2. 3.
Triang
bag. en bois
Cymb. antique
Viol. 1. div. en 2.
Viol. 2. div. en 2.
V-le. div. en 3.
3 Celli Soli
Celli gli altri
Bassi
sim.
2° cor. ingl. to Ob. 4°
4° Fag. to C. Fag. 2°
p sub. e stacc.
pizz.
p sub.
sur le sol
4 Sole
Tutte le altre
30

Clar. picc. (Mib)
Clar. (Sib)
Clar. basso
sempre sf
(in Re)
Viol. 1.
Viol. 2.
4 Solo
V-le.
le altre
3 Soli
Celli
gli altri
Bassi
cresc.
meno f

31
Solo
Fl. picc. 1.
mf grazioso
Oboi
Cor. ingl. 1
C-Fag. 1. 2.
Cor. 4.
Viol. 1.
Viol. 2.
V-le.
Celli
div.
pizz.
(pizz.)
a 2
sff

32
Fl.picc.1.2.
Fl.gr.
Fl.in Sol
Oboi
Cor.ingl.
Clar.picc.(Re)
Clar.(Sib)
Fag.3.
C-Fag.1.2.
Cor.
Tr.(Do)
Viol.1.
Viol.2.
V.le.
Celli
Bassi
f sempre
sim.
arco
mf cresc
32

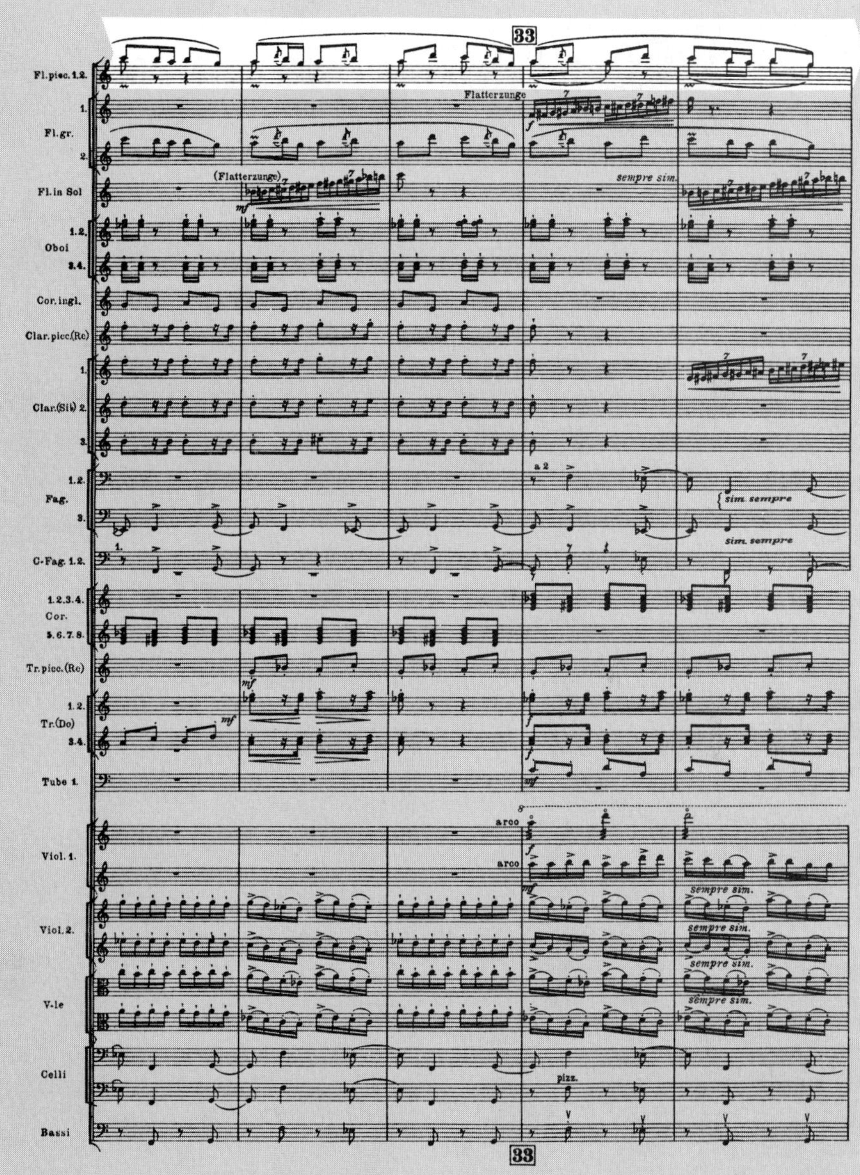

33
Fl. picc. 1.2.
Fl. gr.
Flatterzunge
(Flatterzunge)
sempre sim.
Fl. in Sol
Oboi
Cor. ingl.
Clar. picc. (Re)
Clar. (Si♭)
a 2
Fag.
sim. sempre
C-Fag. 1.2.
Cor.
Tr. picc. (Re)
Tr. (Do)
Tube 1.
arco
Viol. 1.
Viol. 2.
sempre sim.
V-le
Celli
pizz.
Bassi
33

34
Fl. picc. 1.2.
Fl. gr.
Fl. in Sol
Oboi
Cor. ingl.
Clar. picc. (Re)
Clar. (Si♭)
Clar. basso
Fag. 1.2.3.
C-Fag. 1.2.
Cor.
Tr. picc. (Re)
Tr. (Do)
Tr-boni.
Tube
Viol. 1.
Viol. 2.
V-le
Celli
Bassi
sempre sim.
stacc.
Flatterzunge
(Flatterzunge)
a 2
a 3
poco più f
f assai
sim.
arco

35
Fl. picc. 1.2.
Fl. gr.
sempre sim.
Fl. in Sol
Oboi
2.3.4.
Cor. ingl.
Clar. picc. (Re)
Clar. (Si♭)
Clar. basso
Fag. 1.2.3.
C-Fag. 1.2.
1.2.3.4.
Cor.
5.6.7.8.
Tr. picc. (Re)
4. Tr. (Do)
1.2.
Tr-boni
3.
Tube
poco più f
Timp.
secco
Viol. 1.
Viol. 2.
V-le
4 Pos.
div.
Celli
Bassi
35

36
Fl. picc. 1.2.
Fl. gr.
Fl. in Sol
Oboi
2.3.4.
Cor. ingl.
Clar. picc. (Re)
Clar. (Si♭)
Clar. basso
Fag. 1.2.3.
C-Fag. 1.2.
2° C. Fag. to Fag. 4°
gliss.
Cor. 3.4.
5.6.7.8.
Tr. picc. (Re)
4 Tr. (Do)
Tr-boni
come sopra
Tube
Timp.
come sopra
Viol. 1.
Viol. 2.
V-le
Celli
Bassi
36

Ritual of Abduction
37
Presto ♩.= 132
38
Fl. picc. 1.2.
Fl. gr. 1.2.
Fl. in Sol
Oboi
Cor. ingl.
Clar. picc. (Re)
Clar. (Sib)
Clar. basso
Fag. 1.2.
Cor.
Tr. picc. (Re)
Tr. (Do)
Timp. gr.
Gr. C.
Viol. 1.
Viol. 2.
V-le
Celli
Bassi
a 2
ff
ff marcatissimo
2' Picc. to Fl. 3°
trem.
sim.
f ben tenuto
Solo
enharm.
secco
poco sf
non div.
sempre f
pizz.
(pizz.)
(arco)
37
Presto ♩.= 132
38

39
Fl.gr.
Fl.in Sol
Oboi
Cor.ingl.
Clar.picc.(Re)
Clar.(Sib)
Clar.basso
Fag.
Cor.
Tr-boni
Timp.picc.
Timp.gr.
4 Viol. Soli
Viol.1.
Viol.2.
V-le
Celli
Bassi
Flatterz.
Cor.ingl.2
(in Mib)
secco
Soli
a 2
Solo
f assai
glissando détaché
détaché
div.
pizz.
39

40
Fl. picc. 1.
Fl. gr. 1.2.3
à 3
Soli
a 2
Cor.
1. 2.
5.
bouché
Tr. picc. (Re)
Tr. (Do)
Tutti
pizz.
Viol. 1.
Viol. 2.
V-le
p sub. cresc.
Celli
Bassi
40

41
Fl.gr. 1.2.
Fl. in Sol
Oboi
Cor.ingl.
Clar.(Sib)
Clar.basso
Fag.
Cor.
secco
a 3
a 2
Tr.(Do)
Tr-boni
Tube
Timp.picc.
Timp.gr.
arco
Viol.1.
Viol.2.
V.le
Celli
Bassi
41

42 crescendo poco a poco
Fl. picc.
Fl. gr.
Fl. in Sol
Oboi
Cor. ingl. 1.2.
Clar. picc. (Mi♭)
Clar. (Si♭)
Cor.
Tr. (Do)
4 Viol. Soli
Viol. 1.
Viol. 2.
V-le
Celli
Bassi
pizz.
arco
42 crescendo poco a poco

43
Fl. picc.
Fl. gr.
Fl. in Sol
Oboi
Cor. ingl.
Clar. picc. (Mi♭)
Clar. (Si♭)
Fag.
Cor.
Tr. picc. (Re)
Tr. (Do)
Tr-boni
4 Viol. Soli
Viol. 1.
Viol. 2.
V-le
Celli
unis.
arco
a2
43

44
45
Fl.picc. 1
Fl.gr.
Fl.in Sol
Oboi
Cor.ingl. 1.2.
Clar.picc.(Mib)
Clar.(Sib)
Clar.basso
Fag.
C-Fag. 1.2.
Cor.
Tr.picc.(Re)
Tr.(Do)
Tr-boni
Tube 1.2.
Timp.gr.
Viol. 1.
Viol. 2.
V-le
Celli
Bassi
3°Fl to Picc 2°
4°Fag to C.Fag 2°
1.Solo
marc.
p sub. crescendo
p sub.
gliss.
arco

46
Fl.picc.1.2.
Fl.gr.1.2.
Fl.in Sol
Oboi
Cor.ingl.1.2.
Cor.ingl.1.2 : Ob.4
Clar.picc.(Mib)
Clar.(Sib)
Clar. basso
Fag. 1.2.3.
C-Fag. 1.2.
Cor.
(pavillons en l'air)
(pavillons en l'air)
Tr.picc.(Re)
Tr.(Do)
Tr.boni 1.2.3.
Tube 1.2.
Timp.gr.
modo ordin.
Gr. C.
loco
Viol.1.
Viol.2.
V-le
Celli
Bassi
46

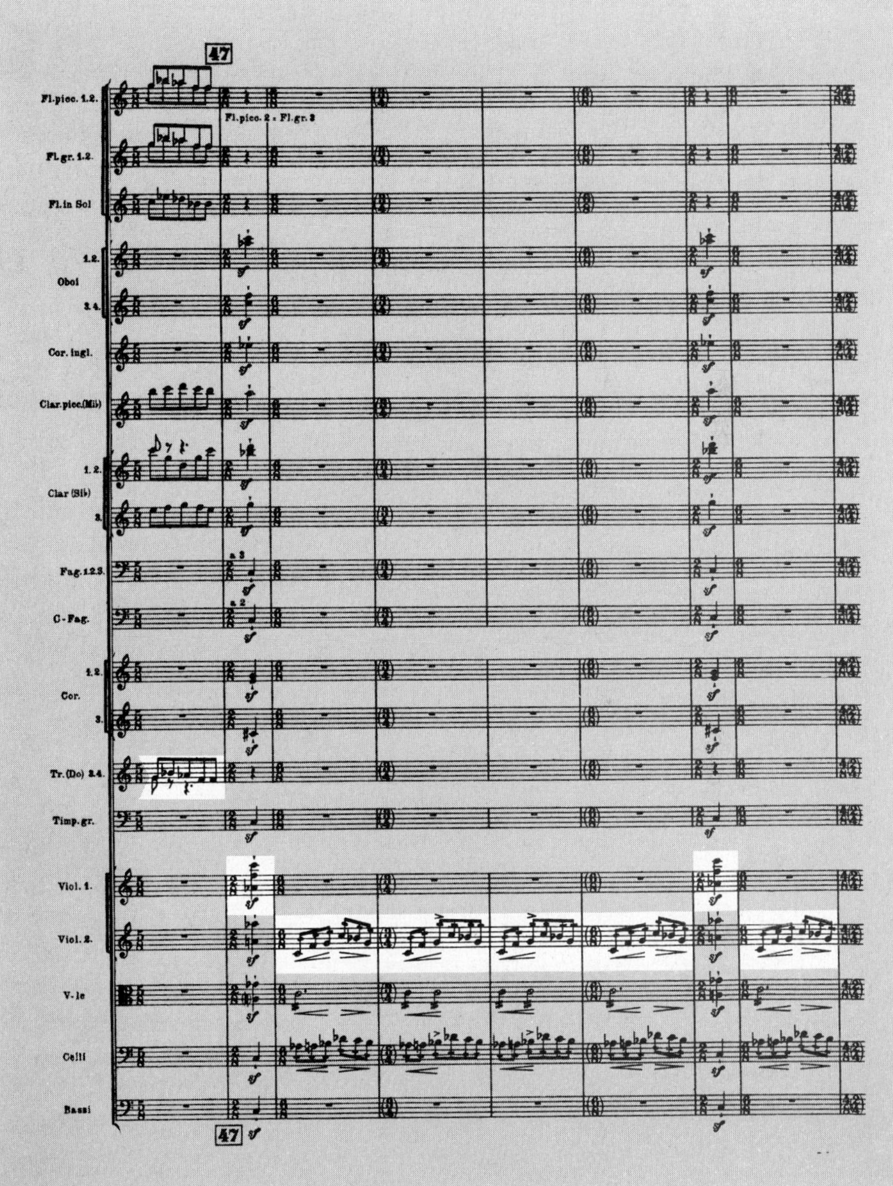
47
Fl. picc. 1.2.
Fl. picc. 2 = Fl. gr. 3
Fl. gr. 1.2.
Fl. in Sol
Oboi 1.2.
3.4.
Cor. ingl.
Clar. picc. (Mib)
Clar (Sib) 1.2.
3.
Fag. 1.2.3.
a 3
C-Fag.
a 2
Cor. 1.2.
3.
Tr. (Do) 3.4.
Timp. gr.
Viol. 1.
Viol. 2.
V-le
Celli
Bassi
sf
47

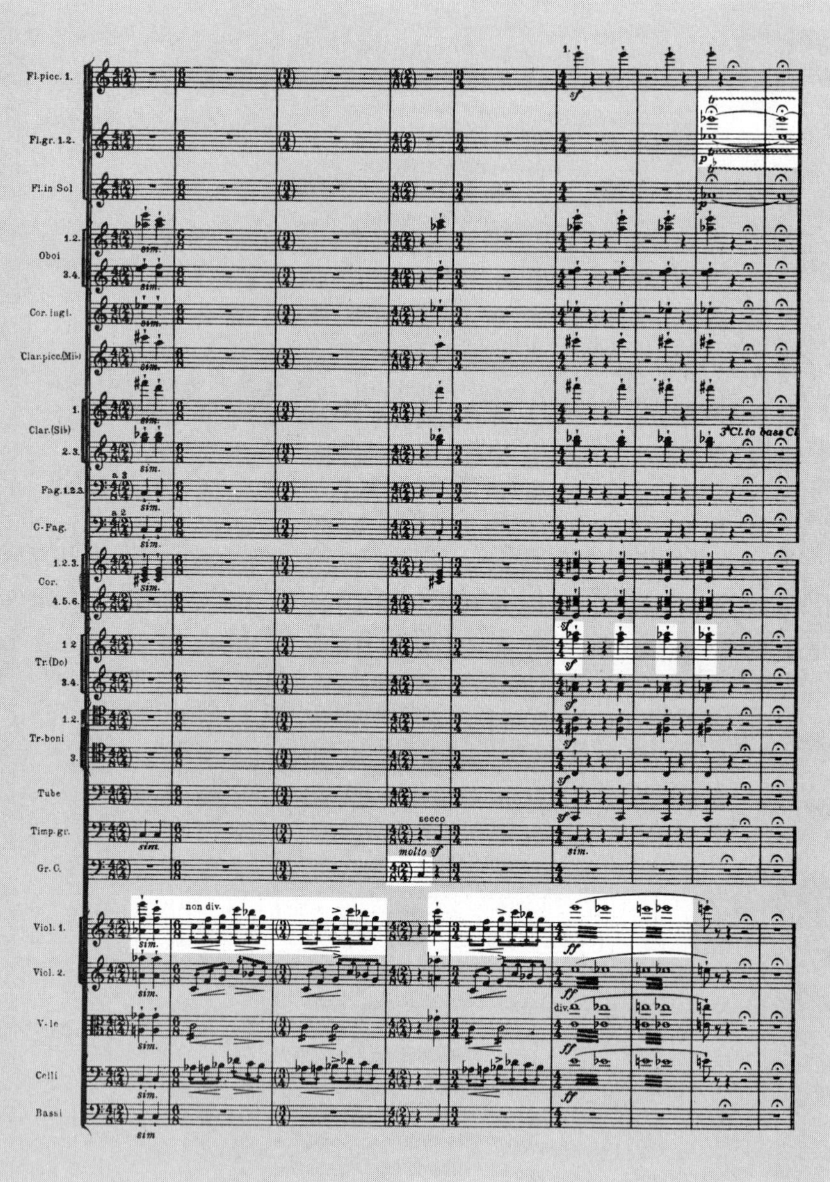
Fl.picc. 1.
Fl.gr. 1.2.
Fl.in Sol
Oboi
Cor. ingl.
Clar.picc.(Mi♭)
Clar.(Si♭)
Fag.1.2.3.
C-Fag.
Cor.
Tr.(Do)
Tr-boni
Tube
Timp. gr.
Gr. C.
Viol. 1.
Viol. 2.
V-le
Celli
Bassi
sim.
non div.
secco
molto sf
div.
3°Cl. to bass Cl.

28. STRAVINSKY, First movement from *Symphony of Psalms* (1930)

1
Fl. gr.
Oboi
C. I.
Fag.
C-Fag.
Tr-ni
Tr-ne (basso)
Timp.
Gr. C.
Arpa
P.-f.
V-C.
C-B.
mf
p

2
Fl. gr.
Oboi
C.I.
Fag.
C-Fag.
Cor.
Tr-ni
Tr-ne (basso)
Timp.
Gr.C.
Arpa
Piano 1
Piano 2
V-C.
C-B.
8va bassa
Arco unis.

cant. espressivo
3
Cor. 1 2
Piano 1
8a bassa
Piano 2
Una corda (secco)
V-Cello Solo
Arco
mf cant.
V-C. Solo
Gli altri V-Celli
Gli altri V-C.
C-B.
4
Oboi
C.I.
Fag.
Cor. 1 2
A.
mf cant.
E - - xau - -
Piano 1
8a bassa
Piano 2
V-C. Solo
Gli altri V-C.
C-B.

Oboi
C.I.
Fag.
A.
-di o - ra - ti - o - nem me - am, Do - mi - - - - ne

5
Oboi
C.I.
Fag.
S.
A.
T.
B.
Tutti V-C. div. a 2
mf
f cant.
Et de - pre - ca - ti - o - nem me - - - - am.
mf cant.

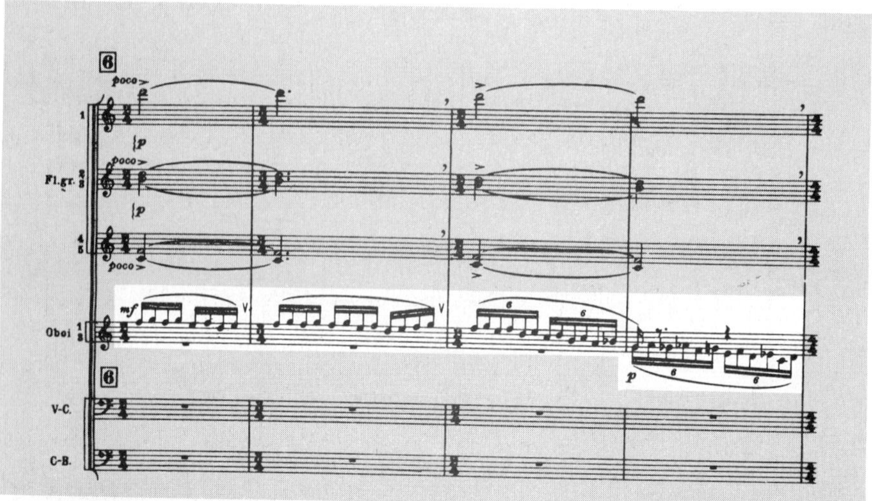
6
poco
p
Fl.gr.
poco
Oboi
mf
6
V-C.
C-B.

7
espressivo
mf
8
Oboi
p
C.I.
Fag.
A.
mf cant.
Au - ri - bus per - ci - pe lac - ri - mas me - -
Unis.
V-C.
C-B.

9
Fl.gr. 1 2
Fl.gr. 3 4
5
ben marc.
a 2
f
mf
sempre ben marc.
Fl.gr.5 = Fl.piccolo
Oboi 1 2
3 4
C.I.
Fag. 1
2 3
C-Fag.
Tr-ne 1 2
Tr-ne 3 (basso)
Timp.
Gr.C.
p
A.
T.
as.
Ne si -
Arpa
Piano 1
Piano 2
V-C.
C-B.
Div. Pizz.
Unis. Arco

Fl. gr.
Oboi
C. I.
Fag.
simili
C-Fag
Tr-ni
Tr-ne (basso)
Timp.
Gr. C.
S.
Ne si - le - as.
T.
- le - as, ne si - le - as.
Arpa
Piano 1
Piano 2
etc. simile
V-C.
Div. Pizz.
C-B.
Div. Pizz.

10
C. l.
mf stacc. e ben marc.
Fag.
mf stacc. e ben marc.
Tr-ni
Tr-ne (basso)
leggiero ma marcato
A.
ben cant.
Quo - - - - ni - - - am ad - - ve - na
B.
ben cant.
Quo - - - - ni - - - am ad - - ve - na

C. l.
Fag.
très court
C-Fag.
très court
Cor.
mf
Solo staccatissimo
Tr-ni
Tr-ne (basso)
Tuba
S.
ben cant.
e - - - go sum a - - - - - - pud
A.
e - - - go sum a - - - - - - pud
T.
ben cant.
a - - - pud
B.
e - - - go sum a - - - - - - pud

11
Oboi
Fag.
C-Fag.
Cor.
Tr-ba picc. Re
Tr-be Do
Tr-ni
Tr-ne (basso)
Tuba
f ben cant.
mf ben cant.
etc. simile
S.
A.
T.
B.
te et pe - - - re - gri - - - nus,

Fl. picc.
Fl. gr.
a 2
cres - cen - do
Oboi
C. I.
détaché et bien marqué
Fag.
C-Fag.
Cor.
Tr-ba picc. Re
Tr-be Do
Tr-ni
Tr-ne (basso)
Tuba
S.
A.
T.
B.
si - - - cut om - - - nes pa - - - tres

12
etc. sim.
Fl. picc.
Fl. gr.
a 2
etc. sim.
Fag.
sempre marcatissimo
C-Fag.
Cor. 1.3. 2.4.
sim.
Tr-ba picc. Re
Tr-be Do
Tr-ne (basso) e Tuba
8a bassa
S.
me - i
Re - mit - te mi - hi,
A.
T.
B.
Piano I
marcatissimo
Piano 2
V-C. unis.
Arco
C-B. unis.

Fl. picc.
sempre sfp
Fl. gr.
sempre sfp
Oboi
sempre sfp
sempre stacc.
sempre stacc.
C.I.
Fag.
sub. p
sempre stacc.
sempre stacc.
S.
re - - mit - te
A.
sub. meno f
re - mit - te mi - hi, ut re - fri -
T.
sub. meno f
re - mit - te, re - mit - te mi - hi, ut re - fri -
B.
re - mit - te
Arpa
mf staccatissimo sempre simile
muta LA♯ in LA♭
V-C.
sub. p
etc. stacc.
C-B.

13
Fl. picc.
Fl. gr. 1
Oboi
a 2
C. I.
Fag.
mf pesante
C-Fag.
mf pesante
13
S.
mi - - - hi, pri - us quam a - be - - -
A.
- - ge - rer pri - us quam a - be -
T.
- - ge - rer pri - us quam a - be - -
B.
mi - - - hi, pri - us quam a - be - -
Arpa
Piano 1
mf
Piano 2
f
V-C.
C-B.
mf e ben pesante

senza dim.
Fl. picc.
Fl. gr.
Oboi
C. I.
Fag.
C-Fag.
Cor.
Tr-ba picc. Re
Tr-be Do
Tr-ni
Tr-ne (basso)
Tuba
senza dim.
S.
A.
T.
B.
-am et ampli-us non e - - ro.
Piano 1
Piano 2
8a bassa
Div. a 2
V-C.
C-B.
Enchainez

Translation

Hear my prayer, O Lord, and give ear unto my cry; hold not Thy peace at my tears; for I am a stranger with Thee, and sojourner, as all my fathers were. O spare me, that I may recover strength: before I go hence, and be no more.

PSALM 39 (KING JAMES VERSION),
VERSES 12-13

29. ANTON WEBERN (1883-1945),
Pieces for Orchestra, Op. 10, Nos. 3 and 4 (1913)

zögernd
drängend - - zögernd molto rit. - - - tempo
5 molto espr.
Kl. in B
Hr. in F m. Dpf.
Pos. m.Dpf.
Harmon.
Mand.
Git.
Cel.
Hrf.
gr. Tr.
kl. Tr.
Glocken
kaum hörbar
äußerst leise
Herden-glocken
kaum hörbar
zögernd
drängend - - zögernd molto rit. - - - tempo
Solo - Gg. o. Dpf.
dolcissimo
Solo - Br. m. Dpf.
pizz. (vibrato)
arco
Solo - Vlc. m. Dpf.

rit.
10
Kl. in B
Hr. in F m. Dpf.
Pos. m.Dpf.
espress.
ppp
Harmon.
verklingend
Mand.
verklingend
Git.
Cel.
verklingend
Hrf.
verklingend
gr. Tr.
ppp
verklingend
kl. Tr.
äußerst leise
verklingend
Glocken
verklingend
Herden-glocken
verklingend
rit.
Solo-Gg. o. Dpf.
Solo-Br. m. Dpf.
Solo-Vlc. m. Dpf.
verklingend

IV.
Fließend, äußerst zart (♩=ca 60)
rit. - - tempo
rit.- 5 - - - - - tempo
Kl. in B
ppp
Trp. in B m. Dpf.
dolce
pp
Pos. m. Dpf.
dolcissimo
sehr gebunden
Mand.
dolce
Zeit lassen
p
Cel.
Hrf.
kl. Tr.
Fließend, äußerst zart (♩=ca 60)
rit. - - tempo
rit. - - - - - - tempo
wie ein Hauch
Solo-Gg. m. Dpf.
Solo-Br. m. Dpf.

30. EDGARD VARÈSE (1883-1965), *Ionisation* (1931)

1
1 Grande Cymbale Chinoise
Grosse Caisse (très grave)
2 Gong
Tam-tam clair
Tam-tam grave
Baguettes Timbales en feutre
3 2 Bongos clair grave
Caisse Roulante
2 Grosses Caisses moyenne grave
4 Tambour militaire
Caisse roulante
5 Sirène claire
Tambour à corde
6 Sirène grave
Fouet
Güiro
7 3 Blocs Chinois clair moyen grave
Claves
Triangle
8 Caisse claire
2 Maracas claire grave
9 Tarole
Caisse claire
Cymbale suspendue
10 Grelots
Cymbales
11 Güiro
Castagnettes
12 Tambour de Basque
Enclumes
13 Piano

2
3
1 Grande Cymbale Chinoise
Grosse Caisse (très grave)
2 Gong
Tam-tam clair
Tam-tam grave
3 2 Bongos clair grave
Caisse Roulante
2 Grosses Caisses moyenne grave
4 Tambour militaire
Caisse roulante
5 Sirène claire
Tambour à corde
6 Sirène grave
Fouet
Güiro
7 3 Blocs Chinois clair moyen grave
Claves
Triangle
8 Caisse claire
2 Maracas claire grave
9 Tarole
Caisse claire
Cymbale suspendue
10 Grelots
Cymbales
11 Güiro
Castagnettes
12 Tambour de Basque
Enclumes
13 Piano
(sec)

4
1 Grande Cymbale Chinoise
Grosse Caisse (très grave)
2 Gong
Tam-tam clair
Tam-tam grave
3 2 Bongos clair grave
Caisse Roulante
2 Grosses Caisses moyenne grave
Baguettes Timbales en Bois
4 Tambour militaire
Caisse roulante
Baguettes Timbales en feutre
5 Sirène claire
Tambour à corde
6 Sirène grave
Fouet
Güiro
7 3 Blocs Chinois clair moyen grave
Claves
Triangle
8 Caisse claire
2 Maracas claire grave
9 Tarole
Caisse claire
Cymbale suspendue
10 Grelots
Cymbales
11 Güiro
Castagnettes
12 Tambour de Basque
Enclumes
13 Piano
Fouet

sec
5
1 Grande Cymbale Chinoise
Grosse Caisse (très grave)
2 Gong
Tam-tam clair
Tam-tam grave
3 2 Bongos clair grave
Caisse Roulante
2 Grosses Caisses moyenne grave
4 Tambour militaire
Caisse roulante
5 Sirène claire
Tambour à corde
6 Sirène grave
Fouet
Güiro
7 3 Blocs Chinois clair moyen grave
Claves
Triangle
8 Caisse claire
2 Maracas claire grave
9 Tarole
Caisse claire
Cymbale suspendue
10 Grelots
Cymbales
11 Güiro
Castagnettes
12 Tambour de Basque
Enclumes
13 Piano
Fouet

1 Grande Cymbale Chinoise
Grosse Caisse (très grave)
2 Gong
Tam-tam clair
Tam-tam grave
3 2 Bongos clair grave
Caisse Roulante
2 Grosses Caisses moyenne grave
4 Tambour militaire
Caisse roulante
5 Sirène claire
Tambour à corde
6 Sirène grave
Fouet
Güiro
7 3 Blocs Chinois clair moyen grave
Claves
Triangle
8 Caisse claire
2 Maracas claire grave
9 Tarole
Caisse claire
Cymbale suspendue
10 Grelots
Cymbales
11 Güiro
Castagnettes
12 Tambour de Basque
Enclumes
13 Piano
Fouet

6
1 Grande Cymbale Chinoise
Grosse Caisse (très grave)
2 Gong
Tam-tam clair
Tam-tam grave
Baguettes Tambour
3 2 Bongos clair grave
Caisse Roulante
2 Grosses Caisses moyenne grave
4 Tambour militaire
Caisse roulante
5 Sirène claire
Tambour à corde
6 Sirène grave
Fouet
Güiro
7 3 Blocs Chinois clair moyen grave
Claves
Triangle
8 Caisse claire
2 Maracas claire grave
9 Tarole
Caisse claire
Cymbale suspendue
10 Grelots
Cymbales
11 Güiro
Castagnettes
12 Tambour de Basque
Enclumes
pouce
13 Piano

1 Grande Cymbale Chinoise
Grosse Caisse (très grave)
2 Gong
Tam-tam clair
Tam-tam grave
3 2 Bongos clair grave
Caisse Roulante
2 Grosses Caisses moyenne grave
Baguettes Timbales en peau
4 Tambour militaire
Caisse roulante
Baguettes Tambour
5 Sirène claire
Tambour à corde
6 Sirène grave
Fouet
Güiro
7 3 Blocs Chinois clair moyen grave
Claves
Triangle
8 Caisse claire
2 Maracas claire grave
9 Tarole
Caisse claire
Cymbale suspendue
10 Grelots
Cymbales
11 Güiro
Castagnettes
12 Tambour de Basque
Enclumes
(pouce)
13 Piano
Triangle
Grelots

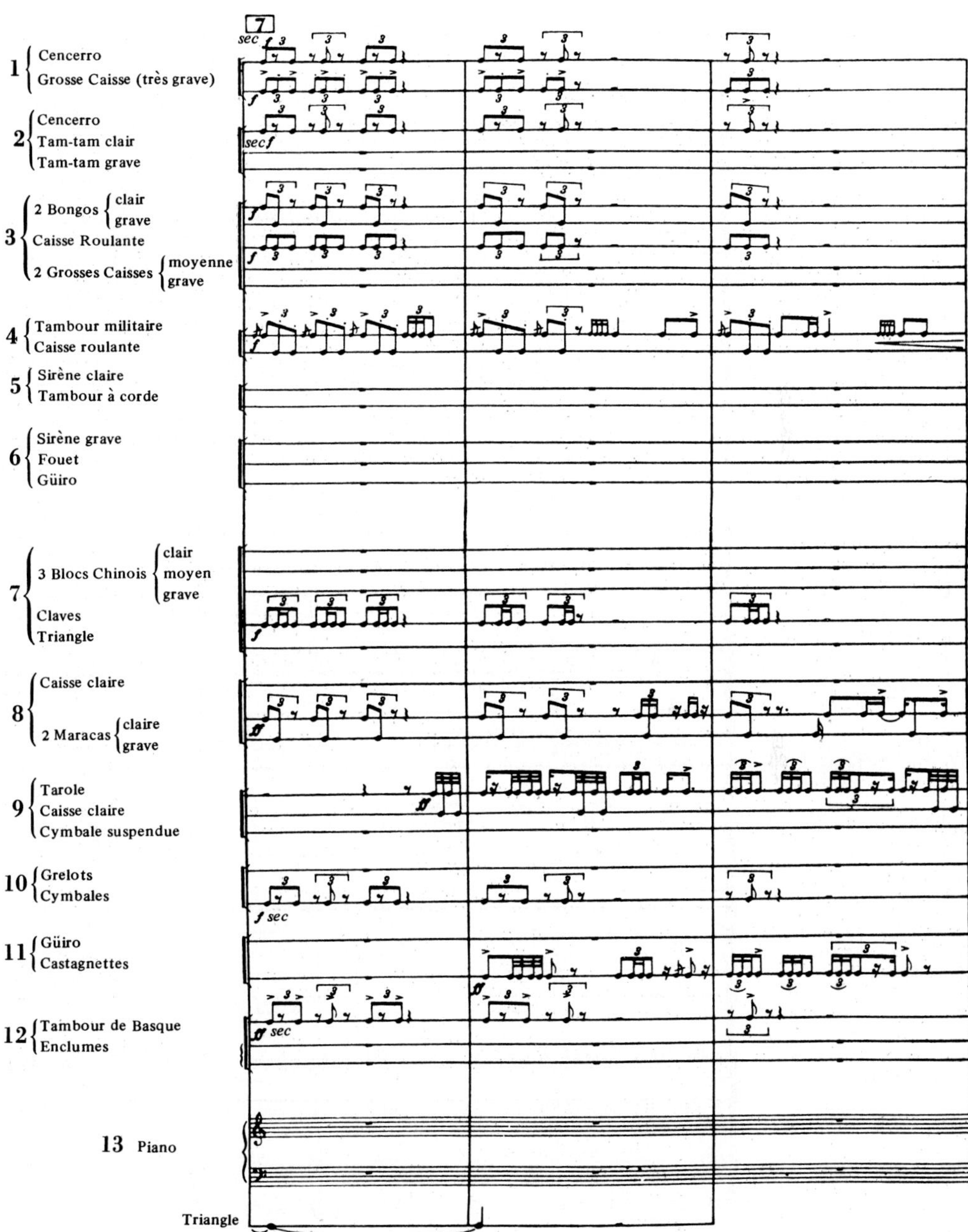
7
sec
1 Cencerro
Grosse Caisse (très grave)
2 Cencerro
Tam-tam clair
Tam-tam grave
secf
3 2 Bongos clair
grave
Caisse Roulante
2 Grosses Caisses moyenne
grave
4 Tambour militaire
Caisse roulante
5 Sirène claire
Tambour à corde
6 Sirène grave
Fouet
Güiro
7 3 Blocs Chinois clair
moyen
grave
Claves
Triangle
8 Caisse claire
2 Maracas claire
grave
9 Tarole
Caisse claire
Cymbale suspendue
10 Grelots
Cymbales
f sec
11 Güiro
Castagnettes
12 Tambour de Basque
Enclumes
ff sec
13 Piano
Triangle

1 Cencerro
Grosse Caisse (très grave)
2 Cencerro
Tam-tam clair
Tam-tam grave
3 2 Bongos clair grave
Caisse Roulante
2 Grosses Caisses moyenne grave
4 Tambour militaire
Caisse roulante
5 Sirène claire
Tambour à corde
6 Sirène grave
Fouet
Güiro
7 3 Blocs Chinois clair moyen grave
Claves
Triangle
8 Caisse claire
2 Maracas claire grave
9 Tarole
Caisse claire
Cymbale suspendue
10 Grelots
Cymbales
11 Güiro
Castagnettes
12 Tambour de Basque
Enclumes
13 Piano
8
sec
Baguettes Timbales en bois

1 Cencerro
Grosse Caisse (très grave)
2 Cencerro
Tam-tam clair
Tam-tam grave
3 2 Bongos clair grave
Caisse Roulante
2 Grosses Caisses moyenne grave
4 Tambour militaire
Caisse roulante
5 Sirène claire
Tambour à corde
6 Sirène grave
Fouet
Güiro
7 3 Blocs Chinois clair moyen grave
Claves
Triangle
8 Caisse claire
2 Maracas claire grave
9 Tarole
Caisse claire
Cymbale suspendue
10 Grelots
Cymbales
11 Güiro
Castagnettes
12 Tambour de Basque
Enclumes
13 Piano

Grande Cymbales Chinoise
9
1 Cencerro
Grosse Caisse (très grave)
2 Cencerro
Tam-tam clair
Tam-tam grave
Gong
3 2 Bongos clair
grave
Caisse Roulante
2 Grosses Caisses moyenne
grave
4 Tambour militaire
Caisse roulante
5 Sirène claire
Tambour à corde
6 Sirène grave
Fouet
Güiro
7 3 Blocs Chinois clair
moyen
grave
Claves
Triangle
8 Caisse claire
2 Maracas claire
grave
9 Tarole
Caisse claire
Cymbale suspendue
10 Grelots
Cymbales
frottez
11 Güiro
Castagnettes
12 Tambour de Basque
Enclumes
13 Piano

10
1 Grande Cymbale Chinoise
Grosse Caisse (très grave)
2 Gong
Tam-tam clair
Tam-tam grave
3 2 Bongos clair grave
Caisse Roulante
2 Grosses Caisses moyenne grave
4 Tambour militaire
Caisse roulante
5 Sirène claire
Tambour à corde
6 Sirène grave
Fouet
Güiro
7 3 Blocs Chinois clair moyen grave
Claves
Triangle
8 Caisse claire
2 Maracas claire grave
9 Tarole
Caisse claire
Cymbale suspendue
10 Grelots
Cymbales
11 Güiro
Castagnettes
12 Tambour de Basque
Enclumes
13 Piano
Baguettes de Timbales en peau
frottez

11
1 Grande Cymbale Chinoise
Grosse Caisse (très grave)
2 Gong
Tam-tam clair
Tam-tam grave
3 2 Bongos clair grave
Caisse Roulante
2 Grosses Caisses moyenne grave
4 Tambour militaire
Caisse roulante
5 Sirène claire
Tambour à corde
6 Sirène grave
Fouet
Güiro
7 3 Blocs Chinois clair moyen grave
Claves
Triangle
8 Caisse claire
2 Maracas claire grave
9 Tarole
Caisse claire
Cymbale suspendue
10 Grelots
Cymbales
sec
11 Güiro
Castagnettes
12 Tambour de Basque
Enclumes
13 Piano

1 Grande Cymbale Chinoise
Grosse Caisse (très grave)
2 Gong
Tam-tam clair
Tam-tam grave
3 2 Bongos clair grave
Caisse Roulante
2 Grosses Caisses moyenne grave
4 Tambour militaire
Caisse roulante
5 Sirène claire
Tambour à corde
6 Sirène grave
Fouet
Güiro
7 3 Blocs Chinois clair moyen grave
Claves
Triangle
8 Caisse claire
2 Maracas claire grave
9 Tarole
Caisse claire
Cymbale suspendue
10 Grelots
Cymbales
11 Güiro
Castagnettes
12 Tambour de Basque
Enclumes
13 Piano
Fouet

12
1 Grande Cymbale Chinoise
Grosse Caisse (très grave)
2 Gong
Tam-tam clair
Tam-tam grave
3 2 Bongos clair grave
Caisse Roulante
2 Grosses Caisses moyenne grave
4 Tambour militaire
Caisse roulante
5 Sirène claire
Tambour à corde
6 Sirène grave
Fouet
Güiro
7 3 Blocs Chinois clair moyen grave
Claves
Triangle
8 Caisse claire
2 Maracas claire grave
9 Tarole
Caisse claire
Cymbale suspendue
10 Grelots
Cymbales
11 Güiro
Castagnettes
12 Tambour de Basque
Enclumes
13 Piano
Fouet

1 Grande Cymbale Chinoise
Grosse Caisse (très grave)
2 Gong
Tam-tam clair
Tam-tam grave
3 2 Bongos clair grave
Caisse Roulante
2 Grosses Caisses moyenne grave
4 Tambour militaire
Caisse roulante
5 Sirène claire
Tambour à corde
6 Sirène grave
Fouet
Güiro
7 3 Blocs Chinois clair moyen grave
Claves
Triangle
8 Caisse claire
2 Maracas claire grave
9 Tarole
Caisse claire
Cymbale suspendue
10 Grelots
Cymbales
11 Güiro
Castagnettes
12 Tambour de Basque
Enclumes
13 Piano
Fouet

1 Grande Cymbale Chinoise
Grosse Caisse (très grave)
2 Gong
Tam-tam clair
Tam-tam grave
3 2 Bongos clair grave
Caisse Roulante
2 Grosses Caisses moyenne grave
4 Tambour militaire
Caisse roulante
5 Sirène claire
Tambour à corde
6 Sirène grave
Fouet
Güiro
7 3 Blocs Chinois clair moyen grave
Claves
Triangle
8 Caisse claire
2 Maracas claire grave
9 Tarole
Caisse claire
Cymbale suspendue
10 Grelots
Cymbales
11 Güiro
Castagnettes
12 Tambour de Basque
Enclumes
13 Piano
Triangle
Prenez Tam-tam clair
sec
molto
Prenez Cloches
Prenez Glockenspiel
pouce
Prenez Tam-tam

♩ = 52

13

1 { Tam-tam clair
Grosse Caisse (très grave)

2 { Gong
Tam-tam grave

3 { 2 Bongos { clair
grave
Caisse Roulante
2 Grosses Caisses { moyenne
grave

Baugettes Timbales éponge

4 { Tambour militaire
Caisse roulante

Voilá

5 { Sirène claire
Tambour à corde

6 { Sirène grave
Fouet
Güiro

7 { 3 Blocs Chinois { clair
moyen
grave
Claves
Triangle

8 { Caisse claire
2 Maracas { claire
grave

9 { Tarole
Caisse claire
Cymbale suspendue

L.V.

10 { Cloches

Sonne à la double 8va

11 { Glockenspiel à clavier
(with resonators)

12 { Grand Tam-tam
(très profond)

attaque sèche (percutée), Laissez vibrer, durée indiquée

13 Piano

Pèdale
jusqu' à la fin

8va bassa

1 Tam-tam clair
Grosse Caisse (très grave)
2 Gong
Tam-tam grave
3 2 Bongos clair grave
Caisse Roulante
2 Grosses Caisses moyenne grave
4 Tambour militaire
Caisse roulante
5 Sirène claire
Tambour à corde
6 Sirène grave
Fouet
Güiro
7 3 Blocs Chinois clair moyen grave
Claves
Triangle
8 Caisse claire
2 Maracas claire grave
9 Tarole
Caisse claire
Cymbale suspendue
L.V.
10 Cloches
Sonne à la double 8va
11 Glockenspiel
12 Grand Tam-tam (très profond)
13 Piano
8va bassa

Lunga
1 Tam-tam clair
Grosse Caisse (très grave)
2 Gong
Tam-tam grave
3 2 Bongos clair grave
Caisse Roulante
2 Grosses Caisses moyenne grave
4 Tambour militaire
Caisse roulante
5 Sirène claire
Tambour à corde
6 Sirène grave
Fouet
Güiro
7 3 Blocs Chinois clair moyen grave
Claves
Triangle
8 Caisse claire
2 Maracas claire grave
9 Tarole
Caisse claire
Cymbale suspendue
10 Cloches
11 Glockenspiel
12 Grand Tam-tam (très profond)
13 Piano
poco
Lunga
morendo
Lunga
morendo
8va bassa

31. ALBAN BERG (1885-1935), Act III, Scenes 4 and 5, from *Wozzeck* (1918-1921)

Berg's *Wozzeck* Act III, Scenes 4 & 5 reprinted through the courtesy of London Records, a Division of PolyGram Classics, Inc.

Wozz
da regt sich was.
whispered loudly
Still!
Cel
As
(frog croaks)
(mp)
230
accel
Etwas rascher
(spoken)
Al-les still und tot.
(shouting)
Mör-der!
Str m D
Trp m D
Holz
Hfe
gliss (quasi Des-Dur)
Mör - der!!
235
again whispered
Ha! da ruft's.
poco rit
gest Hr
Str
gliss (C-Dur)
Ces
(quasi Ces-Dur glissando)
Pos m D

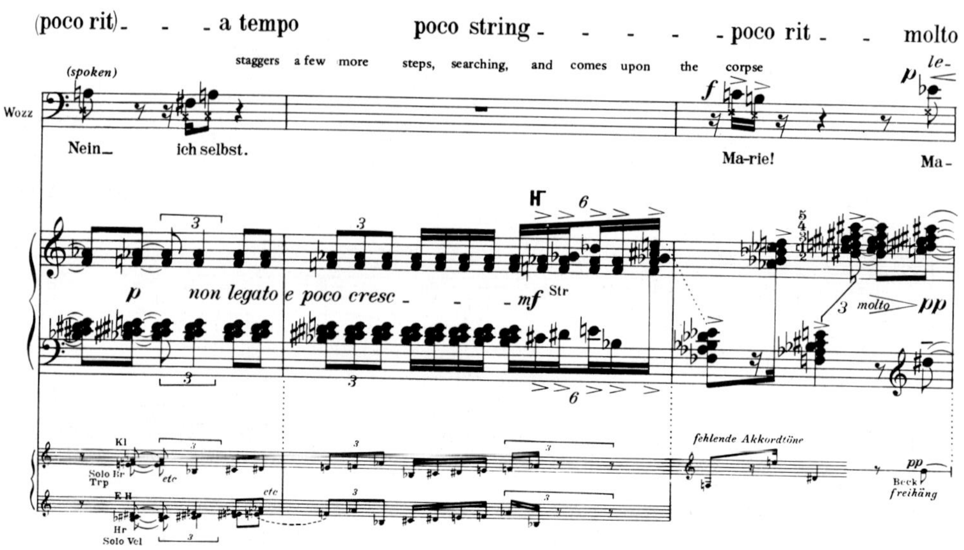
(poco rit) - - - a tempo
poco string - - - - - poco rit - - molto
staggers a few more steps, searching, and comes upon the corpse
(spoken)
Wozz
Nein_ ich selbst.
Ma-rie! Ma-
le-
non legato
e poco cresc - - - mf
Str
molto
pp
Kl
Solo Br
Trp
etc
E H
Hr
Solo Vcl
fehlende Akkordtöne
Beck
freihäng

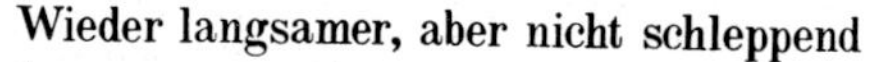
Wieder langsamer, aber nicht schleppend

(quasi Hauptzeitmaß)
gato
240
[quasi
Wozz
rie! Was hast du für ei-ne ro - te Schnur um den Hals?
(Kl)
(Trp)
E H
2 Solo Gg
sempre pp
p espr
Hfe
Kl
E H
sempre pp
Trp
Hr
sempre pp
Solo Br
Solo Vcl
(E H)
espr
(Kl)
Hfe
port
etc

poco string
Walzertempo
(breaking into song)
Wozz
Hast Dir das ro - te Hals - band ver-dient, wie die Ohr - ring - lein,
(2 Gg)
(Hfe) hoch
Kl
Fl
poco cresc
richtige Lage
2 Solo Gg
Kl
poco cresc.
245
sempre string
mit Dei-ner Sün - de!
(spoken)
Rasch (♩ = 100-120)
Wozz
mit Dei-ner Sün - de!
Was hän-gen Dir die
Str
Fl
mf
f
K Bs allein
Holz
250
Wozz
schwar - zen Haa - re so wild_?!_ Mör - der!_ Mör -
(mit oberer 8va)
Holz
Pik
Holz
Xyl
ff
f
(Holz)
Trp
Pauken

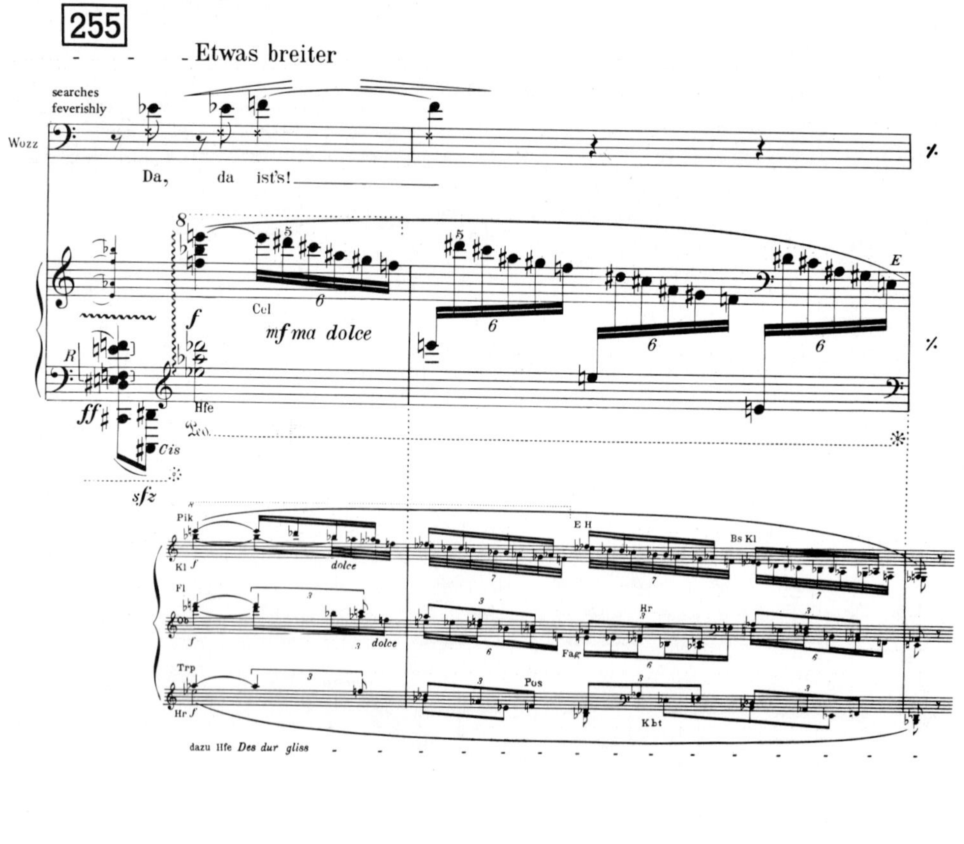

255

- - - - Etwas breiter

searches feverishly

Wozz

Da, da ist's!

Cel

mf ma dolce

Hfe

ff

Cis

sfz

Pik

Kl *f*

dolce

E H

Bs Kl

Fl

Ob

f

dolce

Hr

Fag

Trp

Pos

Hr *f*

Kbt

dazu Hfe *Des dur gliss* - - - - - - - - - - - -

Wie zu Anfang dieser Szene
(♩ = ca 100)
ritard
quasi Hauptzeitmaß
(♩ = 80)
am Teich
throws the knife in
Wozz
So! da hin-un-ter!
Es taucht ins
Holz Blech Holz
ff Str
dimin
p
Hfe
sfz
mf
poco a poco
260
The moon rises blood-red from the clouds
dunk-le Was-ser wie ein Stein.
Holz Blech Holz
Pos Hr
E H Kl
Pos
E H
dimin
Pos
Fag
Hr
verlöschend
Blech Holz Blech etc.
diminuendo
ppp
senza cresc
Hfe
pp
kleines Tamtam
freihängendes Becken
looks up
265
pp
A-ber der Mond ver-rät mich
Der Mond ist blu-
G Gg m D
Pos
alle 1. Gg ohne D
ppp
verlöschen
kl Tamtam
Becken
Hfe
verklingen lassen
gr Tamtam

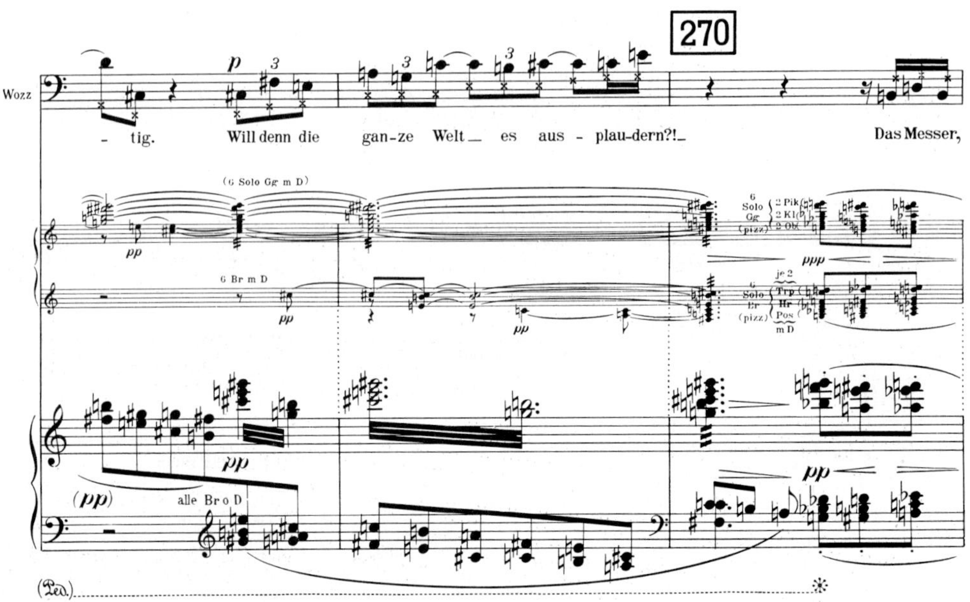
270
Wozz
- tig. Will denn die gan-ze Welt_ es aus - plau-dern?!_
Das Messer,
(6 Solo Gg m D)
6 Br m D
6 Solo Gg (pizz)
2 Pik
2 Kl
2 Ob
je 2 Trp Hr Pos m D
6 Solo Br (pizz)
alle Br o D
(Ped.)

wades into
Wozz
es liegt zu weit vorn, sie findens beim Ba-den o-der wenn sie nach Muscheln tauchen.
etc
Ped.
Ped.

Ganz frei ' a tempo
the pond
(with a somewhat singing voice)
275
(spoken)
Wozz
Ich find's nicht.
A-ber ich muß mich wa-schen.
Ich bin blu-tig.
Gg m D
ppp ged Blech allein.
pp
f Holz
Pkn
mf
pp
tief
Xyl
mf
1.Gg m D richtig
2.Gg col leg gestr
(1.Gg)

moaning :
Wozz
Da ein Fleck- und noch ei-ner.
Weh!
molto espr.
Gg
2 Hfe
Hr
poco f
ff
sfz
hoch
tief
Vcl
K Bs, Pos u Tub
mf
pp
Br
Holz
Kl
f
Vcl

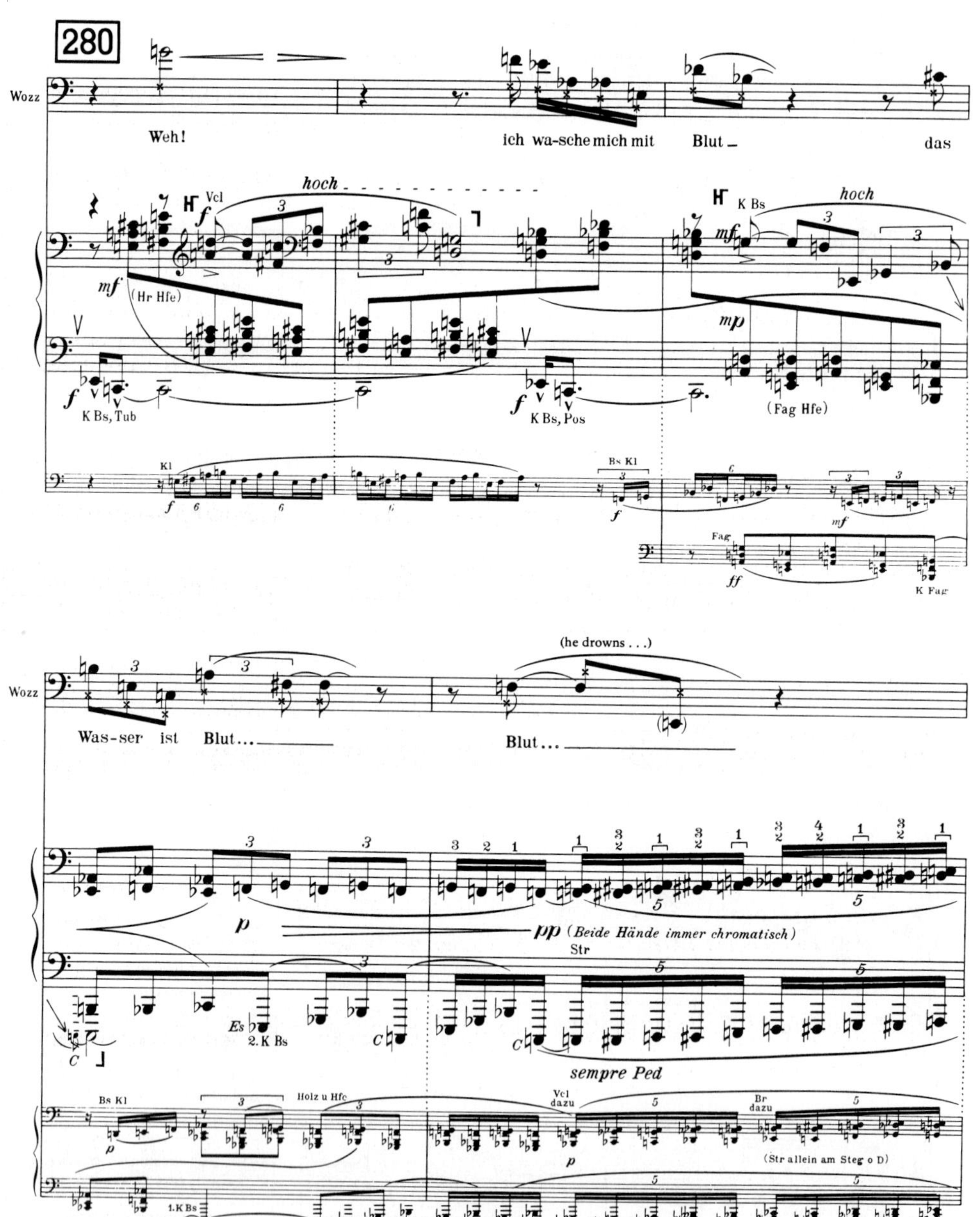
280
Wozz
Weh!
ich wa-sche mich mit
Blut —
das
hoch
Vcl
K Bs
(Hr Hfe)
K Bs, Tub
K Bs, Pos
(Fag Hfe)
Kl
Bs Kl
Fag
K Fag
Wozz
(he drowns . . .)
Was-ser ist Blut...
Blut...
(Beide Hände immer chromatisch)
Str
Es
2. K Bs
sempre Ped
Bs Kl
Holz u Hfe
Vcl dazu
Br dazu
(Str allein am Steg o D)
1. K Bs
3. K Bs

285
sempre pp

sempre pp
(ohne K Bs)

The Doctor enters
sempre pp
Holz
pp Holz
ppp
(ohne Vcl)
p
Kl
Fag
Bs Kl
2 Fag
K Fag

The **Captain** follows the Doctor (speaks)

The **Doctor** (stands still): *p* Hören Sie? Dort!

290 Hauptmann: *p* Jesus! Das war ein Ton. (also stands still)

Doktor (pointing to the lake): Ja, dort! **Hauptmann:** Es ist das Wasser

im Teich. Das Wasser ruft. Es ist schon lange niemand ertrunken.

295

Hauptmann: Kommen Sie, Doktor! Es ist

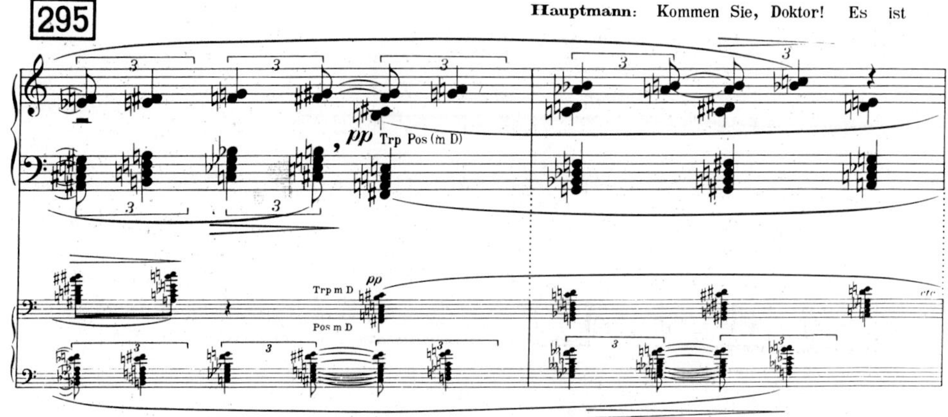

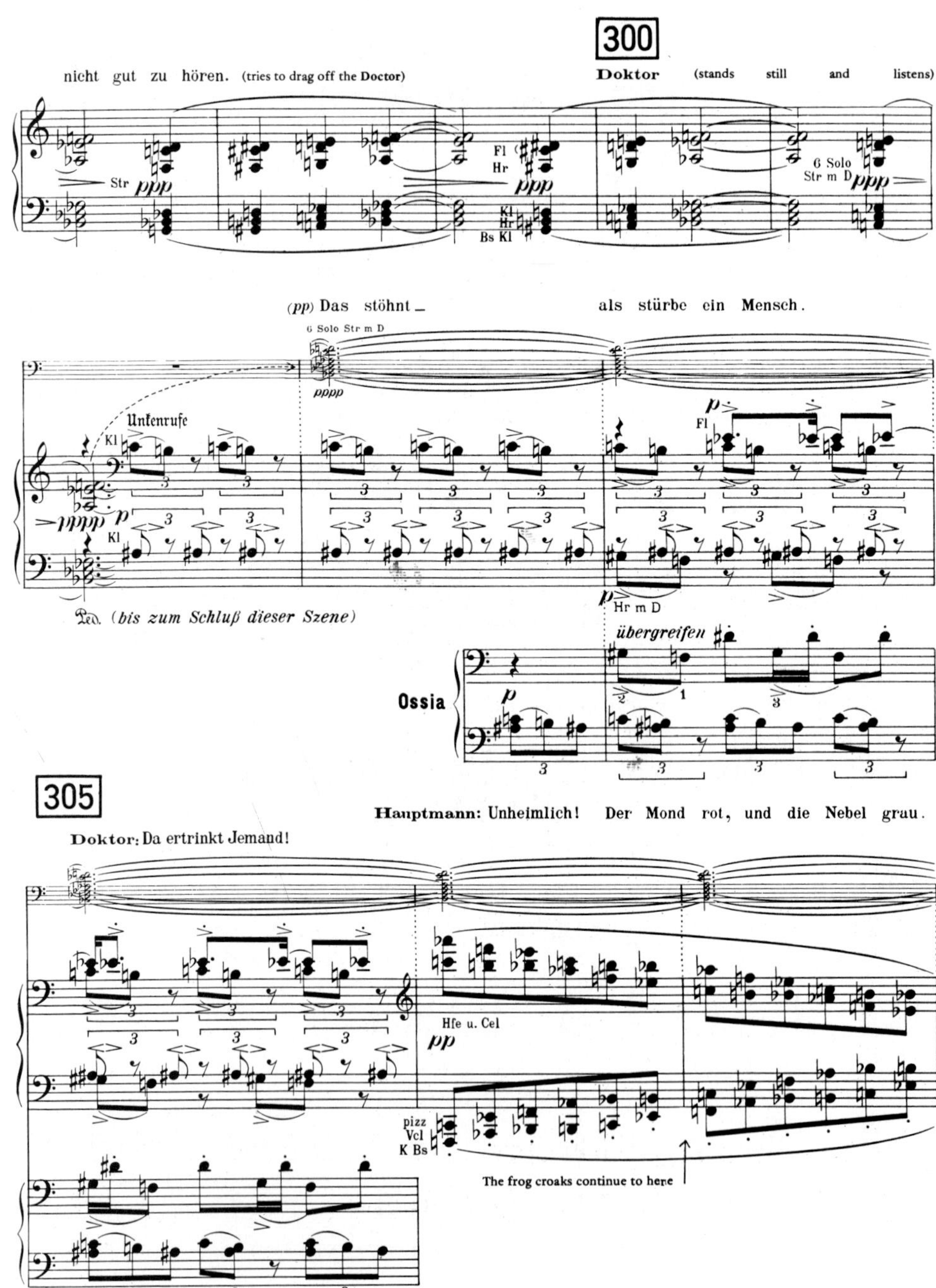
300
nicht gut zu hören. (tries to drag off the Doctor)
Doktor (stands still and listens)
Str ppp
Fl
Hr
ppp
Kl
Hr
Bs Kl
6 Solo
Str m D ppp
(pp) Das stöhnt _ als stürbe ein Mensch.
6 Solo Str m D
pppp
Unkenrufe
Kl
pppp p
Kl
Fl
p
Hr m D
Ped. (bis zum Schluß dieser Szene)
übergreifen
Ossia
305
Doktor: Da ertrinkt Jemand!
Hauptmann: Unheimlich! Der Mond rot, und die Nebel grau.
Hfe u. Cel
pp
pizz
Vcl
K Bs
The frog croaks continue to here

310
Hauptmann: Hören Sie?
jetzt wieder
immer 6 Solo Str m D pppp
Fl
Kl
sempre pp
Kl
p
Hr m D
Immer Ped.
hoch
pp
Ossia
tief
Immer Ped.
das Ächzen.
Doktor: Stiller,
jetzt ganz still.
smorz
Ossia
smorz
315
Hauptmann: Kommen Sie! kommen Sie schnell.
(drags the Doctor off with him)
Doktor (follows the Captain quickly)
Vorhang zu
Großer Auftakt
rit
(2 Solo Gg)
6 Solo Str m D
pppp
Pkn
mp
(2 Solo Br)
molto
K Bs pizz
p weich
K Bs arco
mp
Hfe
p
(B Des)

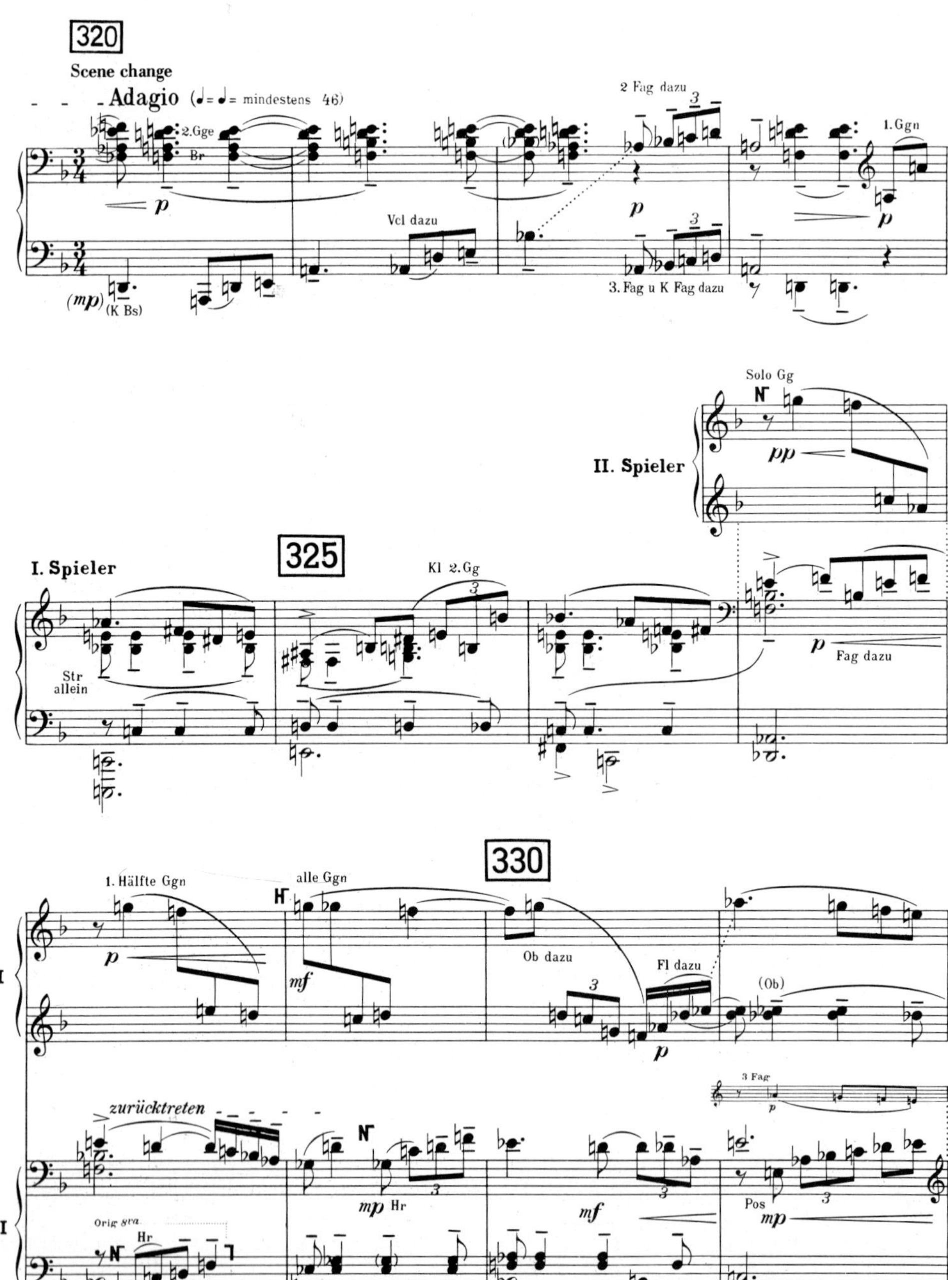
320
Scene change
Adagio (♩= ♩= mindestens 46)
2.Gge
Br
p
2 Fag dazu
1.Ggn
Vcl dazu
(mp)
(K Bs)
3. Fag u K Fag dazu
Solo Gg
pp
II. Spieler
I. Spieler
325
Kl 2.Gg
Str allein
p
Fag dazu
330
1. Hälfte Ggn
alle Ggn
p
mf
Ob dazu
Fl dazu
(Ob)
I
3 Fag
zurücktreten
mp Hr
mf
Pos
mp
II
Orig 8va
Hr
K Bs

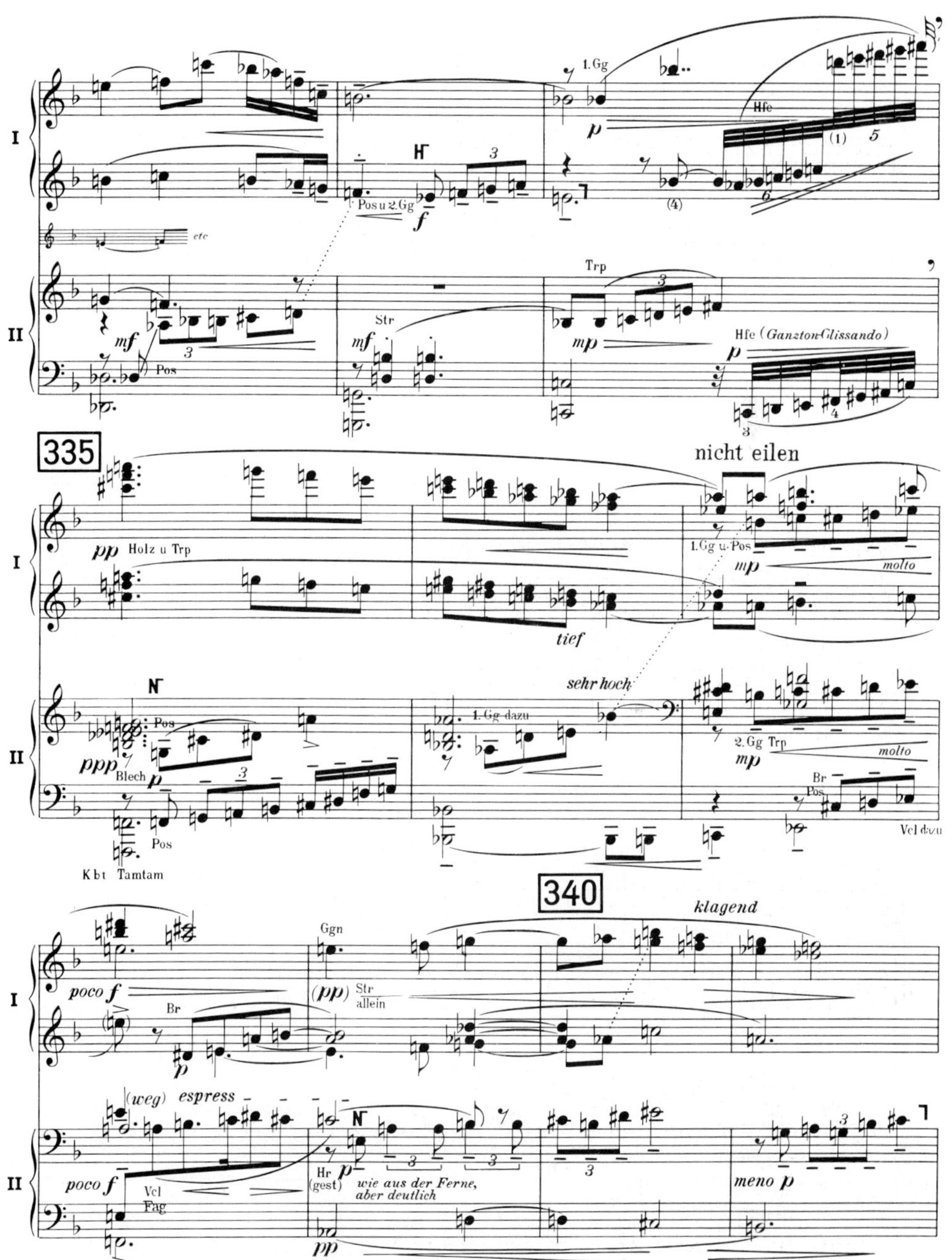

1. Gg
Hfe
Pos u 2. Gg
Trp
Str
Hfe (Ganzton-Glissando)
Pos
335
nicht eilen
Holz u Trp
1. Gg u. Pos
molto
tief
sehr hoch
Pos
1. Gg dazu
2. Gg Trp
Blech
Br
Pos
Vcl dazu
Kbt Tamtam
340
klagend
Ggn
Str
allein
Br
(weg)
espress
wie aus der Ferne,
aber deutlich
Hr
(gest)
Vcl
Fag

string
molto
I
menop
1.Gg u 4 Ob
cresc
mp
Fag
mp
mf
3
cresc
Vel
Holz
II
pp
Vel u. K-B
345
Bedeutend bewegter
(♩= 80-84)
ff furioso
Trp
(pizz)
Ob
(tief)
6
f
Str trem
Pos
f
Pk trem
(gr Trommschlag)
350
je 4
Kl. Fl
(pizz)
pizz
cresc
fp
Hr
f
Trp
f
Str
mf
f
3 Pos
m D
f
cresc

rall
Wieder etwas breiter (Andante)
Fl Kl
Str u Ob
Kl
f espr
Trp
Pos Hfe
rauschend
weg!
cresc
Pke
Hfe
355
Wieder drängend
fp
Kl
Hfe
hoch
Ob
molto fp
col leg
mp
mf
Pos
Hrn u Fag
kl Tromm
tief
Br Vcl K Bs
360
Wieder breiter
Ob
Trp
Gg Xyl
f cresc
Br
alles übertönend
Hr Vcl
Pos
3 Pos
Br Vcl
weg
Hr Vcl
Hr
Holz
Str
Tub
gr Tromm
1 Pos
2 Pos
3 Pos
Fag BB Kl
cresc
etc

365
370
Breit
molto rit
Tempo I
12 Holzbl
Trp
(Tutti)
molto
Fl Kl Gg
Schlagwerk
(4 Pos)
Br
Hr
Hr Trp Br
Pos Hfe pizz 4 Pkn
Schon im neuen Tempo
(ohne Str)
dimin
weg
nicht hervortreten
(ohne Hr)
(ohne Pkn)
meno ff
f espr
(quasi 4/4 Takt
ohne Pos Tb
Vorhang auf
molto p Str
Gg Fl Br
Cel
Ob Ggn
(Kl)
deutlich kadenzieren
Hr Trp
Blech
Hfe
hoch
sehr hoch
Br u. Vcl
Pos Tub
Holz dazu
K Bß

5th (last) Scene In front of Marie's house (bright morning, sunshine)

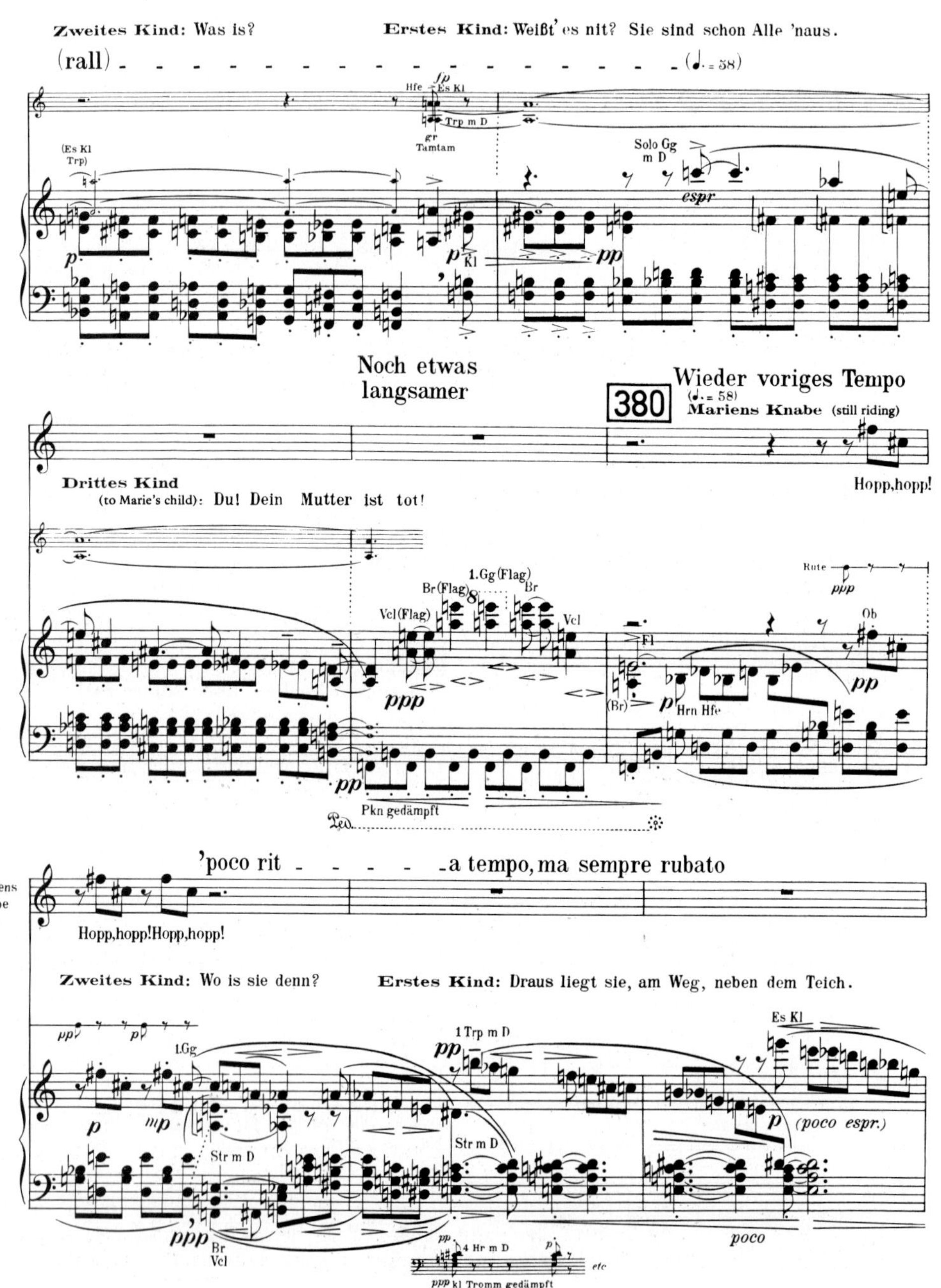
Zweites Kind: Was is?
Erstes Kind: Weißt' es nit? Sie sind schon Alle 'naus.
(rall)
(♩. = 58)
Hfe
fp
Es Kl
Trp m D
gr Tamtam
(Es Kl Trp)
Solo Gg m D
espr
p
Kl
pp
Noch etwas langsamer
380
Wieder voriges Tempo
(♩. = 58)
Mariens Knabe (still riding)
Hopp,hopp!
Drittes Kind (to Marie's child): Du! Dein Mutter ist tot!
Rute
ppp
Br (Flag)
1.Gg (Flag)
Br
Vcl (Flag)
Vcl
Ob
Fl
ppp
(Br)
Hrn Hfe
pp
Pkn gedämpft
'poco rit
a tempo, ma sempre rubato
Mariens Knabe
Hopp,hopp!Hopp,hopp!
Zweites Kind: Wo is sie denn?
Erstes Kind: Draus liegt sie, am Weg, neben dem Teich.
Es Kl
1 Trp m D
1.Gg
Str m D
mp
(poco espr.)
Br
Vcl
poco
4 Hr m D
etc
ppp kl Tromm gedämpft

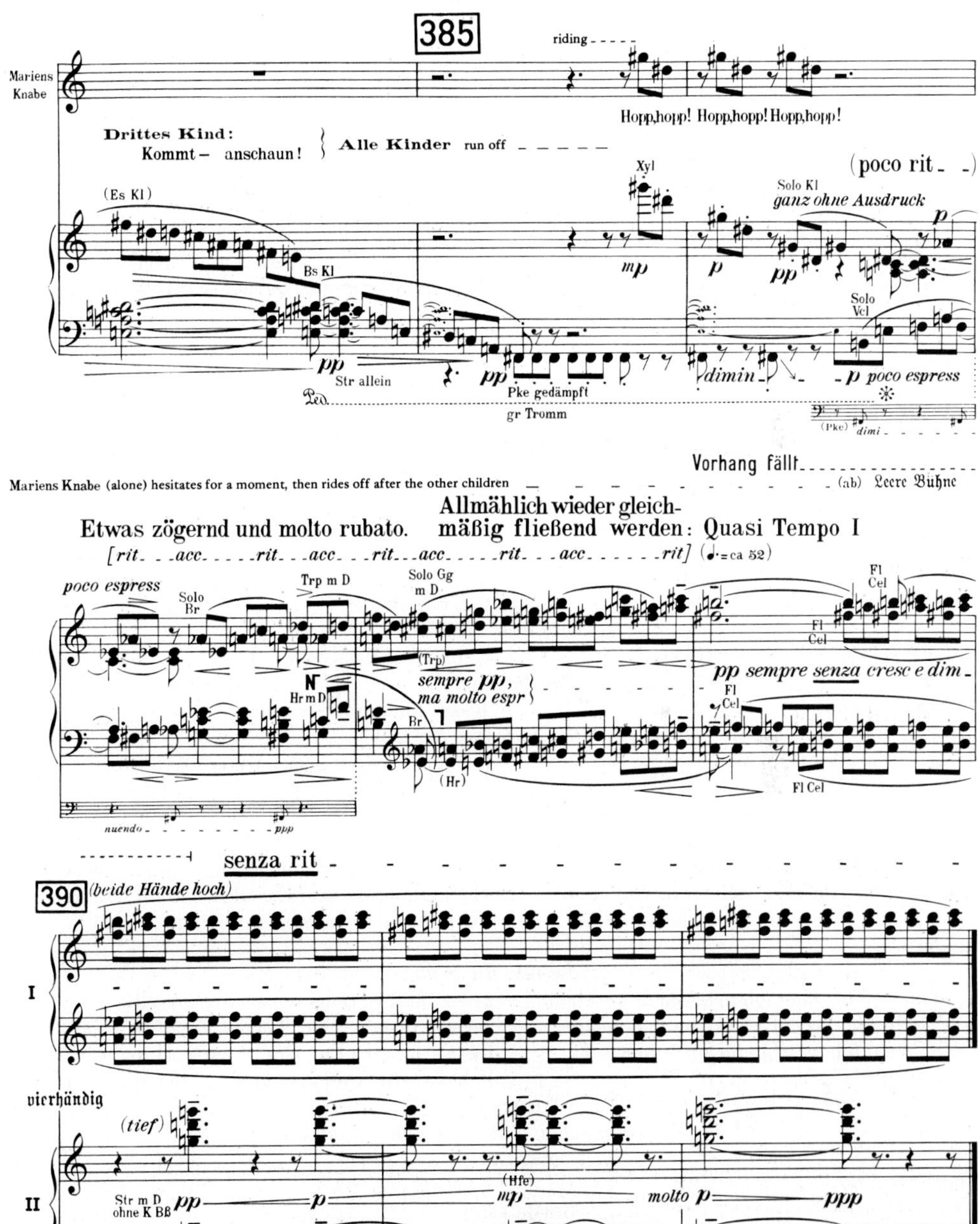

End of the opera

Translation

SCENE FOUR

Invention on a Chord of Six Notes

Path in the wood by the pond. Moonlight, as before.

(*Wozzeck stumbles hurriedly in, then stops, looking around for something.*)

WOZZECK

Das Messer? Wo ist das Messer? Ich hab's dagelassen. Näher, noch näher. Mir graut's... da regt sich was. Still! Alles still und tot.	The knife? Where is the knife? I left it there. Around here somewhere. I'm terrified . . . something's moving. Silence. Everything silent and dead.

(*shouting*)

Mörder! Mörder!	Murderer! Murderer!

(*whispering again*)

Ha! Da ruft's. Nein, ich selbst.	Ah! Someone called, No. it was only me.

(*still looking, he staggers a few steps further and stumbles against the corpse*)

Marie! Marie! Was hast Du für eine rote Schnur um den Hals? Hast Dir das rote Halsband verdient, wie die Ohrringlein, mit Deiner Sünde! Was hängen Dir die schwarzen Haare so wild? Mörder! Mörder! Sie werden nach mir suchen. Das Messer verrät mich!	Marie! Marie! What's that red cord around your neck! Was the red necklace payment for your sins, like the ear-rings? Why's your dark hair so wild about you? Murderer! Murderer! They will come and look for me. The knife will betray me!

(*looks for it in a frenzy*)

Da, da ist's!	Here! Here it is!

(*at the pond*)

So! Da hinunter!	There! Sink to the bottom!

(*throws the knife into the pond*)

Es taucht ins dunkle Wasser wie ein Stein.	It plunges into the dark water like a stone.

(*The moon appears, blood-red, from behind the clouds. Wozzeck looks up.*)

Aber der Mond verrät mich, der Mond is blutig.	But the moon will betray me: the moon is blood-stained.
Will denn die ganze Welt es ausplaudern? Das Messer, es liegt zu weit vorn, sie finden's beim Baden oder wenn sie nach Muscheln tauchen.	Is the whole world going to incriminate me. The knife is too near the edge: they'll find it when they're swimming or diving for snails.

(*wades into the pond*)

Ich find's nicht. Aber ich muss mich waschen. Ich bin blutig. Da ein Fleck—und noch einer. Weh! Weh! Ich wasche mich mit Blut—das Wasser ist Blut...Blut...	I can't find it. But I must wash myself. There's blood on me. There's a spot here—and there's another. Oh, God! I am washing myself in blood—the water is blood . . . blood . . .

(*drowns*)

(*The doctor appears, followed by the captain.*)

CAPTAIN

Halt!	Wait!

DOCTOR (*stops*)

Hören Sie? Dort!	Can you hear? There!

CAPTAIN

Jesus! Das war ein Ton!	Jesus! What a ghastly sound!

(*stops as well*)

DOCTOR (*pointing to the pond*)

Ja, dort!	Yes, there!

CAPTAIN

Es ist das Wasser im Teich. Das Wasser ruft. Es ist schon lange Niemand ertrunken. Kommen Sie Doktor! Es ist nicht gut zu hören.	It's the water in the pond. The water is calling. It's been a long time since anyone drowned. Come away, Doctor. It's not good for us to be hearing it.

(*tries to drag the doctor away*)

DOCTOR (*resisting, and continuing to listen*)

Das stöhnt, als stürbe ein Mensch. Da ertrinkt Jemand!	There's a groan, as though someone were dying. Somebody's drowning!

CAPTAIN

Unheimlich! Der mond rot, und die Nebel grau. Hören Sie?... Jetzt wieder das Ächzen.	It's eerie! The moon is red, and the mist is grey. Can you hear? . . . That moaning again.

DOCTOR

Stiller,...jetzt ganz still.	It's getting quieter . . . now it's stopped altogether.

CAPTAIN

Kommen Sie! Kommen Sie schnell!	Come! Come quickly!

(*He rushes off, pulling the doctor along with him.*)

SCENE CHANGE
INVENTION ON A KEY (D minor)

SCENE FIVE
Invention on a Quaver Rhythm

In front of Marie's door. Morning. Bright sunshine.
(*Children are noisily at play. Marie's child is riding a hobby-horse.*)

CHILDREN

Ringel, Ringel, Rosenkranz. Ringelreih'n, Ringel, Ringel, Rosenkranz, Ring...	Ring-a-ring-a-roses, A pocket full of . . .

(*Their song and game is interrupted by other children bursting in.*)

ONE OF THE NEWCOMERS

Du, Käthe! Die Marie!	Hey, Katie! Have you heard about Marie?

SECOND CHILD

Was ist?	What's happened?

FIRST CHILD

Weisst' es nit? Sie sind schon Alle'naus.	Don't you know? They've all gone out there.

THIRD CHILD (*to Marie's little boy*)

Du! Dein' Mutter ist tot!	Hey! Your mother's dead!

MARIE'S SON (*still riding*)

Hopp, hopp! Hopp, hopp! Hopp, hopp!	Hop hop! Hop hop! Hop hop!

SECOND CHILD

Wo ist sie denn?	Where is she then?

FIRST CHILD

Drauss' liegt sie, am Weg, neben dem Teich.	She's lying out there, on the path near the pond.

THIRD CHILD

Kommt, anschaun!	Come and have a look!

(*All the children run off.*)

MARIE'S SON (*continuing to ride*)

Hopp, hopp! Hopp, hopp! Hopp, hopp!	Hop hop! Hop hop! Hop hop!

(*He hesitates for a moment and then rides after the other children.*)

END OF THE OPERA

LIBRETTO BY ALBAN BERG AFTER GEORG BÜCHNER'S PLAY *Woyzeck*

SARAH E. SOULSBY

32. GEORGE GERSHWIN (1898-1937), *Rhapsody in Blue* (1924)

1 Più mosso
Flutes I II
Oboes I II
Bb Clarinets I II
Bb Bass Clarinet
Bassoons I II
Horns in F I II III
Bb Trumpets I II III
Trombones I II III
Tuba
Timpani
Drums
Piano
1st Sax. Eb Alto
2nd Sax. Bb Tenor
3rd Sax. Eb Alto
Banjo
Violin I
Violin II
Viola
Violoncello
Bass
a 2
mf
tr
arco
poco rit.

2
Moderato assai
Flutes I II
Oboes I II
Bb Clarinets I II
Bb Bass Clarinet
Bassoons I II
Horns in F I II III
Bb Trumpets I II III
Trombones I II III
Tuba
Timpani
Drums
Piano
1st Sax. Eb Alto
2nd Sax. Bb Tenor
3rd Sax. Eb Alto
Banjo
Violin I
Violin II
Viola
Violoncello
Bass
a tempo
Wha wha mute
mf tranquillo
pizz
arco

3 Più mosso
4 Scherzando (commodo)
Flutes I II
Oboes I II
I
B♭ Clarinets
II
B♭ Bass Clarinet
I
Bassoons
II
I II
Horns in F
III
Open
I II
B♭ Trumpets
III
I II
Trombones
III
Tuba
Timpani
Crash Cymbal
Drums
Piano
legato
1st Sax. E♭ Alto
2nd Sax. B♭ Tenor
3rd Sax. E♭ Alto
Banjo
3 Più mosso
4 Scherzando (commodo)
Violin I
Violin II
Viola
Violoncello
Bass

Piano
Pochissimo rall.
A
a tempo
ten.
martellato
poco rall.
17
5 Più mosso
in A
A Clarinets
I
II
poco rit.
B♭ Bass Clarinet
Banjo
Violin II
Viola
Violoncello

Più mosso
A Clarinets I II
B♭ Bass Clarinet
poco rit
p
Piano
Più mosso
(L.H.)
8va
tranquillo
poco rit
Banjo
poco rit.
Violin II
Viola
Violoncello
Più mosso
poco rit.
f deciso
p scherzando
Poco agitato
p poco cresc.
mf
cresc
f
B
ff molto marcato

Tempo giusto
Flutes I II
Oboes I II
A Clarinets I II
B♭ Bass Clarinet
Bassoons I II
Horns in F I II III
A Trumpets I II III
Trombones I II III
Tuba
Timpani
Drums
Piano
1st Sax. E♭ Alto
2nd Sax. B♭ Tenor
3rd Sax. E♭ Alto
Banjo
Violin I
Violin II
Viola
Violoncello
Bass
marcato
Solo
in A
Timp. A-E
non troppo
loco

Flutes I II
Oboes I II
A Clarinets I II
B♭ Bass Clarinet
Bassoons I II
Horns in F I II III
A Trumpets I II III
Trombones I II III
Tuba
Timpani
Drums
Piano
1st Sax. E♭ Alto
2nd Sax. B♭ Tenor
3rd Sax. E♭ Alto
Banjo
Violin I
Violin II
Viola
Violoncello
Bass
7
in B♭
pp legato
cresc.
Sul G

8
Flutes I II
Oboes I II
A Clarinets I II
B♭ Bass Clarinet
Bassoons I II
Horns in F I II III
B♭ Trumpets I II III
Trombones I II III
Tuba
Timpani
Timp C-G
Drums
Piano
8va
1st Sax. E♭ Alto
2nd Sax. B♭ Tenor
3rd Sax. E♭ Alto
Banjo
Violin I
Violin II
Viola
Violoncello
Bass
f marcato
cresc.
a2
flutter tongue
ff

Flutes I II
Oboes I II
A Clarinets I II
in B♭
Solo
Bb Bass Clarinet
Bassoons I II
Horns in F I II III
Bb Trumpets I II III
flutter
Trombones I II III
Tuba
Timpani
Brush
Drums
B.D.
Piano
R.H.
L.H.
simile
1st Sax. Eb Alto
2nd Sax. Bb Tenor
3rd Sax. Eb Alto
Let strings snap
Banjo
Violin I
Violin II
Viola
Pizz. let strings snap
Violoncello
Bass

10
Flutes I II
Oboes I II
Solo (slap tongue)
B♭ Clarinets I II
B♭ Bass Clarinet
Bassoons I II
Horns in F I II III
B♭ Trumpets I II III
flutter
Trombones I II III
Tuba
Timpani
Drums
Piano
slap tongue
1st Sax. E♭ Alto
2nd Sax. B♭ Tenor
3rd Sax. E♭ Alto
Banjo
Violin I
Violin II
Viola
Violoncello
Bass

11
Flutes I II
Oboes I II
B♭ Clarinets I II
B♭ Bass Clarinet
Bassoons I II
Horns in F I II III
B♭ Trumpets I II III
Trombones I II III
Tuba
Timpani
Drums
Roll on Cymb.
Piano
cresc.
1st Sax. E♭ Alto
2nd Sax. B♭ Tenor
3rd Sax. E♭ Alto
Banjo
Violin I
Violin II
Viola
Violoncello
Bass
Pizz.
Arco
mf

Flutes I II
Oboes I II
Bb Clarinets I II
Solo
Bb Bass Clarinet
Bassoons I II
Horns in F I II III
Bb Trumpets I II III
Trombones I II III
Tuba
Timpani
Drums
Gong
Cymb.
Piano
p cresc
1st Sax. Eb Alto
2nd Sax. Bb Tenor
3rd Sax. Eb Alto
Banjo
Violin I
Violin II
Viola
Violoncello
Bass

12 Tempo giusto 𝅗𝅥 = 76

Flutes I II — rall. e dim — a tempo — a 2 — *ff*

Oboes I II — rall. e dim. — a tempo — a 2 — *ff*

B♭ Clarinets I, II — rall. e dim. — a tempo — *ff*

B♭ Bass Clarinet — rall. e dim. — *ff* a tempo

Bassoons I, II — rall. e dim. — *ff* a tempo

Horns in F I II, III — rall. e dim. — *ff* a tempo — a 2

B♭ Trumpets I II, III — rall. e dim. — a tempo — open — *ff* — 1°

Trombones I II, III — rall. e dim. — *ff* a tempo — *ff* — *f*

Tuba — rall. e dim. — *ff* a tempo

Timpani

Drums — rall. e dim — S.D. — *ff* a tempo

Piano — rall. e dim. — a tempo — *f*

1st Sax. E♭ Alto — rall. e dim — a tempo — *ff*

2nd Sax. B♭ Tenor — rall. e dim. — *f* a tempo

3rd Sax. E♭ Alto — rall. e dim. — a tempo — *ff*

Banjo — rall. e dim. — *ff* a tempo

12 Tempo giusto 𝅗𝅥 = 76

Violin I — rall. e dim — a tempo — *ff*

Violin II — rall. e dim — a tempo — *ff*

Viola — rall. e dim. — arco — *ff* a tempo

Violoncello — rall. e dim — arco — *ff* a tempo

Bass — rall. e dim. — *ff* a tempo

Flutes I II
Oboes I II
I
B♭ Clarinets
II
B♭ Bass Clarinet
I
Bassoons
II
I II
Horns in F
III
I II
B♭ Trumpets
III
I II
Trombones
III
Tuba
Timpani
Drums
B.D.
Piano
1st Sax. E♭ Alto
2nd Sax. B♭ Tenor
3rd Sax. E♭ Alto
Banjo
Violin I
Violin II
Viola
Violoncello
Bass
a 2

15 Meno
Flutes I II
Oboes I II
B♭ Clarinets I II
mf con licenza
B♭ Bass Clarinet
Bassoons I II
Horns in F I II III
a 2
B♭ Trumpets I II III
I Solo
Wha Wha mute
Trombones I II III
Tuba
Timpani
Drums
Triangle
Piano
1st Sax. E♭ Alto
2nd Sax. B♭ Tenor
3rd Sax. E♭ Alto
Banjo
15 Meno
Violin I
Violin II
Viola
Violoncello
Bass
Pizz.

Flutes I II
Oboes I II
B♭ Clarinets I II
B♭ Bass Clarinet
Bassoons I II
Horns in F I II III
B♭ Trumpets I II III
Trombones I II III
Tuba
Timpani
Drums
Piano
1st Sax. E♭ Alto
2nd Sax. B♭ Tenor
3rd Sax. E♭ Alto
Banjo
Violin I
Violin II
Viola
Violoncello
Bass
14 Con moto
rit.
a tempo
f marcato
Open
I Solo
Wha wha mute
I Open
Tria
On shell of S.D.
pp
marcato

Broadly Con moto 15

Flutes I II

Oboes I II

B♭ Clarinets I II

B♭ Bass Clarinet

Bassoons I II

Horns in F I II III

B♭ Trumpets I II III

Trombones I II III

I° Solo

I Solo

Tuba

Timpani

Drums

Roll on Cymbal

On shell of S.D

Piano

1st Sax. E♭ Alto

2nd Sax. B♭ Tenor

3rd Sax. E♭ Alto

Banjo

Broadly Con moto 15

Violin I

Violin II

Viola

Violoncello

Bass

Flutes I II
Oboes I II
B♭ Clarinets I II
B♭ Bass Clarinet
Bassoons I II
Horns in F I II III
B♭ Trumpets I II III
Trombones I II III
Tuba
Timpani
Drums
Piano
1st Sax. E♭ Alto
2nd Sax. B♭ Tenor
3rd Sax. E♭ Alto
Banjo
Violin I
Violin II
Viola
Violoncello
Bass
rubato
rit.
mf
a 2
a tempo poco a poco cresc.
S.D.

16 Animato
Flutes I II
Oboes I II
B♭ Clarinets I II
B♭ Bass Clarinet
Bassoons I II
Horns in F I II III
B♭ Trumpets I II III
Trombones I II III
Tuba
Timpani
Drums
Piano
1st Sax. E♭ Alto
2nd Sax. B♭ Tenor
3rd Sax. E♭ Alto
Banjo
16 Animato
Violin I
Violin II
Viola
Violoncello
Bass

Flutes I II
Oboes I II
B♭ Clarinets I II
B♭ Bass Clarinet
Bassoons I II
Horns in F I II III
B♭ Trumpets I II III
Trombones I II III
Tuba
Timpani
Drums
Piano
1st Sax. E♭ Alto
2nd Sax. B♭ Tenor
3rd Sax. E♭ Alto
Banjo
Violin I
Violin II
Viola
Violoncello
Bass
17
pp subito
cresc.
B.D.

Flutes I II
Oboes I II
B♭ Clarinets I II
B♭ Bass Clarinet
Bassoons I II
Horns in F I II III
B♭ Trumpets I II III
Trombones I II III
Tuba
Timpani
Drums
Piano
1st Sax. E♭ Alto
2nd Sax. B♭ Tenor
3rd Sax. E♭ Alto
Banjo
Violin I
Violin II
Viola
Violoncello
Bass

18
Piano
8va
poco
a poco cresc.
L.H.
rall. e dim.
C
19 Meno mosso e poco scherzando (Slower and marked)
espr
pp
20 Solo
I II
Horns in F
III
21
ff
legato

22 Più mosso
Flutes I II
Oboes I II
Solo I
mp
B♭ Clarinets I II
B♭ Bass Clarinet
Solo I
mp
Bassoons I II
Horns in F I II III
B♭ Trumpets I II III
Trombones I II III
Tuba
Timpani
S.D.
Cym
mp
Drums
(Solo)
8va
Piano
1st Sax. E♭ Alto
2nd Sax. B♭ Tenor
3rd Sax. E♭ Alto
Banjo
mp
22 Più mosso
Pizz.
mp
Violin I
Violin II
Viola
Violoncello
Bass

Flutes I II
Oboes I II
I
B♭ Clarinets
II
B♭ Bass Clarinet
I
Bassoons
II
I II
Horns in F
III
I II
B♭ Trumpets
III
I II
Trombones
III
Tuba
Timpani
Drums
Piano
1st Sax. E♭ Alto
2nd Sax. B♭ Tenor
3rd Sax. E♭ Alto
Banjo
Violin I
Violin II
Viola
Violoncello
Bass

23
Flutes I II
Oboes I II
I
B♭ Clarinets
II
B♭ Bass Clarinet
I
Bassoons
II
I II
Horns in F
III
mp
I II
B♭ Trumpets
III
I II
Trombones
III
Tuba
Timpani
Drums
8va
Piano
1st Sax. E♭ Alto
2nd Sax. B♭ Tenor
3rd Sax. E♭ Alto
Banjo
23
Violin I
Violin II
Viola
Violoncello
Bass

Flutes I II
Oboes I II
B♭ Clarinets I II
B♭ Bass Clarinet
Bassoons I II
Horns in F I II III
B♭ Trumpets I II III
Trombones I II III
Tuba
Timpani
Drums
Piano
1st Sax. E♭ Alto
2nd Sax. B♭ Tenor
3rd Sax. E♭ Alto
Banjo
Violin I
Violin II
Viola
Violoncello
Bass

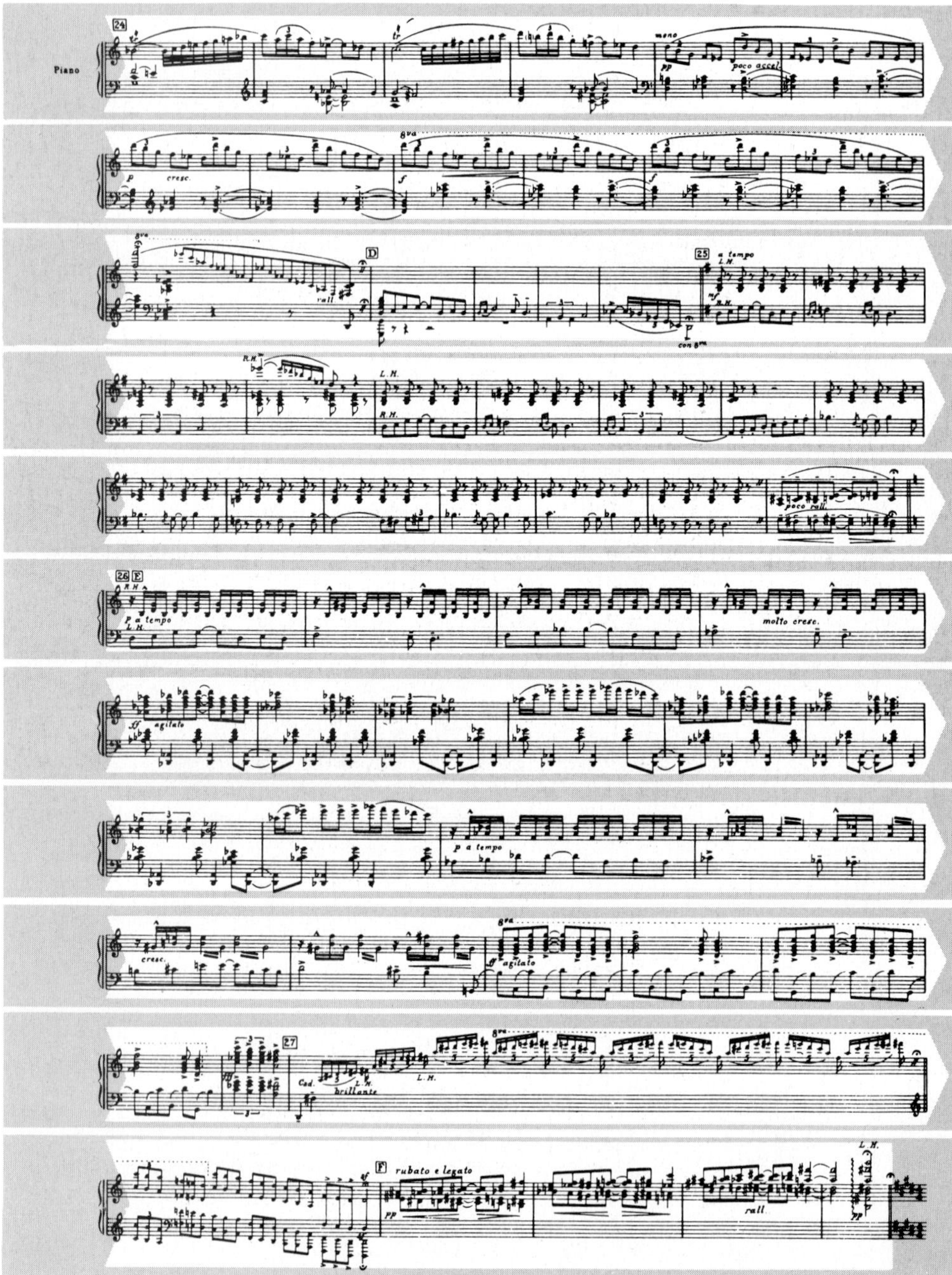

24
Piano
meno
pp
poco accel.
p
cresc.
8va
f
D
rall
25
a tempo
L.H.
mf
R.H.
con 8va
poco rall.
26
E
p a tempo
molto cresc.
ff
agitato
27
Cad.
brillante
F
rubato e legato
pp
rall.

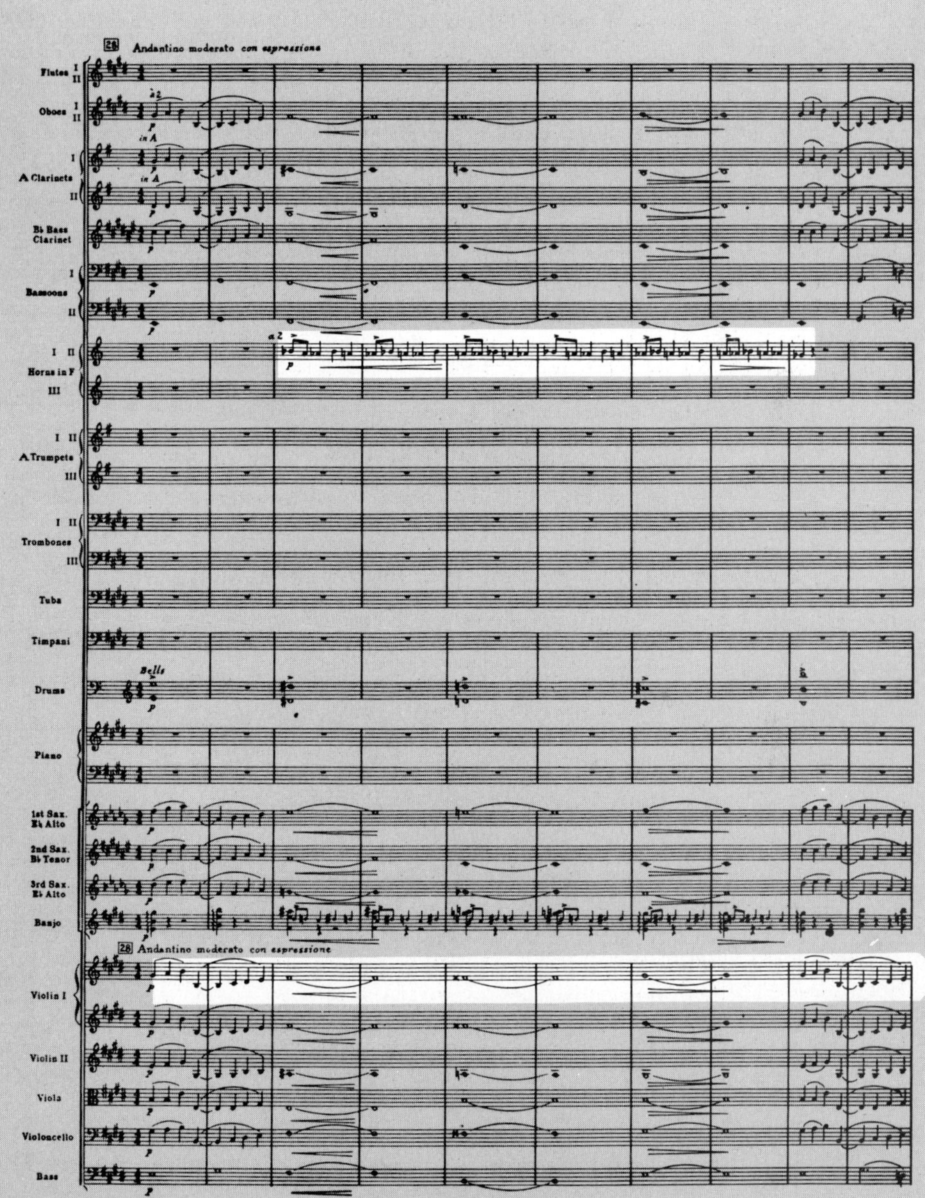
28 Andantino moderato con espressione
Flutes I II
Oboes I II
a2
in A
A Clarinets I II
B♭ Bass Clarinet
Bassoons I II
Horns in F I II III
A Trumpets I II III
Trombones I II III
Tuba
Timpani
Bells
Drums
Piano
1st Sax. E♭ Alto
2nd Sax. B♭ Tenor
3rd Sax. E♭ Alto
Banjo
28 Andantino moderato con espressione
Violin I
Violin II
Viola
Violoncello
Bass

29
Flutes I II
Oboes I II
Solo I
A Clarinets I II
B♭ Bass Clarinet
Bassoons I II
Horns in F I II III
A Trumpets I II III
Trombones I II III
Tuba
Timpani
Drums
Triangle
Piano
1st Sax. E♭ Alto
2nd Sax. B♭ Tenor
3rd Sax. E♭ Alto
Banjo
Solo
Violin I
Violin II
Viola
Violoncello
Bass
mf
mp
rit.

30 Grandioso ma non troppo
Poco rubato
Flutes I II
Oboes I II
A Clarinets I II
B♭ Bass Clarinet
Bassoons I II
Horns in F I II III
A Trumpets I II III
Trombones I II III
Tuba
Timpani
Drums
Piano
1st Sax. E♭ Alto
2nd Sax. B♭ Tenor
3rd Sax. E♭ Alto
Banjo
Violin I
Violin II
Viola
Violoncello
Bass
ff a tempo
Solo
leggiero
stacc.
a tempo

Grandioso
Flutes I II
Oboes I II
A Clarinets I II
E♭ Bass Clarinet
Bassoons I II
Horns in F I II III
A Trumpets I II III
Trombones I II III
Tuba
Timpani
Drums
Piano
1st Sax. E♭ Alto
2nd Sax. B♭ Tenor
3rd Sax. E♭ Alto
Banjo
Violin I
Violin II
Viola
Violoncello
Bass
cresc. ed accel.
ff

Allargando
31
Flutes I II
Oboes I II
A Clarinets I II
B♭ Bass Clarinet
Bassoons I II
Horns in F I II III
A Trumpets I II III
Trombones I II III
Tuba
Timpani
Drums
Bells Solo
Piano
stacc.
1st Sax. E♭ Alto
2nd Sax. B♭ Tenor
3rd Sax. E♭ Alto
Banjo
Allargando
Pizz.
Violin I
Violin II
Viola
Violoncello
Bass

Piano
32
pp legato
poco a poco cresc.
dim.
mp
rall.
con moto, espressivo
p
mf espr.
calmato
33
Leggiero
(L.H.) assai staccato
p
G
Agitato e misterioso
mf sempre stacc.
Start slowly and gradually increase in speed
L.H.
L.H.
Sognando
rall. e dim.
mf a tempo
H
L.H.
f
R.H.

34 Allegro agitato e misterioso
Flutes I II
Oboes I II
B♭ Clarinets I II
B♭ Bass Clarinet
Bassoons I II
2nd Horn only
Horns in F I II III
B♭ Trumpets I II III
1º Solo
Trombones I II III
Solo
Tuba
Timpani
Drums
Piano
1st Sax. E♭ Alto
2nd Sax. B♭ Tenor
3rd Sax. E♭ Alto
Banjo
34 Allegro agitato e misterioso
Violin I
Violin II
Viola
Violoncello
Bass

35 Pomposo
Flutes I II
Oboes I II
B♭ Clarinets I II
B♭ Bass Clarinet
Bassoons I II
Horns in F I II III
B♭ Trumpets I II III
in B♭
Soli
Trombones I II III
Tuba
Timpani
Drums
Piano
1st Sax. E♭ Alto
2nd Sax. B♭ Tenor
3rd Sax. E♭ Alto
Banjo
35 Pomposo
Violin I
Violin II
Viola
Violoncello
Bass

Flutes I II
Oboes I II
B♭ Clarinets I II
B♭ Bass Clarinet
Bassoons I II
Horns in F I II III
B♭ Trumpets I II III
Trombones I II III
Tuba
Timpani
Drums
Piano
1st Sax. E♭ Alto
2nd Sax. B♭ Tenor
3rd Sax. E♭ Alto
Banjo
Violin I
Violin II
Viola
Violoncello
Bass

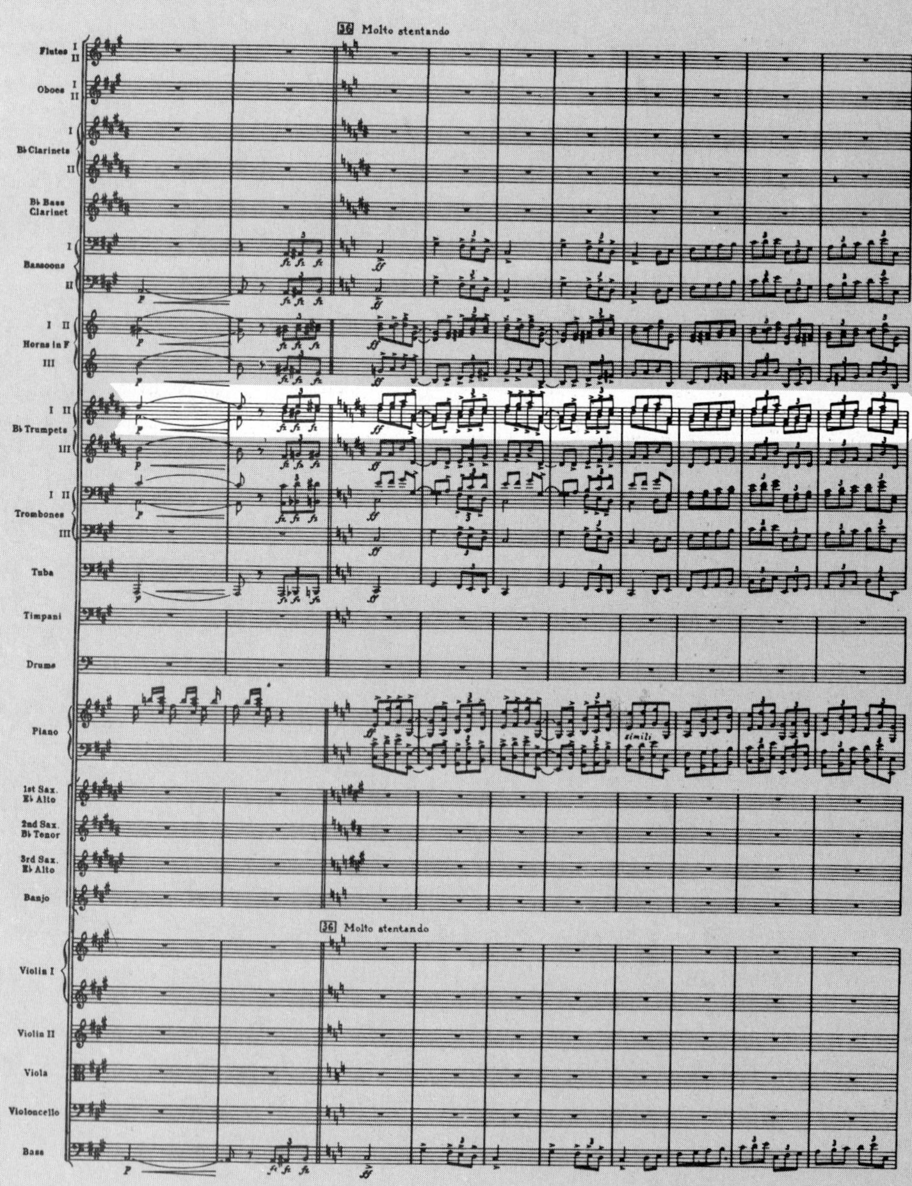
36 Molto stentando
Flutes I II
Oboes I II
B♭ Clarinets I II
B♭ Bass Clarinet
Bassoons I II
Horns in F I II III
B♭ Trumpets I II III
Trombones I II III
Tuba
Timpani
Drums
Piano
simili
1st Sax. E♭ Alto
2nd Sax. B♭ Tenor
3rd Sax. E♭ Alto
Banjo
36 Molto stentando
Violin I
Violin II
Viola
Violoncello
Bass

37 Agitato
poco a poco cresc.
Flutes I II
Oboes I II
B♭ Clarinets I II
B♭ Bass Clarinet
Bassoons I II
Horns in F I II III
B♭ Trumpets I II III
Trombones I II III
Tuba
Timpani
Drums
S.D.
flutter tongue
Piano
1st Sax. E♭ Alto
2nd Sax. B♭ Tenor
3rd Sax. E♭ Alto
Banjo
Violin I
Violin II
Viola
Violoncello
Bass
tremolo

Flutes I II
Oboes I II
B♭ Clarinets I II
B♭ Bass Clarinet
Bassoons I II
Horns in F I II III
B♭ Trumpets I II III
Trombones I II III
Tuba
Timpani
Drums
Cymb. crash
S.D.
Piano
L.H.
1st Sax. E♭ Alto
2nd Sax. B♭ Tenor
3rd Sax. E♭ Alto
Banjo
Violin I
Violin II
Viola
Violoncello
Bass
poco a poco cresc.

38
Flutes I II
Oboes I II
B♭ Clarinets I II
B♭ Bass Clarinet
Bassoons I II
Horns in F I II III
B♭ Trumpets I II III
Trombones I II III
Tuba
Timpani
Drums
Cymb.
crash
Roll on Cymb.
Piano
L.H.
1st Sax. E♭ Alto
2nd Sax. B♭ Tenor
3rd Sax. E♭ Alto
Banjo
Violin I
Violin II
Viola
Violoncello
Bass
div.
poco a poco cresc. ed accel.

Flutes I II
Oboes I II
B♭ Clarinets I II
B♭ Bass Clarinet
Bassoons I II
Horns in F I II III
B♭ Trumpets I II III
Trombones I II III
Tuba
Timpani
Drums
Piano
1st Sax. E♭ Alto
2nd Sax. B♭ Tenor
3rd Sax. E♭ Alto
Banjo
Violin I
Violin II
Viola
Violoncello
Bass
Molto marcato
poco rit.
a 2
S.D.
B.D.
Cymb.
L.H.
div.

39
Grandioso (not too slow)
Flutes I II
Oboes I II
Bb Clarinets I II
Bb Bass Clarinet
Bassoons I II
Horns in F I II III
Bb Trumpets I II III
Trombones I II III
Tuba
Timp E♭-B♭
Timpani
Drums
Piano
1st Sax. E♭ Alto
2nd Sax. B♭ Tenor
3rd Sax. E♭ Alto
Banjo
Violin I
Violin II
Viola
Violoncello
Bass
div

Flutes I II
Oboes I II
B♭ Clarinets I II
B♭ Bass Clarinet
Bassoons I II
Horns in F I II III
B♭ Trumpets I II III
Trombones I II III
Tuba
Timpani
Drums
Piano
1st Sax. E♭ Alto
2nd Sax. B♭ Tenor
3rd Sax. E♭ Alto
Banjo
Violin I
Violin II
Viola
Violoncello
Bass

Flutes I II
Oboes I II
B♭ Clarinets I II
B♭ Bass Clarinet
Bassoons I II
Horns in F I II III
B♭ Trumpets I II III
Trombones I II III
Tuba
Timpani
Drums
Piano
1st Sax. E♭ Alto
2nd Sax. B♭ Tenor
3rd Sax. E♭ Alto
Banjo
Violin I
Violin II
Viola
Violoncello
Bass
40
poco a poco rit.
Timp. F-B♭

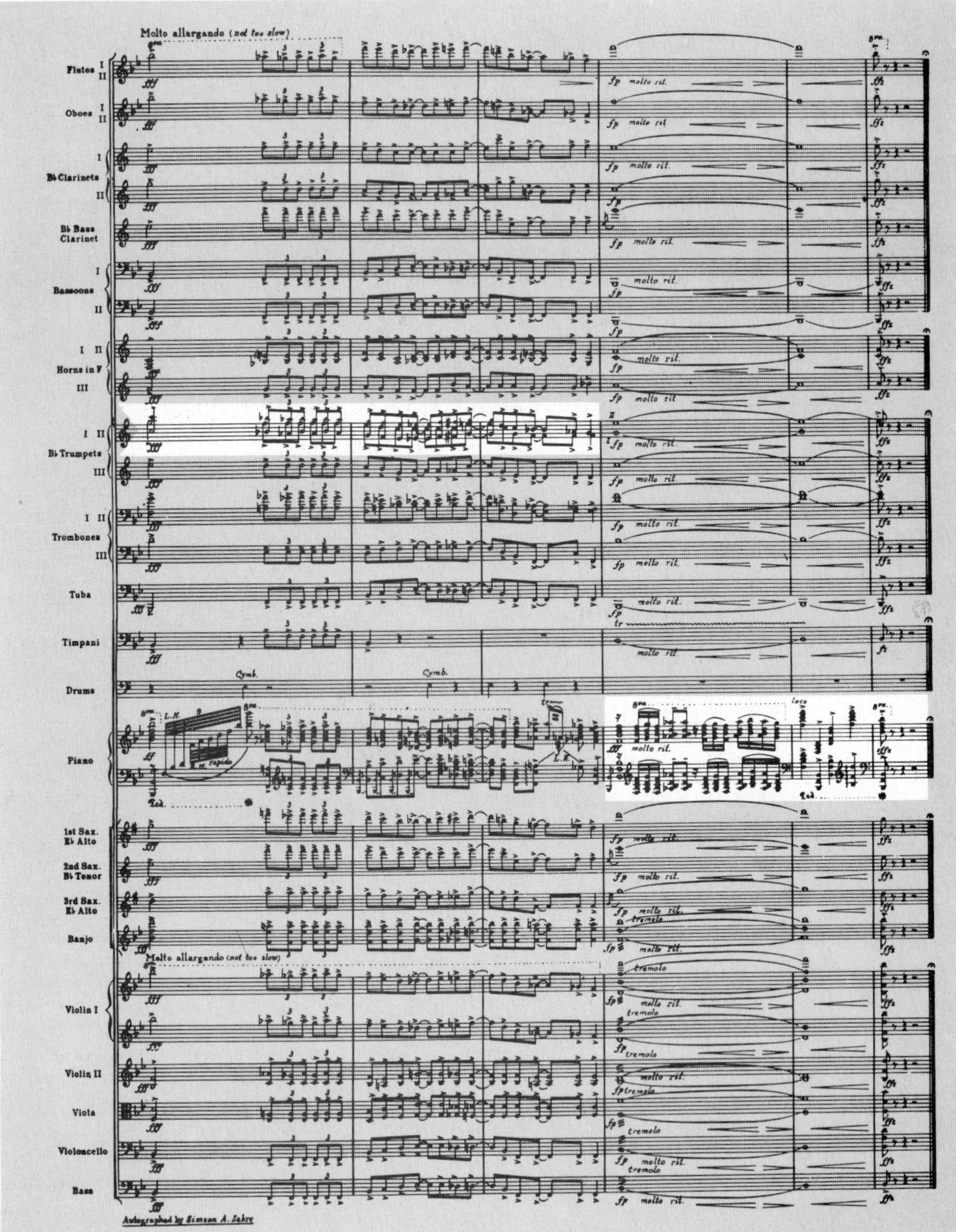
Molto allargando (not too slow)
Flutes I II
Oboes I II
B♭ Clarinets I II
B♭ Bass Clarinet
Bassoons I II
Horns in F I II III
B♭ Trumpets I II III
Trombones I II III
Tuba
Timpani
Drums
Cymb.
Piano
L.H.
rapido
Ped.
molto rit.
loco
1st Sax. E♭ Alto
2nd Sax. B♭ Tenor
3rd Sax. E♭ Alto
Banjo
Molto allargando (not too slow)
Violin I
Violin II
Viola
Violoncello
Bass
tremolo
molto rit.
Autographed by Simeon A. Sabre

33. AARON COPLAND (b. 1900), *Hoe-Down* from *Rodeo* (1942)

I
Picc.
a 2
Flts. I & II
Oboes I & II
C. A.
Clts. I & II in B♭
Bass Clt. in B♭
Bsns. I & II
I & II
Hns. in F
III & IV
I
Tpts. in B♭
II & III
Tromb. I
B. Tromb. & Tuba
Timp.
S. D.
div.
Vln. I
Vln. II
Vla.
'Cello
Bass
marc.

2
Picc.
Flts. I & II
Oboes I & II
C. A.
Clts. I & II in B♭
Bass Clt. in B♭
Bsns. I & II
a 2
I & II
Hns. in F
III & IV
I
Tpts. in B♭
II & III
Tromb. I
B. Tromb. & Tuba
senza sord.
Timp.
W. B.
S. D.
Cym.
hard stick
Piano
sec.
unis
Vln. I
Vln. II
Vla.
'Cello
Bass
pizz.
(pizz.)

3
sec.
Bsn. I
mf
W. B.
Piano
f
3
pizz.
arco
pizz.
Vln. I
pizz.
arco
pizz.
Vln. II
pizz.
Vla.
mf
sec.
'Cello
sub f
Bass

Bsn. I
W. B.
Piano
arco
pizz.
arco
Vln. I
arco
pizz.
arco
Vln. II
Vla.
'Cello
Bass

4
5
Picc.
Flts. I & II
a 2
Oboes I & II
C. A.
Clts. I & II in B♭
Bass Clt. in B♭
Bsn. I
I & II
Hns. in F
III & IV
I
Tpts. in B♭
II
Trombs. I & II
B. Tromb. & Tuba
Xylo.
W. B.
Cym.
hard stick
Piano
Vln. I
Vln. II
Vla.
'Cello
Bass

Picc.
Flts. I & II
a 2
Oboes I & II
a 2
C. A.
Clts. I & II in B♭
a 2
Bass Clt. in B♭
Bsn. I
I & II
Hns. in F
III & IV
I
Tpts. in B♭
II
Trombs. I & II
B. Tromb. & Tuba
Xylo.
Cym.
hard stick
Vln. I
Vln. II
Vla.
'Cello
Bass

6
a 2
Oboes I & II
f non legato
Clts I & II
in B♭
a 2
f non legato
Hns I & II
in F
f
Trombs
I & II
f
6
Vln. I
Vln. II
Vla.
'Cello
Bass

a 2
Oboes I & II
Clts I & II
in B♭
a2
Hns I & II
in F
Trombs
I & II
Vln. I
Vln. II
Vla.
'Cello
Bass

7
Picc.
Flts. I & II
a 2
Oboes I & II
C. A.
Clts. I & II in B♭
Bass Clt. in B♭
Bsn. I
I & II
Hns. in F
III & IV
I
Tpts. in B♭
II & III
Trombs. I & II
B. Tromb. & Tuba
Xylo.
Cym.
hard stick
7
Vln. I
Vln. II
Vla.
'Cello
Bass

8
Picc.
a2
Flts. I & II
sf
a2
Oboes I & II
sf
C.A.
a2
Clts. I & II in B♭
Bass Clt. in B♭
sf
Bsn. I
sf
I & II
Hns. in F
III & IV
mf
I
Tpts. in B♭
II
sf
sf
Tromb. I & II
B. Tromb. & Tuba
Timp.
p
Xylo.
sf
8
Vln. I
sf
mf
Vln. II
sf
mf
Vla.
sf
mf
'Cello
sf
mf
arco
Bass
mf

9
Picc.
Flts. I & II
Oboes I & II
C. A.
Clts. I & II in B♭
Bass Clt. in B♭
Bsns. I & II
a 2
mp
ff
I & II
Hns. in F
III & IV
I
Tpts. in B♭
II & III
Trombs. I & II
B.Tromb. & Tuba
Timp.
Xylo.
Tria.
Vln. I
Vln. II
Vla.
'Cello
Bass
f
p
fff
pizz.

Picc.
a2
Flts. I & II
a2
Oboes I & II
C.A.
a2
Clts. I & II in B♭
Bass Clt. in B♭
Bsns I & II
I & II
Hns. in F
III & IV
I
Tpts. in B♭
II & III
Trombs. I & II
B. Tromb. & Tuba
Timp.
Tria.
Vln. I
Vln. II
Vla.
'Cello
Bass

10
Picc.
Flts. I & II
a2
Oboes I & II
C.A.
Clts. I & II in B♭
Bass Clt. in B♭
Bsns. I
I & II
Hns. in F
III & IV
I
Tpts. in B♭
II
Trombs. I & II
B.Tromb. & Tuba
Xylo.
Hard stick
Cym.
10
Vln. I
Vln. II
Vla.
arco.
'Cello
Bass

11
Picc.
Flts. I & II
Oboes I & II
C.A.
Clts. I & II in B♭
Bass Clt. in B♭
Bsns. I
I & II
Hns. in F
III & IV
I
Tpts. in B♭
II
Trombs. I & II
B. Tromb. & Tuba
Xylo.
Cym.
11
Vln. I
Vln. II
Vla.
'Cello
Bass

Picc.
Flts. I & II
Oboes I & II
C.A.
Clts. I & II in B♭
Bass Clt. in B♭
Bsns. I & II
I & II Hns. in F III & IV
I Tpts. in B♭ II & III
Tromb. I
B. Tromb. & Tuba
Timp
Xylo.
S.D.
Cym.
Vln. I
Vln. II
Vla.
'Cello
Bass
a2
sf
cresc.
fff
ff
f
mf cresc.
dim. molto
arco.

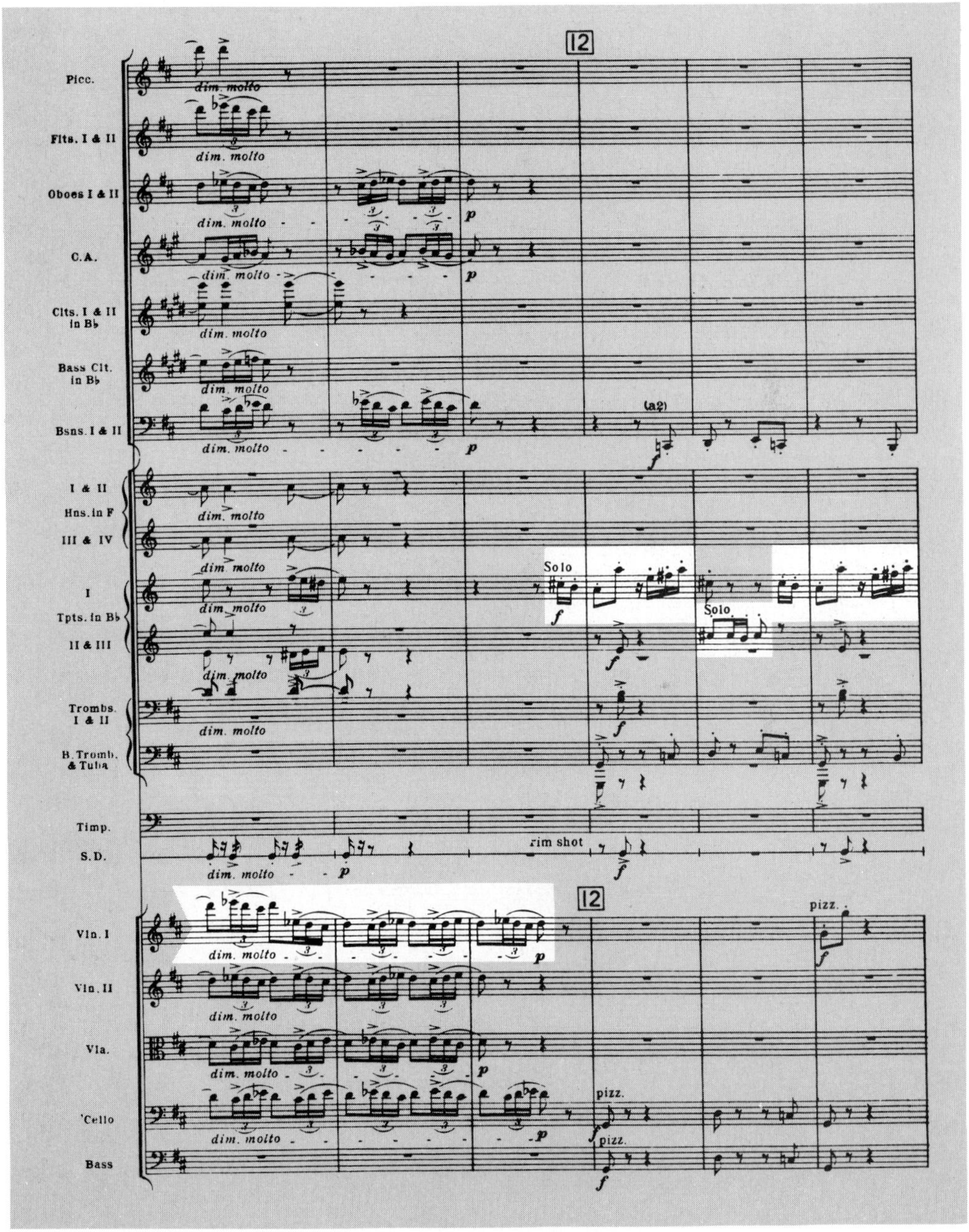

12

Picc. — *dim. molto*

Flts. I & II — *dim. molto*

Oboes I & II — *dim. molto* - - - - - *p*

C.A. — *dim. molto* - - - - - *p*

Clts. I & II in B♭ — *dim. molto*

Bass Clt. in B♭ — *dim. molto*

Bsns. I & II — *dim. molto* - - - - - - *p* — (a2) *f*

I & II Hns. in F III & IV — *dim. molto*

I Tpts. in B♭ II & III — *dim. molto* — Solo *f* — Solo

Trombs. I & II — *dim. molto* — *f*

B. Tromb. & Tuba

Timp.

S.D. — *dim. molto* - *p* — rim shot *f*

12

Vln. I — *dim. molto* - - - - - *p* — pizz. *f*

Vln. II — *dim. molto*

Vla. — *dim. molto* - - - - - *p*

'Cello — *dim. molto* - - - - - - *p* — pizz. *f*

Bass — pizz. *f*

13
Solo
mf non legato
Oboe I
Clts. I & II in B♭
p
Bsns. I & II
I
Tpts in B♭
II
Trombs. I & II
a2
B. Tromb & Tuba
rim
S. D.
13
arco
div. pizz.
f
p
Vln. I
Vln. II
Vla.
'Cello
Bass
Bass Clt. in B♭
Bsn. I
Solo
mf
(arco)
Solo Vln.
Vln. I (div)
Vla. (div)

14
Picc.
Flts. I & II
Solo
Oboe I
mf
C.A.
Clt. I in B♭
Bass Clt. in B♭
a 2
Bsns. I & II
f
I & II
Hns. in F
III & IV
I
Tpts. in B♭
II
Trombs. I & II
B. Tromb. & Tuba
Timp.
rim shot
S.D.
14
unis. arco.
Vln. I
pizz.
arco
Vln. II
unis. arco
Vla. (div.)
pizz.
arco
'Cello
pizz.
arco
Bass

15
Picc.
Flt. I
Oboes I & II
C.A.
Clts. I & II in B♭
Bass Clt. in B♭
Bsns. I & II
a2
I & II
Hns. in F
III & IV
I
Tpts. in B♭
II
Trombs. I & II
B. Tromb. & Tuba
Timp.
S.D
Piano
Vln. I
Vln. II
Vla.
'Cello
Bass
f vigoroso
arco

16
Picc.
Fl. I
Oboes I & II
a2
stacc.
ff
C.A.
Clts. I & II in B♭
a2
stacc.
ff
Bass Clt. in B♭
Bsns. I & II
a2
I & II
Hns. in F
III & IV
sf
I
Tpts. in B♭
II
ff
Trombs. I & II
ff
B. Tromb. & Tuba
ff
Timp.
Piano
16
Vln. I
ff
Vln. II
ff
Vla.
ff
'Cello
ff
Bass
ff

Picc.
ff
Flts. I & II
a 2
Oboes I & II
a 2
C.A.
Clts. I & II in B♭
a 2
Bass Clt. in B♭
Bsns. I & II
I & II
Hns. in F
III & IV
a 2
I
Tpts. in B♭
II & III
Trombs. I & II
a 2
B. Tromb. & Tuba
Timp.
Vln. I
Vln. II
Vla.
'Cello
Bass

17
Picc.
Flts. I & II
Oboes I & II
C. A.
Clts. I & II in B♭
Bass Clt. in B♭
Bsns. I & II
I & II
Hns. in F
III & IV
I
Tpts. in B♭
II & III
Trombs. I & II
B. Tromb. & Tuba
Timp.
S.D. W.B.
Cym. B.D.
Piano
Vln. I
Vln. II
Vla.
'Cello
Bass
a2
a 2
fff
ff
sf
mf
mp
S.D.
W.B.
rubato
(arco)
pizz.

18
Bsn. I
Hns. in F I & II
Tromb. I
Solo
mf
W. B.
Piano
18
Vln. I
p
Vln. II
p
Vla.
p
'Cello
Bass
rit. molto
Clts. I & II (in B♭)
p
Bsn. I
Hns. in F I & II
Tromb. I
Piano
Celesta
p
rit. molto
Vln. I
p
Vln. II
p
Vla.
p
'Cello
(pizz.)
p
arco

19
Picc.
a 2
Fls. I & II
Oboes I & II
C.A.
Clts. I & II in B♭
Bass Clt. in B♭
Bsn. I
I & II
Hns. in F
III & IV
I
Tpts. in B♭
II
Trombs. I & II
B. Tromb. & Tuba
Xylo.
Cym.
(hard stick)
19
Vln. I
Vln. II
Vla.
'Cello
Bass

Picc.
Flts. I & II
a2
sf
mp
Oboes I & II
a2
sf
mp
C. A.
Clts. I & II in B♭
a 2
mp
Bass Clt. in B♭
sf
mp
Bsns. I & II
I
sf
a 2
mp
I & II
Hns. in F
III & IV
I
Tpts. in B♭
II
sf
sf
Trombs. I & II
B. Tromb. & Tuba
Xylo.
sf
Vln. I
sf
Vln. II
sf
p
Vla.
sf
p
'Cello
sf
p
Bass

20

Picc.

Flts. I & II — a2 — *ff*

Oboes I & II — a2 — *ff*

C.A.

Clts. I & II in B♭ — a2 — *ff*

Bass Clt. in B♭

Bsns. I & II

Hns. in F I & II — *ff*

Hns. in F III & IV — *ff*

Tpts. in B♭ I — *ff*

Tpts. in B♭ II & III — *ff*

Trombs. I & II — *ff*

B. Tromb. & Tuba — a 2 — *ff*

Timp. — *ff*

Tria. — *ff*

20

Vln. I — *fff*

Vln. II — *fff*

Vla. — *fff*

'Cello — *fff* pizz.

Bass — *fff* pizz.

21
Picc.
Flts. I & II
Oboes I & II
C.A.
Clts. I & II in B♭
Bass Clt. in B♭
Bsn. I
I & II
Hns. in F
III & IV
I
Tpts. in B♭
II & III
Trombs. I & II
B. Tromb. & Tuba
Timp.
Xylo.
Tria. Cym.
21
Vln. I
Vln. II
Vla.
'Cello
Bass
a2
a 2
f arco.

22
Picc.
Flts. I & II
a2
cresc.
Oboes I & II
cresc.
C.A.
Clts. I & II in B♭
Bass Clt. in B♭
Bsns. I & II
I & II
Hns. in F
III & IV
I
Tpts. in B♭
II & III
Trombs. I & II
B. Tromb. & Tuba
Xylo.
Tria. Cym.
Piano
Vln. I
Vln. II
Vla.
'Cello
Bass

Picc.
Flts. I & II
Oboes I & II
C.A.
Clts. I & II in B♭
Bass Clt. in B♭
Bsns. I & II
Hns. in F I & II
Hns. in F III & IV
cuivré
Tpts. in B♭ I
Tpts. in B♭ II & III
Trombs. I & II
B. Tromb. & Tuba
Timp.
Xylo.
Tria. Cym. B.D.
Piano
Vln. I
Vln. II
Vla.
'Cello
Bass
a2
arco
B.D.

34. RUTH CRAWFORD (1901-1953), Fourth movement from *String Quartet 1931*

20
decresc. poco a poco to meas. 60
p
25
f
mp
mf
30
5
35
fz

40
fz
fz
fz
fz
fz
fz
45
p
f
fz
f
fz
f
fz
fz
fz
fz
fz
fz
fz
50
pp
ff
fz
ff
fz
ff
fz

55
60
65
cresc. poco a poco to meas. 100
decresc. poco a poco to meas. 101
decresc. poco a poco to meas. 101
decresc. poco a poco to meas. 101
70

75
3
5
fz
mf
mp
80
85
mf

90
f
p
p
p
95
più f
100
ff
pp
pp
pp

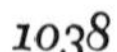

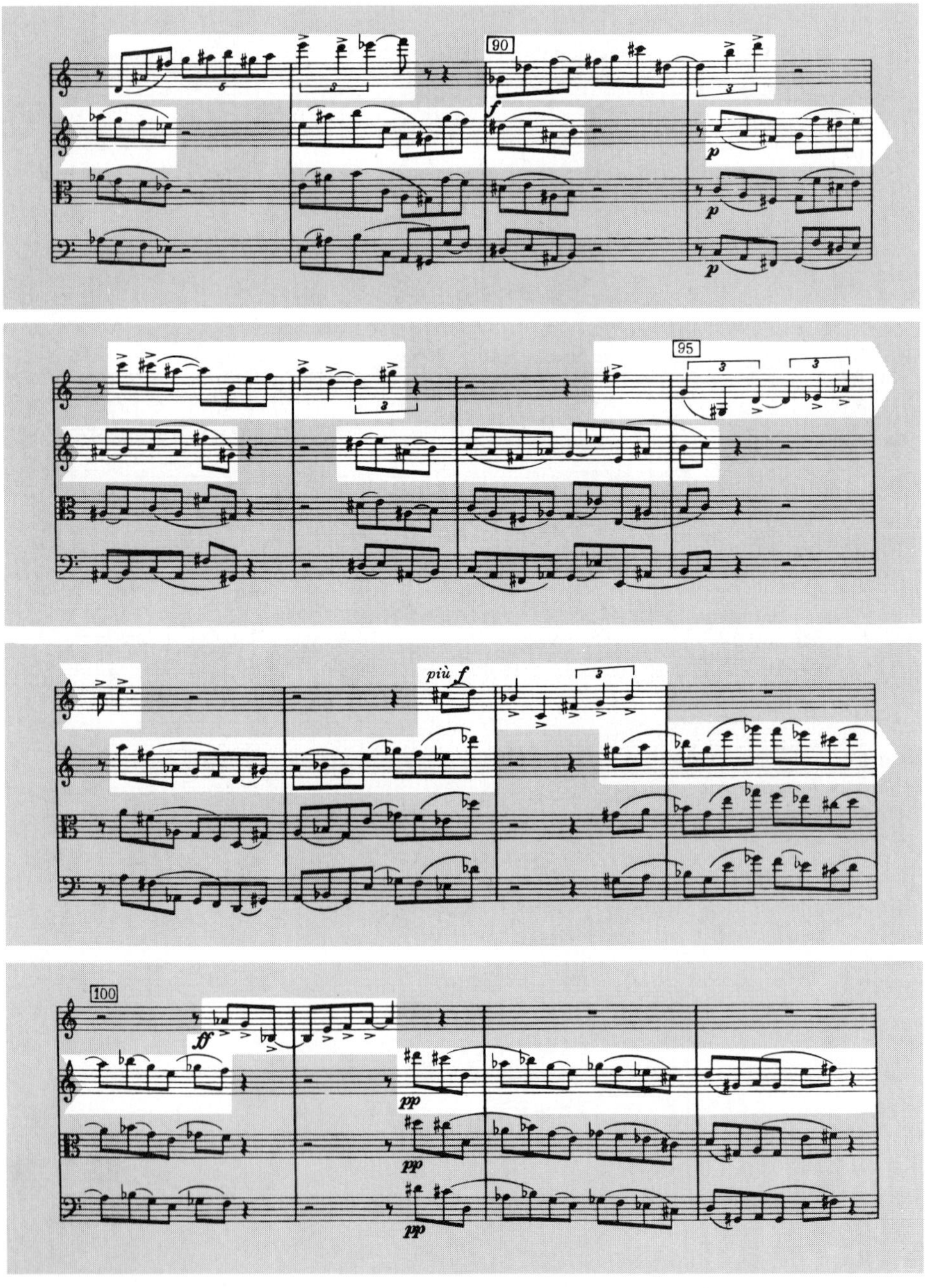

105
sempre ff
sempre pp
sempre pp
sempre pp

3
110

115
ffz
ffz
ffz

35. ELLIOTT CARTER (b. 1908), Etudes 4, 5, and 8 from *Eight Etudes and a Fantasy for Woodwind Quartet* (1950)

IV

20
mf
f
mp
25
più f
p cresc.
p
30
cresc.
35
ff

40
p cresc.
p cresc.
p cresc.
p cresc.
f
45
f
f
f
ff
ff
ff
ff
f
f
f
f
ff
mp
ff
mp
ff
mf
ff
mp
50
mf
p
p
p
mf
mp
mf
mp
mp
mf
mp
(mp)
55
cresc.
mf
mp cresc.
mp cresc.
cresc.
f
p
f
f
p
f
mp
cresc.
p
mp
cresc.
mp
cresc.
p
cresc.

60
p cresc.
p cresc.
p cresc.
p cresc.
65
70
p cresc.
p cresc.
p cresc.
p cresc.
75
mf cresc.
cresc.
mf cresc.
meno f cresc.
mf cresc.
cresc.
mf cresc.
meno f

8
ff
p
mp
ff
mf
mp
ff
mf
pp
cresc.
ff
p
80
pp
mp
mf
ff
mf
p
pp
(pp)
p
mf
ff
(pp)
mf
ff
p
mf
mf
ff
85
mp
mf
p
mf
p
mf
mp
p
pp
p
pp

V
Andante (♩= 60)
Fl.
Ob.
Cl. in B♭
Bsn.
f
f cantando espr.
f non troppo
f non troppo

5
mf
marcato

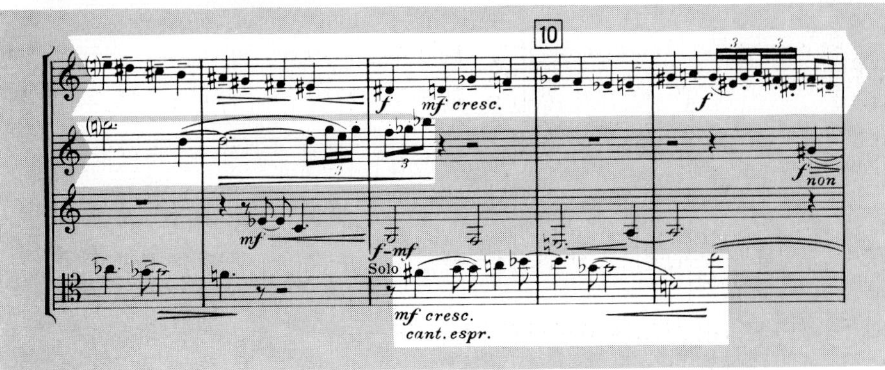
10
f
mf cresc.
f
non
mf
f–mf
Solo
mf cresc.
cant. espr.

troppo
f
mf
non troppo
15
mf
mp
p
20
25
p sub.

VIII
Presto (♩ = 160)
Fl.
Ob.
Cl. in B♭
Bsn.
pp
pp
pp
pp

mf marc.
pp
mf marc.
pp
(pp)

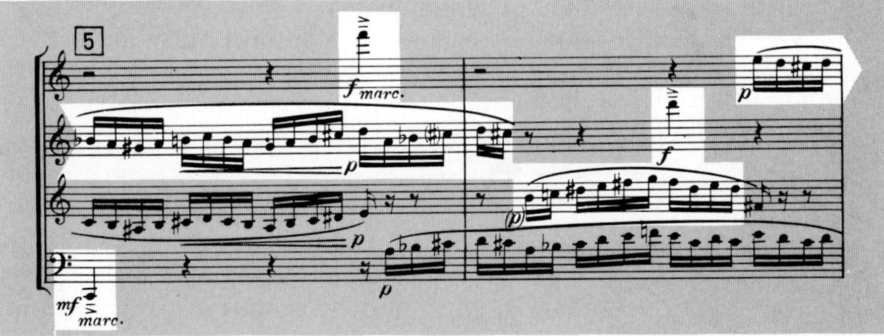
5
f marc.
p
f
p
(p)
p
p
mf
marc.

pp
p
f
mf
pp
(p)

10
mf
p
pp
p
pp
pp
f sub.
f
p
p
f
p
p
f
(p)
(p)
15
8
f
p
f

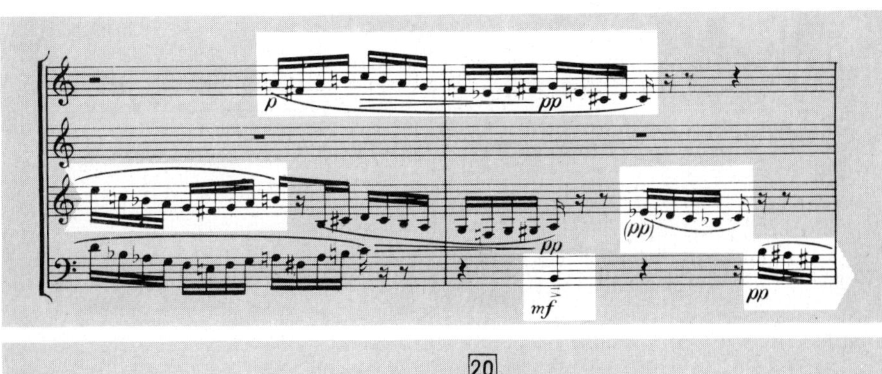
p
pp
pp
(pp)
mf
pp

20
mf
pp

p
f
pp
p
(p)
mf
p
p
(p)

p
f
f
mf
(p)
f
f
mf

25
30

35
40
f
mf
pp
(p)
p
(pp)

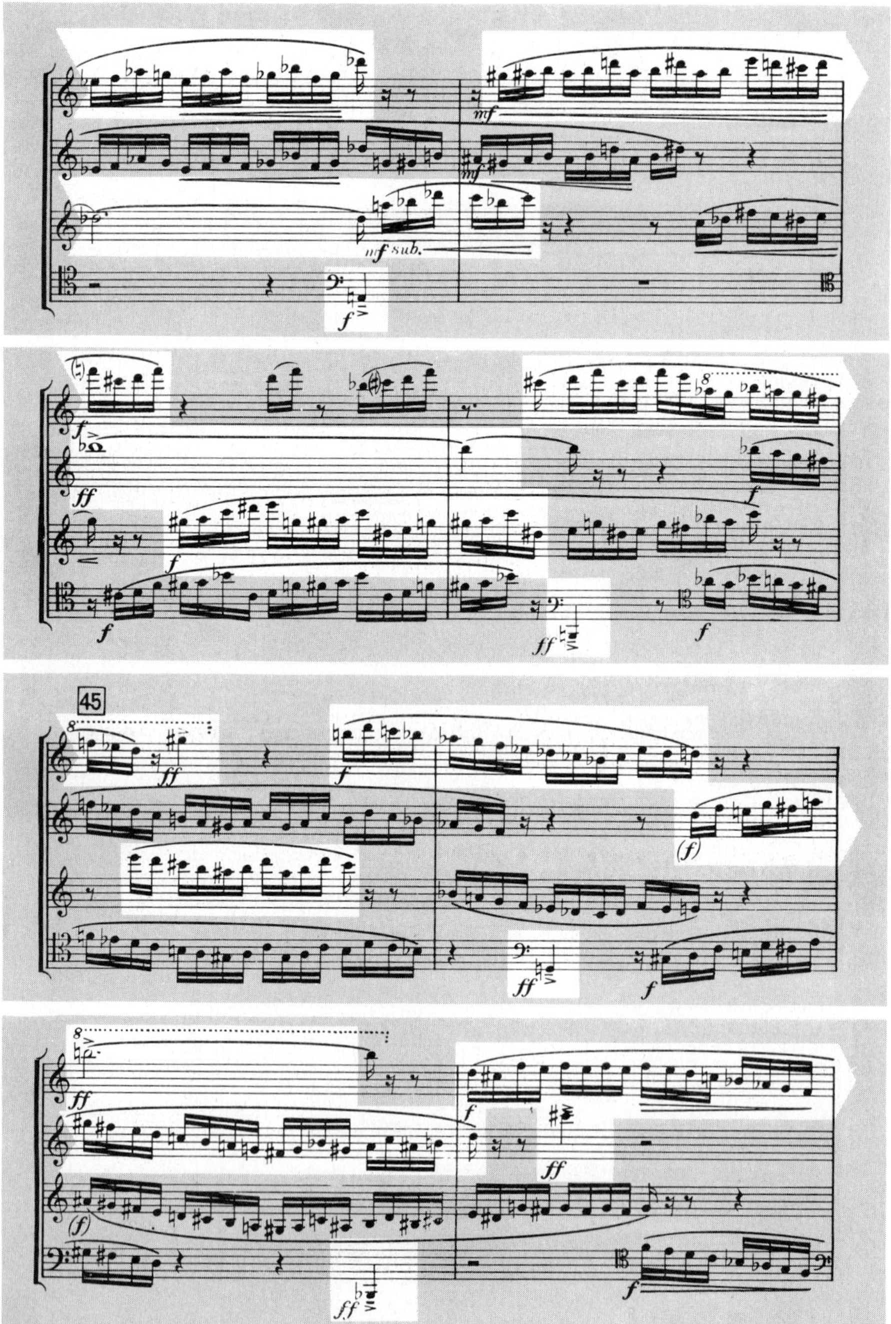

mf
mf
mf sub.
f
f
ff
f
f
f
ff
f
45
8
ff
f
(f)
ff
f
8
ff
f
ff
(f)
f
ff

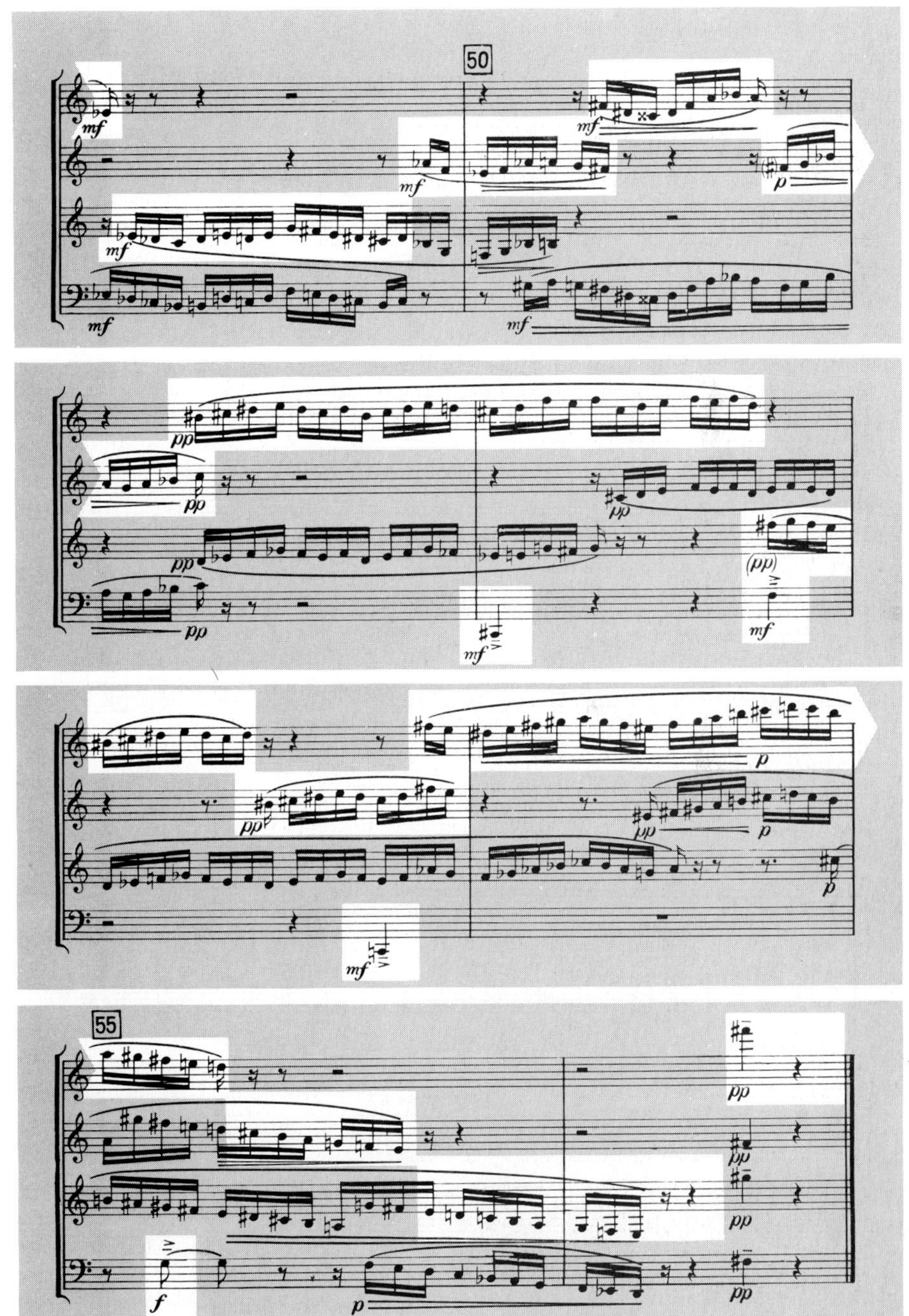
50
mf
mf
mf
mf
mf
mf
p
pp
pp
pp
pp
pp
(pp)
mf
mf
p
pp
pp
p
p
mf
55
pp
pp
pp
f
p
pp

36. PIERRE BOULEZ (b. 1925),
Excerpts from *Le Marteau sans maître* (1954, REV. 1957)

No. 1: *Before "L'Artisanat furieux"*

a tempo
11
Fl. en sol
Vibr.
Guit.
Alto
pizz.
arco
B 10
17
poco rit.
a tempo
p sub.
24
pour 4
pp
p

presser
a tempo
Fl. en sol
Vibr.
Guit.
Alto
arco
pizz.
pour 6
pour 4
poco rit.
cresc.

46
presser - -
Fl. en sol
Vibr.
Guit.
Alto
pour 4
arco
pp sub.

53
a tempo
Fl. en sol
Vibr.
Guit.
Alto
pour 6
pizz.
arco
f sub.

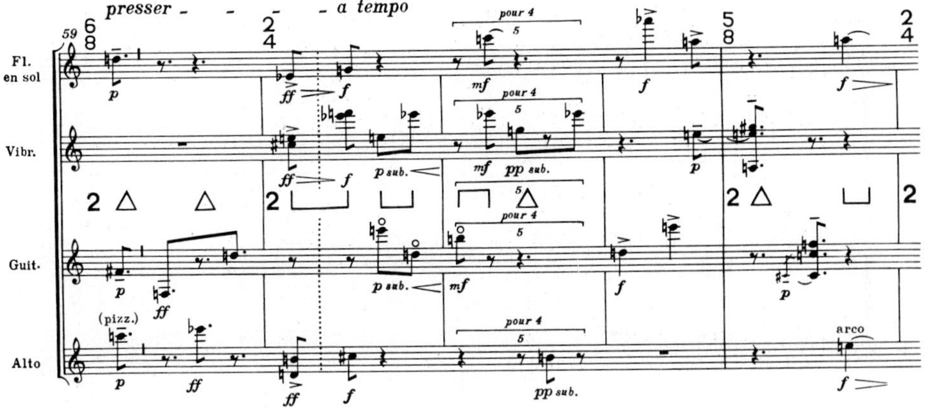

poco rit.
a tempo
Fl. en sol
Vibr.
Guit.
Alto
pour 6
pizz.
arco
ff sub.
poco rit.

a tempo
presser
a tempo
Fl. en sol
Vibr.
Guit.
Alto
pizz.
arco
poco rit. a tempo
pour 4
presser
a tempo
poco rit.
a tempo
presser
arrêt assez court

No. 3: *"L'Artisanat furieux"*

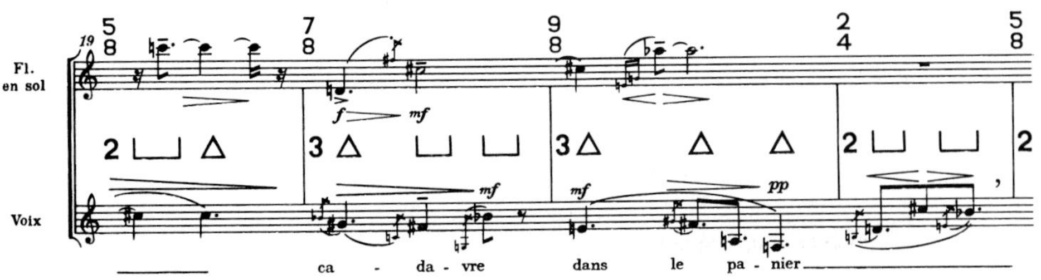
Fl. en sol
Voix
ca - da - vre dans le pa - nier

Fl. en sol
Voix
senza dim.
cresc. al
tenuto senza dim.

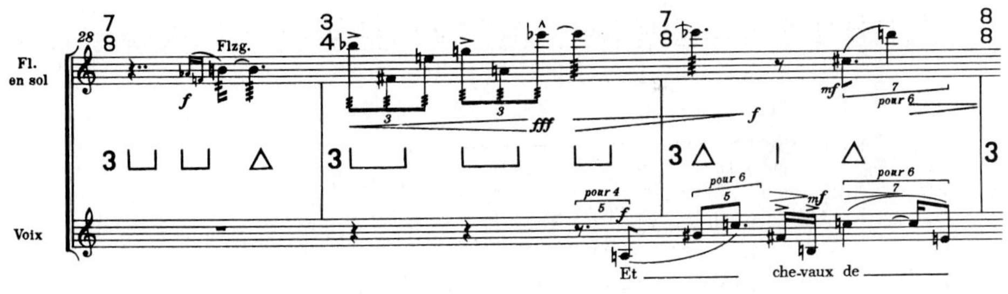
Fl. en sol
Flzg.
Voix
Et che-vaux de

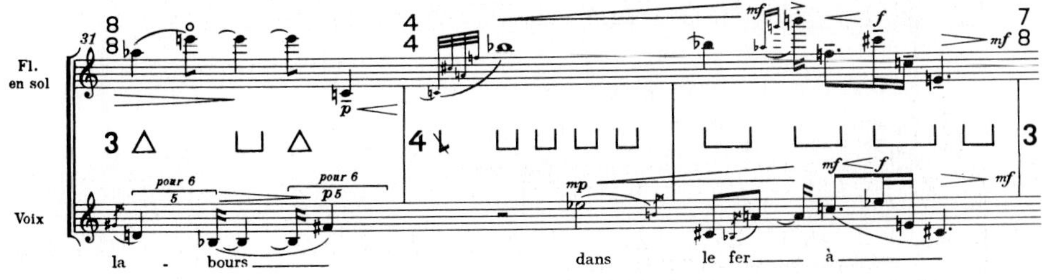
Fl. en sol
Voix
la - bours dans le fer à

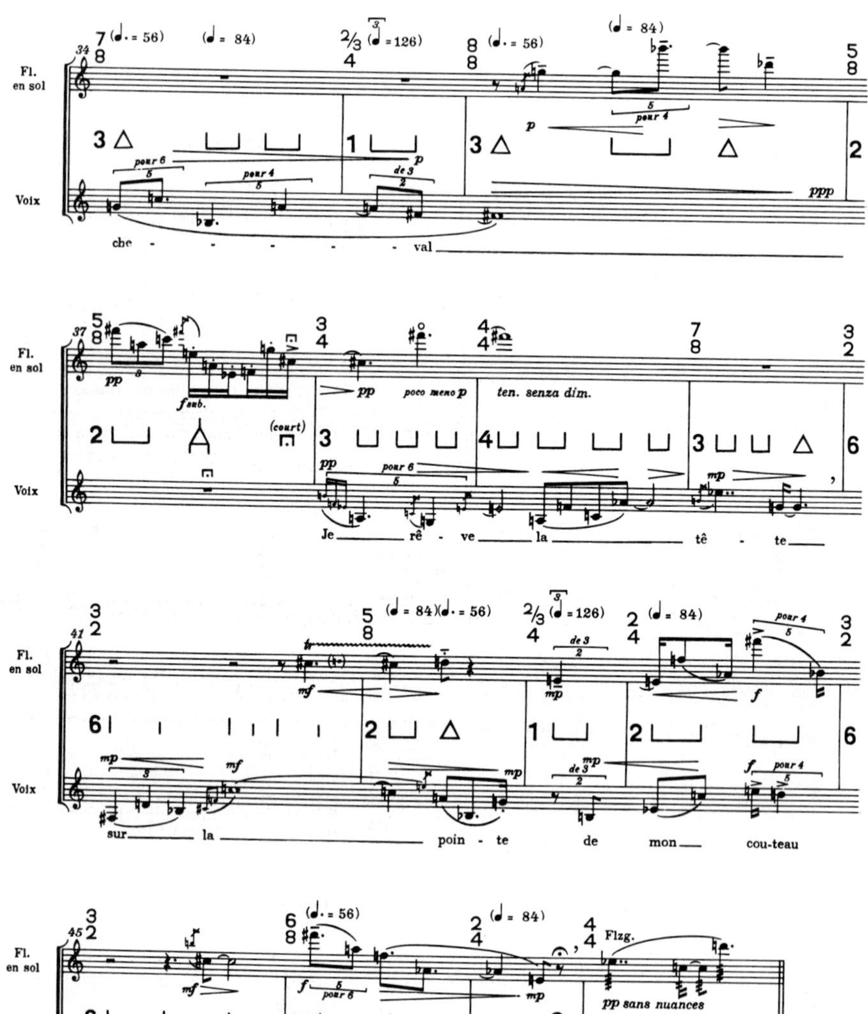

Translation

La roulotte fouge au bord du clou
Et cadavre dans le panier
Et chevaux de labours dans le fer à cheval
Je rêve la tête sur la pointe de mon couteau le Pérou

The red caravan at the edge of the prison
And a corpse in the basket
And a workhorse in the horseshoe
I dream, head on the point of my knife, Peru

No. 7: *After "L'Artisanat furieux"*

sempre accelerando
cédez
Fl. en sol
Vibr.
Guit.
(♩ = 208)
accelerando
molto
A tempo subito (♩ = 168)
très court
pour 4
sec
sempre ff
accelerando
pour 6
sempre f

(♩ = 208)
(♩. = 138)
beaucoup plus vif
poco rit.
accelerando
revenir au Tempo
Fl. en sol
Vibr.
Guit.
B4
B3
rit.
Tempo
più ritard.
accele
court
rando
poco
a
poco
accele
ff sempre
5 pour 6
pp sub.
f sempre
(non accentué)

(♩ = 192)
(♩ = 168)
-rando
molto
Tempo sub.
Fl. en sol
Vibr.
Guit.
pour 4
pas trop long
sec
poco a poco rit.
poco dimin.
p sub.
quasi ff
pochissimo
Tempo sub.
ritard.
sans diminuer
arrêt très court
sempre pp

37. GEORGE CRUMB (b. 1929), *El niño busca su voz* from *Ancient Voices of Children* (1970)

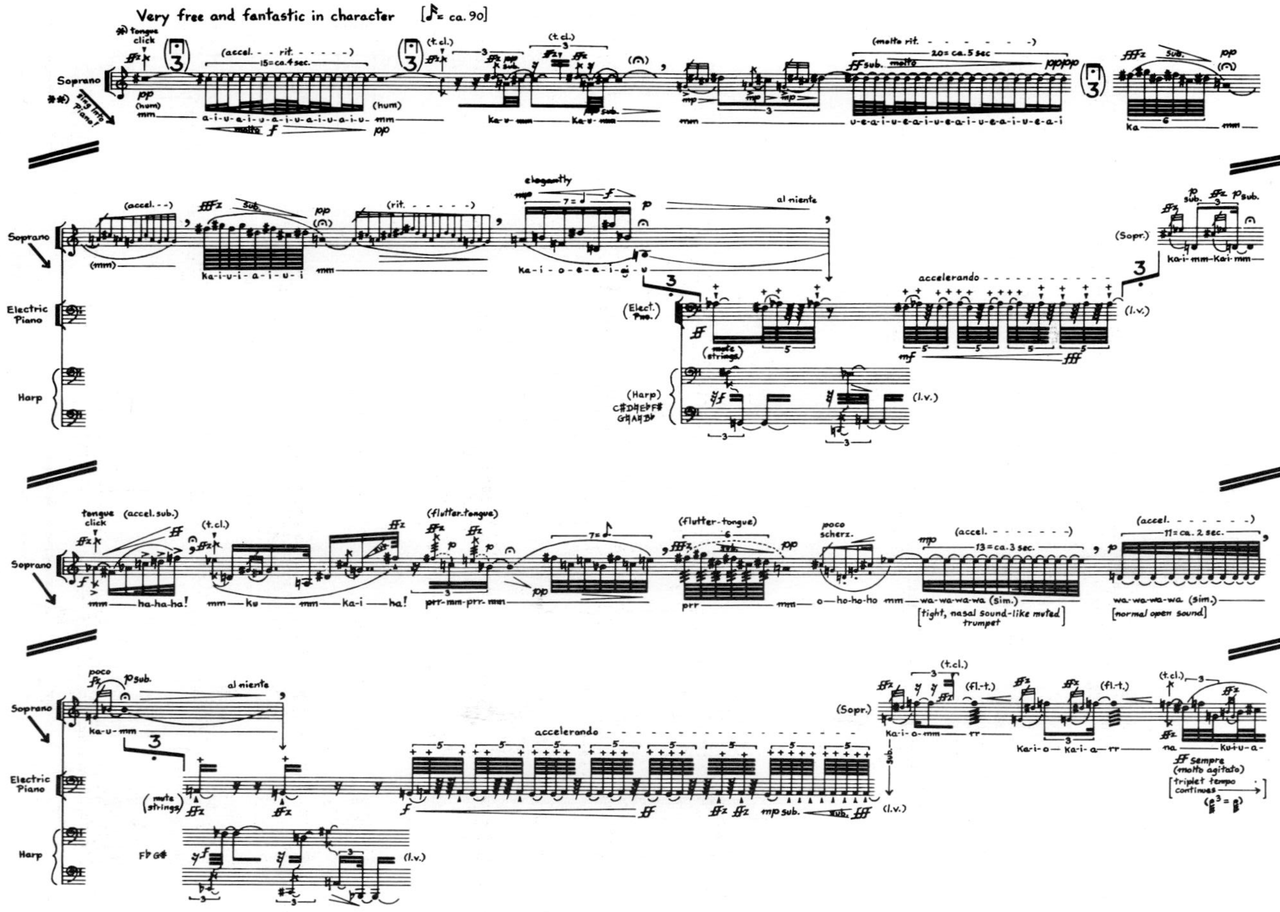

El niño busca su voz from *Ancient Voices of Children* by George Crumb. Copyright © 1970 by C. F. Peters Corporation, 373 Park Avenue South, New York 10016. Reprinted with permission of the publishers who published the score of the complete work under Peters Edition No. 66303.

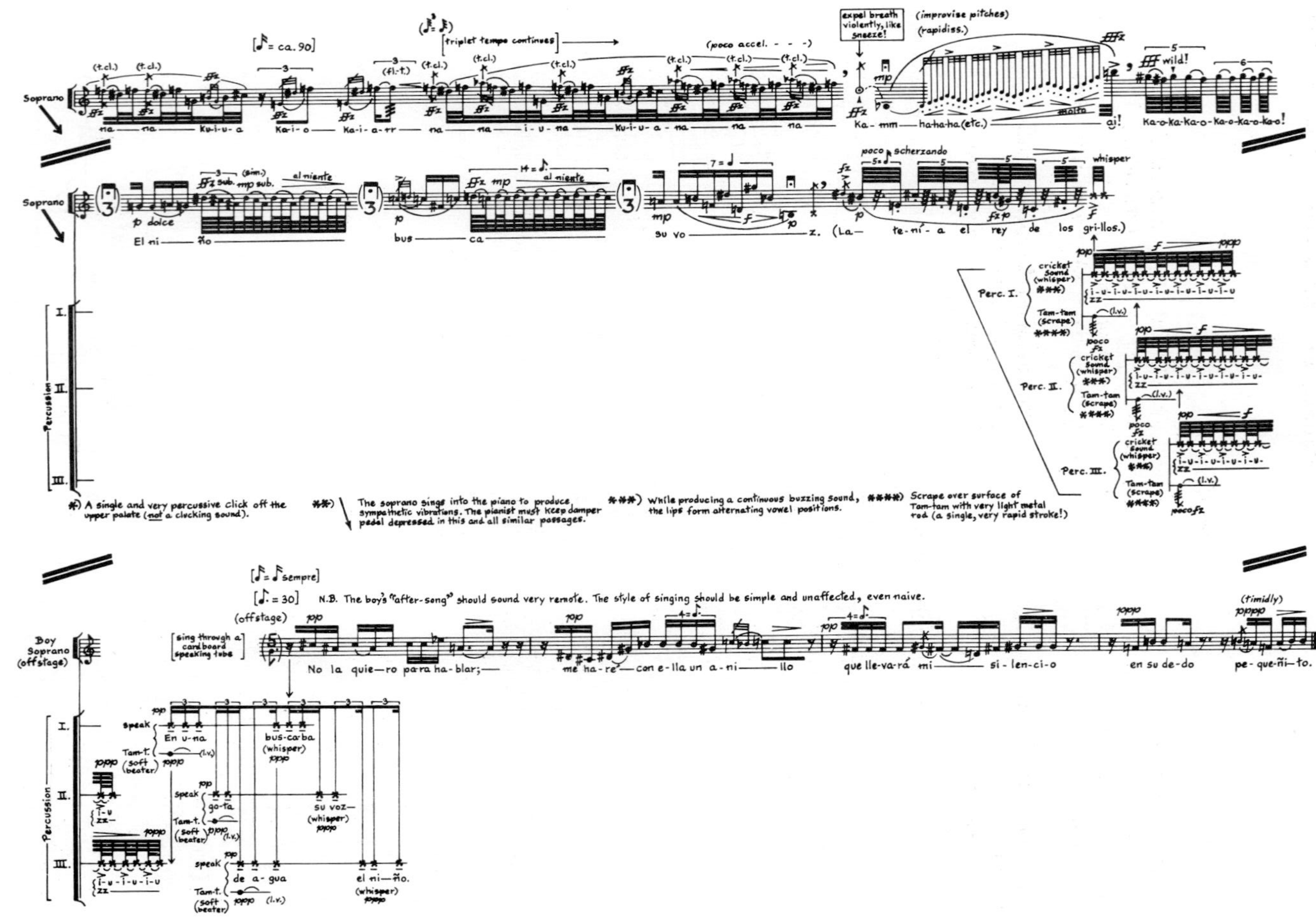
Soprano
Ka-mm — ha-ha-ha (etc.) — aj!
Ka-o-ka-ka-o-ka-o-ka-o-ka-o!
(improvise pitches)
(rapidiss.)
expel breath violently, like sneeze!
triplet tempo continues
(poco accel. - - -)
na — na — Ku-i-u-a — Ka-i-o — Ka-i-a-rr — na — na — i-u-na — Ku-i-u-a-na — na — na
El ni — ño — bus — ca — su vo — z. (La — te-ní-a el rey de los gri-llos.)
poco scherzando
whisper
al niente
p dolce
Perc. I.
Perc. II.
Perc. III.
cricket sound (whisper)
Tam-tam (scrape)
Percussion
*) A single and very percussive click off the upper palate (not a clocking sound).
**) The soprano sings into the piano to produce sympathetic vibrations. The pianist must keep damper pedal depressed in this and all similar passages.
***) While producing a continuous buzzing sound, the lips form alternating vowel positions.
****) Scrape over surface of Tam-tam with very light metal rod (a single, very rapid stroke!)
Boy Soprano (offstage)
(offstage)
sing through a cardboard speaking tube
N.B. The boy's "after-song" should sound very remote. The style of singing should be simple and unaffected, even naive.
(timidly)
No la quie-ro para ha-blar; — me ha-ré — con e-lla un a-ni — llo — que lle-va-rá mi — si-len-ci-o — en su de-do — pe-que-ñi-to.
speak
En u-na
bus-ca-ba (whisper)
go-ta
su voz — (whisper)
de a-gua
el ni-ño. (whisper)
Tam-t. (soft beater)

Translation

El niño busca su voz.
(La tenía el rey de los grillos.)
En una gota de agua
buscaba su voz el niño.

No la quiero para hablar;
me haré con ella un anillo
que llevará mi silencio
en su dedo pequeñito.

FEDERICO GARCÍA LORCA

The little boy was looking for his voice.
(The king of the crickets had it.)
In a drop of water
the little boy was looking for his voice.

I do not want it for speaking with;
I will make a ring of it
so that he may wear my silence
on his little finger.

W. S. MERWIN

38. MARIO DAVIDOVSKY (b. 1934),
Synchronisms No. 1 for Flute and Electronic Sounds (1963)

STOP
START 3
fff
A tempo
Lunga
(ad lib.)
16 sec. 18 sec.
sfff
f
fff
fp sub.
mf
mp
Flutter...
pp
p
p
fff
fff
p
very short pause
STOP
fff
f
pp
ff
sff
pp sub.
32 sec.
ff
pp
ff
pp
f
p
f
ff
pp
ff
pp
Start this part, right after electronic cue ♯ 3, is finished.
⌖ = Air + Percussion
+ = Percussion only.

START
4
ff
pp
ff
f
ff
piu f
sff
pp
sff
pp
fff
fff
ffff
p cresc.
ff
from as fast as possible Rit. poco a poco. ad lib.
11 sec.
mf
fff
p
fff
p
fff
mp
fff
mp
f
fff

percussion like sound
f
ff
ffff
Start slow, accel. po a poco
as fast as possible
28 sec.
STOP
Tacet until the Cue 4 finishes.
pppp
45 sec.
Piu lento (♪ = 72) (Freely)
pp
pp ppp
f
p
pp
ppp
pppp
sf pp
sf pp
mf
pp
p
pp
fff
sff
fff
ffff
sffff
lunga
Piu Lento
p
pp
sff sub.
A tempo
♩ = 50
pp
START 5
STOP
pppp

39. PHILIP GLASS (b. 1937), *Floe* from *Glassworks* (1981)

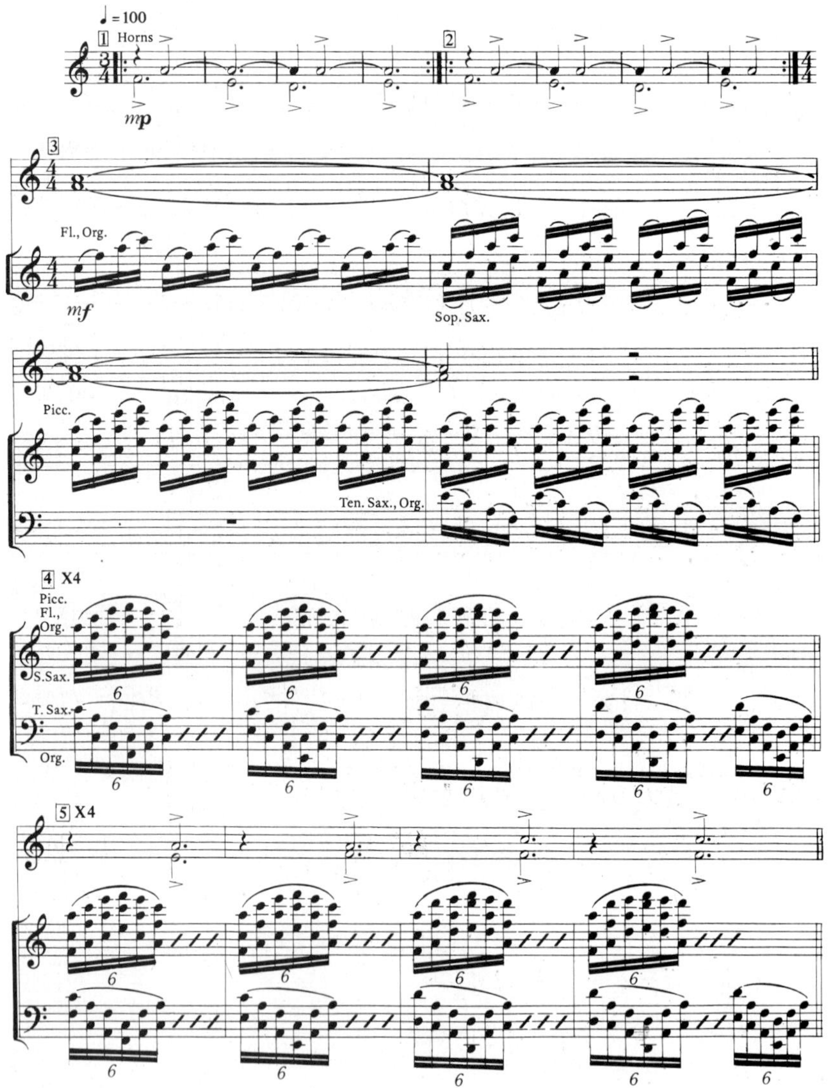

6
7
8
9
10

11
6
12
mp
13
3
4
14
15
mf
16
17 X4
a2
f
18
3

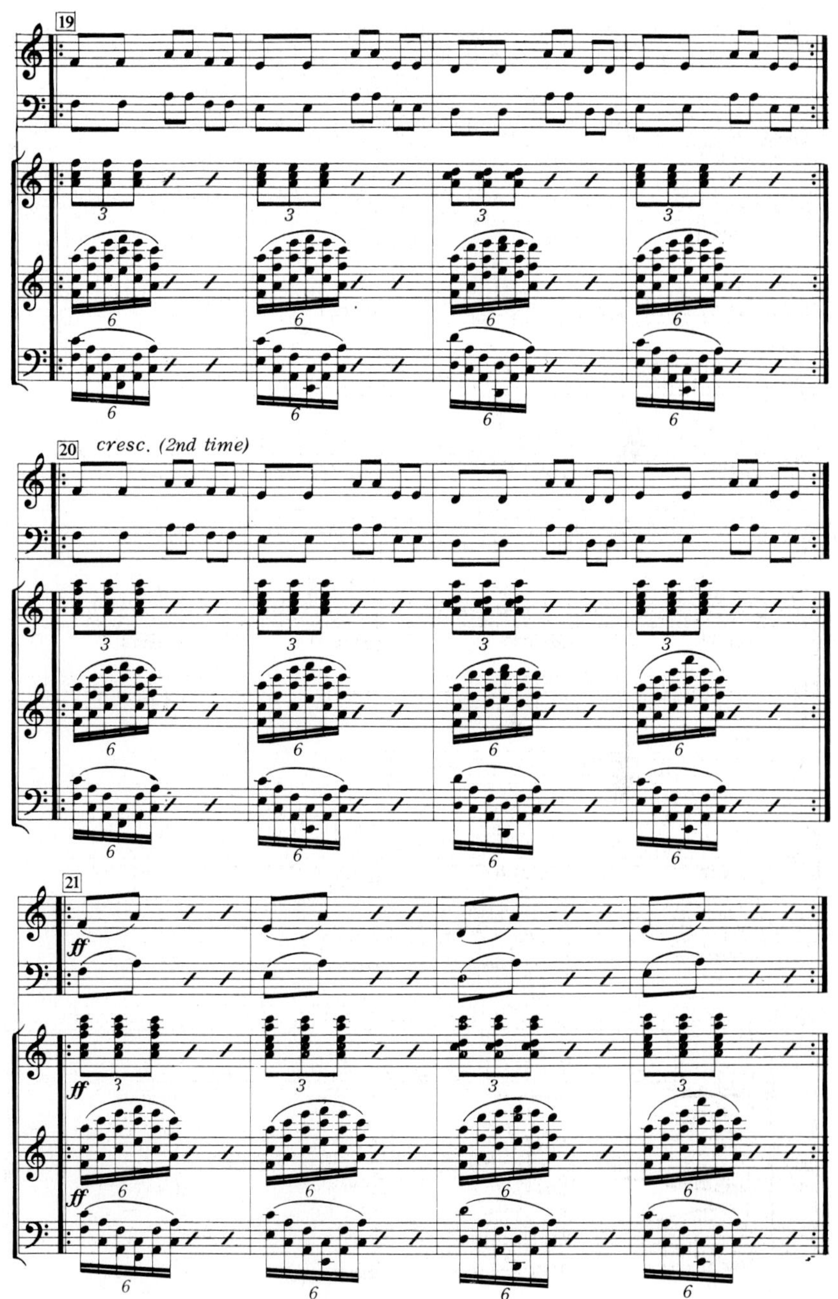
19
20
cresc. (2nd time)
21
ff

Appendix A

Reading an Orchestral Score

CLEFS

The music for some instruments is written in clefs other than the familiar treble and bass. In the following example, middle C is shown in the four clefs used in orchestral scores:

The *alto clef* is primarily used in viola parts. The *tenor clef* is employed for cello, bassoon, and trombone parts when these instruments play in a high register.

TRANSPOSING INSTRUMENTS

The music for some instruments is customarily written at a pitch different from their actual sound. The following list, with examples, shows the main transposing instruments and the degree of transposition. (In some modern works—such as the Schoenberg example included in this anthology—all instruments are written at their sounding pitch.)

Instrument	*Transposition*	*Written Note*	*Actual Sound*
Piccolo Celesta	sound an octave higher than written		
Trumpet in F	sound a fourth higher than written.		
Trumpet in E	sound a major third higher than written		

Instrument	*Transposition*	*Written Note Actual Sound*
Clarinet in E♭ Trumpet in E♭	sound a minor third higher than written	
Trumpet in D Clarinet in D	sound a major second higher than written	
Clarinet in B♭ Trumpet in B♭ Cornet in B♭ Horn in B♭ alto	sound a major second lower than written	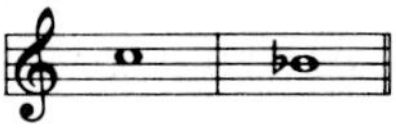
Clarinet in A Trumpet in A Cornet in A	sound a minor third lower than written	
Horn in G Alto flute	sound a fourth lower than written	
English horn Horn in F	sound a fifth lower than written	
Horn in E	sound a minor sixth lower than written	
Horn in E♭	sound a major sixth lower than written	
Horn in D	sound a minor seventh lower than written	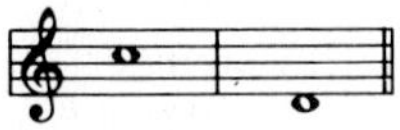
Contrabassoon Horn in C Double bass	sound an octave lower than written	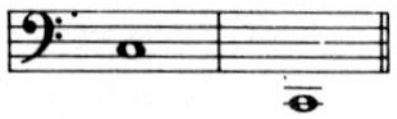
Bass clarinet in B♭ (written in treble clef)	sound a major ninth lower than written	
(written in bass clef)	sound a major second lower than written	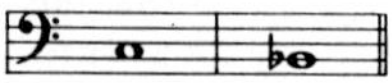
Bass clarinet in A (written in treble clef)	sound a minor tenth lower than written	
(written in bass clef)	sound a minor third lower than written	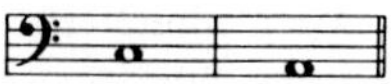

Appendix B

Instrumental Names and Abbreviations

The following tables set forth the English, Italian, German, and French names used for the various musical instruments in these scores, and their respective abbreviations. A table of the foreign-language names for scale degrees and modes is also provided.

Woodwinds

English	*Italian*	*German*	*French*
Piccolo (Picc.)	Flauto piccolo (Fl. Picc.)	Kleine Flöte (Kl. Fl.)	Petite flûte
Flute (Fl.)	Flauto (Fl.); Flauto grande (Fl. gr.)	Grosse Flöte (Fl. gr.)	Flûte (Fl.)
Alto flute	Flauto contralto (fl.c-alto)	Altflöte	Flûte en sol
Oboe (Ob.)	Oboe (Ob.)	Hoboe (Hb.); Oboe (Ob.)	Hautbois (Hb.)
English horn (E. H.)	Corno inglese (C. or Cor. ingl., C.i.)	Englisches Horn (E. H.)	Cor anglais (C. A.)
Sopranino clarinet	Clarinetto piccolo (clar. picc.)		
Clarinet (C., Cl., Clt., Clar.)	Clarinetto (Cl. Clar.)	Klarinette (Kl.)	Clarinette (Cl.)
Bass clarinet (B. Cl.)	Clarinetto basso (Cl. b., Cl. basso, Clar. basso)	Bass Klarinette (Bkl.)	Clarinette basse (Cl. bs.)
Bassoon (Bsn., Bssn.)	Fagotto (Fag., Fg.)	Fagott (Fag., Fg.)	Basson (Bssn.)
Contrabassoon (C. Bsn.)	Contrafagotto (Cfg., C. Fag., Cont. F.)	Kontrafagott (Kfg.)	Contrebasson (C. bssn.)

Brass

English	*Italian*	*German*	*French*
French horn (Hr., Hn.)	Corno (Cor., C.)	Horn (Hr.) [*pl.* Hörner (Hrn.)]	Cor; Cor à pistons
Trumpet (Tpt., Trpt., Trp., Tr.)	Tromba (Tr.)	Trompete (Tr., Trp.)	Trompette (Tr.)
Trumpet in D	Tromba piccola (Tr. picc.)		
Cornet	Cornetta	Kornett	Cornet à pistons (C. à p., Pist.)
Trombone (Tr., Tbe., Trb., Trm., Trbe.)	Trombone [*pl.* Tromboni (Tbni., Trni.)]	Posaune (Ps., Pos.)	Trombone (Tr.)
Tuba (Tb.)	Tuba (Tb, Tba.)	Tuba (Tb.) [*also* Basstuba (Btb.)]	Tuba (Tb.)

Percussion

English	*Italian*	*German*	*French*
Percussion (Perc.)	Percussione	Schlagzeug (Schlag.)	Batterie (Batt.)
Kettledrums (K. D.)	Timpani (Timp., Tp.)	Pauken (Pk.)	Timbales (Timb.)
Snare drum (S. D.)	Tamburo piccolo (Tamb. picc.) Tamburo militare (Tamb. milit.)	Kleine Trommel (Kl. Tr.)	Caisse claire (C. cl.), Caisse roulante Tambour militaire (Tamb. milit.)
Bass drum (B. drum)	Gran cassa (Gr. Cassa, Gr. C., G. C.)	Grosse Trommel (Gr. Tr.)	Grosse caisse (Gr. c.)
Cymbals (Cym., Cymb.)	Piatti (P., Ptti., Piat.)	Becken (Beck.)	Cymbales (Cym.)
Tam-Tam (Tam-T.)			
Tambourine (Tamb.)	Tamburino (Tamb.)	Schellentrommel, Tamburin	Tambour de Basque (T. de B., Tamb. de Basque)

Triangle (Trgl., Tri.)	Triangolo (Trgl.)	Triangel	Triangle (Triang.)
Glockenspiel (Glocken.)	Campanelli (Cmp.)	Glockenspiel	Carillon
Bells (Chimes)	Campane (Cmp.)	Glocken	Cloches
Antique Cymbals	Crotali Piatti antichi	Antiken Zimbeln	Cymbales antiques
Sleigh Bells	Sonagli (Son.)	Schellen	Grelots
Xylophone (Xyl.)	Xilofono	Xylophon	Xylophone
Cowbells		Herdenglocken	
Crash cymbal			Grande cymbale chinoise
Siren			Sirène
Lion's roar			Tambour à corde
Slapstick			Fouet
Wood blocks			Blocs chinois

Strings

English	*Italian*	*German*	*French*
Violin (V., Vl., Vln, Vi.)	Violino (V., Vl., Vln.)	Violine (V., Vl., Vln.) Geige (Gg.)	Violon (V., Vl., Vln.)
Viola (Va., Vl., *pl.* Vas.)	Viola (Va., Vla.) *pl.* Viole (Vle.)	Bratsche (Br.)	Alto (A.)
Violoncello, Cello (Vcl., Vc.)	Violoncello (Vc., Vlc., Vcllo.)	Violoncell (Vc., Vlc.)	Violoncelle (Vc.)
Double bass (D. Bs.)	Contrabasso (Cb., C. B.) *pl.* Contrabassi or Bassi (C. Bassi, Bi.)	Kontrabass (Kb.)	Contrebasse (C. B.)

Other Instruments

English	*Italian*	*German*	*French*
Harp (Hp., Hrp.)	Arpa (A., Arp.)	Harfe (Hrf.)	Harpe (Hp.)
Piano	Pianoforte (P.-f., Pft.)	Klavier	Piano
Celesta (Cel.)			
Harpsichord	Cembalo	Cembalo	Clavecin
Harmonium (Harmon.)			
Organ (Org.)	Organo	Orgel	Orgue
Guitar		Gitarre (Git.)	
Mandoline (Mand.)			

Names of Scale Degrees and Modes

Scale Degrees

English	*Italian*	*German*	*French*
C	do	C	ut
C-sharp	do diesis	Cis	ut dièse
D-flat	re bemolle	Des	ré bémol
D	re	D	ré
D-sharp	re diesis	Dis	ré dièse
E-flat	mi bemolle	Es	mi bémol
E	mi	E	mi
E-sharp	mi diesis	Eis	mi dièse
F-flat	fa bemolle	Fes	fa bémol
F	fa	F	fa
F-sharp	fa diesis	Fis	fa dièse
G-flat	sol bemolle	Ges	sol bémol
G	sol	G	sol
G-sharp	sol diesis	Gis	sol dièse
A-flat	la bemolle	As	la bémol
A	la	A	la
A-sharp	la diesis	Ais	la dièse
B-flat	si bemolle	B	si bémol
B	si	H	si
B-sharp	si diesis	His	si dièse
C-flat	do bemolle	Ces	ut bémol

Modes

major	maggiore	dur	majeur
minor	minore	moll	mineur

Appendix C

Glossary of Musical Terms Used in the Scores

The following glossary is not intended to be a complete dictionary of musical terms, nor is knowledge of all these terms necessary to follow the scores in this book. However, as the listener gains experience in following scores, he will find it useful and interesting to understand the composer's directions with regard to tempo, dynamics, and methods of performance.

In most cases, compound terms have been broken down in the glossary and defined separately, as they often recur in varying combinations. A few common foreign-language particles are included in addition to the musical terms. Note that names and abbreviations for instruments and for scale degrees will be found in Appendix B.

a. The phrases *a* 2, *a* 3 (etc.) indicate that the part is to be played in unison by 2, 3 (etc.) players; when a simple number (1., 2., etc.) is placed over a part, it indicates that only the first (second, etc.) player in that group should play.

aber. But.

accelerando. Growing faster.

accentué. Accented.

accompagnato (accomp.). In a continuo part, this indicates that the chord-playing instrument resumes (cf. *tasto solo*).

accordez. Tune the instrument as specified.

adagio. Slow, leisurely.

ad libitum (ad lib.). An indication giving the performer liberty to: (1) vary from strict tempo; (2) include or omit the part of some voice or instrument; (3) include a cadenza of his own invention.

affettuoso. With emotion.

affrettando (affrett.). Hastening a little.

agitato. Agitated, excited.

agitazione. Agitation.

allargando (allarg.). Growing broader.

alle, alles. All, every, each.

allegretto. A moderately fast tempo (between allegro and andante).

allegro. A rapid tempo (between allegretto and presto).

allein. Alone, solo.

allmählich. Gradually (*allmählich gleichmässig fliessend werden*, gradually becoming even-flowing again).

al niente. Reduce to nothing.

alto, altus (A.). The deeper of the two main divisions of women's (or boys') voices.

alzate. Indication to remove mutes.

am Steg. On the bridge (of a string instrument).

ancora. Again.
andante. A moderately slow tempo (between adagio and allegretto).
andantino. A moderately slow tempo.
an dem Griffbrett (a.d.G.). Played on the fingerboard.
Anfang. Beginning.
anima. Spirit, animation.
animando. With increasing animation.
animato, animé. Animated.
anschwellend. Crescendo.
a piacere. The execution of the passage is left to the performer's discretion.
à plat. Laid flat.
appassionato. Impassioned.
arco. Played with the bow.
arditamente. Boldly.
armonioso. Harmoniously.
arpeggiando, arpeggiato (arpeg.). Played in harp style, i.e. the notes of the chord played in quick succession rather than simultaneously.
arrêt. Stop.
assai. Very.
a tempo. At the (basic) tempo.
attacca. Begin what follows without pausing.
attaque sèche. Sharp attack.
auf dem. On the (as in *auf dem G,* on the G string).
Ausdruck. Expression.
ausdrucksvoll. With expression.
äusserst. Extreme, utmost.

bachetti. Drumsticks (*bachetti di tamburo militare,* snare-drum sticks; *bachetti di spugna,* sponge-headed drumsticks).
baguettes. Drumsticks (*baguettes de bois, baguettes timbales de bois,* wooden drumsticks or kettledrum sticks; *baguettes d'éponge,* sponge-headed drumsticks; *baguettes mi-dures,* semi-hard drumsticks; *baguettes dures,* hard drumsticks; *baguettes timbales en feutre,* felt-headed kettledrum sticks).
bass, basso, bassus (B.). The lowest male voice.
battuto coll' arco. Struck with the bow.
beaucoup. Many, much.
Becken. Cymbals.
bedeutung bewegter. With significantly more movement.
beide Hände. With both hands.
belebend. With increasing animation.
belebt. Animated.
ben. Very.
ben accordato. Well tuned.
bestimmt. Energetic.
bewegt. Agitated.
bewegter. More agitated.
bien. Very.
bis zum Schluss dieser Szene. To the end of this scene.
Blech. Brass instruments.
Bogen (Bog.). Played with the bow.
bouché. Muted.
bravura. Boldness.
breit. Broadly.
breiter. More broadly.
brillante. Brilliant.
brio. Spirit, vivacity.

cadenza. An extended passage for solo instrument in free, improvisatory style.
calando. Diminishing in volume and speed.
calma, calmo. Calm, calmly.
cantabile (cant.). In a singing style.
cantando. In a singing manner.
canto. Voice (as in *col canto,* a direction for the accompaniment to follow the solo part in tempo and expression).
cantus. An older designation for the highest part in a vocal work.
capella. Choir, chorus.
cédez. Go a little slower.
changez. Change (usually an instruction to re-tune a string or an instrument).

circa (ca.). About, approximately.
clair. High.
col, colla, coll'. With the.
come prima, come sopra. As at first; as previously.
comodo. Comfortable, easy.
con. With.
corda. String; for example, *seconda (2a) corda* is the second string (the A string on the violin).
coro. Chorus.
coulisse. Wings (of a theater).
court. Short, staccato.
crescendo (cresc.). An increase in volume.
cuivré. Played with a harsh, blaring tone.
cum quatuor vocibus. With four voices.
cupo. Dark, veiled.

dabei. Thereby, therewith; at the same time.
da capo (D.C.). Repeat from the beginning.
dal segno. Repeat from the sign.
Dämpfer (Dpf.). Mutes.
dans. In.
dazu. In addition to that, for that purpose.
début. Beginning.
decrescendo (decresc., decr.). A decreasing of volume.
descendez le "la" un demi-ton plus bas. Lower the A-string a semitone.
détaché. With a broad, vigorous bow stroke, each note bowed singly.
détimbrée. With snares (of a snare drum) relaxed.
deutlich. Distinctly.
devozione. Devotion; affection, reverence.
dimenuendo, diminuer (dim., dimin.). A decreasing of volume.
distinto. Distinct, clear.
divisés, divisi (div.). Divided; indicates that the instrumental group should be divided into two parts to play the passage in question.
dolce. Sweetly and softly.
dolcemente. Sweetly.
dolcezza. Sweetness; gentleness.
dolcissimo (dolciss.). Very sweetly.
dolente. Sorrowful.
dopo. After, afterwards.
Doppelgriff. Double stop.
doppio movimento. Twice as fast.
doux. Sweetly.
drängend. Pressing on.
duplum. In older music, the part immediately above the tenor.
durée indiquée. The duration indicated.

e. And.
eilen. To hurry.
elegante. Elegant, graceful.
en animant. Becoming more animated.
enchainez. Continue to the next material without pause.
en dehors. With emphasis.
energico. Energetically.
entsprechend. Appropriate; corresponding.
ersterbend. Dying away.
erstes Tempo. At the original tempo.
espansione. Expansion, broadening.
espressione. With expression.
espressione intensa. Intense expression.
espressivo (espress., espr.). Expressively.
et. And.
etwas. Somewhat, rather.
expressif. Expressively.

fehlende Akkordtöne. Missing chord tones.
feroce. Fierce, ferocious.
fiero. Fiercely.
fine. End, close.
Flageolett (Flag.). Harmonics.
flatterzunge, flutter-tongue. A special tonguing technique for wind instruments, producing a rapid trill-like sound.
flebile. Feeble; plaintive; mournful.
fliessend. Flowing.

forte (f). Loud.
fortissimo (ff). Very loud (*fff* indicates a still louder dynamic).
forza. Force.
frei. Freely.
freihäng. Hanging freely. An indication to the percussionist to let the cymbals vibrate feely.
frottez. Rub.
früher. Earlier; former.
fuga. Fugue.
fuoco. Fire, spirit.
furioso. Furiously.
Fuss. Foot; pedal.

gajo. Gaily.
ganz. Entirely, altogether.
ganzton. Whole tone.
gedämpft (ged.). Muted.
geheimnisvoll. Mysteriously.
gesteigert. Intensified.
gestopft (chiuso). Stopping the notes of a horn; that is, the hand is placed in the bell of the horn, to produce a muffled sound.
geteilt (get.). Divided; indicates that the instrumental group should be divided into two parts to play the passage in question.
giocoso. Jocose, humorous.
giusto. Moderately.
gli altri. The others.
glissando (gliss.). Rapid scales produced by running the fingers over all the strings.
gradamente. Gradually.
grande. Large, great.
grande taille. Large size.
grandioso. Grandiose.
grave. Slow, solemn; deep, low.
grazia. Grace, charm.
grazioso. Gracefully.
grosser Auftakt. Big upbeat.
gut gehalten. Well sustained.

H. A symbol used in the music of Schoenberg, Berg, and Webern to indicate the most important voice in the texture.
Hälfte. Half.
harmonic (harm.). A flute-like sound produced on a string instrument by lightly touching the string with the finger instead of pressing it down.
Hauptzeitmass. Original tempo.
heimlich. Furtively.
hervortretend. Prominent.
hoch. High; nobly.
Holz. Woodwinds.

im gleichen Rhythmus. In the same rhythm.
immer chromatisch. Always chromatic.
immer im Tempo. Always in tempo.
incalzando. Pressing, hurrying.
in neuen Tempo. In the new tempo.
istesso tempo. Duration of beat remains unaltered despite meter change.

jeté. With a bouncing motion of the bow.
jusqu'à la fin. To the end.
kadenzieren. To cadence.
kaum hörbar. Barely audible.
klagend. Lamenting.
Klang. Sound; timbre.
kleine. Little.
kurz. Short.

laissez vibrer. Let vibrate; an indication to the player of a harp, cymbal, etc., that the sound must not be damped.
lamentoso. Plaintive, mournful.
langsam. Slow.
langsamer. Slower.
languente. Languishing.
langueur. Languor.
largamente. Broadly.
larghetto. Slightly faster than largo.
largo. A very slow tempo.
lebhaft. Lively.
leere Bühne. Empty stage.

legatissimo. A more forceful indication of *legato.*

legato. Performed without any perceptible interruption between notes.

légèrement. Lightly.

leggèro, leggiero (legg.). Light and graceful.

legno. The wood of the bow (*col legno tratto,* bowed with the wood; *col legno battuto,* tapped with the wood; *col legno gestrich,* played with the wood).

leise. Soft, low.

lent. Slowly.

lentamente. Slowly.

lento. A slow tempo (between andante and largo).

l.h. Abbreviation for "left hand."

licenza. With license.

lieblich. Lovely, sweetly.

l'istesso tempo, see *istesso tempo.*

loco. Indicates a return to the written pitch, following a passage played an octave higher or lower than written.

lontano. Far away, from a distance.

luftpause. Pause for breath.

lunga. Long, sustained.

lungo silenzio. A long pause.

lusingando. Caressing.

ma. But.

maestoso. Majestic.

manual. A keyboard played with the hands (as distinct from the pedal keyboard on an organ).

marcatissimo (marcatiss.). With very marked emphasis.

marcato (marc.). Marked, with emphasis.

marcia. March.

marqué. Marked, with emphasis.

marziale. Military, martial, march-like.

mässig. Moderate.

Melodie. Melody, tune, air.

même. Same.

meno. Less.

mezza voce. With half the voice power.

mezzo forte (mf). Moderately loud.

mezzo piano (mp). Moderately soft.

mindistens. At least.

minore. In the minor mode.

misterioso. Misterious.

mit. With.

M. M. Metronome; followed by an indication of the setting for the correct tempo.

moderato, modéré. At a moderate tempo.

modo ordinario (ordin.). In the usual way (usually cancelling an instruction to play using some special technique).

möglich. Possible.

molto. Very, much.

morendo. Dying away.

mormorato. Murmured.

mosso. Rapid.

motetus. In medieval polyphonic music, a voice part above the tenor; generally, the first additional part to be composed.

moto. Motion.

mouvement (mouvt.). Tempo.

moyenne. Medium.

muta, mutano. Change the tuning of the instrument as specified.

N. A symbol used in the music of Schoenberg, Berg, and Webern to indicate the second most important voice in the texture.

nachgebend. Becoming slower.

Nachschlag. Grace-note that follows rather than precedes the note ornamented.

nach und nach. More and more.

naturalezza. A natural, unaffected manner.

naturel. In the usual way (generally cancelling an instruction to play using some special technique).

Nebenstimme. Subordinate or accompanying part.

nicht, non. Not.

noch. Still.
non. Not.
nuances. Shadings, expression.

oberer. Upper, leading.
octava (8va). Octave; if not otherwise qualified, means the notes marked should be played an octave higher than written.
octava bassa (8va bassa). Play an octave lower than written.
ohne. Without.
ondeggiante. Undulating movement of the bow, which produces a tremolo effect.
open. (1) In brass instruments, the opposite of muted; (2) in string instruments, refers to the unstopped string (i.e. sounding at its full length).
ordinario, ordinérement (ordin.). In the usual way (generally cancelling an instruction to play using some special technique).
ossia. An alternative (usually easier) version of a passage.
ôtez vite les sourdines. Remove the mutes quickly.
ouvert. Open.

parlante. Sung in a manner resembling speech.
parte. Part (*colla parte,* the accompaniment is to follow the soloist in tempo).
pas trop long. Not too long.
Paukenschlägel. Timpani stick.
pavillon en l'aire. An indication to the player of a wind instrument to raise the bell of the instrument upward.
pedal (ped., P.). (1) In piano music, indicates that the damper pedal should be depressed; an asterisk indicates the point of release (brackets below the music are also used to indicate pedalling); (2) on an organ, the pedals are a keyboard played with the feet.
percutée. Percussive.
perdendosi. Gradually dying away.
pesante. Heavily.
peu. Little, a little.
pianissimo (pp). Very soft (*ppp* indicates a still softer dynamic).
piano (p). Soft.
piatto. Cymbal; flat, even; plain, dull.
più. More.
pizzicato (pizz.). The string plucked with the finger.
plötzlich. Suddenly, immediately.
plus. More.
pochissimo (pochiss.). Very little, a very little.
poco. Little, a little.
poco a poco. Little by little.
pomposo. Pompous.
ponticello (pont.). The bridge (of a string instrument).
portando la voce. With a smooth sliding of the voice from one tone to the next.
position naturel (pos. nat.). In the normal position (usually cancelling an instruction to play using some special technique).
possibile. Possible.
pouce. Thumb.
pour. For.
praeludium. Prelude.
premier mouvement (1er mouvt.). At the original tempo.
prenez. Take up.
préparez le ton. Prepare the instrument to play in the key named.
presser. To press.
presto. A very quick tempo (faster than allegro).
prima. First, principal.
principale (pr.). Principal, solo.
punta d'arco. Played with the top of the bow.

quasi. Almost, as if.
quasi niente. Almost nothing, i.e. as softly as possible.

quasi trill (tr.). In the manner of a trill.
quintus. An older designation for the fifth part in a vocal work.

rallentando (rall., rallent.). Growing slower.
rapide, rapidò. Quick.
rapidissimo. Very quick.
rasch. Quick.
rauschend. Rustling, roaring.
recitative (recit.). A vocal style designed to imitate and emphasize the natural inflections of speech.
retenu. Held back.
revenir au Tempo. Return to the original tempo.
richtig. Correct (*richtige Lage,* correct pitch).
rigore di tempo. Strictness of tempo.
rigueur. Precision.
rinforzando (rf, rfz, rinf.). A sudden accent on a single note or chord.
risoluto. Determined.
ritardando (rit., ritard.). Gradually slackening in speed.
ritenuto (riten.). Immediate reduction of speed.
ronde. Round dance; whole note (Fr.).
rubato. A certain elasticity and flexibility of tempo, consisting of slight accelerandos and ritardandos according to the requirements of the musical expression.
ruhig. Quietly.
rullante. Rolling.

saltando (salt.). An indication to the string player to bounce the bow off the string by playing with short, quick bow-strokes.
sans timbre. Without snares.
scena vuota. Empty stage.
scherzando (scherz.). Playful.
schleppend. Dragging.
Schluss. Cadence, conclusion.
schmachtend. Languishing.
schnell. Fast.
schneller. Faster.
schon. Already.
schwächer. Weaker; milder; fainter.
schwer. Heavy, ponderous; grave, serious.
scorrevole. Flowing, gliding.
sec, secco. Dry, simple.
seconda volta. The second time.
segue. (1) Continue to the next movement without pausing; (2) continue in the same manner.
sehr. Very.
semplicità. Simplicity.
sempre. Always, continually.
sentimento. Sentiment, feeling.
senza. Without.
sforzando, sforzato (sfz, sf). With sudden emphasis.
sfumato. Diminishing and fading away.
simile. In a similar manner.
Singstimme. Singing voice.
sino al. Up to the . . . (usually followed by a new tempo marking, or by a dotted line indicating a terminal point).
smorzando (smorz.). Dying away.
sofort. Immediately.
solo (s.). Executed by one performer.
sonator. Player *(uno sonator,* one player; *due sonatori,* two players).
sonné à la double 8va. Play the double octave.
sopra. Above; in piano music, used to indicate that one hand must pass above the other.
soprano (S.). The voice classification with the highest range.
sordino (sord.). Mute.
sostenendo, sostenuto. Sustained.
sotto voce. In an undertone, subdued, under the breath.
sourdine. Mute.
soutenu. Sustained.
spiccato. With a light bouncing motion of the bow.
spiel. Play (an instrument).

spiritoso. In a spirited manner.
staccatissimo. Very staccato.
staccato (stacc.). Detached, separated, abruptly disconnected.
Stelle. Place; passage.
stentando, stentato (stent.). Delaying, retarding.
stesso movimento. The same basic pace.
stimm-. Voice.
Streicher. Bow
stretto. In a non-fugal composition, indicates a concluding section at an increased speed.
stringendo (string.). Quickening.
subito (sub.). Suddenly, immediately.
sul. On the (as in *sul G,* on the G string).
suono. Sound, tone.
superius. In older music, the uppermost part.
sur. On.
suspendue. Suspended.

tacet. The instrument or vocal part so marked is silent.
tasto solo. In a continuo part, this indicates that only the string instrument plays; the chord-playing instrument is silent.
tempo primo (tempo I). At the original tempo.
teneramente. Tenderly, gently.
tenor, tenore (T.). The highest male voice.
tenuto (ten.). Held, sustained.
tief. Deep, low.
tornando al tempo primo. Returning to the original tempo.
touch. Fingerboard (of a string instrument).
toujours. Always, continually.
tranquillo. Quietly, calmly.
tre corda (t.c.). Release the soft (or *una corda*) pedal of the piano.
tremolo (trem). On string instruments, a quick reiteration of the same tone, produced by a rapid up-and-down movement of the bow; also a rapid alternation between two different notes.
très. Very.
trill (tr.). The rapid alternation of a given note with the diatonic second above it. In a drum part it indicates rapid alternating strokes with two drumsticks.
triplum. In medieval polyphonic music, a voice part above the tenor.
troppo. Too much.
tutta la forza. Very emphatically.
tutti. Literally, "all"; usually means all the instruments in a given category as distinct from a solo part.

übergreifen. To overlap.
übertönend. Drowning out.
una corda (u.c.). With the "soft" pedal of the piano depressed.
und. And.
unison (unis.). The same notes or melody played by several instruments at the same pitch. Often used to emphasize that a phrase is not to be divided among several players.

verhallend. Fading away.
verklingen lassen. To let die away.
verlöschend. Extinguishing.
vierhändig. Four-hand piano music.
viertel. Quarter (*Viertelnote,* quarter-note; *Viertelton,* quarter tone).
vif. Lively.
vigoroso. Vigorous, strong.
vivace. Quick, lively.
vivo. Lively.
voce. Voice (as in *colla voce,* a direction for the accompaniment to follow the solo part in tempo and expression).
voilà. There.
vorbereiten. To prepare in advance.
Vorhang auf. Curtain up.
Vorhang fällt, Vorhang zu. Curtain down.

vorher. Beforehand; previously.
voriges. Preceding.

Walzertempo. In the tempo of a waltz.
weg. Away, beyond.
weich. Mellow, smooth, soft.
weiter. Further, forward.
werden. Become; grow.
wie aus der Ferne. As if from afar.
wieder. Again.
wie oben. As above, as before.
wie zu Anfang dieser Szene. As at the beginning of this scene.
wüthend. Furiously.

zart. Tenderly, delicately.
Zeitmass. Tempo.
zögernd. Slower.
zu. The phrases *zu* 2, *zu* 3 (etc.) indicate that the part is to be played in unison by 2, 3 (etc.) players.
zurückhaltend. Slackening in speed.
zurücktreten. To withdraw.
zweihändig. With two hands.

Index of Forms and Genres

A roman numeral following a title indicates a movement within the work named.